CHRISTIANITY IN
INDEPENDENT AFRICA

CHRISTIANITY IN INDEPENDENT AFRICA

edited by
EDWARD FASHOLÉ-LUKE, RICHARD GRAY,
ADRIAN HASTINGS & GODWIN TASIE

INDIANA UNIVERSITY PRESS
BLOOMINGTON & LONDON

Manufactured in Great Britain

Library of Congress catalog card number: 77-26351
ISBN 0-253-37506-1

Typesetting by Malvern Typesetting Services
Printed in Great Britain

Contents

PART 2: TRADITIONAL RELIGION AND CHRISTIANITY: CONTINUITIES AND CONFLICTS

Abbreviations

AFER—African Ecclesiastical Review

AMEC—African Methodist Episcopal Church

AMECEA—Association of Member Episcopal Conferences of Eastern Africa

AMI—African Methodist Independent Church

ARC—African Reformed Church (Zambia)

ARCAM—Assemblée Représentative du Cameroun

BDC—Bloc Démocratique Camerounais

C & S—Sacred Order of the Cherubim and Seraphim

CAC—Christ Apostolic Church

CAFOD—Catholic Fund for Overseas Development

CCAP—Church of Central Africa Presbyterian

CCN—Christian Council of Nigeria

CDA—Calabar Diocesan Archives

CID—Criminal Investigation Department

CMS—Church Missionary Society

CPP—Convention People's Party (Ghana)

CSM—Church of Scotland Mission

CSSp—*Congregatio Sancti Spiritus*, commonly Holy Ghost Fathers or Spiritans

CTC—Catechist Training Centre

CWCN—Catholic Welfare Conference of Nigeria

CWME—Commission on World Mission and Evangelism

ECZ—Eglise du Christ au Zaire

EJCSK—Eglise de Jésus-Christ sur la Terre par le Prophète Simon Kimbangu

ELCT—Evangelical Lutheran Church of Tanzania

ENCC—Eastern Nigerian Catholic Council

ESOCAM—Parti pour l'Evolution Sociale Camerounaise

FO—Force Ouvrière (Cameroun)

FOCA—Faith and Order Conference

FRELIMO—Front for the Liberation of Mozambique

ILO—International Labour Organization, Geneva

JMPR—Jeunesse du Mouvement Populaire de la Révolution (Zaïre)

KANU—Kenya African National Union

KCA—Kikuyu Central Association

KNCU—Kilimanjaro (Native) Co-operative Union

KY—Kabaka Yekka

MPLA—People's Movement for the Liberation of Angola

MPR—Mouvement Populaire de la Révolution (Zaïre)

NAI—National Archives, Ibadan

NCCK—National Christian Council of Kenya

NCNC—National Council of Nigeria and the Cameroons

NUT—Nigerian Union of Teachers

ODA—Onitsha Diocesan Archives

PARMEHUTU—Parti du Mouvement de l'Emancipation Hutu

PCEA—Presbyterian Church of East Africa

RCM—Roman Catholic Mission

RDA—Rassemblement Démocratique Africain

SECAM—Symposium of the Episcopal Conferences of Africa and Madagascar

SES—South-Eastern State, Nigeria

SFIA—School Fees Insurance Agency

SHCJ—Society of the Holy Child Jesus

SO—Stationery Office

SPCK—Society for Promoting Christian Knowledge

SPG—Society for the Propagation of the Gospel

TANU—Tanzania (orig. Tanganyika) African National Union

TTC—Teacher Training College

UCZ—United Church of Zambia

UDI—Unilateral Declaration of Independence (Rhodesia)

UISG—International Union of Superior Generals

UNAR—Union Nationale Rwandaise

UNAZA—Université Nationale du Zaïre

UNC—Uganda National Congress

UNESCO—United Nations Educational, Scientific and Cultural Organization

UNIP—United Independence Party (Zambia)

UPC—Uganda Peoples Congress

UPC—Union des Populations du Cameroun

UPE—Universal Primary Education (Nigeria)

UPP—United Progressive Party (Zambia)

USCC—Union des Syndicats Confédérés du Cameroun

WCC—World Council of Churches

WF—White Fathers

WS—White Sisters

WTBTS—Watch Tower Bible and Tract Society

YCS—Young Christian Students

ZANU—Zimbabwe African National Union

Preface

As Tropical Africa approached independence, it was widely assumed that, since most missionaries were at least partly identified with colonial rule, the influence of Christianity throughout the continent would be dramatically reduced. Was this a misconception, based on Eurocentric conceptions which greatly exaggerated the role of foreign missionaries in the development of the churches in Africa? Did political independence prove to be a decisive watershed, and how have the churches been evolving within the new political climate? What has been the wider cultural significance, both for Africa and the world outside, of the continuing interaction between Christianity and African Traditional Religions? In what respects can developments within Islam in Africa during this period illuminate the Christian experience?

With questions such as these in mind, a research programme has been conducted for over two years at seminars and conferences in eight university and ecumenical centres in Africa and in the universities of Los Angeles and London. Besides these formal occasions, a wide range of contacts was established in most African countries, and in the first week of September 1975 nearly a hundred academics and churchmen met in Nigeria at the Jos Campus of the University of Ibadan to review the findings of this research. These encounters extended across the divisions of academic disciplines, denominational allegiances, ideological viewpoints and ethnic loyalties; together the series constituted an experience and generated a variety of insights which it is impossible to compress within the confines of a single volume. The contributions printed here represent only a small selection of the papers, totalling more than two hundred, presented and discussed during the course of the research programme and at the Jos conference. We are acutely aware of so much that has had to be omitted and of the debt which we and our contributors owe to the other participants in the programme. We hope however that this selection still offers an impression of the far reaching political, social, intellectual and spiritual influences which have been transforming the nature and role of Christianity in Africa during the last two decades.

PREFACE

For financial assistance to the programme, we wish to record our gratitude to The Leverhulme Trust Fund, The Lilly Endowment Inc., The SFIA Educational Trust, The British Council of Churches, The Theological Education Fund, Internationales Katholisches Missionswerk, and the School of Oriental and African Studies, University of London. We wish to thank both Professor E. A. Ayandele, then the principal of the Jos Campus of the University of Ibadan, for the invitation to hold the international conference at Jos and for his opening address included here in an appendix, and also all those whose work enabled the conference to take place. We remember particularly the encouragement advice and help received from the Rt. Rev. Desmond Tutu, then Africa director of The Theological Education Fund, and the Rev. J. Kerkhofs, S.J. of Pro Mundi Vita. We would also like to thank Mrs Yvonne Brett for her translations of the chapters by P. Abega, Diakanua Ndofunsu, J. Mfoulou, Ngindu Mushete and S. Sempore; Dr G. S. P. Freeman-Grenville for his generous and expert assistance in proof-reading, and Mrs Jane Linden for compiling the index.

PART ONE

RELIGIOUS
AND
SECULAR STRUCTURES

Introduction

GODWIN TASIE and RICHARD GRAY

Africa has become the test case of the modern missionary movement and, in a major respect, of twentieth century Christianity. Can the faith of the Jewish apostles, which entered the Graeco-Roman world and conquered that of the barbarians to become so firmly anchored in European culture, be freed from these Western moorings? Can this faith be seen as relevant not merely to modern Western man but also to societies which are modernizing themselves from bases radically different from the assumptions and world view of the Western nations? Africa provides the focus for these issues. South of the Sahara, Christian missionaries have been identified with European cultural and, at times, political imperialism; yet during the modern colonial period nowhere else in the world witnessed so rapid and extensive a process of Christianization.

Admittedly the major distinguishing feature of the modern missionary movement has been its relative lack of dependence on the aid of European states and its freedom from state control, compared with the first three centuries of Catholic missions in Africa shackled as they were by the Portuguese *Padroado*. Even the early eighteenth-century Protestant chaplaincies were intimately dependent on state trade or European settlement. The missionary revival in the early nineteenth century, both Catholic and Protestant, established bases of support and organization largely independent of European governments. Missions therefore were able to move into many parts of tropical Africa far in advance of European traders and administrators, and right across the continent missionaries established schools and independent centres of influence, helping to provide Africa, even if fortuitously, with an essential weapon for the eventual liberation from colonial rule. Thus, although the alliance between Christian missionaries and European colonialism was intimate, it was never complete. The message and impact of the missions could in varying degrees be distinguished from the apparatus of alien rule.

Yet far more significant than these cracks in that alliance was the fact that European missionaries were not the sole representatives of

Christianity in Africa. The equation of missionaries and Christianity was never absolute. There was always a gap between missionaries and African Christianity. The most obvious case was that of the Coptic Church and the ancient Christian kingdom of Ethiopia, and when Africans elsewhere in the continent founded their own independent churches from the late nineteenth century onwards, developing their distinctive response to the Christian gospel, the name of Ethiopia figured among their proudest titles. Less obvious, yet perhaps just as significant, was the situation within the churches established by the missions. On the west coast and elsewhere, many of the pioneer missionaries were Africans: liberated slaves and their descendants returning to their homes; traders whose imports into the tribal hinterland included the new beliefs; migrant workers who brought back Bibles as well as guns and cotton cloth; teachers and evangelists who spread out from mission stations, crossing linguistic and cultural frontiers to propagate the new religion. Through much of the period of European dominance, the cutting edge of primary evangelism remained overwhelmingly African. The catechists, together with the prayer leaders and church elders were the leaders of the new Christian nuclei and it was they who had to interpret the faith at the growing points of the churches.

Africanization then has not by any means been synonymous with the ending of European colonial rule. Its origins stretch far into the past. In many respects, political independence has proved a relatively insignificant factor. In most fields there is still much to be accomplished before it is universally recognized that Christianity has become thoroughly at home in Africa. Yet the structures of the mission-connected churches, and their relations with the state and with secular organizations, have undoubtedly experienced major changes during the last two decades. Part one of this volume seeks to examine the nature and limitations of these developments, while part two investigates the reflections of these facts in the life and thought of the churches and in African culture as a whole.

The most striking change has been the almost universal assumption of leadership by Africans at the head of the churches. In most African territories missions had provided the earliest openings for the first pioneers of the modernizing élite, and in theory all Christian missions looked forward to African control of the churches. Yet despite this early start and ultimate objective which contributed greatly to the origins of African political independence, the missions, with a few exceptions, after World War II fell behind in the transfer of power and it is hard to resist the conclusion that political independence has been the decisive factor in changing the colour of church leadership. Indeed in the Catholic hierarchies of some territories, Africans gained a majority only a decade or more after political independence, (see below p. 33) and even the rapidity of this transfer would have been utterly unimaginable twenty years earlier.

One of the principal consequences of this transformation at the top of the mission-connected churches has been, however, to emphasize the extent to which many of these churches still remain heavily dependent on external assistance. In many areas, the number of foreign missionaries is still as large as, and in some churches larger than, it was at independence. The total number probably exceeds 35,000 without counting wives and dependants and this massive alien presence raises problems of the utmost gravity, as Mr Kendall, writing with authority and wide experience, makes clear. Some African church leaders and their missionary counterparts in the West argue that only a moratorium, a total—if perhaps temporary—cessation of this influx and presence, can give African churches the freedom to develop their own contribution. There is a major distinction here between those churches who have formed the heart of the World Council of Churches on the one side and the Roman Catholics, Pentecostals and conservative Evangelicals on the other. Whereas many of the former are already rapidly decreasing the numbers of their missionaries, the Catholics and others are maintaining or even increasing theirs, arguing that it would be wrong to withdraw assistance at this juncture. With considerable differences between dioceses let alone churches, a uniform, total moratorium, even if feasible, would seem to be inappropriate and, although some of the conference papers at Jos referred to this debate, it is perhaps significant that the proposal was barely if at all discussed at the conference. Yet the sudden withdrawal of missionaries, as, for example, in 1882 in Buganda, or on a much larger scale during both world wars and in the more recent cases of expulsion from the Sudan and Nigeria, has often fostered the rapid growth and maturity of the African church. Transmitting a message, the impact and implications of which they can never be fully conscious, missionaries can seldom correctly judge when it is time for them to withdraw or rapidly change their role.

The presence, whether beneficial or obstructive, of the missionary is but one facet of continued foreign involvement. Finance is another, with the administration of most churches still heavily dependent on aid from abroad. More fundamental than either of these aspects, however, as Bishop Kalilombe stresses, is the fact that the structures of mission-connected churches in Africa were inevitably modelled on alien procedures and practices. The sharpened awareness of all these dimensions of dependence is one of the most significant features of the older churches in contemporary Africa. Under the impetus of the Second Vatican Council, the readiness to modify established structures was universally increased among Catholics, but for Africans, whether Catholic or not, the decisive factor has been their assumption of responsibility and control in the churches' leadership. Already this awareness is strengthening the moves towards new patterns of local leadership and non-ordained ministries. The catechist has been recognized anew as a crucial figure, although his training and role have often still to be resolved, as Dr Tuma points out. Women in religious orders are assuming a far wider range of responsibilities though here again their preparation raises urgent questions. Sister Kupalo describes the formidable legacy of cultural misunderstandings, of male arrogance and financial exploitation, of racialism and tribalism, all of which, she argues, underlines the urgent need for imaginative innovations, particularly in the formation of novices. But above all there is the startling realization that in Africa the effective Christian community is seldom if ever coterminous with the parish or other unit imported by the missions. At the more intimate, local level, where leadership is provided by a respected elder or a voluntary, part-time worker, the distinctions between the denominations are far less obvious and here the churches, as Father Hastings shows, have already virtually liberated themselves from a dependence on overseas aid. In fact at this level, the older churches manifest close similarities with the congregations of the African independent churches, especially as many of the larger independent churches are developing from their charismatic origins to an increasing concern with the problems of wider links and a trained ministry. Indeed, as the papers by Dr Turner, Dr Omoyajowo and Mr Opoku show, the structural challenges facing the larger Christian churches in Africa are becoming strikingly alike: can the mission-connected churches adapt their transplanted structures to reflect the basic grass roots realities, and can the Independents overcome the dangers of isolation without stifling the impetus and spontaneity of their local congregations?

This concern with foundations, with remoulding the churches' structures to the needs and resources of the worshipping community in village homesteads, shanty town or suburb, affects every aspect of Christianity in contemporary Africa. As Dr Kalu argues, effective moves towards church union cannot be contrived by denominational dignitaries but they must embrace local congregations and involve the churches as a whole in renewal and reconciliation. The emphasis on the links between basic units and leadership in the churches, on sensitive communications extending to the summits of power, is also clearly relevant to the most crucial socio-political division in independent Africa: the line which divides the centre from the periphery, the *élite* from the weak, the influential from the underprivileged. Liberation from the encumbrance of imported ecclesiastical structures, freedom for local Christian congregations to shape the life of the churches, could be an integral, essential concomitant to the Church's prophetic response to these fundamental social divisions, and, hence, to the whole relationship of the churches with the states in independent Africa.

At one level the political and social influence of Christianity can be discerned in the actions and pronouncements of church leaders and the response evoked among the politicians and other organized interest groups. Here Church and State meet largely in terms of two structured authorities. At another level, however, the political significance of a church depends on the nature of its contacts with women, rural illiterates, urban unemployed, and other less privileged sections and minorities. In a long-range analysis, the orientation of a church towards this wide spectrum of incipient discontent may well prove to be the most significant element in its contemporary political involvement. But in the short run, in the first decades after independence, attention has been focussed on relationships between the leaders of Church and State. At this level, despite many potential grounds for conflict, in most countries co-operation has emerged as the dominant pattern, and criticism has been muted.

During the colonial period, Christian criticism of government policy had normally been most effective when conducted through private channels. Missionary statesmen, like J. H. Oldham, mobilized their contacts in Whitehall and Westminster, and European missionary bishops informally influenced colonial governors. Although such criticism drew its strength from its close contacts with African opinion and realities, it was largely expressed by expatriates, and the ultimate appeal, if these private representations failed, was to metropolitan public opinion, with missionaries seeking to arouse a Christian, humanitarian conscience in their home bases.

With independence, this active concern of missionaries—albeit merely a minority of them—with the social and political implications of the Gospel became increasingly irrelevant, just as missionaries themselves were becoming far less significant in the leadership of the churches in Africa. The links of the churches with Christian public opinion overseas were no longer an automatic source of strength in any criticism of the rulers of Africa. Often indeed they could be viewed as a liability rather than as an asset, a conspicuous aspect of neo-colonialism, especially where, as with the Catholic hierarchy in Cameroun, examined below by Dr Mfoulou, missionaries had denounced popular nationalist movements in the fear that these would align themselves with Communism. So missionaries caught up in a political crisis after independence were sometimes expelled *en masse*, a disaster for themselves but, as we have seen, not always for the church.

Under African leadership, the churches in Africa had to begin to transform these foreign relationships and to establish new international contacts. These new channels facilitated some notable contributions in the political and social sphere (e.g. the Sudan agreement signed in Addis Ababa or the assistance to the liberation movements in southern Africa), but their ability to strengthen the voice of Christian critics of the governments in independent Africa has yet largely to be proved. Few African church leaders have been as close to the new centres of political power as some of the missionaries were under the colonial regimes. Their opportunities of private influence would seem to have been correspondingly fewer: the regular consultations which President Kaunda has held with clergy in Zambia are an almost unique exception. The political influence of the clergy is also diminished by the fact that, unlike the missionaries with their ultimate resort to a Christian conscience in the home base, African church leaders can seldom appeal to commonly held Christian values across the whole nation. The few attempts which have been made to establish political parties along confessional lines have not, therefore, been marked with notable success, and, Dr Twaddle argues, the actual role of denominational loyalties in the Democratic Party in Uganda has been misunderstood. The channels and resources for prophetic criticism by church leaders are severely limited in independent Africa.

Their room for manoeuvre is further lessened as they find themselves competing with political leaders in the process of moral mobilization. Despite the almost unanimous adherence in the constitutions adopted at independence to the concept of the secular role of the state, virtually no African ruler has been able to adopt a purely secular stance. In part this may be because a rigid division between sacred and secular is alien to most African traditions, where political authority carried with it, or even was in part derived from, sacral functions. Modern leadership often therefore attracts to itself a quasi-religious aura. The example of Nkrumah and the CPP in Ghana, in adopting Christian terminology and in modifying popular texts and hymns to proclaim a political message, has been followed by other leaders and parties. In the cause of nation-building, rulers aim to assert and enforce a lowest common denominator in moral values across the whole religious spectrum. Governments are therefore peculiarly sensitive to criticism which appeals to particular ethical and religious convictions.

The trend towards co-operation between church and state does not, however, stem merely from the obstacles which inhibit the development of criticism by church leaders. More positively, it rests also on a fundamental convergence of ideas and interests. While the missionaries had virtually monopolized the means of exerting a Christian influence on colonial policy, Christianity had also posed a prophetic challenge to the whole system of colonialism. Most notably was this expressed by the Ethiopians—the courageous prophets of independence both outside and inside the mission churches. As Mr Cook points out, in the crucial years in the 1950s in Zambia the African Methodist Episcopal Church could offer a contribution that could be made there by none of the other churches, dominated as they were by the whites. Far more indirectly, yet on a much wider scale, every Christian school was helping in this challenge. Through their contribution to 'modernisation' and their evangelic emphasis on radical freedom and equality, Christian schools disseminated anti-colonial convictions, and Christian congregations often provided a network of individuals, associations and communications of considerable significance to the emergence of modern political movements. Christianity—if not most white missionaries—was thus closely involved in the origins and development of African nationalism.

This basic alliance has been strengthened by the fact that, since independence, African leaders in church and state have been seeking the same objectives. Both have searched for authenticity, have been concerned to re-establish African values in a new, supra-tribal setting. Even in Zaïre, where the exceptionally strong links between the Roman Catholic missions and the colonial regime had left an unusually difficult and dangerous legacy, African bishops and statesmen could find common ground as Professor Ngindu argues, in their re-interpretation of the African heritage. In this task of eradicating neo-colonialism in all its forms and of creating viable national communities, criticism of the state in independent Africa comes to be considered as a dangerous liberal luxury.

To this basic convergence of some social and political ideas has been added the institutional interests of the churches. During the colonial period most missions had made a massive investment in education, so that to be a Christian was often almost synonymous with school attendance and for many Christian communities the school-church complex was the only communal building they possessed. Education and health-care had provided the mission-connected churches with crucial areas of influence and control, so that at a local, grass-roots level the church sometimes appeared as an alternative to the state. Yet no new national state could tolerate willingly a blatant *imperium in imperio,* and in some instances a conflict of interests has resulted in tension and crisis. With the exception of the Jehovah's Witnesses who have been banned in several states and infamously ill-treated in some, the cases of deliberate religious persecution (among which the imprisonment of Archbishop Tchidimbo in Guinea might perhaps be numbered) have been relatively isolated, or, as in Equatorial Guinea, Chad, Uganda or Burundi, have formed part of a broader brutal oppression. Although Christians did suffer during the civil war in the southern Sudan, it would probably again be wrong to class this as part of a systematic policy of religious persecution. Here again the causes of conflict were far wider than the purely religious issue. The experience of the Witnesses, even in Zambia where their treatment proved far more humane and understanding than elsewhere, could prove a significant pointer to an increasing conflict in the future between church and state in Africa, for, as Dr Cross maintains, their fate not only illustrates the difficulties of a prophetic stance, but, on the other hand, also clearly reveals the constraints and consequences of a pusillanimous conformity on the part of other Christians.

In the meantime, however, tension between church and state in independent Africa has but rarely resulted in violence and martyrdom. More often, as for example in Zaïre and Cameroun (see below pp 216–41) the conflict has been confined within the legislative and political process. It has, however, raised issues of the gravest significance for both contenders, most notably in the sphere of education. The nationalization of schools and their total control by the state has been seen by some of the churches as not merely demolishing their vested interests and all that they had contributed to the life of the community, but also as threatening the legitimate rights of Christian families and fundamental religious liberties. Two thoughtful, detailed accounts focus on one particular case study—that of Eastern Nigeria—where this issue has been of considerable significance. Professor Afigbo presents a wide-ranging, penetrating critique based on the arguments of the nationalist politicians, while Dr Cooke shows that the missionaries themselves were by no means unaware of their schools' shortcomings, even if they could not agree on the most effective means of meeting these criticisms and of defending the rights and liberties of Christians. Sometimes this debate has resulted in intransigence and ruthless ultimatums, damaging to both sides and, even more, to the schools themselves. In practice, however, even where there has been rigid confrontation at the policy-making level, local realities have often qualified these consequences. Christian communities in Africa have so much to offer to the educational effort that few authorities can afford to eradicate completely their contribution, though undoubtedly the increasing erosion of the Christian dominance in education has been one of the most notable consequences of the ending of colonial rule.

A realistic appraisal of the damage which unresolved conflict could cause both church and state, together with African traditions of religious toleration and compromise, have generally resulted in a policy of accommodation and alliance by both institutions. In some cases, such as Kenya (see below pp 267-84), the National Christian Council has played a key role in maintaining and expanding this co-operation and in the process its activities have deepened the ecumenical contacts of the churches involved. Nearly everywhere churches have diversified their secular interests. With a decreasing responsibility for education, during the 1960s they increasingly became involved in other nation building activities, especially a variety of rural development projects. The mission education secretary has been succeeded by the Director of Diocesan Development or the *Service Ecuménique Sociale*. At the local level this involvement could greatly increase at least the prestige, and possibly the influence, of the church: the parish tractor, poultry-farm or herd of cows could give the laity a deeper sense of a common Christian co-operation and identity (see below pp 64-5). At the national level, the alliance between church and state has been preserved and reinforced.

This increased attention and concern with development masks, however, a basic dilemma for both ecclesiastical and political establishments. In so far as this involvement in secular structures is seen as providing a sphere of influence, status and even control, the churches' role can be determined by a balance of power, in which governments make use of the churches' resources and churchmen seek to consolidate their position. But if this activity represents a commitment to service, then Christians may be led to challenge the alliance. If the churches take on these tasks not as an opportunity for proselytism but as a response to human problems, inevitably they increase their concern for the under-privileged. If, liberated from educational administration, they establish schools for spastics, clinics for the under five-year olds, village polytechnics for the unemployed school leaver, then they not only provide the state with an opportunity to learn from their experiments but they also extend their contacts with those in need.

How significant have these contacts with the fourth world—with shanty town and depressed rural areas, with unfortunates and hard-pressed women—been since independence? Here those Christian communities which have developed separately or in relative isolation from missionary influence and control have immense advantages, quite apart from their specific theological and religious insights. Most of the charismatic churches and the prophetic movements have, at least originally, no barrier created by a massive involvement in an alien technology and style of living, in great buildings or in programmes needing bureaucratic and professional skills. They had little or no dependence on overseas financial aid, and often all members of the church, both lay and clerical, have participated much more actively in its concerns. (See below pp 56, 99). Some of the major African initiatives within the mission-connected—the Balokole of the East African revival, the voluntary associations in Nigeria and many of the women's fellowships—seem also to have shared in these advantages. And in so far as any church becomes a reality at the local level, its spiritual life results in a fellowship and community which helps to supply the social needs of its members and bring vision and hope to its neighbours.

Often the social and political significance of such communities has been confined to local levels. But in some cases—the African Methodist Episcopal Church in Zambia is a clear example—the church's network has provided an effective bridge between the local communities and the wider, national leadership. (See below pp 288-93). The much greater freedom and respect which some of the independent churches enjoyed with the coming of political independence—notably the Kimbanguist Church—has greatly assisted them in forging these wider links, though it is perhaps too early to say whether their enhanced status and institutional responsibilities will prevent them from acting as effective communicators of the basic interests of their local communities. Undoubtedly however the great festivals and mass assemblies of this and other churches, which regularly bring together thousands of worshippers, have an immensely significant potential as communication foci in a situation where other media tend to be either under strict surveillance or primarily concerned with the interests of the highly educated.

Those churches who inherited a massive institutional superstructure from their missionary connections have a major problem, but also their greatest opportunity, in creating and maintaining contacts with the underprivileged. At times of severe crisis, churches, which previously have been mainly identified with producing a small educated élite, may find themselves suddenly ministering to the needs of a whole population or 'minority' group, and even helping to embody its group consciousness as in the case of the southern Sudan or the Biafran enclave. Then, as the survey by Mr Walls shows, the old barriers and obstacles disappear and signs of a united Christendom emerge. But apart from what have been such rare and temporary circumstances, the problem of transcending social divisions continues to confront most churches. For some, a specific undertaking, such as the involvement of the National Christian Council of Kenya with the shanty dwellers of Nairobi, may provide a set of insights which, if taken up, can challenge many assumptions in church and state. (See below pp 278-9). For others, involvement in credit union schemes, co-operative ventures and other rural development projects may create an awareness of the enormous opportunity confronting every church in the field of rural development. Here, across most of rural sub-Saharan Africa, the nuclei of Christian communities already exist with their organization and enthusiasm waiting to be harnessed to achieve the essential break-through of planning participation and labour mobilization which any development programme must achieve.

But what is perhaps potentially the most radical social contribution of the churches in Africa has been proceeding quietly and almost unnoticed. If the change in social relationships between men and women is to be the greatest world revolution of the twentieth century, altering the nature of human relationships more profoundly than the Russian or Chinese revolutions or even the emergence of the Third World, then the churches in Africa are uniquely placed to take a major part in this. Women are generally the backbone of their membership, providing in many cases much the greater part of the churches' local financial resources. In their schools, hospitals and religious congregations the churches have also provided completely new roles for African women. These new women of course adopt in some respects the elitist viewpoint and interest of their husbands, families or institutions, and often they predominate in the leadership of the women's fellowships and church associations. Yet, as Dr Steady's account of Creole women in Freetown emphasizes, although sharply distinguished by their educational and economic advantages, educated women continue to share acutely in the basic anxieties and insecurity of women in general. Dr Swantz's description of the plight of peasant women caught in the grip of the poverty cycle illustrates how desperate the situation of women can be in contemporary Africa. She indicates how the churches have, at times, dramatically provided the reason and opportunity for the liberation of women, but her analysis also clearly demonstrates how, all too often, the churches' leaders merely conform to male vested interests and collaborate in entrenching the patterns of male dominance. Through their activities in the churches, educated women occupy therefore one of the most strategic positions in contemporary African society. Sensitive to the burdens carried by themselves and even more by their less fortunate sisters, they may yet communicate through the churches an awareness of the problems and fate of not merely women but of the underprivileged in general. And in arousing the conscience of the churches they may help to transform the purposes of the alliance between church and state in independent Africa.

This basic political and social challenge of the under-privileged which now confronts the churches dominates the theological debate which is developing in contemporary Africa. These issues, of Liberation and Africanization, are discussed in part two, but Dr Linden's short case study of the dilemma which has confronted the church in Rwanda points clearly to the practical, secular relevance of this debate. It is not sufficient for Christianity merely to come to terms with African social and political institutions. While freeing Christianity from its purely

Western trappings, Africans are also called to rediscover and proclaim the Gospel which will challenge and transform the bonds of evil, balancing the demands of justice against the needs of reconciliation and peace.

Two final contributions in part one point to the parallel, and in some ways divergent, developments experienced by Islam during this period. Unlike Christianity, Islam has not in twentieth century Africa been identified with alien political rule. Although in some areas Islam expanded and prospered during the colonial period, this advance rested not so much on an alliance with colonialism but on the ability of Muslims to exploit the increased mobility and other opportunities provided by the railways, motor transport and modern urbanization of colonial Africa. Muslim traders, soldiers, clerics and migrant workers moved into new areas bringing with them a faith which had already become thoroughly at home in great stretches of tropical Africa. Modern technological developments presented, however, not only an opportunity but also a challenge to Islam. While Christian schools increasingly provided at least the rudiments of a modern-oriented education, Islamic education remained overwhelmingly traditional in outlook. Some Muslims, notably including the Aḥmadīs, vigorously sought to establish a modernized system of Islamic schools (see below pp 326-7), but during the colonial period their impact was limited and largely restricted to those coastal areas of West Africa where Christian missions had already established an ascendancy.

Political independence has brought far-reaching changes for Islam. The attempts to combine modern and traditional forms of Islamic education have intensified, and, as Professor Doi reports, in some cases the erosion of Christian dominance has encouraged Muslims to greater participation in the government schools. But along with these advances, Islam like Christianity finds itself confronted with increasingly secularist tendencies in school, state and society. Dr Sanneh describes the response of Muslims in Freetown to the basic challenges of urban social change, and emphasizes the extent to which Muslims there have been influenced by Christian examples. African Muslims and Christians may find that their ancient rivalry is being superseded by their common concern in a religious view of the world. Yet by far the greatest change has been black Africa's increased involvement with the Islamic world. Independence has enabled Africans and Arabs to strengthen their mutual contacts, a process greatly accelerated by the Oil Revolution. The fact that the principal Arab beneficiaries have been the more traditional Muslim states led by Saudi Arabia has already influenced the nature of Islam in Africa. Both in Uganda and in West Africa the Aḥmadīs have found themselves under pressure. The growing power and influence of Saudi

Arabia and the traditionally-oriented Muslim states may also create a potential responsiveness to a political resurrection of Islam in Africa. At a time when African Christians are seeking radically to reduce their dependence on overseas links, African Muslims may be entering a period of exposure to a greatly intensified external influence. Each may have much to learn from the other's experience.

The missionary factor in Africa

R. ELLIOTT KENDALL

The Western missionary presence in Africa is a remarkable phenomenon when viewed historically and in terms of the whole continent. It is almost 200 years since the first missionaries left Europe for Africa as part of the modern missionary movement, although there had been earlier attempts at evangelization in Africa which had almost entirely disappeared. During this period an ever-increasing number of Westerners from Europe and North America, men and women, have established themselves in all parts of Africa in the cause of the foundation of the Church and the propagation of the Christian religion. During the whole of this century there has been an uninterrupted increase in the expatriate missionary presence. The latest available statistics suggest that the over-all number is higher than at any time in the past. If Roman Catholics and Protestants are included the total is in the region of 36,000.

It is commonly supposed that the number has been drastically reduced, because of political independence or by reason of the outbreaks of conflict. There has been a definite decrease in the missionaries from the old missionary societies of Britain, but they represent only a small proportion of the whole. Any decrease has been more than compensated by an increase in those from the conservative-evangelical bodies in North America, though there are grounds for believing that statistics will begin to show a decline, because of events such as political independence in Mozambique and Angola, and political changes in countries like Ethiopia. The decline in seminarians in Europe also suggests that new recruits for the Roman Catholic Church will be reduced of necessity.

The question is not merely of historic interest, although the influence of this phenomenon on the development of modern Africa is apparent throughout the continent. For among Western Christians there is a fundamental difference of policy. Some bodies, as evidenced for example at the International Congress on World Evangelism (1974), seek to send an ever increasing number of missionaries. Older missionary bodies, involved in Africa for almost 200 years, are steadily adopting a policy of reducing the missionary element in the churches of Africa. There is a movement of African missionaries to other countries, and of non-European missionaries to Africa, but both movements are numerically small compared with the traditional pattern.[1]

The present time can be regarded as the end of the colonial period although there are still areas dominated by the aftermath of the conditions which it created, such as Namibia, Swaziland and Rhodesia. It is therefore an appropriate time to assess the missionary factor and consider its place in the future. The churches in Africa, and some governments, are impatient for this to be done. The heritage has good and bad in it and needs to be examined objectively by African church leaders.

The modern missionary movement in Africa, 1774-1974

The Portuguese exploration and settlement on the coasts of Africa from the fifteenth century had included serious attempts at evangelization. Churches were established at the coast settlements and in extensive areas now covered by Zaïre, Angola, East and Central Africa. By the end of the eighteenth century the evangelistic thrust had ceased and little visible remained in the form of worshipping congregations. There were ruins of buildings in many places, but no African church existed. The Christian movement had come to an end and there were now only historic remains.

At that point in history the great, earlier missionary period of the Roman Catholic Church was in the past and the modern missionary societies of Britain and Europe had yet to come into existence. In Britain the Society for Promoting Christian Knowledge (SPCK) was in operation, and the Society for the Propagation of the Gospel (SPG) did some work among settlers and slaves in the West Indies.

The year 1775 may be considered the turning point in the development of the modern missionary movement, especially in relation to Africa. The context of its birth was the struggle in British society regarding the rights of slave owners and of slaves in England. In 1772 Chief Justice Mansfield gave judgement that a slave-owner did not have the right to remove a slave unwillingly from English soil. The slaves in Britain, perhaps 20,000 or more, were not set free by Lord Mansfield's judgement, but the propaganda surrounding the public discussion, and the philanthropic work, were primary factors in the birth of the modern missionary movement. Together with the dynamism and the attitudes created by the Evangelical Revival, an environment was produced conducive to the growth of a missionary commitment.

There were other factors in the remarkable explosion of the missionary concern, apart from a fundamental theological explanation. The voyages and writings of Captain James Cook and Joseph Banks stimulated the imagination of people towards a new world peopled by different races. In 1774 Cook was on his second voyage in the Pacific and on his return became the most popular hero in Britain. In the same year James Bruce returned from his extraordinary journeys in Abyssinia. Interest in a bigger world coincided with a measure of rejection from the West in the Declaration of Independence by the American colonies (1776) and the subsequent War of American Independence. At the same time and in the background, secular thinking in Europe and in N. America was explaining and defending the newly articulated concepts of the Rights of Man.

The agitation surrounding black slavery in England led directly to the plan to create a 'land of freedom in Africa' and establish a Christian settlement at Sierra Leone. The scheme launched in 1787, with black and white settlers and chaplains, was the beginning of the modern missionary involvement with Africa. The chaplains called for missionaries to come and begin evangelization of the indigenous people. Additions to the black settlers from N. America and Nova Scotia brought numerous Christians and many denominations. The sons of some local African chiefs were sent to England for education. The missionary encounter with Africa had begun.

The last decade of the eighteenth century witnessed the creation of the missionary societies in Britain. In 1792 William Carey and his Baptist colleagues left for Serampore; in 1795 London Missionary Society workers left for the Pacific and Sierra Leone; the first Church Missionary Society missionaries reached Sierra Leone in 1804. At its inauguration the CMS had recorded 'there seems to be still wanting in the Established Church a society for sending missionaries to the continent of Africa, or other parts of the heathen world'. Methodist overseas work from Britain had begun at an earlier date under the leadership of Dr Coke, and under the authority of the Methodist Conference; the London Committee was formed in 1804. Missionary bodies were formed in Scotland in the same period. A similar pattern developed on the Continent. There was the well-established overseas work of the Moravians; then came the birth of missionary societies at the turn of the century. In the early years of the CMS the majority of missionaries were recruited from the new missionary training centres of Germany and Switzerland.

In the first fifty years of the missionary involvement with Africa, particularly with the West Coast and South Africa, the numbers were small. Roman Catholic participation did not begin again until around 1840. The second half of the nineteenth century was the great period of exploration and of the numerical increase in missionary presence. Statistics are not available. It was not until the World Missionary

Conference at Edinburgh in 1910 that missionary statistics were provided. The missionary atlases for the conference show that in Africa there were 4,534 Protestant missionaries and 6,312 Roman Catholic missionaries. From the two chaplains with the expedition to Sierra Leone in 1787 the total had thus grown to over 10,000 in 1910.One third of the Protestant missionaries were from Britain.

During the whole of the 200 year period until the present time the number of expatriate missionaries in Africa has grown. On the eve of World War II the total had increased to 22,000. Statistics provided by missionary bodies in Europe and North America give the figure of 36,000 for 1970.

The present
While it is true that population figures have changed so drastically in the two hundred year period, so that comparison of numbers from one generation to another is not as straightforward as it might appear, and moreover the categories of expatriate workers in Africa have changed so much that 'missionaries' is a very uncertain term, nevertheless the aggregate figure is of importance as signifying the 'overseas personnel' element in the life of the church.

The presence of foreign missionaries in the African churches is a lively and contemporary issue. Similarly the degree to which missionaries should be sent overseas is a highly relevant question in Western churches, not simply as a matter of policy but as expressing different understandings of the fundamental Christian calling to world mission. What is the nature of the Christian's response to the world now?

In Africa there is a deep questioning about the appropriateness of continuation into the future of the old pattern of numerous missionaries. This is expressed, for example, in the manner in which the moratorium concept has arisen from African leaders and has been defended by the All Africa Conference of Churches. Young African writers generally assume that the old pattern is disappearing and some accentuate the mistakes and failures of the missionary past. African politicans, professionals and academics generally would welcome a reduction in the missionary presence; it is probable that most large church assemblies of Africans would react similarly. The practical difficulties for church executives are related to concerns for filling vacancies, retaining qualified local personnel and maintaining a skilled and experienced team. These are among the main reasons why the process of reduction does not proceed. The churches are growing and developing more sophisticated needs; often the personnel requirements can more easily be met and financed from overseas.

The group of churches included in the rather ambiguous category of 'independent churches' has grown in all parts of Africa, particularly in Southern Africa. They form the third great sector of the Christian church in Africa and are growing at least as rapidly as the other two. None has been dependent on overseas personnel and few, if any, give evidence of a strong desire to have missionaries.

The withdrawal of missionaries is at times being spoken of as a witness for righteousness, or as a significant step towards a greater commitment by the African church to mission. For example, the withdrawal of the White Fathers from Mozambique was seen in the former perspective and the moratorium idea is defended from the latter point of view. The missionary situation is, however, complex and full of dilemmas. For example, the old pattern has produced so many senior personnel that it would be extremely difficult to move them to other types of work. Some churches are dependent on outside resources, and they are to a degree conditional on acceptance of missionaries. It may be noted that there are an increasing number of areas in Africa where local political crises create an emergency situation in which, at some point, the decision is made to exclude or restrict foreign missionaries; the southern Sudan, Ethiopia, Eastern Nigeria and Mozambique are examples. On the whole, post-colonial Africa has been remarkably tolerant of the Western missionary, particularly in the light of the entanglement of the Christian movement with the colonial powers. It may not be too much to claim that it is the African recognition of the intrinsic quality of Christian life and work which has been responsible for this phenomenon.

The sending agencies in Europe and North America represent several points of view. On the one hand the Roman Catholic and conservative evangelical bodies generally maintain the 1910 position of sending a large number of missionaries and base policies on the assumption that similar, if not larger, numbers will be required in the future. In some bodies the measure of achievement is the actual number of missionaries. The growth numerically in missionaries from conservative evangelical bodies in N. America has been remarkable (See appendix on p. 25.)

On the other hand, the older missionary agencies in the West have seen a steady decline in numbers, partly due to policy decisions and partly due to a change in the sense of evangelistic commitment by the established churches to world mission. There is a different emphasis in the concept of mission, and a new emphasis on the integrity of the churches in younger countries. At one time there was unquestioned belief in the appropriateness of expatriates pioneering and leading every aspect of Christian witness in the Third World. This is no longer so and most of the long-established missionary agencies would now be sensitive to the adverse effect which this might have on the maturity of the local church.

Nevertheless, the older missionary bodies all act on the assumption that they have a continuing role which includes the sending of people. There is some perplexity as to how a church can fulfil its essential obligation to world mission without sending people. An inherent difficulty is that this understanding comes dangerously near to the attitude that sending people overseas is of primary importance for the well-being of the sending agency itself, and not in respect of whatever they may accomplish.

Consideration of the question of the missionary in Africa at this point in history brings into focus the important and far-reaching difference between a traditional understanding of mission as evangelism and the founding of churches, and an understanding which has grown in recent decades that mission has much wider connotations related to all aspects of human life. The fact of the establishment of autonomous churches in most countries, with the primary responsibility there for witness and service, and their association with the ecumenical movement, has produced a new emphasis in mission. The former understanding was tied more closely to geographical thinking and the latter to a greater awareness of the relevance of the Gospel to the challenges and complexity of man in his total environment. Christian mission in the world is seen as proclamation of saving truths, but equally as truth which can only be shared with the world by coming to grips with the actual problems which the world faces. The issue could be expressed differently as that between the assertion that God is Love and the conviction that this profound insight can most appropriately be responded to by engaging with man in his total earthly predicament.

If from this point in history we review the last two centuries of church growth in Africa we are faced with this extraordinary missionary phenomenon. It is criticized very severely within and without the church. It was full of foibles and weaknesses, and yet produced a remarkable result, which is not only a testimony to something profoundly true at its heart, but indicates that the African mind has seen deeply into the phenomenon. The parallel African experience of European colonialism damaged the African soul, almost as much as the slavery which had preceded it. The religious phenomenon of the grafting of the Christian church on to Africa has had a very creative influence on the development of society in the whole continent.

The future of expatriate missionary service in Africa
As has already been indicated there are difficult questions arising from the past and which project themselves into the present. Large policy issues are posed for both the churches in Africa and the missionary

agencies in Europe. Can one have any confidence that they are being studied?

Tragic experiences are sometimes caused by a failure to recognize early enough the inherent tensions in a situation and to take appropriate action. The fissiparous nature of the Christian movement often makes action difficult. An experience like the missionary *débacle* in China can eventuate where questions have remained unanswered for a long period. In the West there are visible two major rifts already referred to in this area of concern, apart from theological and ecclesiastical divisions. The first is the policy of the older established churches and societies to limit the overseas missionary element, and secondly the immense pressure of new and conservative evangelical groups, with many older bodies too, to work for an ever-expanding Western missionary presence in the world. The second rift is more fundamental. This century has seen a far-reaching development from the concept of mission associated with the old International Missionary Council, as expressed for example at Edinburgh in 1910, resounding with all the chords of the nineteenth century. The new dimension of Christian response is more clearly expressed in ecumenical concerns, calling Christians to respond to the wholeness of human experience with the fullness of Christian salvation. The old missionary style fits into the former but not the latter.

We may suspect that in Africa the pace of political change, and the frequency of upheavals in young nations, is quickening rather than slowing down. Changes which are difficult in normal times become possible in times of emergency. The missionary factor in, for example, Mozambique and in Rhodesia, may be dramatically altered, not by ecclesiastical planning, but by mundane events. Within a space of two years Mozambique has lost most of the Roman Catholic and Protestant missionary element. It would be difficult to alter the missionary factor in Rhodesia, yet political developments may precipitate a very different situation. The accumulative effect of these events in Africa is going to alter the missionary map for non-theological reasons.

Discussion of missionary policy often appears to be taking place in isolation from the real situation of the younger churches. Their well-being as a primary consideration seems to get pushed into a subsidiary position. There is a constant danger that the institution of the Western missionary agency gains its own momentum, instinctively seeks to perpetuate itself, and, in part, serve its own interests and protect itself with a theological rationale.

Changes in the modern world and in the ecclesiastical scene are so profound and far-reaching that we must face the question of whether or not an entirely different Christian response is needed to the world than the old Western missionary response. Western Christians need to wrestle with what this new beginning is, and what are its implications. This exercise is now in its elementary stages. For the majority of Christians the fact of a major shift has not yet been realized. The difficulties and resistance to change is shown, for example, in the limited success of the major WCC initiative under the heading of Ecumenical Sharing of Personnel.

It is not easy to see the way in which change will be satisfactorily accomplished, how the objectives will be defined and how agreement will be reached on procedure. The old International Missionary Council has disappeared, the national missionary councils are losing support or are themselves disappearing and the Commission for World Mission and Evangelism is not in a position to provide the leadership. Those individuals who are alert to the serious problem which missionary service now presents to the church in Africa can perhaps be of greatest assistance in securing consultation both nationally and regionally. Consultation is only relevant if it includes all the main participants. The problems are formidable and are only likely to be met by well-structured consultations related to limited geographical areas, rather than global assemblies. The pattern of diversity in Africa and in the Western World is so complex that a totally unified and co-ordinated response to the situation is impossible of attainment.

In conclusion, reference may be made to three particular occasions, each with special relevance to this subject. At the Bangkok Assembly of the Commission on World Mission and Evangelism in 1973, with the Conference on Salvation Today, some attention was given to the catholicity of the local church. The Western missionary is no longer seen as the main symbol.

'A Christian from outside—who may be a new immigrant, a foreign student, a layman or woman from abroad temporarily employed in the country, or a missionary from another church—also represents the catholicity of the church and the wholeness of the world and prevents the local church from becoming self-sufficient and inward looking . . . Churches that have a long tradition of "sending" their missionaries elsewhere need to take deliberate steps to accustom their members to the idea that without the presence and witness of the foreigner they themselves are deficient. For these reasons we urge all member churches of the WCC to explore more urgently the various ways in which the sending and receiving of missionaries may become completely mutual and international, a universal enrichment of the church for its mission in all six continents. We particularly commend the principle of an ecumenical sharing of personnel in whatever form may prove to be most effective in any situation.'[2]

[2] *Report of the Bangkok Assembly*, p. 101.

In an important section,[3] the report outlined criteria for sending of Western missionaries to areas such as southern Africa, but this careful analysis has received little serious attention in the West.

Secondly, the Fifth Assembly of the WCC at Nairobi in November 1975 gave a great deal of time to the nature of Christian mission in the modern world. It was understood as something far wider and deeper than the sending of individuals from one country to another. There was serious attention given to the significance of dialogue with other faiths and ideologies. The whole history of the ecumenical movement was seen in terms of witness to Jesus Christ in the world. Bishop Mortimer Arias from Bolivia, for example, claimed that the whole WCC programme has a 'missionary and evangelistic potential'. The record of the Assembly as a whole points the way towards a greater understanding of the implications of involvement in Christian world mission.[4]

Finally, an occasion in 1976 provides a significant and fitting climax to this consideration of 200 years of Christian witness in Africa. It offers the vision of African churches with a deep sense of their heritage and a profound responsibility for Mission in the Continent. In February the General Committee of the All Africa Conference of Churches met at Alexandria and adopted an historic document, 'The Alexandria Confession'. The missionary period is at an end. The churches recognize the work of Christ in their midst and express concern for the total liberation of men and women from every form of oppression and exploitation and for peace in Africa. Member churches pledged themselves to search for authentic responses to Christ as Lord over the whole of their lives.

Missionary statistics for the world, including Africa
(i) The continuous growth of Protestant missionaries is shown in this table from *Map of the World's Religions*, Stuttgart, 4th Edition, 1966.

1903	—	15,288
1911	—	21,307
1925	—	29.186
1952	—	35,533
1958	—	38,606
1963	—	42,952

[3] ibid, pp. 91-2.
[4] Kenneth Slack, *Nairobi Narrative*, SCM, London, 1976.

(ii) Protestant missionaries from the USA to the world. (Taken from *Christianity Today*, November 1971)

	1958	1971
American Baptist Convention	407	290
United Presbyterian Church	1,293	810
Presbyterian Church US	504	391
United Methodist Church (incl. EUB)	1,453	1,175
Episcopal Church	395	138
United Church of Christ	496	356
	4,548	3,160
Southern Baptist Convention	1,186	2,494
Evangelical Foreign Missions Assoc.	4,688	7,479
Inter-denominational Foreign Mission Assoc.	5,902	6,164

In the USA there is thus a steady decline in the number of overseas missionaries from the long established, major societies. There is a substantial increase from the smaller societies and from those with a conservative, evangelical theology.

'It is important to remember that the USA deploys more than 60% of the Christian missionary force around the world, and the resources which go with it, while Western Europe and Australasia account for the remaining 40% or so of missionary and Christian service involvement.'

Dr Philip A. Potter
Report to CWME 1973. Bangkok Assembly.

The ministry of the Catholic Church in Africa, 1960-1975[1]

ADRIAN HASTINGS

Any realistic study of the structures of a society must first take note of the size and spread of that society. The Roman Catholic Church is spread throughout almost the whole of Africa, but it is extremely thin in the northern Moslem countries, where it generally consists of a vicariate or two serving small groups of expatriates with expatriate clergy. Elsewhere it is almost everywhere a fairly extensive body including from 5 to over 50% of the population within its nominal membership. Statistics of church membership may, of course, refer to a number of things—(a) active members, (b) people whom ministers of that particular church 'have on their books', (c) people who, if asked in a census, would claim to belong to that church. As regards (c) David Barrett has estimated for mid-1972 an all-Africa Catholic population, including Madagascar, of 59.6 million—16.27% of the continent's population. How reliable this is I do not know, but it does not appear improbable. The Church herself, however, would certainly not claim so many. In 1966 I calculated the total Catholic population of Africa on Church estimates at 27-28 million, plus catechumens, that means just over 30 million if the latter be included. The rate of numerical Church growth in these years has been very rapid in most places, though it may well now be falling. I would suggest that 20 million in 1960 and something over 40 million in 1975 is a sound estimate according to (b) above—that is to say, the baptized plus active catechumens. 40 million was the figure given by Bishop Sangu of Mbeya in his report to the Roman Synod of 1974. It was in fact the 1973 figure; intended to cover the whole continent, including Madagascar and

---

[1] This study is based on (1) a range of official and semi-official church publications—the annual *Status Seminariorum Indigenarum* published by the Society of St Peter in Rome, various local church directories, *African Ecclesiastical Review,* the Amecea Documentation Service, the Newsletter of the Pastoral Institute of Bodija, etc; (2) David Barrett, *Frontier Situations for Evangelisation in Africa,* 1972; A. Shorter and E. Kataza, eds., *Missionaries to Yourselves, African Catechists Today,* 1972; A. Shorter, 'Marriage, Celibacy and Ministry in Africa', *Clergy Review,* July 1975, pp. 444-52; (3) a number of earlier studies by me, in particular: *Church and Mission in Modern Africa,* 1967, pp. 188-237; *Mission and Ministry,* 1971, pp. 108-43; *Church and Ministry* (Gaba, 1972), pp. 27-52; *Christian Marriage in Africa,* 1973, pp. 103-5, 172-5; 'Celibacy in Africa', *CONCILIUM:* October 1972, pp. 151-6.

other islands, it was probably on the low side. But we will work from it. If one excludes Africa north of the Sahara (Mauritania to Egypt), Ethiopia, Madagascar and the other islands, one is left with 36,750,000 for Africa from the Cape to the Sahara. To this can be added ten million or more 'adherents', 'census Catholics', that is to say unbaptized and unclaimed people who consider themselves in some way Catholic Christians because of family connections, some attendance at a Catholic school, a discontinued catechumenate.

The problems involved in obtaining reliable figures for the number of priests are almost as great as those for the church population as a whole. Are missionaries on long leave included or excluded? Is the bishop included in the number of diocesan priests? White secular priests from abroad easily get included in the figure for black diocesan priests—this has completely bedevilled the figures for Mozambique and Angola where white diocesan priests from Portugal have been placed in the category of native diocesans. In all, there appears to have been rather over 12,000 Catholic priests in all Africa (excluding north of the Sahara) in 1960. By 1966 this figure had risen to something like 15,000. Since then it has not risen significantly, indeed it may have fallen a little. For 1973 Bishop Sangu gives 17,180 as his total figure. For Africa from the Cape to the Sahara he gives 14,618. Of these some 3700 are black, the other 10,900 white.

African priests were a little over 2000 in 1960; their number has risen fairly steadily throughout the period, while the number of missionaries continued to rise fast in the early 1960s, just as it had risen throughout the 1950s. 1967 was probably the peak year; since then there has been some over-all decline. The following table offers a rather approximate picture:

Date	Catholics	African priests	White priests	Total	Priest/ people ratio
1960	20,000,000	2100	10,000	12,000	1:1652
1966	27,000,000	2,800	12,200	15,000	1:1800
1973	36,750,000	3700	10,900	14,600	1:2509

For the number of dioceses, vicariates and prefectures we can be more exact. The *Status Seminariorum Indigenarum* for 1959-60 lists 184 dioceses and archdioceses and 41 vicariates and prefectures for those parts of Africa served by the Congregation of *Propaganda Fide* (which is everything except Portuguese Africa, Algeria, Tunisia, and the Oriental rites), while the *Status* of 1969-70 lists 273 dioceses and archdioceses and 37 vicariates and prefectures: an increase of 85 in all in ten years. There are nine dioceses in Mozambique and eight in Angola; of these 17 seven were set up after 1960. This means that from the Cape to the Sahara there are now at least 327 separate Catholic ecclesiastical units, 92 of which were established since 1960.

Each has its own bishop or prefect apostolic, its own territorial organization, and is supported on an individual basis to a greater or lesser extent with personnel and funds from abroad. Zaïre alone now has 48 dioceses, Nigeria 25, Tanzania 24. On an average each diocese will have some 112,000 known Catholics, 44 priests (of whom some 12 may be African), 100 sisters (half of them African), twenty parishes or mission stations, several hundred catechists. In fact, of course, dioceses vary in scale from Kampala archdiocese with over 600,000 Catholics, 200 priests (half of them African) and 550 sisters (three-quarters African) to Arusha with some 10,000 Catholics, twenty priests and a dozen sisters, of whom only two sisters are African.

The total number of nuns is about twice that of priests. The number of brothers, on the other hand, is small—probably about one quarter the number of priests. While in many countries the majority of nuns is now African, the brothers are predominantly expatriate. Their number has declined rather fast over the last decade.

These general figures provide a sense of dimension for an analysis of the real pattern of ministry as it works out in practice and for some understanding of the very considerable changes which have taken place in the last fifteen years. These changes have come as a response to, first, the altered political condition of Africa and the increasingly uncertain status and future of the expatriate; second, the immense increase in the number of church members, no longer balanced by a comparable increase in the number of priests; third, new church directives and theological and pastoral priorities, deriving in particular from the second Vatican Council and the upsurge of thinking that went with it.

In 1960 almost all the bishops were white and nearly all posts of influence above that of parish priest were also held by white people (vicar general, rector of seminary, headmaster of diocesan secondary school, university chaplain. . .) The dioceses were grouped to a very considerable extent according to the missionary society to which they had been farmed and the instructions from the superior generals of those societies were often the most decisive directives that existed. Within the diocese almost no parish councils and certainly no elected diocesan councils existed. Very few sisters were engaged in general pastoral or social work, the vast majority being employed full time in school or hospital—apart from the considerable number engaged in domestic work, often serving the fathers. In almost every parish there were a dozen, or even dozens of, catechists, but few had received much training for almost nowhere was there a catechist training centre in operation.

Those of the past had almost all been closed or transformed into teacher training colleges. There were just four such training centres active in the five countries of eastern Africa in 1960, and two of those had been recently opened. Nonetheless the local ministry of the church had continued to hinge upon the catechist, supported by some of the teachers in the church's primary schools and by various lay organizations such as the Legion of Mary, the YCS, and the Xaverians, whose strength varied greatly from area to area.

In these fifteen years this picture has changed on almost every point. The expatriate missionary indeed doggedly survives. He has been expelled from the southern Sudan, Guinea and the east central state of Nigeria, but elsewhere he is present almost as in the past. Indeed one of the most striking aspects of these years is his survival. Overall numbers continued to increase until at least 1966 since when they have decreased a little, but the number of foreign priests, sisters and brothers remains massive. If the number has fallen in Nigeria, Zaïre, Tanzania and Burundi, it has actually risen in Kenya and Zambia. To some extent this is due to redeployment from elsewhere. Thus, of the 281 Irish Holy Ghost Fathers who could not return to eastern Nigeria after the civil war, 10 have since gone to Malawi, 12 to Zambia, 14 to Kenya, 15 to Sierra Leone and 12 to Ghana, but the large majority have not and most probably will not return to Africa. If the Verona Fathers had not been expelled from the southern Sudan they could not have increased their strength in Uganda during the later 1960s as they have done. But these factors are essentially temporary. With the sharp decline in recruitment for missionary societies in nearly all countries since the middle 1960s and the withdrawal of a significant proportion of younger members, overall missionary numbers are bound to decrease steadily and increasingly in the future. Nevertheless one important characteristic of these fifteen years has been the tenacity of Catholic missionaries in staying on in large numbers unless forcibly excluded. This can be illustrated from the five countries of eastern Africa:

Expatriate Missionary Personnel (other than lay)

	Kenya	Uganda	Tanzania	Zambia	Malawi	Total
I. Expatriate priests, 1961						
	415	447	900	289	206	2257
II. Expatriate missionaries, 1967						
Priests	554	531	876	352	226	2529
Brothers	144	170	324	148	91	877
Sisters	738	447	829	425	228	2667
Total	1426	1148	2029	925	545	6073

III. Expatriate missionaries, 1973

Priests	646	508	794	381	242	2571
Brothers	111	116	254	162	100	743
Sisters	785	340	765	647	241	2598
Total	1542	964	1813	1010	583	5912

IV. Increases and Decreases, 1967-73

Priests	+102	-23	-82	+29	+16	+42
Brothers	-33	-54	-70	+14	+9	-134
Sisters	+47	-107	-64	+42	+13	-69
Total	+116	-184	-216	+85	+38	-161

V. Increases and Decreases in expatriate priests, 1961-73

+231	+61	-106	+92	+36	+314

Kenya, then, increased its total foreign ordained personnel by 55% on 1961 figures — a remarkable achievement for the decade of independence; Tanzania's, on the other hand, decreased by nearly 12%. On the other hand it has to be observed that the 1961 figures show that at that time Tanzania had been rather over favoured by Catholic missionaries. Even after twelve years of change Tanzania still had over a hundred more foreign priests than Kenya. In general while the total for sisters and—still more— brothers has fallen significantly, the stability of the foreign priests is the most striking impression: the 1973 figure is considerably higher than that for 1961 and slightly higher than that for 1967.

Up to the late 1960s missionary priests also continued to fill almost their old role in most dioceses, holding nearly all key leadership posts. It is only after 1968 that this changed. Once it did, the position was reversed fast and drastically. They are now excluded in the majority of dioceses from almost all positions of authority above that of parish priest. The small number of African priests in most dioceses means, however, that the leadership in most parishes remains in expatriate hands.

The number of African clergy has slowly but steadily grown throughout these years: from about 2100 in 1960 to, perhaps, 3700 in 1975. The number of major seminarians in the thirty to forty 'major seminaries' of Propaganda Fide's Africa was 1661 in 1960. Of these almost 400 were in Zaïre. The total changed little until the late 1960s when it started to rise, cautiously at first but then rapidly. It passed the 2000 mark in 1967; it reached 2775 by 1971 and 3650 in 1974. The largest rise has been in Nigeria which reached 500 in 1971 while that same year Tanzania went over 400. By 1974 Nigeria had over 800 and Tanzania over 500. Major seminary courses are now nearly all of six years length. In the past probably 50% of the students left the seminary without being ordained; with the increase in seminary numbers, the proportion of those leaving without ordination has also increased, but it varies considerably. In Benin (Dahomey) few students are admitted but nearly all of them reach ordination. In Kenya quite the contrary is the case.

The number of ordinations to the diocesan priesthood over fourteen years has been as follows in eleven selected countries. The total refers to the whole of *Propaganda Fide's* Africa.

	Cameroun	Benin (Dahomey)	Ghana	Ivory Coast	Kenya	Malawi	Nigeria	Tanzania	Uganda	Zaïre	Zambia	Total
1959	11	1	—	5	2	—	4	18	9	34	—	110
1960	10	2	3	1	3	1	6	12	13	27	1	111
1961	5	—	2	5	7	4	12	15	8	14	1	119
1962	12	6	6	1	7	5	13	10	7	27	1	157
1963	1	1	6	7	6	3	22	17	11	27	2	178
1964	—	2	1	5	5	1	18	13	10	37	1	158
1965	—	1	11	2	7	7	22	27	15	19	6	160
1966	7	4	5	3	4	—	33	29	10	26	5	181
1967	2	3	6	3	1	3	21	8	14	12	1	102
1968	1	7	3	2	10	—	25	24	11	16	3	135
1969	10	8	3	1	—	2	19	19	15	21	1	146
1970	14	—	2	4	—	3	22	37	18	13	—	155
1971	5	5	10	5	9	5	23	31	13	15	1	176
1972	—	1	10	5	7	3	54	26	9	3	4	168
Total	78	41	68	49	68	37	294	286	163	291	27	2056-

It is striking that there was no rise in the total number of ordinations between 1962 and 1972. The massive growth in numbers in Nigeria (mostly the dioceses of the East Central State) was for long offset by decline elsewhere, notably in Zaïre. In some countries, such as Kenya and Uganda, while the number of major seminarians has greatly increased, the number of ordinations has not. Elsewhere, Zambia most notably, neither seminarians nor ordinations have increased. Tanzania is the country which has done most consistently well. While it already had many local priests in 1960, it has steadily advanced the number of its annual ordinations. Nigeria, on the other hand, had rather few African priests at the start of our period; today its record (but that means mostly the East Central State) constitutes the one great success story of these years in this field. Its ordinations are now proceeding at the rate of fifty or more a year. It is striking that for 1972 Nigeria and Tanzania by themselves account for almost half the total of Africa's ordinations.

While the total number in these fourteen years was over 2000, that does not mean an increase of 2000 in the number of priests. It has to be set against deaths and departures from the priesthood; these together now seem to constitute about one quarter of the number of those ordained: so 2000 ordinations bring a rise of some 1500 priests.

Since 1972 there has been a marked rise in ordinations and in 1974 there was a total of 237, of which 84 were in Nigeria. Of these 53 were for the four Igbo dioceses of Enugu, Onitsha, Owerri and Umuahia. It is probable that future years will show at least as high figures, though it has at once to be noted that this increase hardly affects the large majority of African dioceses.

While the number of African priests has grown steadily but not stupendously, the kind of work they do has changed far more decisively. There has been a complete reversal of roles vis-à-vis foreign missionaries. In 1960 there was still only one African bishop in Uganda— Joseph Kiwanuka of Masaka, appointed as far back as 1939. Only in 1962 was he joined by a second, Adrian Ddungu, his successor in Masaka when he himself was moved to the archbishopric. In 1960 there was only one African bishop in Kenya, Maurice Otunga; an auxiliary bishop since 1957, only that year did he receive a diocese of his own, Kisii, newly established. In Nyasaland (Malawi) there was one—Chitsulo of Dedza; in Northern Rhodesia (now Zambia) there was none. In Tanganyika by the end of 1960 there were 6 (4 diocesans and 2 auxiliaries) but 3 of them had been appointed that year; there were at the same time 14 white bishops. In Zaïre, the end of the following year, December 1961, there were still 32 white diocesan bishops and 4 Africans, with an additional 4 black auxiliary bishops.

This position altered remarkably little for another six years. In Togo a black majority (3–1) was established in 1965, but this was quite exceptional. The Dutchman Joseph Willigers could still be appointed to the Ugandan see of Jinja (the second town in the country) in the second half of 1967, though the appointment did indeed produce something of a shock both in ecclesiastical and political circles. With it there were 7 white bishops in Uganda as compared with 5 black, one of whom was an auxiliary. That was the position at the start of 1968; in Kenya at the same time it was still 9–2, in Zambia 8–1; in Tanzania there were still 14 white bishops as there had been in 1960 while the Africans had only increased from 6 to 9.

Very soon after this, however, the position changed decisively. White bishops were finding their role increasingly difficult and—perhaps also for reasons of wider ecclesiastical policy—Rome switched to a policy of rather rapid Africanization of the episcopate. A spate of resignations and African appointments followed. A black majority was established in Zaïre (24-22) before the end of 1968, in Tanzania and Uganda in 1969, in Cameroun in 1970, in Zambia in 1971, and in Nigeria in 1972. In Kenya, however, (if Prefects Apostolic be included) it was still not attained at the beginning of 1975, while Malawi remains 3-3. Whenever it is attained, it really constitutes the crucial change. Only when local bishops form a majority in the country and at the meetings of the episcopal conference is it really clear in theory and practice that theirs is the decisive responsibility. If at the beginning of 1968 Tanzania had 14 white bishops and 9 black, at the beginning of 1975 it had 5 white and 19 black.

In the same years, 1968 and after, there was a steady changeover in regard to most other senior posts. African priests replaced foreigners as rectors of nearly all the seminaries, on the staff of the national secretariats and elsewhere. This process has naturally gone much further to date in Tanzania where there are over 500 local priests than in Zambia where there are not more than 60. But in Tanzania too a few white enclaves remain. It is probably of some importance for the smooth achievement of the take-over that the process should be staggered and that some white missionaries and a handful of white bishops should remain well after the decisive change has taken place. In 1975 Tanzania, the most Africanized of Catholic churches to date, still has four white bishops (all in less developed dioceses) out of 24.

In some countries the number of African sisters has increased far more considerably than that of priests. Uganda in 1969 claimed 279 local priests but 1322 local sisters; Kenya 68 priests, 515 sisters. The same does not appear to be the case in West Africa. In a number of cases in the east there are now far more local than expatriate sisters, which is never the case for priests. The training and role of these sisters vary greatly. In some congregations all have had a secondary or equivalent education and are expected to do skilled jobs, in others a large proportion have had only primary education and in each house of sisters more than half will devote themselves to house-keeping, gardening and cleaning the parish church. In some places the sisters have been expected to concentrate their attention upon feeding and caring for the priests; this seems to be particularly the case in South Africa. In general since 1960 there has been both a very considerable upgrading in the training of sisters and an enlargement of their roles. They are entering far more widely than previously into pastoral and catechetical work. There are three parishes in the west Ugandan dioceses of Hoima and Fort Portal where, there being no resident priest, the local congregation of Banyatereza do almost all the work the latter would do—conducting Sunday services, preaching, distributing holy communion, parish visiting.

In 1960, above the diocese in the ecclesiastical structure the most effectively important bodies were still what they had been for many years: the missionary societies. There was very little national co-ordination in the church except in education and medicine where relations with government and dependence upon government subsidies necessitated it. It is striking too how the training of the diocesan clergy was carried out almost entirely on missionary society lines. Thus in Uganda there were three major seminaries, one run by the White Fathers, one by Mill Hill, one by the Verona Fathers, each for its own area. The Mill Hill seminary also catered for Kenyans coming from the Mill Hill area there; Katigondo, the White Father one, also catered for some Tanganyikans from neighbouring White Father areas over the border. African diocesan priests were thus divided in their training and even in their dress. For missionaries it was still almost unthinkable for different societies to share in a common work and it was rare for them even to meet socially. In 1960 a White Father who had worked for years in Uganda wished to visit Kenya to see what it was like before returning to Europe to take up another appointment; he was forbidden to do so by his Regional Superior on the ground that it was a pointless expense seeing that there were no White Fathers at work in Kenya. The dioceses served by a single society all across Africa sometimes appeared as a great empire linked to one another but almost oblivious of what was going on elsewhere. Each received its marching orders from a generalate in Europe, and even the bishop had often to be careful not to get out of step—or he would be sent no reinforcements for a year or two.

Most of this has now gone. The power of the generalates is vastly reduced, and they themselves co-operate far more closely. Today you can find men of different societies living together within a single institution and still more often within a single diocese. With the appointment of African bishops the differences of approach between the dioceses has decreased and the African clergy themselves have formed or are forming national associations which express their common identity. As the power of the generalates is reduced, so has that of the national episcopal conferences increased and so has the size of the national secretariats. Beyond these national organizations there are international ones, such as AMECEA, the association of the episcopal conferences of Kenya, Malawi, Tanzania and Zambia with its office in Nairobi. At the continental level the structures of the church have been crowned by SECAM, the association of all the episcopal conferences of Africa set up at a meeting of the archbishops in Kampala in July 1969 to coincide with the Pope's visit. Cardinal Zoungrana of Ouagadougou is its president and it has its own secretariat. While its achievements up to now have not been great, though its costs must have been considerable, its existence is symbolic in expressing the increasing sense of unity of the Catholic Church in different parts of black Africa both in relation to its own internal problems and towards the rest of the world. The fruit of this greater sense of unity has certainly appeared in the co-ordination of African participation in the various episcopal synods in Rome.

Such structures sound impressive but they are, finally, of limited significance, though there is a danger that church leadership pay too much attention to almost delusory macro-structures, thus avoiding the hard challenge of workable micro-structures. In analysis, at least, we must not succumb to this temptation and will therefore return, first to the diocese, then to the parish and the sub-parish.

Among the three hundred or so dioceses of black Africa we may distinguish, very roughly, two different types. The first kind is those areas where a fairly extensive African ministry now exists from top to bottom. They comprise the Igbo dioceses of the East Central State of Nigeria (Onitsha, Owerri, Enugu and Umuahia), the Ganda dioceses of Uganda (Kampala and Masaka), four or five Tanzanian dioceses (Bukoba, Moshi, Songea, Sumbawanga), a couple of Sotho dioceses (Maseru and Leribe), and some others, notably in Benin (Dahomey), Rwanda and Zaïre. A number more have moved fairly far in the same direction, even though they may still have a majority of foreign priests—Mbarara in Uganda, Tabora and Morogoro in Tanzania, Dedza in Malawi are a few examples. In all no more than fifty out of the 300 dioceses and prefectures of black Africa should be put in this group. They have on average at least 40 African priests each, which is more than half the total number. These fifty dioceses are mostly by no means self-supporting either as to personnel or as to finance, on the contrary, but they can claim a fairly strongly rooted local ministry and church leadership. If all foreign missionaries left, they could survive (some with very considerable difficulty) while sticking basically to the accepted Catholic system of the priesthood. They are mostly old evangelized areas, often ones of fairly high population density, and many of them have in fact already very bad priest/population ratios.

The second group comprises the other 250 dioceses. Some are small in the number of their church members—new areas of Catholic evangelization, perhaps only begun during the last twenty-five years; some of these have still no local priests at all, and perhaps no more than twenty or thirty missionaries. But others are large and important dioceses, even old areas of evangelization in which a numerous African clergy has never developed. They include all the Kenyan dioceses; those of western Nigeria; most of those in Zambia. Many in every country. In some of these the number of ordinations is progressing and may have built up well in another ten years. In others there is still little sign of this happening. On an average these 250 dioceses have just seven African priests each.

One can consider a rough comparison between the positions of Archbishop Nsubuga of Kampala and Archbishop Milingo of Lusaka. The former has some 600,000 Catholics in his diocese—probably the biggest diocesan figure in Africa—and a very bad priest-people ratio. Nevertheless, he has 100 priests and over 400 sisters of his own nation and language behind him; he has some 60 local brothers, many hundreds of catechists and a number of well established lay organizations of one kind and another. His clergy have a notable *esprit de corps*; he was himself for years a parish priest and then vicar general of the diocese before election. He knows his people and has a very considerable instrument at his disposal for their mobilization. Archbishop Milingo has almost none of this in Lusaka. A much younger man brought in from a different diocese, he has now just ten African priests and fewer sisters or brothers. Even his catechists are few. Surrounded by a group of expatriate Jesuits who cannot become too involved in any critical issue, his ability to mobilize people will depend almost wholly upon his personal charisma and very little upon any structure of ministry below him.

The figures for African and missionary priests from four Tanzanian and four Kenyan dioceses illustrate the contrasts. They also show well enough what has been happening over the last few years: how the increase of local clergy seldom compensates numerically for a decrease of missionaries, once the latter really gets under way; how elsewhere missionary figures can rise even in the 1970s.

Diocese	1967			1973			Increase or Decrease
	Africans	Expatriate	Total	Africans	Expatriate	Total	
TANZANIA							
Bukoba	59	33	92	79	16	95	+3
Mbeya	9	44	53	10	38	48	-5
Mwanza	31	62	93	33	52	85	-8
Morogoro	25	63	88	36	37	73	-15
KENYA							
Eldoret	2	46	48	2	49	51	+3
Kisii	14	24	38	12	39	51	+13

| Mombasa | 4 | 46 | 50 | 6 | 46 | 52 | +2 |
| Nyeri | 21 | 61 | 82 | 26 | 77 | 103 | +21 |

The Catholic Church in Africa is predominantly a rural church, and it is the ministry at village level, where the great majority of its members actually live, which is finally important. Most dioceses consist of fifteen to twenty missions or parishes. Each of these consists of (a) a central church and priests' house with its schools, possibly a sisters' convent and dispensary, and a group of people living in its immediate neighbourhood, maybe even on mission owned land, (b) scores of villages beyond in a radius of up to 100 miles, among which there will be fifteen to a hundred 'out-stations', 'sub-parishes', or 'basic Christian communities'. In some dioceses each of these sub-parishes will have its own little church and most will have a part-time catechist too; in others there may be no church but a small school building. Here the local Christian community, from a dozen to many hundreds of people, will gather for worship and instruction. A priest from the central mission may hope to visit it from time to time: once a month for important and accessible places; perhaps only once a year for many of the smaller and more inaccessible ones, if even that. He comes as an outsider to hear confessions, give some solemn instruction, discuss such human problems as are brought to him particularly in regard to marriage, arrange for people to go to the central mission for baptismal instruction, confer with the catechist.

The real life of this local church is a very different thing from the theoretical and official model of the mission-parish as directed by its priest, white or black, and centred upon the daily celebration of Mass, the traditional focal point of Catholic observance. As Bishop Kalilombe has written:

'Our system in the diocese as in practically all the sister dioceses around us, represents a sort of anomaly. We think and work in terms of "parish" and yet nobody is duped. In actual fact, as far as real Christian life is concerned, it is on the sub-parish level that the real thing is going on. Grouped under the rather broad umbrella of parish are several (in most cases quite numerous) basic Churches. These are led really by the resident Church elders, laymen, while the priests do their best to make the presence of the ordained minister felt at longer or shorter intervals. Such a situation is one that cannot be avoided in the state of affairs actually obtaining. What is happening is actually this that several local Churches, which are entitled to their own resident ordained minister, share a single minister between them, which makes the presence of this minister in each local Church rather infrequent and transitory'.[2]

[2] P. A. Kalilombe, *Christ's Church in Lilongwe Today and Tomorrow,* Likuni Press, Lilongwe, 1973.

Here at the grass-roots the pattern of church ministry has in many places changed little enough in the last twelve years. 'Africanization' was not possible or meaningful here for the simple reason that it had already largely taken place before 1960. Only the external priest hurrying in on his motor cycle would still probably be white. But just at that point—the point of intersection between the real thing and the official pattern—the system has been falling apart. The number of church members has doubled, there are more village churches than ever, but the total number of priests in active rural ministry has decreased, and even main mission stations are being closed in many dioceses. New types of work in town and school and administration have sucked up the young African priests. The one place a young priest is unlikely to stay for long in the great majority of dioceses is a rural parish. The reason is simple enough. 300 dioceses mean 300 bishops, 300 vicars general, 300 priests to administer the cathedral parish, 600 or more to teach in seminaries, 300 directors of diocesan catechesis, 300 chaplains for secondary schools, a 100 or so for national ecclesiastical administration, another 100 to study, two or three hundred more sick or old. How many are left for regular rural pastoral work?

It is here that the missionaries remain, but they are growing older and fewer. Where there were three fifteen years ago, there will now be two, yet having to cope with twice the number of people. Inevitably the outstations are visited more and more irregularly, personal links diminish, the whole orderly structure of the system crumbles. Two elderly men may be struggling to provide pastoral care for 20,000 nominal Catholics scattered over 60 different inhabited areas.

To assist, and then effectively replace, the dying missionary has been the great theme of these years. The official conservative view is to replace the white seminary trained priest by the black seminary trained priest, full stop. As this has proved in practice impossible, at least outside a handful of dioceses, there has been a series of other initiatives which together constitute the most creative side of the history of the Catholic ministry in these years.

The first major initiative, the characteristic response of the 1960s, was the campaign to reinvigorate the ministry of catechists. Where there were four Catechist Training Colleges in 1960 in eastern Africa, there were twenty-two by 1969. Five new ones were built in 1966 alone. Nearly all these centres offer a two year training course for married men, who must at least have more or less completed primary schooling. At many of these colleges the wives also attend courses of various kinds. By the early 1970s such schools in eastern Africa alone were training on average 394 catechists a year. Nothing perhaps better shows the determination of the Catholic Church in Africa than this vigorous attempt to redevelop an intermediate ministry, more adapted than the seminary priesthood to the conditions of society. Yet it at once creates its own problems. Intended to supplement the ministry of priests, in practice it has tended more to replace it; yet it cannot do just that function which Catholic teaching consistently stresses as the central work of the priest: preside at the Eucharist. But it still needs to be paid. A full time two year course at a Training College can be expected to lead to a full-time, and therefore a paid, ministry. But very few African parishes can afford more than a couple of full-time paid catechists, and few sub-parishes really need a full-time minister—though they do need someone of very real dedication able to give quite a few hours of his time each week.

By about 1970 while the valuable work being done by catechists, particularly the newly trained catechists, was widely appreciated, more and more attempts were surfacing to devise a still more lay and flexible pattern of local ministry. The catechist by himself can become too much of a lone clerical, rather autocratic figure. The balance is found in the development of councils and the multiplication of lay ministries or responsibilities. Not only the parish gets its council but also the sub-parish; indeed the parish council becomes a sort of federal assembly of sub-parish councils, just as a diocesan council (where established) becomes an assembly of the representatives of parish councils. In areas, and they are not few, in which this system has really developed, the Catholic Church has been going quietly but effectively congregationalist beneath its public hierarchical super-structure. In the parish of Mbogora, Burundi, for instance, every bigger out-station is now regarded as a parish of its own and is directed by a ten-member committee: six men and four women. These committees have overall responsibility for pastoral work, for baptismal and marriage instruction, for the admission of catechumens, the mutual-aid fund for the poor. As such these out-stations still cover a considerable area, so each is divided into separate hills or other localities, each of which has a four-member committee responsible to the main one. The large committees of the outstations in turn send their representatives to the old parish committee wish is composed of a president, his assistant, the sub-parish representatives and the priests.

Similar patterns can be found today in many African countries. An overall shape of ministry is emerging different from that which has been taken for granted by the Catholic Church in the past. Its immense strength is the wide participation of the laity and sharing of responsibilities; its weakness is the peripheralizing of priest and Eucharist. But in many other places there has as yet been little change at local level in these years, except that a priest may visit more and more rarely. It would be of great interest to make a wider study of the shape of church life, worship and ministry in such Catholic village communities.

We might find that they differ less than we imagine from what is to be found in a Protestant or 'Independent' church.

Whether the stress be upon the training of catechists or a network of village councils, the problem of the celebration of the Eucharist is not resolved. Since apostolic times the Catholic ideal and—except in emergencies—Catholic practice has been weekly celebration. Never in history has the Catholic Church deviated from the view that this is normative and the second Vatican Council, while modifying many other practices, increased rather than diminished insistence upon the Eucharist as the focal point of Christian living and the local church. As it is also unswerving Catholic tradition that there must be an ordained priest to preside over the Eucharist and proclaim the words of institution, there has been more and more unease with the situation in the church in Africa in which the priest and the Eucharist are becoming a rural rarity, and Catholic practice diverting further and further from Catholic theology.

With this in mind I appealed in October 1964 in the *African Ecclesiastical Review* for 'a radical reappraisal of the training and conditions required for a local ministry' and proposed 'the widespread ordination of tried and tested married men, such as the better trained catechists' (pp. 293-4). I was asking whether in principle the Catholic Church was right to go on refusing an ordained ministry of a type accepted by all other churches. It cannot be denied that this became the central point of debate for the next ten years. I myself urged the same thing at greater length in *Church and Mission in Modern Africa* (1967), *Mission and Ministry* (1971) and *Church and Ministry* (1972), but of course many other people have called for the same thing in different parts of Africa. In July 1968 the bishops of Zambia resolved to ask Rome for permission to ordain married men, while later the same year Fr Mosmans, the general secretary of the episcopate in Zaïre, wrote to Bishop Kabangu of Luebo proposing 'the priestly ordination of the best among the lay pastors' and stating that Cardinal Suenens would certainly support this in Rome. Bishops in South America were asking for the same thing. In July 1969 the hierarchies of five countries (Gabon, Chad, the Central African Empire, Congo-Brazza and Cameroun) voted in favour of a request to Rome for permission to ordain married men as the only possible way 'to answer the most elementary pastoral needs'.

The opposition to these proposals has been equally clear, dating at least from Pope Paul's encyclical upon priestly celibacy of June 1967. At Kampala in 1969 Cardinal Zoungrana declared that the whole celibacy issue was an 'imported question', produced by foreigners. In June 1970 the bishops of Tanzania asked for no more discussion on the subject 'for the present'. 'It is our intention to wait and see how such experiments of ordaining married men, if approved and undertaken on the suggested scale, work out first in other countries.'

There was undoubtedly strong pressure from the Roman nuncios upon the national episcopates to prevent this discussion continuing; but so considerable was the demand in various parts of the world, that the matter was finally placed upon the agenda of the Roman synod of September 1971. There Cardinal Malula of Kinshasa, Bishop Dayen of Chad, Bishop Sarpong of Kumasi spoke among others in favour of the ordination of married men, but a small majority of votes against change was obtained and nothing further was done. Since then there has been less public discussion—probably because it is recognized that it is temporarily useless to argue about it. While those in favour believe that public opinion in the church at large and the needs of the pastoral situation are steadily advancing towards change, there is in Africa as elsewhere a strong body opposed to any ordination of the married.

This point of view is well represented among the hierarchy and particularly in those areas where a considerable number of vocations of the traditional type are forthcoming. It sees the present shortage of priests as a temporary phase which can be overcome, it feels that the spiritual arguments for celibacy are objectively sound and important, that a married priesthood would be a heavy extra financial burden for a poor church, and that if it existed there would be danger of a deep division within the priesthood. Clearly, while much of the argument must depend upon the objective analysis of the present situation both in Africa and beyond, much depends too upon whether one considers the modern Catholic system of a wholly celibate priesthood in itself the best (or even a right) pattern of ministry; or whether, quite apart from the acute present shortage, one does not recognize considerable theological and practical advantages in a pattern of ministry closer to that of other churches, both Eastern and Western. It would be outside the scope of this paper to go further into this theoretical discussion, but it has been necessary to consider it because of the light it throws upon the state, the problems and the new initiatives of the Catholic ministry in Africa in the 1960s and 70s.

Finally there is one development which comes quite close to putting into practice the proposals which we have just considered and which probably represents the most advanced point reached hitherto in the wider structural revolution in local ministry which we have been observing from various angles. For while it has not been permissible to ordain married catechists to the priesthood and the considerable debate on the subject might therefore seem to have achieved nothing, rather the opposite is true, for by sheer necessity a new ministry has been bursting forth in various places across the continent which in almost all but name is the very thing that was asked for eleven years ago.

In 1964 the Vatican Council agreed to the re-establishment of a married permanent diaconate—of the ordination of men for all pastoral and sacramental work other than the celebration of Mass and the giving of absolution after confession. It is striking that though at the time the Council had the needs of Africa and South America most in mind at this point, Africa is today the continent which has made least use of it. There are still today little more than fifty deacons of this kind in Africa in contrast with many hundreds who have been ordained elsewhere, particularly in Germany and the United States. In black Africa Cameroun has the most with eleven and in the diocese of Douala they are now playing an important pastoral role.

The small number of deacons in Africa may surprise one and it certainly does not suggest that the continent is moving in the direction I have suggested. This, however, is deceptive. A better explanation would rather seem to be that most of those bishops in Africa who are interested in such a development do not wish to be tied down by any fixed formula, or by the restrictive conditions Rome has attached to the diaconate in the matter of age. At the same time many dioceses are now moving to the selection of a proportion of the catechists or other outstanding lay leaders for a special pastoral cum sacramental ministry only one step short of the priesthood. From country after country there is now news of such men being specially appointed, particularly of course to be ministers of communion. Thus in 1975 Bishop Agre of Man in the Ivory Coast appointed two catechists, Thomas Mahan of Beoue and Toussant Oulai of Seambly to be guardians and distributors of the holy sacrament in their village. Just a few months earlier the first two men, Luigi Aderobo and Paolo Adiga, were chosen for a similar task in Arua diocese, Uganda. In Gulu diocese, next to Arua, Bishop Kihangire has now appointed a considerable number: men who have qualified after training to be ministers of the Eucharist and who have a white cassock and a cross as their ministerial dress.

Such men are not simply people who distribute communion. They are mostly senior catechists, already entrusted with the regular care of a village or group of villages, men who preach and baptize. They are similar to the 'Bakambi' whom in September 1974 Cardinal Malula appointed as pastors of eight parishes in Kinshasa archdiocese after special training. But the most thought out example of the new pattern of the married pastor catechist is probably that of the archdiocese of Kisangani, as developed by Archbishop Fataki. There are now some thirteen in the archdiocese. The pastor catechist is required to be married; he has completed at least four years of secondary schooling, and he and his wife have followed a two year course at the catechetical institute and a year of probation before entering on their full ministry.

Each year he and his wife make a six day retreat and they take part in regular refresher courses. They preside over all the prayer meetings of the faithful in church, distribute holy communion, catechize the children and adults, organize the catechumenate, prepare adults for marriage and children for confirmation, keep up the parish registers, visit the sick, preside over funerals.

Clearly, in all but the celebration of Mass—which has still to be done by someone else from outside hurrying in and then out again from time to time in what is essentially a non-pastoral and hence an aliturgical way—they are parish priests, and the time is surely not very far distant when the many hundreds of such people who are now emerging in the Catholic ministry throughout Africa will be ordained priests. It is interesting that the Archbishop of Kisangani insists that they should be married: for the rural pastorate of the future, celibacy it seems may be the exception rather than the rule. On a cautious estimate some 30,000 priests of this type may be needed in the coming years.

Since 1971 this type of ministry has been emerging all across Africa except in the few dioceses where priests of the traditional type are rather numerous. Perhaps the church in Africa has been wise. It saw no point and some danger in a theoretical change of the law before a sure new way had been found in hard local practice. All the evidence suggests that this is now spreading fast and one may hope that the debate of the 1960s—focusing as it did upon the breakdown of the existing system and the need for a new way forward—contributed not a little to the pragmatic breakthrough of the 70s.

Patterns of ministry and structure within Independent Churches

HAROLD W. TURNER

The coverage of the vast and complex field of independent African Christianity is patchy, and particular studies in depth or detail are still few. Much harm has been done by hasty generalizations and superficial theorizing, and we shall therefore concentrate upon analysis of the issues and possibilities, illustrated by examples, rather than assert too many firm conclusions as to what has occurred among African independent churches since the colonial period.

We may, however, venture one general statement to the effect that there seems to have been no decline in the appearance of new movements nor reduction in the growth of existing movements since the ending of the colonial situation and the accompanying weakening of the missionary presence. Indeed, it might well be that the greatest growth has been in Ghana, where independence first arrived in Black Africa, and where estimates in the nineteen-seventies speak of some 500 different bodies. This could be contrasted with South Africa (despite the fact that this is by no means a typical colonial situation) where some falling off in the membership of the Bantu independent churches was reported in 1972. We are therefore warned against over-simple theories of a direct relationship between colonial rule (or missionary control) and the rise of independent churches. Likewise whatever we may discover by way of new developments or significant changes in the post-colonial period is not necessarily due to political independence; much of it may well have occurred in any case.

It must also be remembered that political and religious colonialism (a term that is unfair to missions but perhaps allowable in this context) are not identical. In the formal sense of church government or independence, autonomy as over against the Western Christian parent body both ante-dated and post-dated political independence in different areas; in the more substantial senses of influence and inheritance religious colonialism may be said in certain respects to continue, and even to be found in countries such as Liberia and Ethiopia which have been outside the colonial situation in the usual sense.

Armed with these cautions against simplistic explanations we may proceed to an analysis of the relationships of independent churches with other bodies and with one another, and of their membership structures, social forms, and leadership patterns.

External Relationships: Relationships with the Older Churches
In the sixties a distinct change in the attitude of the older to the independent churches began to emerge, with sympathetic enquiry replacing hostility or indifference. The kinds of article on independent churches that appeared in the *Nigerian Christian,* the (then) *Congo Mission News,* and in East African religious journals at the end of the decade, would have been inconceivable ten years earlier. This change has been matched by an increasing ecumenical interest on the part of the independents, who were usually the more generous of the two parties in their earlier attitudes. Even the Harris churches of the Ivory Coast, who had little love for their older churches, were reported to be more ecumenically minded. Independent churches which had their applications for membership in national Christian councils rejected at the start of the decade were members of the same Council a few years later. They are now to be found in the national councils in Sierra Leone, Ghana, Nigeria, Zambia, Kenya, South Africa and other countries, and this means a very great deal to them. Some, such as the African Brotherhood Church of Kenya, are now also members of the All Africa Conference of Churches, and the admission of the *Eglise de Jésus Christ par le Prophete Simon Kimbangu* to the World Council of Churches in 1969-70 has been much publicized; others were admitted by the WCC at Nairobi in 1975. Several have been welcomed into the International Council of Christian Churches; these include the *Eglise Chrétienne Evangélique d'Afrique* of Zaïre, and the *Eglise Reformée Indépendante de Madagascar*, but membership in this smaller rival body to the WCC is probably less stable.

There has often been an informal and unstructured relationship of inter-dependence between the older and the independent churches, whereby they performed different services for each other's members. Those from the older churches often sought the services of a prophet or healer among the independents, and usually somewhat secretly, while the independents used church or mission schools for the education of their children, church bookshops and journals for their literature, and even retained a second membership in order to secure a proper church burial or for other specific services. These mutual services have probably increased rather than declined in the last dozen years, except where the older churches have lost their schools to the state or the independents have started their own.

Other somewhat loose relationships have taken the form of affiliation with or sponsorship by an older Christian body from overseas. It might be thought that with independence this would give way to similar relationships with older churches within Africa, but there is very little sign of this as yet, apart from the tentative use of theological and Bible colleges for training ministers. In recent years the independents in the Central African Empire known as the *Comité Baptiste* invited Şwiss missionaries to assist them; the Kimbanguist *EJCSK* has had help from European Moravians and Reformed and from American Mennonites; the Christ Apostolic Church of Ghana has had 'fellowship agreements' with two different American bodies within three years; and a group of Cherubim and Seraphim in Nigeria have sought substantial aid from the Greek Orthodox Church in Athens. The American Mennonite Church Mission Board located in Elkhart, Indiana, has had more experience of this kind of relationship than any other body. After answering a call for sponsorship from an independent leader in eastern Nigeria in 1959 it helped local independent churches to form their own association, with a Bible school; in 1970 it began helping the Church of the Lord (Aladura) to establish its own theological seminary near Lagos by providing the main teacher; in the same period it was the chief agent in assisting Ghana independents to establish a co-operative Good News Training Institute for preparing leaders at various levels; other sponsorship discussions were held in Dahomey and the Ivory Coast, and similar relationships commenced in Botswana in 1974 and in Swaziland in 1975. The Canadian Baptists have had a team of four married missionaries working fraternally since 1970 within the body in Kenya known as the African Christian Churches and Schools.

A somewhat different kind of relationship occurs through the increasing attendance of African independent leaders at international gatherings. Thus Yeboa-Kurie of Ghana's Eden Revival Church and others visited the World Pentecostal Assembly in Texas in 1970, and independent leaders are now likely to be present at some World Council of Churches meetings.

The effects of these ecumenical and other contacts on the independents, whether formal or informal, are somewhat mixed. The benefits of recognition by the world Christian community, of a wider experience and broader outlook, are sufficiently obvious. Less obvious is the reinforcement of the existing tendency to model themselves on the older churches and in their most Western forms, to place their own financial independence at risk after seeing the relative affluence of Western Christians, and to become ecumenical tourist curiosities or showpieces—soon every Western church visitor to Africa will want the 'experience' of worshipping in an independent church, preferably of the more exotic kind. Financial assistance is probably the most dangerous of all forms of help; already it has initiated a project in Ghana at a level the independents cannot easily maintain, and in South Africa it has been a major factor in splitting the African Independent Churches Association.

Relationships between the Independent Churches

The surface view presents a picture of constant division and secession, of a hopelessly fissiparous mass of smallish churches unable to organize effectively for life in modern Africa. There is plenty of truth in this, in spite of the contrary evidence of the amalgamation of distinct bodies or the subsequent return of secessionists. Both processes have been at work throughout the history of African independency. In the post-colonial period there seem to be more frequent and more serious attempts to establish what H. J. Becken has called 'summit organizations', associations that represent the independents' own ecumenism parallel to that of the older churches. Eastern Nigeria has already been mentioned; there have been several such associations in Ghana, including that which Yeboa-Kurie attempted, and the Ghana Evangelical Fellowship of four apostolic-type churches in the seventies; in Zaïre some twenty-eight independent churches were gathered into an association around Luluabourg in 1965; in Kenya there have been associations of Spirit churches in the western area, and the *Kenya Christian Handbook* lists no fewer than fourteen attempts to form an all-Kenya association. South Africa has seen several such developments, especially the African Independent Churches Association that worked with the Christian Institute of Southern Africa for some years, and the Assembly of Zionist Apostolic Churches that affiliated with the Christian Council in 1966. Since 1972 Marthinus Daneel has been assisting with the establishment of a standing association among the southern Shona churches, and by 1974 the possibility of a relationship with the Christian Council of Rhodesia had arisen. In 1972 the Botswana Association of Inter-Spiritual Churches had some twenty member bodies.

This persistent attempt to form associations stems from several sources: the increasingly ecumenical climate in general, the desire for Christian recognition that a single small church cannot achieve on its own, and the practical problems of developing a strong influential church able to make itself visible in the life of the new nations. Here also the effects are liable to be ambivalent. The very attempts at greater unity can provide new divisions, leading to two rival associations as has happened in Ghana and South Africa, or divisions within one of the denominations concerned over the question of membership itself, or over some policy of the new association, as was threatened in Rhodesia. It is probable, however, that the effort at co-operation will continue and increase, even though it is weakened by the continuing divisiveness at other points.

Membership Structure

It is plain that many independent churches begin within one tribal people. The question is whether their membership expands beyond this limit, and whether there are secessions by tribal groups from trans-tribal churches. Some churches have shown considerable growth without expanding into other tribes. Thus the African Brotherhood Church numbers perhaps 60,000 but these are almost all Kamba in Kenya despite the desire of the church to include other peoples. Similarly the Maria Legio Church of perhaps 50,000 is open to all and the leaders are quick to declare its inter-tribal nature, but in fact it is very largely confined to the Nilotic Luo in Western Kenya who are unpopular with the surrounding Bantu peoples. These are two examples of churches that are not inherently tribal in their convictions but are limited by factors they have been unable to overcome. Most churches showing considerable expansion have achieved this by drawing other tribes into their membership. Divisions or tensions within a church then often have a tribal basis, but actual secessions on this basis do not seem to be as numerous as one might expect. In general it would appear that there is no necessary inherent connection between independency and tribal peoples in the sense of tribalism, and that these churches are not inclined to foment the latter as some politicians have done.

Many independent churches aspire to a national scope and influence, even if remaining substantially tribal in membership. Political independence has almost certainly encouraged this, just as at an earlier stage some independents were influential in nationalist movements. Occasionally since national independence politicians and independents have tried to use each other for their own ends but this has seldom lasted, and the striking thing is the widespread spiritual independence among these churches as over against politics. The desire for national influence is that of a free agent able to embrace all the peoples within the nation and to offer them a Christian church suited to national needs and culture. There does not seem to be any case of a single independent church becoming the dominant church embracing most of the Christians in the nation; the Kimbanguist Church might have had such thoughts at one stage in the early sixties, but deliberately rejected this possibility. Most independents, while coveting a national extension, or even after achieving this, seem content with a situation of religious pluralism.

Even more striking and more significant is the extent to which churches which began in a particular tribe have extended beyond national boundaries and achieved an international structure. This has occurred even where they may have remained predominantly within the tribe of origin in their own country. Thus the Church of the Lord (Aladura) began among the Yoruba of Nigeria and has spread into other areas of Nigeria, mainly among migrant Yoruba without any great response from eastern or northern peoples; yet in Ghana it has substantial expansion among Fante, Ga and Ashanti, in Liberia it includes many Bassa and Americo-Liberians and others, in Sierra Leone its membership is Creole and Mende, with a sprinkling of other tribes, and it has also a foothold in Togo and branches in London and New York, where members maybe of any West African or even other peoples. Here is a comparatively small and ill-endowed church with a remarkable dynamic, that has always seen itself in international terms. The Christ Apostolic Church and the Cherubim and Seraphim of Nigeria have also expanded into other countries, likewise a number of East African independents. Those in South Africa that have extended into Central Africa have seldom maintained any overall structural unity but have produced autonomous churches similar in nature. The Kimbanguist Church of Zaïre claims branches in some ten Central African countries, while the Vapostori of Rhodesian origin are reported to be established also in Zaïre, Congo, Malawi and Mozambique (before 1974).

The last example suggests that this international expansion can occur irrespective of whether the areas concerned are in a colonial or a post-colonial situation, and in fact much of the expansion outlined above, except that of the Kimbanguists and the Vapostori, had occurred before political independence. It would be difficult to support any statement about international expansion increasing in a post-colonial area, although it is certainly continuing. We should also note signs of new strains felt by such international churches due to the formation of independent nations, strains that were probably less evident in the colonial period. The advent of independence in Ghana saw increasing restiveness among Church of the Lord members at being under Nigerian authority, and this has led to a series of more or less overt rebellions in the Ghana branches, which have sufficient strength to match that of the church in Nigeria. Likewise there has been tension within the African Methodist Episcopal Church (if we can regard this as virtually an independent church) in Central Africa where Zambia, Malawi and Rhodesia each wanted to have the residence of the bishop they shared located in their own country. (See also below, pp. 294-5).

It may well be that we are observing the decline of a pan-Africanism nourished within a common colonial situation and the emergence of new and stronger national loyalties. It remains to be seen whether any independent church can maintain and develop a strong international organization over a period of time and in face of the shifting patterns of tension between the new nations. At most we can observe a missionary zeal and an intention to transcend the limits of tribe and nation that appear authentically Christian.

As for the socio-economic aspects of membership, P. J. Dirven has reported that the followers of the post-colonial Maria Legio in Kenya have been drawn from the 'liminal individuals' in society—the poor, the sick, the insecure and the disaffected. This corresponds to the popular image of the independents, if extended to include illiterates, unemployed, and the lowest socio-economic classes in general. It is well known that something similar obtained in the appeal of the Christian missions in their earlier stages, unless the initial response came from the traditional rulers as in Uganda or the *élites* in some other areas. And M. L. Daneel has reported that, in the 1960s, forty per cent of the members of all churches among the southern Shona, both older and independent, came from the lowest classes.

On the other hand Daneel has also shown that, contrary to the common suggestion, there is no correlation between membership in an independent church and low degree of education. We shall return to the question of education at a later point, but may comment here on the extent to which educated people, with a corresponding higher social status, are to be found among the independents of West Africa, which is probably ahead of other areas in this respect. On a visit to the Celestial Church of Christ in Ibadan in 1973 I found myself in conversation before and after the service with four people—the first two worked in the administrative offices of the University of Ibadan, the third was a lecturer there, and the fourth (who earlier had been observed leading a Bible class in his white robe and bare feet) proved to be the Deputy Vice-Chancellor of the University. Some might say this merely illustrates the proverbial saying about birds of a feather; in fact it indicates the social range to be found in the independents, or that is potentially present. My own impression is that churches may commence with an appeal to the more liminal members of society, although exceptions are to be found, as in the early Faith Tabernacle forms of the Nigerian Aladura movement. As firmer structures are established these churches appeal increasingly to members of any social class, and this in spite of the prestige, equipment and trained ministry possessed by the older churches. This process is probably accentuated in the post-colonial situation for several reasons—the decreasing reliance on the educational and medical services of the older churches as these are replaced by public services, the increasingly inadequate level of their ministry without the compensating charismatic powers of the independents, and the more conscious emphasis on African cultural forms in religious matters.

It would also be difficult to demonstrate whether the independents were predominantly rural or urban in their membership, for some are one and some the other and some combine the two. If there is an increase in urban membership this is because that is where the population is flowing and where the independents are able to offer a ministry relevant to urban problems; they are not left behind as suitable only for rustics. If their strength is still in the countryside it is for the same reason—that is where the people are, as with the southern Shona studied by Daneel. Some churches retain a rural base and headquarters, but have more sophisticated leaders and members in the towns where they deal with government offices. This obtains perhaps more in South Africa where migrant workers in the cities maintain their own rural roots. Sometimes the wealthier city congregations contribute through central funds for the financial support of the poorer rural branches, as with the AME Church in Zambia. Where there are 'holy cities' these will almost of necessity be in a rural area, but few seem to have been founded since about 1960. In one case at least, the Church of the Lord in Nigeria, the headquarters established by the founder in a small bush town in the thirties was shifted in the late sixties to the Lagos metropolitan area; the necessary justification was established by comparing Nazareth to Jerusalem. Whether this is the forerunner of a general trend it is too soon to say.

Evidence is also lacking when it comes to other questions such as whether membership is becoming more stable or continues to reveal the great fluidity whereby members pass from one independent church to another; where there is a constant succession of new bodies, as in Ghana, it would appear that there is still considerable fluidity. The sources of recruitment are not likely to exclude the existing independent churches, but what proportions come from primal religions, the older churches or other independents has been little studied. Similar ignorance prevails about any difference in the appeal to and retention of men as against women in the membership; the common image features a predominance of women, and this is probably usually the case. At the same time one can find congregations very much the reverse, and Daneel has shown that his southern Shona churches have a distinctly greater appeal to men than have the older churches or missions.

Forms of Social Organization, Leadership and Authority
If we adopt the familiar Western spectrum of sect, denomination and church then the basic questions will be where the African independents start and which way they tend to move along the continuum. In general it might be said that the Ethiopian type of independent body commences

and remains as a denomination, but that the prophet-healing type more often starts as a sect and frequently develops into the direction of a denomination. This process is usually associated with increasing size, greater ecumenical interest, the desire for recognition on public occasions, more members from the upper socio-economic classes or involved in public life, a concern for their own social and economic development, for education and a better trained ministry, and for similar development in society at large. In their own self-understanding they have no desire to be a 'sect' in the Western sense, but possess the intention of being the real Church of God, reformed as against Western mission Christianity, and with a message and mission to the whole world. This confident and open attitude is strikingly apparent in so many of these bodies.

On the other hand, there are some though perhaps less frequent signs of a movement in the opposite direction, towards a more typically sect form. This has been observed in Zaïre and the Congo Republic where some of those who trace an inheritance from Simon Kimbangu have dissociated themselves from the main Kimbanguist Church, turned their backs on politics or concern with medical or educational services, and retired into their own world of spiritual healing and power sought through an elaboration of ritual. These developments are to be found in the Mayumbe and other groups that broke with the *EJCSK* Kimbanguists at the beginning of the sixties, and in the Churches of the Holy Spirit described by Janzen and by MacGaffey. Bastide has also discussed this possibility inherent in what he calls messianic movements; these may further modernization under a colonial regime by strengthening the demand for independence, and then come into conflict with the new African regime and withdraw into a more rigid and sectist position of separation from the world. In view, however, of the overwhelming concern for development in so much of ex-colonial Africa this second tendency would seem to be much less common.

The Western sect-church spectrum is under fire from sociologists, has never been satisfactory theologically, and probably oversimplifies or distorts the African phenomena like so many other Western categories or analyses. Our own replacement consists of five categories derived descriptively from the wide range of phenomena; prophet movement (more inchoate primary form), church (organized in congregations like the older churches), community (with comprehensive activities in a new village or holy city), clientele (individuals dealing with a practitioner but not themselves a continuing community), and ancillary cult (alongside other forms, for special benefits or purposes). If these are arranged in a circle, rather than as a linear continuum, then we can depict the variety of developments that occur, from almost any one form across the circle to almost any other form.

A comprehensive examination of the tendencies since the colonial period ended cannot be attempted here, but some observations may be made. Firstly, there do not seem to be many new large-scale prophet movements since 1960, with the exception of the Maria Legio under Simeon Ondeto and Gaudencia Aoko from 1963 in Kenya; there have, however, been plenty of minor ones which have either faded out or quickly condensed into a small church. Nor do there seem to have been any new communities of the holy city or New Jerusalem kind; the fourteen notable examples in our list were all founded by 1959; the communal villages of the utopian Kingdom movement in Ghana are too small and recent to form a substantial exception, but there are probably others as yet unreported. The famous Aiyetoro community in Nigeria in the mid-sixties repudiated the idea of daughter communities, but in the early seventies there were a number of these along the lagoons. It may be that in the freer atmosphere of independent nations there is less reason to withdraw into communities of this kind, less persecution, and a greater involvement in expanding national services and activities. If so then we can expect a profound change in the ethos of these communities, or they may become places of pilgrimage and commemoration set over against administrative headquarters with associated services located in more urban or metropolitan settings; the Aiyetoro community, for example, has a headquarters for its commercial enterprises in Lagos.

Apart from these two observations it is difficult to make any other general statements about social forms since independence. The mission model of congregations organized in a denomination is widely followed, and increasingly so as independent groups become larger and more stable, like the Christ Apostolic Church in West Africa or the African Brotherhood Church in Kenya. It is possible that the main new initiatives occurred in the colonial period and that these independent churches have begun a process of consolidation and of re-alignment of existing bodies which is replacing the continuing emergence of new ones. This of course does not apply to those areas where independency has not yet occurred or is still small in scale.

The range of forms here may be thought of in terms of the letter Y and of three main types, charismatic, organizational and ritualistic, placed one at each of the terminal points; then any one form can be examined in terms of its relationship to the other two.

The charismatic form is represented more especially by the prophet-healing churches, and by the earlier stages of their development. In the light of what was said above about new prophet movements it is not surprising if we find this form of leadership in decline, and observe the paucity of major new charismatic figures in the sixties. Who should be added to Ondeto and Aoko already mentioned? Josué Edjro, the Ivory Coast healer who attracted mass pilgrimages, remained within the Methodist Church and so represents no more than a clientele or clinic form. One can perhaps observe a loss of influence on the part of earlier figures such as Reuben Spartas, Alice Lenshina, and Christianah Akinsowon of the Cherubim and Seraphim. Gaudencia Aoko has already lost her charismatic appeal and by 1973 belonged to no church; Simeon Ondeto remained the Spiritual Head of the Maria Legio but the future seemed to lie with its Cardinal Mumbo, the practical business man who dealt with the government authorities. Prophet Wovenu of the Apostolic Revelation Society in Ghana presented the rare combination of high charisma with great organizing ability, and showed no loss of influence.

The organizational form seems to replace the charismatic, in good Weberian manner, as these movements become more 'routinized'. Charismatics are less needed and less valued once the initial impetus has been given and a tradition established. Educated organizers are required, on the model of bureaucrats, professional and business men in independent Africa. It has been suggested by Janzen that independent governments are not so suspicious as were the colonial powers of a strong centralized organization, and may even encourage this development in the interests of order, stability, and ease of dealing with the church; charismatic prophets and secular rulers have never comported well together. It is not surprising therefore to find the sixties marked by such organizational leaders as Joseph Diangienda of the *EJCSK*: Adeleke Adejobi of the Church of the Lord (Aladura), Yeboa-Kurie of Eden Revival Church (later Feden Church), and, in East Africa, Bishop Ajuoga of the Church of Christ in Africa.

The ritualistic form seems to provide an alternative to the bureaucratic organizational type when the charisma declines or is superseded. If power is not found in the spiritual qualities of the gifted leader, or in the strengths of a larger and probably hierarchical organization, then it is sought through the elaboration of ritual regarded as operative in itself, or perhaps by the dispersal of charisma across a wide section of the members who can become possessed by the Spirit within the ritualistic framework. Some of the Cherubim and Seraphim societies in Nigeria should perhaps be classified in this way, for they have lost the originating charisma and have never achieved a strong central and unified organization. The clearest example seems to be that of the Churches of the Holy Spirit in the lower Zaïre region which share the Kimbanguist tradition but have turned away from all the new developments that have strengthened the *EJCSK*. They have experimented with commerce and then rejected this, they possess no paid ministry—every male member is a potential prophet, for the structure is egalitarian rather than hierarchic, and elaborate rituals form the main activity. Especially in the local cultural context this is potentially a return to magic. When we examine the organizational types we find that the *EJCSK* has a restricted and controlled use of rituals and resembles a Baptist church, that the 'best organized church in Kenya', the African Brotherhood Church, has very simple worship forms, likewise the strongest and largest of the Nigerian independents, the Christ Apostolic Church; in all of these 'pentecostal' phenomena are strictly controlled.

Another dimension of the charismatic/organization alternatives may be mentioned. It is seen in the tension between what may be called the charisma of age and wisdom, expressed in a gerontocracy so characteristic of traditional Africa, and the organizational demands of the more modern youth—the young men of some education who want schools and a national organization for their church. J. D. Y. Peel regards the Cherubim and Seraphim as, on the whole, representing the first position, and the Christ Apostolic Church the second, although even here Yoruba cultural influence led to the re-establishment of some degree of gerontocracy in the sixties with the ageing of the group of leaders who had controlled the church over its first forty years. Marie-France Perrin Jassy in her study of the Luo independents noted that all responsible posts were held by men aged 25-45, and the old men were simply members; the new religion had so completely replaced the ancestor cult with its ritual roles for the elders that their very position in society had been undermined. The degree of this tension between the old and the young, and its outcome, will of course vary across the different cultures, but we may hazard the opinion that the voice of youth has been more influential since independence.

A further dimension of the internal structure of authority and leadership is found in the sources of revelation that are recognized. The first form is often the vision, dream, or death-resurrection trance of the founder. He may later deposit the revelation so received in a book of rules and rituals that is not capable of further development after his death and so becomes a canonical authority that guides the organizational men who replace him. This happened with Johane Maranke's 'New Revelation', the book of his visions accepted by the Vapostori since his death in 1963. In default of this the leaders in the hierarchy may claim their own revelations as the basis for their decisions, even if not notably charismatic, or simply proceed under their own wisdom. A different source of authority appears where there is emphasis upon prayer and Bible study by all members, for this is liable to produce a critique of decisions by the hierarchy. The same result occurs where there is regular group discussion, as with most matters in the East

African Revival movement, and at this stage the system has become democratic rather than hierarchical. Our own limited experience suggests that there is an overall tendency among African independents to develop the kinds of criteria for revelation manifest in the last two forms, where biblical study and reasoned discussion provide a new critique both of revelations and of leadership. This is not incompatible in the African mind with continuing respect for leaders and for authority, although it has also been responsible for some secessions.

The structural relationship to traditional patterns should also be examined. No one has set out more fully the various ways in which these independent churches represent a radically new form as over against traditional culture than Perrin Jassy. She observes that here is a private and voluntary group, not coterminous with the whole community, replacing the blood ties of lineage and clan by a spiritual basis of association, introducing a more fluid system in place of fixed roles and status, and providing new roles for youth and for women and a measure of equality for everyone, together with a potential universality that transcends the boundaries of clan or tribe, collective forms of religious expression that were unknown in traditional religious practice, and centralized organization in an acephalous society. While she was describing the contrast for the Luo many of her features apply in varying degrees elsewhere.

In spite of the extent to which a church is a new institutional form it is remarkable that so many independents still reflect the patterns of their tribal society. Sundkler made much of this point in relation to the Zulu, and it is evident elsewhere, as in two of the bodies already mentioned: the African Brotherhood Church which has a hierarchical structure and system of councils very like that of its own Kamba society, and, in contrast, the Holy Spirit Churches in Zaïre which continue the more egalitarian and loosely structured pattern of their own traditional people. In spite of this the latter maintain a sense of communality with similar churches beyond their own cultural areas, so that the traditional and the innovative (i.e. this degree of trans-tribal universality) are not necessarily incompatible.

The problem of succession to leadership upon the death of the founder presents a particular instance of the relationship between old and new forms. Succession from father to eldest son (sometimes disputed by another son) has been not uncommon, as with Isaiah Shembe to his son J. G. Shembe in 1935, and Jehu-Appiah to Matapoly Moses Jehu-Appiah in 1948 in the Musama Disco Christo Church; in the Kimbanguist Church it was Joseph Diangienda, the youngest child, who was chosen by Simon Kimbangu when only three years old to succeed him. Likewise when E. B. Lekganyane died in 1966 he left instructions for his thirteen year old son to succeed him in Zion Christian Church, as he himself had succeeded his father in 1949. Other examples are Johanne Maranke followed by his son Abel in the Vapostori in 1963, and Gideon Urhobo by Emmanuel in the Nigerian God Kingdom Society late in the 1950s; in this case the succession failed because this Judaistic movement rejected the son who had transferred to a Christian position while being educated in Britain. Oshitelu of the Church of the Lord would have liked his son to follow him but the son felt unsuitable and avoided the issue by leaving the church, so that Oshitelu chose his ablest organizer, Adejobi, who became primate in 1966. It is probable that family succession is becoming less common as churches become larger and therefore have more senior leaders to provide candidates for the headship, and as the access to better education which the son of the head of church has more than other children opens up a wider range of occupations and so undermines the hopes of his father.

Leadership Training and Education

Ethiopian types of independent church displayed a substantial concern for education from the beginning and have maintained this along with the growth of demand for education in the community at large. They have sometimes used the facilities of the older churches for ministerial training but have remained weak at this point; even the AME Church in Zambia, in spite of its American connections, is still without provision for training a ministry, and its leaders are only self-trained. The prophet-healing types of independent have been more African in orientation, and therefore less involved with education, which has usually meant westernization at the same time. Some have been hostile to education and, as with their opposite numbers in Western society, have depended on the resources of the Spirit.

All churches, however, have shared in the increasing African concern for education in the post-colonial era, and there has been a significant increase in the quantity and quality of ministerial training. More young people have been sent to Bible schools abroad, and even Adejobi himself, while second in the leadership of the Church of the Lord, spent 1961-3 at the Glasgow Bible Training Institute. Others have begun the possibly more difficult practice of sending men for training to the institutions of missions or older churches within Africa; thus eastern and western independents in Nigeria have used the Mennonite Bible school at Ilorin, and the Holy Spirit Church in Kenya sent its first student to St Paul's College, Limuru, in 1970, and has since sent others to the Friends' Bible School.

The West African-wide Church of the Lord (Aladura) may serve as representative of the general tendencies. In the first thirty years from its foundation in 1930 there were no educational activities apart from a sketchy training for its ministers, carried on in three countries in the form of the traditional apprenticeship system. In the sixties it had begun a primary school in Monrovia, and was the recognized religion in a few Ghana private schools owned by members of the Church. In the present decade it has launched out with a secondary boarding school and a theological seminary near Lagos, and warmly supports the grammar school being established in memory of the founder in Oshitelu's home town, Ogere.

The principal tutor in the seminary has been provided by the Mennonite Church Missions Board, assisted by the Theological Education Fund for the World Council of Churches. Similar assistance has been given in other training programmes—to the *EJCSK* in its large seminary operating at a very respectable level at N'Kamba, to the African Independent Churches Association's own seminary by the Christian Institute of Southern Africa and others, to the southern Shona churches by M. L. Daneel, to Ghana churches by the Mennonites and others in the Good News Institute already mentioned, and to some other programmes. This is undoubtedly one of the most significant developments since independence, and is almost certain to expand, however mixed its blessings will eventually prove to be.

The motive behind the increasing concern with general education and the establishment by independents of their own schools deserve some comment. Among the complex reasons we find a sense of discrimination—real or imagined—against their own children in mission or church schools, or fear of their children being won over to the faith of the other church; this situation, however, changes with the increasing take-over of education by the new governments. There is also an expectation of financial help for the work of the church to be derived from school fees or government asistance; this also vanishes with state education. In addition there is a declining reliance on their own spiritual dynamic and an over-estimation of education as the key to everything, together with a genuine concern for the religious dimensions of education. Finally we note the influence of missions and older churches in suggesting that schools belong to the proper model of a Christian church; the prestige and status accorded in the community to 'proper' churches on this model exercise a powerful influence on the independents.

The saddest feature of this concern with independent church schools is the failure to realize that the day of the church school is rapidly passing in much of Africa, and the imitation of a model that is increasingly archaic in the more developed areas of the new nations. It is difficult to blame bodies less experienced in such matters when even the older churches often fight a rearguard action against a development they should be welcoming as a sign of the success of their own pioneering of education. It would be equally unfortunate if the new developments in ministerial training were to imitate models that have been only too Western, but some at least of the Western sponsors involved are keenly aware that their own patterns are unsuitable.

In all the other areas, such as polity, where Western patterns and structures have been adopted by the independents, it is usually found that while the terminology may remain unchanged a considerable degree of Africanization has occurred in substance and in actual operation; to this extent, whatever be the new developments in the post-colonial era, these churches are remaining true to their most common designation, as both African and independent.

Select Bibliography

BECKEN, H.-J., 'Patterns of organizational structures in the African independent churches movement in South Africa', *Africa Marburgensia* 1(2), 1968, 17-24.

———, 'The African independent churches' understanding of the ministry', in D. Bosch (ed), *Ampsbediening in Afrika* (Lux Mundi, 5), 1972, 134-144.

DANEEL, M. L., *Old and New in Southern Shona Independent Churches.* The Hague: Mouton, vols. 1 and 2, 1971 and 1974.

JANZEN, J. M., and MacGAFFEY, W., *An Anthology of Kongo Religion.* Lawrence: University of Kansas Publications in Anthropology 1974.

PEEL, J. D. Y., *Aladura: A Religious Movement among the Yoruba.* London: Oxford University Press 1968.

PERRIN JASSY, M.-F., *Basic Community in the African Churches.* New York: Orbis Books 1973.

SHENK, W. R., 'Mission agency and African independent churches', *International Review of Mission* 63(251), 1974, 475-91.

TURNER, H. W., 'African independent churches and education', *Journal of Modern African Studies* 13(2), 1975, 295-308.

WEST, M. E., 'Independence and unity: problems of co-operation between African independent-church leaders in Soweto', *African Studies* 33(2), 1974, 121-9.

Major changes and developments in Christian leadership in Busoga Province, Uganda 1960-74[1]

TOM TUMA

The Church Missionary Society, which first opened a missionary station in Busoga in February 1891, encouraged—in accordance with its established policy—some of the newly converted Basoga to serve in the church. This led to the development, by the end of World War I, of a pyramidal structure of church leadership and organization.

The European missionaries in the field, who, incidentally, were not very keen on sharing responsibilities and powers with their African colleagues, were at the top of this structure while the lower strata were filled by the indigenous people. For the Roman Catholics the most important ecclesiastical division was the missionary district[2] which was manned by one or two European missionaries assisted by a head-catechist and a host of about sixty Basoga catechists. Each of these catechists would be in charge of a village church and, possibly, a village school.

The Protestant church organization was similar, in as far as it took a pyramid form, to that of the Roman Catholics. But the main difference between the two was that the Protestants, because of their policy of creating a 'native Church' rapidly, had by 1918 four Baganda pastors (Musisi, S. Namunyenga, E. Mukasa, Y. Kiwavu) serving in Busoga. Each village church and school was run by a catechist and six to eight of these churches formed an *omuluka* (plural—*miruka*) or sub-district. The senior catechist or lay-reader was in charge of the *omuluka*. About six to ten *miruka* formed an *obusumba,* a pastorate in the charge of an ordained clergy. Lastly there were four missionary stations which were run by the European missionaries.[3] For administrative purposes, the pastorates run by the Baganda pastors came under these missionary

---

[1] It is only the Roman Catholic and Church of Uganda (Protestant) leadership which is discussed in this paper.

[2] In 1918 there were four RC missionary districts namely, Kamuli, Iganga, Jinja and Budini.

[3] The Protestant missionary stations were located at Kamuli, Iganga, Jinja and Kaliro.

stations.

It should be noted that by the beginning of the inter-war period, a good deal of the work of the Christian church in Busoga rested mainly on the shoulders of the Basoga church workers either in their capacity as catechists or chiefs. However, the established pattern of church organization under which they laboured encouraged them to look to the centre (the missionary station) for leadership and guidance in their work, thus imposing on the lower strata the relationship of continuous tutelage from above. However, with the changing situation in inter-war and post-war Busoga, various developments, many of which are still unfolding, occurred in the Christian leadership there.

AUTHORITARIANISM AND CLERICALISM

As early as 1918 the Protestants in their efforts to create a 'native Church' ordained the first Musoga, Nasanaeri Wabuleta, a deacon. This policy of ordaining some of the Basoga to reinforce the already over-worked European and Baganda missionaries soon gained momentum. By 1940 a total of eleven Basoga had been admitted to holy orders.[4]

The Basoga clergymen, whose number was growing gradually, in-creasingly assumed more pastoral responsibilities. This was because in the inter-war and post-war periods, the European missionaries were progressively concentrating their efforts on more specialized work, namely teaching in schools—which had become very popular with the Basoga—and in theological colleges and working in hospitals. Secondly, by the 1930s Baganda pastors were no longer posted to Busoga since it was felt that the Busoga church was of age and could, therefore, recruit its own clergymen. Lastly, because of increasing political pressure the chiefs who had been instrumental in promoting Christianity in the first three decades, were loosening their grip on church affairs.

The assumption of more responsibilities by the Basoga pastors meant that the policy of continuous tutelage was losing its vigour; it also helped to enhance the high social status or *ekitiibwa* which the ordained clergy enjoyed. The early Basoga clergymen, by and large, adopted the life-style of the Basoga chiefs. Naturally most of the later clergy tended to imitate their predecessors. Indeed as late as 1952 Fallers observed that the Basoga clergymen modelled their behaviour upon the chiefly pattern.[5] The main danger with this practice was that it contributed to the growth and sustenance of authoritarianism and clericalism in the Busoga church.

It is well known that the Roman Catholics had a long and rigorous

---

[4] Information derived from relevant issues of *Ebifa mu Buganda* (News in Buganda) and *Ekitabo Ky'ebitesebwa Olukiiko lwe Gwanga*, NAC, Busoga.

[5] L. A. Fallers, *Bantu Bureaucracy*, Chicago University Press, 1965 edition, p. 198.

training for their African priests. They did not therefore have any Musoga priest until 1940 when Tomasi Kasadha was ordained a priest at Gaba. By 1960, the number of Basoga priests had risen to three.[6] Although the Basoga Roman Catholic priests do not seem to have modelled their behaviour upon the chiefly pattern, the highly centralized system of their church, their training and the awe they inspired among the Basoga Roman Catholics, encouraged them—like their Protestant counterparts—to maintain a good deal of authoritarianism and clericalism.

In the last fourteen years, however, the image of the chiefly, authoritarian priests has been fading steadily, particularly among the Protestants. A majority of the Basoga clergymen who were interviewed indicated that they were acting as servants of their congregations and not, as in the pre-independence period, as Christian bosses.[7] Asked why this was so, my informants attributed the change to the theological schools which have, in the recent past, increasingly placed emphasis on training servants rather than bosses of the church. While this is true, the factors responsible for the change are rather more complex.

First, since the visit of the well known Phelps-Stokes commission to Uganda in 1924, the Protestant and Roman Catholic churches began to invest a lot of money and manpower in the development of institutions, particularly schools. As the Rev. Canon Waibale, who has since died, recalled, the Basoga church workers especially the *basumba* (clergymen) were deeply involved in the organization and administration of the church schools. The *musumba* (singular) acted as the chairman of the schools' committees in his pastorate. It was his responsibility to ensure that the members of staff were well behaved and he paid regular visits to the schools to inspect their work. Waibale claimed that this was done because the schools were seen as an extension of the church and the pupils were regarded as 'tomorrow's Church'. Hence the emphasis placed on the development of schools.[8]

With the acquisition of independence in 1962, the Uganda government, interested in promoting national unity, took over the administration of most of the schools in the country. Evidently this came as a major blow, particularly to the Protestants, who had pinned almost all their hopes for growth and expansion on the schools. It was now clear that schools could no longer be used as instruments of evangelization. Secondly the loss of the schools also meant the loss of some substantial church revenue. Lastly with some of his 'empire' collapsing, the

[6] Interview with Fr Kasadha on 25 March 1972, at Kyebando.

[7] This view was expressed, for example, by the Rev. E. Kamira and the Rev. A. Kadali, interviewed on 18 February 1975.

[8] Interview with Canon Waibale on 11 March 1972, at Namutumba.

clergymen or priest may well have had some of his *ekitiibwa* eroded.

It seems that it is partly these developments which have encouraged the church leadership, both Protestants and Roman Catholics, to shift their emphasis from the schools to the parishes where the parishioners have to be persuaded, rather than 'coerced' either directly or indirectly, into supporting the church. But, as the young and progressive Protestant Bishop of Busoga remarked, the Christians have tended to support the church whole-heartedly only on realizing that the church is their own institution and not—as in the pre-independence days—a 'personal' possession of the clergy.

IT IS THEIR CHURCH

The bishop further pointed out that one of the most effective ways of achieving this has been to encourage lay participation in church affairs at every level. He observed that the laity was heavily represented in the various Protestant church committees. Indeed in many of these committees the laity overwhelmingly outnumbered the clergy. For example, the Planning and Development committee of the diocese whose total membership was sixteen had only three clergy on it; the rest of the members were laymen.[9]

The importance of the growing participation of the laity in church affairs has not only been to inject new life into the church but also to minimize the authority and power of the clergy. Indeed a majority of these committees which are dominated by the laity make decisions which affect the Protestant Church at every level. As might be expected, some of these decisions are not popular with the clergy. For example, in 1974 the St James parish council at Jinja refused to accept a catechist who had been given a job in the parish by the vicar before he had consulted the parish council.[10] This open defiance of the clergy's decision would have been most unusual in church circles twenty years ago. It seems, however, that incidents of this kind are likely to occur more frequently as the Christians increasingly realize that the church is their church; they belong to it and it belongs to them.

By contrast, there has not been any spectacular decline in the authoritarianism and clericalism in the Roman Catholic Church in Busoga. But some of the recent developments in the Roman Catholic Church indicate that a change in this direction is already taking place. The establishment of the parish councils, the diocesan pastoral councils

---

[9] Interview with Bishop Cyprian Bamwoze on 24 February 1975 at his home at Bugembe.

[10] Ibid.

and the Episcopal Conference at the beginning of the 1960s are some of the major milestones in this direction. It is true that these committees are still dominated by the clergy. For example, in 1966 the diocesan pastoral council consisted—and no significant change in representation has occurred since—of six priests, three sisters and three laymen.[11] It is also true that these committees, unlike the Protestant ones, are advisory rather than decision-making committees. However, their existence gives the laity—at least a section of it—a sense of participation in the affairs of their church. This may well be helping to consolidate the loyalty of some of the laity to their church.

Secondly, following the shift of emphasis from the schools to the parishes, the Roman Catholic leadership has introduced in almost all the parishes various farming projects which have generated a good deal of interest among the Roman Catholic population in Busoga. Using funds from the Catholic Fund for Overseas Development (CAFOD), the Roman Catholics, unlike the Protestants, started in 1968 three poultry farms at Nawanyago, Wesunire and Kamuli. At Kyebando a group farming scheme was started for growing sugar cane, and asparagus was introduced at Itanda.[12] More recently (1970) a rice growing scheme has been started at Nambale where a swamp has been cleared and planted with IR8 miracle rice from the Philippines.[13] Whereas the main reasons for introducing these schemes have been to encourage the laity to work and to improve the quality of their products, those who have participated in these projects have also improved their financial positions. According to one of the leading Christians in Itanda area, Tito Muwumba—who had himself shown some considerable interest in the asparagus project—by introducing the farming projects the Roman Catholic leadership clearly demonstrated that it cares about the laity which in turn has responded with respect for their leadership and commitment to the church, their church, since it cares for them.[14]

It should be noted that the Protestant leadership has not—until very recently—been very keen on introducing projects similar to those described above for the benefit of their followers. This is because the Protestants do not have the money to finance such projects as they hardly receive any funds from overseas. Secondly—and possibly more important—the Protestant leadership, with its scattered remains of the evangelical tradition, tends to frown on such developments. But even among Protestants this attitude is fading. For example the Bishop of

---

[11] Diocesan News Letter published by Jinja Diocese, November 1966.

[12] Diocesan News Letter, June 1968.

[13] Diocesan News Letter, June 1970.

[14] Interview with Tito Muwumba on 20 November 1971 at his home at Itanda.

Busoga keeps many head of cattle at his place at Bugembe. Further, Iganga parish has plans to start a small cattle ranch on the vast church land there.

These recent developments indicate, among other things, that a new kind of church leader who is well trained, sensitive to the various needs of his parishioners, broad-minded, ready to experiment and accept change, is beginning to evolve. But the situation in Busoga is changing so rapidly that there is a very urgent need for this type of new church leader to provide effective leadership in a rapidly changing situation. The church in Busoga has realized this, and various serious attempts are being made to produce the new type of church leader quickly.

ATTEMPTS TO IMPROVE THE QUALITY AND INCREASE THE QUANTITY OF CHURCH LEADERS

(i) The Ordained Clergy

Busoga, like the rest of Uganda, has a rapidly growing population. In 1959 the total population was 660,507. Ten years later, it had risen to 949,384,[15] an annual increase of nearly 5.0%. As the rapidly growing population has to be evangelized, the attempts to do this create a major strain on the church's leadership which does not seem to have grown much in the last two decades.

Secondly, in this period the churches (Protestant and Roman Catholic) have been faced with the new and rapidly growing problem of the secularization of human life in which human experience is increasingly withdrawn from direct reference to religion. The growing number of schools, particularly boarding schools, were partly responsible for this development, but other factors were also involved. By 1940, Jinja, the capital of Busoga, had become an important urban centre in the Eastern region. In 1948 Jinja's population was 4,400.[16] But according to the 1969 census, the population of Jinja had grown to 52,509. This rapid rise of the urban population may well have accelerated the process of secularization as the Church's leadership cannot cope adequately with the rising numbers and the urban environment does not encourage the practice of African traditional religion.

Thirdly, the Christian population has also been growing rapidly. For example, the Roman Catholics numbered 135,000 in 1966. Eight years later, their population had risen to 181,928.[17] Evidently, the rapidly

---

[15] Uganda census books 1959, 1969.

[16] Cyril and Rhona Sofer, *Jinja Transformed,* Kampala, 1958, p. 14.

[17] Catholic Directory of East Africa, 1966, 1974-6.

rising Christian population has also caused considerable pastoral problems. For example, the Protestant parish of Gadumire (East Busoga) had a total of twenty churches in 1972 and the average annual growth of Christians there was just over 3000. However, the parish had only one ordained clergyman and seven catechists to work in the twenty churches.[18] It is clear that this staff is too small to do a satisfactory job.

Lastly , the 1969 census revealed that Busoga had a reasonably high percentage of people (65.1%) who had received some form of education. 11.1% of the 'educated' Basoga were above 45 years of age and many of them would be dead now. However, the next age group.16-45, had a high percentage (43.8%) of 'educated' men and women. This is the group which would probably have a large number of highly educated and sophisticated people who would need an equally sophisticated church leadership to minister to them. Similarly the last group 6-15, also calls for a modern and well-educated church leadership, since 72.5% of this group was going to school in 1969. Many of these people are still schooling either in secondary schools or universities. Soon they will be working in various fields where they will need an intelligent church leadership to minister to them. Moreover, it is well known that the number of 'educated' people rises every year in Busoga. If the church leadership is to remain effective, it must raise not only the standard of the church leaders but also increase their number.

The Protestants, as already implied, ordained their clergy—unlike the Roman Catholics—after only a short course lasting about two years. Their main recruiting ground for the supply of the ordinands was the group of catechists who formed one of the rungs of the professional ladder in the Protestant Church. The catechists were tried and faithful men who had had little or no formal education. This unsophisticated method of recruiting Protestant clergymen had the advantage of creating a substantial indigenous ministry quickly. But one of its main disadvantages has been that the Protestants have hardly benefited from the rising tide of schooling and educational institutions in the last forty years because they have continued recruiting poorly educated catechists to the priesthood.

However, in 1955 the Protestants took the initial steps to improve the quality of their clergymen. A meeting of the Inter-diocesan Theological Committee (ITC) of the Dioceses of Uganda and Upper Nile was held on 30 July 1955 to discuss ways and means of improving the quality—and probably the quantity—of the ordained clergy. Two of the major recommendations were that recruitment for the ministry should be made 'at full secondary level' and that a theological department should be established at Makerere College as this would help to promote

[18] Information from church statistics book, Iganga, Busumba Archives.

theological education.[19] In response to the new proposals Mukono, in 1958, introduced a two year pre-ordination course in English. The students admitted to the course had to have had six to nine years of formal education. After two years, the students were sent to work in the villages as lay-readers[20] for two or more years. They would then return to Mukono on the recommendation of the parish, to complete their course of ordination. This would take another three years.

Unfortunately this new scheme does not seem to have worked well. This was mainly because the people who ended up in a theological school after six or nine years of schooling were, on the whole, those who had failed to find places in other—possibly better—institutions. In other words the ministry was not their initial choice and most of them were rather poor in the academic field, thus providing a somewhat shaky foundation for improving the quality of the clergy. Secondly, there was a great weakness of lack of proper help and supervision from the elderly ordained Basoga clergy. Some of these senior clergy may well have been jealous of the younger men who would soon replace them. But others may simply have failed to relate to young men who, because of their knowledge of English, tended to act as if they were far better than the old clergy. It is said that the first Musoga to train under the scheme behaved in this way and he was not recommended to go back to Mukono for the ordination course.[21] It appears that several other Basoga catechists met the same fate and only one or two were ordained through this scheme.

In 1961, another interesting development occurred when Buwalasi college started to offer a diploma course in theology. However, seven years later, Buwalasi which had run into serious financial and staffing problems, was forced to close down.[22] Although Mukono was now offering both the certificate and diploma in theology courses, it is clear that the closure of Buwalasi was a major blow to the Protestant efforts to improve the quality and quantity of their clergy. With only one college offering higher training to the ordinands, the competition for places is very keen with the result that the number of people who get access to these courses is very small. This apparently is one of the major reasons for the absence, in Busoga, (with the exception of the bishop who has a BA degree) of a single Protestant clergyman who has obtained a diploma

[19] Minutes of the Inter-diocesan Theological Committee of the Dioceses of Uganda and Upper Nile, meeting on 30 July 1955, kept in Buwalasi File at Mukono Theological College.

[20] The Basoga called them *Ababulizi Abo'Luzungu,* meaning lay-readers who knew English. This was done to distinguish them from the majority of elderly lay-readers who did not know English.

[21] Interview with Bishop Cyprian Bamwoze on 24 February 1975 at his home at Bugembe.

[22] Buwalasi File.

in theology. There are, however, several Basoga clergymen who have obtained the certificate in theology and the 1975 student list at Mukono includes four Basoga diploma candidates. So that in the next two years the Protestant Church in Busoga will have its first diploma clergymen.

The dilemma which the Busoga church leadership faces is that the church is confronted with a situation, as already described, which calls for a rapid increase of well-trained church leaders, particularly the clergy. But the output of the theological colleges is extremely small. This is true not only of Mukono, but also of the Roman Catholic seminaries. For example, between 1940 and 1974 only nine Basoga have been ordained priests.[23] The theological colleges have limited funds and facilities. This makes it difficult for them to increase their intake and therefore their output. Also—in the case of the Roman Catholics—the ordination course is so long that only a handful of people ever persist to the end.

In the last fourteen years, while the churches have tried to improve the quality of some of the clergy, somewhat desperate measures have also had to be taken to see that the situation caused by the increasing number of Christians does not get out of hand. The first and obvious step has been for the church leaders, particularly the clergy, to spread out more thinly on the ground in order to meet the needs of the growing body of Christians. The main weakness with this arrangement is that the clergy are able to give only very minimal pastoral care to the Christians. And it may well be that very often when the clergyman is needed, he is unable to come, as he would be visiting some distant church in one corner of his big parish.

Secondly, the Roman Catholics have retained a big expatriate staff. For example, in 1974 Busoga had thirty-seven priests and brothers. Twenty-nine of these were European priests; six European brothers; one Muganda priest and one Muganda brother.[24] But the European priests are getting old. Moreover, their presence in huge numbers is somewhat embarrassing in an independent African state. It is certain, therefore, that at least some of the expatriate priests will soon have to be replaced. Indeed this would be in line with the thinking of the Vatican because during his visit to Uganda in July 1969, the Pope, when closing the All Africa Bishops' Symposium in Rubaga Cathedral declared, 'By now, you Africans are missionaries to yourselves . . . you Africans must now continue, upon this continent, the. building up of the Church.'[25] In Busoga this task will have to involve a growing number of Basoga church

---

[23] 'Diocesan Staff 1966–74', list in Diocesan Archives, Jinja. File S/2 statistics.

[24] Diocesan Staff list, 1966–74. File S/2 Statistics.

[25] Discourse of His Holiness at the closing of the symposium in the Cathedral of Kampala, 31 July 1969.

workers and a diminishing number of expatriate missionaries. In contrast to the Roman Catholic Church leadership, the Protestant leadership has been completely Africanized or Basoganized. There were forty ordained Basoga clergymen in 1974.[26] But their number was still too small to cope with the work. Consequently, the bishop ordained in 1974 three lay-readers without any pre-ordination training. Their only qualification was that they were, according to the bishop, 'able men of integrity'. The three men namely, E. Wapali, S. Magulu and Y. Kigenyi have now helped to reinforce the already overworked and small ordained ministry.[27] The danger here is that if this practice became a regular one, it would frustrate the original Protestant efforts to improve the quality of the clergy.

Thirdly, the Basoga Christian women (both lay and religious) have since the 1910s played an important role in church leadership in their country. Before the 1960s a majority of the women church workers were employed as school teachers, while others worked in the medical field. But with the assumption of the administration of schools by the independent Uganda government, there has been less emphasis on recruiting women church workers as professional teachers. Instead the tendency has been—at least in the Roman Catholic Church—to rechannel their services to the parishes where, as already discussed, there is a serious shortage of church workers.

In the Roman Catholic Church the women church workers, mainly sisters, teach in the Sunday schools, but a good deal of their time is also spent in womens' clubs in which they teach personal hygiene, reading, writing, sewing, making mats and baskets, and performing plays.[28] Further they visit homes, hospitals and even prisons where they deal with various pastoral problems. In the Western region of Uganda an experiment was started in 1968 in which some of the sisters were posted to out-stations where they did the type of work an ordinary lay catechist does.[29] The Jinja diocese has not started a similar experiment yet. But the success of the experiment in Western Uganda and the continuing shortage of staff are likely to encourage similar developments in Jinja diocese, and elsewhere, in future.

The Protestants, on the other hand, have watched quietly the number of their women church workers grow thin over the last two decades without making any serious attempt either to retrieve or breathe new life into this group of church workers. Staff lists of Iganga, Kaliro,

[26] 1974 Staff List (Protestant), Diocesan Archives, Jinja.

[27] Interview with Bishop C. Bamwoze on 24 February 1975 at his home, Bugembe.

[28] Diocesan News Letter. December-January, 1967-8.

[29] A. Shorter and E. Kataza (eds.), *Missionaries to Yourselves,* London, Chapman, 1972, p. 181.

Namutumba and Busesa deaneries in the period 1967 to 1973, for example, hardly include any women church workers. It was only Iganga and Busesa which listed eight and six women respectively and it is likely that these are only voluntary Sunday-school teachers. It is rather difficult to account for the diminishing number of Protestant women church workers. It appears, however, that since the withdrawal of the Protestants from the schools, the Christian women teachers there have found it increasingly difficult to identify with the Protestant leadership. Consequently they have developed an indifferent attitude to church activities and responsibilities. Secondly many of the women church workers have become Balokole (saved ones) and they prefer to work with the Balokole as evangelists than with the 'official' Protestant Church which may not allow them to exercise their full potential as leaders.[30] Lastly marriage has also taken a heavy toll of the Protestant women church workers. Many active single women church workers tend—perhaps understandably—to become passive as far as church work is concerned on getting married. In spite of these factors the Protestant Church would benefit enormously by recruiting more women workers to work mainly with the women and children in the rural areas. Two Basoga girls, Miss P. Kadhumbula and Miss Bawaya have recently been ordained deaconesses, thus laying the foundation for a strong ministry of women in the Protestant Church in Busoga. This is an encouraging development, but what is needed more urgently is a big group of voluntary but committed women church workers to play their role of complementarity which has steadily weakened in the last two decades.

Fourthly, the Roman Catholics and Protestants have during the last decade increasingly used either voluntary or part-time church workers. A few of these—the Protestants—are ordained men, but a majority of the part-time workers are laymen who are respectable in their communities and faithful to their Christian calling. Part-time workers have done an excellent job in providing leadership in Christian communities which would otherwise be fragmented. Part-time workers have been in such high demand that they have, at times, outnumbered the full-time workers. For example, the Roman Catholic staff list for 1969 listed sixty-five full-time catechists and ninety-six part-time workers.[31] At present it seems that the part-time worker is not a permanent solution to the problem of shortage of trained church workers. Admittedly their status would be considerably enhanced if the suggestion of making part-time workers deacons[32] is taken seriously and followed up. As this has not

[30] For further information on the Balokole see p. 74.

[31] Staff list 1969. Diocesan Archives, Jinja.

[32] A. Hastings, *Church and Mission in Modern Africa,* London, Burns and Oates, 1967, p. 227.

happened yet, the only major advantage of the part-time arrangement is that it helps the church to keep various Christian communities going while urgently needed church workers are being trained.

(ii) The Catechists

Since the introduction of Christianity in Busoga, the catechists, as already indicated, played a very important role in both the expansion of the church and in leading the young, but growing Christian communities in the country. Although the catechists had these important pastoral functions to perform they were neither well educated nor well paid. During the inter-war and even post-war periods the catechists were further ignored because there was no attempt made to improve their conditions of service and both the Protestants and Roman Catholics diverted their resources from catechist training to the schools and teacher-training colleges. The result was that the bright and ambitious catechists were forced to look for employment elsewhere, where they were better paid,[33] while the hopeless condition of the catechists tended to discourage good new candidates from entering the catechist ministry. As the good and able catechists were leaving, the Protestants and Roman Catholics increasingly employed men of inferior quality as catechists. It is little wonder that as late as 1953 Fr Saraber of Wesunire (North Busoga) remarked

> They [catechists] have too little knowledge of our faith so that they cannot even explain the Sunday Gospel. They have no religious training. There has not been any development since the early beginning. There are no or certainly not sufficient books explaining the faith. They have no primary education so that many hardly know [sic] to read and write. The lack of wages keeps many young men back from this beautiful work.[34]

The Protestant catechists were not as poorly trained as the catechists Fr Saraber described; the Protestants would at least know how to read and write. One thing remains clear, however, and that is that the catechist ministry in Busoga, as elsewhere in Uganda, had not—by the beginning of the 1960s—benefited from the various educational changes in Uganda. Their salaries and education remained ridiculously low and their quality, influence and *ekitiibwa* had suffered a serious decline.

In the 1960s the serious problem of lack of adequate manpower

---

[33] Tom Tuma, 'The Introduction and Growth of Christianity in Busoga 1891-1940: with particular reference to the Roles of the Basoga Clergymen, Catechists and Chiefs', University of London Ph.D. Thesis 1973 p. 299-301.

[34] Fr C. Saraber to Bishop Billington, 10 Jan 1953. File, XIV History. Diocesan Archives. Jinja.

encouraged the Protestants and Roman Catholics to realize that the declining catechist ministry could be revived and made to play a more active role in the church. It was with this realization and, in the case of the Roman Catholics, with financial help from various overseas missionary organizations,[35] that the church undertook either to build or upgrade various catechist training centres (CTC) in Uganda. The Jinja diocese (Roman Catholic) sends its catechists to both Mityana (Buganda) and Kidetok (Bukedi) catechist training centres to receive further training. As one of the aims of the catechist training centres is to raise the intellectual level of the catechists, Mityana and Kidetok require a candidate to have had some pastoral experience and at least seven years of formal education. The course lasts two years during which the students are instructed in spiritual, liturgical, biblical and doctrinal material. This training helps the catechist to improve his knowledge and to equip him for teaching religion in schools. It is interesting to note that Kidetok admits only married men who have to take their wives with them. This gives the wives the opportunity to learn some new skills, but it seems that the most important reason for this arrangement is to enable the students to live in a real community. It should be remembered that since Vatican II there has been a growing understanding of the church as a community in which the church workers provide the necessary leadership. In other words, the newly trained catechist is also expected to act as a leader of his community.

These developments are new and their impact on the catechist ministry and the church is still largely undetermined. However, the difficulties which the revival of the catechist ministry has raised are clearer and are worth mentioning. First, the question of ordaining some of the worthy catechists to a permanent diaconate has caused several protracted debates in Roman Catholic circles. Some say the ordination will help to alleviate the problem of the shortage of priests, but others have argued that ordination of the catechist will introduce a double clergy: one group would be highly educated and celibate and the other would be married and poorly educated.[36] This is a valid point to raise. But if double standards are accepted in the catechist ministry, why shouldn't they be accepted in the priesthood? The ordination of some of the catechists will be an experiment and, like all experiments, it may or may not work, It is perhaps in this light that the ordination of some of the catechists should be seen.

The Protestants have rather belatedly reopened (February 1975)

[35] B. Joinet, 'The Training of Catechists and its Financial Implications' in *Missionaries to Yourselves,* A. Shorter and E. Kataza (eds.), London, 1972, p. 83.

[36] M. Rooyackers, 'Catechists and the Future of the Christian Ministry', in *Missionaries to Yourselves,* pp. 138-142.

Bishop Hannington catechist centre at Iganga. The reopening of the CTC may well have been partly influenced by the vigorous catechist programme of the Roman Catholics and partly by the need to train more third certificate candidates some of whom would eventually be upgraded to the rank of ordained clergy. [37] The course will last one year and the minimum entry requirement is possession of the second catechist certificate. It seems that one year is too short a period for the students to experience any reasonable intellectual growth. It is also doubtful whether the training of the third certificate catechist, who might eventually be ordained, will help to improve the quality of the ordained Protestant clergy. Further, the Rev. E. Kamira who is in charge of the catechist centre is also the *omusumba* of Iganga and has no intention of giving up this post. It is therefore unlikely that he will satisfactorily combine the two jobs. It is also worth mentioning that the staff of the CTC consists of only two people, the Rev. E. Kamira and his assistant S. Isabirye. Although only about twenty students will be admitted, the staff seems to be rather too thin to do a good job. Moreover three days before the CTC was reopened, neither of the staff members had a clear idea of what was going to be taught to the new students. In view of all this, it seems that the Protestants have few chances of making any significant improvement in, say, the next ten years to the quality of their catechists, while the catechist programme of their Roman Catholic counterparts appears to be well-organized and adequately financed.

It should also be noted that throughout the last decade the Protestants and the Roman Catholics have not provided any facilities to train the untrained catechists who, incidentally, are more numerous than the trained catechists: according to the 1972 staff list, the Roman Catholics employed 16 trained and 183 untrained catechists. A similar pattern is also recognized in the Protestant parishes. For example, Namutumba parish had 17 trained and 36 untrained catechists in 1972. In the same year, Kiringa parish had only two trained and 11 untrained catechists.[38] Lack of money to build new buildings and pay improved salaries of well-trained catechists; little enthusiasm for further training; poor academic background are some of the factors which make it difficult—if not impossible—for improvement in quality of all the catechists to be realized. Admittedly the Roman Catholics offer their untrained catechists some simple training during their monthly meetings and annual retreats but it is doubtful whether such piecemeal—and probably not well planned—training has any great impact on the untrained catechists. On the whole, the untrained catechists have been left on their

[37] Interview with the Rev. E. Kamira on 18 February 1975 at his home at Iganga. The Rev. E. Kamira has been named to run the Iganga CTC.

[38] Church Statistics. Iganga Busumba Archives.

own, by both the Protestants and Roman Catholics, to fare as best they can. This necessarily means that for a long time to come, the catechist ministry in Busoga, and probably elsewhere in Uganda, will consist—as it has always done—of the two categories of trained and untrained catechists. And as long as these categories remain distinct, with the trained catechists in the minority, the old catechist image—in spite of the reopening of the CTC—is likely to remain unchanged.

The Balokole and Dissent

One of the most interesting developments in Busoga church history in the past fourteen years has been the split into the awakened and non-awakened groups within the Balokole or revival movement. This development is new and is still unfolding, therefore whatever conclusions are arrived at will be tentative. The history of the beginning of the Balokole movement is well known and need not be repeated here. However, it is worth remarking that by the 1940s the revival movement had already taken root in Busoga where it was introduced and spread mainly by a small, but highly mobile, fearless and vocal group of committed Basoga namely, (Mrs) M. Mwavu and Mika Mwavu, Mesulamu Waiswa, Aloni Isabirye, Firimoni Kireri, E. Wakobi and T. K. Mukabire.[39] In spite of some fierce initial opposition from the Protestant established leadership in Busoga, the revival movement did not secede and they remain, to this day, members of the Protestant Church, although they enjoy a separate and distant identity from the rest of the Protestants. It is rather surprising, therefore, that the split should have occurred in the revival movement itself. What are the factors which led to this development?

The issue of awakened and non-awakened Balokole started in Kampala and it is from here that it has spread throughout East Africa. Although every unit or group of Balokole has almost complete autonomy, Kampala—being an old Balokole centre and the seat of nationally recognized Balokole leaders, for example S. Nsibambi—has tremendous influence over the different Balokole units scattered all over the country. Moreover, the monthly Balokole meetings in Kampala are attended by Balokole from the various units in the country. This makes it possible for a reliable channel of communication

[39] The seven people named here were all school teachers except Kireri who was Gombolola Chief at Namalemba and Isabirye who was already a CMS catechist. He is now an ordained minister. Mika Mwavu 'Obulamu Bw'owoluganda Tomasi Mukabire 1910–39', (The life of our brother Tomasi Mukabire). Mwavu was a close friend of Mukabire and this short paper he wrote was based on his personal recollections.

[40] Interview with Yona Mondo 16 July 1975 at his home, Kawempe.

to be established between Kampala and the Balokole units in the country, and the various units of Balokole outside Kampala are informed about the developments there.

In the 1960s, according to several informants, some of the Balokole led by Yona Mondo and the Rev. Y. Matovu began to feel that the movement had gone off course as it was compromising on many issues with the modern world. For example Balokole girls were seen wearing long hair and short dresses and respectable Balokole were involved in borrowing money which they sometimes failed to pay back. Mondo had also observed that Nsibambi, who was an invalid and was not attending their regular fellowship meetings, could no longer give the Balokole movement the strong leadership it needed.[40] The dissenting group believed that what was needed to put the movement back on its right course was to rekindle the spiritual vitality of the movement. But how would this be done? The clue to the answer was discovered in Ephesians 5:14 'Awake, Sleeper, rise from the dead, and Christ will shine upon you!' For Mondo and his followers, the Balokole had been sleeping and he called upon them to awake. He, however, took an either/or stand on the issue and claimed that either one was awakened and a Mulokole or non-awakened and not a Mulokole.[41] This claim disturbed, as would be expected, a large number of Balokole who did not share Mondo's position. Indeed the elderly, respectable and recognized leader of the Balokole in Uganda, S. Nsibambi pleaded on three occasions with Mondo asking him to apologize for the stand he had taken and for lack of respect for the 'abakulu mu Revival', leaders of the revival movement. But Mondo rejected these pleas,[42] thus, demonstrating openly his readiness to defy recognized authority. Nsibambi, who was thoroughly upset by Mondo's insubordination, attributed this strange behaviour to Mondo's desire to acquire 'wealth, power and fame'.[43] Mondo denied these claims vehemently.

The non-awakened who were led by Kabaza, Bujimbi and Kigozi were also concerned about the theological implications of stressing awakening. They argued that the awakened group were putting Jesus Christ second and 'awakening' first. This meant 'taking away the pre-eminence of our Lord Jesus and the salvation through him is no longer important without awakening'.[44] The non-awakened were further disturbed by the awakened group's narrow and negative attitude to some

[41] S. Nsibambi's letter addressed to Ab'oluganda (brethren) on 8 September 1971.

[42] S. Nsibambi to Ab'oluganda.

[43] S. Nsibambi, 'The Nature of Revival and how the Grace of our Lord helped us to receive it here in Uganda and East Africa and the danger that can destroy it if it is not safeguarded.' Paper privately circulated.

[44] S. Nsibambi, paper privately circulated.

African traditional customs. For example, the ceremony of introducing a boy to the parents of the girl he intends to marry and the payment of dowry were singled out as some of the wicked customs which Balokole should not practice. Lastly, the non-awakened did not like the fundamentalist and legalistic stand which Mondo had taken. For example, that the awakened should not keep dogs because God takes care of them; they should not have life insurance policies because this expresses lack of faith and trust in God's protection.[45]

The awakened and non-awakened were fast drifting apart in spite of Nsibambi's attempts to bridge the gap between the two groups. Moreoever, there was growing antagonism and incidents of violence between the two groups. This development clearly indicated that reconciliation between the two groups was not possible—at least for some time. Therefore to minimize the clashes between the awakened and non-awakened, the latter began in 1974 to hold their weekly meetings at Kyambogo instead of Namirembe where the awakened group held their meetings. The split was now a sad reality which the Balokole had to learn to live with. In a final display of authority, Nsibambi expelled Mondo, Matovu and their followers from the Balokole movement until they refrained from their schismatic tendencies and apologized publicly to the rest of the Balokole.[46] It appears that by doing this, Nsibambi simply played into Mondo's hands; this was exactly what he wanted so that he could establish his own leadership in a new group, the awakened.

It should be noted that the split did not occur for seven years, during which period the various Balokole units in and outside Uganda were also drawn into the dispute. In Busoga, the debate was centred on the same issues as already discussed but the struggle for power there featured rather prominently. Before the secession, Mika Mwavu was recognized as the leader of the Balokole particularly in central and southern Busoga. Further north, however, the Balokole there tend to recognize Mesulamu Waiswa, one of the founders of the movement in Busoga, as their leader. Indeed when asked, five years ago, who was the leader of the Balokole movement in Busoga in the 1940s, Mika Mwavu replied:

> We did not have a leader in the proper sense of that word. But in a way Mesulamu Waiswa and myself could be said (still are) to have been the leaders. We decided when and where to meet. We also acted as advisers and guardians to the rest of the *Balokole*. Generally, however, every *Mulokole* (singular) is a leader. What I mean is that every *Mulokole* is expected to act both as a responsible person and to proclaim the Gospel.[47]

[45] S. Nsibambi to Ab'oluganda.

[46] S. Nsibambi to Ab'oluganda.

[47] Interview with Mika Mwavu on 22 October 1971 at Iganga.

Mwavu's statement makes one point clear and that is that the structure of authority is not well defined among the Balokole. Also, it should be noted that the leader is not appointed but he evolves. Yet once he has emerged, he does not, as already indicated, have any machinery to enforce his decisions or policies. Further, there is no device which can be used to change the leadership, once this is established. This situation encourages rather than discourages rivalry and the emergence of alternative leaders. In Busoga, then, Waiswa and Mwavu were recognized as leaders and, inevitably, a state of 'natural' rivalry has always existed between them. The awakened issue arrived to find a situation which was open to division. When Mwavu identified himself with the awakened group, Waiswa sided with the non-awakened among whom he would easily manoeuvre into an unrivaled position of leadership. Indeed he is now recognized as the leader of the non-awakened group in Busoga while Mwavu is the leader of the awakened group,[48] thus clearly illustrating that in Busoga the split has occurred along old cracks in the Balokole movement.

It is too early to determine the impact of these developments on the revival movement. However, the impression one gathers from many people is that the revival has been discredited by the split. For some time, therefore, its influence on the people is likely to grow weak. Secondly as long as the structure of authority in the Balokole movement remains vague and undefined, further splits are likely to occur in the near future.

Conclusion

By and large, post-independence Busoga has been characterized by a rapidly growing population; a rising number of literate people; increasing sophistication and secularization. The church in Busoga is aware of these developments and attempts have been made to respond to the demands of the new situation. The raising of the standards of the Protestant clergy; opening of new catechist centres; increasing lay participation and the subsequent change in the image of the clergy are some of the major changes which have been introduced or encouraged to develop in response to the demands of the new situation. It must be pointed out, however, that these changes have not been sufficiently far-reaching to make any significant impact on the situation in Busoga. The church will have to introduce more radical and far-reaching reforms in order to respond effectively to the new and rapidly changing situation in Busoga.

Another problem is that some of the recent developments, for example, the split in the Balokole movement may have adverse effects on

[48] Interview with Mrs Mwavu on 18 February 1975 at Iganga.

the church leadership (Protestant) in Busoga. However, this is a very recent development which is still unfolding and it may be unwise to determine how it is going to affect the church and its leadership. But if there are any further splits—and this is likely to happen—within the movement, this may well have serious repercussions in the Protestant leadership.

The African local churches and the world-wide Roman Catholic communion

Modification of relationships, as exemplified by Lilongwe Diocese

P. A. KALILOMBE

The *Report on the Experiences of the Church in the Work of Evangelization in Africa,* prepared by Bishop J. Sangu for presentation at the 1974 Synod of Bishops in Rome, had this to say:

One of the most important developments in Africa in the last 20 years has been the process of de-colonization. Between 1957 and 1969 no less than 42 countries became independent from colonial rule.

A parallel development has taken place in the Church. Formerly the missions were entrusted to Missionary Institutes which received from the Sacred Congregation for the Evangelization of Peoples the *'jus commissionis'.* During the last 20 years most of the missions have become dioceses and the hierarchy has been established bringing to an end the *'jus commissionis'.* The missions have become local Churches, although they still remain 'under' the Sacred Congregation for the Evangelization of Peoples.

This 'coming-of-age' of the Churches signifies a turning point in the history of the Church in Africa. It is the end of the missionary period. This does not mean the end of evangelization, even first evangeliza-tion. But it means, in the words of Pope Paul VI during his visit to Uganda: 'You Africans may become missionaries to yourselves'. In other words, the remaining task of evangelization of Africa is primarily the responsibility of the African Church itself.

This fact implies a radically changed relationship between the Church in Africa and the Sacred Congregation of the Evangelization of Peoples, the Missionary Institutes, and the other Churches in Europe and North America.[1]

One cannot but agree with this assessment of the situation concerning

[1] *Report on the Experiences of the Church in the Work of Evangelization in Africa;* The African Continent's report for the 1974 Synod of Bishops on 'The Evangelization of the Modern World' pp. 15-16. A mimeographed text distributed to the Bishops from African delegates to the Bishops' Synod. Henceforth referred to as 'Africa Report'.

relationships between the world-wide communion of the Roman
Catholic Church and the local churches now developing in Africa. The
statement is seen to be all the more weighty when we realize that the
Africa report was prepared from a fairly large and representative number
of national reports from episcopal conferences all over Africa. It is
therefore a summing up of a definite feeling which is gaining ground in
Africa, and thus deserves careful study.

In this paper I propose to begin by examining the situation of
Lilongwe Diocese as it was towards the end of 1972, the year that a first
African (Malawian) bishop was ordained for the diocese. This is in the
hope that the exposition can serve as a 'case study' of the relationship
between a developing local church in Africa and the world Catholic
communion. Admittedly conditions vary in the different countries and
dioceses of Africa. But it can validly be assumed that the case of
Lilongwe is to some extent typical of a large number of 'local churches'
on the continent. Secondly, I wish to draw some conclusions from this
case study, and situate these conclusions on the wider plane of Pan-
African Catholic consciousness as evidenced by what has gone on in
meetings of African Catholic church leaders in recent years.

THE DIOCESE OF LILONGWE

Lilongwe Diocese, which today comprises most of Malawi's Central
Region, is one of the seven ecclesiastical territories of the country. It was
raised to the status of a diocese in 1959, and Bishop J. Fady, WF,
became its first titular bishop. From the very start this territory was
entrusted to the White Fathers, and they have been the majority among
the pastoral workers ever since. It was to their society that Rome had
granted the *'jus commissionis'* for the territory, a sort of 'charter'
putting on the society the exclusive responsibility of building up the
church there and administering it. But, when the hierarchy was
established in the country, other missionary groups could join the
diocese. On 10 December 1963 a group of Carmelite Fathers from Spain
arrived in the diocese and have been taking part in the mission work until
now. There are also a couple of expatriate secular priests, who together
with the local diocesan priests complete the number of clergy in the
diocese.

There are several women's religious congregations working in the
diocese. The earliest were the White Sisters (Sisters of Our Lady of
Africa). They were later joined by the Sisters of Charity of Ottawa (Grey
Nuns), and then the Carmelite Sisters of Luxemburg and of Spain. A
local congregation, the Teresian Sisters, had been started in the 1930s.
They now form the majority of the local religious, although the Grey

Nuns and the Luxemburg Carmelites have also local recruits among themselves. In recent years the contemplative Poor Clares started a monastery in Lilongwe. [See also below, p. 569.] They have been highly successful in finding local vocations who are now by far the majority among them. As for men religious, there are a number of Marist Brothers who are mostly engaged in education work in post-primary institutions. All these religious, except the Poor Clares, are in fact engaged mostly in education, health, and social services. But a certain number among them are full-time pastoral workers in the parishes.

When I was ordained Bishop of Lilongwe in August 1972 and succeeded Bishop Fady, the situation of the diocese was something like this: the total population of the area was 1,400,000 (Malawi's population was estimated at about 5,000,000); the number of baptized Catholics stood at 189,000, while that of catechumens was 50,900.

The diocese consisted of 16 parishes and one quasi-parish which were served by an average of 3 priests per parish. Each parish is normally subdivided into outstations and smaller prayer-churches. These are served by trained and non-trained catechists and a large number of lay church elders. It was estimated that the number of remunerated or full-time catechists was 87, while that of non-remunerated (voluntary and often only part-time) catechists was 268.[2]

The Church was managing three secondary schools, one teacher training college, and one nursing school, plus a number of domestic science centres. In all these a number of brothers and sisters were engaged in the name of the diocese, because, although these schools are state-aided, the Church is responsible for their management. The same is true of the three main hospitals and the other smaller dispensaries and health centres which the religious congregations run in the name of the Church, even if the government offers substantial aid in the way of salaries, equipment and personnel. There was also a large number of primary schools which fall under the management of the diocese. In actual fact, however, the Church's burden for these, both personnel-wise and finance-wise, is very limited in that the government is almost fully responsible for them.

There can be no doubt that the running of the whole diocesan machinery calls for a large number of qualified and full-time church personnel. The system is such that the parishes could not function properly without an adequate supply of priests and religious. The schools and health services need a team of highly qualified church personnel working in the name and under the responsibility of the Church if the

---

[2] Details and statistics taken from the Diocesan Archives and from texts prepared for the Lilongwe Diocesan Mini-Synod (1973-5). The statistics are valid for the year 1972.

diocese is to continue its management of these specialized services.

In 1972 the total number of priests in the diocese was 76: 51 White Fathers, 13 Carmelite Fathers, 2 expatriate secular priests, and 10 diocesan (Malawian) priests. Not all these were actually or actively involved in parish work. Only 44 priests were in active service in the 16 parishes. Three other priests were professors at the inter-diocesan major seminary; two others were teaching at the minor seminary, two were taking care of the language centre, and one priest was full-time chaplain for sisters. Two other priests were engaged in mass media work (printing and journal), one priest was full-time chaplain for secondary schools, and two priests were in administration work for their congregation. Moreover, at that time 16 were on home leave, and two were studying overseas. It may be of interest to note that of these 76 priests, 15 were over 60 years of age, 14 between 50 and 60 years, 17 between 40 and 50, and only 30 were under 40 years of age. It could be said, therefore, that the majority were of an advanced age. This is not an idle remark when it is realized that already at that time the crisis in priestly vocations in the 'feeding' missionary congregations was very acute. It was to be foreseen that when, for any reason, one or the other of these missionary priests were to leave or to retire, they would be very difficult to replace. As for the local priests the prospects were that we had 16 students on the 6-year course at the major seminary. The most we could optimistically hope for, then, was that we might have 16 more priests in the coming 6 years.

Religious Brothers were 20: 9 Marist Brothers engaged in education work, and 9 White Father Brothers and 2 Carmelite Brothers working as auxiliaries especially in 'material' work. Religious Sisters were far more numerous, a total of 132: 45 Teresian Sisters, 30 Sisters of Our Lady of Africa, 24 Sisters of Charity of Ottawa (about 10 of whom were African), 11 Luxemburg Carmelite Sisters (4 of them Malawians), 4 Spanish Carmelites, and 18 contemplative Poor Clares (12 of them Malawians). Since most of these religious were working in schools and hospitals, as far as strictly parish work is concerned, their number is in itself immaterial, since only a handful are full-time pastoral workers.[3] And yet this large number is crucial as far as the diocese itself is concerned. On these religious falls the heavy commitment of the church in the network of schools and health services which are highly complex and expensive.

I was evidently interested in the finances of the diocese. I thought I should have an idea what was needed to keep such a complicated thing as the diocese going every year. What could possibly be the annual budget? How much money was needed annually, and for what? Where did the money come from? What were the prospects of such money forthcoming

---

[3] This was the situation in 1972. In most cases the numbers have subsequently tended to diminish rather than increase.

every year? For a new bishop, on whose inexperienced shoulders the burden of the local church was falling, these questions were vital.

A look at the diocesan treasurer's statement for 1971 made me tremble. It was little consolation to learn that the financial year ended happily with a credit balance of 1,297 Kwacha (K1,297). N.B. the Malawian Kwacha is equivalent to 10 English shillings. The receipts for the year, plus the credit balance left over from 1970, had amounted to some K 96,650. But the expenses were K 95,353.[4] These expenses were analysed to include such headings as: budgets for the parish (priests') communities (to the tune of K 23,517!); travel (home leaves for missionaries, and journeys within the country); expenses on seminarists (a total of K 6,416), and expenses for studies for priests; salaries for catechists, pensions, taxes, rents, insurances; constructions and repairs of houses and churches; salaries and pocket-money for lay missionaries, some brothers and some priests; administration, etc. . .

This was an eye-opener as to what the diocese needs money for. I could see that the schools and hospitals did not figure on the diocesan budget. It was explained that this was because these institutions were expected to be self-supporting in the sense that they depended on government aid, fees, and gifts which it was the responsibility of those who run the institutions to find on their own initiative. The religious were also largely excluded because each congregation is supposed to take care of its own houses and members with the aid of salaries received, help from mother-houses overseas, or from benefactors. If this was cause for relief, I could not but wonder what the diocesan expenses would amount to if this burden was some day to be thrown on the diocese also.

It was more interesting, and revealing, to examine the analysis of the receipts. As was to be expected, help coming from 'Rome' (Pontifical allocations: Propagation of the Faith, St Peter Apostle, Holy Childhood, etc.) was preponderant: K 35,768 or more than a third of the whole receipts. Another important heading was: 'Gifts from Christians abroad': K 12,209. Other sources of income included gifts from the WF, Mother House and grants from government (salaries).

What was of special interest for me, however, was what we may call local resources. One item was listed as 'Local Farming and Industry', things like the printing press, mills, farms, etc. owned by the diocese. That this amounted to some K 7,440 is a proof of serious efforts towards self-support. But here the initiative comes from the institution itself. What was more revealing was what the local Christians had contributed by way of church tithes. Apparently tithes for 1970 (4 parishes) and 1971 (10 parishes) plus an extraordinary collection, had given the sum of

---

[4] Details taken from the Diocesan Treasurer's office: statement for 1971 and budget for 1972.

K14,753. Other church collections (again for 1970: 3 parishes, and 1971: 10 parishes) came to K 1,635. This total of K 16,388 for the year 1971 and part of 1970 is really not impressive when compared with the whole receipts: K 96,650. I was left wondering how 189,000 baptized members and 50,900 catechumens could only manage to contribute this sum over the whole year. The conclusion was obvious: the diocese was not running with local resources but almost exclusively with 'charity' from abroad.

A DEPENDENT CHURCH

This situation of a 'local church' running with the help of other churches was, after all, not such an extraordinary one, nor was Lilongwe an exception in this regard. The church in Malawi and indeed in most 'mission lands' came into being when missionaries from abroad were sent to evangelize the territory. Understandably these missionaries had to start from scratch: to preach the Gospel to people who had not yet heard it, to set up structures for church life and mission in the area, to formulate policies for so doing, and then find ways and means of realizing those missionary policies.

The only personnel they could initially count on was that coming from other sister churches which had already attained a consistency and vitality strong enough not only to take care of themselves but also to send missionaries abroad to set up the church in other lands. Only later on were they in a position to find and train indigenous church workers and involve them in the task of building up the local church. And indeed it is to the credit of the early missionaries that from the very start they realized that it was their urgent responsibility to train local church workers and thus set the foundations for a truly local church. We see that practically from the start they formed lay teachers and catechists as auxiliaries in their evangelical work, and soon afterwards built seminaries for the training of local priests and houses of formation for local religious.

In the same way the resources needed for the work of the church had initially to be obtained from abroad, precisely through the initiative of those same missionaries who knew how and where to find the needed aid. Thanks to this external help the work of evangelization was made possible and the structures of the local church could slowly take shape. Admittedly the missionaries realized that as the local church emerged, this church should be taught to make more efforts to find its own resources. There is no denying the fact that serious efforts in this respect have been made over the years.

And yet looking at the facts in 1972 one had to admit that the Church of Lilongwe was still basically a dependent church,—and this after more than 70 years of missionary work in the area. As the statistics show, out of the 76 priests who kept the diocesan structure running, only 10 were Malawians, and a full 66 expatriates. Of the 20 religious Brothers, only one was Malawian and the rest expatriates. The situation for the Sisters may look much better since of the total number of 132, 71 were local. But we must not forget that the 61 expatriates were among those charged with the most complicated and expensive concerns of the diocese: post-primary schools, major hospitals, and basic administration organizations. And as for resources there is no comparison between the K 16,388 contributed by the local people and the K 80,262 which had to be obtained from abroad. In both personnel and resources therefore Lilongwe Diocese was running almost completely on external aid.

I was led to ask myself: Suppose tomorrow all the expatriate church personnel were to leave this diocese, would we be able to run the church as it is with only 10 local priests, 1 brother, and the 71 local sisters? And suppose all external aid were stopped, could we make do with only K 16,388 where K 96,650 are actually needed? These are evidently rhetorical questions. You could not possibly hope that in such an eventuality the diocese could continue in its present state or be able to achieve what it was achieving then,—and in the same way. The diocese could carry on only on condition that there was a continuing help from abroad in both personnel and resources. But for how long could we expect to receive such help? Already it was clear that the missionary congregations on which our hopes were founded were suffering from a dramatic drop in priestly and religious vocations, so much so that it was vain to expect reinforcements from that quarter. And as for overseas financial help, it was becoming more and more difficult to get, because in most of the former benefactor churches the attitude towards 'Missions' and 'Missionaries' was definitely becoming cool, not to say downright negative. But even had the prospects been brighter in those respects, that would not have been sufficient reason for unqualified optimism.

In 1972 there were other reasons for second thoughts. In various parts of Africa (e.g. Guinea, Eastern Nigeria, Uganda, parts of Mozambique, the Sudan,—just to mention some outstanding instances) events had demonstrated that the continuing presence of expatriate missionaries could not be lightly taken for granted. What was happening in those parts of Africa could very well happen elsewhere. For, after all, those events were symptomatic of a growing sense of dissatisfaction spreading widely in Africa. At this time, when most of the countries that formerly were colonies have achieved their political independence and are hard at work to consolidate this independence in all other aspects of national life, is it not anomalous that the local churches alone should continue to depend for their very existence on the charity of sister churches abroad?

RELATIONSHIPS OF DEPENDENCE

The quotation from the Africa Report which was given at the beginning of this paper suggests that in the recent developments of African history there is a parallelism between what has taken place in the political field and what has happened in the church. Such a parallelism has often been decried as inexact and confusing on the ground that colonialism and the missionary movement are really two very different phenomena. To some extent this is true: it is not legitimate to assimilate purely and simply these two movements because the basic aims and motivations of colonialism were different from those of evangelization. But there is no denying the fact that in the minds of many people mission work has tended to be thought of in similar terms as the colonial enterprise. It has been fashionable to say that the Cross of Evangelization prepared the way for the Sword of Colonialism. But let us be fair. It is perhaps not exact to say that everywhere missionary activity preceded or came in the wake of colonial expansion, or to say that the church was necessarily in collusion with colonial powers. There are many instances where this was certainly not the case. And it is a pity that today, in retrospect, people tend to make unfavourable generalizations about the church being the instrument of colonialism.

Nevertheless it is to be admitted that missionary activity has been influenced for quite some time by the colonial reality. In any case, in the mind of the people the two movements, coming as they did at about the same time, were bound to be construed as two versions of one and the same type of human encounters, in which a foreign way of life came to invade the local one with the definite intent of modifying the latter. The assumption was that the local way of life was going to profit by being thus influenced and modified by the foreign one, which comes down to saying that the foreign way of life was superior and better. In the case of colonialism the assumption was that Western civilization was better and should come to improve the more backward and primitive local cultures. As for the church, the superiority came from the fact that she was the bearer of the Gospel of Christ, which was God's final answer to man's inarticulate and erring gropings. Since the missionary happened to belong to the same Western civilization, he naturally tended to assume that the Western interpretation of Christ's Gospel was the right and standard one. Western culture and the Christian message could thus be in danger of being identified.

It is perhaps salutary to examine briefly what the exact relationship has been between the developing local churches and the world-wide Catholic communion through the Congregation for the Evangelization of the Peoples (formerly *Propaganda Fide*), the Missionary Institutes and the older churches of Europe and America.

Prior to the 1960s most territories in Africa belonged to what were called 'mission lands'. This means that the work of evangelization there, and the task of setting up and running the church was the responsibility of overseas churches, mostly through the missionary organizations. The Roman Congregation of *Propaganda Fide* was finally responsible for this missionary activity. It was the department charged, in the name of the Pope and the Universal Church, with the task of organizing these activities all over the world. These mission areas were called Vicariates or Prefectures Apostolic. In other words, they were not dioceses on their own, they were not yet really local churches but dependent churches. In principle it was the Supreme Pontiff himself who was Bishop of these ecclesiastical territories. The bishops or ecclesiastical heads who actually administered them did so in his name and under his direct responsibility through *Propaganda Fide*, which called upon one or other missionary organization to take on the responsibility of evangelizing the territory.

It is important to point out that both the congregation and the missionary institutes working under its supreme authority and direction are the concrete expression of the universal Catholic Church's co-responsibility in the accomplishment of her God-given mission. It is the whole church that is charged by the Divine Missionary with the task of 'going out into the whole world to make disciples of all nations' (Matt. 28, 19). The Church Catholic subsists in and through the communion of local churches spread all over the world. These local churches render the Universal Church present and operative in the concrete local societies, cultures, and situations in which they are found. The local church is not an isolated or self-contained entity. She is indeed a consistent and concrete presence of the church through her insertion in the local context, but to be really part of the Universal Church she has to remain open to the other local churches with which she is in communion. The tasks, successes, failures, needs, growth or drawbacks of one local church are the concerns of all the other churches in the communion. Therefore wherever and whenever one local church is in need she has the right to be helped by sister churches who are in a position to do something about it. The Roman Congregation, working in the name of the Pope who is the sign and factor of this catholicity, actually facilitates and concretizes the involvement of all the local churches of the world in the creation of new local churches in new territories. And in fact this Roman Congregation was created in the 17th century precisely in order to make sure that the 'expansion' of the church in new territories was the common work of the whole church rather than the project of one national church, or indeed a means of making the church serve the secular or colonial interests of some nations. As a central body in a presumably neutral and non-nationalistic situation, the Roman Congregation is in a better position to serve as an acceptable and impartial recipient of world-wide charities for the missions and a distribution centre with a universal out-look.

To a certain extent the same can be said of the missionary organizations. It is indeed true that most of these organizations or congregations have arisen through the charismatic initiative of individual members of the church, often within the context of a definite local church with inevitable cultural and even national overtones. There are even missionary institutes that are 'national' in the sense that their membership, methods, and support depend mainly on one specific nation or country. Many other institutes however are international. All the same, because of the supreme responsibility of the Roman Congregation over the activities of all these missionary bodies, there is a certain guarantee that through these institutes the whole church is really involved, rather than just one local church or one nation.

And yet we have to admit that the involvement of older churches in the building up and running of mission churches, even if expressed through the agency of the Roman Congregation and the missionary organizations, does involve a danger: that of trying to build the missionary local church to the image of the older 'parent' churches. In other words, there is the danger that the young missionary church might remain for too long a dependent church, a sort of appendage to the overseas churches that have given her birth and continue to support her. We have pointed out, in the case of Lilongwe Diocese, that she was a 'dependent church'. And we tried to show that this was because, in the situation, the type and amount of personnel and resources needed to keep the local church running were such that it will always be necessary to make appeal to overseas or older churches.

In the final analysis such a local church is still just a 'transplanted church'. The shape or form of this local church is still too much a copy of overseas churches. The ways and methods followed in running her are very much those used in the churches abroad where the missionaries come from. So that in order to keep the church going it will be necessary to use the same 'instruments' as those of the overseas churches, and to employ the same methods and ways with the help of the same type and quality of expertise and experience. If you want to maintain the same system and the same kind of enterprise then you need adapted 'equipment' and similar 'technicians' as those required for the original 'standard': the overseas church.

In fact, the basic problem in our young churches of Africa is not the need for more priests, more sisters and brothers, and more money to run our churches as they have run up till now. This would be just begging the question. This problem of staffing and resources as expressing itself now is not the basic one: it is just the consequence of a more fundamental problem. If we need more and more of these it is because we are assuming that the actual system has to continue in the same way, just because this is how things are done in other churches elsewhere. Now, as long as such a transplantation of the church continues, it is evident that our churches will be dependent on the churches in Europe and America, our 'prototypes' and the source of our very being. It is illusory to hope for a really 'local' church in Africa unless we are prepared to question even the system itself. The question should be this: If really we want to make the church local in Africa, what has to be done? But this question calls for another preliminary one: What is a really local church?

WHAT IS A REALLY LOCAL CHURCH?

When AMECEA[5] Bishops met in plenary session in Nairobi in December 1974 for a special study session on *'Planning for the Church in Eastern Africa in the 1980s'*,[6] they realized that what was needed was to plan for a really 'local' church in Eastern Africa. They took time to describe what for them would be a really local church. Their way of thinking can be taken as representative of the thinking that is going on in most parts of Africa today. In the Preamble to the 'Guidelines' which emanated from this session we find this description:

'While the Church of Christ is universal, it is a communion of small local Christian Churches, communities of Christians rooted in their own society. From the Bible we learn that such local Churches are bosn through apostolic and missionary preaching. But they are meant to grow so that with time they become firmly rooted in the life and culture of the people. Thus the Church, like Christ himself, becomes incarnated in the life of the people. She is led by local people, meets and answers local needs and problems, and finds within herself the resources needed for her life and mission.

We are convinced that in these countries of Eastern Africa it is time for the Church to become really "local", that is: *Self-ministering, self-propagating and self-supporting.* Our planning is aimed at

[5] This abbreviation stands for: Association of Member Episcopal Conferences of Eastern Africa. AMECEA comprises the episcopal conferences of Uganda, Kenya, Tanzania, Malawi and Zambia. Every three years the bishops of these five countries meet in plenary session to share experiences, plan ways of collaborating on a number of points of common interest, or study together one or another point.

[6] A full report on this Session is found in *AFER,* Vol. XVI, Nos 1 and 2; 1974.

building such local Churches for the coming years.'[7]

What the bishops meant by these basic characteristics of a really local church had been amply discussed during the session itself.

A self-ministering church

A local church is self-ministering when all the essential services needed for the life and work of the church are actively assumed by members of that local church, and not mainly by helpers from outside. As long as these services are heavily dependent on missionary or external aid, the church is not yet self-ministering. In the context it was insisted upon that when we talk of 'ministry' and 'ministers' we should not think only, or even mainly, of priests or ordained ministers. We should rather consider 'ministry' in its broadest sense.

> The ordained ministry is just one (the most basic, I grant) of the indispensable ministries in the Church. There are many other ministries needed for the proper functioning of the Body of Christ. And these ministries are not necessarily 'ordained': they can be exercised by lay people—often better by them! Thus we have ministries of teaching religion, organising and executing liturgical functions and prayer, leading and ordering Christian communities, sanctifying Christians in all sorts of ways, including the celebration of some sacraments, taking care of the material side of Church administration, etc. For these and other ministries, the clergy is admittedly mainly responsible because of their role in the Church. But Christ's will is such that the *clergy alone cannot fulfil them adequately.* And that, not just due to their small number, but *because the proper running of these services calls for a variety of charisms and gifts that are not found among the clergy alone.*[8]

In order to build a self-ministering church in the context of our African communities it is necessary to involve the whole church in the active ministry. And evidently the decisive factor will be a more enlightened and involved laity since by far the majority of church members will be the laity.

> 'Until such time as the laity have been fully involved, and a realistic redistribution of ministries, ordained and non-ordained, has been made, it is impossible to say whether we have too few priests or too many! There is plenty of room for a large number of non-ordained ministries, which could be assumed by the laity. And perhaps, if they

[7] Ibid. pp. 9-10.

[8] P. A. Kalilombe, *Christ's Church in Lilongwe Today and Tomorrow*, Likuni Press, Lilongwe, 1973, pp. 20-1. It will be seen that the thinking in all this section is tributary to what A. Hastings has written about extensively, e.g. in *Mission and Ministry*, Sheed & Ward, 1971, *Church and Ministry*, Gaba Publications, 1972.

were, we would find out that the shortage of priests that is talked about is not of the same type as we tend to assume.' [9]

A self-propagating church

A living and effective local Church should possess the outgoing dynamism to attract new members. A self-propagating Church is one that does not rely for this attracting of new members only or mainly on outside missionaries, but on her own members, her own initiatives, her own methods and means.[10]

Where the whole church membership is actively involved in the life and witnessing of the church in an area, this local church not only succeeds in attracting new members, but also exerts its influence on the whole society. Being the bearer of Christ's mission to preach the Good News, it is inevitable that an active church will become the leaven in the mass of mankind: helping the Gospel values to permeate the day to day life of the total community. A self-propagating church is one which becomes this salt, light, or leaven through the agency of the members who are actually sharing in the life of the area. In this case the methods used will be those within the range and comprehension of the local people, and the areas of men's life and activity where the message of Christ will be made to bear will be those relevant to the conditions of the people. In other words, when and where those mainly responsible for the spreading of the Gospel are the local people, there is much chance that the church will 'scratch where it itches' rather than give nice answers to problems that are not there or that pose themselves differently from what the answers presuppose.

A self-supporting church

A self-supporting church is one that depends *mainly* on the local members to find money and other material goods to maintain and run her essential services, to support her pastoral workers, and to expand those services that the church needs to develop.

No one can doubt that richer countries have a grave duty to give economic assistance to poor countries, and rich churches to poor churches. The question is how to implement these principles without undermining the real character of a local church and the ecclesiastical reality of subsidiarity and self-reliance. The people of God are an earthly, eating, drinking, buying, selling people. It is not only practically advantageous, it is theologically necessary that a local

[9] *AFER,* XVI, p. 59.

[10] Kalilombe, *Christ's Church,* pp. 23-4.

church be itself an economically viable unit.[11]

A self-supporting church is one which depends more on the local people than on outside help. One important consequence of such a dependence on the local contribution is that the material aspect of church life and work will be determined mainly by the local possibilities and the real local needs. In other words it is the 'local pocket' that should dictate what type and size of material realities the church is going to possess and use. A church that intends to become really 'local' must resist the ever-present temptation of becoming a slave to imported needs and standards. This is a point that missionaries will want to remember.[12]

This description of a self-ministering, self-propagating, and self-supporting church must be rightly understood. A truly local church is one in which the ministry, the missionary activity, and the material support is *mainly* local. This word 'mainly' is being used deliberately. It is on purpose that we have avoided the word 'exclusively'. A church that would strive towards becoming exclusively local is doomed to atrophy and death. A healthy and developing church must be open to communion and collaboration with other sister churches, or else she becomes isolated and dies a natural death. In speaking about a self-reliant or truly local Church the AMECEA Bishops were far from advocating an isolated or self-sufficient church. They only wanted to find out under what conditions our young African churches could hope to develop from dependent churches into self-reliant ones.

Building Small Christian Communities
The three characteristics of a truly local church are a tall order, and one would wonder whether they are feasible in the circumstances of our African churches. The bishops believe that they are possible, but they pointed out on what condition. The Preamble to the Guidelines continues with these words:

> We believe that in order to achieve this we have to insist on building Church Life and work on basic Christian communities in both rural

---

[11] A. Hastings, *Mission and Ministry*, p. 14.

[12] 'It is perfectly true that missionaries have stressed the importance of paying church tax in season and out of season, even going as far (too far) as refusing the sacraments (including baptism for their children) to those who fail to pay. The question one has to ask is whether this constant endeavour has not been largely vitiated by the context within which it has operated, especially of recent years. A context in which, first, local christians can see perfectly clearly that missionaries have in fact access to sources of money beyond their wildest dreams; secondly, church institutions have been created and ways of clergy living established which the local church—with the best will in the world—could not support financially. The local christians draw the obvious conclusion: if you choose to erect institutions totally beyond our means, you can provide the financial support yourselves and not look to our meagre resources.' Ibid. pp. 14-15.

and urban areas. Church life must be based on the communities in which everyday life and work takes place: those basic and manageable social groupings whose members can experience real inter-personal relationships and feel a sense of communal belonging, both in living and working. We believe that Christian communities at this level will be best suited to develop real intense vitality and to become effective witnesses in their natural environment.

In such authentic communities it will be easier to develop a sense of community whereby the Church can exist as Christ's Body, consisting of 'many parts' (clergy, religious, laity) with many charisms, but making one Body in the one Spirit (I Corinthians, 12). We want to see collaboration and co-ordination in the life and work of all the different parts of the Christian community.[13]

The forming of such smaller Christian communities has become a major preoccupation and a decisive programme for the church in Africa. The AMECEA territories decided to make it the topic of their plenary meeting in 1976. Already at the 1974 Roman Synod of Bishops the Africa Report was able to state that 'many Bishops' Conferences in Africa strongly recommend that present Church structures and attitudes be modified by establishing basic Christian Communities.'[14]

At the root of all this pre-occupation with small Christian communities is the conviction that, to be realistic, the formation of a true local church has to start from the bottom, that is by the building up of smaller Christian communities. Because when it comes to real feeling of community and a possibility of on-going community tasks, the community in question must be of such a size, territorial proximity, and sufficient similarity of interests as to draw its members into a feasible entity. Such a small Christian community is the only level at which 'the Church' can concretely live and work. It is at this level, that the church will be really present in the society at large and will be able to act.

Communities of this type can be built up by grouping people who live in such a geographical proximity that they can meet at regular intervals, can know one another sufficiently to have a feeling of 'family', can pray together, and can experience together joys, sorrows, successes, failures, problems and solutions. They must be able really to work together, plan together, train one another and help one another. They should group a sufficient number of adherents and variety of ecclesial charisms to be able to assure the ordinary non-ordained ministries that keep the local church alive and active in day-to-day life. It is evident that for such local communities the presence of local, trained and efficient lay leaders is basic. These leaders would support, animate and lead the community in

[13] *AFER*, XVI, p. 10.

[14] 'Africa Report', p. 12.

its various needs and services. A local church council, composed of leaders of various aspects of the community's life and work will serve as a co-ordinating, animating and directing organ of the local church.

In most territories of Africa this is not something completely new. Although on paper and in juridical terms we in Africa have adopted the language of older churches with their tradition of dioceses, deaneries, parishes, etc, the reality is quite different. We talk indeed in terms of 'parish', but in actual fact, as far as real Christian life is concerned, it is on what we may call sub-parish level that the real thing is going on. Grouped under the rather broad umbrella of 'parish' are several basic churches which are the real units of *the* Church. They are usually led by some resident catechist or church elders—laymen—while the priests do their best to make the presence of the ordained ministry felt at longer or shorter intervals.

The African bishops would like everyone to realize that this state of affairs is not a second-best solution, but perhaps the only realistic basis of church existence in our territories. They would like therefore to exploit to the full the potentialities latent in this type of church existence. The conviction is that if the church's life and work is based first and foremost on this level, self-ministering, self-propagation and self-supporting of the church will be possible. At this local and rather restricted level, the needs, problems, structures, and required techniques are of such a simple type that the majority of the faithful can be expected to get involved and feel really part of the church. At the higher levels of parish, diocese, or conference, things get so big and complex that only a minority can be usefully involved, and this minority needs to be specially selected and highly trained. Were we to base the church's life and work on this higher plane, we would need a multitude of such specialized personnel and a lot of complicated instruments and much money to keep things going.

Evidently these higher structures are needed and important. They are necessary as unifying, organizing, directing and animating structures. They serve to insert these smaller churches into the authentic stream of the one and Catholic Church, assure vitality and guarantee authenticity and rectitude. Without them the local churches would disintegrate into sects devoid of real links with the Apostolic Church, and thus unable to represent the Church of Christ. But the point is that once the real thing is going on at the grass-root level, it will be easier to run and maintain the higher structures. It might be that with far less priests and external financial aid we could eventually realize more than we actually are doing. Anyway this is the hope of the African bishops. They feel that our relations of dependence *vis-à-vis* the older churches would be modified deeply if we succeeded in building thriving smaller or basic Christian communities.

CONCLUSION

During the first phase of missionary work it was inevitable and quite normal that the young churches growing up in the mission lands were dependent especially in personnel and financial resources on the older churches that had given them birth. This visible dependence has, however, been accompanied by a deeper and more subtle form of dependence: the fact that the older churches have tended to model the young churches on what was going on in the older, overseas, churches. In a way, this might be seen as an attempt to transplant the overseas church on to the African soil.

In the circumstances, there was nothing really wrong in that. But with the growth towards maturity of these young churches, and especially in the recent context of decolonization and political independence, it is being realized more and more that a second phase of development is overdue. The young churches will have to become really 'local' churches, self-reliant, standing on their own feet, and rooted in the life and culture of their country. When this happens, new relations will develop between the older churches and these younger ones. One should see in the current re-thinking of structures by the African bishops and their preoccupation with self-reliance, not a desire to break with the older sister churches of Europe and America, but rather the desire for new and more authentic relationships of collegiality, co-responsibility, and ecclesial communion in the total life of the Church.

The Aladura Churches in Nigeria since Independence

AKIN OMOYAJOWO

The Aladura churches are those indigenous churches which began to emerge in Nigeria from the second decade of this century. They are quite different from the traditional or mission-oriented churches and those which broke away from them. They are churches which began as indigenous churches, founded by indigenous persons and run under indigenous leadership. They have always regarded themselves as independent especially of European or foreign domination and, therefore, had no manifest cause to look forward to the political independence of this country to foster their growth, expansion and influence. Their development since the attainment of independence has however been highly significant: in their growth, their ecumenical position, their sociological outlook, and their attitude to both society and state.

EXPANSION AND CONVERSION

Churches belonging to the Aladura group have expanded phenomenally since independence. Statistics are not available, but from general observations one can safely conclude that the churches are expanding more rapidly in post-independent Nigeria than in the days before independence. For instance, it has been suggested that within the first five years of independence, the Christ Apostolic Church founded fifteen churches in Ibadan town alone.[1] Similar expansion can be documented of the other Aladura churches, especially the Cherubim and Seraphim Church which is noted for its proliferations, and the Church of the Lord Aladura, not to mention the hundreds of other smaller Aladura churches.

One significant development that must be clearly noted is the rapid emergence of the Celestial Church of Christ which has easily become the most popular, the most attractive and the most influential Aladura church today. It was founded in Porto Novo, Dahomey [Benin], in 1947

[1] J. D. Y. Peel, *Aladura: A religious movement among the Yoruba*, London, 1968.

by Mr S. B. J. Oschaffa, a carpenter who was a member of the Methodist Church before he received his revelation. His message was that the world is full of vices because Christians had departed from the Truth of God. He was to call everybody to a life of repentance in order to avoid hell fire.

By 1952, the message of Prophet Oschaffa had found its way to Nigeria through some fishermen who had joined the church in Dahomey. The first branch was organized under Senior Evangelist S. O. Ajanlekoko formerly a sales manager of Nigerian Brewers Limited. From 1962, when Alexander A. Bada became its evangelist, it has spread to virtually all parts of the country and within the last five years has become the most dynamic, the most fanatical, the most mysterious and the most vigorous indigenous church in the country. It has 150 branches in Nigeria. In Lagos alone there are strong branches in about eleven centres, and Ibadan has twelve branches. Even in the northern states of Nigeria, branches have been established in Kaduna, Kano, Maiduguri and Jos. Its connections internationally are very strong as active branches are said to have been founded in Britain, France, Germany and the United States of America. There has therefore been a steady drift from the established churches into the indigenous churches. And this raises the whole question of conversion. What type of people get converted into the indigenous churches?

In the colonial days those who were won into the churches were mostly the under-privileged. Professor Ayandele observed some years ago that the impression was that while the mission-connected and African churches captured the cream of society like top civil servants, engineers, lawyers, doctors, skilled workers, university teachers, and wealthy businessmen, the Aladura sought out the types of people beyond the attention of mere churches—those who were the least socially and materially privileged.[2] In those days, enlightened people generally did not want to show interest in the Aladura churches openly. How could they when the powers-that-were, the colonial administration, in a way regarded these churches as *religio illicita*? For instance, Captain W. A. Ross, the Resident at Oyo, wrote in August 1930 that 'they are not recognized Christian missions and they should be regarded as enemies'.[3]

The reaction of enlightened Nigerians to these churches which white government officials described as 'not fully recognized and not under the control of responsible authorities' and against the establishment of

[2] E. A. Ayandele: 'The Aladura among the Yoruba: A Challenge to the "orthodox" Churches', a review article in *The Nigerian Christian*, ed. T. Vincent, Vol. 3, No. 7, Ibadan, July 1969, p. 16.

[3] National Archives Ibadan, Oyo Prof. F., 662, Letter to Childs, Asst. District Officer, Ilesa.

which strong measures were recommended because there was going to be a great danger if they became established and strong,[4] was naturally one of contempt. They preferred the more socially dignifying, and more sophistication-conscious mission-connected churches to the spiritually-oriented Aladura churches which were almost exclusively patronized by the poor, the illiterate, and the sick. This situation generally prevailed while colonial rule lasted. No one worth his salt wanted to stake his prestige on association with such a church movement whose very leaders were either pure illiterates or semi-illiterates. Those who had reasons to visit their leaders did so normally under cover of darkness like Nicodemus.

But with the attainment of independence, the situation changed. First, it was an opportunity to escape the unfavourable and spiteful attitude of the white overlords. Apart from the Apostolic Church which accepted white missionaries to escape cold persecution from government officials, all the other Aladura churches refused to yield to such temptations. One is not surprised that it broke that alliance with the British Apostolic Church within a decade of its entering into it. This culminated in the formation of the Christ Apostolic Church in 1941 by the more prominent members of the Apostolic Church, I. B. Akinyele, Joseph Babalola and Odubanjo. Then, with the attainment of independence of Nigeria, the psychological fear of belonging to a church that was 'not recognized' by the government because it was not under 'proper control' disappeared. Those government officials and members of other churches who had nursed a secret interest in the movement began to manifest adherence openly.

This conclusion is justified by one of the statistics of Peel in which he examined the previous religion of converts into the Christ Apostolic Church, and the Cherubim and Seraphim Church, the largest Aladura churches in Nigeria. Against the 63% of converts into the Christ Apostolic Church and the 66% of converts into the Seraphim Church from the Anglican Church alone, conversions from Islam into the two churches were 4% and 2% respectively and from the traditional religion only 4% into the Christ Apostolic Church and none at all into the Seraphim Church. These statistics were compiled in Ibadan City.[5]

Children of the earliest Aladura members who became members not by conversion but by virtue of their birth, and were therefore oblivious to the fear of the adults, brought new life into the whole movement. They had the advantage of good education like any other citizen and they became in a way a source of attraction to young educated elements like

---

[4] N. A. I. Oyo, Prof F. 662. Letter to Resident Oyo 5.9.31.

[5] Peel, op. cit. p. 205.

themselves who had been outside the church. There developed also adherence in consequence of lineal affinity. Members of a whole family might join the church of the most influential person in the family. Such kinsmen, whatever their status or standard of education no longer regarded it to be degrading to attend Aladura churches. It has often been emphasized that the Aladura churches have essentially a this-worldly orientation. There is, of course, the universal human concern about the future and one's lot on earth, and so it would not be entirely fair to posit a this-wordly tendency for the Aladura churches alone. It is, however, true that people in distress flock into them in search of solution to their spiritual problems, for the care of their diseases, for protection from both their physical and spiritual enemies and for the fulfilment of their ambitions and hopes. Consequently, we now find among the members of the Aladura churches, persons of varying social and economic positions. There are engineers, lawyers, magistrates, medical officers, university lecturers, top civil servants, senior police and army officers, etc. One prominent post-independence feature was the frequent consultation of Aladura prophets by top politicians, ministers of state or members of Parliament. When the writer visited Northern Nigeria on a research tour a few years ago, he was lodged with a senior magistrate who was a leading member of one of the Aladura churches. We are therefore not very much surprised that the mode of conversion today has changed radically from what it used to be.

ECUMENICAL MOVEMENT

An attempt was made before writing this paper to sound the opinion of a number of Aladura churches on the ecumenical movement. In other words, what has been their relationship to one another and to other churches since independence? Generally, all agreed that since independence there has been more understanding among all Aladura churches than ever before; a general recognition of a sense of mission and an awareness of a common goal, viz., to bring Africans to Christ via media that are understandable to Africans and more relevant to the African milieu. But they all admit also that every effort so far made to bring them all together has failed. The sections in Lagos of the Eternal Sacred Order of the Cherubim and Seraphim all complained that union has been impossible mainly because an agreement could not be reached on the question of leadership. This is, however, not peculiar. One of the major reasons for the failure of the 1965 projected union of Anglican, Methodist and Presbyterian churches in Nigeria was the distribution of episcopal offices. [See also below, pp 167-9] St Stephen's Christ Apostolic Church at Effon Ekiti, the seat of the late Joseph Ayo Babalola, held that the CAC does not like other Aladura churches because 'they have no good organization, because they use candles and because some of their leaders use magical means to see visions'. This was also the view of Pastor J. F. Ayeni the minister in charge of Oniyanrin Christ Apostolic Church in Ibadan. This feeling is understandable because the CAC is very close to the mission-connected churches in organization and even in administrative arrangement.

Pastor Durojaiye of Oke-Itunu CAC, Ibadan, who alone felt that relationship among Aladura churches is generally cordial, is not involved in the administrative bureaucracy of his denomination because his church is independent of the central body, which controls the other branches. The fast developing Celestial Church and the well-organized Church of the Lord saw relationships among all Aladura churches as generally cordial. We should look at the point a little more closely.

A few attempts were made before 1960 to bring all the Aladura churches together. There was, for instance, Aiyelabola's 1941 effort to initiate a 'Prophets' Union' for the promotion of 'the unity of the Aladura ministers in that area' and for bringing the churches together. It failed mainly because Oshitelu, who probably feared that his position was being threatened, backed out.[6] Eleven years later, the Federation of Aladura was formed at Ibadan and this again failed to achieve anything before it went into oblivion in 1956 because the CAC 'refused' to co-operate. Also in 1952, the Nigerian all-Prayer-men's Union was formed at Egbado with its headquarters at Ilaro. Each of the Participating churches—the CAC, the Church of the Lord (Aladura) and the Cherubim and Seraphim—kept its identity while services were conducted and baptisms performed uniformly.

The first bold attempt made after the Nigerian attainment of independence was the formation in 1961 of the Spiritual Union of Aladura churches at Ibadan by certain leaders of the Church of the Lord. The fact that the other Aladura churches were not to be invited until a later date was due only to the wish to 'avoid the mistakes of the earlier Federation of Aladura.'[7] This body has continued to exist and other Aladura churches participate actively in its activities. The supreme head of the Cherubim and Seraphim Church in Western State is its current chairman. The ultimate goal is to find means of uniting all Aladura churches into one dynamic and virile church. This is a dream, and it might die as such for one must not under-estimate the differences that exist among the Aladura churches.[8] Some of them are so hopelessly

[6] H. W. Turner, *African Independent Church,* Oxford, 1967, Vol. 1., p. 70.

[7] Turner, op. cit., Vol. 1, p. 102.

[8] One useful thing the organization has been doing is to check the excesses of the

fragmented within themselves that any hope of uniting them into a unit cannot be envisaged now. It must, however, be admitted (as some of them have said) that relationships among them have been remarkably cordial. In fact non-members usually regard all of them as one and the same group. This was probably one of the reasons why Mr E. Olu Runshewe, of the UNESCO project co-ordinator's office in the faculty of engineering at Lagos University, a Cherubim and Seraphim member, embarked on a project of trying to create a forum for a dialogue between the three major Aladura churches—the Cherubim and Seraphim, the Christ Apostolic Church and the Church of the Lord, Aladura. In a memorandum submitted by him to one of the churches in 1967, Mr Runshewe suggested that a general meeting of the three churches throughout Nigeria be summoned to discuss

> 'among the other things, general matters concerning the upliftment of the status and the integrity of the society in general, in order to curb all excesses and various abuses and to finalize other important issues that may be brought by other members of good thoughts'.[9]

He then issued twenty-four proposals embodying the structure of the new body. Nothing substantial has come out of Runshewe's proposals, but they at least highlighted the burning enthusiasm of the youths within Aladura churches, especially those who had had the advantage of good education, to bring the churches to the same level of development as the other churches, and the success of the Egbado group which has continued its loose association of all Aladura churches in that division, bears evidence of the possibilities that exist for co-operative efforts among them.

Turning to the Aladura churches' relationship with the other churches especially the established or 'Western-related' churches, we have already indicated that the relationship in pre-independence days was far from being cordial. We have also tried to give reasons for this. There was the rather intimate relationship of some of the established churches (whose leaders were mostly white missionaries) with the colonial government. There was also the spiteful attitude of the Colonial officials to the Aladura churches. The foreignness of the mission churches was, to the Aladura churches, intolerable. However, by 1960, most of the 'Western-related' churches had come under native leadership and the gap between them and the Aladura churches began to diminish. The established churches also became objective in their estimation of the Aladura churches. For instance, a report published in 1960 by the Christian Council of Nigeria on *Christian Responsiblity in an Independent*

self-styled prophets who parade the streets in their flowing robes with their messages of doom.

[9] Olu Runshewe memorandum of November, 1967.

Nigeria, admitted that the Aladura 'groups have arisen out of dissatisfaction with the life of the Church (or its lack of life) and, as so often happens in such circumstances, there is over-compensation for the felt lack, so that what was missing was elevated to undue importance'.[10]

The mission churches have realized the need to learn from the independent churches. Praying bands after the manner of the Aladura churches have been organized in many 'mission-oriented' churches; musical instruments have been introduced to put life into their worship. The Aladura churches themselves have been trying to bridge the gap between them and the other churches. For instance, the Apostolic group of churches, the Church of the Lord and some sections of the Cherubim and Seraphim Church, have adopted the church-type system of administration even with the posting and maintenance of workers. It is no mere coincidence that in the year of independence the Aladura churches began to apply for membership of the Christian Council of Nigeria. The first application dated 29 August 1960 came from the Supreme Spiritual Father J. O. Atansuyi of Ikare, who claimed he was the successor of Moses Orimolade, the Late Founder of the Cherubim and Seraphim Church. E. Olu Coker, another Seraphim leader, wrote on 2 September 1960 and claimed to have over 300 churches with over 500,000 members and ten branches in Ghana. S. Ade Johnson also wrote in the month of independence on behalf of Captain Abiodun, the living founder of the Cherubim and Seraphim Society. The general secretary of the Christian Council of Nigeria (CCN), Rev. W. S. Wood replying, called on the Aladura churches to get united first before forwarding further applications.

The ecumenical spirit was demonstrated in 1962 when the Christian churches in Lagos organized a week of revival services and invited all Christian socieites to participate—all mission churches, the African group of churches and all Aladura churches in Lagos participated. The inspiration received from this revival and the 1960 applications probably prompted officials and representatives of the CCN to initiate in August 1963 a consultation whose aim was outlined by the late Rev. T. A. Adejumobi, then general secretary of CCN, as 'the traditional desire' of his organization to help churches not yet within the CCN 'to realise their calling and to fulfil their mission as part of the Lord's body to the world'. The ultimate aim of the CCN, he further stressed, was to bring together into one united body all the factions within society. This initiative consequently led to the formation of the Christian Peace Committee in 1965 under the chairmanship of Prince S. B. O. Sajowa, an Anglican churchman.[11] The Committee has continued to hold regular

---

[10] *Christian Responsibility in an Independent Nigeria,* Ibadan, 1961, p. 103.

[11] Other members and observers at their meetings included leaders of many

meetings at the Anglican Bishopscourt in Lagos, even though the prospect of achieving the anticipated union remains very uncertain.

The older churches, therefore, no longer look down on the Aladura churches as irretrievably inferior to them. Indications point to their readiness to do what Welbourn has recommended: 'to accord to these groups the same right to exist as we claim for ourselves . . . for we cannot escape the condemnation of preaching Christ from envy and rivalry'.[12] Here, it must be empahsized that the time is long overdue when the CCN should relax its policy a little bit and make its membership open to the Aladura churches. It is absolutely necessary, as Professor Idowu has suggested, that the mission churches should swallow their pride and receive the message which these (Aladura) movements give, as well as accept the lead which their resultant churches are offering with regard to the urgent matter of an indigenous church in Nigeria.[13] Happily, the true spirit of ecumenism is already at work. Their interdependence has become crystallized in their 'borrowing' of various elements from one another. The testimony of the Aladura churches with regard to this issue is very encouraging. Captain Abiodun's man at the Okesuna Cathedral said: 'The Orthodox Churches are co-operative. They not only invite our head to worship in their churches, they made her (Captain Abiodun) the President of the interdenominational Christian Women Association of Nigeria.'[14] And E. Olu Coker, the Baba Aladura of the Seraphim section based at Rufai Street, Surulere, Yaba, had nothing against the older churches. 'The relationship has been very cordial,' he said, 'especially since Independence.'[15] In fact, it could be said now that the mission churches have begun to 'swallow their pride' and are now putting life and vitality into their worship with ideas and forms of religious expressions taken from the Aladura churches.

ISLAM

The geographical location of the Aladura churches has on the surface reduced considerably the contact that might exist between these churches

Christian denominations in Lagos.

[12] F. Welbourn, *East African Rebels,* London, 1961, p. 206.

[13] E. B. Idowu, *Towards an Indigenous Church,* OUP, 1975, p. 47.

[14] Interview in Okesuna, Lagos on 14 August 1975.

[15] Interviewed in Lagos on 13 August 1975, the Pastor of Effon-Alaye CAC, the Cherubim and Seraphim Apostle at Okebola Ibadan, Pastor J. O. Durojaiye of Oke-Itunu Ibadan, Pastor J. F. Ayeni of CAC Oniyanrin Ibadan, Samuel Popoola of the Celestial Church of Christ, Yemetu, Ibadan, etc, all claimed that the Orthodox Churches are friendly to them, and often invite them to exchange pulpits or to attend the Pastors' conference.

and Islam. The north which is a predominantly Muslim area has very few Christians. On the other hand, in the south, the west has more or less equal numbers of Christians and Muslims. But in the eastern states, Islam is virtually non-existent. There seems therefore to be no cause for any encroachment on each other's influence and area of jurisdiction. But when we realize that the Aladura churches have recently succeeded in penetrating the thoroughly Islamized north which was once declared by the colonial administration to be forbidden ground to Christian missionaries, and the fact that it is the predominantly Muslim centres of the west that have the largest concentration of Aladura prayer houses, any generalizing assertion must be made with extreme caution. The Aladura churches themselves admit that in the past they have not succeeded in winning converts from Islam as much as they have from the older churches and Peel's statistics which we cited before confirm this. We shall try briefly to account for both these situations. First, we shall suggest reasons for the failure of the Aladura churches to win Muslims in large numbers before independence, a failure which persisted until recently, and then we try to explain why the situation has changed rather drastically especially in the north.

The colonial government's policy of 'not supporting Christian missions in the north'[16] was well-known. While this constituted a great barrier to the mission churches, there seemed to be much that Islam in Nigeria had in common with the Christianity of the Aladura churches. Both have ceased to be alien as both have always had African rather than alien evangelists. Both did not demand 'race suicide' as an accompaniment of conversion. Both have ideas that are in harmony with the culture of the convert: both allow him to marry more than one wife. In both, the African remains essentially an African; he does not have to become an imitation white-man aping every aspect of European life. Both have certain ritual practices in common, e.g. distinctive flowing robes or garbs worn by every adherent; removal of shoes before entering places of worship, wearing of caps in places of worship,[17] use of emblems, praying at set periods in the day. There is also the use of tongues in church services by the Aladura in somewhat the same way that the Muslims use Arabic.[18] Our argument here is that if both have so much in common, there is a basis for a kind of unintentional compromise whereby there was not such a conflict as would, under normal circumstances, generate the need for mutual conversion.

---

[16] J. S. Coleman, *Nigeria: Background to Nationalism,* p. 133.

[17] It is not in all Aladura churches that this is practised.

[18] I have actually seen cases in Aladura churches where the Prophet or Prophetess spoke some words of Arabic when they claimed to be speaking in tongues.

On the other hand, these same reasons seemed to have paved the way for the recent invasion of exclusive Muslim territories by the Aladura churches. The turning point was after the *coup d'état* in which Ahmadu Bello, the Sardauna of Sokoto, who was both the political and the religious leader, was killed and the north was broken into six states in 1967 in consequence of which the religious hegemony was virtually destroyed. It was not too difficult for the kettle of water for ablution to become the kettle for consecrated water, the turban to become the praying cap, the flowing toga to become the praying gown, etc.

TRADITIONAL RELIGION

The Aladura churches' attitude to traditional religion is very interesting. All Aladura church leaders interviewed for the purpose of this research, vehemently rejected any suggestion that they have anything to do with traditional religion. As far as they were concerned, all traditionalists are pagans and idol worshippers who should be converted. Mrs Adejobi, wife of the Primate of the Church of the Lord, Pastor F. O. Esela of Effor-Alaaye C.A.C. and Apostle A. A. Adegbite of Okebola C & S went on to declare unequivocally that the attitude of their churches to the traditionalists is one of uncompromising hostility. Samson Popoola of the Celestial Church of Christ, Yemetu, Ibadan made a delightful distinction: 'They (traditionalists) bow down to Idols while we bow down to God and to Jesus Christ.' The problem here is that any observer of these churches might readily come to the conclusion that they owe so much to traditional religion that they could be taken as practising paganism with a borrowed Christian veneer. In traditional religion, there are elements of magic, divination, veneration of ancestors, belief in spirits, the use of elements and symbols all of which have parallels in Aladura practices; divination in the consultation of prophets, in the telling of visions in the interpretation of dreams; magic in the instantaneous healing of the sick, raising of the dead, smelling out of witches and in other related activities. There is no gain-saying the fact that the Aladura have incorporated many features from the indigenous forms of worship. There is the use of local musical instruments, lyrics, hymns composed to local tunes, dancing and clapping during worship as is the practice in the traditional worship.

But it seems obvious that what the traditional society has provided through its religious expressions and cultural setting is the outward form of service; it has not made much impact on the inner value of the members' faith. Their concern is to remove the stigma of foreignness from Christianity in this land. The way they have done this was to incorporate such elements from the traditional society and religion as are not necessarily diametrically opposed to Christian faith and doctrine in order to make Christianity more meaningful and more at home here. If in the process of doing this, they are suspected of practising syncretism, there is nothing dishonest about it, for syncretism is a feature of every religious form without which any religion cannot be dynamic. Oosthuizen has stated this point very vividly.

> Sociologically, the Church must take hold of the main aspects of the African cultural patterns, otherwise it will remain foreign and without roots. This does not mean adaptation or accommodation or seeking point of contact, but rather taking possession of what can be utilized in the indigenous culture to the advantage of the proclamation of the Christian message.[19]

In these days of cultural renewal what we find is that more and more · Christians flock to the Aladura churches; for in them they discover that they are not only Christians, but sincere African Christians.

THE ALADURA CHURCHES: IN SOCIETY AND IN THE STATE

Much has been said already about the Aladura's position in society and his attitude to society. Writing about the Aladura in Yorubaland, Peel observed that 'their aim is to be good Christians within Yoruba society, whose general terms they accept, to change it as far as they can, and to intercede with God for it'.[20] This summarizes the role of the Aladura in Nigerian society. It is their determination to be good Christians within society which prompts them to 'show off'—in public preaching, in their distinctive dresses, in their austere and sometimes ascetic living. It is their determination to change society which inspires them to preach even if at odd and 'unholy' hours, to tell prophecies and visions. It is their role as intercessors that is symbolized by their prophetic ministry, their incessant call for prayers and repentance, their well-known prophecies of doom, and their claim to give material comfort in the form of healing, and spiritual solace, to the depressed in mind.

The pre-independence hostility toward Aladura adherents which originated from the colonial authorities and was inherited by Nigerian government officials and Christians, began to disappear after the attainment of political independence. In fact more attention was given to their prophecies. An illustration of this is the prophecy of Captain Abiodun for the year 1970:

> More children will be born this year than in any year in the

[19] G. C. Oosthuizen, *Post-Christianity in Africa*, London, 1968, pp.3-4.

[20] Peel, *op. cit.*, p. 237.

past . . . there will be an acute shortage of drinking water this year. Violence will be on the increase. There will be more cases of armed burglary and highway robbery. There will be an alarming rate of unemployment. Two top leaders will die this year and there will be many fatal motor accidents on Nigerian roads. There will be a famine in 1970 as well as an epidemic of plague, though smaller than in 1918. Plenty of money but scarcity of goods.[21]

We might quickly add here that, though some of these prophecies were quite obvious, every one of them came true. No more were such prophecies dismissed as frivolous, rather, there was a general call for prayers for the aversion of calamities. This is in tune with Nigerian traditional practice. We must not be oblivious to the claim of the Aladura churches that in them man can find solutions to his existential problems: his health problems, his fear of witches and other spiritual enemies, his economic and social problems, etc. If he came to them, his barren wife would become a mother, he himself would land a lucrative job if he was jobless, or secure promotions in his place of work, etc. There is no end to what they claim God can do through them. All this meets the aspirations of the typical Nigerian, whatever his learning and whatever his status. These roles have, therefore, continued to boost the prestige of the Aladura in Nigerian society.

Since the Aladura do not reject society, the good government of society is of paramount interest to its members. Independence was welcomed by all with great enthusiasm and thanksgiving services. From 1962, when the political unrest in the then Western Region plunged the whole country into a series of crises, Aladura churches found themselves being called upon to play the role of the Old Testament Prophets, to warn the people of this country against the evils that lay ahead, and the grave consequences of the injustices that prevailed in the political arena. While the 'older' churches exercised great restraint in making statements that had political implications, the Aladura became very vocal in their condemnation of politicians, who, they alleged, made life very difficult for the common man.

When the first *coup d'état* took place on 15 January 1966, many Aladura prophets claimed that it had been shown to them in visions. For instance, a C. & S. prophet in Kaduna asserted that he saw the event in the form of an open combat between Jesus and Muhammad. Jesus fought and won with a sword, while Muhammad used a spear.[22] This vision was said to have taken place at a vigil on the night of 14 January 1966—the night of the coup. When the last bloody civil war broke out in Nigeria, most Aladura churches pledged their support for the unity of

[21] *Drum Magazine.* June, 1970.
[22] Story from the C. & S. leader in Kaduna. It was seen as a victory of Christianity over Islam, the predominant religion of Northern Nigeria.

the nation and condemned without any disguise Odumegwu Ojukwu, the 'rebel' leader and prayed openly for his defeat. While mission churches refrained from value-judgments, most Aladura churches characteristically saw the war from the humanitarian if not subjective point of view. They blamed Ojukwu for the suffering of millions of Nigerians and so, in characteristic Old Testament manner, prayers were said always for the complete vanquishing of the enemies. Substantial donations were made to the Troops Comfort Fund while the women's sections, led by Captain Adiodun, donated various articles at the Dodan Barracks, the residence of the Head of State.

Asked what their reaction was to the 29 July 1975 change of government in Nigeria, a number of prominent Aladura leaders expressed the view that they knew it was forthcoming, because it had been shown to them in visions. They saw it as God's inevitable intervention and a manifestation of his wrath on national leaders who had departed from His ways and His ordinances. They claimed that theirs is a dual role of praying for the govenment and of warning it when it is found to be going astray. Thus, today there is a growing sense of responsibility in matters of national interest by all Aladura members. They continue to call for prayers for the welfare of the people of the country and pay occasional visits to the rulers to pray for them and to relate visions. In this country, where freedom of worship is safeguarded by the constitution, the government does not discriminate between religions and so on every important occasion and during any crisis, calls are made to Christians and Muslims alike, to offer prayers in their churches and mosques, for the unity of the nation. Occasionally too, Aladura churches (more than other churches) order their members to observe some days in fasting and in praying for the State and the people.

The concept of Church and State held by Aladura churches is one of harmony, with the Church having the spiritual oversight while the State exercises the temporal authority. But the Church must reserve the right to direct the State with revelations received in visions, in matters of public interest, and to criticize or even condemn the government whenever it enacts policies of oppression and injustice. The Aladura believe that society must be freed from all the besetting problems of sickness, fear, insecurity, etc, so that the spirit of God could freely in-dwell it and ultimately manifest the Kingdom of God. In this way, the Aladura churches have remained more dynamic and more virile than the 'older' churches.

CONCLUSION

The Aladura churches in Nigeria have become a force to reckon with since independence. In a way, they have become organization-conscious like the 'older' churches. Administratively, they are increasingly tending towards the 'older' churches. They have indeed borrowed many elements from them. This is most obvious in their vestments. One can hardly distinguish between the robes of a C. & S. Baba Aladura and an Anglican or Roman Catholic Bishop today. Nevertheless, as Grimley and Robinson have observed 'they [the Aladura] followed the basic pattern of organization of African communities. This included less hard-and-fast application of principles and rules, great dependence upon and adherence to the strong personality of their leaders, group decision by arriving at conclusions through general consensus of opinion,[23] and at the same time considerable freedom for individuals to express themselves and indulge in personal idiosyncracies'.[24]

One fact that must always be kept in mind is that the Aladura churches came into existence because of the 'older churches' failure to meet the needs of the indigenous people spiritually, morally and even materially, and because of the churches 'refusal' to be African in worship, in theology and in understanding.[25] The African failed to see the direct relevance of Christianity to his life. To him, the Christian Church was overtly an arm of the colonial government. The result was the development of an ambivalent spiritual life. In time of crisis he would revert back to non-Christian solutions. The impact of the church on society was generally weak; its method of evangelization, which was individualistic, failed to recognize the cherished African communal living. Conversion came to mean rejecting one's family (in polygamous cases, dismissing all wives but one) and ethnic associations; the social balance was upset and the rhythm of society was disturbed. The Christian lived in two worlds: that of traditional religion, in which he had been brought up (but with which he could not openly associate himself lest the colonial master took offence), and that of Christianity, (with which he was not at proper grips). There was, therefore, a conflict within the individual Christian. A spiritual revolution was necessary to restore harmony and this was promptly provided by the Aladura churches. The Holy Spirit descended, as on Pentecost day, to proclaim afresh the Gospel message in languages which Nigerians understood and so through revelations manifested in trances, dreams, visions and prophecies, established the universality and the all-embracing, and all-saving power of Jesus Christ.

[23] The 'older' churches are in fact beginning to learn from their congregational form of worship.

[24] J. B. Grimley, and G. E. Robinson, *Church Growth in Central and Southern Nigeria,* Michigan, 1966, pp. 300-1.

[25] T. A. Beetham, *Christianity and the New Africa,* London, 1967, p. 45.

Perhaps Tai Solarin's prophecy of 1961,[26] an illustration of the attitude of certain educated Nigerian nationalists immediately after independence, that 'Christianity has no future in Nigeria' and that by 1984 the numerical strength of Protestant Christians would have decreased by half of what it was in 1954 and the Roman Catholics by one third, would have come to pass had the Aladura churches not emerged. Not only have they re-interpreted Christianity in a meaningful way to Nigerians, they have taught the older churches how to worship the Deity. One would agree, therefore, with Grimley and Robinson that 'Solarin was very conservative in his estimate of growth for the "indigenously African" churches', which he predicted would have doubled if not trebled their number, and entirely wrong in his prediction for other churches.[27] The common characteristic of the church in independent Nigeria is a tendency towards the Aladura churches' liturgical system in which the unfulfilled emotional needs in the western-oriented churches have found ample fulfilment. All those existential problems which give form to the traditional worship, have found alternative and adequate solutions in the church. The obvious conclusion that one can logically reach is that the Aladura way of worship is the true African expression of the Christian religion. This accounts for why they have stopped being apologetic especially in matters relating to their most glaring weaknesses, and are taking positive steps to remove them. These are evident in their struggle to have their leaders well-educated and in the establishment of strong and effective administrative machinery which would, hopefully, take care of the usually glaring abuses. Say what we may, the survival of the Christian Church in Nigeria today lies mainly in the direction of the Aladura churches. Their phenomenal evangelistic success is one of our proofs. Our enthusiastic attempt at re-interpreting theology in an African context, would yield positive results if the Aladura churches' expression of Christianity is taken as the springboard. This is what Apostle A. A. Abiola, leader of the Cherubim and Seraphim Church in Western State, Nigeria, was saying in effect when at the opening session of the synod of another Aladura church on 7 December 1974 he declared:

> We Aladuras in Nigeria are a peculiar church. We want to remain peculiar. We want to remain indigenous. We represent God's own way of revealing Himself to Africa: this is why we are peculiar. Many people who do not understand us ridicule us. They say that we are not sophisticated, that we are not educated. We know these things, but we are happy that we are an indigenous church, practising Christianity in the indigenous way and worshipping God by this means. God does hear us in this indigenous way and has been doing marvellous work through our hands, Halleluiah!

[26] *Daily Times,* Lagos, 16 September 1961.

[27] Op. cit., p. 363.

Changes within Christianity: the case of the Musama Disco Christo Church

KOFI A. OPOKU

The main thrust of European Christian missionary activity was to 'Christianize' Africa in the manner and fashion of the European appropriation of the Christian Evangel; and much of missionary endeavour was based on the presupposition that African ways were necessarily pagan and had to be done away with. Dietrich Westermann's statement amply underscores the missionary position of the nineteenth and early twentieth centuries *vis-à-vis* Africa; he wrote:

> 'However anxious a missionary may be to appreciate and to retain indigenous social and moral values, in the case of religion he has to be ruthless . . . he has to admit and even to emphasize that the religion he teaches is opposed to the existing one and one has to cede to the other'[1]

Thus an uncompromising attitude towards African culture became synonymous with the propagation of the Gospel, and salvation in the missionary sense, became a rescue operation from the thraldom of African culture. The establishment of 'Salems' by the early Basel Missionaries in Ghana as opposed to 'Mau mu' (pagan quarters), was concrete proof of this attitude, and those who converted to Christianity came out from among their people and became separate, leading a life which was patterned largely after that of the missionary.

The negative attitude towards African culture which led to an intolerant rejection of African experience, has become a heritage of the church in Africa and up to the present time, when most of the churches are in African hands, there is still the feeling that too much familiarity with African culture would sap the essential Christian flavour from the church's being and existence; and there is the constant insistence that the church must maintain its distinct identify and be different from the cultural environment in which it finds itself. Evidence of this may be found in the church's overcautious attitude, bordering on fear, and its grudging acceptance of elements of African culture into its life and worship.

[1] *Africa and Christianity*, Oxford University Press, 1937, p. 94.

This unjustified fear of African culture is a decided lack of trust and confidence in God and His power to make all things new, and to bring every culture, considered to be either man's own achievement or God's gift to man, to His service. Moreover, it is also an unwillingness to recognize the fact that God has made Himself manifest in the African experience and that the easy assumption that there is a *tabula rasa* in Africa and that God has made Himself known to others but hidden Himself from us here in Africa, must be abandoned. Such recognition would compel an attitude of humility in the face of African culture which should contrast sharply with the arrogant and disdainful attitude of yesteryear and from which the church is still trying to free herself. It will also lead to the conviction that a Christian society can be built on the foundations of African culture here in Africa.

It is in the light of the above consideration that the Musama Disco Christo Church (Army of the Cross of Christ Church) merits attention as an example of a new form of Christianity in Africa. The Musama Disco Christo Church is one of the oldest Pentecostal churches founded in West Africa. It was founded by a former Methodist catechist, Joseph William Egyanka Appiah, who later became the Prophet Jemisimiham Jehu-Appiah. It started as a prayer group within the Methodist Church at Gomoa Ogwan, in the Winneba District of the Central Region of Ghana in 1919, and was known as the Faith Society. In 1922, the Faith Society was established as a full-blown church, the Musama Disco Christo Church, after J. W. E. Appiah and his followers had been asked to leave the Methodist Church.[2]

Prophet Jemisimiham Jehu-Appiah did not only found a church and become its General Spiritual Head; he also established a dynasty and became its progenitor with the title of *Akaboha* (King) I, and his son, the *Akasibeena* (Prince), became, according to the constitution of the church, 'entitled to hold this line of succession as a divine right, as ordered by the Holy Spirit.[3] The wife of the Akaboha, the Prophetess Natholomoa Jehu-Appiah, became the *Akatitibi* (Queenmother) of the church; and the King and Queen therefore became the supreme authorities in the Musama Disco Christo Church. As a prophet and leader of a spiritual movement, Jemisimiham Jehu-Appiah laid down the foundations of the Musama Disco Christo Church as an 'indigenous Christian Church, founded to serve as our humble present—a "Myrrh" from Africa to Christ, which is our divine and precious gift, not caring whether others are offering "Gold" or Frankincense'.[4]

---

[2] For a fuller account of the founding of the church, see C. G. Baëta, *Prophetism in Ghana*, London, 1962.

[3] Constitution of the Musama Disco Christo Church, 1959, p. 11.

[4] ibid, p. ii.

The new church bore the marks of the parent church, the Methodist Church, with its circuits, camp meetings, deacons and its use of the Christian Asor Ndwom, the Fante Methodist hymnary. But it also deviated from her Methodist heritage with the introduction of the *Yinaabi*, rosary, the introduction of its own liturgy which is contained in the *Bagua Mu Som Ahorow Nye Mpaayi*, and the establishment of the Holy City of Mozano, first near Gomoa Fomena, and later, after the death of the founder, the New Mozano near Gomoa Eshiem established in 1951. In Mozano every church member has full privilege as a citizen of this citadel. The church also differentiated itself from the parent church by its emphasis on divine healing, the founder having instructed his followers 'not to use any medicine for any treatment for the Lord is Thy Healer'. The church also introduced heavenly names to its members and these names are believed to be given by God and each person's heavenly name is peculiar to him. (From the founding of the Church up to 1972, the founder and his successor had given 90,000 heavenly names and no two of them were alike). A language peculiar to the members of the church was also introduced, and is used in greetings and salutations and entry into houses. Members also used copper rings and crosses to set themselves apart. Furthermore, the church is distinguished by its own special rules and its creed, in which members affirm belief in the Holy Musama Disco Christo Church, and by its special prayers in tongues which members recite whenever in difficulties.

The church's adherence to the Bible, as her unerring guide in matters of administration and general worship is noteworthy, but more especially, the influence of the Old Testament, and particularly the rituals and history of ancient Judaism constitute a veritable prototype for this church. The church has an Ark, with the same degree of sacredness as the Ark of the Israelites, located in the *Kronkronbea Sanctum* or Holy Place, and the Ark is kept in the *Sanctum Sanctorum* where only the Akaboha enters once a year to offer prayers. Occasionally, there is Burnt Offering, reminiscent of ancient Judaism, and the blood of the sacrificial animal is used in marking the entrances to all the houses in Mozano (this takes place during the Mercy Seat Meditation, which is a period of fasting and prayers three weeks before the church's annual festival, *Asomdwee Afe*, Peace Festival, which falls on August 24 each year). On other occasions, the blood of the sacrificial animal is used in marking the foreheads of pastors and prophets with the sign of the cross, and the ashes are distributed to all the pastors to take back to their stations to mark the foreheads of all the members as a sign of the bond of unity that binds them together as *Musamafo*, members of the Musama Church.

The church also sees its own history made up of persecutions and trials, and the small band of followers who accompanied the founder on his journey from Gomoa Ogwan, to Onyaawonsu and to the old Mozano, and finally to the New Mozano, are seen as a modern-day re-enactment of the journey of the Israelites from Egypt to Canaan. At the southern entrance to the New Mozano, the church has erected the *Nokwarbo* (literally the Stone of Truth) in honour of God who has fulfilled all His promises which He made to the founders of the church. The New Mozano, therefore, is a Canaan, a promised land, the fulfilment of the prophecies of old.

But the church remains in many respects thoroughly African and has succeeded in blending various heritages together. In its very organization, the pattern is the traditional Akan state structure, based on war organization. The General Head Prophet of the Church bears the title of *Nana,* a title used by Akan kings and chiefs, and under the Akaboha (King) are right wing chiefs, left wing chiefs, rearguard, scouts, advance guard etc. As a king, the Akaboha has his own regalia including umbrellas, swords, palanquins, and linguist staffs; he also has his drummers, horn-blowers, and elders. The Queenmother has her own court officials and regalia, just as in Akan tradition, and these aspects of African culture and tradition are faithfully combined with the Gospel of Christ.

The church's attitude to marriage follows the general acceptance of polygamy in Akan society and the church's Constitution states: 'as an African church polygamy is not a moral sin', and for further support of its position references are made to Biblical personalities who practised polygamy and yet are fathers of our faith. The church also teaches that open marriage is more divine in Christian life than secret concubinage. Polygamy therefore, does not disqualify a person from being accepted into membership of the Musama Disco Christo Church, neither does it debar a member from partaking of the Sacrament of Holy Communion.

In the matter of public worship, use is made of African music and traditional chants are sung with Biblical events as lyrics; the history of the church, like that of some African societies, is recited in song by a leading cantor and responded to by the congregation. African musical instruments predominate in worship services, and the prominence which the church attaches to Ghanaian languages is reflected in the instructions for public worship, the first of which states explicitly, 'vernacular shall be used in all church services wherever possible'.

The Church's Notion of Itself
The Musama Disco Christo Church regards itself as an African Church which has received a special revelation from God through its founder,

Prophet Jemisimiham Jehu-Appiah and his successor, Prophet Matapoly Moses Jehu-Appiah, whose birth was prophesied as the one who would build the church. The birth of the 'promised son' was regarded as a sign of the ultimate victory of the church, which was at that time (1924) going through a period of persecution, and was greeted with the ringing of bells and great jubilation, marking the first Peace Festival of the church. Through the celebration of the Peace Festival every year, the church reminds itself of the promise which has been fulfilled and assures itself of victory over persecutions, and its continued victorious fight in God's strength. The founder and his wife were given the title, *AYEMIDI-KUSIDI,* (Double-Pointed Sword) by a direct voice from heaven, to denote their spiritual power and they regarded themselves from the founding of the church as the double-pointed sword with which God carries on His fight against evil in the world.

The church regards itself as a divine creation, and its very name, Musama Disco Christo (the Army of the Cross of Christ), is derived from the heavenly language or the language of angels. The headquarters of the church, Mozano (My Town) is the name by which the church believes God calls the town, and is indeed God's town. The heavenly names given to members of the church further confirms the divine origin of the church, for the names are peculiar to the church and a name once given is never repeated.

The founder of the church and his successor had a direct experience of God and His power and this is the basis of the church's awareness of itself as a *spiritual church.* Members also have a direct experience of God, as Holy Spirit, reflected in faith healing and prayers, and supported by fasting and the performance of 'systems'—recommended rituals accompanying prayers. This direct experience also accounts for the church's original stand, though greatly modified in recent years, against the use of medicine.

The church through its sermons and writings sees itself as the true, original church which has been refounded for Africans. In a speech to visiting Afro-American Scholars and pastors on 30 July 1972 the Akoboha II said:

> . . . much as Kwegyir Aggrey once restored the lost Black Man's intelligence on the academic map of the world, much as Marcus Garvey once more repaired the shattered economy of the Black Man on the trade map of the world, much as Kwame Nkrumah once more reconstructed the sleeping Black Man's Empire on the political map of the world; so Jehu-Appiah rediscovered an Old Time Religious Life for the Black Man as you see today. In the domain of human intellect, there is no colour line.

But the discovery of the 'Old Time Religion' is not exclusively for black men; the rediscovery imposes a mission of universal dimension on the church, as the Akoboha II stated in the preamble to the church's Constitution in 1959: 'I entreat all brethren that are members of my church, to preserve this God-given heritage—this Pentecostal Blessing, once delivered to the Saints and ask you further to call the other Christians of all races and denominations to a common understanding and united front to proclaim Christ . . .'

Church Organization and Structure
Baëta wrote in his book *Prophetism in Ghana*:[5]

> . . . the prophetic leaders and their helpers . . . have on the whole, followed the basic pattern of organization of African communities . . . it centres round the strong personality of its leader, who is its real pivot, though use is made of all sorts of councils as well; above all it gives more scope to individuals to express themselves freely.

The organization of the Musama Disco Christo Church follows the pattern described by Baëta. At the pivot of the organization is the General Head Prophet or Akaboha, who has spiritual and temporal power and is the final authority. He acts on the basis of his spiritual authority, but he works through councils which have been established by the church, and the structure is hierarchical.

In practice, the General Annual Assembly of the Church, called the I'Odomey Conference, is the actual governing body of the church and of this conference the Akaboha is the life chairman. At the I'Odomey Conference, declarations by the Akaboha are openly discussed and then a decision is arrived at through consensus in the traditonal manner of arriving at decisions, and these are regarded then as binding. Below the I'Odomey Conference are the circuit and quarterly meetings and the station and leaders' meetings. These deal with more local problems of the church and important matters are referred to the I'Odomey Conference and the Akaboha. The office of the General Head Prophet is hereditary, according to the church's constitution, and below him are pastors and prophets in a descending order. Appointment of pastors and prophets are made by the General Head Prophet; and a pastor or prophet can rise through the ranks from the bottom to the top, on the basis of criteria established by the church.

The ecclesiastical structure is as follows opposite:

[5] pp. 128-9.

General Head Prophet (and Queenmother)	
Prophets	Pastors
1. Senior Prophet	1. Senior Pastor
2. Regional Prophet	2. Regional Pastor
3. Prophet Grade I	3. Pastor Grade I
4. Prophet Grade II	4. Pastor Grade II
5. Prophet Grade III	5. Pastor Grade III
6. Prophet Grade IV	6. Pastor Grade IV
7. Non-Grade Prophet	7. Non-Grade Pastor
8. Junior Prophet	8. Deacon or Deaconess
9. 1st Class Male and Female Healer	9. 1st Class Catechist
10. 2nd Class Male and Female Healer	10. 2nd Class Catechist
11. 3rd Class Male and Female Healer	11. 3rd Class Catechist

Lay Leaders and Traditional Organization

On a more fundamental level, and undergirding the ecclesiastical organization of the church, is the traditional Akan state (*Oman*) structure, which allows laymen to wield power in the affairs of the church. The importance of the Akan state structure lies in the fact that it is tied up with the history and development of the church, and the church's sense of mission and destiny are reflected in the divisions.

On the traditional level, the Musama Disco Christo Church is like an Akan state, *Oman*, at the head of which is Nana Akaboha (King), who combines both spiritual and temporal power. The position of the Queenmother, *Akatitibi,* originated from the fact that she is a co-founder of the church; and her position became even more important during the reign of the Akaboha II (1948–72), because she was the mother of the king, and presently she is the grandmother of the Akaboha III.

The Akaboha has his wing and divisional chiefs who are all laymen, and each chief has sub-chiefs under him; the arrangement follows the traditional Akan war organization. The first division of great importance is the *Obaatan* (Mother), which is the name given to the Abura circuit, the first area where the church was established outside of the Old Mozano. The founder of the church hailed from Abura Edumfa in the

Cape Coast district, and the circuit elder in that town holds the position of the *Obaatan* of the church.

The divisional chiefs of the church with their sub-chiefs are as follows:

1. *Obaatan*	Abura, Eguafo, Cape Coast, Assin
2. *Nifahene* (Right wing)	Ajumako
3. *Twafohene* (Scouts)	Breman, Ekumfi, Saltpond, Enyan
4. *Adontenhene* (Advance Guard)	Agona
5. *Benkumhene* (Left wing)	Awutu, Eastern Gomoa
6. *Kyidomhene* No. 1 (Rear Guard)	New Juaben, Nsawam, Kibi
7. *Kyidomhene* No. 2 (Rear Guard)	Akwamu, Krobo, Adidome, Hohoe, Ho, Accra, Tema

These divisions come to the fore during Piodama, when the entire church sits as an Akan state, to hold a durbar during the annual Peace Festival.

During the reign of Akaboha I, 1922-48, when the church had no written constitution, the church had the First and Second Committees, made up of divisional chiefs and circuit stewards (also laymen), who served as the executive council, a council of elders for the king.

The Musama Disco Christo Church as an OMAN

The *Oman* of Musama is headed by the Akaboha (King) who is called *Nana* by his followers and he is every bit an Akan chief. His titles are the same as those given to Akan chiefs and he is greeted with salutations reserved for chiefs and kings. He is greatly revered, and as a sign of the reverence accorded him, sandals and footwear are removed in his presence, and women kneel in greeting him.

As a king, he never goes anywhere unaccompanied by his elders and attendants, including a linguist and an umbrella bearer. He has his own regalia, including swords, umbrellas, palanquins, linguist staffs, gilded sandals and hats, horns and drums. The Akaboha's position as a chief is recognized by traditional chiefs in the area who invite him to their state functions and are in turn invited to attend the church's annual Peace Festival at Mozano.

The ceremonies surrounding the death and installation of the Akaboha follow closely the Akan traditional procedures regarding the death and enstoolment of chiefs. The Akaboha is laid in state with swords, linguist staffs, sandals, gilded hats, etc. as decorations on the bed. And as in the case of a dead chief of an Akan state, the pastors, prophets and circuit elders swear an oath to the Akaboha lying in state at midnight. Each person swears to carry out his appointed duties and responsibilities faithfully and to remain loyal to the church, even though the Akaboha, who appointed him to the position, is dead. All who file past to pay their last respects remove their footwear as a sign of respect; and sheep are also slaughtered as in Akan tradition.

Before the installation of the Akaboha, he is confined for a period of forty days, which coincides with the *Apatam* of the Akan, during which chiefs-elect are instructed and groomed by the elders. During the last three nights prior to the Akaboha-elect's installation, he is taken to the *Sanctum (Kronkronbea)* of the church at midnight and there the most important ceremonies are performed by the elders of the church, headed by the Senior Prophet. In Akan tradition the principal officiant during enstoolment ceremonies is the Chief Stool Bearer and the ceremonies take place in the Stool House. In the installation ceremonies for the Akaboha-elect, the Senior Prophet plays the role of the Chief Stool Bearer (*Nkonguasoafohene*) and the *Sanctum* becomes the Stool House, where the Akaboha-elect is brought into contact with his predecessors and is anointed seven times as their successor. The public part of the installation ceremonies are held outside the *Sanctum* on the day of installation and it includes the putting on of official vestments performed by the Senior Prophet; and the administration of the oath of office on behalf of the entire church is done by the Senior Pastor who functions as Senior linguist on this occasion. The Akaboha then rides triumphantly in his palanquin from one end of the town to the other amidst horn blowing, dancing, drumming and singing before entering the temple to preach his inaugural sermon. From the temple the Akaboha enters his official residence where, immediately upon arrival, a spotless white sheep is slaughtered. In Musama tradition, just as in the Akan, it is only after the installation that a date may be fixed for the final funeral obsequies of the late Akaboha.

The town of Mozano, where the Akaboha resides, functions as an *ahenkro*, capital town of the *oman* of Musama. It is from Mozano that all major decisions affecting the church emanate and it is here that the annual festival, the Peace Festival, is held. As an *ahenkro*, there are shrines and holy places where the faithful may pray and receive healing. Here smoking and drinking are strictly forbidden. Like the usual Akan town, Mozano has its wards and quarters. There are four wards in town: Ahembrom (Royal Quarters) where the Akaboha, the Akatitibi, and the royal family live; Atsefo ward, where the emigrants from the Old

Mozano settled. In addition to these there are the Kokooase (Under the cocoa trees) and Anaafo (valley area) wards.

The church can furthermore be identified as a distinct *oman* whose members are distinguishable from others by the wearing of copper rings and copper crosses, which serve as 'tribal marks'. The heavenly names which are peculiar to the church may also serve as 'tribal names'. In the *oman* of Musama, which in fact has become an extended family, there is an additional sense of belonging, security and identification. For members are not only supported and given guidance and advice on problems which confront them, but they also receive a code of conduct and discipline. Furthermore, each member of the church is entitled to a full burial by the church and one's family does not have to bear the expenses of his funeral. And in addition to the above, the church's own language, though not very extensive, contributes in no small measure towards its distinctiveness as an *oman*.

Membership of the *oman* of Musama is not restricted to one ethnic group but embraces people from other groups, and the same pattern is reflected in the leadership of the church, and especially the ethnic distribution of the pastors and prophets reflects a wide base. Furthermore, membership is not restricted to a particular status group, but cuts across all status, and the high and low, rich and poor, educated and uneducated, business executives and junior civil servants, university students and graduates, head of state and politicians all belong to, or come to the Church for assistance. Membership is tied up with the understanding of the role and the practice of, religion in African society. Bishop Sarpong wrote: 'The African's religion concerns his whole person, not just his soul. It helps him to have children, to get rich, to avoid sickness, to get back his health, to grow old and to prosper'.[6] Religion in the *oman* of Musama fits this description by Bishop Sarpong and, like traditional religion, the Christianity practised in the *oman* of Musama is a religion of being and doing, and represents a rejection of missionary Christianity which was largely a religion of mental culture. It is a religion which is meant for day to day living and which provides satisfying answers to the problems of contemporary life. Unlike missionary Christianity which denied the existence of demons, witches and evil spirits, the Musama church recognizes the existence of such spirits but demonstrates the power of God over them.

The Musama Disco Christo Church, then, draws heavily on traditional Akan religion and culture in its search for more satisfactory answers to the problems of contemporary life and combines elements of Methodism with a strong African policy. The self-awareness of the church, as a divinely-established institution, matches that of Ancient Israel; and the

[6] Catholic Voice, Vol. 46 No. 2, February, 1971, p. 23.

church regards itself as the recipient of the 'faith once delivered to the saints', a faith which leads to the practice of the 'old time religion'. Through divine healing, which is the church's most effective weapon of evangelization, a new *oman* has come into existence and its members are admonished to abandon recourse to traditional gods and other sources of succour and to turn to God in the firm belief that 'Christ is not only a God of Salvation but also a Father who is prepared to meet all our needs'. The abandonment of recourse to traditional gods does not, of course mean the rejection of traditional values. The traditional world view of spirits, demons, witches, etc. is upheld and it is within this milieu that the church makes its message of salvation meaningful. Indeed the church offers solutions to both traditional as well as contemporary problems.

Although the Musama Church is a modern phenomenon of twentieth century origin, it cannot be looked at exclusively from the point of view of social change. The church shows a considerable degree of cultural continuity. Although the Church is a 'spiritual church', its membership is not limited to people on the 'fringe' of society. As an *oman*, its membership cuts across all sections of Ghanaian society. At the pivot of the *oman* is a king, the Akaboha, who fulfils the role of a king in the Akan tradition. As a king in the Akan tradition, the Akaboha has both spiritual and political duties to perform. The Musama Disco Christo Church meets the criteria for a Christian church and may be regarded as a further extension of Christianity in Africa based on the conviction that a Christian society can be built on the foundations of African culture.

African Sisters' Congregations: realities of the present situation

ANCILLA KUPALO

Many articles have been written about African sisters for various publications. In most of them the focus has been on the statistics within dioceses, country or region. The content is extended to the good work that is being done by the sisters in different fields.

The general impression given of African sisters is therefore a very successful one. For anyone who has taken an active part in the foundation and formation of African sisters, there is much they can rejoice over. No one can deny that there was hard work and self-dedication put into the training of the indigenous sisters, as well as many sacrifices offered, given the circumstances of the time. However, it is not fitting that we should spend our time congratulating the foundresses on their good work, or admiring the African sisters for their response to religious life. We can certainly admit that there is still much wanting and much to be desired in the life of the African sisters. It is therefore my concern in this paper to take a good look at the present situation of the African sisters. This cannot be done independently of the past. It is necessary to take a look at the historical background in order to understand the present.

This historical background will consist in the foundations of African sisters' congregations as I know of them from first-hand-information given by African sisters at Gaba Pastoral Institute 1971-5, sisters coming from the five AMECEA countries, (being the abbreviation for Members of the Association of Episcopal Conferences of Eastern Africa, i.e. Kenya, Uganda, Tanzania, Malawi and Zambia), and from other countries of Africa, for example, Swaziland, Rhodesia, South Africa, Gambia and Cameroun in West Africa.

Following the historical facts, I will next deal with the most burning issues in the African sisters' congregations, problems which have been repeatedly sounded in seminars, meetings of the Association of Sister-hoods—and especially during the African Sisters' Study Conference in Limuru, Kenya in September 1974. And finally I will end with some recommendations, suggestions geared towards what the African sisters are craving for, what should be their priorities and pre-occupations if they want to make religious life more meaningful and relevant to their members.

The historical background and composition of the congregations

The early missionaries started settling in eastern Africa in the 1870s. Their intention was to evangelize the African people then living in 'darkness' but this was not an easy task. The language, customs, values and thought patterns of the African people presented big obstacles to the missionaries. Along with these, the lack of preparation on the part of missionary societies for the important work of evangelization added to their incompetence. This has left an impact on the African Christians. They lack conviction in their Christian faith as a result of a poor approach. On the one hand the missionary was challenged by a situation very different from his home, and on the other hand the African was confused by the new doctrines. Also, the urgency of evangelizing posed a problem. Some missionaries carried out a crash programme and baptized people in great numbers in order to snatch these African souls which were being 'plunged into hell'. The time for real good formation in Christian values was not long enough. Worse still, the contempt for African values by missionaries made the comprehension of Christianity impossible because there was no reference to African thought patterns.

As a result, Christianity for a great number of Africans can be compared to a coat that one puts on at one's convenience. This fact has great importance for the African sisters' congregations, because the recruits for religious life came precisely from these Christians whose formation in the Christian faith was the very minimum.

It was at the turn of this century that missionary sisters came to eastern Africa as a response to requests from bishops to come and help with the work of evangelization. They too experienced the same obstacles in their work of teaching the Christian message. Culture and tradition were not consulted—they fell short in making use of the richness that lay in the African way of life. However their presence had an impact. Young girls were observing their total dedication in whatever they were doing. They considered it good to give such a life a trial. This was the beginning of God's work in the hearts of the African girls. To give them a trial, the missionary sisters would take them in as house maids, gardeners, dhobis. They were illiterate and shy but very hard-working in manual labour. This was the general picture. Young girls living with missionary sisters for an indefinite length of time. But in fact these girls became the first members of the congregations we have today.

In the AMECEA countries alone, there are about 4844 African sisters according to the statistics of 1974. Of these, the greatest number belong to African sisters' congregations. It also appears that the foundations of these congregations were begun between the 1920s-30s with very few in the 1940s. There are however two exceptions: the Sisters of Our Lady Queen of Africa at Karema in Tanzania founded in 1907, and the Daughters of Our Lady known as the Bannabikira of Uganda, founded in 1910.

Another observation about these congregations is that almost all were founded by bishops although the training was later entrusted to the missionary sisters. Some of the very few congregations actually founded by missionary sisters are those of the Little Sisters of St Francis in Uganda; and the Holy Cross Sisters in Zambia and Rhodesia.

With the lack of a real encounter with African culture comes the problem of the composition of the different congregations of African sisters. Due to primitive means of communications in the past, tribalism in Africa was very strong at the time of these foundations. There were tribes which considered themselves 'superior' to others in the same country. Authority would therefore be in their hands. The typical example of the Tutsi and Hutu of Burundi, the Ganda and the other tribes in Uganda, the Tonga in Zambia, and the Shona in Rhodesia. These circumstances showed clearly that the founders were not aware of the possibility of clashes in the congregations. Sometimes taking sides created even stronger tribal ties between the African sisters and the grudges still exist up to this day. In some congregations the self-conceited tribes have continued to rule the congregations until the other sisters got tired of it and finally walked out. This problem extended to the methods of recruitment and education of the young aspirants. Some tribes were considered unintellectual and were restricted to unskilled labour while other tribes were put into school. This created distinctions, a problem facing many African congregations today. This was not, of course, the case in exclusively tribal congregations.

In Uganda, 'Bannabikira' sisters, mentioned above, are almost exclusively Ganda. No doubt such a tribal gathering lacks the benefit brought by a mixture of cultures. The dangers are that they can be too much wrapped up in their own traditions to the extent of closing in on themselves. Although the Bannabikira have many houses all over Uganda they lack that unity in diversity within their communities. In Kenya, too, there is the Congregation of Sisters of Mary Immaculate which is exclusively Kikuyu founded by a Consolata bishop and trained by Consolata sisters.

Given the mentality of the African people and especially that of the women, the relationship between the bishop founder and the African sisters was one of: superior to inferior, power to weakness, father to child, benefactor to receiver. This was the only way the African sisters could relate. And, even after the African sisters were entrusted to the missionary sisters for formation, this attitude continued because of the frequent reference to the bishop or mother superior who was better educated, and better informed than they were. Consequently, tension and fear overpowered the African sisters. In order to cope with the situation (because of their conviction of God's call) they developed a 'yes yes' mentality and took refuge in the virtue of 'conformity' confusing it with 'obedience'. That was the standard by which they were judged as fit members for religious life. It was also very much in conformity with the mentality of the colonial era, that is superior-subject relationship. This certainly poses two big questions. First, what kind of obedience did the African sisters pledge at their profession? And second, what sort of obedience did the superiors expect from the African sisters? These questions are of vital importance. Even after ten or fifteen years of self-rule repercussions are still visible. Only recently, during a profession ceremony in East Africa, I was shocked by the bishop's sermon in which he strongly appealed to the sisters that their obedience must be like that of the civil servants who always go wherever they are appointed without questioning, without consultation. This was in December 1974. The ideal obedience set before the whole congregation! In short, the way authority was exercised did not give the African sisters a chance to grow up. And as a matter of fact, the struggle for authority in African congregations has as its basis the power—weakness, master—servant, and mother—child relationships, especially in societies where monarchy was the way of ruling. The dialogue which is the result of recognition of equality and co-responsibility is still a long way off.

During the study-conference of African sisters from AMECEA countries, it was pointed out that 'some African sisters become Religious before they become Christians.' This statement confirms what was said above about the early missionaries' insufficient approach. Christianity was hardly introduced to the African people when recruitment to religious life was started. The content in formation programmes did not help either, for it consisted in rules and obligations. Blind obedience was the recommended attitude. The virtue most appreciated was 'childishness', shown by always waiting for approval from superiors. Common sense was condemned, and taking a decision proved one's pride and independence and was qualified as the loss of one's vocation.

Thus the essence of the girls' search was lost on objects. Intelligent African girls, who entered the religious life well aware of what they were looking for and who felt the sting of abandoning the beauty of an 'African Woman', failed to get the right orientation. What these young women were giving up was that human relationship in the normal African traditional setting, as well as the new relationships which would have been created by their marriage. This value was badly neglected by the missionary sisters engaged in formation. Instead of human relationships, the African girls were presented with objects. There was a great lack of that orientation which could have given the candidates a more positive outlook, thus helping them to be like a householder who brings out from his storeroom things 'both new and old'. (Matt. 13:52). It was the lack of complementarity between African values and 'Religious' values which made religious formation fall short of its purpose, with the result that there was no depth in the spirituality of the African sisters. What they were given was another coating of a foreign way of life, unrealistic sometimes, and artificial most of the time.

All this time, the African sisters led a life of submission and conformity. They were on the receiving end, while the missionary sisters monopolized the giving end. Administration was not the African sisters' concern. Financial worries were inconceivable. They were given what they needed, provided they asked for it. The 'how' of getting these materials was a private dealing, a ground on which they should not trespass. On the whole, life seemed pretty easy as far as administration was concerned. If there were projects to be carried out, they knew about them because they had to pray in order to obtain the necessary financial help from benefactors. But the planning for the project and the correspondence involved were hidden talents. Secondly, the ruling body was made up of missionary sisters without representation of the indigenous sisters. As a result, misunderstandings between the two groups were inevitable. Leadership in schools and hospitals was also monopolized.

Then came the era of independence. The early 1960s saw East African states resume responsibility one after the other. The people of the country used this situation to convince the African sisters that they too should resume independence in matters pertaining to the ruling of their congregations. The initiative therefore came from outside. Some congregations of expatriate sisters did their best to prepare the African sisters for this step. But others felt threatened and the transition period was not always a very happy one for both parties. The Teresian sisters of Malawi have grateful memories of their transition period, because the White Sister who helped to prepare them for their first chapter worked with them very co-operatively. But there are examples where the African sisters were left to find their own way to self government. There were other sad incidents whereby houses were emptied and goods sold by the trustees. On the other hand, African sisters also fell short in trying to understand the attitude of the missionary sisters. For most of them

Africa had become their home where they had spent their youth, their energy and talents without reserve, and here they were—being asked to let go what they had worked for all their lives. Certainly, there should have been better mutual understanding.

In short one can say that some of the missionary sisters granted self-government to the African sisters begrudgingly and with the minimum of preparation. There was little help given regarding job-description, and, as a result, African superior generals were at a loss and are still confused even today.

Even though many African sisters' congregations obtained their independence after the Second Vatican Council, the method of community and administration is still the old one. It is therefore not surprising to come across communities that are stifled and closed. The pattern which they are following is one of 'central government' and they are scared of trying out any other ways. In this regard, finance presents a major problem. The bursars are not qualified accountants, so they are apt to make big mistakes. To safeguard this, the bishops' houses find an excuse to involve themselves in the finances. Some African sisters' congregations are deprived of their small earnings. Diocesan sisters fall under the authoritative hand of the hierarchy and the slightest reaction against such treatment is immediately hushed up. In short, whether out of sympathy for incompetence on the part of the superiors or for other reasons, the bishops and priests meddle in the affairs of the African sisters. This interference in internal matters makes havoc of the efforts of the young African congregations.

However, problems in administration are not only external. On the contrary: the lack of co-responsibility among the superior generals and their councils is even of greater concern in the congregations.

'A problem shared is half solved'[1]
The creation of Associations of Sisterhoods in every country deserves high praise. For it offers a round table where individual congregations can air their problems and find ways and means of solving them. Much more so for diocesan African sisters' congregations which tend to be under the monopoly of bishops or their founders. Equally so, the existence of the UISG (i.e. the International Union of Superior Generals) in Rome gives the sisters even more security in matters concerning the spiritual welfare of the religious sisters. It is within this setting that I wish to take up the second part of this paper.

Both at the 1972 and the 1973 meetings of the UISG in Rome, the need for discussions on open dialogue concerning common problems was

[1] An African proverb.

discussed by superior generals and other representatives of African sisterhoods. A partial fulfilment of this was realized when twenty-four African sisters from Kenya, Uganda, Tanzania, Malawi and Zambia met in Limuru, Kenya, in September, 1974. The purpose of this meeting was first to endeavour to discuss the role of the religious woman in evangelization today, both in the local situation and in the countries of eastern Africa as a whole. Secondly, they tried to discover what can be done to improve the opportunities of African sisters in order to carry out their responsibility as committed women of the Church today. From a talk given by Bishop J. Odongo, Chairman of AMECEA, entitled 'The Role of AMECEA in the service of the Church, and the participation of Sisters in the same service', the following words were extracted: Vision, Challenge—and Collaboration. The sisters saw this as a call to take an active part in the service of mankind at local and regional levels. But in order to meet this challenge they realized that there were many problems which make their participation difficult if not impossible.

From private discussions, questionnaires and during the five-day study-conference referred to above, the African sisters discovered that it was a common experience to have little communication between themselves and their bishops. Paternalism still exists in many dioceses. And, as a result, African sisters are not consulted in planning for the diocese. Interference in the internal affairs of the congregation reduces the superior generals to mere figure-heads. Some bishops will nominate or manipulate the election of superior generals for personal interests. Suppression of the sisters' educational development impedes the sisters' apostolate. I know of bishops who limit the education of the African sisters to junior secondary. In some dioceses African sisters are abused as cheap labourers who win no remuneration. Other dioceses take the sisters' income for the diocese at the cost of the sisters' welfare. The relationship between African sisters and African priests was seen in terms of business: function came first and sometimes at the expense of persons. It was also remarked that indigenous sisters themselves are not always harmonious, often due to regional or tribal differences.

Compared with these problems of external communication, other problems are mainly internal. As mentioned earlier, recruitment of candidates for the religious life was open to any good Catholic girl. Education was not considered. But when the African sisters resumed self-rule the question of who should be accepted for religious life became a crucial point in their deliberations. Most congregations demanded at least full primary education, others would only accept candidates with secondary education. There are however practical problems involved in accepting primary leavers. Such candidates may have to continue with their secondary education. They are thus delayed two or four years before they enter formation. If they start with their noviciate, they will be two or four years behind in their academic learning and this has its difficulties too. Financially congregations spend a lot of money educating these young girls at their own risk. Sometimes a congregation may have more sister students than those engaged in the apostolate. Where sisters run private secondary schools like the Little Sisters of St Francis and the Bannabikira sisters in Uganda, the number of the aspirants at the end of four years is much smaller than that at the beginning. It also requires a lot of personnel to staff the school as well as the noviciate. This may not always be possible.

The greatest obstacle discovered is the lack of well-informed and informed personnel for the work of formation. Until now, the less educated lower grade teachers have been considered good enough to take charge of the formation of novices, with the result that formation programmes are neither suitable nor relevant for the young girls. These sisters approach religious life in the old rigid way, or if they try otherwise, they do not have the training needed to make them self-confident. The vows are mostly presented in a negative way. There is also still too much conformity which leads to a stereotyped spirituality. All these points can be observed in the way professed sisters conduct their lives.

Religious life is not taken seriously. Prayer life is too casual. Community living lacks sufficient concern for each other. The practical aspects of the vows, especially the vow of poverty, are not very visible in the lives of some African sisters. Many sisters think that this vow is a contradiction to their own lives among their people. Others go in for helping to educate their relatives. They are confounded by the problem of 'how to become poor' with so much at their use, be it community, hospital or school property. Some sisters refuse to accept their limitations regarding academic learning, and aspire to higher education without considering the other sisters' opportunity and the apostolate they are being prepared for.

The liturgy which is the expression of the faith and bond of unity of a Christian community lacks vitality and meaning in many African sisters' convents. The increasing 'early retirement' from hard work affects their spiritual life. There does not exist that constant searching for God and Christian values. For most of the African professed sisters, especially those with final vows, the impression one gets is that they are waiting passively for the 'Parousia'. That is one reason why African sisters' congregations lose so many of their highly educated sisters. For during their academic training, their spiritual life does not receive equal nourishment. Most often they are left uncatered for. Their isolated lives add to their loneliness. There is little effort from the superior general or sisters of their own communities to keep the sense of belonging in them and sustain their prayer life and spirituality in general. With the result that they find it difficult to re-adjust themselves back to normal religious community life after their studies. Consequently some leave the convent. For these intelligent sisters will not just sit and wait! They would rather find something else worth living for immediately. What these sisters need is more challenge and a deepening of their religious life.

To sum up, then, one can say that whether it is the novice in formation, the professed sister in her community or at work, the superior general and her council in their administration or in their relationships with each other, the one point which seems to come up in seminars, in study-conferences or discussions as the most crucial problem in the African sisters' congregations is 'Formation'.

The need for solid spiritual formation

In the study-conference referred to above, the African sisters felt the need for a real solid spiritual formation if the members are to carry out their responsibilities effectively in the various kinds of apostolate. There has been too much emphasis on the competence of African sisters as teachers, nurses, intelligent and outstanding young superiors general outspoken in big assemblies of cardinals and bishops, and what have you! Granted, all these are necessary, but that is not the essence of religious life. After all, sisters are a very small number of African educated women who have taken greater responsibilities in their societies. The fact that African sisters may have been pioneers of education for girls does not qualify them today.

What the people expect of them is that they live what they profess. Competent and efficient women, yes, but first and foremost women grounded in faith; women full of love; women overflowing with Christ's goodness permeating those around them. Women who know how to give; who become poor by sharing what they have with their fellowmen and women for whom obedience means 'Freedom'. Freedom to say 'Yes' which makes them mature women, who take responsibility for their actions. The Africa of today does not need the meek and humble children closed up in their own world; on the contrary, Africa expects her daughters to reflect her values well embodied in the Christian values and attitudes. It is therefore high time that the African sisters realize their responsibility of incarnating Christ in their culture. To witness to Him here and now. To proclaim Him within the African values, and in short, they have the duty to make the Christian faith relevant to their people, and religious life meaningful to their fellow young women.

Therefore, it follows that the African sisters must be well informed in

Christian doctrine, theology, scripture, liturgy, catechetics and pastoral anthropology. For, without good knowledge of these disciplines, the implementation of African values will lack depth and lose ground. Until they realize the need for constant searching by reading of such materials, it remains absurd to talk about 'adaptation' in African congregations or on local or wider levels. It has already been remarked that some indigenous bishops, priests and sisters are too westernized. And as a result, they do not know their own culture and customs, nor do they understand their people.

It is essential that priorities be established to get a good spiritual formation; short annual renewal courses for novice mistresses and other forms of on-going formation should be organized at all levels. Bishops should be aware of their great responsibilities to provide women religious with chaplains who are well trained, interested and in good health. The spiritual formation of the sisters should be included in their priorities, and they ought to stop giving to the convent old, sick, and difficult priests; this is a great offence to the sisters' beliefs, expectations and convictions.

Religious superiors on the other hand should be more adventurous in utilizing institutions which offer good courses in any of the above mentioned subjects. So often African congregations remain irresponsive in sending their sisters to courses pertaining to spirituality, while they are ready to send six, eight, ten sisters at one go to UK or USA for academic learning. Not that there is anything wrong in that, but their vision is somehow unbalanced. The continuous exodus from their congregation of African sisters who have been abroad clearly shows a fault somewhere. The opportunities they are offered for secular studies are not balanced by their spiritual formation. The two should go hand in hand. To come back to our point, superiors general of African sisters' congregations should start preparing scripture theology personnel among their sisters. This can be done as a joint effort on diocesan, national or regional level.

What can African sisters today offer to young girls that will really be meaningful? How relevant to Africans are the formation programmes in noviciates? If I were to suggest a programme, I would put first on the list, the meaning of 'vocation'. It is vital that the novices understand from the start what 'vocation' means. 'That is, "vocation" is not a thing given, possessed, retained or lost, but rather it is a continuous relationship between the soul and God.'[2] It is not a once-for-all possession. So often African sisters tend to take vocation as something one has, just because one has answered the first call. This results in passivity in the sisters. Therefore it is important that the novices understand that God continues

[2] E. F. O'Doherty, *Consecration and Vows*, p. 18.

to call his people, and the individual has continually to respond. Furthermore, this constant renewal and re-choosing is often done implicitly by the conscientious observation of rules, prayer life and community love.

The second point I would emphasize would be 'Community Life', such as can be understood in the African context. This would demand from the novice mistress a knowledge of African values which could be integrated into those of religious life, which are the three vows. In the *New Catechism*, the evangelical counsels are summarized like this:

'1. Man is ordained for marriage according to the structure of his mind and his body. But there are people who deliberately and gladly remain unmarried. They do it "for the sake of the Kingdom of Heaven". (Mt 19:12).
2. Man is allowed to call certain things in this world his own. He needs them in order to be independent as a human being should be. But there are people who undertake to possess nothing personally.
3. Man develops by being able to follow his own initiative. But there are people who freely vow obedience.
   Those who renounce these three human values are trying to follow the example and counsel of Jesus.'[3]

How can these values be made relevant for the young African women who are aspiring to the life of evangelical counsels? It would take me too long to deal with all the three values, what I will take is the first value. Let us look at what an African girl gives up in this respect when she responds to the call to religious life. What would she have been, had she chosen to get married? Besides the marriage itself, an African girl gives up a whole network of relationships: the role she would have played as a respected mother, and wife; a link between two clans, relating as daughter-in-law and sister-in-law to the other. What can one draw from this as a useful approach in explaining the vow of celibacy to novices in formation? There is certainly a richness in what I referred to as 'Network of relationships' in the African context. This network bears the fruit of the 'extended family'. And although some societies look upon an extended relationship as an oppressor and exploiter of nuclear families, it has nonetheless many positive aspects to be desired.

While she gives up the extended family created by marriage and procreation, the candidate on the other hand enters into an even wider family by joining a congregation of sisters. Such a community may consist of several tribes, all different in their customs and taboos: tribes which were alien one to another, and which could never relate on friendly terms, superior tribes which oppressed the small ones and terrified the weak ones. In Kenya, a congregation which is composed of members from

[3] *The New Catechism*, p. 410.

Kikuyu, Luo, Luyia, Kamba, Kalenjin, Teso, Kisii, and Gisu of Eastern Uganda has a witness to give. Such a composition should be seen as: a breaking of tribal barriers which separate and divide men; a break-through in suspicions and prejudices; a break-through in fears that exist between tribes.

Just as in marriage, peace and harmony are created between two tribes so a religious should work towards creating one tribe that is a Christian community without imposing any one set of cultural or tribal customs but, on the contrary, making good the contribution brought in by all the members for the growth of that 'Africanness' in the expression of religious life. The one community wherein all are accepted for what they are and respected for what they want to become. A community in which the members exist for one another without favouritism. A community which, because of its composition, is able to draw all men into unity. The Luo-Luyia-Kikuyu-Kalenjin-Kisii-Kamba-Teso-Gisu. The unity which Christ brought us on the Cross. A community of real African women whose delight will be to live for the 'other', that 'other' Christ being found in the fellow sister. Life devoted to the growth of the people of God.

The network of relationships growing between the sisters themselves and extending to the people of the local community, and eventually permeating the wider, universal 'Brotherhood', thereby living the very same hope and purpose that Christ died for. Thus their fulfilment will consist in knowing that they are sisters to Christ by their service to their fellow men according to Jesus' own words:

'Anyone who does the will of God, that person is, my brother and sister and mother.' (Mark 3:35)

These are ideals which should be pursued in formation. Christian values married with the African values of an African woman. The aim of formation should be to help these young girls in their growth into 'womanhood'. But these ideals are worth aspiring to only if the adult members of the group, in this case 'the congregation', live authentic lives. Perhaps there is something for the African novices to be referred to in the initiation rites in African traditions.

The youth to be initiated may be compared to the novice in religious life. Both are persons who are seeking their identity within a larger and more stable community. Though their age-group may seem stable, it is none the less incomplete by itself until it is recognized by society. This society may be the clan or the tribe according to the integrity of each. In the religious life the society consists of the professed members of the congregation. So both the African initiate and the novice for religious life have a community into which they aspire to be initiated as adult members.

What preparation is there for the novice? As with the secular initiates, there is need for separation from people and things. Like the former initiates, the novices are introduced into the art of communal living. This life entails hardships caused by tribal differences and individual characters. Much is made of self-effacement in order to promote mutual understanding. It demands surrendering one's will, and acceptance of other people's wishes. Indeed if we cannot find a comparison of the physical pains inflicted on the initiates according to tradition, we can none the less find similar hardships, perhaps even more painful in the noviceship which they learn to endure with mutual support. Furthermore,

> All these are accepted as the response to an interior need, a conscious and willed search for a state of the deepest recollection necessary to hear the voice of the Master and learn from Him His words and ways.[4]

Each of the societies, as mentioned above, is unique; each has its standard and principles, and everyone wishing to be initiated into them has to abide by these principles and live up to the standards thereof. In the case of the novices, they are taught such things as will enable them to live up to the demands of the congregation. Moreover, the mistress of novices will instruct them on how they may achieve the integration in their lives of contemplation and action. How to acquire a closer union with the Lord and their relations with their fellowmen. It is during this time that the three evangelical counsels are unfolded to them and the contents and significance of these counsels explained.[5]

Now although the two communities mentioned form the large group in which the individual initiates or novices find their identity, they are far from self-sufficient as groups. In the case of a clan or a tribe into which the youth are incorporated, the initiation finds meaning only in as far as her clan/tribe related to other tribes. Her life as an adult in her own tribe should widen into the neighbouring clans/tribes around, which in turn will find in her a worthy character to be integrated into their society. This will make the girl an instrument by which her own clan will extend its relationships and her own personality embrace a new family, clan, tribe to which she will devote her life and service all the days of her life.

---

[4] *The Way*, No. 7, June 1969, p. 20.

[5] A word on programmes. I would highly recommend the use of the Post Primary Syllabus known as 'Developing in Christ' and 'Christian Living Today' (Chapman, London) in formation programmes. The content in these books is adapted to the African situation—the method used is life experience, and the Christian message is presented as 'A Way of Life', with up-to-date scriptural, theological and pastoral anthropology materials. These and other books will certainly meet the needs of the African sisters in their search for self-identity.

What implications have we for the novice in the religious life in the above statement? The religious society into which the novices will be initiated by the three evangelical counsels is not an individual group. Of itself it is also insufficient. Its integrity consists in its relation to the larger community: the Church. The religious by their vows will find an identity with the whole people of God. Their service will of necessity embrace every people. It is quite clear therefore that religious profession is no longer considered a private affair of the community, their relatives, and a handful of selected friends. It concerns the Church because religious life is a service of the Church into which the individual has given herself in perfect charity. In this charity they will find a meaning to their giving up the three precious human values in Christ's own words

A man can have no greater love than to lay down his life for his friends. You are my friends, if you do what I command you. (John 15:31-14).

Church and the changing role of women in Tanzania

MARJA-LIISA SWANTZ

In considering the position of women in Africa, the Christian contribution is on the one hand exalted and on the other played down with accusations that mission-led education was too one-sidedly directed toward the male population. Yet the Christian influence on the position of women cannot be evaluated in general terms. As with the role of the church in the history of Africa in general, so also its role in relation to women requires a detailed study of individual missions and individual societies with their particular histories. In societies under direct pressures from international trade and slave agents the consequent social dislocation provided a different scene for entering missionaries than societies with established social and political structures.[1] The time during which the Christian church has been influential in shaping the social scene in Tanzania can be divided into three periods, referred to as the formative period, the period of entrenchment and the period of emancipation. Of these, the latter two form the main focus of this discussion.

The formative period
The history of the churches on the coast of Tanzania tells the story of freed slave women who—together with freed men—became the first pupils in mission schools and who became leading members of the first congregations and teachers for others. The position of these women, detached from their societies of origin, facilitated their taking up of new roles.[2]

---

[1] E.g. Marcia Wright, *German Missions in Tanganyika 1891-1941*, Clarendon Press, Oxford 1971, makes this kind of analysis. Bengt Sundkler, *Bara Bukoba, Kyrka och miljo i Tanzania,* Verbum, Stockholm 1974, also pays attention to social, cultural and individual factors affecting men and women as the Church is born.

[2] S. von Sicard, *The Lutheran Church on the coast of Tanzania 1887-1914 with special reference to the Evangelical Lutheran Church in Tanzania*, Synod Uzaramo-Uluguru, Gleerups, Lund 1970. 138, 214; A.E.M. Anderson-Morshead, *The History of the Universities' Mission to Central Africa*, Vol 1, 1859-1909, London 1955, 18, 31, 236, 270.

The degree of acceptance of women in leadership positions in various missions and churches depended both on the initial attitudes of particular missions and missionaries toward women's roles and the feedback from the social environment in which the work was carried out. For example, in 1931 the German Berlin mission working on the coast and in the Southern Highlands reported having as many as 72 female workers, 432 paid indigenous male workers and 10,634 Christians. The Bethel mission, reported the same year, on the other hand, in its Usambara mission 179 paid male and 36 female workers and 5,131 Christians while in Bukoba area they had only one female worker and 64 male workers and 4,428 Christians. Similarly the Leipzig mission working in the strongly male dominated Chagga society had not employed any female workers while the number of male workers was 262 and Christians 21,652.[3]

It is interesting to note that the same attitude did not prevail in relation to girls' education among the Chagga, where the value of education was quickly recognized for male and female children alike. In 1931 the recorded numbers of children in Leipzig mission schools were 1,842 boys and 1,897 girls, while in Berlin mission schools there were 4,942 boys and 2,783 girls.[4] However, when the level of girls' education was raised and special girls' middle schools were established following the same pattern as the boys' schools, there was much resistance from the parents. It required great determination on the part of missionary teachers and individual parents to break through public opinion. The church played in this an innovating role in offering women new opportunities of learning and leadership and, at least in principle, stressing the equal value of man and woman.

But in spite of her innovating role the church has also affirmed traditional values and practices. In areas where societies were less affected by external interventions and the social relations were less disturbed, women's conversion to Christianity came only after that of men. The first Christians in them were young men who were more mobile and had few binding social ties as yet. The women's membership in such congregations grew when girls had to be taught as wives for Christian men who rejected polygamy, a fact which was not always welcomed by women because it meant a greater workload for them.

---

[3] W. Gerber, *Lutherisches Missionsjahrbuch fur das Jahr 1933*, Wallmann, Leipsig, 1933, 86.

[4] Ibid.

The period of entrenchment

The introduction of a cash economy in Tanzania as in other African countries had a profound influence on the position of women. The exodus of men to towns and estates, either as labour recruits or forced by tax demands, left the women with the responsibility to manage their farms and care for the children alone. There were areas in which the pattern of young men leaving the villages became so common that a youth's initiation to life needed at least a temporary stay away from home, and in many cases this has become a permanent pattern.[5] It was also the way a young man obtained the needed bridewealth money which then gave him the impression that he worked to 'buy' his wife. The phrase 'I have paid for her' is still often repeated and gives a man a sense of having a right to the power which he exercises over the woman.

The pressure on women who wanted to make independent decisions and become Christians apart from their families resulted from fear that they would be alienated from the social behaviour and norms expected from them and thereby lose value in marriage. This made girls' education in the early congregations a slow process.

When women were left alone to manage the farms they gained a degree of independence and new skills. For example, in a coffee-growing area like Kilimanjaro many women have had to learn how to prune and spray the coffee trees and to take care of the sales and purchases. Yet, studies from Moshi and Bukoba show that there are cases in which the woman is obliged to set the money aside for the husband, because the coffee belongs to the husband who has inherited the land and the trees.[6] Transportation expenses as well as any tractor ploughing is paid by the husband whereas the manual work of hoeing and weeding is not counted in terms of money, unless paid workers are used. The wife's work has been purchased by paying the bridewealth.

Man's power through his use of money was initially a result of the husband's earlier entry into the money economy . This took him out of the social scale within which even the public roles had been earlier fitted, and gave him control of money and purchased goods. The man was no

---

[5] G. Philipson, *Sociological Report on Some Ujamaa Villages in Njombe District*, University of Dar es Salaam, Sociology Dpt Mimeo. 1972, 6; Monica Wilson, *Communal Rituals of the Nyakyusa*, Oxford University Press, London 1959, records that in 1937 women members outnumbered men by two to one in Moravian Nyakyusa congregations because of labour migration to the south.

[6] A student study from Kangabusharo and Lugaze villages in Bukoba district (R. Mutembei) and a malnutrition study in Moshi (M-L Swantz, U. Henricson, M. Zalla, Socio-economic causes of Malnutrition in Moshi District, BRALUP, Univ Dar es Salaam, 1975) gave data which verified this statement. The use of coffee money was the prerogative of the husband, but he could in some cases delegate the wife to take care of it. More usually he gave some part of it for a purchase of clothes and other necessities, or the care of the household as such.

more as dependent on the wife's work input as before, but could manage independently from her. When cash crops were introduced, the homegrown cash crops became the domain of men, who were taught the required skills and learned the basic facts about growing these crops. Thus, the whole cash economy belonged to the sphere of man and gave him a sense of power.

Another result of the cash economy was that the fathers of girls could demand part of the bridewealth in cash. When the girls began to obtain an education the fathers could again raise the bridewealth requirements and the girls themselves could expect gifts. This in turn meant that educated men often preferred to marry less educated girls. Another reason for the latter was man's need to feel his superiority in relation to his wife.

In areas where the church became a dominant institution, as in Kilimanjaro, the novelty of the Christian message and of the economic and educational opportunities it offered began to wear thin. To be a Christian was a different matter for the second and third generations.[7] The missionaries and indigenous church elders and teachers fought for the abolition of some of the traditional customs, but at the same time they enforced some of the values. For instance, the German missionary Gutmann's emphasis on preserving the Chagga social system intact had also the effect of maintaining the male dominated authority pattern. The emphasis on man's superiority and woman's absolute duty to obedience toward her husband were supported by the way the Biblical teachings were interpreted.

The whole colonial period, particularly after the introduction of Indirect Rule in 1926, meant a consolidation of ethnic units. This has been called a period of neo-traditionalism by some historians. In the Lutheran Church in Kilimanjaro, under the Leipzig mission, the period of ethnic consolidation coincided with the emphasis on ethnic values and preservation of cultural forms. A similar emphasis was found also in the Anglican and Moravian Churches. The conflict present in today's development efforts in finding a balance between cultural continuity and development was already the problem of the early missionaries. In the provincial conferences of missions working in Tanganyika, in 1911 and 1930, the missionaries were divided between those who thought in terms of Christianization of traditional customs and building on the traditional social system and morality, and those who recognized modern conditions as fundamentally different from traditional life.[8] African participants tended to take the progressive view, as some of them did also in the same kind of confrontation in the Masasi Diocese where Bishop Lucas became

[7] A good account of the differences is given by M. Wilson, 1959.
[8] Wright, 1971, 106, 115, 127, 130, 169.

the protagonist of cultural preservation.[9] The division between the progressives and conservatives went through all the main missions, the dividing line being drawn between individuals rather than missions.[10] The church contributed to tribal consciousness through the use of vernacular in its teaching and preaching and later through leadership structures when larger church units began to emerge. In areas where the church was a dominant institution the total pattern of peoples' lives was more and more affected by the demands as well as the privileges the church set for them. The issues which had caused conflict initially were eventually settled, and tribal and church ceremonies were fitted into a settled pattern of life.[11]

In relation to the position of women this had its consequences. Whereas initially, women's position was seen by the missions as an issue and women's rights were defended when the question concerned her independent opportunity to become a Christian, to follow the Christian way of life and to choose her own marriage partner, now the church became the guardian of traditional Christian virtues. Missionaries, local catechists and later pastors were bound by their own traditional concepts about the place of woman, which tended to consider obedience above all as the womanly virtue. This period in the life of the church helped in entrenching the woman's position in homes and congregations, as being a servant to man. In a legal and social sense, the woman was treated as a minor, just as a child was a minor, requiring the same forms of protection and punishment in order that she would recognize her position and duties.

To summarize, the church has been instrumental in opening up opportunities for women through roles of leadership, formal education and work opportunities. At the same time, however, within the church discriminatory practices have been upheld with divine authority. Christianity had come to Tanzania at a point of history when social conditions were unsettled and the economic well being of the people shaken. It offered both material benefits and an ideology to support the new forms of life. It changed some basic values and enforced some of the existing values. But when institutional forms were developed they began to undermine the innovating role of ideology, which became a force in

[9] T. O. Ranger & Isaria Kimambo (eds), *The Historical Study of African Religion*, Heinemann, London 1972, 247.

[10] In the Moravian mission Bachmann versus Gemuseus; among the German Lutherans Gutmann, Knak etc versus Axenfeld and Klamroth. Another example was Mumford's attempt to establish Malangali school to complement the Indirect Rule and to support an ideology committed to social conservation. The resistance from the missionaries and the students alike brought down the experiment. Wright 1971, 168.

[11] Wright, Ibid, 180. Wilson, 1959, 177-123.

support of the existing social values. The combined ecclesiastical-tribal ideology interpreted reality in a way which became generally accepted by the society. With the growth of cash crop economy, individualistic capitalistic ideals of progressive entrepreneurs were incorporated into this situation.

With the developments that have taken place in Tanzania and its declared socialistic programme, the leading sector of the Chagga society has found itself out of step with the officially accepted ideology of the country. Class differentation has emerged as a dominant feature in the formerly clan and kin based society with the growth of capitalistic economy. The cash economy has deprived the people of sufficient land for food crops, pushing part of the population off the land or making them virtually landless. Along with this development, the affluence of the wealthy and the flourishing business of the traders have become conspicuous, when compared with the grass and mud huts of poor neighbours. The traditional ideological basis is no longer relevant for the total population. It has become obvious that the part of the population who have felt the strain the hardest are the peasant women of the poorer class. This was clearly revealed by a malnutrition study which was conducted by the writer in Moshi District.

A study was made of families whose children had been to a nutritional rehabilitation centre in Kilimanjaro Christian Medical Centre. The area covered was in the central Kilimanjaro just above Moshi town in Kibosho and Uru (Catholic) and partly in Machame (Lutheran). The reason for the study was the increasing incidence of protein calorie malnutrition and the need to understand its causes. These were found to be largely economic, in that other constraints—poor health of the parents, frequent births or excessive drinking—became an unbearable burden in families whose financial resources could not tolerate any extra strains. The nutrition problems also focussed on the weak structural position of the woman and her limited opportunities to deal with a crisis situation.

Men and women alike expressed the view that a woman should not aspire to tasks which would challenge the male authority in a home. Both knowledge of the economic position of the husband and care of coffee sales were considered tasks for the man. In the same way, it was considered unsuitable for a woman to speak in public meetings since such public roles belonged to the man who knows how to handle such matters, although a few women were recognized to be exceptions to the rule. It was also considered a threat to the husband's authority if the wife were to have an income of her own. In an interview, the secretary of the marriage reconciliatory board in Kibosho told of cases in which an unemployed husband had brought accusations against his wife who had an independent income from beer brewing. This caused the wife to think of herself as equal to her husband and to show it by coming home as late as the husband did. A wife who was found to consider herself equal to her husband was warned by the board and made to pay a fine so as to be kept in her place. The teaching of the church accorded with the traditional teaching in making the man the unquestionable authority in the household, even when unable to support the family. Individual cases, of course, should not be generalized, However, the spreading news of incidents does deter the woman from taking household initiatives beyond those means allotted to her by custom.

The means which are considered legitimate are the care and selling of bananas and beans, and the brewing of beer if it is done on a small scale. As already indicated, coffee is considered a man's crop, as is maize, the proceeds of which the man has the right to keep for himself. Further, meat is man's prerogative. If there is meat to be eaten, it is slaughtered and usually bought and brought home by the man. However, to see women in the meat shops is a common occurence because, in many instances, men are employed away from home. In such ways Chagga society tries to keep distinct the roles and rights of men and women. The roles are not only conceived as distinct but also accord with value judgements. There seems little questioning among the men about the superiority of the male roles. In patrilineal Chagga society this superiority is seen as a necessity to provide the continuity and health of the lineage.

The women's workload is affected by the inequalities in landholdings and educational standards alike. It hardly needs to be said that the strains on the wife of a poor peasant far exceed those experienced by the more wealthy women. A simple description serves here to point out the existing differences. The woman's workload in a wealthier homestead is lightened through hiring help in the household and using paid labourers in coffee picking, in cultivating and in harvesting the maize and beanfields below the mountain. The wealthier woman can make use of the available transportation facilities; riding on a bus or a truck. At cultivation time, she is helped by a tractor hired to cultivate the plot. The plot can be much larger, consisting of ten or more acres because labour is not the major constraint. At harvest time, there is paid labour to harvest the beans in a day and means to transport them up the hill where the thrashing and cleaning can be done without a great rush. In harvesting the maize, the crop can be transported straight from the field by lorries to the buyers. Further, fertilizers can be used to enhance the yield and, in the case of coffee, the recommended sprays can be utilized. A wealthier household can get a loan to buy a grade cow or two and obtain a regular milk supply. It is possible to have more cattle and goats because the grass can be transported from the plains on pick-up trucks and women paid to cut the grass along the roadsides and river valleys. In fact, evidence shows that cattle loans acquired from the Cooperative Union are not often paid back, or the repayments have been very small. This in turn means that part of the wealthy farmers' cattlekeeping is paid by the smallholders from whose coffee returns the price of the cattle is cut off before the money is returned to the Primary Society from coffee sales.[12] The poor peasant woman is left without any of these privileges and is caught up in the poverty cycle of lack of land, labour, frequent births, malnutrition, and unemployment. The burden of this poverty falls on the woman.

What opportunities are left open for a peasant woman in the present situation? The opinions of women reveal a general sense of resignation to the constraints upon them. There is an awareness of deprivation but any efforts at self-improvement seem to lead nowhere. The women's resignation results in alcoholism, severe malnutrition of pre-school children and infant mortality, which although the lowest in the country in the northern zone, is, in the low income group, higher than the national average.[13] One thing preventing women from any efforts at improvement was the realization that men had the power to make women suffer for such efforts. In the records of the conciliatory board in Kibosho were women's complaints of maltreatment by the husband; cases of beating were mentioned particularly often. If it could be demonstrated that the wife was at fault, the board had recognized the husband's right to punish the disobedient wife, although the husband may have been warned not to mistreat his wife. Because the woman's position is that of a minor, the husband has the right to expect obedience from the wife and has the duty of punishing her. These values are inculcated in the society in the traditional value system as well as within the teachings of the local church. Therefore the woman feels helpless in confronting them, and has been taught to accept them herself. The women experienced the hierarchical structure of the Catholic Church as being too powerful to allow individuals to question the prevailing local teaching or their interpretation of that teaching, even though it may have been against

---

[12] Of cattle loans given by Kilimanjaro Cooperative Union (KNCU) since 1969 the amount of payments due at the time of checking 1974, was 140,000/- and payments made amounted to 42,800/- (30.6%), Tom Zalla, *Herd Composition and Farm Management Data on Smallholder Milk Producers in Kilimanjaro; Some Preliminary Results*, University of Dar es Salaam, Economic Research Bureau, 1974, Paper 74.8.

[13] I. D. Thomas, 'Infant Mortality in Tanzania', *East African Geographical Review*, No 10, 1972, 9. The malnutrition study in Moshi District showed that in the studied 42 families with severe malnutrition problems, 29 our of 210 children had died (13.8%), which is a median rate for the whole country. For the zone in general the aggregate value is 102/1000.

orthodox lines of the church at large.[14] On the other hand, the parishes have helped in creating work opportunities, in teaching both female and male youth in trades,· and have offered work to those known to be especially in need of income even though they may not have been Christians themselves.[15]

The churches support the women in principle and through their women's work; in practice, the acute problems of women have not been sufficiently analysed nor their prime causes sufficiently recognized. The church has failed to see that the traditional social system no longer has the built-in forms of protection which earlier compensated for the woman's weak structural position. Sufficient consideration has not been given to the fact that although women may be well cared for, a woman is limited in her rights if she remains within the existing social custom. She is dependent on the good will of the men who stand for her rights. For example, if a father deserts his wife and children, leaving them without support, the father's family may not be willing or able to support them, especially if the wife has not had a male child on whose behalf she could claim land. There are more and more cases in which there is no land or property to divide, even if a claim were made and a legal course followed. There are more and more women whose complaints fall into the category of social welfare, needed temporarily, until more decisive structural changes have been made which enable a woman to cultivate land regardless of whether she has a husband.

One can naturally question how far the responsibility of the church goes and how far can it help. It seems, however, that the church has been slow to recognize these needs. The leaders point to traditional ways of family support and dislike any introduction of Western forms of welfare. They may be right, but at the same time we lack sufficient analysis of the structure of the society and the prevailing power structure within it.

It seems that the church continues to perpetuate an ideological basis which, on closer analysis, may well turn out to be a denial of the basic Christian teachings. The general social and political conservatism has had both direct and indirect effects on the woman's position. Thus, what is here called the period of entrenchment is one of solidification and increased immobility within the congregational social and economic structure. Women's position in such a situation cannot be considered as separate from the total socio-economic situation. The malnutrition study demonstrated that the church as an institution with close contact and influence in the lives of the people might well consider the matter of the poorer peasants as their own and help to mobilize them on communal and co-operative levels. Many leading members of the congregations

[14] The actual teachings were not studied; only people's own interpretation of them.

[15] This was observed in Uru mission.

belong to the class of entrepreneurs. Whether this prevents the church from identifying itself with the poor is a crucial question.

Emancipation

In the vocabulary of the church we can speak about renewal and liberation. The history of a church illustrates the process which Victor Turner has analysed in terms of structure and anti-structure, a dialectical process involving experiences of *communitas* and structure.[16] In church history, the liminal times are the times when the spirit-experiences change the regular rules and patterns of life, giving individuals or groups a freedom of behaviour directed by an immediacy of the experience of the spirit. Such periods can be discerned both in the churches and in the lives of individuals. Thus, in examining the changing role of women, examples of individual conversion or of women joining communities like the Legio Maria[17] are experiences of liminality, *communitas*, whereby a woman has been torn away from the structure and is in a process of becoming a member of a new social group with new social rules and sanctions.

The East African Revival Movement had a profound effect on the position and role of women. My information is particularly from the Evangelical Lutheran Church in Bukoba, but one assumes that the same examples could be repeated from the Anglican Churches, where the same revival movement existed. From 1950 onwards, revival in the Bukoba church meant that women, who had always been quiet in public, began speaking in meetings and at small gatherings. Women, who had never before been consulted about financial matters in the homes were drawn to common consultation by their husbands about the family's use of money. Whereas men had previously felt free to exercise sexual liberties, women were now witnessing a new kind of fidelity on the part of their husbands. The women seized the initiative in caring for the sick, organizing meetings and appearing before other people with more spiritual freedom.[18]

The same practices continue, but in the church where such freedom for women has been recognized in important matters, there has come still another period of 'structure' when the rights given to women have been institutionalized and frozen. The situations in which the women can act and speak have become part of a pattern. The same awareness and alertness is no longer there to transfer the spirit of this freedom along with the demands of the time. For example, the north-western diocese of

[16] Victor W. Turner, *The Ritual Process, Structure and Antistructure*, Aldine Publishing Co. Chicago 1969, 97.

[17] Marie-France Perrin Jassy, *Basic Community in the African Churches*, Orbis Books, New York 1973.

[18] Oral information. Also Sundkler, 1974, 197.

the ELCT had up to the time of writing, not allowed women to apply for jobs in the church unless the husband did it for her, neither had the church permitted married women to keep paid employment. In many cases the obvious imbalances have not been sufficiently considered. Perhaps it is a sign of another period of renewal that the church in question has decided to launch a large scale self-research project on the role of women and youth in the church. This promises the needed spirit of self-examination which may bring new insights and more desire to move ahead again. If successful, the study should lead to a possible renewal of the structural position of the woman as far as the church can help to bring it about.

The Lutheran Church of South-Western Tanzania had a period in the 1960s when the women were on the move. Women examined their own traditional ways of life and made decisions as to what they should reject in view of the Christian teachings. They would then form small groups and go to other villages teaching Christian and non-Christian women. They would meet with them in groups and discuss questions which were considered a hindrance to faith and development. These Nyakyusa and Bena women accustomed themselves to speak in churches, even in front of large gatherings. It is common to see a Nyakyusa choir being directed by a woman, with half dancing movements. What started as a new kind of *communitas* experience has now become part of the church structure. Women's organizations are in operation in all the churches. They have become a training ground for leadership as every village congregation has its women leaders and in larger women's gatherings these women have gained sufficient confidence to appear in leadership roles.

A study of women conducted in Bukoba district showed how several women's leaders in the studied Ujamaa village had received their training in the church women's group and could now offer their help for the political women's movement. This is a feature common in most areas where the church has been active. A moving example of this is a life history of a Haya women's leader who had to go to prison because of her position as a TANU committee member, where she had to suffer a collective punishment for a deed of another committee member.[19]

However, more basic measures will be needed so that women's economic position in rural areas will improve. The church is part of a social system with crude inequalities and shares the responsibility to bring about needed structural changes. Women's opportunities to earn cash income have been limited. Women have sold surplus foodcrops, sell handicraft or pastries and brew beer, but seldom have they seen any cash returns from labour spent on cash crops like coffee or cotton. If a

---

[19] Sundkler, 1974, 236-7.

woman is divorced or left a widow without a male heir in strongly patrilineal socieities, she is often left without any land or with a very small plot which does not support her and her children, and in any event she is dependent on the good will of some male members of her own or her former husband's families. This has led to women's exodus from rural areas which can be considered a conscious form of emancipation and rejection of an inadequate social situation in which they were forced to live under conservative male dominance, without a right to land. Many have gone into overt or covert prostitution, which until recently has been practically the only way open for women to become economically independent.[20]

Tanzanian society is at present thrusting forward a political programme of Ujamaa socialism which aims at creating structural changes. With political pressure, the ideological position of a number of people may change in such a way that the traditionally held ideological supports of male chauvinism become inadequate and the designed programmes offer women more equitable returns from their work. This is the case in those Ujamaa villages where women are paid individually for their work. If the husband thinks he can depend on his wife's work to cultivate his share in the communal field, he is disappointed because he finds his wife reaping the financial benefits from her own agricultural inputs. A similar structural change is conceivable in Kilimanjaro Region as well; for example, banana sales and beer-brewing could be made a co-operative enterprise controlled by women, since the system assigns both of these tasks to the woman. Outside intervention could then bring such economic pressure on the men that they would have to check their own ideological position.

In spite of the hopes that the Ujamaa policy has raised, the pessimistic attitude commonly adopted by the women has some justification, in that the change of values cannot be brought about by the people who themselves tenaciously adhere to, and are entrenched in, the existing value system. Just as it is difficult for the wealthy farmers to start working against themselves—that is, to voluntarily change their private enterprises to co-operate efforts—so it is difficult for the men to work for a change in the system of banana-selling or beer-brewing. They know that it would affect one of their most vital social institutions, the beer-club and beer-drinking. Yet the economic pressures created by an economic practice which forces sectors of the people to the periphery, whether they are women or poor peasants, may become the effective force for change necessary in a situation such as that in the Kilimanjaro Region.

[20] M-L. Swantz, *Strain and Strength Among Peasant Women in Tanzania*, Research Report BRALUP, Univ of DSM, 1976.

Studies made in Ujamaa villages provide evidence that, if the village becomes a viable economic unit, women will greatly benefit from it. They will have membership in the village and right to hold land, even if they are divorced and living alone, and they will be paid for their daily labour. It requires, however, a conscious struggle on the part of women, since conservative attitudes can become dominant also in new villages. It will also be harder for the young girls to settle in villages than for older women with established life and work patterns.

One of the issues that has to be settled in Ujamaa villages is the age at which both boys and girls will begin to earn their own income instead of working for their families, if it is hoped that the young people will stay in rural areas. The age is officially set as being eighteen years, but this is not followed in practice. There is evidence, both from studies in Moshi District and on the coast, that a mother can depend more on her daughters than her sons for receiving cash or gifts. For this reason girls' employment is rather encouraged than discouraged.[21]

The official policy of the TANU party recognizes equality of both sexes and this finds expression in decisions which have been taken. There are more and more occupations open for both sexes and this gradually helps to change distorted ideas about the inferiority and weakness of women. Yet opportunities for women's employment continue to be relatively few. In all types of employment Christian women are in a majority because their marriage age is higher than that of the Muslim girls and their educational opportunities have been better.

The dominant Muslim culture on the Tanzanian coast has restricted the Muslim women's lives forcing them to marry at an early age and consequently keeping them from outside employment. At the same time, easy divorces have given the individual women considerable freedom. The coastal woman marries several times in the hope of strengthening her financial position. Eventually she may have built a house for herself, her children would have grown up and would be giving her some support. She may have risen to the status of a respectable woman in her own social group and could now use her position as a wedge against men. Men have to approach such a woman with due respect, even at times hoping to gain economically. A middle-aged coastal woman with some personal ambitions uses the way for emancipation open to her through divorces and new marriages and avoids the road of open prostitution. Easy divorce also averts mounting pressures in a family since the marriage pattern does not anticipate permanent unions. Simultaneously, however, women as well as men easily lose an attitude of trust in a fellow human being.[22]

[21] Ibid.
[22] Ibid.

In contrast, a Christian Chagga woman, as became evident from the study in Moshi area, commonly suffers and bears the hardships. The formal tie of a Christian marriage is still relatively strong, although the wife may use her right to run back to her father's house and wait for her husband to come and settle the problem with her father. Of the sample of 42 Catholic peasant women, 34 had had all their children from one marriage and were still living with their husbands. Considering the hardships which those women were facing, one can draw the conclusion that the religious sanction of marriage being insoluble was still a strong binding force.

The official policy of Tanzania supports marriage as a stable institution. The Marriage Act of 1971 gave a woman legal protection: a husband cannot take a second wife without the first wife's consent; no divorce can be granted unless the matter has been before a conciliation board; a husband has to support his divorced wife; a Christian marriage may not be converted to a polygynous marriage as long as the partners confess the Christian faith; a person cannot inflict bodily harm of any kind on his or her spouse, etc. The influence of the church in formulating the marriage law was considerable since the first unsatisfactory draft was left open for debate and correction, an opportunity which the religious bodies seized.

A law can be of support to women only if women are aware of the rights it offers them and if the social environment enables the women to make use of the law. In this the church would have a decisive role to play if the matter of women's rights were taken seriously. The church has tended to look at the issue of marriage as a spiritual matter, not being aware that acute marital problems arise from the prevailing concept of inequality of man and woman. Still less has the church confronted the material and economic base of this inequality.

Conclusion

Christianity has had a significant role in opening up new roles for women, in giving them more freedom as individuals and considering them as equals to men. Both in individual life histories and in the history of the churches, the initial stages offered new social patterns of integration and assimilation.

The growth of the churches with ethnic identifications coincided with the period of Indirect Rule which strengthened ethnic identities and affirmed traditional values. The period of stabilization in the churches meant a period of entrenchment in regard to women's position in rural societies. This has, in some strongly Christian areas, converged with the development of entrepreneurship and capitalistic patterns of economy leading to a growing class distinction. The position of women cannot be considered apart from the problems of poor peasantry on the whole, especially in rural areas.

Women who have lived under pressures have found ways of emancipating themselves. For some it has come through a spiritual experience of renewal in the home. For others it has meant resorting to prostitution. The new employment opportunities in the city and towns are the answer for divorcees and young girls. Ujamaa villages give women right to land and monetary returns for their labour, both basic rights which rural women have earlier lacked. Still for others, life continues as a hardship along with the determination to live through the struggle.

In the lives of all subjugated people there is a growing consciousness of basic human rights. The church may be so adherent to the existing structures that it may not be able to use the opportunity to struggle openly for the fulfilment of womanhood as a more liberated and dignified state of life. There is a possibility, on the other hand, of renewal within the spiritual processes of which the church has historically been a part. The church has the weapon of the word in teaching week by week. The church dominates the conciliation boards and could make a closer examination of the equity of the boards' rulings and advice as well as other discriminatory practices. Such questions as women's right to hold land and right to family inheritance as well as equal educational opportunities are basic in order that women would gain full respect within the family and society.

The role of women in the churches in Freetown, Sierra Leone[1]

FILOMINA CHIOMA STEADY

In studies of Christianity in Africa the primary interest has been on the impact of this religion and its colonial association on traditional African religious systems. Investigations have been geared toward the adjustment the African has to make from his or her own religion to a new religion with its associated Western ethics and culture. Where the result of this contact has led to the formation of schismatic religious movements these have received much attention because of their political significance as protest movements.[2] The emphasis on adjustment has tended to eclipse the importance of Christianity for a group of Africans for whom Christianity and Western culture are as old as their very existence as a group. For the Creoles of Freetown, Sierra Leone Christianity *is* the traditional religion, and Western ethics and culture form part of their multi-faceted life-style and ideology. Observing that Christianity in its Western forms has been a part of Creole society and culture for well over a century and a half, a Creole clergyman has declared:

If both the leaders who decide the policy of the churches and the members of the churches are Africans, it is . . . absurd to suggest that the Freetown churches are not native churches. Even so-called Western services have a distinctive quality of their own, which is not

[1] Excerpted from 'Protestant Women's Associations in Freetown, Sierra Leone', in *Women in Africa: Studies in Social and Economic Change*, edited by Nancy J. Hafkin and Edna G. Bay, with the permission of the publishers, Stanford University Press. Copyright © 1976 by the Board of Trustees of the Leland Stanford Junior University. Data for this article werre collected during a period of field research on women's associations in Freetown, Sierra Leone from July 1970 to September 1971. I wish to thank the Wenner-Gren Foundation for Anthropological Research for their financial support.

[2] E. Bustin, 'Government Policy toward African Cult Movements: the case of Katanga' in M. Karp (ed.) *African Dimensions*, Boston, 1975 examines 'the relations between secular authorities and religious nonconformists under colonial rule and after independence in Katanga' and suggests that 'the relationship is characterized not so much by mutual suspicion as by lack of a common base of reference. This hampers the process of communication, and so long as it does, a certain amount of misunderstanding is bound to continue between church and state' (p. 135).

imported from Europe![3]

This article examines the role played by women of a settled, urban and Christian community in fostering certain Christian values in their religious associations, and attempts to determine the extent to which some of the functions of these associations promote a conservative female ideology.

Freetown Creole Society

The theoretical importance of the Creoles of Freetown for African studies was pointed out a quarter of a century ago,[4] but anthropological field research in Sierra Leone has largely ignored them.[5] Even when noteworthy field studies have been conducted in Freetown, the main focus has been on tribal immigrant life in the city. Scholars have tended to see the Creoles primarily in terms of their relations with other ethnic groups. Consequently the theoretical interest has been in comparative analysis or minority—and ethnic-group studies.[6] The neglect of the study of Creole institutions is a serious oversight, since the Creoles represent an excellent example of cultural synthesis on the African continent.

Freetown did not become a city—it was planned that way. The various groups of repatriated former slaves that settled in Freetown between 1787 and 1863 came from very different places—England, Nova Scotia, Jamaica and Africa, especially Nigeria. These people were for the most part already exposed to urban and Western patterns of behaviour.

The early settlers were Christians—predominantly Wesleyans, Baptists, and members of the Countess of Huntingdon's Connection. The Church Missionary Society, an Anglican body that received material and moral support from the British colonial government, was active in promoting Christianity among subsequent groups arriving at Freetown, as were missions of other denominations. For the Creoles, a group whose members were of diverse backgrounds, Christianity—especially the Protestant Christianity adopted by the majority—became a vital integrative

---

[3] E. Fashole-Luke, 'Religion in Freetown' in C. Fyfe and E. Jones (eds.), *Freetown: a symposium,* Freetown, 1968, p. 132.

[4] K. Little, 'The significance of the West African Creole for Africanist and Afro-American Studies', *African Affairs,* 49, 1950, pp. 308–19.

[5] One notable exception is A. T. Porter, *Creoledom: A study of the development of Freetown society,* London, 1963, an excellent study that is sociological as well as historical.

[6] There are eighteen ethnic groups in Sierra Leone, seventeen of which are represented in Freetown. Of Freetown's population of 128,000, Creoles constitute about twenty-five per cent and are the second largest ethnic group in Freetown (*1963 Population Census of Sierra Leone,* vol. 2, p. 13).

catalyst. Moreover, Protestantism was consistent with urban values since it encouraged such concepts as individualism, thrift and industry. Furthermore, Creole Protestantism emphasized self-improvement. This was ultimately linked with the Calvinist doctrine of salvation, for much of this self-improvement was aided by what Creole society regards as 'blessing'. The person who has blessing can only prove this by advancing himself or herself in society; but more important is the fact that if a person has blessing he or she is bound to advance in society. This is usually possible as a result not only of divine predestination but also of the opportunities for achievement and innovation through individual effort in Creole society. Much of this self-improvement is made possible through education,[7] which is of supreme value in Creole society. To be a good Creole one has to have attended school regularly. Consequently virtually all Creole women have received formal schooling, and some have distinguished themselves by attaining high positions through promotion within their chosen profession. The first secondary school for girls, Annie Walsh Memorial School, was founded in 1849 by the Church Missionary Society, succeeding the Female Institution established two years earlier.

Freetown Creole society therefore has marked Christian and English characteristics which are apparent in its religious and educational institutions. It must be added, however, that there are also important retentions of African and Caribbean influences. A significant but not exclusively African feature is the Creoles' strong identity with their ancestors, expressed in after-death rituals such as *swujo* and graveside libations.[8] Most *rites de passage* have strong African elements as does the complex bilateral kinship structure. Caribbean and African influences are apparent in Creole architecture and music (*gumbe*),[9] in the traditional dish *fufu*,[10] and the female ethnic dress—*print en enkincha* or its forerunner, *kabaslot en kotoku*. That Creole culture represents a blend is readily apparent in its language, *Krio*.

Christianity, the most important feature of Creole society, enabled the early settlers and their descendants to withstand the vicissitudes of

---

[7] See D. L. Sumner, *Education in Sierra Leone,* Freetown, 1963. G. Harding 'Education in Freetown' in Fyfe and Jones, (eds.) op. cit. 1968, attributes the early attention given to education by the Church Missionary Society to two factors—religious zeal which saw education as a means of spreading the Christian religion, and philanthropic ideals which considered that the knowledge acquired through education would lead to a better way of life.

[8] See: H. Sawyerr, 'Ancestor worship—the mechanisms', *Sierra Leone Bull. of Religion,* 6, 1964, pp. 25-33; Fashole-Luke op. cit.; J. Peterson, 'The Sierra Leone Creoles: a reappraisal' in Fyfe and Jones (eds.) op. cit.

[9] Little, op. cit., 1950 discusses some similarities between Creole and Caribbean music.

[10] Porter, op. cit., p. 104, discusses the origin of the dish *fufu*.

political and economic life in Freetown.[11] The Christian religion also provided a common identity and a basis of solidarity. It engendered a system of beliefs, outlined a code of morality, served as a means of social control and encouraged self-improvement and philanthropy. All of these ideals were considered worthy of inculcation and preservation. Hence communities developed around churches. The church provided the inspiration to practise these ideals in everyday life and served as a potential link for all the members of the parish. In short, Christianity became a way of life. Associational recruitment on the basis of religion was therefore highly desirable, since this would strengthen ties based on common beliefs and purposes, and help to preserve Christian ideals.

Religious Associations

The prevailing influence of Christianity in the way of life and identity of the Creoles caused religion often to take on a formal meaning pertaining directly to church organization and worship. Associations which are classified as religious in this chapter are those attached to churches. In Freetown society it is important to behave in a religious manner. For women, religious piety is extended through participation in one or more of the women's associations attached to the church. The really pious woman not only knows the whole order of service and most of the hymns by heart; she also belongs to several religious associations. Most of the Christian associations in Freetown are women's associations.

It has been estimated that there are 50,000 Muslims and 40,000 Christians in Freetown. There are seventeen mosques and sixty-five churches representing fifteen different Christian denominations and sects. However, the associations studied are Protestant associations mainly because the majority of the churches in Freetown are Protestant churches. Of the sixty-five churches in Freetown only three are Roman Catholic.[12]

Not all Creole women join religious associations, and the number of active participants is usually smaller than the enrolled membership. In

[11] Fyfe, *A History of Sierra Leone,* London, 1962, is a monumental work that gives a detailed history of the Freetown settlement and the difficulties encountered in establishing this settlement. J. Peterson, *Province of Freedom,* London, 1969, examines the resilience of the settlers in the face of some of these difficulties. A. T. Porter, *Creoledom,* London, 1963, analyses Creole attainment to and subsequent loss of a position of dominance in Freetown on account of political and economic changes. M. Banton, *West African City,* London, 1957, discusses tribal life in Freetown and comments on the nature of intergroup tensions. M. Kilson, *Political Change in a West African State,* Cambridge, Mass., 1966, is an authoritative work on the political history of Sierra Leone and gives an insight into the politics of ethnicity there, though J. R. Cartwright, *Politics in Sierra Leone,* Toronto, 1970, examines the ethnic dimension more closely. L. Spitzer, *The Creoles of Sierra Leone,* Madison, 1974, is a study of Creole responses to colonialism.

[12] Fashole-Luke, op. cit.

addition, the most active participants tend to be in their middle years (forty-five to sixty). But the concern of this article is with institutional structure and function and not so much with the degree of participation or with statistical variables. It is significant enough that some women are active.

These associations, variously styled as bands, committees, groups, guilds, unions or societies, are autonomous bodies within each church. Some, however, such as the Mothers' Union and the Women's Volunteers (Anglican) and the District Women's Work Committee (Methodist) operate at national and local levels. This is also true of the Women's Society for World Service of the Evangelical United Brethren denomination which is multi-ethnic in composition. In spite of the autonomous nature of these associations there is a similarity in their functions—a factor underlying the points being discussed.

The main functions of the associations can be discussed under three headings, two of which clearly indicate the associations' conservative nature. First, these associations support the church. Second, they contribute to the maintenance of the male-dominated clergy (the status quo) by providing alternative avenues for the development of female religious leadership, instead of their seeking to become members of the clergy themselves. Third, they help to maintain a double standard of morality. The last two functions are most significant in terms of female emancipation within the church.

Supporting the church
Since the church symbolizes Christian values, one of the main functions of these associations is to ensure that this religious edifice is preserved in a physical and material sense. This is done primarily through fund-raising activities such as luncheon sales, bazaars, fêtes, and thansgiving services. The proceeds go toward the general maintenance and renovation of the church, or toward the purchase of some particular item, e.g., a silver chalice or a stained glass window. In some cases, associations, such as Women's Guilds and Women's Volunteers, have been formed for a special fund-raising project—to purchase a pipe organ or to help the church clear some of its debts. Once the equipment has been purchased or the debt cleared, they may cease to function. As a result there is much proliferation of women's religious associations, which consequently constitute the largest type of women's association.

A number of religious associations guarantee the general upkeep of the church by setting aside a maintenance fund for minor repairs and renovations. One association, the Ladies' Working Band, is found in all Anglican churches (except for St George's Cathedral), and functions in a direct caretaking capacity. The members of each Band regularly clean the church premises, and they decorate it on ceremonial occasions. In the Methodist churches the Ladies' Guild, Silent Worker, Ladies' Union, Ladies' Industrial, and Ladies' Auxiliary usually perform similar functions. Members of a number of other associations act as sideswomen (ushers) during services.

Not all fund-raising and caretaking efforts are directed toward the church. In keeping with Christian teachings on philanthropy, and with the tendency in Creole society to link generosity with kindness and goodness (quite apart from implications of status and reciprocity), a portion of the funds collected are donated to charitable organizations. In addition, association members visit hospitals, orphanages, and homes for the handicapped at Christmas to sing carols and to present gifts to the inmates. Members of the Dorcas Association formerly made clothes and purchased food and religious books for others less fortunate than themselves.

Providing alternative avenues for the development of female religious leadership

Needless to say, the record of Christianity in terms of the development of female clerical leadership is a poor one. Historically, women have been the scapegoats of Christian asceticism and have been viewed as the contaminating force of sin, especially for the male clergy. Reflecting the strongly patriarchal family law of the Old Testament, Canon Law institutionalized male dominance. This legacy is still reflected in the suspicion of the all-male clergy toward female emancipation in the church. A function of religious associations therefore is to provide avenues for the development of religious leadership among women who hold no formal position in the clerical hierarchy in Freetown.

Women's desire for religious leadership is legitimate, since Christian doctrine promises equal spiritual dignity to all; and women's need to express this dignity through leadership is logical. Meetings usually have periods devoted to the reading of passages of scripture, to Bible study, to prayers, and to hymn singing. Most women enjoy this devotional aspect of meetings because of the pleasure they derive from 'feeding the soul' through religious songs, studying the scriptures, and praying. Some of the associations, such as the Martha Davies Confidential Benevolent Association, and Mrs Pinkney's Spiritualist Association—named after their founders—are essentially prayer groups that have become formalized. These groups offer a revival type of worship, faith healing and extemporaneous prayer—popular kinds of devotional expression among some Freetown women. Whereas in many cases in Africa this mode of worship results from a complete break with the orthodox church and the development of separatist churches, which in some cases have women priests,[13] in Freetown members of these prayer groups have not severed links with the traditional churches.[14] This may be because 'orthodox' Christianity is already a meaningful religion whose values have become internalized to such an extent that they are an integral part of Creole everyday life. Those desiring a less formalized type of worship in the churches have tended to become affiliated with one or more of the American evangelical churches and pentecostal groups in Freetown, such as the Evangelical United Brethren denomination and the Assemblies of God.

In Creole society prayer is often regarded as a powerful force in solving problems and in assuaging anxieties; the prayers offered by prayer groups can be seen as an extension of this view. Though Creole belief systems accommodate other forms of metaphysical power, such as those derived from the ancestors, and though some Creoles occasionally consult the occult power of the sorcerer, prayer is generally regarded as the more continuous and sustaining force. Prayer provides women with a weapon in the fight against hardship. Creole women often 'take their troubles to God' and rely heavily on His justice, saying '*lef gi God*' (let God decide). They believe that their faith and reliance on God gives them the strength to withstand the 'trials and tribulations' of life. Creole society prescribes that troubles should be borne bravely if one is to remain alive and sane, for hardship is seen as part of life. 'It is not trouble that kills you, but how you take it.'[15] There is a tendency to identify with Biblical stories of suffering and persecution because life in Freetown has been difficult for many. Women in particular believe that their lot is a hard one, and that the burden of maintaining the health, happiness and unity of the family falls heavily on them. Although high morale and levity are often apparent, women live with the constant threat of family illness, death, burglary, and economic hardship. For many, the only consolation is their religion, which promises salvation and offers comfort. Religious associations offer women an opportunity to enjoy devotional fellowship with others who share similar problems.

[13] B. Jules-Rosette (ed.), *The new religions of Africa: priests and priestesses in African cults and churches,* forthcoming.

[14] D. B. Barrett in *Schism and Renewal in Africa* London, 1968, credits Freetown with the first ecclesiastical schism south of the Sahara (p. 18). This occurred in 1819 when settlers seceded from the Wesleyan mission. Despite this early start separatist bodies have not developed much in Sierra Leone. Fashole-Luke, op. cit., gives some reasons for this. The separatist groups that do exist were imported from Nigeria, and the most successful of these is the Church of the Lord (Aladura), which forms the subject of H. W. Turner *History of an African Independent Church,* Oxford, 1967.

[15] Mrs Etta McEwen, personal communication, 10 October 1970.

Where an American woman might consult a psychiatrist, the Creole woman's first move would be to pray. Reliance on prayer is learned early in childhood through the institution of family prayers. The parlour in Creole homes is traditionally an important religious sanctuary where the family Bible and other religious books are kept on the centre table. The room is symbolic of the paramount importance of religion in the life of the family and serves as the site of worship. In many families prayers are said every Sunday morning, and in the more devout families every day or even twice daily. Prayers also mark significant occasions in the lives of family members and figure in the opening of a new house or in the welcoming of a student who has returned home after years of study abroad. Such prayers are often led by a minister who is a relative or a close friend of the family. Although women often lead a family group in prayer, and, by virtue of their role in the family, are often responsible for the religious instruction of the young, they do not usually lead others in prayer at these ritual gatherings or during formal religious devotion.

There is evidence from historical sources that in the early days of settlement Creole women often had experience in church leadership. According to Fyfe 'they preached and testified in Nova Scotian churches'.[16] One woman had her own congregation in her house in Water Street. However, the development of such female leadership was not encouraged by the Church Missionary Society nor by the Methodist missionaries. Nor did the African clergy that later assumed the leadership of the missions allow the development of female leaders.[17]

Religious leadership tends to command a large measure of automatic respect even outside the church hierarchy, and this accounts for its importance to men and women alike. It was apparent at most business meetings of these associations that the chairman or president had very strong administrative and decision-making powers in addition to ceremonial leadership. For example, the president often issued directives to resolve formal debates instead of inviting a motion from the members who willingly accepted and even expected such directives.

Association leadership not only makes a woman an 'exceptionally good Christian' but also adds to her status in the community, and secures for her the ultimate glory of a grand funeral. The greatest honour a Creole can receive after death is to be laid out in church and to have a

---

[16] Fyfe, op. cit., 1962, p. 378.

[17] The AME (African Methodist Episcopal) Church was an exception. One woman, Jane C. Bloomer, rose to the rank of Deacon (minister) and was pastor of a church. She was also head of the Martha Davies Confidential Benevolent Association, and was considered a religious leader with enough inspiration to induce a state of spirit-possession ('*fen soirit*', finding the spirit).

well attended funeral spilling over into the churchyard and adjacent streets. A cortege of association members in uniform marching at a woman's funeral procession is testimony to a life well lived as a Christian. Only very active church women (usually leaders of religious associations) receive this great honour. In Creole society it is not only important to have lived well but also to die well.

Preserving a double standard of morality
A third function of these religious associations is that of preserving a system of morality based on Christian marriage. In keeping with Christian doctrine and statute law, Creole marriage is monogamous. This may provide another explanation for the relative absence of separatist churches among the Creoles. Oosthuizen observed that polygamy is a significant feature of these churches. 'Polygamy is practiced in the nativistic movements throughout Africa.'[18] An explanation offered by Hodgkin is that monogamy is frequently regarded not as a Christian institution so much as a specifically European one, lacking spiritual sanction.[19]

The archetypal example of an association preserving what has come to be regarded as Christian marriage is the Mothers' Union, a worldwide body that seeks to be the guardian of Christian marriage and morality. The Mothers' Union of Sierra Leone is organized on two levels —diocesan and local. Each branch, headed by the 'enrolling member', is attached to a church, and at a local level each branch functions separately. However all branches meet together once a year in October to mark the opening of the Mothers' Union year. At this annual meeting members reinforce their commitment to uphold the sanctity of Christian marriage and family life.

According to the association's secretary, the Mothers' Union is open to married women, but it also wishes to expand its membership to 'reach as many women as possible; to bring them into the moral fold; and to offer them moral uplift and spiritual guidance for family life.' She was certain that if the rules pertaining to Christian marriage and family life were applied too rigidly, i.e., if membership were restricted to married women, half of the present members would be ineligible, for divorced and separated women have been accepted as members. Some women are defaulters in Christian marriage through no fault of their own, and as the secretary noted, a large number of them are 'tormented with problems of family life in a rapidly changing city where nearly every conventional

---

[18] G. C. Oosthuizen, *Post-Christianity in Africa,* Grand Rapids, 1968, p. 180.

[19] T. Hodgkin, *Nationalism in Colonial Africa,* London, 1956, p. 103.

mode of conduct is being challenged and threatened.' The Mothers' Union therefore fills the need for moral support and advice when marriage and family life seem threatened. The following is part of a prayer sometimes offered:

O Lord Jesus Christ
Who has taught us that if the house will stand
It must be built upon a rock
For otherwise it falls,
Grant us in the Mothers' Union
To stand firm on the rock of Thy word—
That those whom God hath joined
May not by man be put asunder,
That love must never fail;
Grant us in our inward faith and outward witness
To bring encouragement and hope
To those who falter
Through ignorance, or weakness, or despair . . .

In addition, marriage counselling is usually provided through the Mothers' Union workers and the 'enrolling members'. These women are dedicated to the ideals of Christian marriage and family life, and are seen as having invaluable wisdom in helping to resolve marital problems. In addition to holding individual consultations they frequently address branch meetings on various topics concerning the home and family.

In Freetown society, as elsewhere, Christian monogamy in its truest form (marital fidelity) is only an ideal and not the norm. Oosthuizen has observed that 'the great danger in Africa . . . is the impression that is often given that monogamous marriage is automatically good—in spite of immoral developments within it in modern urban society.'[20] In Freetown several forms of unorthodox sexual liaison among Christians exist, the two most customary being (1) faithful concubinage of single people and (2) *om na trit* (outside home)—the keeping of long-standing mistresses, with or without children, by some men before and after marriage. From interviews with married men it would appear that pro-stitution—defined here as 'an *on the spot* exchange of sexual services for money'—has never played as significant a role in providing a 'safety valve' for the shortcomings of monogamy as it has in the West. Alter-natives to prostitution are provided by a category of women occasionally refered to as 'surplus women'—usually mature spinsters, women who are divorced or separated, or widows—who may enter into a liaison with a married man. There may be very strong economic reasons for this, especially among widows with no independent financial resources. In the absence of welfare-state benefits and the institution of the levirate, an

[20] Oosthuizen, op. cit., p. 182.

om na trit (outside home) relationship may be the only alternative to destitution. Other sociological reasons for the institution of *om na trit* among the Creoles have been discussed elsewhere.[21]

Affairs in the Western sense of 'temporary flights into fantasy' were rare in the past, but are increasingly becoming fashionable among young professional men who do not appear to want the additional economic burden of supporting an outside home. Apparently their desire for a higher standard of living and their more receptive attitude toward modern contraceptive methods help to ensure that these affairs remain transitory. Very often these transitory extramarital liaisons progress to more stable relationships and may threaten the stability of the legal home; for the more permanent they are, the greater the risk of family disintegration. Although divorce is rare, it does occur among the highly educated, especially those who have been abroad.[22] Young married women with good careers feel less dependent on a spouse and can therefore initiate a divorce and free themselves of an unreliable husband.

The tensions that some of these deviations create are brought out from time to time in the association's deliberations. The dilemma of the Mothers' Union is the difficulty of reconciling ideals and practices. The ideals, dictated by the church, are supported chiefly by women. The practice is dictated by men, whose behaviour in the majority of cases does not conform to the Christian ideals of family life and marriage.[23] The paradox of the Mothers' Union is that it is a women's association seeking to uphold the sanctity of an institution that involves both men and women. In its attitude toward sexuality, the Mothers' Union follows traditional Creole views. Chastity before marriage and fidelity after marriage have always ranked higher in the system of merit for women than for men. Formerly a bride had to be proved a virgin on her wedding night—the prestige of her family depended on it. A married woman who commits adultery is severely reproached by her husband and by Creole society—the severest criticism coming from other women. Indeed, a married woman can easily fall from grace among members of her own sex if she is even alleged to have committed adultery, or if she is seen flirting with another man. But such fidelity is not demanded nor expected of men.

It is clear then that a double system of morality exists for men and women. The Mothers' Union promotes this double standard, for the onus of maintaining sexual 'chastity' before and after marriage in practice falls on women alone. By manipulating each other to conform to

[21] F. C. Steady, 'Male roles in fertility in Sierra Leone: the moving target', in *Marriage, Parenthood and Fertility in West Africa*, forthcoming.

[22] Fashole-Luke, op. cit., p. 137.

[23] Ibid.

the moral code Creole women hope to preserve the moral integrity of their own domestic group. Those women who do not conform are seen as belonging in fact to the other side, 'the male side', which in Creole women's sexual categorization stands for 'the wild', 'the unrestrained'. Women on the wrong side are either treated as social deviants who should be brought back to the 'moral fold' or are abandoned as 'lost souls' if they resist conformity.

Some of the problems which erode the objectives of the Mothers' Union are widespread and are being discussed at meetings of the Mothers' Union all over the world. At its World Council Meeting held in Great Britain in 1973 the worldwide body altered its rules and divorced women were generally allowed to become members. The admission of men was proposed and is now under review. This, of course, would necessitate a change in the association's name, and this change is also being considered. Both issues are likely to feature in the next World Council meeting. A change that includes men in the membership would be more realistic, since any attempt to 'uphold the sanctity of marriage' and to 'affirm the Christian principle of permanence in the relationship between husband and wife' should be directed at both men and women.

Conclusion

A study of Protestant associations among Creole women of Freetown, and the relations of these associations to the social structure has yielded some new insights and alternative interpretations for studies of Christianity in Africa. The associations we have examined are not transitional institutions, but are extensions of institutions that are already part of Creole social organization. Thus to a great extent they preserve and promote Christian values already entrenched in Creole society.

It may be argued that some of these associations are imported from Europe. In a study of associations in Mexico, Dotson observed that 'acculturation will loom large as a complicating factor in cross-cultural studies'.[24] But acculturation is not the relevant concern in the Creole context. Religious associations here must be seen not as results of acculturation but as consequences of a cultural synthesis that has become a way of life. The important point is not that they are imported, but that they have become adopted by and have acquired intense relevance for Creole society.

The fact that these are women's associations may have relevance on a psycho-social level. In their attempt to preserve and promote standards and values considered 'good' in Creole society, these associations

[24] F. Dotson, 'A note on participation in voluntary associations in a Mexican city', *American Sociological Review*, 18, 1953, p. 386.

develop solidarity among their members. This group consciousness takes on symbolic manifestations on ceremonial occasions through the custom of dressing identically. The Creole custom of wearing the *ashuobi* (dresses of identical fabric and design—originally a Yoruba custom) at weddings as a means of identifying a group of women who are usually, but not necessarily, related by kinship ties, has often been extended to celebrations of other kinds. Although on the formal level each association has its own distinctive uniform (usually a white dress, a sash, straw hat with the association ribbon, and membership badge) it is not unusual for members of the same association to wear *ashuobi* on ceremonial occasions. These uniforms tend to emphasize the fact that each woman is working toward a goal shared by other women. This leads in turn to the development of a collective system of ideas—a kind of female ideology. Through this ideology women manipulate each other to conserve, promote and conform to society's values and standards. The fact that these values may be inconsistent with social reality (as in the case of Christian morality) or may endorse institutions that do not recognize women's needs or potentials for religious leadership is often overlooked.

Church unity and religious change in Africa

OGBU U. KALU

Judging from the reports of the Faith and Order Commission of the World Council of Churches, there are more negotiations for church unity going on in Africa than in any other continent.[1] The desire for church unity must, therefore, be an important ingredient in the current ferment within the churches in Africa. The irony of our age is that church unity is more talked about than consummated. Both the remarkable degree of interest and the failures demand closer attention and perhaps provide a clue to the nature of the church in modern Africa.

In the first place, church union movements in Africa constitute an aspect of missionary strategy. Faced with inhospitable climate, hostile receptions, the strains of survival in foreign cultures and places far from home, missionaries made efforts to sink their differences and tolerate or even co-operate with one another. The increasing cost of expansion and the realization that competition could be wasteful and even undignifying for messengers of the Gospel led through comity and co-operation to discussions on organic unity. The only line which was strictly drawn, even in the face of these adversities, was that between Roman Catholics and Protestants. The implacable war in Europe among these confessional groups was continued in the most far-off colonies.

Otherwise, the exigencies of the mission fields forced the missionaries from casual relationship (comity) to more deliberate, conscious effort to act together (co-operation) in order to tackle common problems and even to discuss unity. Within this perspective, church union movements in Africa started as a survival tactic when the various missionaries could no longer cope effectively alone. Protestant missions huddled with Protestant missions and defined themselves in contradistinction against Roman Catholics.

This is not to deny that the missionaries made appeals to the theology of unity especially with the growth of the ecumenical movement in Europe. The ripples from the Edinburgh Conference of 1910 reached the African shores. But amidst the proof-testing were stresses on the pragmatic and beneficial dimensions to unity. This can be seen from early

[1] Report of the Faith and Order Commission, 10 February 1974.

missionary conferences in Nigeria. The resolutions of the Senior African Agents during their third meeting in 1931 were replete with defensive notions like 'the desirability of preserving a *united front*' and the emphasis on the 'weakness' of their ministry created by 'divisions among us'. Earlier in 1905, representatives of Church of Scotland, the Niger Delta Pastorate and the Church Missionary Society had met in Calabar to delimit spheres of mission work so as to avoid overlap and duplication. As the country was opened (or as the British would rather say, pacified), missionary activities increased. So did operational costs. Mobility to higher income areas among church members created further necessity for concerted action. The Presbyterians, for instance, allowed the CMS a chaplaincy at Calabar for the benefit of those Anglicans who followed the expansion of the Cross River trade to the entrepôt, Calabar. Only the bumptious Primitive Methodist, who wanted to establish a mission instead of a chaplaincy, drew the rebuke of the Presbyterians. A certain Mr Luke, a member of the Council Committee of the United Free Church Mission, Scotland, moved that

> with reference to the proposal of our brethren the Primitive Methodists to begin work in Calabar this Council sympathizes with them in their need of a base and a rest house in this port. In the belief that it is possible to arrange a base without having a man stationed here and that ground may be procured for a Rest House, the Council would urge their P.M. brethren (sic) not to think of anything that would suggest overlapping. In view of how small a bit of Southern Nigeria Christian Missions have yet touched it would be little less than a crime for another Society to start work in Calabar Town.[2]

Four years later, Reverend Wilkie, a Presbyterian, stressed the same point in a paper read to the 1909 Conference of Missions in Eastern Nigeria. The interesting point is that Wilkie saw the conference as a meeting of 'generals to discuss plans for campaign.' Union movement was a strategy designed to ensure greater effectiveness.

This conference was only one in a long series. The discussions reveal opposing undercurrents in the missionary enterprise—a tendency towards rivalry and a serious effort to counteract this tendency with negotiations for co-operation and unity for the survival of all. The origin of the church union movement affected the fortunes of the ideal in Africa. It was initiated by whites as an aspect of missionary strategy. It was conceived in ecclesiastical terms, uniting some missions for greater capability, and was an incomplete process since the great barrier between Protestants and Roman Catholics was assumed as a given datum. For Africans, the church union movement came as an external force just like

---

[2] *Council Minutes*, 11 April 1905. The Primitive Methodists were advised to move to Akwa Effy River, which ran into the Cross River estuary, opposite James Town.

the denominations it was trying to destroy. This explains the paradoxical situation in Nigeria where the white missionaries appeared to be more anxious to consummate the church union in December 1965 than many Africans were. The whites brought denominations and the whites wanted to take them away, but some blacks demurred.

It must, however, be pointed out that the failures of the church union ideal in Africa could not be merely explained by its foreign origin. Many change-agents in Africa are from external sources. The degree of their success as catalysts for change is a function of the feasibility in domesticating these change-agents. Could it be that the nature of the missionary enterprise in Africa made it impossible for the church union ideal to trigger off religious change, or is it that the church union question has been posed in non-creative terms?

Besides, black attitudes towards church union have been complex. In the nineteenth century, nationalist churchmen wanted it as an effort to create an African church, expressing that chimera, African spirituality. Alexander Crummell would have such unity as an aspect of the 'redemption' that would

> wrest a continent from ruin; . . . bless and animate millions of torpid and benighted souls; . . . destroy the power of the devil in his strongholds, and to usher therein light, knowledge, blessedness, inspiring hope, holy faith and abiding glory.[3]

Crummell and many others believed in the power of Christianity as a force for the emancipation of man and for African salvation. He swallowed hook, line and sinker the European's image of the dark continent. He called on black exiles to return as agents for Christianizing Africa. Through the years, some blacks saw church union movement as an indigenization project (with all the woolly conceptions of indigenization). Others, still, have accepted the theological perspective in Christ's call for union. Smaller denominations under black leadership took the pragmatic view. Some nationalists mistook the destruction of denominations for the rout of the church and the renaissance of African culture and religion.

This paper will re-examine the fate of the church union ideal which arose from such complex origins. The *débacle* in Nigeria provides a good case study. A comparison with the failure in Zambia provides an insight in the dilemmas of the ideal and the predicament of the church in this continent. One is led to ask whether church unity could make the church in modern Africa more effective. Is it capable of causing religious change?

[3] Crummell, A., 'The Relations and Duties' in E. O. Uya (ed.), *Black Brotherhood: Afro-Americans and Africa* (Boston: D. C. Heath & Co, 1971), 70.

The Nigerian Débacle

There has been a curious silence on the history of church union movement in Nigeria. Yet, the discussions ranging from comity to organic unity started at the turn of the century and encapsule the essential aspects of the penetration into and interaction of Christianity with Nigerian culture and religions.[4] For some tantalizing period it appeared that the union would be consummated. An inaugural date was fixed for 11 December 1965. The arrangements were made in great detail: representatives of the uniting churches (Methodists, Anglicans and Presbyterians) were to meet at Anglican Girl's School, Broad Street, Lagos on 10 December to sign the Deed of Union. There was to be an International Book Exhibition on that day too. The following day would feature two services of inauguration and unification followed by a thanksgiving service in the evening. Green sashes for the clergy, buntings and vast quantities of educational literature were prepared; and so the arrangements went on. But the minutes of the meeting which finalized the arrangements contain the information that

> A telegram was read from Rev. E. B. Idowu addressed to the chairman calling for the postponement of the inauguration of Church Union. The committee regretted the intemperate language in which the telegram was couched and particularly the reference to the Secretary of the committee. A motion of complete confidence in the Secretary was adopted unanimously and it was agreed to pass from the matter.[5]

That was on 3 November 1965. Three weeks later, the chairman brought an emergency meeting of the committee to a close at Ibadan after a resolution to postpone the inauguration.[6] It was a very agonizing situation and just as embarrassing since some guests were due in Lagos already and various overseas church headquarters had contributed financially to the new venture.

A tree does not crash without rustling. It had become common knowledge that there was trouble in the Methodist ranks. The Tinubu and Olowogbowo societies had sued the leaders in court in an effort to block the inauguration. On 21 November the Agbeni society threatened a court action in sympathy while a fourth, Ago-Ijaye, filed their suit without hesitation.[7]

Some churchmen surmised that the postponement would be short-

---

[4] See my forthcoming book, *Divided People of God: Church Union Movement in Nigeria 1875-1966* (New York: NOK Publ. Ltd).

[5] Inaug. Cottee. Min. 157-8. See, Exec. Cottee. Min. 136 for the details of the arrangements.

[6] Inaug. Cottee. Min. 155 (6, 8).

[7] In the High Court of Lagos, Suit No. LD/59/65.

lived, and in fact frantic surgical efforts were made to save the infant but to no avail. A decade later, the ideal is more muted than seriously discussed. One hears the prophetic words of R. M. Macdonald at the Ibadan meeting:

> 'postponement could in the circumstances only be indefinite post-ponement, and it might be years before a new generation of negotiators could reach again the point to which we had been led by the Holy Spirit.'[8]

His bitterness is understandable. A Presbyterian missionary at Itu, Macdonald had served the merger cause for a long time, from the first halting steps in the Eastern Region of Nigeria to this final national phase. He served as secretary through some of its most difficult years, and con-summation would have been a fulfilment of a life's labour. The cup of victory was snatched from his lips. He concluded that the union ideal failed because certain Methodist societies sabotaged it out of 'completely worldly motives'. The judgement reflected a view shared by some that the collapse could be explained by 'a clash of personalities and fears about property' and did not involve theological or ecclesiastical isues. On the contrary, commented T. S. Garrett in a post-mortem appraisal,

> 'Church union in Nigeria had a remarkably easy passage when it was a scheme on paper . . . The deeper searching of heart and the more spirited debates have been sparked off by practical decisions.'[9]

The situation was more complex than this and though the disunity within Methodism burst the balloon, their situation was a microcosm of the state of the church in Nigeria.Archbishop Patterson himself attested in a speech at the Synod of the Niger Diocese that his fellow Anglicans should not deceive themselves into believing that all the faults lay with the Methodists.[10] One must still ask why the noble enterprise failed amidst the profuse protests about its desirability and roots in Biblical theology. Yet the aim is not mere diagnosis of a lost cause but concern whether such a union as was proposed would have been capable of causing religious change in Nigeria.

The collapse itself was due to a combination of four factors. The dif-ferences within the Methodists were the most ostensible cause. Behind this lay a personality clash within her leadership, structural faults in her organization and differing views on goal and process. The concern over church property among some Methodist societies in Lagos might smack of the pursuit of worldly things but actually it reflects another source of

[8] Inaug. Cottee. Min. 155 (8).

[9] YES (CMS Member Bulletin), January 1966. Garrett cited a speech by Archbishop C. J. Patterson (Province of West Africa) made at Onitsha to same effect.

[10] Frank Curtis, Sec. CMS: Circular Letter 2, 28 June 1966.

the collapse, namely, conservatism. Years of missionary rivalry left deep imprints. Poor communication took its tolls: lack of proper education and conscientization of the people on the meaning of church union, the structural gap between the activities of executives, and the participation of local congregations whose reference tended to be parochial, are only a few of the communication problems. The situation was exacerbated by wild rumours. Acute man-power problems made it difficult to ensure that those who represented the various localities were sufficiently well-trained to understand and convey the message accurately. The air was rife with half-truths in the last year of the negotiations. Protagonists made appeals to ethnic jealousies and every base instinct they could use. A fourth category of causes refers to the criticism of the actual content of the proposed constitution. Related to this is the pattern of negotiation which appeared to be concerned with resolving or patching ecclesiastical differences rather than taking an eschatological perspective.

We shall restrict our comments to the last three categories. Years ago, the Faith and Order Commission devoted a series of studies to the institutional factors which militate against mergers.[11] The gap between executives operating from the headquarters and local congregations with limited frame of reference could wreck the most ingenious merger plan. In the Nigerian context this is very cogent because most traditional political cultures are participant. Though there may be much resemblance to the parochial culture in the sense that attachment and loyalty are still to the primary groups in conformity with the small scale polity of the traditional society, it differs from the parochial culture in that it is not marked by the type of alienation depicted in Almond and Verba's definition of the term.[12] On the contrary, it is marked by a high level of congruity between structure and culture. Everybody feels himself part and parcel of the polity within limits set by custom and the traditional code. To operate without due reference to local bases in such a community is to court failure. There was a considerable resentful opinion that union was negotiated above the heads of the masses. Some churchmen warned about the dangers inherent in such negotiations. For instance, the editor of *Church Union News* had ominously noted in 1963 that

it is widely believed that the failure of the churches in North India to reach unity is due in part to the fact that discussion has only been held at the top level and ordinary church members have been in the dark.[13]

[11] *Institutionalism and Church Unity* (New York: Assoc. Press, 1963).

[12] G. A. Almond and S. Verba, *The Civic Culture, Political Attitudes and Democracy in Five Nations* (Princeton, NJ, Princeton University Press, 1963), p. 13, 18-26.

[13] *Church Union News* (Nigeria), 2, (1963), 4.

Worse still, the people were not properly educated about the meaning of church unity; hence the tendency to see it as mere amalgamation and the failure to pose the question of union in a broader, eschatological perspective.

The most ironical by-product of the historical missionary enterprise is that the messengers of a God of peace and love should have reproduced such rancorous rivalry between denominations. The simple facts about denominationalism in Nigeria are firstly, that it is a product of non-African histories, carried over during the expansion of Europeans. Secondly, there is no polity prescribed in the Scriptures. As Archbishop Whitgift argued against Thomas Cartwright, in an effort to prevent the introduction of Genevan presbyterian polity, each community has to choose a church polity which suits her culture. Presbyterian polity went as well as with monarchy as the Devil did with God, intoned King James I. Put in another way, church polity was strictly one of the *adiaphora*, 'things indifferent'. Each of the world peoples must work out her own mode of religious expression.

There is nothing new in this idea and yet most Christian groups in Africa believe firmly that the church must remain faithful to the tradition passed on by the first missionaries and converts.[14] There is a stylized view, almost a legend, concerning the early period of the church's life which continues to direct the thought and action of the present generation. The evidence of traditionalism is easily found in the liturgy, homiletic and exegesis of local congregations. The roots, perhaps, lie in the conservative traditionalism of African societies. Levi-Strauss observed that the dominant characteristic of primitive societies is their determined attempt to 'remain faithful to the past conceived as a timeless model'. Malinowski and Hendrik Kraemer concur.[15] Ecclesiastical conservatism, therefore, has its roots in social as well as historical factors and breeds an uncritical attitude towards forms, ecclesiastical or otherwise.

At the village level, social conservatism could explain the ability of denominations to establish such a strong hold on people's minds. The equal adherence of educated lay people emphasizes the success of the missions' socialization process. Their control of schools, hospitals and other social welfare facilities provided vast opportunities to orientate

---

[14] J. V. Taylor made the observation on the hold of tradition, *The Growth of the Church in Buganda* (London, 1958), 19 and Philip Turner has underscored it in his 'The Wisdom of the Fathers and the Gospel of Christ: Some Notes on Christian Adaptation in Africa', *Journ. of Relig. in Afric.*, IV, 1 (1971), 45-68.

[15] C. Levi-Strauss, *The Savage Mind* (London, 1966), 217-69; B. Malinowski, *Magic, Science and Religion* (London, 1948); Hendrik Kraemer, *The Christian Message in a Non-Christian World* (London, 1938), 150-1.

neophytes towards the narrow pursuit of the denominations' interests. A recent study on the role of the Church in the politics of the former Eastern Region of Nigeria shows clearly that the Protestant-Roman Catholic rivalry permeated the running of the government, elections, allocation of amenities and other aspects of politics.[16] It reached the point when the making of a Cabinet, promotions into the higher echelons of the Civil Service, had to be fought in an ecclesiastical version of the scramble for the national cake. Each denomination established communicative links through those it had indoctrinated at school, formed pressure groups and intensified the strains in the body politic. The boundary delimitations of the 1900s ensured that certain denominations predominated in certain geographic and ethnic parts of the country. The political involvement of the church coupled with the parochial dosage in the political culture to intensify ethnic jealousies. A church which should be the sign of Christ's reconciliation in a divided society became the axle of ethnic-oriented politics and national disunity.

Religious conservatism and denominationalism seriously hindered the forging of a liturgy which expressed the intensity of African spirituality. T. S. Garrett, who headed the committee on liturgy, observed that while there was evidence of adaptation in the Nigerian church 'an equally prevalent phenomenon which deserves the investigation of the student of missionary history is that of resistance to change.'[17] All were agreed on the necessity for union but proved reluctant to give up their liturgies. Consequently, the committee did not progress beyond a liturgy for the unification ceremony.

Intense denominational loyalties marred the spirit of the negotiations. Anglicans were openly accused of insensitively pressuring for a united church in their own image. The two classic cases concerned that knotty issue, episcopacy. The intense haggling over Bishop S. O. Odutola's residence and the posting of bishops in Eastern Regional dioceses were undignified and created a lot of bad blood.[18] Some camouflaged the rigid loyalty to their denominations by insinuating that the product-content would be a mammoth organization inimical to individual spiritual freedom or freedom to worship as one wishes. They argued that Christ's call for unity was a unity of the spirit precisely because all forms of unity before the eschaton would remain imperfect. There is no doubt that denominationalism has, like a cankerworm, sapped the resources and viability of the church in Nigeria. It contributed to the failure of the

[16] E. C. Amucheazi, 'Church and Politics in Eastern Nigeria, 1945-1966', MA Thesis, Univ. of Nigeria, 1972. See also his article, 'A Decade of Church Revolt in Eastern Nigeria, 1956-1966', *ODU*, 10 (July 1974), 45-62.

[17] T. S. Garrett, 'Conservatives and Unionists', *Theology*, 68 (1965), 417-22.

[18] For details, see Chapter Five of my *Divided People of God*.

union ideal.

Besides a negotiation process which left too much mark of bargaining, some criticized the product-content. It was unlikely that the Plan for Union would please all. As has been mentioned, there was both consonance and tension within the church union movement from the initial impulse. Various groups wanted the union for different reasons: obedience to Christ's desire that 'they may be one', an ingenuous strategy for survival, anti-Roman Catholic sentiment, nationalism and a means of building an indigenous church.

The advocates of an indigenous church criticized the lack of a creative expression of 'what we believe' (as the East Africans suggestively termed their statement of doctrine) and the incomplete liturgy and various Western Christian residues in the Book of Constitution. Unionists retorted that a great effort had been made to devise a constitution typically Nigerian however dependent on the Church of South India and Ceylonese models. The real argument of the opponents of union was that the whole goal of church union should be stated differently. Bishop C. J. Patterson aptly summarized the lesson from the Nigerian *débacle* when he observed that

> 'Maybe this was a shock that many people needed. There was real danger that we might unite on a very superficial level with much sounding of drums and mutual congratulation, to the accompaniment of music and dancing, without any real understanding of what union involves and costs.'[19]

Comparisons

The remarkable thing is that the situation in Nigeria is very typical of the rest of Africa. None of the numerous union projects, has worked out. In Kenya, Zambia and Ghana the efforts are bewitched. Zaïre may have more success with the support of the government and the ideology of *authenticité*. But government intervention raises difficult issues of the 'bounds of either sword' (as Milton would say).

The church union saga in Zambia is perhaps the best known because Dr P. Bolink has produced a book on it. In the final stages, it boiled down to a discussion of union between the United Church of Zambia and the only other two Protestant bodies who had so far resisted union overtures—the Anglicans and African Reformed Church. As usual, all the parties concerned showed interest in church unity. But the basic structures became important. The leadership of the African Reformed Church was African and, as Dr Bolink said, 'in all the ruling bodies of

[19] YES (CMS Members Bulletin), January 1965.

the Reformed Church, the simple, often uneducated village church elder, not knowing a word of English, played an important role and could do so in his language'.[20] They considered the church union project an expatriate affair, felt lost in proceedings taking place in English and unenthused with the breadth of a programme which envisaged eventual union with Roman Catholics. The Protestant ideology of yesteryears was sustained.

The Anglicans, on the other hand, enjoyed expatriate leadership, formed a part of an inter-state ecclesiastical province and were High Church or Anglo-Catholic in orientation. The ARC refused to negotiate with the UCZ if the latter negotiated with the Anglicans. However, since both the UCZ and the Anglicans had an expatriate leadership, they were able to open talks. It was at this point that the bane of church union talks with Anglicans (Low or High) became palpable, namely the issue of episcopal succession and unification of the ministry. In Nigeria, Kenya, Ghana and Zambia those with non-episcopal polities quickly compromised to accept an episcopal polity. However, they still had to fight to protect the validity of their own ministries. In Ghana and Zambia this was exacerbated by the High Church leanings of the Anglicans and their concern to include Roman Catholics in the talks. The UCZ considered the Anglican goal unrealistic, hence their enthusiasm was dampened. In Ghana, the Anglican diocese of Accra withdrew from the talks on the issue of episcopal succession. One must hasten to add that other factors contributed to the failures in Zambia and Ghana. In Zambia, the personalities of the leaders of either party kept the momentum, and the death of the Anglican Archbishop deflated the morale. Also, the UCZ members suffered from what their leader termed 'built-in-inertia'. The church was a product of an earlier union and the continued discussion of further unions and unsettled constitution bred weariness. Otherwise, the issue of apostolic succession need not produce so much bile in Africa. In the United States the Theology Section of the Roman Catholic/Presbyterian—Reformed Consultation produced a sensible solution in 1971.[21] The Roman Catholic theologians affirmed 'a positive recognition of the "ecclesial reality" of the churches and communities of the Reformation and that these communities are sources of grace'. Moreover, both sides rejected a tactile, genealogical understanding of apostolic succession as a proper understanding that prevailed in the early church. Following the lead of Vatican II a re-appraisal is under way.

The mood and the ethos in the union discussions have so far been

[20] P. Bolink, 'Towards Church Union in Independent Zambia', Unpublished Paper, Jos Conference on Christianity in Independent Africa, p. 13.

[21] Ministry in the Church (A Statement by the Theology Section of the Roman Catholic/Presbyterian Consultation). Richmond, Virginia, 1971, p. ix.

bedevilled with similar problems as in Nigeria. The efforts have appeared to be what Morris called 'ecclesiastical plumbing'.[22] Failures at least provide the opportunity for reflection. The deer that escapes the hunter only provides an opportunity for another hunting day.

Shifting Perspectives

The union ideal in Africa gathered momentum at a period when the goal of ecumenism was still the resolving of the dilemmas of denominational separation. It was also a strategy at a certain stage of missionary expansion. Later, more pressing issues of human divisions and issues of human liberation from forces which oppress and divide overtook the movement. Therefore, the ideal needs to be re-thought on two fronts: the new theological understanding of *henosis* (union) and the specific meaning of *henosis* in an African context.

The challenges of our world need the response of a united church. But church unity is not merely the merger of institutions, it entails an understanding of the meaning of the *kerygma* for us as Africans (in particularistic terms) and for the whole *oikoumene* (in universalist terms). Unity should be a process of establishing a community in order that a humane future may be developed. The goal is to provide the churches with the capacity to confront alienations and injustices, not merely as issues to be resolved, but as part of the process leading toward a renewed Christian community. There must be a shift of perspective from ecclesiastical divisions to human divisions and this will need an inter-contextual method to highlight pressure of unity in church and the world.

This is not to sit lightly on theological issues as some anti-unionists contend.[23] On the contrary, this perspective on the goal and process of union movement is radical in Biblical theology. Christ prescribed oneness as the *esse* of His Church, the people who know and celebrate His task of reconciling the world to His Father. He celebrated this union in the Eucharist and the outworking is palpable in His living and dying for others. The response to the question of John's disciples, pointing to the sight He had given to the blind and mobility to the lame, indicates what should constitute the priority for the church.

Organization and traditional heritages of various denominations are not unimportant. Rather, the attempt here is to point to the ideology which serves as focus and backbone for change and by which forms or traditions should be criticized. The Biblical account of God's activities in

---

[22] P. Bolink, op. cit. p. 17.

[23] John Macquarrie, 'Is Organic Union Desirable?', *Theology*, 73, 604 (October 1970), 437-44; 'Secular Ecumenism', *The American Eccl. Rev.*, 161 (November 1969).

history portray Him as constantly judging and shattering forms and traditions created by man for security. Denominationalism or divisions in the church must be recognized as products of cultural and intellectual factors.[24] Men are called to seek consistently the unity model of the eschaton in the here and now period and never pretend that any particular polity is the true face of the church.

A church that has the correct perspective of her *raison d'être*, which is mission, will live as a visible sign of reconciliation under the various conditions of human interdependence. For us as Africans, church unity can only cause a religious change if it serves as a means of re-understanding ourselves as a people open to God's liberating at-one-ment; if it offers the possibility of shaking off the chains of denominationalism; if it brings a clear perception of our mission, call to discipleship and the mobilization of our resources for effective evangelism, and if the confession, liturgy and polity of such an united church will reflect our new understanding of the meaning of Christ's mission to our culture.

The by-products of rivalry in the historical missionary enterprise have been churches incapable of achieving a unity which was also a renewal. In conclusion, the ideal of church unity in Africa must not be posed as an end in itself but as a first stage in the quest for a religious change in our continent and a renewed Body of Christ in the whole *oikoumene*. Evidently, it will require an outpouring of the Spirit to flush men off their old denominational securities towards the realization of Christ's promise of a new heaven and a new earth.

---

[24] This point is elaborated and put in clear perspective by V. C. Samuel, 'How the Unity of the Church Can Be Achieved', Paper read at Faith and Order Conference, Legon, July 1974 (FOCA/74:13). See also, John Deschner, 'The Unity of the Church and the Unity of Mankind', FOCA/74:18.

The missions, the state and education in South-Eastern Nigeria, 1956-71

A. E. AFIGBO

When in 1970 the government of the East Central State took over sole responsibility for public education in the state, the action came to many observers as a complete surprise. In fact, so surprised were some people that they tended to explain the policy of excluding the Christian missions from participation in education in terms of an attempt by the victorious party in the Nigerian civil war to punish the missions operating in Igboland for their alleged involvement in that tragedy on the side of the defeated party. Indeed not a few people were inclined to resurrect the old bogey of Muslim conspiracy against Christian Igboland which had featured prominently in war-time Biafran radio broadcasts. The argument went something like this: the real victors in the war were the Muslim oligarchy of the North whose long-term policy was the Islamization of the whole country, especially of Igboland where hitherto Islam had enjoyed no foothold. The exclusion of the missions from participation in education, which was glibly equated with the secularization of education, was only a first step in a carefully laid plan to uproot Christianity and plant Islam.[1]

Many explanations can be offered for the above misunderstanding of the state take-over of schools and education. First, the measure was imposed without discussion or consultation immediately after the collapse of Biafra—a time when the defeated party still feared severe reprisals from the victors in spite of assurances to the contrary. Second, education had come to occupy such a central place in the life and work of the missions especially in Igboland, that any attempt to deprive the missions of their schools and of the right to active involvement in (or rather to the domination of) education could only look like a diabolical plan to undermine Christianity. Third, few of those who had to contemplate the meaning and import of the new policy and draw their own conclusions were able to appreciate the historical background. Even

[1] Hardly anything of this kind of reaction to the takeover found its way into the pages of the newspapers or pamphlets of the day. But it did crop up for a time again and again in oral discussions of the takeover amongst groups whose members could trust one another.

though most of them had attained adulthood by the 1950s when the debate on the role of the church in public education started taking a critical turn, they had failed, like the Christian missions themselves, to appreciate the full implications of the increasingly embittered dialogue. And to make matters worse there was at the time no sound historical study of the developments in educational policy in Eastern Nigeria, especially for the period since the coming of self-government in 1956, to guide them.

It is this gap in our knowledge that the present paper seeks to make good somewhat. Its central thesis is that the East Central State Public Education Edict of 1971 was not, in spite of popular belief, a bolt from the blue. On the contrary it was the long-delayed result of an educational policy that had been in gestation for long. A study of the numerous policy papers available on this matter shows that, for a long time before 1970, a limitation of the role of the Christian missions in education, or indeed their complete exclusion from participation in education, had been seen as the much-longed-for 'divine' event which would usher in the millenium of economic and technological development as of cultural reawakening. If this was so, then the take-over could not have been aimed at punishing the Christian missions in Igboland for allegedly supporting rebellion. Nor could it be an attempt to carry out the secret anti-Christian designs of a so-called Muslim oligarchy using supposed crypto-Muslims.

The colonial origins of the problem
A criticial study of the history of educational policy and administration in South-Eastern Nigeria would seem to suggest that the involvement, indeed the dominant role, of the Christian missions in public education, though tolerated and at times encouraged by the secular authority, was never considered as a very good thing either for government or for the people. Indeed it can be said that the colonial authority accepted large scale missionary participation in education partly because by 1891, when effective colonial rule came to be established, missionary domination of the educational field was already an accomplished fact, having existed in a place like Calabar for nearly half a century. What was more, even after coming into being in 1891, secular authority spent the next two decades or so conquering the people and establishing a colonial *pax*. Thus pre-occupied, secular authority was in no real position to provide social services other than those like a communications network or administrative and judicial institutions which either directly aided conquest or contributed to the maintenance of law and order as a follow up to conquest.[2]

[2] For the attitude of the colonial government to missionary control of education in

In such a scheme of things education occupied at first a relatively secondary position and so could be left mainly to the missions within whose scheme it enjoyed, from the beginning, a place of first importance. Yet there can be no doubt that the colonial authority saw it as its proper responsibility to provide public education. Hence even during those early days when it found itself in no position to implement an alternative educational programme in the territory, it undertook not only to subsidize the educational work of the missions but also to lay down conditions which each mission school must fulfil to qualify for a subsidy. This was the earliest assertion, by secular authority, of supreme power in the matter of education and it goes back to about 1894. The next stage was reached in 1899 when the same authority started insisting that not only should it lay down the conditions which a mission school should satisfy to deserve a subsidy or grant, but that it had a duty to set up an educational inspectorate to ensure that the prescribed conditions were fully met. From here it was but a short step to the next stage in which the government asserted its right to close down schools which fell far below prescribed standards. Indeed it would appear that the colonial authority would have preferred, if it had the capability in terms of money and personnel, to take over full responsibility for education in the territory. In any case it believed that only schools built and run by government could be completely satisfactory. In the event it decided to build a few primary, secondary and teacher training institutions to serve for the missions, as some kind of the ideal they should aim at in their educational work.

The truth is that the government was never really satisfied with the results of missionary education. In theory both it and the missions would appear to have aimed initially at attracting a small fraction of the people out of the mainstream of indigenous life and occupations and training them for new kinds of jobs, for clerkships, the teaching profession and for junior positions in the church. But in practice the missions who controlled most of the schools were not very much interested in the training of clerks or even highly qualified teachers and at times adopted measures to forestall that happening. They were more concerned with raising pious low-grade teachers and mission hands and with using the schools in effecting the mass conversion of children and, may be, their parents.[3]

This conflict between secular authority and the missionary bodies over

the former Eastern Region and the present Midwestern State of Nigeria see Afigbo, A. E., 'The Background to the Southern Nigerian Education Code of 1903', in *Journal of the Historical Society of Nigeria*, vol. 4, no. 2, 1968, pp. 197-225.

[3] For this aspect of education in early colonial Nigeria see Ajayi, J. F. A., *Christian Missions in Nigeria* (Longman, 1965), and Afigbo, A. E., 'The Background to the Southern Nigeria Education Code of 1903'.

the purpose of public education in our area of concern, as in Southern Nigeria generally, has remained a live issue ever since. Writing in 1900 on missionary education in the coastal portions of South-Eastern Nigeria Mr Henry Carr had said

> The aim of the missionary societies in establishing schools is entirely different from that of the government or practical men. The missionaries look upon schools as instruments for making converts, other men view them as instruments for making good and useful citizens.[4]

Twenty eight years later the annual report of the Southern Provinces of Nigeria referring to the same issue said:

> It must always be remembered that it is not easy for a missionary to see eye to eye with an official educationist in the matter of schools and education. The one has his duty to his mission, and his interpretation of that duty must be realized and respected when considered with the purely secular outlook of a Government Superintendent.[5]

In fact the gap between the government and the missions widened as time went on. While the missionary societies stuck to their original idea of the role of education in colonial Africa, the secular authority modified its position somewhat from the 1920s. A policy which aimed at producing clerks, teachers and the other junior hands needed in the colonial bureaucracy had emphasized education of a literary kind. Long after this initial need for clerks, etc., had been more or less satisfactorily met, the original literary model of education remained. The result was the production of swarms of young men whom the government did not want, and who were in no position to employ themselves or to re-integrate themselves with indigenous society. To this development secular authority attributed much of the political and social discontent which was becoming noticeable in many parts of southern Nigeria from the 1920s. On this it said:

> Much of the discontent and many of the social problems of present times in Nigeria . . . can be identified with a system of education which was, and in a measure still is, foreign to the lives of the people, and which is formulated without true perspective and, being alike for rural and urban areas, caters for neither.[6]

As a solution government began more seriously, than hitherto, advocating using education to make the young more useful members of their traditional communities. This was to be achieved by introducing a

[4] Carr, H., *Special Report on Schools in Southern Nigeria* (Old Calabar, 1900), p. 7.

[5] National Archives Ibadan (hereinafter NAI) C.S.O. 26/2 No. 11852, vol. VI (Annual Report on the Southern Provinces of Nigeria) paragraph 14.

[6] Ibid.

curriculum that would emphasize education in crafts, agriculture, moral responsibility and local leadership.

The missions, however, did not share in this ideal or if they shared in it they did nothing noteworthy to realign their institutions to realize it. The result was, as the Rev. A. G. Frazer put it, that

> a country dependent largely on land has seen its schools train the rising generation for vocations unconnected with the land, and almost entirely for work in relation to a small ruling group of foreigners, whose local interests are necessarily of comparatively narrow range.[7]

It must, however, be observed that in their refusal to disavow the original system and curriculum geared towards a purely literary training, the missionary bodies had the support of the *élite* who suspected that the would-be new policy in education was a kind of wicked plot to keep Africans down eternally.

At the inauguration of the new policy the Colonial Secretary had ponderously declared:

> Government welcomes and will encourage all voluntary educational effort which conforms to the general policy. But it reserves to itself the general direction of educational policy and the supervision of all educational institutions, by inspection and other means.[8]

Yet the fact remains that no matter what the colonial authority did to ensure supervision and inspection, it failed—owing to lack of either will or sufficient commitment or funds—to wheel the missions into line. Indeed if anything the government would appear to have followed the missionary example in the matter. On this Professor J. F. Ade Ajayi has written:

> The cartoonist might well picture His Excellency the Governor, reading out a speech condemning literary education as he was laying the foundation of yet another grammar school on the abandoned site of an old industrial institution.[9]

In the event the thankless, and in fact tricky job of getting the missions to conform or face exclusion from participation in education was left by the colonial authority as a legacy to its nationalist successors. These latter had to face and solve the problem if their dream, of evolving a strong,

[7] NAI C.S.O. 26/3 No. 20071 Report on Education in the Southern Provinces by Rev A. G. Fraser, paragraph 8.

[8] *Education Policy in British Tropical Africa*, cmd. 2374, (HMSO 1925), p. 3.

[9] Ajayi, J. F. A., 'The Development of Secondary Grammar School Education in Nigeria', *Journal of the Historical Society of Nigeria*, vol. 2, no. 4, 1963, p. 517.

[10] Okpara, M. I., 'Education for a Living Society' an address delivered on 19 June 1962, Appendix 'B' of *Report of the Conference on the Review of the Educational System in Eastern Nigeria* (Enugu 1964), p. 40.

virile and meaningfully sovereign nation state was to be realized.

The missions, the state and education 1956-1971

In 1956 South-Eastern Nigeria, then known as the Eastern Region, attained internal self-government. This meant, among other things, that the determination of policy in issues of purely domestic concern passed to an executive body made up of members of the nationalist *élite* who were in their turn responsible to a legislative assembly chosen from amongst the most enlightened and most politicized sections of the region's population. The regional government had in fact attained full control over education within the region in 1954. With this development in the political sphere, and sovereign independence for the Nigerian nation already clearly visible on the not distant horizon, the question of education—its form, its curriculum, its objectives, its control and administration, who had the right to participate in it and in what way, on what conditions and to what extent—came aggressively to the forefront of policy and politics.

In spite of its brawls with the missions and mission schools over education, the colonial government had never evolved more than a basically conservative educational policy. True it wanted an educational system fitted to indigenous society, but this was not for the purpose of changing the inner springs of society, nor for bringing about a social, economic and political revolution, but for keeping indigenous society in its traditional groove. But the nationalists, especially in the Eastern Region, thought of, or saw, education differently. They wanted education suited to indigenous society for revolutionary reasons. While not imposing alien ways in a wholesale manner, or rather while preserving what was good in indigenous culture, education was to be used to inaugurate a revolution in the Eastern Region, mainly a scientific and technological revolution geared towards industry, health and agriculture. Dr M. I. Okpara spoke for members of this class when he argued that:

> Education is . . . the main-spring of all national action. Unless it is right and purposeful the people either crawl or limp along. But we are a people in a terrific hurry to bridge the gap created by centuries of neglect.[10]

If, with its conservative educational policy, the colonial government felt deeply worried about and dissatisfied with the educational policy of the Christian missions, the nationalists, with their radical educational programme and insistence on rapid development, were bound to be even more deeply disappointed with the colonial heritage in education which

[11] *Report of the Conference on the Review* . . . (1964), p. 7.

was largely the work of the missions, or in any case was seen by the nationalist *élite* as the work of the Christian missions. Members of this nationalist *élite,* speaking through the Eastern Nigerian Government as through commissions and review panels appointed by that government, thus criticized this colonial heritage in education not only on those grounds highlighted by the colonial authority, but on other grounds as well.

There was, for example, the question of a dominantly literary curriculum which had incurred the ire of the colonial government from very early days. Here the government of Eastern Nigeria and its many committees and policy papers on education from 1954 vehemently criticized the mission-dominated educational heritage for not placing adequate emphasis on science and technology generally, and on agriculture, the mainstay of the region's economy, in particular. For this reason, it was argued:

> the colonial type of education . . . did not adequately meet the needs of the country . . . The result is that manual, agricultural and technical education have come to be associated with inferior status and to be accorded low instead of high regard in the scheme of things.[11]

In contrast to this the government decided that:

> We must now evolve a policy, a system of education which will produce men and women who will not be out of place in a technological age . . . a system which will feed our industries with personnel . . .[12]

To this end it was going to effect 'a shift in emphasis from Primary and Secondary Grammar School Education to Technical and Scientific Education.'[13] In the primary schools, for instance, the curriculum was going to be 'completely over-hauled and re-oriented' with the introduction of science subjects.[14]

One reason for the emphasis on science and technology was to promote the study of agriculture in the schools unlike hitherto. For instance, it was argued that if the new government emphasis on agriculture was going to capture the imagination of school boys 'it must be both scientific and mechanized'.[15] To the government the neglect of agriculture by the colonial educational system was particularly serious as it was, at the time, the mainstay of the region's economy. Not only did it provide much-needed food, it provided export goods and industrial raw materials and could be made to provide jobs for the thousands of school leavers

---

[12] *Policy for Education* (Enugu 1963), p. 1.

[13] Ibid., p. 1.

[14] Ibid., p. 4.

[15] *Report of the Conference on the Review* . . . (1964), p. 4.

whom the government, the missions and commercial houses were in no position to employ. In spite of these obvious arguments for laying emphasis on agriculture in our educational system, asked Dr M. I. Okpara, did agriculture occupy any significant place in the inherited system of colonial education? The answer was, of course, 'hardly'. To such an extent was agriculture neglected that even schools which pretended to teach rural science had no demonstration farms. What was worse those teachers who were trained in rural science tended to abandon the teaching of the subject after it had helped them to obtain their Senior Teachers' Certificate.[16] In order to break with this tradition the government determined to introduce the teaching of agriculture in the primary schools, and to make that subject compulsory for the first three years of the secondary school where hitherto it had been optional.[17]

As pointed out above, this brand of education geared towards technical and vocational training had been resisted in the 1920s by the missions with the active support of the educated *élite*. Thus in a sense this later criticism of the missions by the *élite* does look like a stab in the back. But it must be pointed out that the political, social and intellectual climate of the 1950s and 1960s was very different from that of the earlier decades of the century. But whereas the *élite* adjusted themselves to changing needs and circumstances, the missions remained immobile and unmoved.

It was not only the curriculum of the inherited educational system that drew the criticism of the Government of the Eastern Region and its agencies. There was also the question of the excessive duplication of schools and their programmes which was partly responsible for the high cost of education in the Eastern Region. Because the churches used the schools mainly for the recruitment of members, and because of the existence of sectarian or denominational rivalry amongst the different missionary bodies, each did what it could to establish as many schools as possible. The more schools a mission controlled the greater the chances it had for converting many children (and maybe their parents) and the more chances it had of standing up to the challenges of rival missions. One result of this was the uncontrolled proliferation of schools without any regard for their viability or even for the real needs of the communities on which they were at times imposed.

This aspect of missionary education policy had also been denounced by the colonial government. It was largely to discourage it, that government inspection and supervision of schools became more scrupulous, while the conditions which a school had to fulfil to qualify for government recognition and grant became increasingly more

---

[16] Ibid., p. 17.

[17] *Policy for Education*, p. 4.

rigorous. But while the colonial government could without qualms close down some of the unrecognized schools and thus deny the former inmates education, or allow such schools to exist without financial support and thus condemn the children in such schools to education of a third rate kind, the nationalist governments of the 1950s and 1960s could not do the same. All the children in those schools being fellow Nigerians deserved equal treatment with their luckier colleagues either in the government schools or in the approved or assisted schools. One outcome of this line of argument was that government expenditure on education mounted by leaps and bounds. In 1959 it was estimated that the Government of the Eastern Region was spending 'about a third of the revenue of the Region' on education by 1957.[18] By 1963 it was estimated that between 1957 and 1962 the government spent on education 'an average of forty-three per cent of the Region's Recurrent Expenditure'.[19]

It was not only the government but also the villages that felt the burden of this mounting cost of building and running these schools many of which duplicated one another unnecessarily. On this it was observed that:

> Almost every village in the Region has one or more primary school, built entirely . . . by communal effort . . . The same applies by and large to the construction of secondary school buildings by voluntary Agencies, where the bulk of the money used in the construction . . . is mainly found by the local people themselves, Government and other outside assistance playing a minor role.[20]

The villages raised all this money by means of so-called voluntary contributions but detailed investigation shows that the contributions were not so voluntary and that they imposed severe hardships on many families. Even the government itself, which tended to be effusive in its prais of voluntary contribution and local initiative, noticed this fact as early as 1953. A policy paper on education issued that year argued:

> It is in no spirit of disparagement whatever that it is suggested that in recent years the system (of voluntary contribution) has fallen into difficulties. Where in a village two schools are maintained by voluntary contributions from two sets of people, there has been bitterness and trouble engendered.[21]

It is therefore understandable that by the 1960s some communities were

---

[18] *Report on the Review of the Educational System in Eastern Nigeria* (Enugu 1962), p. 41.

[19] *Policy for Education*, p. 1.

[20] Ibid., p. 1.

[21] *Policy for Introduction of Universal Primary Education*, (Sessional Paper No. 9 of 1953), p. 6.

beginning to call upon the voluntary agencies working amongst them to bury their denominational rivalries and merge some of the existing schools to make them more viable and to lessen the burden of voluntary contributions on poor peasants. But, as would be expected, the voluntary agencies ignored the call.[22] So manifest was the financial strain of running these many schools that some people began to fear that the mounting cost of education was likely to usher in, amongst the masses, an 'era of swing back from the universal popularity of and belief in, education to a scepticism as to its value, and doubt as to whether it justifies the value set on it and the sacrifice it entails'.[23]

Government looked upon the proliferation of schools as an inevitable concomitant of missionary involvement in education and of the tendency for missions to see the school as the main agency for conversion. If, therefore, the government wanted to curtail expenditure on non-viable schools it had either to limit missionary initiative in education, or, where that was not possible, to exclude the missions altogether from participation in that area of social service. One other feature argued in favour of total exclusion. This was the fact that denominational rivalry in education tended to create splits and divisions in towns and villages. It was invariably the case that a village that had two or more schools run by different missions found itself split along sectarian lines to the detriment of joint endeavours in social development.[24]

The other major criticism which the government and its agencies levelled against the existing system of education was its arrogant disregard for our indigenous culture which it sought to replace with cultural bits and pieces taken from Western Europe. This, the government considered an anachronistic policy in an independent Nigeria. It was argued that

> the present political and social status of Nigeria demands a reorganisation of the existing educational system which would better reflect óur spiritual, moral and cultural values and at the same time meet the challenge of the growing needs of the nation.[25]

To achieve this cultural re-awakening, many innovations in the school

---

[22] *Report of the Conference on the Review* . . . (1964), p. 2.

[23] Ibid., p. 1.

[24] One of the missions tried to counter this point by arguing that if it was necessary to abolish things making for division, we should also abolish 'villages, towns, clans, divisions, states, languages etc.'. See *Education 1971* Easter Joint Pastoral Letter by the Catholic Bishops of the East Central State. The reply to this argument, of course, is that if we cannot abolish all factors making for division, we can at least abolish those it is possible to abolish. Politics, it has often been said, is the art of the possible.

[25] *Report of the Conference on the Review* . . . (1964), p. 7.

curriculum were suggested. For instance it was insisted that 'in every Secondary School History should be taught by a qualified, preferably Nigerian, teacher' and that in teaching both this subject and Geography 'emphasis should be placed on the detailed study of the History and Geography of Nigeria before anything else'.[26] The study of Nigerian languages was also to be introduced and every student made to take at least one such language. Even the syllabus in English literature was to be modified to meet the needs of Nigeria for an independent cultural identity. This was to be achieved through the inclusion of suitable texts written by West Africans. In this regard it was pointed out that 'Achebe's *Things Fall Apart* is more meaningful and helpful . . . than *The Mayor of Casterbridge*'.[27] Games and physical education were also to be modified and enriched through the inclusion of indigenous games. A panel which reviewed education in the Region in 1962 claimed that:

> In the souls of most of us engaged in this brief review there lurks an aching void for the games and pastimes of our childhood days, for the joys of the village green. Most of these have been ousted by imported games which are not bad because they are imported, but which should remain side by side with those of our own culture and mode of expression.[28]

The Christian missions with their alien base in Western culture and their past performance in this matter could not be trusted to subscribe fully to this programme of promoting indigenous cultural nationalism through education. If, therefore, the government meant to implement this programme it had to find a way of breaking the missionary stranglehold on education.

There is no doubt that the government and the nationalist *élite* in general had serious and well-founded criticisms against the mission-designed system of education which we inherited from the colonial era. But it would be misleading to think that it was just dissatisfaction with the actual performance of the missions in this field that exposed them to unrelenting attack from the nationalists. The fact is that this group saw colonialism with which for decades they had been locked in conflict, as a hydra-headed monster whose grip on our national life went beyond just the control of our political and administrative institutions. Its control extended also to our economy, to education as to our religious and cultural life. The Christian missions had played an important role in promoting the stability of the colonial regime through the kind of education they inculcated. The nationalists therefore saw the control of

---

[26] Ibid., p. 21.

[27] Ibid., p. 20.

[28] Ibid., p. 4.

education as a vital adjunct to political sovereignty for only by taking it into their own hands or by forcing the missions to put state needs in education first, could they use it to create the kind of men, the kind of citizens and the ideological atmosphere they considered necessary for consolidating the sovereignty of a newly independent state. Thus the struggle for the control of education was merely another dimension of the nationalist movement, just as is the recent attempt in the economic sphere to ensure that our economy is under indigenous control.

In this sense among the factors which made the missions highly suspect and vulnerable were the facts that they had been part and parcel of the colonial regime, that their bases lay outside the frontiers of Nigeria and that until recently their upper hierarchies were dominated by non-Nigerians whose loyalty to the nationalist ideal could not but be questionable. With respect to the last point, that is the loyalty of the expatriate missionary to the newly independent Nigerian state and his ability to appreciate our problems should he even be loyal, the attitude of the Eastern Nigerian Government to the use of foreign experts in the review of our educational system is very illuminating. On this the Minister for Education, Dr S. E. Imoke, said:

> In quest for the right solution we have commissioned many experts to study and advise. Generally such commissions have been manned by non-Nigerians. The findings and recommendations of those commissions have been extremely helpful to us . . . But no foreigner, no matter how sincere, knowledgeable and objective can see or feel our problems in exactly the same way as we ourselves; for they are bound to be influenced by circumstances and conditions which, while relevant in their own countries, may not be quite applicable to our set of circumstances and conditions.[29]

That the government of the Eastern Region took very seriously the whole question of revolutionizing and indigenizing the inherited colonial system of education can be seen from the number of policy papers which it issued, as from the number of commissions of investigation which it set up on various aspects of the problem. Among the policy papers were those on the introduction of Universal Primary Education in 1953 and another on education generally in 1963. Among the commissions of investigation were that headed by Professor K. O. Dike of the then University College, Ibadan and another headed by the late Mr Alvan Ikoku, a well-known educationist and school proprietor. These were in addition to commissions or investigations or policy papers on the issue emanating from the centre. One of these, and a remarkable one at that, was the Adefarasin commission of 1965 on aspects of teachers' demands.

---

[29] 'Foreword' by S. E. Imoke to *Report of the Conference on the Review* . . . (1964).

Many of these policy papers and commissions gave broad hints of the need for government to reconsider the role of the missions in education, especially by making its own intervention and participation more direct and more effective. In other words it was generally considered unsatisfactory and absurd that the government and the people should bear all the cost of education, while the so-called voluntary agencies controlled the actual day to day running of the institutions, especially since these agencies, in particular the missions, did not share the views of the government regarding the new social role of education in a modernizing state.

In 1947, that is about nine years before the coming of self-government to the Eastern Region, Governor Sir Arthur Richards had conceded that it had become essential 'to redefine the relationship between Government and Voluntary Agencies so that in future, the Government, the Voluntary Agencies and their respective staffs would know their several and related responsibilities'.[30] Later still the Adefarasin Report, also a Federal document, considered it strange that 'education was financed almost wholly by the Governments (of the Federation) even though they exercised no direct control.' It therefore insisted that 'there was . . . a case for the reappraisal of the proper role of Voluntary Agencies under present conditions'.[31] Coming nearer home in terms of geography and time, the Dike commission, after reviewing what series of historical accidents led to the existing situation in which the missions exercised an unhealthy control of our education, insisted that

> an historical series of events does not relieve the state of the responsibility to concern itself directly with education and to ensure that all children, regardless of religious or social background, shall have equal opportunities for an education related to their aptitudes and abilities.[32]

The question, of course, arises as to what was the reaction of the missions to these open and extensive criticisms of their more than a century of domination of education in Eastern Nigeria and to the above broad hints of an eventual government take-over of direct control over schools? A full investigation of this question has to be done on two broad fronts. The first front is concerned with the ill-advised attempt of the missions to make the question of the control of education a political issue over which they were prepared to challenge the government and the

---

[30] Quoted in *Report on the Review of Educational System in Eastern Nigeria*, p. 6, from Legislative Council Debates for August 1947.

[31] *Report of the National Joint Negotiating Council for Teachers 1964-65* (Lagos 1965), p. 11.

[32] *Report on the Review of Educational System etc.* (1962), p. 34.

NCNC openly through inflamatory press publications and statements from the pulpit, through rowdy women's demonstrations, through the injection of religion into elections, and even through opposing the scheme for universal primary education, etc. This has been dealt with in detail by Mr Elochukwu Amucheazi and does not need to be repeated here.[33]

The second and more relevant front is concerned with what they did to ensure that the education they gave in the schools met the criticisms raised above and therefore satisfied the needs of the nation thus making it unnecessary for the state to intervene directly in this their ancient preserve. Here there is no evidence that the missions did anything noteworthy even though some of them, for instance the Roman Catholic missions, had come to concede the outrageous anachronism of the kind of education they had given and were continuing to give to Nigerians. The Joint Pastoral Letter issued by the Nigerian Catholic Hierarchy in 1960 admitted that:

> The time has come to revise generally our entire educational system to fit it better with the circumstances of the country. For too long our ideal has been based on models hastily imported from abroad.[34]

In fact, if anything, some of the actions taken by the missions in the general area of education helped to emphasize some of the shortcomings in their education which angered the nationalists. Thus, for instance, in the region the period between 1953 and the coming of the Nigerian Civil War was the great age of school expansion. The missions went into this with such zeal and determination that nothing the government could do could stem the tide. This, of course, meant that the problem of proliferation, duplication and rising cost became more glaring. It also meant that the schools graduated more students than the economy could find places for. And since these new schools were cast in the mould of the grammar schools of the colonial era, it meant that the social irrelevance of the education they gave became more manifest. It was this that the government of the East Central State referred to as the lack of 'rational relationship between investments and expansion in education and the absorptive capacity of the economy'.[35] It is a measure of the extent to which the missions had failed to adjust the education they gave to the needs of the times that in 1971 it was still possible legitimately to criticize the existing educational system on the old grounds of inter-denominational

[33] Amucheazi, E. C., 'Church and Politics in Eastern Nigeria 1946–1965' (MSc thesis, Ibadan 1972).

[34] *The Catholic Church in Independent Nigeria* (Ibadan 1960), p. 11.

[35] *Policy on Public Education*, Official Document No. 3 of 1971, East Central State, p. 1.

rivalry, dissipation of community efforts and resources, social irrelevance, cultural alienation and so on.

Indeed the missions were peculiarly unresponsive to criticisms and admonitions in the field of education and it is doubtful whether any amount of harangue or pleading could have led them to recognize the force of the argument which Mr Henry Carr addressed to them in 1900 that they must recognize that 'the children whom they are training to live in heaven have first to get through this world.'[36] Probably this unresponsiveness derived from the belief, not unusual in such men, that in the final analysis they are accountable not to any human agency but to God. But it is also likely that they considered the differences in their ranks—between the RCM and the Protestants—more serious than the rift between them as an interest-group and the emerging Erastian state. There is evidence to show that the post-1953 uncontrolled expansion in schools was to a large extent a result of the old rivalry between the missions for converts, especially as all the missions continued to depend almost wholly on the schools for recruitment. Pre-occupied with interdenominational rivalry the missions did not understand the full implications of sovereign nationhood, of the coming of age, politically, by the indigenous *élite*. It is this that helps to explain why the East Central State Public Education Edict of 1971 took them by surprise and why it caught them still mentally unprepared to consider other means for membership recruitment than public education.

From the foregoing it is thus quite clear that the policy of direct state control of education in the East Central State cannot be explained only or even mainly with reference to the civil war, though there is no doubt that the civil war, by helping to disorganize the missions in the former Eastern Region, helped to make the take-over possible. In fact state control of education has since become more or less a national policy. The Second National Development Plan (1970-4) prepared long before the civil war ended had declared that 'a country like Nigeria cannot afford to leave education to the whims and caprices of individual choice'.[37] Had the former Eastern Region emerged from the civil war still as an administrative unit, the Public Education Edict of 1971 would have applied to the whole area. In any case other states are now following the example set in 1971 by the East Central State.

One can, of course, if anxious to console the missions, argue that the state take-over of public instruction is a sign of the success of the missions in education—a sign that within the short period of one hundred and twenty-four years (1846-1971) they had successfully

---

[36] Carr, *Special Report on Schools etc.*, p. 7.

[37] *Second National Development Plan 1970-74* (Lagos 1970), p. 235.

brought their own children (i.e. the educated *élite* who run these states) to adulthood. For it is this alone that had made it possible for these *élites* to take into their own hands their political destiny, including the control of public education. The missions, however, did not see it in this light. And in any case there was no formal hand-over.

One other point which deserves mention here is the fact that when the missions were unceremoniously elbowed out of the educational arena, no section of the society concerned came out significantly in their defence. The reasons for this are still to be uncovered by intensive field research. But here one can suggest that the timing of the take-over was probably important. The fact that it happened immediately after the civil war when most people, as already mentioned above, were afraid for their lives may well explain this. But it is also quite likely that even more important was the fact that the missions had not actually succeeded in building up an organic link between them and indigenous society at large. Somehow they were still considered as some kind of adventitious outgrowth. As a result not everything that happened to them could be seen as touching the vital interests of society as such. This way of looking at the missions had been, paradoxically, reinforced by the image with which the missions had emerged from the collapsed Biafran experiment. Vast elements in society still bore grudges against the missions which, in their management of food and medicaments meant for the poor, had shown beyond all doubt that they were at bottom human organizations (in spite of the wide claims to divine inspiration) and so were still subject to the usual human failings of corruption, nepotism, double-dealing, callousness, selfishness, etc.

Also probably important was the fact that the swarms of teachers who had worked as employees of the missions, had not much love for them as employers of labour and preferred to come under the government which was expected to offer, and has since offered, far better conditions. With these people spread all over the countryside and pointing out to their relations and friends, the possible advantages of state takeover, it is probably not surprising that the missions did not have many voices to sing their chorus that the state takeover is synonymous with the secularization of education, and that the secularization of education means certain moral chaos in this world and damnation in the next.

And, finally, there is one complaint of the missions about the state takeover of public instruction which is bound to amuse the *élite:* this is the fact that the missions were not consulted.[38] Here it may be pointed

---

[38] (i) *The Church in Education* (Statement by the Eastern Area Committee of the Christian Council of Nigeria) May 1971, p. 2.

    (ii) *Education* 1971 Easter Joint Pastoral Letter by the Catholic Bishops of the East Central State of Nigeria, p. 5.

out that the missions had not distinguished themselves during the colonial period by their defence of democratic political rights. Nor did the internal organizations of the missions, with their so many hierarchies, set a shining example of democratic government. In fact the common Christian image of the shepherd and his flock, used in describing the relationship between the priest and his congregation, is basically anti-democratic. It conjures up a situation in which the shepherd rules his flock without consultation, without question, without dissent.

Church, state and education: the Eastern Nigeria experience, 1950–67 *

COLMAN M. COOKE

The threat of a government take-over of the schools hung like a Damoclean sword over the Catholic Missions in Nigeria from the early nineteen-fifties. This chapter examines this debate in the context of Calabar diocese, which is situated in south-eastern Nigeria with an Ibibio-speaking population.[1] Unlike the Igbo dioceses, Catholics there were very much a minority in comparison not only with the followers of traditional religion but also with the Protestant missions.[2] This minority position strongly influenced Bishop James Moynagh in his stand on the schools debate, Catholic opinion was not as united nor as monolithic as many were led to believe. Moynagh's position differed from that taken by Archbishop Charles Heerey of Onitsha and the majority of the Nigerian hierarchy. That it was a minority view in no way invalidates his argument: with hindsight one might well argue that had it been followed, dialogue would have replaced confrontation and co-operation, threat.

Despite.the increasing role of Local Authority schools and the known government bias in their favour, the Catholic schools system in Calabar peaked between 1957-9.[3] In 1957 one third of the school-going

* Archbishop F. Arinze (Onitsha) and Bishop B. Usanga (Calabar) gave me not only access to their diocesan archives but the hospitality of their homes. Bishop James Moynagh made personal papers available to me and was patient with my questions. To all of them I owe a debt of gratitude which I am glad to be able to acknowledge. Of course the responsibility for the views presented is my own.

[1] Calabar mission was founded in 1903. It remained part of the Vicariate of Southern Nigeria until 1934 when Calabar and Ogoja provinces were made into the Prefecture of Calabar with Mgr James Moynagh as first prefect. In 1938 Ogoja was separated from Calabar. Made a Vicariate in 1947, Calabar became a diocese in 1950. In March 1963 the Province of Annang was detached from Calabar diocese to become the diocese of Ikot Ekpene with Mgr D. I. Ekandem as its first bishop. Members of St Patrick's Missionary Society (Kiltegan Fathers) worked in both dioceses.

[2] Church of Scotland Mission (1846); Qua Iboe Mission (1887) and the Primitive Methodists (1896) were the pioneering Protestant missionaries.

[3] Calabar Diocesan Archives (CDA); File-Sacred Returns 1957-9. Cf also E.

population opted for primary education under Catholic sponsorship. Pupils increased from 44,028 in 1957 to 87,345 in 1959. Teachers numbered 2433. The number of schools had decreased from 470 to 293 owing to government regulations and the mission's own policy of consolidating plant and equipment with a view to greater administrative efficiency. Mission input in terms of personnel and finance was considerable. From a total of fifty-three priests Moynagh deployed twenty-two in full-time educational work while seventeen others, parish priests, spent the greater portion of their time administering the parish schools in their role of school managers.[4] The entire resources of the Society of the Holy Child Jesus, an international order engaged in girls' education, and the young Nigerian congregation, the Handmaids of the Child Jesus, were also directed to education. The mission's main contribution was in terms of effective administration; the literary bias of education handed down from Enugu, as indeed the many decisions on educational content, were efficiently executed and seldom questioned.[5] This was the price of continuing grants-in-aid. Moynagh's pioneering work in agricultural science and experimental dairying received no official support. Total disinterest and even hostility was the reaction of Enugu officials to the diocese's proposals on technical education made in the late fifties. The SHCJ did innovate and explore curriculum development. Their name was 'synonomous with excellence in education'.[6] Yet while 'officialdom' admitted the excellence of the SHCJ product, it thought it a little too expensive for the generality.

CHURCH-STATE CONFLICT ON EDUCATION

In March 1951 the Apostolic Delegate to British Africa, Archbishop David Mathew, drew the attention of the Nigerian bishops to developments in the Gold Coast and Northern Rhodesia where

'proposals have been made for the cession *en bloc* of large numbers of mission primary schools to the control of the Local Native Authority. In the case of N. Rhodesia the Director of African Education on receiving a joint protest from the Ordinaries, withdrew the proposal which he described as "premature" '.[7]

Fitzgibbon, the Catholic East of Nigeria, *Africa*, November 1961, pp. 5–10. (*Africa*, monthly publication of St Patrick's Missionary Society.)

[4] CDA File—Sacred Returns (1957).
St Patrick's Missionary Society, Archives (SPS) Moynagh/Gilmartin, 10 February 1957.

[5] Personal communication: The Rev T. Lucey, Supervisor of schools (1958–62) and his predecessor the Rev. J. Gilmartin.

[6] Interview Mr Francis Archibong 13 October 1972 then Secretary to Ministry of Education, South Eastern State, subsequently Secretary to SES Government.

At the request of the Advisory Committee on Education in the Colonies, Mathew had submitted a report on the relations between Voluntary Agencies (i.e. missions) and Government in the matter of education. Mathew argued that the Catholic Church would be in a position to exercise efficient control of schools of all types and guaranteed the professional competence of its teachers. While accepting the growing increase in the number of government schools Mathew was emphatic on the need for voluntary agency schools:

'I look on a Catholic school or a Moslem school as something rooted in the African scene. Our increasing number of family units have a right to a Catholic school for their children, and the African parent of any religious affiliation has the right to send his children to the type of school of his choice.'[8]

It was this right of choice that would be contested.

Forewarned by Mathew and briefed by Archbishop Porter of Accra on the schools question in the Gold Coast, the Nigerian bishops sought a concerted plan by which they might ride out the gathering storm.[9] That there would be a crisis was tacitly accepted. They presented their case in 1953 with the publication of *'The Bishops' Joint Circular on Education'*.[10] Considerable overlapping occurs in education between the functions of the family, the Church and the State. Catholic social teaching is quite clear on the respective rights of each competent party, and it received its classic expression in the encyclical *Divini Illius Magistri* of Pius XI in December 1929.[11] It was this and the many commentaries subsequent to it that formed the philosophy behind the bishops' stand.

Man is both spiritual and physical; only religious values can supply the integrating principle that unifies these diverse but inseparable elements. In education the rights of the family and the church are prior to those of the state 'and this by natural and divine law'. An education that does not

[7] Onitṣha Diocesan Archives (ODA) Mathew/Heerey 2 February 1951, and for what follows. Mathew's letter was circularized to the bishops in March.

[8] CDA 1/3 copy of *Statement on Catholic involvement in Education* made by Mathew to R. J. Harvey, of the Advisory Committee on Education in the Colonies, 1 February 1951.

[9] ODA Porter/Heerey 27 October 1951. Due to public support and sympathy given them during the Parliamentary debate and a remonstrance presented to the Government by the Catholic bishops, schools legislation in the Gold Coast had been modified. Porter insisted that the future of mission schools depended on the good will of the Local Authorities.

[10] The Joint Circular was issued under the name of Archbishop Charles Heerey of Onitsha, President of the Board of Bishops of Nigeria and the Cameroons. CDA. 2/3 Minutes of the Meetings of Ordinaries May 1952, January 1953 give the background.

[11] English translation under title of *The Christian Education of Youth* in Selected Papal Encyclicals and Letters 1928-31. (London 1932).

enable the individual to understand the purpose of his life on earth and realize his destiny in the life to come is both incomplete and unreal to the Catholic. The supernatural-eternal cannot be sacrificed to the natural-temporal. It is this uncompromising supernatural base of the Catholic position in education that is such a scandal to secular man or the nation state. The role ascribed to the state in education by Catholic social teaching 'is twofold, to protect and to foster, but by no means to absorb the family and the individual, or to substitute itself for them.'[12] Its role is to protect 'the prior rights of the family as regards the Christian education of its offspring, and consequently also to respect the supernatural rights of the Church in the same realm of Christian education'.[13] On the basis of distributive justice the state is acting unjustly when it insists on an educational monopoly 'which physically or morally forces families to make use of government schools, contrary to the dictates of their Christian conscience, or contrary even to their legitimate preferences'.[14]

While subscribing fully to the policy of Nigerian self-government and expressing a sincere willingness to co-operate with all interested parties, the Nigerian bishops insisted on the respective rights of family, Church and State.[15] It could only be in exceptional circumstances that Catholic children could be permitted to attend non-denominational schools. This was a matter of conscience. On the vexed question of Local Education Committees the bishops saw the latter's role as pertaining to the provision of educational facilities 'in a measure commensurate with the education taxes raised by the county'. The missions would help the LEC in providing trained personnel, in eliciting local support and in the provision of the religious basis necessary for genuine education. The bishops feared a growing cleavage between mission schools and state ones. They argued that 'Every school, if it is to fulfil its highest aim, must be *both,* a religious and a state school'. Religious in the sense that 'the religious tradition inherent in its foundation' must be adhered to while a state school in that it is open to every child 'in full freedom of conscience' and meets the requirements of the educational authorities regarding standards, curriculum, etc.

Reaction to the bishops' proposals was quite different in the West—and East—Regions[16] Legislation in the Western Region (1954)

---

[12] The Christian Education of Youth.

[13] Ibid.

[14] Ibid.

[15] The Bishops' Joint Circular and for following discussion.

[16] For a detailed study of the education issue see D. B. Abernethy: *The Political Dilemma of Popular Education* (1969) hereafter cited as Abernethy (1969), in particular Part II: The Era of Universal Primary Education. A brief study is found in Abernethy's article: *Nigeria* in D. G. Scanlon's: *Church, State and Education in*

while supporting Universal Primary Education (UPE) none the less apportioned a not ungenerous role to the mission schools and heeded the undoubted experience of the voluntary agencies. In return they received acceptance by the missions who put their proven expertize at the disposal of the Western Region. Such a balanced approach was not, however, followed in the East.

UNIVERSAL PRIMARY EDUCATION IN THE EAST 1953-8

In 1953 R. I. Uzoma, Minister of Education in the Eastern Region, outlined future developments in primary education.[17] An eight year primary course was proposed; the four initial years would be universal and free by 1956. This was provisional on the local rating authorities meeting forty-five per cent of the cost. Facilities in the TTC's would have to be greatly increased to meet this expansion but the graded proposals had good hopes of implementation and were welcomed by the Catholic missions.

In the phased general election for the Eastern House of Assembly in December 1953, the National Council of Nigeria and the Cameroons (NCNC) won seventy-two seats; Dr Nnamdi Azikiwe assumed the premiership while I. U. Akpabio became Minister of Education. Abernethy makes fair comment on the attraction of UPE to politicians:

'The politicians who launched the universal primary education programs acted to benefit their regions and their country. But they also acted to protect their own political careers.'[18]

This was particularly so in the East. The Action Group had got UPE underway in the West. The popular support needed by NCNC and Azikiwe could only be maintained if innovative legislation were introduced: UPE would meet the needs for progressive legislation. On 17 August 1956 the Eastern Region announced its plans for UPE which was to take effect from January 1957.[19] While the plan was introduced over the heads of the civil service and ignored the problem of meeting the financial demands of UPE, its most peculiar aspect is noted by Abernethy:

Africa (1966) hereafter cited as Abernethy (1966). For discussion of the situation in the Western Region, see Abernethy (1969) pp. 144-50. He stresses that many individuals within the Action Group had had experience of working within the Methodist and Church Missionary Society hierarchy prior to entering politics.

[17] Abernethy (1969) pp. 161-2.

[18] op. cit. p. 133.

[19] Eastern Region: Universal Primary Education; Statement of Policy and Procedure for the Guidance of Educational Officers, Local Government and Voluntary Agencies. (1956).

'But one of the most remarkable aspects of the Eastern Region's universal primary education program was the absence of such consultation either with the voluntary agencies or with the Nigerian Union of Teachers'.[20]

Relations between the voluntary agencies and the ministry for education were such that in January 1955, all mission education secretaries protested as to their standing with the ministry.[21] The Regional Board of Education did not meet in 1956-7, while unrest among the teachers was such that they came out on strike in June 1956.

Anxiety on the part of the Catholic bishops was increased by the fact that there was no Catholic representation among the upper echelons of the party while grassroots NCNC support was predominantly Catholic.[22] The perspective from which NCNC leadership would view education if not stridently anti-Catholic would at least be in tune with the Protestant background of its upper echelons. Lacking informal contact with NCNC leadership, the Catholic mission was limited to the access given to Father John Jordan, CSSp, in his capacity as Catholic Education Secretary. At a meeting with the Education Minister in January 1955, Jordan was informed that an Eastern Education Ordinance was being drafted by the Permanent Secretary, Powell.[23] Beyond confirmation of the number of Native Authority Training Centres being allocated (twenty-four) Jordan had to content himself with effusive though banal ministerial pleasantries on the 'fine work' done by the Catholic mission. It would appear that this was the last consultation that took place; thereafter information was by ministerial decree. Debarred from precise information on future legislation, the Eastern bishops issued *A Short Note from the Catholic Bishops on Universal Primary Education* in May 1956.[24] This simply alerted Catholics to the fact that the mission was concerned about two crucial areas: the right of parents to choose the agency and where possible the school which would educate their children; and secondly the right of parents to unite together in providing school accommodation

[20] Abernethy (1969) p..165. Abernethy (pp. 165-9) stressed how much this failure to consult eventually weakened the Eastern Region's capacity to provide UPE.

[21] Ibid.

[22] The Catholic Mission lagged behind the Protestant missions in the matter of secondary education. It was not until the mid 1940s that they began to seriously challenge this Protestant dominance. There was one Catholic in the Azikiwe cabinet of 1954.

[23] CDA Circular of 10 January 1955 to all Proprietors (Catholic) from Fr Jordan giving the substance of the discussions between Imoke & Jordan.

[24] This was a brief outline of the rights of parents in the matter of the education of their children. It was issued (24 May 1956) under the imprint of the four eastern ordinaries: Heerey, Moynagh, McGettrick and Whelan. It was probably occasioned by the government's ban on the construction of classrooms for first year primary school pupils issued in May 1956.

should this be deemed necessary.

Finally on 17 August 1956 the ministry showed its hand with the publication: *The Eastern Region: Universal Primary Education—Policy Statement*.[25] Its main provisions were:

1. The missions retained proprietorship of existing mission schools while their previously unassisted schools would be aided for UPE purposes. First year intake could be expanded to three streams.

2. Proprietorship of unopened mission schools and all future new schools would be in the hands of the Local Authority whose schools alone would receive building grants.

3. Children who had registered for UPE but were unable to obtain admission in existing schools would be assigned to other schools by the Education Officer.

4. Trained teachers would be posted only to schools that earned grants in 1956 and it was hoped that 'in the near future' teachers would be bonded directly to the government.

5. Children would be free to absent themselves from religious instruction in all schools and in Local Authority schools religious instruction would be in accordance with the wishes of the parents.

The Protestant missions generally welcomed the proposals and appreciated the positive aspects of the plan.[26] Due to the past experiences of the home churches, there were different attitudes among the Protestant missions to education. The Church of Scotland Mission was most at ease in education in the East; its home experience, as a result of the 1918 Education Act, revising Scottish education, had given it ownership and management of schools and the appointment of teachers while the State met capital and current expenditure. The CMS appeared content in grammar school education which remained untouched by UPE but its primary schools were of poor quality in the East. This unease with primary education may well have been a reflection of the Church of England's attitude which from 1870 onwards had handed over her schools to the state. Given the great strides made by Catholics in primary education which had overtaken previous Protestant dominance, and in the context of interdenominational rivalry in the East, many Protestants felt that while UPE proposals would curtail their own work, it would affect Catholic control of primary education much more.

The proposals were discussed by the Catholic hierarchy at their September meeting in Kaduna, when they decided that 'a statement of Catholic policy should be prepared and circulated' and 'that protest should be made here and at home' . . .[27] The Eastern bishops had

[25] For a synopsis: Abernethy (1969) pp. 171-2.

[26] Ibid. p. 172.

[27] CDA 2/3 Minutes of Meeting of Nigerian Ordinaries, Kaduna, 4-5 September

already decided, the meeting was informed, 'to make diplomatic approaches to the Premier and the Minister and if these failed to arrange a protest campaign'. Premier Azikiwe declined to meet Archbishop Heerey when the latter, as Metropolitan Archbishop, requested a meeting.[28] In October the hierarchy issued their reply in: '*The Catholic Case in the East: Statement from the Catholic Proprietors, Eastern Region.*'[29] The bishops welcomed 'the splendid project of universal primary education' but proposed certain amendments on the grounds that:

> The desire to make amendments is of the very essence of democracy. Every councillor can propose amendments to every bill on its way through the House. Why should the Catholics, to whom fifty percent of what has been achieved in Eastern Education is due, be deprived of this fundamental right?[30]

The bishops sought more consultation between the ministry and the missions so that the latter could be kept informed of educational policy, as without advance warning they could scarcely be ready to implement such policy. To work effectively within the new framework the missions needed representation on the educational planning committees. The bishops wanted mission schools built in 1956 to be used for UPE, and they sought official guidelines that would spell out the implications of UPE in contentious areas of new schools, use of available school accommodation and financial discrimination against mission schools. Finally county councils should be given definite rules of procedure regarding staffing and management of their local authority schools.

Receiving no redress in the matter of these proposals, the Eastern Nigerian Catholic Council began a series of organized protests in the Igbo dioceses. Such were in line with the general decision of the bishops that protest should be made.[31] It was precisely on the matter of public protest that Bishop Moynagh differed from the general attitude of the bishops. Three factors greatly influenced Moynagh's position in the entire education debate.[32] Firstly there was the fact that the Catholic

1956. Of the seventeen present, including the Apostolic Delegate, Archbishop Knox, there was no Nigerian-born bishop.

[28] CDA 9/3 Moynagh to Heerey 28 March 1964; Moynagh recapitulates the development over previous years.

[29] The statement was issued on 20 October 1956. The September meeting had agreed 'that the eastern bishops and some representatives from the West should meet at Onitsha'. The statement was a result of that meeting.

[30] 'The Catholic Case in the East' and for following. Such amendments had been made in the education Bill in the Gold Coast. (footnote 9).

[31] cf. footnote 27. Moynagh opposed the ENCC then; for his continuing opposition to and reservation about the ENCC cf. ODA: Moynagh/Heerey 3 November 1961.

[32] Personal communication from Bishop J. Moynagh.

community was very much a minority in Calabar compared to the longer-established Protestant missions, Church of Scotland, Qua Iboe Mission and the Primitive Methodists. Secondly there was a multiplicity of voluntary agencies running schools: over forty in Calabar. Moynagh believed that the government would have to intervene in the matters of multiplicity of agencies and of small schools, and he was not unsympathetic towards such intervention. Finally and perhaps the most crucial consideration was that the mood among young Nigerian graduates and professionals favoured some form of welfare state with its concomitant of state control in education.[33]

Moynagh opposed any direct political action on the part of Catholics in the education debate. He believed that the Catholic case should be heard; initially in 1952-3 he had proposed a federation of Catholic parents who would put the case.[34] He was more successful in organizing a Catholic Teachers' Federation within his own diocese specifically as part of Catholic Action but eschewing politics.[35] He regarded the ENCC as being too politically minded and forbade demonstrations either under its aegis or any other group on the grounds that such could only increase tension and further polarization. He realized that Igbo Catholics were champing at the bit for a fight; this he entirely opposed on the grounds that it would even further divide the East on Catholic-Protestant lines. With his appointment in 1956 as Chairman of the Catholic Welfare Conference of Nigeria,[36] Moynagh increasingly became a man with a brief for the entire country, not just upholding his own diocesan interests and perhaps more importantly, insisting that the Catholic Church was not co-extensive with the Catholic Church in the East, still less with the Igbo dioceses.

In the last analysis it was not the protest of the bishops nor of the ENCC but the threat of a general election in the East that made the government come to some arrangement. NCNC leadership feared for their grass-roots support among Catholics. Opposition candidates were being advanced and there was much talk of a Catholic opposition in Onitsha-Owerri.[37] The threat of a Catholic opposition proved to be a

[33] This concern with the outlook of the young Nigerian professionals and intellectuals was a constant theme in Moynagh's letters and articles. Cf. J. Moynagh, 'The Church in Africa' in *The Furrow*, 3, 1 January 1952.

[34] ODA Moynagh/Heerey 3 March 1953; CDA 2/3 Minutes of Meeting 13 January 1954.

[35] Cf. *Constitutions of the Federation of Catholic Teachers Associations,* Calabar Diocese, (Calabar 1956). Moynagh handed over this area to his Auxiliary, Bishop D. I. Edkandem.

[36] The CWCN was set up by resolution 8 of the Meeting of Nigerian Ordinaries at Kaduna, September 1956.

[37] Apropos NCNC Abernethy (1966) p. 231 commenting on its activities, describes it

damp squib, but in view of the elections, concessions were offered to the voluntary agencies which amounted to an almost complete removal of barriers to further expansion. While the March 1957 elections were a clean sweep for the NCNC, yet the Catholic grass-roots support was recognized when six Catholics received cabinet posts. Later in the year G. E. Okeke succeeded Ukpabio as Minister of Education. The Catholic viewpoint could now be heard in the corridors of power though it would be foolhardy to expect that it could oppose the main thrust of education policy. None the less proposals concerning Local Authorities and the bonding of teachers were not pressed.

With the election over 'a truce of sorts was reached over the religious issue'. However, UPE was running into increasing difficulty. The lack of planning, the refusal to heed civil service advice as to the costing of UPE, the political immaturity and brashness that had led NCNC to increase their enemies rather than their friends—all now came home to roost in a breakdown of UPE.[38] In January 1958 school fees were introduced at a level three times greater than pre UPE days; over a quarter of a million children were withdrawn from school due to inability to pay fees. This was the real tragedy of the situation. The comedy was provided by sundry politicians attempting to place the blame on everyone but themselves, a comedy made more ironic in that now it was a Catholic Minister of Education who was attempting the explanations.

The mid fifties *débacle* with government had shown the Catholic mission its vulnerability from the point of view of public image, in that no Nigerian-born bishop was engaged in the discussion though Onitsha had ordained its first priest as early as 1930. Archbishop Mathew had been pressing the matter of advancing some Nigerian priests to the episcopate.[39] In 1954 Monsignor Dominic Ekandem was consecrated

as 'a rather secretive organization of lay Nigerian Catholics who in many ways were more vehement in opposing the government than the Irish Fathers'. It was among these that there was talk of Catholic Independents. Abernethy (1969) pp. 175-7 treats of the influence of the oncoming election in the entire crisis.

[38] Abernethy (1969) pp. 179-85: B. C. Okwu, Acting Minister due to the illness of Education Minister Okeke, who had previously opposed UPE on religious grounds was now defending the changes and cutbacks on economic grounds. At one meeting Okwu gave as 'his personal views as a Catholic, that the (UPE) programme was a trick devised by white civil servants to embarrass the NCNC'.

[39] The CSSp were admitting Nigerians to membership of their congregation. Naturally they looked forward to CSSp succession in their own dioceses. This, however, prevented Nigerian secular (diocesan) priests from being advanced to bishoprics. While Mgr John Anyogu—the senior Igbo priest—was made auxiliary bishop to Heerey in 1957, he did not receive a diocese until 1962 when he became bishop of Enugu. Mgr Antony Nwedo, CSSp was made bishop of Umuahia in 1959 and Mgr Godfrey Okoye CSSp of Port Harcourt in 1961. The question of the promotion of Nigerian CSSp as against Nigerian diocesan priests was an extremely sensitive one.

auxiliary bishop to Bishop Moynagh, the first West African bishop in modern times.[40] By the sixties he was joined by Bishops Nwedo, Okoye and Anyogu from the Igbo dioceses. These now became the spokesmen for the Church. Together with representatives of the Catholic laity they attended a round table conference on education on 30 March 1962 called by Premier M. I. Okpara.[41] While representatives of all interested parties attended they achieved little more than an exchange of views. Moynagh lamented the lack of accord between government and mission on education.[42] Since 1957 government policy had excluded the missions from consultation on future plans. Some within the government, including the Minister of Education, favoured nationalization of schools. The bishops were divided on the issue: some would depend on the pro-mission element among the politicians to prevent a take over; others, including Moynagh, favoured negotiations that would give guarantees for the future, the minimal being access to schools for religious teaching. Moynagh sought for some understanding with the government and a long term plan for education. He decried the negative attitude of the bishops which rejected 'a possible take over without any plan of our own for rational cooperation'. The reality was that the government could squeeze out the missions: in his own diocese a quite minor official closed twenty-eight Catholic schools in Uyo and the mission had no redress.[43] Moynagh felt that while there were many thousands of Catholics who would support the mission in a crisis, such a confrontation could only play into the hands of politicians who would use the Protestant-Catholic rivalry for their own ends. He was uncertain as to whether the Catholic teachers—the younger ones—would support the missions in a crisis with the government.

A Common Religious syllabus and the NUT Strike, 1963-4
In late 1963 Minister S. E. Imoke presented proposals for a common religious syllabus. Given the evident strains and tension already present, which it can be presumed had been made known at the Okpara meeting in March 1962, the decision to introduce such proposals was ill-timed to say the least. Heerey opposed the syllabus which led Imoke to claim that the Catholics

> did not even look at the proposed syllabus before rejecting it. There is no question of my backing down on the proposal to introduce a

[40] At the time of his consecration he was the only Nigerian priest in Calabar diocese. Bishop Ekandem has now (May 1976) been created Cardinal.
[41] CDA 9/3 Heerey/Moynagh 21 March 1962.
[42] CDA 3/3 Moynagh/Pignedoli 13 January 1963.
[43] CDA 9/3 Moynagh/Whelan 22 June 1963.

common religious syllabus for schools since, I am convinced, this is in the best interests of proper and planned educational development in this region.[44]

Heerey circularized the Eastern bishops with relevant correspondence between Imoke and himself and proposed that the Catholic ministers should be apprised of the correspondence.[45]

Moynagh objected to the use of the Catholic ministers 'to bring political pressure to bear in favour of the church' and further contended that Imoke's proposals deserved discussion and debate which they were not given.[46] Furthermore Imoke had been given no room to manoeuvre; the church cannot and should not, Moynagh argued, publicly corner a minister of government and leave him without an honourable exit. Collective responsibility among the bench of bishops ensured that no individual broke ranks. Moynagh's protests were made privately to the bishops, but not to the press.[47] However, in 1964 the four Nigerian-born bishops of Ikot Ekpene, Port Harcourt, Umuahia and Enugu publicly protested to Premier Okpara.[48] They called on the Premier to state openly if government policy was intent on secularizing education or not; the government should not attempt to do it by stealth. It must be added that the bishops were working under strained circumstances as the Vatican Council was meeting (October 1962–December 1965): this meant frequent and prolonged absence from Nigeria and the difficulty of keeping in touch with a changing and complex situation.

The significance of the NUT nation-wide strike in October 1964 lay in the hope that it would pressure the Federal Government into establishing a commission charged with settling teachers' salaries and conditions of service on a national basis. In this it was successful. It was the NUT's insistence on the national aspect that prompted Moynagh to propose a national policy on the part of the Catholic church with regard to education. His proposal took the shape of an 1800 word submission to the bench of bishops: *Education in the East, June 1965*.[49] He

[44] ODA 9/3 Imoke/Heerey 13 February 1964.

[45] ODA 9/3 Heerey/Moynagh 21 January 1964; Heerey/Circular to Bishops with copies of Imoke correspondence 22 February 1964.

[46] ODA Moynagh/Heerey 26 January 1964.

[47] A point made to me by many clerics in Nigeria was that the bishops had agreed on collective responsibility for all statements issued. They agreed that despite the difference of opinion among themselves that it would be fatal if the government could claim the support of any one or more bishops against the hierarchy.

[48] CDA File 9/3. Among correspondence on the education crisis there is an undated letter of these four bishops to Premier Okpara protesting government discrimination against the mission in the matter of grants since 1957.

[49] CDA. Education in the East dated 21 June 1965, and for following discussion.

spoke as one who had spent thirty-five years in Nigeria and had made a substantial contribution to education. He interpreted the NUT's demands as being symptomatic of growing federal influence in education and increasing state control of schools. Increasingly decisions would be made on a federal basis. The NUT was a national body and so they would claim unified national conditions of service. The Eastern bishops must appreciate the national aspect of the case now emerging. To fail to do so would be a cardinal error:

> If the Catholic Church in the East is made to appear as the enemy of national unity, and as an obstacle to national planning, then the image of the Church among progressives in all regions will be that it is a body hostile to Nigerian unity—a 'retrograde neo-colonialist' organisation which impedes the march of Nigerian unity.[50]

The final decision must be with the bishops, for he saw it as an 'abdication of their duties if they were to pass on that decision to a group of laymen'. He accepted that many of the bishops favoured the present *status quo* but doubted that this could be preserved with the present march of events.

Three considerations suggested to him that the mission lacked the support essential to preserve the *status quo*. Firstly, it could only be done with the full co-operation of the entire Catholic teaching profession. Such co-operation could not be expected. The Catholic teachers could hardly be expected to turn their back on the NUT which was fighting for better conditions of service etc., on a national scale. Secondly, the mission could not count on the fullest support of Catholic school committees, etc., in the East quite simply because many Catholic members of local government etc. 'have a vested interest in local education . . . they are quite happy to exert control at local community level'. Even local Catholic school committees would welcome the financial relief that would come with government intervention: these committees had been shouldering a heavy financial burden for the last decade and they were anxious to get rid of it. But the crucial group, Moynagh argued, were the young graduates and intellectuals:

> These men, whether Catholic or Protestant, are all filled with the idea of a Socialist State in some form—call it African Socialism or what you will—and an essential feature of all Socialism is control of education. They will insist that Africa must have a type of education geared to the new African states and conditions. Our system of control they regard as 'foreign', 'neo-colonialist' etc.[51]

[50] Ibid.
[51] Ibid.

In those circumstances Moynagh made a final appeal for some agreement with the government in the matter of state control of schools which would guarantee by law the mission's essential demand—the right of access to schools for religious instruction. The bargaining position of the mission was still strong enough to achieve such an agreement. He feared

> It will not be strong if we wait to suffer defeat in a bitter conflict which cannot be won. Even if it were won *now* it would come up again in three, five or seven years time when a new breed of men take over.[52]

Indeed it could be hoped that if initiative for discussion and agreement came from the bishops that much more than 'access to schools for religious instruction' would be agreed upon and safeguarded by law.

No hard decisions were come to on the submission before the bishops left for the final session of Vatican II.[53] Political events were to overtake them. Few of them had returned from Rome when the January 1966 coup occurred. Military government now came to each region. The role of the Church in a situation of civil conflict is never an easy one. The image of 'Biafra' as 'encircled Christendom' was a gross over-simplification of a very complex situation. Such over-simplifications become popular equations in emotive times. In the post-war situation it was equally popular to portray the Church in the East as the enemy of national unity. This view saw the state 'take-over' of schools as the final 'getting even' with the missions. Yet the main thrust of government from the fifties onwards had been towards growing state control. The question really was 'When would state control take place' rather than 'Would state control occur?' The post-war situation made such a 'take-over' relatively simply in the absence of an organized opposition that in other circumstances the Catholic mission might have provided.

[52] Ibid.

[53] A factor militating against any decision was the illness of Archbishop Heerey. He died in February 1967. In practice the *status quo* position of facing each issue as it occurred was retained.

Religion and the press in 'the Enclave' in the Nigerian Civil War

A. F. WALLS

'Biafra is a Christian country, we believe in the ability of the Almighty God to come to the aid of the oppressed and give us victory as he gave victory to young David over Goliath.'—*Lt-Col S. M. Ojukwu, in a lecture to Theological Students 16 January 1968.*

'Lt. Col. Odumegwu Ojukwu our beloved Moses
Hail our Freedom, BIAFRA! Freedom
With joy and determination we fight
Together to keep our hard won freedom
With God's Blessing and Guidance.'—*Verse printed on a Christmas card* ('Christmas War Greetings')

This note is deliberately restricted to one limited aspect of the part religion played in the Nigerian Civil War, and in the full consciousness that there are much larger and more important parts of the story which should be considered. Since the writer left what was then Eastern Nigeria two weeks before the January coup of 1966, and next set foot in what was by then the East Central State six weeks after the end of the war in 1970, he is not in a position to assess the significance of some of the things which deeply interest him personally: the part, for instance, played by diviners, whether of the old religion or the new[1] in influencing fighting on the ground; the way in which churches which had long seen their principal and normal involvement with the community as being in the sphere of education suddenly found their schools gone and the absolute necessity of involvement in relief work;[2] and perhaps above all, the way in which church life not only carried on under wartime conditions—as a mountain of synod agendas, service programmes, special prayers, minutes of discussion on practices which might or might not

---

[1] There are several stories that prophecies played a crucial part, especially in the surrender of one Biafran division; and a senior member of the administration recalls the constant visits of prophets instructing him ('by revelation') to call a fast or to take specific actions.

[2] An Igbo Catholic priest records as his principal reflection on the war that Catholics in his country had never produced a charitable order, and that so much relief work fell on expatriates.

arise from the exigencies of the wartime situation[3] bear witness—but burst out in some new directions.[4] One would like to assess the statement made by more than one informant that at least the early part of the war was marked both by a moral renewal[5] and the virtual disappearance of traditional religious practices;[6] and then there is the still more vital question of the relations of Christians within Nigeria since the war. The scope here is much humbler: it is to look at Christianity and the Christian expressions through the eyes of the press of the Biafran enclave during the war period—those flysheets under a variety of titles, printed on whatever came to hand—wrapping paper and ruled SO books included—bearing various imprints from Enugu, Onitsha, Umuahia, Port Harcourt, Nnewi, Aba and Owerri. Only a scatter of these has been available; and the sample gives out, not surprisingly, before the final contraction and collapse of Biafra. There is a sufficient spread of papers, however, to give a fair basis for discerning certain common themes, and for deducing something of the 'Biafran' self-consciousness.

The first thing which must strike the reader is the prominence given to religion, to church themes and to churchmen. The quasi-official *Sunday Sun* of 23 June 1968, for instance, (published by the Biafra Information office) is not untypical in devoting most of one centre page to a weekly sermon ('Give Thanks for Everything') and a reader's letter on 'Spiritual Leadership'. On the other centre page the regular columnist raises the question 'Has Satan taken over Wilson's government?' and answers it with reference to church opinion and theological comment, and a poem is contributed called 'God's workshop'. News items on the two other pages refer to the Presbyterian Church of East Africa, two London based Catholic organizations (who are quoted as attacking Chief Enahoro for attacking Cardinal Heenan) and an Igbo priest's advocacy of industrial co-operatives as the basis for the economy of postwar

[3] An episcopal circular to clergy in the Niger Diocese mentions the use of yam in communion where wafers were unobtainable and the growing practice of lying in state before burial services.

[4] Some examples are given by an expatriate missionary who spent most of the war in the enclave: Bill Roberts, *Life and Death Among the Ibos*, London 1970.

[5] 'All the corruption and self-seeking seemed to drop away', was one expatriate's impression.

[6] A minister in the South East, in an area which was radically divided in sentiment, speaks of the way in which, in the emergency the churches filled and people who had maintained the old practices gave them up, to resume only well after the war. See also *Biafra Sun* 1 January 1968. It is interesting to compare the statement of the Rev. E. A. A. Adegbola of Ibadan: 'When all our troubles came upon us, what did we decide to do? We decided to pray. We turned religious overnight . . . Were we trying to bribe God? Or to deceive one another?' (*Christian Concern in the Nigerian Civil War*, Ibadan 1969, p. 7.)

Biafra. This could often be paralleled: and at a solemn time—New Year or one of the Christian festivals—the proportion is higher still. An Easter Issue, the *Sunday Sun* for 14 April, devotes a whole page to an open letter to the Archbishop of Canterbury, another page to an Easter sermon, quotes a speech by a high ranking officer under the headline 'Biafra is like Christ' and an Easter message from the Head of the Civil Service, together with a moving little poem ('A Soldier's Prayer'), a letter from an apostle, and a collection of Easter messages under the omnibus headline 'Top Men of God exhort Biafrans'; and in this case the regular columnist bases his article on passages from a book by the American Catholic writer Fulton J. Sheen.

This prominence of religious themes provides one obvious if somewhat trite, comment: that a self-conscious Christian profession was part of the self-identity of Biafra. From the beginning the civil war was for Biafrans a religious war, to an extent which puzzled Western observers who had forgotten what it was like to belong to a religiously self-conscious community, and exasperated Nigerian Christians who lived in a plural community and saw the unity of One Nigeria as a separate issue from that of the survival of the faith. But Biafra was not a plural community, or at least there was nothing to force its religiously plural-istic aspect into the open. Few Biafrans had Muslim brothers-in-law. Biafra could claim a Christian identity as neither the Federation nor any state outside the former Eastern Region could do. Religion could once more be a binding, a cohesive force in a community, instead of a sign of its basically divided character. And, as Christianity gave self-identity of Biafra, so a Muslim identity was bestowed upon the Federal Nigeria. 'Islam—main cause of the war. Moslems have no regard for others' proclaims a headline in the *Biafra Sun* for 1 January 1968, and the item reports a speech by a member of the 'Solidarity Delegation' on the theme that 'religion is one mighty gulf separating Biafra and Nigeria'. Islam—'from which Biafra was naturally insulated'—was the main cause of the war. 'Just as Christianity and Islam can never be bedfellows, so will Biafra and Nigeria never become one country again'. A writer in *Daily News International* for 16 April 1968 takes up the same theme: at the eleventh hour before the conflagration, he says, the Nigerian and Biafran churches did try to save the situation, and failed. 'Islamism ex-ploited that opportunity to become deadly partisan and has in fact been the diabolical force behind Nigeria's savagery, which has been propped up not only by Russia and Britain but also by Moslem states in Africa and Asia'. The editorial in *The Mirror* of 20 February 1968, under the headline 'Islamism vs. Christianity' sees Lagos 'acting as a tool of the world moslem league and in conjunction with the Nigerian Moslem organizations' in 'a Jihad against Biafrans, the core of Christianity in this part of Africa.' The less sophisticated *Standard* (5 February 1968) complains of 'Godless northerners' looting churches, hawking sacred vessels, and using church cloths for their 'dirty women'. The Christian and anti-Muslim self-identification of Biafra took colour from the pre-1966 situation of the Sardauna's tours, and the uninhibited proclamations of militant Islam which they reflected.[7] They also explain why it was necessary for Federal Nigeria to stress not only its plural character but its compatibility with Christianity.[8]

What then had the Biafran press to say about Nigerian Christians? Much wickedness is ascribed to General Gowon—neither a Fulani, a Hausa nor a Muslim—but references to his outspoken Christian profession are rare.[9] Chief Awolowo is described (*Sunday Sun* 17 December 1967) as a necromancer whose claims to be a Christian and a Methodist are a sham. Nor are such accusations confined to politicians: an article in the *Biafra Sun* of 18 April 1968 is headed 'Nigeria's Church Leaders Debase Religion' and begins with the hymn verse

Men scorn thy sacred name,
And wolves devour thy fold;
By many deeds of shame
We learn that love grows cold.

The proof of this lies in the way in which Nigerian churchmen condone, and even praise, the Federal Government's actions; and one well-known Yoruba church leader, who had told a BBC reporter that he anticipated a speedy end to the war, is said to belong 'to a religious gang that usually worship and invoke Mammy Water at the Victoria Beach, Lagos'. 'It may be therefore that it was the water goddess to whom he referred in his prediction to the BBC and not the true God of the entire world.'

The identification of Biafra and the Christian cause led to a problem that created much heartsearching. The sympathy of the Papacy was obvious, as was that of opinion in many Western countries, sympathy which was frequently expressed in concrete form through explicitly Christian organizations. But for many Biafran Christians, and for the

[7] Cf. H. W. Turner, *Christian Century* 10 September 1969, p. 177: 'If the late President John F. Kennedy had made personal evangelistic tours on behalf of his Roman Catholic faith, had offered to rebuild certain delapidated Catholic churches, and had announced that a foreign government had given him funds to build two big new Catholic churches in, say, Washington and Boston, we can guess at what the reactions of many citizens in the United States would have been.'

[8] Cf. *Unity in Diversity* published by the Federal Ministry of Information Lagos (1967?) which is concerned to show, *inter alia*, the large number of Christians in the Federation, and their strong representation in Government, administration and judiciary. 'From its inception, Nigeria has never mixed religion with politics' (p. 3).

[9] *The Mirror* 20 February 1968 says that he 'claims to be the son of a missionary preacher and yet fosters the evil ends of the Islamic north'.

overwhelming majority of Protestants, Christianity was associated with Britain. Why, then, was the British Government so unequivocally committed to the support of the Federation? Time and again the press, through articles, reports and letters, returns to this theme—sometimes with outrage, sometimes with sheer puzzlement. 'One hopes that Satan has not completely taken over Wilson's government' says one columnist (*Sunday Sun* 23 June 1968); and he even reflects whether that government is so obsessed with its guilt that they think they can never atone for the past in Biafran eyes. In which case, let them take heart from the amnesty recently given to people who had acted disloyally. 'How much easier would it be to forgive our foreign enemies.'

Christian Britain under the leadership of 'Herod' Wilson (alias Alhaji Wilson, *Sunday Sun* 14 April 1968) had joined with atheist Russia for the destruction of a Christian country (*Daily News* 16 April 1968). The only possible explanation was the moral and spiritual bankruptcy of Britain. Britain was losing her place in the world, said the *Daily Standard* (25 January 1968) because she was now concerned only with economic and no longer with moral and religious considerations. (*The Standard* lamented in particular that 'Dr Ramsey, the head of the C.M.S.' was silent.) The lesson could be enforced with news stories. *The Statesman,*[10] had a series 'No Country is Civilized'. An example is the entry for 5 February 1968 which featured a nasty court story involving bigamy and a bogus clergyman in Warwickshire. And some asserted that it had ever been so. A columnist in the *Mirror* (10 February 1968) asks 'How Christian are the British?' The reason British missionaries were sent was 'so that the British trader could have an easy run of trade'. The interesting thing about this article is that despite the reiteration of this well-known thesis it is neither anti-Christian nor anti-missionary—it is simply anti-British. There *were* good missionaries 'whose only aim was the saving of souls', 'men who helped to build our faith in God'—but they were continentals. Britain declares herself a Christian nation by the pageantry of the Coronation, but her low church attendance, the recruitment of bishops and clergy from the wealthy and well-connected, and the very presence of the Church's leader in the House of Lords proves her age-long hypocrisy. 'How many missionaries of English origin are in Biafra today?' The Okigwe Provincial Commissioner (speech reported *Biafra Sun* 18 January 1968) reflects the same conviction that 'Britain's brand of Christianity is a mere cloak for sin, an instrument of colonialism and imperialism', but for him there was an important rider. The re-evangelization of Britain will be one of the tasks facing the Christian Church in post war Biafra—and Biafran Christians

---

[10] *The Statesman* had some enterprising features: one series on 'War is ending in Biafrans favour' had the by-line 'By Bing Crosby'.

should 'mobilise their energies towards the achievement of this great mission.'

A marked change occurs after the archbishop's speech in the House of Lords Debate in February 1968 and still more the visit of the delegation from the British churches in March 1968. 'Here at last—British Churchmen' proclaims the main headline of the *Daily Flash* (8 March 1968), and the *Sunday Sun* (10 March) describes the motorcade into Owerri. Part of the pleasure in the events was due to assumptions about the significance and importance of the Church in Britain. 'For the first time in eight long months, a massive body of the British public opinion, championed by the Church, one of the wealthiest and most powerful institutions in the United Kingdom, has arranged itself against the one government which has the power to stop this war'. (*Sunday Weekly Times* 19-20 February 1968.)

This last underlines part of the importance of the religious question for people in the enclave: the link which it afforded with the outside world. So many of the visitors were churchmen, so many of the sources of aid were Christian, church bodies were so prominent among the expressions of support, as to reinforce the self-consciousness of a Christian state facing a Muslim *jihad* supported by the household of faith. 'Pope Worried over Biafra, Wishes Us Well' is the main headline of the *Daily Standard* (23 July 1968) 'All over Biafra: Deafening Applause Greet Papal Envoys' is the main outline of the *Mirror* (12 February 1968), with the significant extra line: 'They promise to be our voice to the world'. The papal envoys, indeed, receive abundant attention (and countless photographs) in all the papers—and it is only fair to say that their cautious utterances about the non-political and non-diplomatic nature of their mission were included in the reports. The same is true of the British churches' delegation. The headline 'We Will Do Our Best—British Clergymen make a Promise' (*Sunday Sun* 10 March 1968) again marks the main news story. The main story in *Sunday Weekly Times* (motto: The Voice of God is the Voice of Man) for 19-20 February 1968 is the Archbishop of Canterbury's speech in the House of Lords on 17 February, supported by other churchmen quoted on BBC interviews, a commendation of the Pope for his 'humanity, nobility and bravery' and a photograph of the two papal envoys, the whole with the caption 'Christian Efforts to Stop the War'. The joint statement in March 1968 from the Vatican and the World Council of Churches calling for a ceasefire was naturally another major focus of interest; the *Daily Flash* (22 March 1968) quoting Voice of America for the statement that the two bodies jointly 'had influence and the authority over more than eighty countries in the world'. It was such news as this that enabled Biafrans to feel that they were acting on a world stage, not hidden away in a corner.

But whatever the importance of the international links forged by religion, the main significance of what the press reveals remains the place of religion in the Biafran self-understanding. Some of the themes which emerge are worth a moment's consideration. First the identification of Biafra with Biblical Israel becomes a commonplace. The elect people are both resisting enslavement in Egypt, and are destined to enter the promised land. The Christmas card (1967?) quoted at the head of this paper, with its picture of Biafran soldiers with guns at the ready and its verse saluting 'Ojukwu our beloved Moses' bears on another page the verse 1 Peter 2: 9: 'Ye are a chosen generation, a royal priesthood, an holy Nation, a peculiar People; that ye should show forth the Praises of Him who hath Called you out of darkness into His Marvellous light'. The same theme runs through articles, speeches, sermons, poems. A headline in the *Sunday Sun* (18 February 1968), 'Biafrans are God's own People' introduces a report of a sermon in Umuahia. God's choice of Biafra, said the preacher, had been demonstrated by the arrival of Ojukwu, the emergence of Biafra, the discovery of the counter-coup, the survival after so many attacks—He will deliver them as He delivered Israel in Egypt. A provincial administrator (*Biafra Sun* 1 January 1968) also saw the manifestation of the power and grace of God in Biafra's sur-vival—as a result of which, he said, 'heathens have cast their idols away and acknowledge the efficacy of the power of the Almighty God'. The regular sermon in the *Sunday Sun* for 28 January is on the theme 'The Lord will uphold Biafra' and its text Isaiah 41: 10 'Fear not, for I am with you . . . I will help you, I will uphold you with my victorious right hand', and a poem on the same page begins 'Courage, Biafrans, Courage!! Canaan in sight.'

The references just quoted are from a period of the war when Biafran forces were doing rather well. As the war went on, another dimension to election occurs—the significance of suffering. The Easter message of the Officer Administering the Government was on the theme 'suffering and death for the cause of humanity can be the gateway to glory and life.' Christ, whose sufferings had been the subject of our meditations for the past few weeks—the general was, of course, referring to Lent—was the victim of conspiracy and injustice, but by his death humanity was saved and a dark world given the light of love, peace and dignity. Biafra was also the victim of conspiracy and injustice 'As a Christian nation, let us be like Christ.' (*Sunday Sun* 14 April 1968). The regular Sunday sermon in the *Sun* at that time added to the well-known note 'God has taken our cause into his hands' the fact that He was the defender of the weak and defenceless, and the regular columnist heads his article 'The Fast before the Feast' and provides a meditation on defeat turned into victory. (*Ibid.*) The sermon in the *Sunday Sun* for 23 June 1968, on 'Give thanks for everything' gives as a cause of thanksgiving the privilege of suffering for the truth, and the friends God has given the nation in its suffering in an unfriendly world.

The identification with the Biblical nation elected to suffer and triumph leads to an analogy with the battle with Amalek, in which Israel or Amalek prevailed according to whether Moses' hands were raised or lowered (hence let us keep Moses' arms raised by prayer and fasting, says an evangelist to 'saints and priests of Biafra' in *Daily Flash* 27 March 1968), and to a quotation of Joel 2: 17 in which 'Muslims' slips into the place of the heathen (*Sunday Sun* 10 March 1968). It can be applied in somewhat grotesque ways (witness the 2,000 schoolchildren who sent 2,000 pebbles 'for onwards transmission to the Head of State, Lt. Col. Odumegwu Ojukwu, whom they described as "Little David" to use in killing Gowon'—*Biafra Sun* 18 January 1968). But it is clear that it was more than superficial from the other ways in which the identification was applied. Behaviour proper to a Christian nation is a recurrent theme. The sermon in the *Sunday Sun* for 28 January, for instance, already referred to, makes clear that the promises to Israel were for a nation turning from its sins. The preacher in the *Sunday Sun* for 14 April 1968 is more specific—justice must be given to minority peoples within Biafra. 'The superior weapons of Nigeria have not given them any right over Biafra. So also the superior right of any town in Biafra does not give them any right over a weaker village. God will deal with the one as with the other.' 'In this War' says the same preacher in the issue for 10 March, 'we have to do with a holy and righteous God . . . It does not help us to compare ourselves with Nigeria and from that to conclude we are a Christian nation. We are a Christian nation only as we do the will of God.' This theme is taken forward particularly with reference to the necessity of forgiveness. This is taken into straightforward propaganda. In a public address in January 1968 Col Ojukwu concluded 'Please God have mercy on Gowon', and this is taken up and elaborated in a broadcast reprinted in the *Mirror* for 20 February 1968 under the title 'May God forgive Gowon'. It is war propaganda, rather than devotional meditation; but the fact that propaganda could be cast in this form is itself significant. The head of the civil service, however, can send a message looking forward to a Christian nation ready to forgive even as Christ did at His dying hour (*Sunday Sun* 14 April 1968).

The best known feature of Nigerian church life in the period immediately before the emergency was the anticipation of a United Church of Nigeria from the union of the Anglican, Methodist and Presbyterian churches, a scheme which collapsed so close to its intended consummation in December 1965 that articles appeared in the Church press on the assumption that the union had taken place. There are few ripples of this in the Biafran press.[11] Catholic, Protestant and Cherubim and Seraphim sources are all quoted; and prominence is given to the appeal of a minor group, the Full Gospel Churches ('Help to Save Lives of Millions') to their American counterparts. Even the National Church of Biafra (the successor of the old National Church of Nigeria and Cameroon) appears—in the unlikely role of commending the Pope and urging Christians throughout the world to follow his example (*Daily Flash* 8 March 1968). A provincial administrator (addressing a delegation of the Sacred Order of Cherubim and Seraphim) looked forward to 'One united and national Church of Biafra' after the war, and forecast that 'there would be no heathens' because they would have been converted by the evidence of God's power (*Biafra Sun* 1 January 1968).

The Biafran episode, then, provides us with an unusual modern African example to set within the typology of relations between church and State; one in which church leaders can be charged—in an ordination sermon—'to use their position as spiritual leaders of the nation to ensure that all enemies of the nation are exposed' (*Times of Onitsha* 19 December 1967); but in which also a senior administrator can inculcate the necessity of charity and forgiveness in imitation of Christ (*Sunday Sun* 14 April 1968). Perhaps the last word should be with an ordinary Lance-Corporal, who contributed the following to the *Sunday Sun* of 14 April 1968:

My shoulders ache beneath my pack:
Lie easier Cross, upon His back.
I march with feet that burn and smart:
Tread, Holy Feet, upon my heart.
Men shout at me who may not speak,
They scourged Thy back and smote Thy cheek.
I may not lift a hand to clear
My eyes of salty drops that sear.
Then shall my fickle soul forget
Thy Agony of Bloody Sweat?
From Thy pierced palm red rivers come:
Lord! Thou did suffer for me more
Than all the hosts of land and sea:
So let me render back again
This millionth of Thy gift.

---

[11] Nabo Graham-Douglas, *Ojukwu's Rebellion and World Opinion* n.d. [*c*. 1969] p. 8 sees a *rapprochement* with the Roman Catholic Church following the dispute with the Eastern Region Government in 1962 over educational policy and giving 'the prospect of creating a virtual Roman Catholic state'.

The Catholic Church and Camerounian nationalism: from misunderstanding to opposition

J. MFOULOU

It is hard to deny that the Christian churches have been an agent of progress in Cameroun. Missionaries have not only built schools and hospitals, but in their fight against the dowry and for the emancipation of women, for example, they militate in favour of social justice. Some of them went so far as to oppose forced labour, thus openly pitting themselves against the colonial administration. Very soon after World War II, and shortly before independence, priests, both missionaries and Camerounians, took part in territorial or local politics with or without the consent of their bishops; Abbé Melone and Father Déhon sat in the *ARCAM* (*Assemblée Représentative du Cameroun*); Abbé Nkonda was elected mayor of Mbalmayo. This shows that the churches had not lost interest in politics; indeed, the opposite was the case.

From that time the attitude of the churches and churchmen towards Camerounian nationalism was open to question: would they give it a warm welcome as a progressive element, one of the logical results of their work of awakening consciences? Or, on the contrary, would they disapprove of it as dangerous, if not harmful? My research on this subject leads me to assert now that the relationship between church and nationalists has gone from misunderstanding to opposition by way of disagreement.

This statement is accurate only if one takes a very limited definition of the church and refers mainly to the relations between the Catholic church and the *Union des Populations du Cameroun* (*UPC*). I will try, in conclusion, to return to a definition of the church. As for the second aspect of the problem, my study is indeed concerned essentially with the Catholic church and the *UPC*. Why the Catholic church rather than any other Christian church? The reason is that the activities of the Catholic church with regard to Camerounian nationalism are easier to study. Firstly the official positions taken up by the church on this subject are ascertainable, because they were made public. Secondly the Catholic church had much more freedom for action, since it was run by missionaries largely of French nationality. The Protestants, especially the Presbyterians, if they were to act, would have had to do so much more discreetly since they were mostly of American nationality. Moreover the rise of nationalism created a situation somewhat embarrassing for Protestant missionaries: in the early days, nationalist leaders were largely of the Protestant obedience; one of them, not the most unimportant, was one of their former pupils; the words and music of the nationalist rallying song, later the national anthem of independent Cameroun, were composed by the Protestant teachers of Foulassi and their pupils.

As for the choice of the *UPC*, it is justified by the simple fact that the *UPC* was the party which for ten years (from its founding in 1948 to its disintegration into rival factions in 1958-9) symbolized and embodied Camerounian nationalism. Speaking of Um Nyobé, George Chaffard writes: 'For all progressive youth, whatever their ethnic origin or religion, the Secretary General of the *UPC* is the undisputed leader of Camerounian patriotism, the man who raised the standard of independence.'[1] I believe that this remained true right through the period with which we are concerned, not only for Um Nyobé but also for the party that he led. The formation of moderate parties occurred later, certainly not before 1951, often with the encouragement of the Soucadaux administration, as a counterweight to the *UPC*.[2] Only gradually were some of these parties converted to certain nationalist principles. Thus the *BDC (Bloc Démocratique Camerounais)* adopted the principle of independence at its 1953 congress, but considered the idea of re-unification fallacious.[3] Indeed it must be added that in adopting these nationalist positions, the other parties modified them profoundly to such an extent as to render them, if not unrecognizable, at least unacceptable to the nationalists. Thus some favoured independence within interdependence, others independence in stages at a time when the *UPC* was talking of immediate independence and the reunification of the two Camerouns.

The misunderstanding: The strike at Douala (September 1945) and its consequences.
The origins of the break between the Catholic church and Camerounian nationalism can be traced back to the strike of railway employees

---

[1] In *Les Carnets secrets de la Décolonisation*, Vol.II, 360.

[2] David E. Gardinier, *Cameroon: United Nations challenge to French policy*, London, 1963.

[3] *Ibid*. 67.

organized at Douala on 24 September 1945. For lack of written documents[4] we are unfortunately unable to reconstruct this event exactly; the oral sources we have been able to consult are largely agreed on what follows. To protest against their low living standards, the railway workers belonging to the *USCC (Union des Syndicats Confédérés du Cameroun), 'regetist'* in inspiration and obedience,[5] went on strike. As was to be expected the reaction of the administration and the colonial police was extremely brutal: the strikers were charged. To escape the gunfire, some fled to take refuge in the cathedral: according to oral sources, the Bishop of Douala allegedly allowed the strikers who had taken refuge in the cathedral to be shot. Still worse, his vicar-general, Father Albert Krummenaker, ran over one or two people in his haste to return to his mission house at Edéa: at once popular opinion credited him with the intention of running over these victims on purpose.[6] True or false, these stories (perhaps merely rumours) made the unionist strikers believe, rightly or wrongly, that the Catholic church was against them, and ranged on the side of the exploiting colonialists.

It may be asked why the Bishop of Douala gained this reputation. Without trying to excuse him, it is quite possible that he honestly and sincerely believed that strikers of this kind must necessarily be Socialist, and Socialist automatically meant Communist. This hypothesis is all the more plausible in that at the same period the following clarification of the attitude to unions can be found in *Le Cameroun catholique:* 'The church is in favour of the establishment of the trade unions, but not any sort of union: only Christian unions, that is to say by Christians, for Christians and between Christians.'[7] Then in May 1946 the same monthly journal condemned Socialism in words which made quite clear the attitude of the Catholic church towards that system: 'It is clear that this Socialist, philosophical system of marriage, the family, education and religion (or, rather, the negation of it), can in no way be admitted by Catholics. It is in all respects absolutely opposed to Catholic dogma.'[8] Moreover at this period this Catholic journal undertook a major campaign of vilification of Communism and Russia.[9] If this

---

[4] All the journals of the period that I have been able to consult in the national archives maintain, on this event, a silence, which could in itself be eloquent.

[5] A certain Donat, a *CGT* militant, was both its inspirer and advisor.

[6] According to other sources it was not Father Krummenaker, but a teacher named Zimmerman, who ran over someone as he tried to flee the scene of the fusillade.

[7] In number 11, March, 1945 (pp 2 and 7) under the title 'Que penser des syndicats?'

[8] *Le Cameroun Catholique*, May 1946, 'Y a-t-il opposition entre socialisme et catholicisme?' 7.

[9] See for example *Le Cameroun Catholique*, No. 11, March, 1945, already cited;

hypothesis is born in mind one can see that from the very beginning there has been a fundamental misunderstanding between the Catholic church and the Camerounian nationalists, with the church thinking the latter dangerous Communists to be combatted energetically, and the nationalists interpreting the anti-communist hostility of the church as a colonialist reaction. All that remains is to show how this misunderstanding was transformed first into open disagreement, then into violent opposition.

The disagreement: the condemnation of the UPC and the troubles of 1955

The year 1955 was decisive in the development of the relations between the Catholic church and Camerounian nationalism. Firstly in April of that year the bishops of Cameroun published a document on the *UPC,* attacking it not on account of its nationalist programme, but on account of its Communist links and tendencies. (At the time there was a rumour that the bishops had done this at the request of the High Commissioner, Roland Pré, and that he had gone in person to the premises where the bishops' meeting took place. Gardinier claims that the *BDC,* a party founded and led by the Catholic Aujoulat, also asked the Catholic church to condemn the *UPC.*)[10] What is certain is that this condemnation appeared to be the logical conclusion and a normal outcome of a vast campaign against Communism launched by the Catholic church of Cameroun, and prosecuted in all the media at its disposal. Thus in July 1954 the *Cameroun Catholique* sounded the alarm by revealing a 'plan of world conquest by Communism'.[11] In September of the same year Father Pierre Pichon warned Christians against the prophets of Communism in an article entitled 'Les faux prophètes',[12] a title which reveals clearly the atmosphere reigning between the Catholic church and the nationalists. In many educational establishments run by Catholics, *L'Etoile contre la Croix,* a book about the persecution of the Catholic church by the Chinese Communist regime, was required reading. At the same time

No. 2, June, 1946; 'Le Paradis soviétique: jugez-en vous-même.'; No. 4, August, 1947: 'Menaces!'; No. 3, July, 1948: 'Le rideau de fer en Allemagne de l'Est'. Finally there should be noted a special number whose title, 'Le Communisme contre l'Eglise', speaks for itself, and in which *Le Cameroun Catholique* denounces as Communist Camerounian students who had accused a bishop of being colonialist. There are analogous anti-Communist campaigns in the years 1955 and 1960.

[10] *Op. cit.,* 68.

[11] p.6.

[12] See *Le Cameroun Catholique,* No. 8, September, 1954. The article in question is the French translation of the article 'Beprofet medugan', published by P. Pichon in the Catholic weekly in the vernacular *Nleb Bekristen* (The Christian Counsellor), which has a very large circulation among the faithful.

courses on Communism were multiplied and intensified in the seminaries, with a presentation and interpretation that can easily be imagined. All this aroused a real collective phobia among Christians with regard to Communism; and the bishops' stance must be seen in this psychological context if its full significance is to be appreciated.

Before setting ourselves a few questions about this action by the bishops of Cameroun, we should make clear that the latter ordered all their priests to communicate their position to the faithful from the pulpit during the Easter ceremonies, as if to etch more deeply in the minds of their parishioners the gravity and seriousness of the indictment, thus making a greater impression on them.

Now one could first ask oneself whether the *UPC* really was Communist, as the bishops' declaration claimed. We shall try to return to this question in conclusion, when I shall attempt to demonstrate in what sense the *UPC* can be said to have in fact been Communist, and in what sense it certainly was not.

It seems to me more important to find out first what was the effect of this indictment by the Ordinaries of Cameroun on Camerounian nationalism. We have seen that in putting Christians on their guard against the *UPC* the bishops took great care to make clear that they were doing this, not on account of the nationalist ideas of the party, but only because of the movement's links and tendencies. Now it is conceivable that this was precisely the best way to break the *UPC:* following the anti-communist campaign already described, and in the midst of a collective phobia that held sway among the Christians, was it not the most telling argument, and thus the surest means, for making any Christian adhesion to the *UPC* impossible?

And would not the breaking of the *UPC* in this way deal a heavy blow—at the very least—to Camerounian nationalism, at a time when the other parties and the leaders of the country were reluctant to believe in independence and reunification? Indeed those who made up a delegation to the United Nations at that time did so to argue against the views of the *UPC*. Douala Manga Bell went to represent France and the French point of view.[13] Jules Ninine, another Cameroun deputy to the French National Assembly, called independence a 'dangerous illusion'.[14] Guillaume Bissek of *Esocam (Parti pour l'Evolution Sociale Cameroun-*

[13] Ref. Gardinier, *op. cit.*, 63. See also Chaffard, *op. cit.*, 365, 357 and 358.

[14] In *Le Cameroun Libre*, No. 466 of the first fortnight of March 1954, 1-2; see also Gardinier *op. cit.*, 48.

[15] See, for example, *Le Cameroun Libre*, No. 471 of the second fortnight of May, 1954, 5: 'Un hommage à la France de Monsieur Charles Assalé'. If Georges Chaffard is to be believed (*op. cit.* 354), Assalé left the Communist CGT for FO at the instigation of the High Commissioner Soucadaux.

aise) and Charles Assalé of *FO (Force Ouvrière)* were full of praise for France.[15] Okala, who criticized French administration in Cameroun, demanding, as a good socialist, 'more social justice', was nevertheless opposed to the views of Um Nyobé.[16]

What is more, to break the *UPC* in this way might deal a fatal blow to revolutionary nationalism, thus handing over the political arena to the moderate parties led by Catholics: the *BDC (Bloc Démocratique Camerounais)* with Aujoulat, Mbida and Fouda, amongst others, in leading positions;[17] the Cameroun Socialist Party of Charles Okala; *Esocam* with Guillaume Bissek, etc. Thus the *UPC's* resentment against the Catholic Church which favoured its political adversaries in this way is easily understood. One might even wonder whether the position taken up by the Catholic Church did not place it in the same camp as the political enemies of the *UPC* and the Protectorate colonialists. In fact the *BDC* also condemned the *UPC* for its Marxist philosophy and its links with the French Communist Party.[18] *Le Cameroun Libre*, the paper of the French in the colony, did the same[19] and gave a solemn warning: 'Cameroun is entering upon a dangerous path: the inescapable consequences of the rise of nationalism.'[20]

Lastly was this position not indicative of a coalition or at least a certain collusion between the Catholic church and the colonialists? And did it not, voluntarily or not, prepare the ground and public opinion for the condemnation and dissolution of the *UPC* by the French National Assembly on 13 July 1955? As Gardinier noted at almost the same time: 'it *(UPC)* saw the *BDC,* the Roman Catholic hierarchy and the administration taking measures against it.'[21]

In May 1955, Moumié, the chairman of the *UPC,* launched an appeal to the workers to demonstrate their lack of confidence in the French administration. This rallying cry was perhaps intended to create an atmosphere of uncertainty in the country as the time of the visit by a mission from the United Nations Trusteeship Council approached, or simply to give an idea of the popularity enjoyed by the *UPC* among the people. The fact remains that the movement received little support: demonstrations took place only in a few large towns in the south of the country.

---

[16] Ref. Gardinier, *op. cit.*, 64–5.

[17] Ref. Chaffard, *op. cit.*, 355.

[18] Ref. Gardinier, *op. cit.*, 68.

[19] In No. 416 of February 15th, 1952, 2.

[20] In No. 473 of the second fortnight of June, 1954, 1–2.

[21] *Op. cit.*, 69. In an attempt to counter the evil effects of this condemnation by the Catholic Church, Um went on two occasions to see the General Secretary of the Presbyterian Church, asking him to influence his church to make a public declaration of support for the *UPC* (this information was kindly given me by the Reverend Pastor Anderson).

But this was enough for the French colonial administration which took advantage of this opportunity to get rid of the over troublesome *UPC*.

The exclusion of the *UPC* from the political arena left its enemies a clear field and, in particular, allowed the Catholic André Marie Mbida to form the first government of an autonomous Cameroun in May 1955. It also marked the beginning of open disagreement between the Catholic church and Camerounian nationalism. Indeed Mbida, the Prime Minister, adopted an obstinate, intransigent attitude towards the *UPC*, and this ended all hope of a national reconciliation. What is more, together with the other deputies from Cameroun, he opposed the amnesty of the *UPC* by the French National Assembly.[22]

Meanwhile the *UPC* continued its activities clandestinely. Thus it issued a directive to boycott the elections of 1956; once more its directives were not carried out. Therefore it had no hesitation in turning to violence to prevent the elections' taking place in the areas it believed to be under its control. Thus in the Eséka region two already elected candidates, Dr Délangué and Samuel Mpouma, were killed in particularly tragic circumstances. But the *UPC* fought most violently against the Catholic missions as centres of resistance to its influence. In Bamiléké territory nuns were terrorized and priests abducted; in Sanaga-Maritime, the mission at Mom underwent a regular siege, and its priest, Abbé Vgote, spent a dreadful week-end shut in the parish church with his curate and a few of the faithful. The Catholic mission at Lokbikoy suffered the same fate a little later, the *maquisards*[23] (outlaws) going as far as setting fire to the mission church.[24]

These acts of terrorism and vandalism perpetrated against Catholic missions can be understood as hostile actions, revenge against a force and people opposed to the influence of the *UPC*. Indeed we have seen the nationalist party, on the eve of its dissolution, in opposition to political formations led by Catholics. In Sanaga-Maritime it was a priest, Abbé Maloné, who for a long time won the elections against the *UPC* candidates. And in the centre in general, particularly in Nyon and Sanaga, it appears that after playing the Aujoulat card, the missions played the Mbida card, another Catholic. These missions acted as centres of resistance to the *UPC* through the moral and psychological ascendency they possessed over their congregations. Finally there were rumours that

[22] Ref. Chaffard, *op. cit.*, 367, 373, 376. At the time, some people even reported that he had stated in a Catholic mission that if he were given a hundred *UPC* members, he would take the gun himself and shoot them one by one.

[23] This is the term generally used to designate the *UPC* members who, after the dissolution of their party, decided to take refuge in the forests of Sanaga-Maritime and the Bamiléké, and operate from these hideouts.

[24] Ref. Gardinier, *op. cit.*, 80, 94; Chaffard, *op. cit.*, 390, 396.

the priests were acting as informers to the Camerounian government and the army of pacification on the activities of the *maquisards* by means of Confession. This would explain in particular the abduction of priests. But the situation became worse and worse in the *maquis* zones. So the auxiliary bishop of Douala, Mgr Mongo offered to approach Um Nyobé, the *maquisard* leader, with the aim of stopping the spilling of blood, and bring back Um himself within the law. With the agreement of the High Commissioner, Messmer, the prelate did indeed spend two days with the leader of the rebellion. He returned, bearing a message in which Um laid before the High Commissioner his conditions for a return to peace in Cameroun. These conditions did not meet with the approval of the representative of France, with the result that when Mgr Mbongo returned to Um, he was accused of having been party to the game played by the colonial administration. But matters were coming to a head. Messmer yielded his position as High Commissioner in Cameroun to Ramadier. In February 1958 the government of Mbida was overthrown, and Ahmadou Ahidjo, the deputy prime minister, formed the second government of the Protectorate of Cameroun. Seven months later—13 September 1958 to be exact—Um Nyobé was surrounded and killed in the *maquis* by the army of pacification. A few weeks later the Ahidjo government decreed an amnesty for the *UPC:* high-ranking leaders of the party did in fact come out of the *maquis*, but this response did not succeed in returning the country to a state of peace. It was in these circumstances and in this atmosphere that the French Protectorate of Cameroun acceded to national sovereignty on 1 January 1960.

What is of interest here however is the nature of the relationship that the *UPC*, having left the *maquis* and operating legally, would maintain with the Catholic Church.

The opposition: Christian-Democracy and UPC opposition
Mbida, the fallen Prime Minister, had gone into exile, and settled at Conakry, where he had encountered other Camerounian political exiles, mostly *UPC* leaders and militants who had left the country at the time of the dissolution of the *UPC* in 1955 and had refused to return after the amnesty granted by Ahidjo as Prime Minister. At Conakry, Mbida made no secret of his sympathy for the *UPC* ideas, and from the capital of Guinea proclaimed that he was 'in favour of immediate independence for Cameroun'. Was this a genuine conversion, or merely a political stratagem? Whatever the answer the former Prime Minister soon left his comrades of one day to return to his country immediately after independence, on the eve of new legislative elections. His numerous supporters gave him a triumphal welcome on his arrival at Yaoundé.

The return of Mbida from exile restored courage and hope to all the Christian Democrats and to Catholics in general. The party immediately set about reorganizing itself for the elections. The Catholic journal *L'Effort Camerounais* gave it column space and, according to its adversaries, the auxiliary bishop of Yaoundé, Mgr Etoga, acted as chaplain to the party or at any rate afforded it spiritual support.[25] Mbida and his party won a resounding victory in Nyon-et-Sanaga in the legislative elections of 1960, taking all the seats.[26] Meanwhile the Christian Democrat leader seemed to have forgotten utterly his Guinean flirtation with the *UPC*, and thought only of consolidating his own party.

The control of the Yaoundé region by the Christian Democrats put a stop to any serious *UPC* influence there; and the obvious collusion of the former with the Catholic church was the starting point of a campaign of attacks and vilification conducted against the church and organized mainly by the *UPC* journals in the area.[27]

We can distinguish three main themes in this literature aimed at the Catholic church, generally not of a very high standard. Firstly the church was accused of preaching hostility to the *UPC*, totally unconnected with its spiritual mission. For this reason beneath the title 'To those who see the "red menace" everywhere' Sende Jean-Paul, the general secretary of the *UPC*, violently attacked *L'Effort Camerounais*, 'the paper of the local papists', and its editor, Father Fertin, for their anti-communism and their opposition to the *UPC*. The author had no doubts about likening the activities of the Catholic management to Roland Pré's efforts to combat the *UPC*.[28] And, in another article, a certain Jérémie William Singantawinz [29] maintained that instead of being concerned with things spiritual, bishops, priests and catechists spent their time telling their congregations who not to vote for because of his adherence to the *UPC*, 'presented as a Communist party and an atheistic organisation'. And as supporting proof of his allegations the author cited the case of two catechists from Abong-Mbang who were struck off the list of catechists by a certain Rev. Fr Guillaume Wang-Sonk for having made known their sympathy with the *UPC*.[30]

Next the *UPC* accused the Catholic Church of supporting openly, if not publicly, their political opponents, in the shape of the ex-Prime

[25] See, for example, *Abolege*, No. 7, November 22nd, 1960, 6-9.

[26] Henri Effa, the well-known editor of *L'Effort Camerounais*, thus entered the National Assembly under the banner of the Christian Democrats.

[27] A perusal of the various publications of the *UPC*, legal at the time, leaves the impression that the publications of the regions represented in the legislative assembly by the *UPC* do not attack the church as much as the publications of the Yaoundé region. This is important for our subject.

[28] See *Abolege*, No. 4., October 1st, 1960, 6.

[29] Probably a pseudonym.

[30] *Abolege*, No. 18, n.d., 5-6.

Minister Mbida and his Christian Democrat supporters. This was the most frequent complaint of the contributors to the papers which supported the *UPC*, and this demonstrates clearly in my opinion the political nature of this party's opposition to the Roman Catholic Church. Thus we learn for example that one Abbé Mengsgrissa had no hesitation in gathering together members of his tribe in his presbytery to give the Democrat leader the opportunity to 'practise his policy of lies'.[31] We learn also that 'during the elections of 10 April 1960, Mgr Etoga recommended all the Catholic missions of Djoungolo to vote for a polygamous Catholic Democrat, a casual new adherent, because he was the brother-in-law of the bishop' and that 'the party of the Catholic Betis, called Christian Democrats, is a tribalist and tribal Beti *"staff"* (sic), its fundamental doctrine being the *"Etogaic Law"* laid down by Mgr Paul Etoga, the Chaplain of the Party'.[32] In another unsigned article in *Abolege* we find the following question-and-answer sequence:

Question: Whom should we ask for our political direction?
Answer: We should ask Mgr *Etoga* and Nti Kayser *Mbida* Ndgana 1st to give us a political direction which is correct: in this way we receive from the former a Vaticanistic and anti-atheist direction, and from the latter a demotheocratic and anti-UPC direction.[33]

These few examples are enough to confirm what we stated above, that the opposition of members of the *UPC* TO THE Catholic church was chiefly of a political nature. The third accusation made against the church in the writings of members of the *UPC* was that churchmen had a colonialist manner which was at variance with the religion that they preached. Thus beneath the title 'L'épouvantail et les missionnaires' (The scarecrow and the missionaries) Okala Abene asserts that the so-called Christian countries and churchmen support barbarous deeds perpetrated against colonial peoples. And the author concludes:

To say that it is the duty of a minister of the church of Christ to defend egoistical, criminal and immoral interests, is to proclaim the decadence of that ignoble ethic called Christian. The role of the evangelising mission is ended. Let the missionaries go home, where much remains to be done.[34]

There is no need to add that the Catholic church did not remain indifferent to all these attacks, while at the same time they provided it with additional 'proofs' that the *UPC* was well and truly Communist.

[31] O.M.O., 'Les Mbidalogies d'un philosophe juriste', in *Abolege*, No. 6, 15 Oct, 1960, 10.
[32] Serna Kangan Gani, 'Voulez-vous aller au ciel?' in *Abolege*, No. 6, 15th October, 1960, 10.
[33] 'Catechisme de Mbidalogie', question no. 8, in *Abolege*. No. 7, 22nd November, 1960, 6-7.
[34] In *Abolege*, No. 9, 9th November, 1960, 4.

When attacked, the church thought it its duty to counter-attack. Nevertheless the public reaction of the Catholic church was calmer than that of its opponents. In number after number the *Catholic Weekly* showed conclusively to its readers that the party of Mayi Matip, Kamden Ninyim and Sende was incontestably an atheist, Communist organization which, in attacking the church, aimed to separate the hierarchy from the faithful, and finally destroy all Christian influence in the land.[35] The editor of *L'Effort Camerounais* published a short work in which he tried to show that a priest, like any other citizen, has a right to hold political opinions and let them be known.[36] And Abbé Jean Zoa—who later became, and still is, the Archbishop of Yaoundé—wrote a pamphlet whose title alone says enough: *Pour un Nationalisme chrétien.*[37]

By way of a conclusion
At the end of this very limited study there can be no question of conclusions as such. Therefore I would prefer us, in concluding, to ask ourselves whether the Catholic church really was anti-nationalist and whether the *UPC* was in fact Communst and anti-church. The reply to the last question does not appear easy, especially when it is a matter of whether the *UPC* was against the church. The mass of literature mentioned above appears to establish incontrovertibly that there was in fact a fundamental opposition between the *UPC* and the Catholic church. Yet Um Nyobe and Moumié, the two leaders of the nationalist movement, greeted the consecration of the first Camerounian bishops as a great national event. And when *UPC* members attacked the missionaries, they never went so far as to bring into question the presence of the Catholic church itself in Cameroun. Thus in an article, which was nonetheless very virulent, a certain Serna Kangan Gani confined himself to demanding the replacement of Mgr Graffin by Abbé Jean Zoa, the departure of the missionaries and even the creation of a '*National Catholic* Church'.[38] At no time was there any question of putting an end to the activities of the church as such, even less of replacing Roman Catholicism by another belief or another sect. In the same way, all that they blamed the hierarchy for was turning the faithful against the *UPC,* and Mgr Etoga in particular for his leanings towards the Democrats. In short, we are dealing with anti-colonial reactions and political

[35] See, for example, J. Mfoulou, 'L'U.P.C. est-elle communiste?', *L'Effort Camerounais*, 1960.

[36] P. Fertin, *Le Prêtre et la Politique*, Editions St. Paul, Yaoundé, 1960.

[37] Editions St. Paul, Yaoundé, 1960.

[38] 'Voulez-vous allez au ciel?', *Abolege*, No. 6, 15th October 1960, 8–10; my italics.

opposition, rather than an anti-religious attitude.

As for whether the *UPC* was Communist, we stressed at the proper place the affiliation of the movement to the French Communist Party—at first through the intermediary of the *Rassemblement Démocratique Africain, (RDA)* then on its own account—and the influence of the *CGT* and the sympathy of the Communist world towards the movement. That said, nothing in the writings of the leaders which I have consulted leads me to declare that the *UPC* was an organization with an ideology that was atheist, anti-religious or simply of Marxist inspiration. It is only among *UPC* members living abroad, that we find disputes between factions quoting as authorities different Marxist tendencies. Lastly one can say, with no danger of error, that the Catholic church of Cameroun was not against nationalism as such. As I have tried to show, the Catholic hierarchy had indeed a different conception of nationalism—'independence within interdependence with France' for example—and it would have liked to see that conception win. Therefore it showed itself anti-*UPC,* since the *UPC* was in favour of another point of view.

Authenticity and Christianity in Zaïre*

NGINDU MUSHETE

THE SOCIO-RELIGIOUS CONTEXT

If there is one major problem facing African churches today, it is the problem of Africanization. An answer must be found to the very real and urgent questions that a changing African society poses with regard to evangelization. The question therefore that must be asked, and that we are asking here, is in what circumstances evangelization can really achieve penetration in Africa in these times of a return to ancestral springs for nationalistic reasons. It is in the context of this pastoral imperative that we wish to place and to comprehend the ideology of recourse to authenticity launched in Zaïre by President Mobutu.

Our intention, in this paper, is not so much that of analysing and examining the various aspects of the Zaïrean ideology of authenticity as that of producing some sort of inventory, of necessity schematic, something more personal, or even subjective: to subject ourselves to a historical self-examination. To analyse the current situation without at least linking it to what has immediately preceded, would be to juxtapose symptoms without reaching a diagnosis. To understand the ideology of authenticity, it must be placed in context. Our aim therefore will necessarily be threefold yet unified: to show what gave rise to it, to make clear its aims and analyse the forms it takes, and finally to determine the tasks facing the church.

The concept and ideology of authenticity bear the marks of their relationship with the 'colonial situation', and the 'State Commission for the Orientation of the Nation', (*La Commission d'Etat à l'Orientation Nationale*) expresses it as follows:

'What has come into being is not authenticity as such, but the doctrine which assigns to authenticity the role of prime mover in the construction of the Nation. The steps taken in the mind of the father of his country (President Mobutu) in the erection of this doctrine were purely pragmatic. They were the fruits of prolonged meditation on the

* A rather longer version of the original French text of this chapter has appeared in *Cahiers des Religions Africaines*, VIII, no. 16, July 1974, pp. 209–30.

realities of Zaïre, some permanent, others due to the present situation . . . The urgent reality was first of all the decolonization of the mind. In the life of Zaïrean society the phenomenon of colonialism had lasted a relatively short time, a man's lifetime, but had been particularly potent. The acculturation which it caused was virtually a total upheaval which still today greatly hampers the life of our nation . . .

This powerful force which is no longer exercised must be matched, by the *MPR,* by a force of at least equal if not greater power to overcome the obstacle of acculturation. It is this which explains and justifies the unprecedented vigour and extent of the campaign for a recourse to authenticity. Zaïre intends to rediscover its soul as quickly as possible.'[1]

Thus absolute priority is given to the cultural revolution which will restore a Zaïrean soul to the population as a whole; and this implies total decolonization, even religious . . . And why not underline it? By its extent and the degree of intensity it reaches, the struggle against the West, and in particular the Christian West, appears to be the first dialectical moment of realization by Christians in Africa of the problem of their autonomy, and the related problem of access to the faith. For liberty in the state and liberty in the church are for Africans a single fundamental problem. It cannot be too often reiterated that, for a great number of Africans, the Christian West represents and denotes the privileged civilization which, having had some success historically as the incarnation of Christianity, appears to be the only one capable of fulfilling the role adquately. It denotes also the universal church, it holds virtually all the important positions in the central government of the church, and it is the criteria of its particular culture alone which determine the formulation of doctrine, the conception of morals and the form of worship.

This is the fundamental criticism formulated by Africans against the Christian West; essentially it denounces, as being profoundly unjust and unjustified, what could be called the cultural imperialism of the West, which purposely or not, consciously or not, seems to reduce Christianity to the dimensions of its historical realization in the West. There is thus no doubt that the difficult problem to be faced as a matter of urgency by African churches today is that of the apparently foreign character of Christianity. This formulation of the problem is stated particularly clearly by the new generation of Zaïrean intellectuals. These are the words of Professor V. Y. Mudimbe:

'By what right should one give one's faith to a foreign religion? Be it Catholic, universal, anything you like, the problem remains:

[1] Sakombi Inongo, *Authenticité*, n.d., p.l.

Catholicism is a religion with the imprint of the West upon it even as regards the understanding of its messages.'[2]

In Zaïre, as everywhere else in Africa, the Church has spoken in languages that were foreign or only partly understood. Christianity has been incapable of embodying itself in African cultures. It has remained apart from, parallel to society.[3] In particular it appears in individualistic guise, whereas traditional religion was and is essentially social. It pervaded the whole of life: individual, family, political and social; it allowed people to understand each other, to be aware of each other's worth, to be an integral part of society, tolerate their circumstances, master their anxieties, reach a state of equilibrium sufficient for themselves as individuals and as members of the group.[4]

Like many other African countries, Zaïre is in search of its true path. It is imbued with the desire to display before the world its real personality and integrity, as well as with the will to make a contribution through its own specific nature to the construction of the community of mankind.

Zaïrean nationalism or the philosophy of authenticity[5]

According to the Manifesto of the *Mouvement Populaire de la Révolution (MPR)*, Zaïrean nationalism displays the following characteristics: the glorification of the national entity, the maintenance of territorial integrity and national sovereignty, the affirmation of the greatness of the state and the policy of developing the power of the state, mastery and control of the material and human resources for the economic and social development of the nation, and the incorporation of regional diversities in the national entity.[6]

---

[2] V. Y. Mudimbe, *Entre les eaux. Dieu, un prêtre, la révolution*. Paris, 1973, p. 35.

[3] See on this point a most enlightening work: Marie-France Perrin Jassy, *La Communauté de base dans les Eglises africaines*, Kinshasa, 1970.

[4] cf. *Les Religions africaines comme source de valeurs de civilisation*, colloquium at Cotonou held 16-22 August 1970, Paris 1972. See also the work of Professor Mulago, *La Religion traditionelle des bantus et leur vision du monde*, Coll. *Bibliothèque du Centre d'Etudes des Religions Africaines*, Kinshasa 1973. See in particular part IV: 'Vision bantu du monde ou communion-participation vitale', 121-46.

[5] On the genesis, development and scope of Zaïrean authenticity, the reader may consult: *Le Manifeste de la N'sala* or *Le Manifeste de Mouvement Populaire de la Révolution*, Kinshasa, 1970; the speeches of President Mobutu, in particular the address given on 4 October 1973, at the United Nations; also the lectures given by Sakombi Inongo, Commissaire Politique et Commissaire d'Etat à l'Orientation Nationale; D. Kamembo, J. Kazadi, H. Mpinga, *Le Nationalisme congolais*, Kinshasa 1971; Elungu Pene Elungu, 'Authenticité et Culture', in *Revue Zaïroise de Psychologie et de Pédagogie*, 1973, vol. 2, 5-10.

[6] *Manifeste de la N'sala*, foreword, p. 6.

Made explicit in this way, the ideology of authenticity appears in the first place a political philosophy, with the aim of confronting the various political, social or cultural challenges of the contemporary world. 'Zaïre, which has made the transition from indescribable chaos to a country with organisation and government, has, on the basis of its unfortunate experiences, come to recognise its true friends. The Zaïrean experiment has been worked out on the basis of a political philosophy which we call authenticity.'[7] In this context the authentic person is someone freed from all forms of mental alienation.[8] For President Mobutu, authenticity is another name for radical decolonization, total political, economic and cultural freedom.[9] To be converted to authenticity is in practice to renew contact with those free men, our ancestors, who were free in that they were creators of culture and civilization.[10]

Authenticity and Christianity in Zaïre

Thus our task is to extract the historical and religious (theological) significance of the 'recourse to authenticity'. But let us first take a look at the events which have a significant bearing on the changing relationships between the Catholic church and the state of Zaïre since 1971, the year in which the Zaïrean authenticity campaign was launched. We shall restrict ourselves to essentials.[11]

[7] United Nations speech of President Mobutu, 4 October 1973.

[8] cf. Mabika Kalanda, *La remise en question de la décolonisation mentale*, Brussels. See also the short work by m'Buze Nsomi, *Révolution et humanisme*, Kinshasa, 1974, which clearly outlines the essential aspects.

[9] 'Le MPR proclame que son but est de libérer les congolais et les congolaises de toutes les servitudes et d'assurer leur progrès en édifiant une République vraiment sociale et vraiment démocratique.' Manifeste, 8.

[10] One cannot speak of rich and poor cultures. 'Conceptions of the world,' said Dilthey, 'are based on the nature of the universe, and the relationship of our finite spirit to that universe. Thus each one of them expresses within the limits of our thought one aspect of the universe. Each one of them is true, but all are limited.' Reflecting on African philosophy Mabika Kalanda formulated this interesting observation: 'No system of philosophy is more complete than all the others; no philosophy contains the whole truth about the nature of man and his destiny: one may and does find wise men in any philosophical system.' op. cit. 151.

[11] On the changing relationship between the Catholic church and the state of Zaïre, consult: *L'Eglise à l'aube de l'indépendance*, the Declaration of the VIth Plenary Assembly of the Episcopate of the Congo, Kinshasa 1962; *L'Eglise et l'Etat, L'Eglise au service de la Nation Zaïroise*, the Acts of the XIth Plenary Assembly of the Episcopate of Zaïre, 5 March 1972, Brussels, Ed. Marx Arnold, 1972, p. 226. The book is in three sections. The first part gives a resume of the relationships between Church and State from June 1967 to February 1972, and the memorandum, Church and State, communicated to the head of State on 6 March 1972. The second part sets forth positive modalities of collaboration proposed by the Church to the State of Zaïre. The third part deals with relations between the Church and the *MPR*. Further reading: P. Chauleur, 'L'Eglise et l'Etat en Afrique noire', in *Etudes*, Paris, May 1973, 645-8; *Informations Catholiques Internationales*, 1 October 1970, 13; *Pro Mundi Vita*, special note no. 34: 'l'Eglise dans les Etats Africains'.

In January 1971 the Permanent Committee of the Bishops of Zaïre provided doctrinal clarification of the action of the Church in the temporal domain.[12] Two principles were affirmed: firstly the authority of the State which alone is responsible for the organization and management of the 'earthly kingdom'. The Permanent Committee declared and affirmed: 'The Church shall lay claim to no rights in this domain, which is the prerogative of the State. There can therefore be no possibility of perceiving the situation as that of two parallel powers, and even less as that of two rival powers'. Secondly, regarding the mission of the church, it stated that 'the Church must assist men to live according to the Gospel. As the essence of its message is charity, the Church must serve the world, and in this particular situation, must serve the Zaïrean community', and it specified 'but in accomplishing this mission, it is the duty of the Church to itself to remain faithful to the message of the Gospel, to do its utmost to see that it is understood and lived out in a given socio-cultural context.' Since every human society is a living organism and thus in perpetual evolution, the church cannot link itself to a given political regime, and at the same time remain faithful to its mission.[13]

August 1971 witnessed the nationalization of the Catholic University of Lovanium and of the institutions of further education,[14] the fusion of the three existing universities (Catholic, Protestant and official) into a single National University: The National University of Zaïre, and the nomination of a Zaïrean bishop,[15] priests, monks and nuns as officials of the new National University.

4 October 1971 saw the campaign for 'authenticity'. On 5 January 1972 the government reorganized the youth section of the *Mouvement Populaire de la Revolution (JMPR)* and made obligatory the introduction of a *JMPR* Executive Committee not only in all educational establishments, but also in all private institutions which exist for the religious training of church personnel (seminaries, novitiates, scholasticates).

In a letter dated 17 January 1972 the President of the Conference of Bishops, Monsignor Lesambo, informed the heads of institutions of religious instruction that it was a matter of extreme delicacy, which fell within the competence of the conference of bishops.

The Permanent Committee considers that it is not authorised to

---

[12] *L'Eglise au service de la Nation Zaïroise*, 20 ff.

[13] Ibid. 20.

[14] At that time Catholic education in Zaïre accounted for sixty-eight per cent of teachers in primary education, and forty-four per cent in secondary education.

[15] The person in question is Monsignor Tshibangu Tshishiku, the auxiliary bishop of Kinshasa and a former Rector of the Catholic University of Lovanium.

commit the episcopacy and religious superiors in this way by tolerating the establishment of the *JMPR* in this precise form within establishments whose purpose is to train priests, monks and nuns for whom all political activity is forbidden both by the Holy Office and by the Council of Vatican II, given that 'men of the Church' are held to belong wholly to all men. (. . .) The permanent Committee considers that in such a delicate matter any valid solution can only follow investigations in discussion with the highest authorities of the land. It has therefore convoked a plenary meeting of the episcopacy for the beginning of next March.[16]

On 6 February 1972 the nationality law banned the use of Christian first names in favour of authentically Zaïrean names. 'None of my ancestors had these sonorous first names,' said President Mobutu, 'I admire those who love and fear God; not the God of the Westerners, but the Supreme Being revealed to us through our traditions.' In a note made public in the Catholic Agency *DIA* on 18 January 1972 the Episcopal Commission for Evangelization affirmed and declared that Christianity is the source of authenticity, and that the Christian name denotes a change in the personality of the newly baptized.[17]

On 12 January 1972 the Catholic weekly *Afrique Chrétienne* published an editorial on the subject of authenticity in which the editorialist noted that what is at stake is 'our greatness and dignity as a free people', but that there can be no question of 'disinterring from the night of the past an original African philosophy which, if it ever existed, can have been no more than the expression of a social situation, now completely out of date.' This text, considered subversive by the Political Bureau of the *MPR*, was erroneously attributed to Cardinal Malula, the archbishop of Kinshasa. The cardinal was expelled from his residence, the publication of *Afrique Chrétienne* suspended, its director, a native of Zaïre, and the editor responsible, a Scheut Father missionary, were closely questioned.

On the day before President Mobutu returned from his rest in Switzerland, Cardinal Malula regretfully left Kinshasa for Rome, at the invitation of the Holy See. The Eleventh Plenary Assembly of the Episcopate of Zaïre took place from 28 February to 5 March 1972 on the theme: 'The Church in the service of the Nation of Zaïre.'[18] The importance of the theme was underlined in the following manner:

The rapid strides made in the organisation of the State of Zaïre constitute an important turning point in the history of the Church in Zaïre. Having been a missionary church, closely associated with the

---

[16] *L'Eglise au service de la Nation Zaïroise*, 25.

[17] Ibid. 209.

[18] cf. supra note 11.

work of the colonial power, it must now take its place in a sovereign state, sovereign in every sense of the word. Since the Church of Zaïre is one of the largest in Africa, the decisions of the Plenary Assembly will have important repercussions throughout the whole of Africa.[19]

After the Plenary Assembly a delegation of bishops handed to President Mobutu, on 6 March 1972, a memorandum on relations between Church and State,[20] and a note on the relations between the Church and the MPR-JMPR,[21] Christian first names,[22] evangelization,[23] students, the periodical, and the exile of Cardinal Malula.[24] The documents were rejected by the Political Bureau 'both as regards form and content'.

The government decided on the setting up of JMPR committees in all seminaries before 1 April 1972; failure to do so would result in prosecution. Moreover thenceforth it was forbidden for all state officials to attend religious ceremonies in their official capacity. Simultaneously all mention of religious ceremonies was deleted from the official programme of state functions.

On 8 March Monsignor Lesambo, the chairman of the Episcopal Conference of Zaïre, decided on the closure of the major seminaries to avoid the setting up of JMPR committees. The Archbishop of Kananga, however, accepted the formation of JMPR Committees in two of the major seminaries in the ecclesiastical province of Kananga, and, following negotiations with the government, the bishops accepted the formation of JMPR committees in the major seminaries on the express proviso that they should respect the purpose, orderliness and specific nature of these religious establishments. This was accepted by the Political Bureau on 17 April.

On 9 November 1972 the government banned all confessional organizations and gave to the JMPR alone the task of organizing the young people of Zaïre, for 'Zaïre is a free country, the youth of the country should be one and indivisible, and all training has as its first task the formation of good citizens.'

On 8 February 1973 the government banned thirty-one confessional newspapers and periodicals, the majority of these being Catholic. The following day the Political Bureau of the MPR dissolved the Episcopal Assembly of Zaïre (i.e. plenary assembly, permanent committee, provincial conferences, general secretariat) as a subversive organization, and forbade bishops to travel outside their diocese for the purpose of

[19] *L'Eglise au service de la Nation Zaïoise*, 26-7.

[20] Ibid. 57-90.

[21] Ibid. 171-204.

[22] Ibid. 209.

[23] Ibid. 209-12.

[24] Ibid. 213.

mutual consultation or the adoption of common policies.

In an interview granted by President Mobutu on 6 April 1973 to the paper *Le Soir*, he declared:

There will never be in Zaïre, in my lifetime as Head of State, any problem between God, Mobutu and the people of Zaïre. But between God, Mobutu, the people of Zaïre and churchmen there will be. Let me explain. We provoke no one. The human institution, I repeat human, that we call the Church, and that exists in the Vatican, has no connection with Zaïre, or with Mobutu . . . I say that this country and the party have nothing in common with the outside world, that is to say with all institutions foreign to our Republic, be they political, economic or spiritual . . . We can no longer accept political, economic, religious or spiritual domination imposed from without . . . Before independence people spoke of the three powers: the Administration, the Companies and the Church. The two former have had to give way; there is no reason why the same should not apply to the Church . . . I have never had any problem with Protestants or Kimbanguists, because they do not get their orders from outside. But the bishops of Zaïre do receive such orders, as is proved by that famous 200 page document.[25] They are the agents of a foreign power.

Breaking with a tradition virtually unbroken since the Lateran Agreements of 1929, in May 1973 President Mobutu made an official visit to Italy without calling on the Pope. He declared on that occasion that this convention was conceived and established for Europeans, and had nothing to do with him, and that the Pope was a Head of State whom he could only visit if he had been formally invited.

On 24 June 1973 before 200,000 *MPR* militants President Mobutu declared that the differences with Cardinal Malula were definitively over. 'All that we ask of our bishops is that they should be on the side of authenticity with us.' A statement by the General Secretary of the*MPR*, which appeared in *Le Monde* on 30 June 1973 clarified the above facts: 'The Church must submit to *MPR* discipline . . . This submission may not be simply an act of faith, a benevolent promise, it is a constitutional duty.'

At the end of November 1973 President Mobutu authorized a meeting of the archbishops of Zaïre. Accompanied by Monsignor Tshibangu Tshishiku, they met at Lubumbashi from 12 to 15 December. There were two points on the agenda: on the one hand the lifting of restrictive measures concerning the Conference of Bishops of Zaïre, and on the other a re-examination of the status of the Catholic church in Zaïre, the structures of its organization, its operations and its methods. The Zaïrean archbishops stated their convictions as follows:

[25] An allusion to the *Actes de la XIe Assemblée Plénière de l'Episcopat du Zaïre*.

Bound to Zaïre by bonds of blood and by divine vocation, we welcome the true value of the *détente* officially declared by the head of State on the 24th June last.[26] We believe in the strength of our common Bantu wisdom, which will smooth away family quarrels and direct us to new horizons, relying on each other's support . . . The request that we are making is dictated by our urgent desire to see the Catholic Church fulfil more efficaciously its role as servant of the world in the heart of our great nation. For firmly rooted in this country, the Church cannot conduct herself as a stranger, but must feel at home in Zaïre. She takes as her own the ideals of the country as expressed in the slogan, 'peace, justice and work', together with that of cultural renewal and integration; she contributes to the wider influence of the country by her participation in African and worldwide congresses, and desires to work out new modalities of presence and action within the community of the nation. In the colonial period we witnessed the collaboration of religious and civil authorities. This collaboration was certainly fruitful; but it bound the Church too closely through its official representatives to the colonial regime. As regards ourselves, we are anxious for the same collaboration, in the fullest confidence and with the most total sense of participation in the life of the nation, without however reaching a situation that implied direct intervention in the political domain.[27]

This request and the intentions expressed by the archbishops of Zaïre received a favourable reception from President Mobutu, who made known at the end of March 1974 his decision to lift provisionally 'the ban on meetings of the Episcopal Conferences throughout the territory of Zaïre.' The Permanent Committee of the bishops of Zaïre held its first meeting at Kisangani from 24 April to 4 May 1974, and on 4 May the government authorized the creation of three faculties of theology, Catholic, Protestant, and Kimbanguist, within *UNAZA*.[28]*

Doctrinal Clarification and Suggestions for Research
We indicate here some urgent theological problems which the ideology of a recourse to authenticity poses for the Christian conscience.

Questions of personality, a struggle for influence, a leftward political turn: many hypotheses have been formulated in an attempt to explain

[26] The reconciliation between President Mobutu and Cardinal Malula.

[27] The presence and action of the Church within the integrated national community are thus fully confirmed.

[28] In fact only the Catholic and Protestant faculties are in operation on the university campus of Kinshasa.

* Since May 1974 the relationships of church and state in Zaïre appear to have continued to fluctuate in much the same rhythm as indicated by Professor Ngindu. In December 1974, following the President's visit to China, 'the radicalization of the revolution' was launched, but in November 1975 Cardinal Malula was reinstated in the National Order of the Leopard. (Ed.)

and understand the Church-State problem in Zaïre. Certainly the experience of China in bringing about the liberation of man outside the churches and even in opposition to them constitutes a challenge for the young churches of Africa which must be taken up in all its dimensions. But we think it necessary to go even further. Beneath the difficulties of the state, there is also a question of vocation. The preoccupations which find the expression in the slogan of authenticity are not new. Indeed the government's critical stand springs from a very general sociological problem: the cultural monopoly of the West and its three series of consequences, for the people, for culture, and for the relationship between the people and religion. Thus the problem posed here is both historical and practical and very circumscribed: the training of the people by and through 'authentic action', seen as the source of and vehicle for values and civilization. This problem has been perceived and well analyzed in a note in *Pro Mundi Vita,* devoted to Church-State relationships in Zaïre. The note states:

> It is not primarily a question of an ideological or specifically religious conflict, nor of a conflict on the subject of authenticity as a cultural and political philosophy, but above all a confrontation of forces, or the impossibility of peaceful coexistence between two different social 'systems'. The Catholic church—and in a smaller degree the other Christian churches—is the only firmly established organisation which still has the courage to pass judgment and issue directives independently of the political party. The *MPR,* under the leadership of Mobutu and seeking its inspiration in 'Mobutism', is firmly resolved to concentrate power entirely in its own hands, and suppress all trace of European influence in the life of society. The determination to de-Westernise the social life of Zaïre cannot be achieved without the surrender of the spiritual power. The regime feels itself closely watched, and even condemned by the international character of the Catholic church. Such a limitation cannot be accepted by an absolute power of the sort envisaged by Mobutu and the *MPR.* It must also be said that the philosophy of authenticity has a certain importance in the sense that Christianity in Zaire was the cause of a degree of disacculturation because it showed little understanding with regard to traditional societies and religions.[29]

Another strong reason for the conflict between Church and State in Zaïre is to be found in the separation in the secular West between religion and politics. 'The drama is rooted in the Catholic "system" itself, in the centuries old separation between the Church and the people . . . in the clericalised institution developing its own culture, its own works, its own language, its own structures, having a monopoly of what is religious and

[29] *Pro Mundi Vita,* Note spéciale no. 39, 1975, 25.

of the Gospel.'[30] The 'reign of the spirit' for the people is religion. An intellectual can be made spiritual without being religious, without being a Christian. But for the masses it is different. For them the same situation applies for the spiritual life as the moral sense: in principle it is possible to conceive of a basis other than religion for them; in practice only religion is strong enough to sustain them.

From this point of view, as can be understood, the pastoral task of the Church is inseparable from social criticism. Religion has no right to turn someone into a stranger in his own land, make him indifferent to the lot of his people. The famous statement by Karl Marx: 'religion, the opium of the people', was made in a precise historical context. Even if it was justifiable at the time, it can by no means be given the status of a dogma valid for all times and all places. In any case it is up to us to prove to everyone that religion, properly understood, is a source of dynamism, and of a lucid, disinterested commitment to the service of one's country and one's brothers.

In this context, if it is right to suggest some directions our thoughts might take at this time of tentative searchings, whose importance is clear to all, I will present two claims which seem to me particularly important: we expect from the Christians of Africa that they should be clear-sighted about the situation of their country and demanding as regards themselves. A striving for lucidity and the will to be involved, these are the two fundamental aspects of our mission in independent Africa. The first task we must fulfil is that of lucidity. Indeed, confronted by the widespread confusion of ideas experienced by post-colonial Africa, it appears particularly important that we African intellectuals, we who are responsible for the cultural heritage of our countries, should select a new horizon for our thoughts. This should go beyond the contradictions of the present, for which the ruling ideologies certainly bear a heavy load of responsibility, but in which also Africans have made the mistake of cramming too easily all the dogmatisms of Western and Eastern ideologies. This striving for lucidity is seen to be all the more indispensable, in that Africa must now ward off the danger of conformism. It seems as though we are afraid of leaving the beaten track and making innovations. Instead of putting blind trust in slogans taken from France, China or the USSR, which express French, Chinese or Russian realities, we must resolutely take up the task of analyzing our own data.

From all the foregoing, it appears clearly that the major problem of the church in Zaïre is the problem of the authenticity of its message, taking account of the transcendant nature of the Gospel message, the inadequate presentation of this message by non-African missionaries, and

---

[30] Henri Maurier, 'Commentaire sur les Actes de la XIe Assemblée Plénière de l'épiscopat du Zaïre de 1972', in *Cultures et Developpement*, 1973, no. 4, 878.

also the fact that this presentation coincided with a period of confrontation of cultures and cilizations. Here we have the whole problem of the originality and specificity of Christianity laid before us. If it is not to perish, the church of Zaïre is called upon to Africanize itself as regards the personnel of the hierarchy and the laity, its mode of expression, its liturgy and more profoundly, its theology.[31]

Faithful to Africa's past and to the authentic traditions of the church, African theologians must undertake the task of taking stock, analyzing and selecting. They must for their own sakes throw a bridge between yesterday and tomorrow by finding a valid situation today. This is to say that the present situation in Africa demands from them continuous boldness and lucidity.

But the African world today has need of more than abstract ideas; it has need of examples, men who embody and thus illustrate their ideals, who feel themselves responsible for the transformation of their country. As we have already remarked, the African is more willing to follow a person than an idea. This means that the presence of the Christians must be first and foremost a witness to life spent in the service of the integral development of man.

We must however remember that Zaïre intends itself to be a secular state, in which tolerance and religious freedom are considered normal, and in which every aspect of religion is in principle banned from public life.[32] Religion there has become a strictly private matter. All religious festivals, including the Nativity, have been deleted from the official calendar of the state. This cannot but pose problems of conscience for the Christian.[33] In Zaïre we are now less inclined than in the past to affirm the presence of the church in society by means of the classic

[31] See my article: 'Unité et pluralité de la Théologie', *Revue de Clergé Africain*, 1967, 22, 593-615.

[32] The word secularity or *laïcité*, given its meaning in the XIXth Century, is not easy to define. Etymologically *laïcité* is linked to laicism and laicization. In French usage the word has two fundamental meanings: 1. a neutral meaning, which designates the doctrine whose aim is to give a non-confessional, non-religious character to state institutions; 2. the word also designates the doctrines hostile to the Christian religion, or indeed any religion, to the extent of making a religion of denying all religion. Cf. A. Manaranche, art. 'Laïcisation, Laïcisme, laïcité', in *Catholicisme*, vol. VI, 1965, col. 1643-66; H. de Lubac, *Le drame de l'humanisme atheé*, Paris, 1945; H. Chatreix, *Au-delà du laicisme*, Paris, 1946.

[33] The bishops of Zaïre studied this problem on the occasion of their XXIIth Plenary Assembly, held at Kinshasa from 6 to 17 January. In a communique entitled: 'Declaration de l'Episcopat face à la situation présente', the bishops of Zaïre made the following observation: 'The principle of the laicity of the state does not in itself pose a problem for the Church if it is understood and practised in the sense of the Constitution, where it means that the state does not give a privileged position to any religion, that there is not and shall not be any religion or form of religion, imposed on all its citizens as the State religion . . . The principle of laicity appears to be understood in Zaïre as having an anti-religious meaning, or at least a meaning opposed to the Christian religion. This appears to be the sense of several official

works: schools, hospitals, almshouses etc . . . The presence of the church has to be maintained in a manner which is much more supple, more 'prophetic', based rather on interpersonal relationships, which are moreover more in keeping with African wisdom. The priests, monks and nuns who run these establishments, work henceforth within the framework of the institutions of the state, or directly as apostles of the church, at the level of the parish or diocese. Let us be aware of this historic conjuncture and keep it so.

Thus the recourse to authenticity brings us to reconsider, or even revise the Christian theology of the relationship between the church and the world. We have stressed as we went along that traditional African wisdom seems to give little importance to the dualities of temporal and spiritual, political and religious, natural and supernatural, as they have been elaborated and understood by numerous western Christians before the Second Vatican Council and before *Pacem in terris*. In this respect, the Christian theology of the supernatural needs to be very carefully and precisely reconsidered. The opposition between nature and the supernatural is simplistic. It prevents our reading the Holy Scriptures profitably. In its deepest meaning the supernatural world of the Christian cannot be seen as something added to our nature from outside, juxtaposing itself to it or superimposing itself upon it. It is, on the contrary, a relationship in depth with God and other men. If it is not to rest on erroneous premisses the theology of the supernatural should start from the dogma of the Incarnation and end there. We should emphasize the theme of the recapitulation of all things in Christ, the Perfect Man (Ephesians 1.10), and the theme of Christ as the Alpha and Omega of the universe and of history (Revelation XXII. 12-13), to which might be added the theme of a new heaven and a new earth (Romans VIII. 14-21), and that of Christ, the Image of the invisible God (Colossians I. 15).[34]

By any standard Zaïre is a secular one-party state. The church's task is not to develop its own design for society, a Catholic design.[35] On the other hand, the church in Zaïre can collaborate actively in the

measures and declarations regarding the Christian Churches: the suppression of Christian first names with a non-African origin; the suppression of confessional youth movements; the suppression of means of expression, in particular the Christian publications; the suppression of crosses and crucifixes in public places; suppression of religious instruction in schools; the suppression of the Faculties of Theology at UNAZA, and finally the proclamation of the *MPR as a church.*'

[34] cf. the excellent article by Y. M. J. Congar, 'L'Influence de la société et de l'histoire sur la développement de l'homme chrétien', in *Nouvelle Revue Théologique*, 1974, vol. 96, 673.

[35] It should be noted that the Catholics of the United States—the largest of the religious denominations—have an American point of view, not a Catholic one. Polish or Cuban Catholics under a Socialist regime, or Algerian Catholics in an Islamic country have problems other than the inauguration of a 'Christian social order'. The prospect of a Christian design for society has in any case been overtaken

development of this country by producing a change of mentality, for it can give a solid foundation to human experience, and a real meaning to progress; and it cultivates and encourages the virtues necessary for development: a sense of justice and human fraternity. The church would be betraying its mission if it appeared to be a foreign body in the country, unmoved by the real questions that trouble the general population. The Africanization of Christianity in Zaïre is thus a serious problem, and perhaps the most serious problem today.

by Vatican II which puts the Church in the midst of the world, not over against it: it is the problems of people of our time that grip the Christian and the Church. The latter does not pretend, with universally accepted authoritative solemnity, to provide a ready answer, but is prepared to try with all men of good will, according to the happy phrase of John XXIII, consenting not only to learn from specialists the technical aspects of the problem, but also to share with all those who reflect on our times, her own reflections inspired by the Gospel of Jesus Christ. (Cf. *Gaudium et Spes*, nos. 1, 2, 7, 13, 16, 40 . . .)

The Roman Catholic Church in social crisis: the case of Rwanda [1]

IAN LINDEN

L	Were you in agreement with Catholic social teaching as it was taught at that time (1950s)?
Dr Grégoire Kayibanda	Frankly, I have never been in complete agreement with traditional social teaching because the people were still poor and I thought that this teaching had a tendency to support capitalism.
L	You saw it as capitalist?
Kayibanda	Yes, it saw change coming from the capitalists themselves, whereas, looking at it from the viewpoint of the poor, what was needed was a completely new system.
L	Do you think that in the 1950s the Missionary Church was as concerned with the poor as much as today? Or were they relying on the powerful?
Kayibanda	I wouldn't like to give exact dates but by 1950 there was still the tendency to be involved with the establishment, but I don't think it was necessarily the wish of the whole Church—it was only the wish of some of the Church leaders in their attitudes to African affairs. It's forgiveable. One can understand it. I don't think you should see it in the light of the Church as a whole . . . There were certainly two phases from the Church's point of view. In the first phase the BaTutsi refused the Church. They didn't want any of it. In the second phase they saw that it started to become important. Unhappily the Church was being 'pulled along by' (vehiculé par) the Europeans. There was no way of doing otherwise as only the Europeans were priests. You must distinguish between these two phases. Usually the BaHutu are very open; if a movement comes along, they go in, they try to understand the ideas. If a movement comes along the Tutsi study it from the outside; they do not go in, they try to sabotage it, get it into

[1] This article will be inadequately footnoted to safeguard the security of informants.

a corner, then corner it for themselves, they manipulate it politically and financially; for them it is a
matter of financial manipulation. The Church
walked into the trap, into the Batutsi's trap. Then
afterwards in the third phase the Church
thought . . . no, when I say the Church I am
going wrong, the heads of the Church, not the
Church as such . . . that all the same you were
obliged to work with the *responsables*, with the
chefs d'équipe, with the nobility, if you wanted
things to run smoothly. They worked with them.
In the fourth phase, the one you are living now, as
far as I am concerned it is very delicate . . . sensitive. Now, I want you to see this. Is the Church
both for the rich and for the poor? Is the Church
for the *élite*? That's the real question. Is it for the
Europeans in the country? *Or is it for the Nation?*
I am not suggesting a National Church. You
know, I've studied a bit too much theology for
that. National Church, that spells the destruction
of the Church; it's a useless idea, the Church is
Catholic. I feel it is absolutely vital that you
understand this; the period we are going through
at the moment, this transition period, we have to
watch out that the Church is the Church of the
people.

Interview with the President of the Republic of Rwanda, 27 June
1973.

If the success of Christianity in Africa is measured by the extent to which
a world religion in its Western trappings has become part of, incarnate
in, African societies, there are many success stories. Catholicism in some
areas of northern Rwanda is the 'traditional' religion. Television
commentators in Togo at Christmas speak without any sense of the in-
congrous of 'our traditional midnight mass'. Christian churches grow up
like palm trees in Yorubaland. It is a truism that Christianity is now an
African religion, perhaps more than a European one, and it is a mistake
to imagine that this is significantly less true of the institutional churches
than the Independent churches.

Yet the very success of this Africanization, whether at the level of
African bishops at the Vatican or the faith-healing of the Aladura, has
thrown the Christian church from the seminary and theological college
into the stark realities of life in the new nation states. Here the demand is
'seek first the political kingdom'. The penalty for refusal, paid in recent
years by the terrible sufferings of the Jehovah's Witnesses in East-
Central Africa, can be reminiscent of the first Christian centuries. The

distinction between a secular and a religious world is not readily accepted in Africa. If the church is to be incarnate, it is to be incarnate in whole men, whole societies; the political dimension cannot easily be put on one side. This much has been clear in practice and may well emerge as a theme in a new African theology that escapes from the Cartesian dualisms of Western philosophy. And it is perhaps in the political kingdom that the Western missionaries failed the young African churches most grievously. The lack of a prophetic voice, a consistent official critique of European class society, meant that no coherent social philosophy was handed on. Only the trauma of Nazism and the contribution by Russian communist troops to the salvation of Europe shocked the Western churches into articulating goals of social reform relevant to the modern state.

So it was that the mission churches appeared before World War II as accomplices of colonialism, and Africanization could seem to African Christians an end in itself. The model of mission-colonial administration relations was rarely one that could serve a young church in seeking Christian solutions to social conflict and relations with the state. When the Christian churches did move into the political arena, as in their support of the Biafran cause in the Nigerian Civil War, it was more with an emotional commitment to their 'flock' than with any thought-out theology of society. Similarly the concerned but tortuous pastoral letters of Bishop Donal Lamont, committed to social justice in Zimbabwe yet keeping the church out of 'politics', demonstrate how much a new theology of revolution is needed in the African church.

If the question of social theory is important, that of practice is no less so. The missions seemed to be the handmaid of colonialism because the missionaries appeared as part of white colonial society. As long ago as 1910, the missiologist Mirbt, pointed out that the essential weakness of Christianity in relation to Islam was its failure to overcome racial and ethnic differences.[2] European missionaries had good relations with their Christians, sometimes championed their cause; they hardly ever intermarried. The period of change-over from European to African clergy has invariably been one of tension. Similarly the hierarchy of colonial society and European class distinctions were rarely transcended in the daily life of mission stations. 'Incarnation' meant the acceptance of ethnic and social distinctions in African societies, sometimes the creation of new ones; their disappearance in a new Christian unity and brotherhood was proclaimed from the pulpit; but the task could hardly be begun in the gross inequalities of the colonial period.

The case of Rwanda is particularly striking since it was *par excellence* a

---

[2] Mirbt, C. *Mission und Kolonialpolitik in den deutschen Schutzgebieten,* Tübingen 1910, 210-211.

success story in the conventional sense that led at independence to tragedy. Rwandan society was rigidly stratified in a caste-like system and the missionaries naturally thought in terms of De Nobili's methods amongst the Brahmins. Yet the ruling Tutsi adamantly refused to convert until the 1920s with the result that the majority of Hutu farmers formed the body of the mission church. After the conversion of the nobles and finally the young king, Rudahigwa, in the 1930s, the Hutu church, which now had its own priests, was slowly dominated by the Tutsi. By the 1950s, Catholicism was the state religion. There was a Catholic court, culture and chiefs under Belgian tutelage.

While in the early days, the missionaries tended to support the Hutu against the exactions of the Tutsi, despite warnings from the Vicar-Apostolic and German authorities to keep out of politics, the heady success of the Tutsi conversions pushed revolutionary ideas of social reform into the background. After World War II, though, the new generation of priests with their European experience of social Catholicism championed the Hutu cause. The Hutu social democrats, mainly teachers and ex-seminarians, were able to use existing church institutions, newspapers and societies, to disseminate their ideas and gain support. Many of the older missionaries, however, disapproved of movement and sided with the Tutsi clergy.

By the end of the 1950s, the Catholic Church was split and the intransigence of the Tutsi conservatives at court exacerbated the situation. Both sides legitimated their position by quoting Catholic social teaching. Finally in November 1959, a peasant revolt sparked off by Hutu propaganda gave vent to grievances about land shortage and generations of Tutsi exactions, and suddenly added powerful momentum to the Hutu movement. With the Belgians keeping any Tutsi counter-revolution in check, *PARMEHUTU* was able to organize under the leadership of Kayibanda and gained power in 1961. Although many Tutsi fled the country Rwanda entered the post-independence period with the anomalous situation of a Hutu state with a Tutsi-dominated church. At the head of the Rwandan hierarchy was Archbishop Perraudin, a Swiss White Father, whose social encyclicals in the 1950s were now looked on by the Tutsi as treachery of the worst sort.

The first major crisis after the Rwandan revolution of 1959-61 took place after attacks on Rwanda led by Tutsi guerillas, the *Inyenzi*, at the end of 1963.[3] The Red Cross estimated that 5,000-8,000 Tutsi were killed in the subsequent repression. Sporadic outbursts of violence against Tutsi in the wake of guerilla attacks had occurred since the revolutionary jacquerie of 1959-61. Letters from the Rwandan episcopate condemning

---

[3] Lemarchand, R. *Rwanda and Burundi,* London 1970 197-228.

violence were sent out on 24 August 1961, and an appeal against 'these odious crimes' at Easter, 1962. At Christmas, 1963, the killing of innocents after guerilla raids was again condemned; it could 'only draw down on our country the curse of God'. A letter dated 1 January 1964 was sent out which, while deploring the terrorist attacks, continued that it 'cannot be silent either on the repression'. Four Tutsi priests, suspected by the government of having contacts outside Rwanda, Abbés Gérard Mwerekande, Narcisse Rwasubutare, Ferdinand Marara and Vianney Kivovo, were temporarily imprisoned.

The Tutsi case against the government of Grégoire Kayibanda was presented to the Vatican by J. B. Kayonga and Michel Kayihura, a leader in exile of *UNAR*, the Tutsi-dominated Independence party, and brother of Mgr Gahamanyi, the Bishop of Butare in southern Rwanda. Kayonga had been *Econome-Général* of the Rwandan Josephite Brothers but had left to become a Trappist at Mokoto, Léopoldville. After taking his vows, he went in 1957 to do refugee work but failed to return. On 4 February 1964 *Le Monde* published an article by a Swiss technical assistant of UNESCO from Nêuchatel, M. Vuillemin, allegedly a Marxist, who had resigned as a lecturer at the *Groupe Scolaire* in Butare on the grounds that he was unwilling to be an accomplice to genocide. In it he claimed that genocide of the Tutsi was taking place in Rwanda and he intimated that the church's main interest was to safeguard its position and only intervene discreetly although slaughter was taking place. On 10 February 1964, Vatican Radio broadcast an impassioned message to Mgr Perraudin, head of Rwandan hierarchy, using such inflated language as 'Since the genocide of the Jews by Hitler, the most terrible systematic genocide is taking place in the heart of Africa'. On the same day the Rwandan episcopate sent a telegram to the Vatican in 'protest against false information broadcast on 10 February', requesting that Red Cross estimates be broadcast and adding that the comparison with Hitler is monstrous and gravely offensive to a Catholic Head of State'. The telegram was not acted upon and no reply was apparently received. A letter sent by Mgr Perraudin correcting the grossly inflated estimates of *Le Monde* was never printed.

The implications of the European press, e.g. *France-Soir*, 4 February 1964, and *Le Figaro*, 11 February 1964, was that Rwanda was a clerical state whose church leaders did not wish to rock the boat by protest: 'Le mince vernis du christianisme a craqué', gloated *Le Figaro*. But the hierarchy had protested in unequivocal terms. Monsignor Rwabigwi, Archbishop Perraudin's Vicar-General, had written a passionate appeal for peace and order on 2 February 1964. The combined bishops were equally explicit in January 1964.

Knowing of certain violent reactions by the population in some regions of the country: murders of innocents, arson, personal vengeance killing, robberies and other disorders, we condemn them absolutely not only as unworthy of Christians but also quite simply as shameful and degrading . . . We wish to draw the attention of those responsible in the public forum to the duty which is incumbent on them to always respect the human person even and above all in the exercise of justice.[4]

In March, a tour by Anastase Makuza, President of the National Assembly, in which he gave several press conferences to European journalists, finally put the tragic events of 1963 into perspective.

Since the clergy of the Catholic Church in Rwanda were, owing to the inheritance of the colonial period, still largely Tutsi, the progressive purging from the republic of the Tutsi class was bound to have profound effects on ecclesiastical institutions. The racial tension—'racial' since the class differences of Tutsi and Hutu had for some time been articulated popularly in terms of ethnic affiliation even though intermarriage over a period of five centuries had made such distinctions largely spurious—was somewhat relaxed by the creation of Nyundo Diocese in 1952 under Bishop Aloys Bigirumwami, a Tutsi from the Rwanda vassal state of Gisaka of whose royal lineage he was a member. The Rwandan clergy had been allowed to choose in which diocese they should serve, with the result that the majority of the Tutsi clergy moved north to Nyundo while most of the Hutu stayed in south-central Rwanda. The process of finding Hutu priests who were *episcopabile* was not easy; owing to the cultural impoverishment of the peasantry under Tutsi rule, the Hutu had no tradition of scholarship and leadership. The great names of the Rwandan church, Kagame, Bushajiya, Janvier Mulenzi, were all from aristocratic Tutsi families. The brilliant Hutu priest, Bernard Manyurane, who was ordained Bishop of Ruhengeri on 28 January 1961, fell ill on 11 February and died in Rome on 8 May. It seems probable that he was poisoned.[5]

Thanks to the academic pre-eminence of the Tutsi abbés, they took up key positions in seminaries and, since so much of Rwanda's education was *de facto*, though after 1964 not *de jure* in clerical hands, it seemed as if the church controlled secondary education as a whole. The culturally conditioned disdain for *le petit Hutu* meant that Hutu pupils in the minor and major seminaries experienced the humiliating contempt of their superiors and this acted as a brake on their attainment. They were expected to be inferior to Tutsi pupils and, as recent educational experiments on black children in the States have shown, such predictions tend to be self-fulfilling even in conditions of unconscious dis-

[4] All such letters are published in French and Kinyarwanda.
[5] Unattributable interview.

crimination. Whether Hutu pupils had 'a chip on their shoulder', or whether their Tutsi teachers deliberately tried to humiliate them into failure, is of secondary importance to the fact that in the post-colonial period the Hutu experienced no psychologically satisfying academic success and attributed this continued failure to the continuing prominence of the Tutsi in positions of power within the education system.

What is not in dispute is that a disproportionately high percentage of Tutsi seminarians passed through siminary education in the dioceses of all bishops save that of Mgr Perraudin who tried, according to government policy, to peg the intake of Tutsi to the 10-15% level of the population as a whole. This may seem shocking but the Tutsi were undoubtedly trying to regain through the church what they had lost in the revolution in the state: positions of power and influence through which they could dominate national life. However little active support Mgr Bigirumwami gave for conservative, reactionary Tutsi priests in Nyundo diocese, they were tolerated and their presence was deeply resented by the predominantly Hutu population who had historically never been fully brought into the Tutsi feudal system. The Tutsi of Nyundo seminary formed, if not a political, certainly a cultural caucus, that was deeply antipathetic to the Hutu. Attempts to form councils of priests had to be abandoned since they polarized Tutsi-Hutu opinion in the diocese, and the resulting lack of communication between priests and bishop facilitated a process in which the Tutsi clergy became increasingly seen as alien oppressors.[6]

At the beginning of 1973 for a number of reasons including the simple one that many Hutu had left the seminaries to enter government employment where they were favoured, Rwanda's seminaries stood out, in popular opinion, as havens of Tutsi ascendancy, and the education system as the threatening stronghold of undiminished Tutsi power. The Hutu pupils, frightened that they would be cheated out of the revolution's fruits, and having tasted precious few of them anyway, reacted violently by expelling their Tutsi colleagues and teachers from educational centres, convents, noviciates and seminaries. It was initially a social reaction to diminishing job opportunities and the continued presence of Tutsi in important administrative posts, but grew into an attempt at a minor revolution within the Catholic Church which had come to epitomize for young Rwandans the wily retention of power by their former overlords, now disguised in soutanes.

On 22-23 February, the bishops of Rwanda met in extraordinary session to discuss the problem of the racial violence that had erupted in the country's education system. Tutsi pupils were being expelled from almost all secondary institutions after violent demonstrations against

[6] Unattributable interviews.

Tutsi at the university of Butare had given the lead. In their pastorals, the bishops spoke unequivocally of racialism:

These troubles aimed at eliminating the pupils of one ethnic group. Some went as far as wounding and pillage. In the last few days these menaces and the taking of the law into their own hands has grown to include employees and workers in private enterprise. Rumours are spread against priests and even prelates . . . The law of God as well as the declaration of the Rights of Man to which Rwanda subscribes, also the Rwandan constitution, are fundamentally opposed to these procedures of eliminating people and this persecution with its racial roots . . . If there are social problems to be resolved, and there is no lack of them, let those who are responsible, and not individuals and anonymous groups, do so by means of dialogue.[7]

On 25 February, the pupils at the St Pius X Seminary at Nyundo divided up into 'ethnic groups' and by the evening the Tutsi had fled to their villages. Two days later the pupils at the Ecole d'Art, opposite the seminary, were circulating a list of people who were to leave. During the night of 27-28 February the Tutsi teachers at the seminary fled to Zaïre via Goma together with twelve Tutsi major seminarists. Several hundred Tutsi were attacked in the prefectures of Kibuye and Kisenyi. On 12 April, Nyamasheke Mission was attacked by school pupils and Abbés Robert Matajyabo, Modeste Kajyibwami and Mathias Kambali wounded. On 27 April, Abbé J. Kashyengo of Kisenyi Mission fled to Zaïre, the twelfth Tutsi abbé to flee since the beginning of the troubles.[8]

Throughout March tension was high around Nyundo and anonymous notices were put on the church door calling for the departure of Mgr Bigirumwami with all his Tutsi clergy. On 26 March, the seminary head Mgr Matthieu, was dismissed and his place taken by Major Alexis Kanyarengwe and four days later the same 'secularization' took place at the Mater Ecclesiae Juvenat at Muramba; it was made into a girls' collège under the direction of Sister Twagiramariya Euphrasia.[9] On 4 April, after a message calling for calm had been broadcast to the nation on 22 March, the President, Dr. Grégoire Kayibanda, presided over a meeting of the Conseil du Gouvernement which condemned the violence in terms reminiscent of the bishops.

Thus the Government in conformity with the Party Manifesto of MDR-PARMEHUTU cannot tolerate that an individual or group of individuals set themselves up as able to take the law in their own hands (judging) people by reason of their racial origin, and will repress in conformity with the laws now in vigour, all infractions against goods or persons.[10]

---

[7] 10-11 March La Libre Belgique.
[8] Civitas Mariae Nos. 181, 180, 179, March to May 1973.
[9] ibid.
[10] Communiqué de la Présidence de la République Kigali, 4 April 1973.

The fact that the church condemned the racial violence one month before the government did not escape attention and drew down on the hierarchy the wrath of Rwanda students, studying in Belgium, almost all of whom were Hutu, although 65% of the university of Butare was still Tutsi (until the expulsions). They condemned the church for controlling education, ignoring the social problems of Rwanda and engaging in politics. Mgr Perraudin, the great champion of social justice during the struggle for Hutu emancipation, was described as 'the brake on all attempts at development and growth by the Rwandan people'. The document was answered point by point by Fr Dominic Nothomb emphasizing the social teaching of the church in pastoral letters throughout the period 1958-73.[11]

The wheel had turned full circle. From 1958-64, Mgr Perraudin had been the *bête noire* of the Tutsi and even as the anti-clerical students in Rwanda were criticising him for being pro-Tutsi, Radio Bujumbura was denouncing him for his role in the break-up of Tutsi feudalism. By calling for social justice and condemning racial violence the church had drawn the fire of both Hutu and Tutsi extremists. The same Hutu who had been immeasurably aided by Catholic support for a social justice platform in 1959, with the result that the revolution was seen by the Tutsi as an externally contrived Belgo-Catholic plot, now criticised Perraudin for demanding justice for the remaining Tutsi in revolutionary Rwanda, many of whom had reconciled themselves to life under a new regime.

Many observers felt that the hierarchy had gone too far in the February pastoral in calling the disorders 'racial' and failing to elaborate on the social dimension.[12] On the other hand, it was difficult to find any other word for a situation in which 'pure' Hutu students checked noses and fingers of their colleagues to ascertain their ethnic origin, and the hierarchy did list several pastorals to its credit on social justice. Even the government spoke of attacks on people 'en raison de leur appartenance raciale'. Nonetheless, it was certainly the 'racial' epithet which triggered the student reaction since it brought an African state, founded on a moral cause, into the innermost circle of political hell reserved for South Africa. Yet the way Hutu girls chased out their Tutsi colleagues from schools, and even some noviciates, indicates that a purely social aetiology of the events was inadequate. Sexual fears and jealousies, an element which perhaps more than any other indicates an added psychological dimension of racism in social conflict, were as relevant in the Hutu-Tutsi confrontation as in White-Black interrelations. It seems reasonable to suppose that racial language started as a type of ideological

[11] Nothomb, D. 'Note concernant la "Motion des Etudiants Hutu en Belgique" sur le problème Socio-Ethnique au Rwanda' 10 April 1973.
[12] Communiqué de la Présidence.

shorthand to communicate a more complex, and barely comprehended social analysis, but that after 1959 it achieved a certain autonomy to motivate finally an irrational level of social violence; such a conclusion is surely born out by the events of February-March 1973. It was, it seems to me, the pointing out of the irrational that so disturbed the Hutu intelligentsia in Belgium. Forgetful as they must have been in the materialist paradise of Brussels of the fragility of a social order based, as they saw it, on the highest principles of rationalism and democracy.

Apart from the real social conflicts within Rwanda, the growth of a racism was greatly facilitated by the widespread slaughter of Hutu in neighbouring Burundi; with a death toll reaching around 200,000 by May 1973, this could only be seen for what Radio Kigali proclaimed it to be, a systematic genocide of educated Hutu in Burundi.[13] It is known for certain that seventeen Hutu priests were executed in 1972 including the writer Michel Kayoya. The country's two Hutu bishops, Bihonda of Muyinga Diocese and Kaburungu of Ngozi Diocese, spent May 1972 under house arrest after a rebellion, led by the Hutu against the Tutsi regime of Michel Micombero, was ruthlessly repressed. The immediate public reaction of the Tutsi bishop of Bujumbura, Ntuyahaga, was to support the government line. He published a pastoral on 7 May and it was followed shortly by a pastoral from the Tutsi bishop of Gitega, Makarakiza, on 10 May in which the situation was represented as an attack by a foreign power. Only in the joint letter of the Burundi hierarchy signed on 24 May 1972 was there any reference to the severity and extent of the repression: 'Those who assume that a whole tribe had revolted and should therefore be exterminated are no different from those ruthless rebels and are guilty of grave injustice to a vast number of people'. Yet despite the previous record of Bishop Ntuyahaga, there was no mention of social justice nor the social causes of the rising. [He had discussed the appalling conditions of the Hutu at a council of priests in October 1969 and the Lenten Pastoral of all the bishops in 1970, *Charity and Peace through Justice*, dwelt at length on the social problems of Burundi.]

Despite the widespread realization by August 1972 that genocide was being committed and that the original rebellion of April had been an internal attempt at revolution, Burundi's five bishops instructed their clergy on 12 August according to government mythology.

> It would be wrong to see the problem as a classic instance of internal politics, a conflict between Hutu and Tutsi. It is rather a diabolical plot to deceive the people in order to foster racial hatred so that, in the process, some could get rid of those that stood in their way.

[13] Unattributable interview.

Almost exactly similar statements could be produced from spokesmen for the Tutsi party *UNAR* in Rwanda during the revolutionary period 1959-60. By 1973 the deportation of White Fathers from Burundi had become common and the animosity of the Tutsi clergy in Burundi towards the missionary personnel far exceeded anything experienced in Rwanda before the revolution. Again, in December 1972, the permanent secretariat of the clergy in Burundi published a booklet about the repression which white-washed the government and played down the gravity of the situation. In May 1973, after a raid by refugees from Rwanda, the repression gained momentum in Ngozi diocese with the estimated deaths of 25,000 Hutu.[14]

This type of mirror-image situation in Burundi in which the Tutsi-led church reacted to the most severe systematic extermination of the literate members of a racial group ever known to Africa, and the execution of seventeen of its Hutu clergy, with explanations amounting to demonology, and a refusal to denounce openly the government's hand in the repression, must have greatly contributed to the tension which exploded into an anti-Tutsi, anti-clerical movement at the beginning of 1973 in Rwanda.

The Tutsi vision of the Catholic Church after independence was strongly Platonic in its outlook. After the shock and disorder of the *jacquérie*, they appointed themselves guardians of the cultural heritage of the old kingdoms. They were modern men in the sense that no feudal substratum was necessary to support this new claim to power. In place of the dynastic *abiiru*, the guardians of the esoteric code that provided the legitimation for kingship and Tutsi class society, were to be the Catholic guardians of the new moral code, a Tutsi clergy whose rationality and cultural pre-eminence would qualify them for a new moral dominance in the Republic of Rwanda.

This dominance had characterized the role of the missionary church in Belgian Rwanda and its limitation as a qualification for supremacy had been pointed out by Abbé Alexis Kagame. He called it aptly *politicisme*.

C'est un système de sa nature inavoué, latent, qui, sous prétexte d'assurer les intérêts religieux réels, veut en réalité asseoir des bases solides à l'emprise dominatrice 'd'un corps culturel sur l'esprit des autochthones.[15]

---

[14] Unattributable interview.
[15] Kagam, A. *Le Colonialisme face à la doctrine missionaire à l'heure du Vatican II*, Butare 1964 (Written 1955), 144.
'It is a system which by its very nature is latent and unacknowledged; under the pretext of assuring the interest of Religion, or even on some occasions genuine religious interests, it wishes in reality to establish a solid foundation for the ascendancy and domination of a cultural framework over the Native mind.'

He was reacting at the time to the *politicisme* of a European-led Church which was supporting radical Hutu seminarians and priests. *Je vous ai compris, je comprends ce que vous avez voulu dire.* Who better than an *umwiiru* and Roman Catholic priest to characterize the nature of white imperialism for it differed in its cultural-religious dimension so little from the *politicisme* of Tutsi sub-imperialism. The post-independence 'Tutsi church was as *politiciste* as the pre-independence white church.

On the other hand, the Hutu clergy, trained largely under Tutsi auspices where they felt more keenly than anyone the *emprise dominatrice* could either passively accept a felt inferiority and hope for honorary membership of the Tutsi guardian class by reason of their priesthood, or like Alöys Nzamwita, Director of Education before the coup in 1973, leave a priesthood they saw to be corrupted by Tutsi ideas of guardianship. The model of the French revolution with a national clergy versus an old aristocratic clergy clinging to ancient privilege provides some insights into the Rwandan situation.[16] Many of the Tutsi saw the events in Rwanda as a local aberration which did not have Rome's approval; implicit in their judgement was the belief that theirs was the true Catholic Church while the Hutu had become prey to the social heresy of Mgr Perraudin. The felt inferiority of the Hutu priests was largely explained by the force of the Tutsi argument that they, the Tutsi abbés, were not only more Roman but more Rwandan in their Catholicism. They had the high culture of Rwanda and Rome. When Radio Bujumbura, more sophisticated in its propaganda than Radio Kigali, derided the Rwandan Hutu for being pawns of the Belgians and Monsignor Perraudin, it seemed true.[17] The position of the large missionary church was not to be envied.

In short the Rwandan experience has demonstrated the inadequacy of 'Africanization' as an end in itself. The overriding issue was which Africans, Tutsi or Hutu? In other words, what was the church: a custodian of ruling-class interests and culture, an embodiment of social inequality, or an agency for the transformation of society, a generator of social justice? Is the Christian church in Africa to be the prisoner of ethnic particularism, a passive mirror of state and society, as in Rwanda before the Second World War? Rwanda's stratified society asked these questions of the young church with an immediacy rarely encountered in other African nation-states. But nothing is surer than that in the next

---

[16] Some Tutsi abbés made virtually no accommodation to the new political ethos after independence, though this was rare.

[17] Radio Kigali and Radio Bujumbura engaged in a verbal battle between June 23-27, 1973 after attacks of Burundi in the Organisation of African Unity over alleged army assistance to Burundi refugees in the May border incursion. I believe Rwanda participated in this slanging match to divert attention from the north versus south-centre regional tension that finally ended in the coup of July 1973.

decade the African church in other states. will confront the same
question.

Was the Democratic Party of Uganda a purely confessional party?

MICHAEL TWADDLE

When Uganda achieved independence from Britain on 9 October 1962, it did so after an eventual struggle between three main political parties: the *Kabaka Yekka* ('the king alone') movement based upon Buganda and the Uganda Peoples Congress with support outside Buganda on the one hand, and the Democratic Party which campaigned in both areas on the other. In the first general election of March 1961 the Democratic party triumphed over the Uganda Peoples Congress, but this victory was greatly assisted by a boycott of territorial elections by the quasi-federal government of the Buganda kingdom. In the elections held during the following year, DP succumbed to the joint opposition of UPC and the recently-formed *Kabaka Yekka* movement. Since then, KY has excited considerable interest amongst scholars as an intriguing example of a neo-traditionalist party, and UPC has benefitted academically too from its period of political dominance. The Democratic Party, on the other hand, has been sadly neglected by political analysts. Emerging first as a tribal faction in Buganda during the early 1950s, it contested the first country-wide elections of 1958 as a territorial party, fought the 1961 and 1962 general elections as a genuinely popular movement, survived as a largely extra-parliamentary group during the years of UPC dominance before being temporarily suppressed by President Milton Obote in December 1969, and enjoyed a few days of glory immediately after the seizure of power in January 1971 by General Idi Amin before eventually being similarly crushed by Amin's arms. Clearly both UPC and KY deserve scholarly attention, but what is less clear is why DP should be so utterly neglected as a problem in political analysis. Yet when it has been considered at all by political scientists DP has tended to be dismissed as an institution 'predominantly Catholic in inspiration, leadership and support'.[1] Apart from these three aspects of DP, little else has struck scholars as requiring especial study in its highly variegated short history.

Superficially, the prominence accorded to politico-religious questions in the Uganda of President Idi Amin would seem to confirm the stress

---

[1] Thomas Hodgkin, *African Political Parties* (Harmondsworth, 1961), 206.

commonly put upon them in the earlier rise to power of Milton Obote. After all, Obote frequently referred in his speeches to 'religion' as well as 'tribe' constituting serious obstacles to Ugandan national unity, and statistics as well as history have appeared to many observers to confirm that Obote's warnings here were as academically correct as they were politically necessary. But there is a world of difference between a religious denomination providing the sociological material for political parties to work upon, and between that denomination also determining the character and course of party conflict. It is the main contention of this paper that the assumption (for it is really no more than an assumption) that DP was a Catholic party pure and simple neglects the crucial transformation that came over it once Benedicto Kiwanuka became its President in October 1958 and pays excessive attention, not only to some highly debatable statistical correlations, but also to an evolutionary view of history and a misplaced anxiety about the political influence of expatriate priests in non-Western societies during the latter phases of decolonization.

To be sure, there is an unfortunate history of earlier political antagonism in Uganda between Catholic and Protestant that most political scientists have felt unable to ignore. When British officials in the 1890s seized control of the nuclear area of what would shortly become the Uganda Protectorate, they did so at a time of considerable tension between Catholic and Protestant chiefs in the Buganda kingdom. Several years before the same men had fought off an attempt by Muslim Baganda to transform their kingdom into an Islamic state, but the necessity of formulating alternative policies to the Muslims precipitated the formation of separate Catholic and Protestant successor parties. As British rule expanded outside Buganda during the early years of this century, and as Christianity too extended into these areas through the agencies of the Church Missionary Society and its principal Catholic rivals, the White Fathers, the Mill Hill Fathers and the Verona Fathers, there was a marked tendency for politico-religious conflicts to be replicated throughout the Uganda Protectorate. When DP was founded during the 1950s only a few years after the Uganda National Congress had been successfully launched throughout the Uganda Protectorate, political scientists were not surprised. It seemed a further projection of an earlier trend.

Besides earlier politico-religious tensions, a further explanation for the success of DP has been sought in priestly inspiration. Much play has been made here of the initial naming of DP as the 'Christian Democratic Party', and of the various European nationalities of many Catholic priests working in Uganda. There are also certain proof texts that tend to crop up repeatedly in introductions to studies of other Ugandan political parties. One such document is the pastoral letter issued by the Catholic bishops of Uganda shortly before the first countrywide elections of 1958, stating that 'Catholics may not give their vote to any party or candidate whose programme is directed against God's law' and advising those with doubts about particular cases to consult their local priest. Other proof texts are the two pamphlets written by Father Tourigny while he was national director of Catholic Action in Uganda in 1956. There Tourigny remarked among other things that whereas DP had been 'received with enthusiasm in all Catholic quarters' the Uganda National Congress needed close watching ('the religious authorities strongly disapprove of the adhesion of Catholics to the Congress although no direct condemnation of it has been issued by the hierarchy'). While such remarks must indeed be deemed unfriendly to UNC, it is the office held by their author that has struck scholars as being the most significant thing about them. 'Not surprisingly', writes Colin Leys,[2]

> The Catholic hierarchy, working through Catholic Action, saw the opportunity which a democratic franchise would provide for giving an end to their sixty-year-old disability [before Protestant chiefly ascendancies in so many parts of Uganda] and between 1954 and 1956 they launched the Democratic Party throughout the districts and kingdoms; the fact that it was originally to have been called the Christian Democratic Party indicates the analogy with European Christian Democratic parties which guided the thinking of the founders of the DP. Building on the mission and mission-school system throughout the country the party soon had a considerable following, and in the years before independence established itself as the leading party in local elections in Ankole, Kigezi, Acholi and West Nile. It ranged itself sharply against the other principal political party, the Uganda National Congress formed in 1952, castigating it as communist and ungodly.

To be sure, Leys admits that by the time he personally observed DP in action in Acholi district during 1964 it 'had become a coalition of personalities and areas which, though certainly Catholic, was no longer dependent on the Church for either leadership or funds', but even this admission is qualified by the remark that 'it is hard to believe that any party formed after the UNC was established could have atracted much support but for the initiative and backing of the expatriate priests in the missions'.[3]

Nevertheless, to all who have mentioned DP however briefly in view of the pressing interest of other Uganda political parties, its Catholic character is chiefly assumed because of the nature of its presumed

[2] Colin Leys, *Politicians and Policies, an essay on politics in Acholi, Uganda, 1962-5* (Nairobi, 1967), 5-6.
[3] Ibid. 18.

support. To David Apter the success of DP in recruiting members outside Buganda is primarily explicable in terms of its 'overwhelming Catholic membership'.[4] To Colin Leys too DP-UPC competition is considered to have been 'based upon religion':[5] but whereas Apter simply assumes Catholic support, Leys does mention some statistics relating to the 1961 election:

> The greater the percentage of Protestants in a district, the higher the vote for the UPC. The greater the percentage of Catholics, the higher the vote for the DP. The relation between the DP and Catholicism, however, was considerably closer than that between the UPC and Protestantism. Thus the UPC was considerably more successful in expanding beyond its religious base.[6]

It is principally upon this correlation between religious allegiance and voting behaviour in Uganda that the assertion that:

> unlike nearly all other multi-party systems in Africa, the UPC-DP struggle was not a competition between ethnic groups with their characteristic regional bases. It was a competition between the adherents of the Roman Catholic church, wherever it was established, and, in effect, everybody else[7]

is based, and it is with this statistical correlation that our critique of DP having been purely a confessional party must start.

Analytically the basic trouble with taking seriously the correlation between voting support for a political party and denominational numbers in the case of DP is that it imputes a relationship between action and belief that is at best tautological and at worst disdainful of the real nature of political conflict in late colonial Uganda. To be sure, many early and late DP members were Catholics, but so then were many Ugandans; many more, in fact, than were Protestant, a fact that is conveniently not allowed for in the customary correlation between voting behaviour and religious affiliation in late colonial Uganda.

Below district level in Uganda statistics on religious allegiance are not available, but what little evidence there is about constituency contests between DP and UPC during the 1961 and 1962 general elections does not confirm the wisdom of making any mechanical correlations between religious allegiance and voting behaviour. For upon closer inspection in the Bukedi district of eastern Uganda, such correlations dissolve into a myriad of patron-client relationships linking aspiring notables to a

[4] David E. Apter, *The Political Kingdom in Uganda* (Princeton and London, 1961), 309.
[5] Leys, *Politicians and Policies*, 11.
[6] D. Rothchild and M Rogin, 'Uganda' in Gwendolen M. Carter, ed., *National Unity and Regionalism in Eight African States* (Ithaca and London, 1966), 380.
[7] Leys, *Politicians and Policies*, 11.

multitude of local coalitions of voters that defy classification in purely religious terms.[8] To be sure, Bukedi district may be atypical of Uganda as a whole because of its supposedly unusually complicated local politics,[9] but Bukedi is one of the few districts in Uganda where an attempt has been made, on the basis of voting support for all Catholic candidates in the 1958 election and for only DP ones in the 1961 district council elections, to see evidence of DPs success in 'organizing' the Catholic vote more effectively as time progressed.[10] True also, eastern Uganda as a whole may be suspect as a basis for any wider generalizations about the political action of religion in Uganda because of the supposedly more detached attitude towards politics of the Mill Hill Fathers compared with their colleagues in the White Fathers and Verona Fathers. Personal research suggests otherwise (Father Lyding of Budadiri mission in Bugisu district was surely as 'political' an expatriate priest as any other in late colonial Uganda); but one must agree with Professors Mackenzie and Robinson that at best individual constituency studies can only be illustrations of electoral tendencies, not conclusions.[11] However, in the almost complete absence of other data about UPC-DP conflict at constituency level elsewhere in Uganda, the evidence from Bukedi may perhaps be allowed to suggest at least one alternative hypothesis to the accepted wisdom. This is the suggestion that, but for outbursts such as those of Father Tourigny and the analytical convenience of an evolutionary view of history, it is most unlikely that religious allegiance as such would have been granted such a high status in scholarly explanations of the decolonization process in Uganda.

It was perhaps to be expected that some historians would explain the present in terms of the past, but political scientists ought to have known better. Too much has been assumed from the fact that the first president of DP was Matiya Mugwanga, a leading Catholic chief in Buganda and erstwhile candidate for the post of chief minister in the Kabaka's government: too little from the transformation that came over DP when Benedicto Kiwanuka became its president in October 1958. Whenever this switchover has been mentioned, Kiwanuka's appointment of leading Protestant Ugandans to executive positions in DP during 1960 has been dismissed as political window-dressing, and his ideology (stressing

---

[8] See Michael Twaddle, 'The politician as agitator in eastern Uganda' in W. H. Morris-Jones, ed., *The making of politicians: studies from Africa and Asia* (London, 1976).

[9] Rothchild and Rogin, 'Uganda', 382.

[10] Martin Lowenkopf, 'Political parties in Uganda and Tanganyika', MSc dissertation, London University, 1961, 91.

[11] W. J. M. Mackenzie and K. E. Robinson, *Five Elections in Africa* (London 1960), 487.

nationalism and democracy) dismissed as an epiphenomenon of Catholic theology. Instead of concentrating upon the crucial political developments emanating from October 1958, essence has been inferred from origin and the enduring Catholic character of DP deduced from its early history as a parochial faction of mostly Catholic chiefs operating in the Buganda kingdom during the early 1950s. This is not only bad history but bad political science, for only by treating the Democratic Party that contested the 1961 and 1962 elections as the mindless prisoner of its pre-1958 past can the most militant nationalist party to arise in late colonial Uganda be dismissed as merely the Roman Catholic Church at the polls.

To be sure, there is also subjective suspicion about expatriate priests at work here. But had DP really been established quite so firmly as a confessional party on the European Christian Democratic model in the early 1950s, one would expect more philosophical underpinning than just a few unfriendly remarks by one expatriate priest and just one pastoral letter ostensibly designed more to protect Catholic interests in schools than to foster the development of any one political party. To be sure, an attempt has recently been made to document a sustained 'programme of political indoctrination' in favour of DP supposedly conducted in the pages of two northern Ugandan missionary journals,[12] but the actual evidence adduced to substantiate this supposed campaign seems ambiguous at best. *Lobo Mewa*, a Lwo newspaper, and *Leadership*, an English magazine, were scanned for references to political events in the three crucial years 1958, 1961 and 1962. For 1958—the year by which DP is supposed to have been assiduously spread throughout Uganda by ecclesiastical stealth, but a year in which only one MP was elected to Legislative Council on the DP ticket (Gaspare Oda of West Nile District)—very few references to politics of any sort were found. There was also an 'almost virtual absence of political controversy' in *Lobo Mewa*. *Leadership* did refer to a conviction that 'the Catholics as a group were not getting their due share from the Government, both central and local, when it comes to the allocation of public resources, notably public offices, aids to schools and scholarships', but these grievances do not seem to have been especially related in print to the Democratic Party. In sum, only three grounds of 'partiality for the Democratic Party' are in fact suggested:

(i) a few general articles on the dangers of world communism in each year;

(ii) a statement in 1958 that DP was not a Catholic party, but that Catholics were free to join it and also to encourage others to do so too;

[12] A. G. G. Gingyera-Pincycwa, 'The Missionary Press and the Development of Political Awareness in Uganda 1952-62: A Case Study from Northern Uganda', *Dini na Mila* iv, 2 (May 1970).

(iii) a comment on the 1961 elections, replying to the UPC allegation that DP had only won them because of the 'active participation of a religious denomination'. ('The explanation [for UPC failure] lies in the open attacks which Mr Obote made in North[ern] Prov[ince] against the Church. No wonder now if Catholics want to defend their faith and their institutions; and they have done so with the ballot. "Leadership" has always encouraged people to defend Catholic institutions').

To treat such statements as evidence of political indoctrination really seems slightly dotty, since all that one may legitimately deduce from them is that the Catholic Church in Uganda was openly concerned to defend its interests in schooling and to encourage Catholics to make the most of the opportunities provided by democratic politics.

None of the supposed grounds for DP being a purely confessional party—inspiration, leadership or support—therefore seem especially conclusive, and Obote himself appears to have acted accordingly in the run-up to the 1962 elections: UPC entered those elections with a manifesto pledging non-interference with voluntarily-run schools as well as with almost as many Catholic notables amongst its candidates for parliament as there were Protestants on the DP side. Granted this latter-day switch in electoral tactics by UPC, it is hardly surprising to find a much smaller statistical correlation between Protestantism and UPC support in overall terms. Vote-catching was more a matter of producing attractive patrons and policies in these elections than a mindless positioning of the faithful.

In the second (and, as yet, last) general election in Uganda, Obote proved much more adept at trimming his electoral sails to changing political winds than did Kiwanuka, and doubtless part of the reason for this lay also in the contrasting character of UPC as a political party: not a largely extra-parliamentary party like DP but an intra-parliamentary clique of MPs initially mostly elected as independents in the 1958 elections. Various explanations have been advanced for the comparatively late development of nationalist parties in Uganda (tribal differences, few Africans educated abroad, small indigenous urban population, no *lingua franca*, the policy of indirect rule), but the suggestion that it was Catholicism which irretrievably split the nationalist movement seems the least plausible of all. We have it on the authority of one of the early UNC militants most respected by David Apter for his intellectual calibre that 'we could have arrived at 9 October [Independence Day, 1962] some four years ago but we made the fatal error of splitting the party and we were where we had started'.[13] It seems

---

[13] Erisa Kironde, 'Before' in *Transition* (October 1962).

unnecessary to turn human error here into an act of God.

Certain political scientists, of whom David Apter is undoubtedly one, have tended to assume otherwise, and before proceeding further we should perhaps note why. When Apter studied Ugandan politics the very idea of tracing the development of any political party in institutional terms seemed somewhat old-fashioned; it was informal structure rather than formal organization that provided the best key to political understanding, and where informal structure was concerned nothing seemed more important than religion. Apter's three-fold division of African political parties into mobilization systems, consociational systems and modernizing autocracies assumed that in each of them religion performed a function in politics comparable to cement in building-construction: it bound political systems together. In modernizing autocracies like Buganda it was tradition itself that became the 'political religion' filtering change through the medium of traditional institutions. In mobilization systems like Ghana, African socialism played a comparable but much more radical role. With consociational systems, which fell somewhere in-between, religion also performed crucial integrative functions and in the Ugandan case it was clearly Catholicism that was most important in this respect, both positively and negatively. Not that Apter is unkind to priests. The 'main impetus' behind DP he detected, not in priestly conspiracy, but in the generally 'aggrieved views of Catholics [in Buganda] who find themselves restricted to an obsolete system of awarding chieftaincies on the basis of religion, while the total Catholic membership of Buganda is larger than that of any other single group'.[14] One trouble with this particular suggestion is that what is true of factional politics in the Buganda *lukiiko* is also assumed to be true of wider African constituencies both inside and outside Buganda; but did every Ugandan peasant really want to become an appointive chief on the Buganda model? Apter's approach also distinguishes insufficiently distinctly between religious belief-systems and political ideologies.[15]

It would be extremely foolish to deny that Catholicism had no influence upon DP ideology as it was refashioned in Kiwanuka's hands, but it is a very different matter to conclude that the two are indistinguishable. The stress on 'democracy' as well as 'nationalism' in DP ideology certainly appealed to the constituency of Catholics in Buganda who felt themselves oppressed by undemocratic practices in the Buganda *lukiiko*. But so too did it to Muslims beyond as well as within Buganda, and the story of Muslim participation in DP has only just

---

[14] Apter, *Political Kingdom*, 342.

[15] This point is elaborated in my essay on 'Ganda receptivity to change', *Journal of African history* xv (1974).

begun to be told.[16] The strain of anti-communism in DP ideology also owes much to Christian missions in Uganda, albeit to Protestant as well as Catholic ones, but this particular strain has tended to give DP a misleadingly moderate image when compared with UPC. In fact, DP was by far the most militant and radical of the political parties contesting the 1961 and 1962 elections in Uganda. The Uganda National Congress had certainly been a radical party, effectively combining popular support in Buganda during the period of the Kabaka's deportation (1953-55) with a populist programme of attacks upon arbitrary government elsewhere in Uganda. But long before DP became a real political force in Uganda (during 1959, if Bishop Russell is to be followed [17]) UNC had split irretrievably over the issue of the leadership qualities of Ignatius Musazi, and younger educated militants in UNC had left to found a diversity of other abortive political parties. Benedicto Kiwanuka was the true heir of Ignatius Musazi, combining support in Buganda with the role of agitator in other parts of Uganda in a fashion that most political scientists have found totally incomprehensible. Not only did Kiwanuka successfully retain the support of younger intellectuals which Musazi had so lamentably failed to do, but he also acquired considerable support amongst poorer urban Africans in Uganda because of his militant stance on both Africanization and economic development. In large measure Kiwanuka was able to do this because his position as a successful Kampala lawyer gave him financial independence, whereas his earlier experience as a schoolboy of life in South Africa stiffened his stance on Africanization and the need for a swift transition to independence. In comparison, Obote seems a distinctly conservative figure, as perhaps befits a party president who first came to power as leader of an intra-parliamentary clique. Kiwanuka's stress upon 'democracy' was deeply subversive of those local networks of notables which formed so much of the political backbone of UPC as well as KY. That DP won the general election of 1961 seems less surprising in retrospect than that it lost the 1962 one.

In the literature on Uganda the first of these elections is usually considered a moral defeat for DP, though it was DP that seized most seats in the Legislative Council. But this was largely because the Buganda government boycotted the elections, and DP won 19 of the 22 seats allotted to Buganda on a tiny poll:

> Thus, in spite of polling fewer votes than UPC in the whole count, 415,000 to 495,000, DP won forty-four of the eighty-two elective seats in the Legislative Council, thanks to their one-sided victory in

[16] See footnote 8.

[17] J. K. Russell, *Men without God? A study of the impact of the Christian message in the north of Uganda* (London, 1966), 41-2.

Buganda . . . Considering DPs defeat up-country and their inability to count upon winning even half of Buganda's twenty-one seats [in a straight contest], the position of the Government party at the London conference was indeed tenuous.[18]

Or so it appeared to most outside observers. The *Kabaka Yekka* party did not make the same mistake. Even after it had been agreed that MPs from Buganda would be indirectly elected by a majority of the Buganda *lukiiko* (the *lukiiko* itself being chosen at fresh elections in February 1962 at which Buganda government officials would act as both registration officers and returning officials), KY organisers were unhappy. A KY report on *lukiiko* constituencies compiled only a month before the *lukiiko* elections actually took place 'expressed doubts about the Kabaka's prospects in nearly half of them'.[19] In fact, KY won all but three seats, and it is difficult not to sympathize with Kiwanuka's accusations of widespread vote-fixing by returning officers.[20] It is also difficult not to sympathise with Kiwanuka's suggestion of a Protestant priestly plot at the London conference of 1961. After all, it was there that Mutesa II was 'most insistent . . . that the local chiefs [of Buganda] should be election officers' and also there that the Buganda government delegation successfully persuaded the British government to impose indirect rather than direct elections upon Buganda.[21] This involved the British Colonial Secretary concerned (Iain Macleod) reneging on an earlier assurance to Kiwanuka that all elections to the new Legco would be direct ones, and the likelihood of an Anglican plot here in the form of supporting advice as to the wisdom of indirect elections seems much more likely than supposed priestly inspiration behind DP could ever appear. Nevertheless while the first conspiracy has been almost universally pooh-poohed by scholars (M. S. M. Kiwanuka seems the only one to take it seriously[22]), the second one has passed into the standard accounts as a straightforward matter of fact.

If Kiwanuka was justifiably disappointed to win only three seats in the Buganda *lukiiko* elections of February 1962, he was even more surprised when DP gained so few seats outside Buganda in the general election two months later. Nor was Kiwanuka alone in this surprise: as we shall shortly see, the magazine *Africa Confidential* expected DP to win a small

---

[18] M. Lowenkopf, 'Uganda: prelude to independence', *Parliamentary Affairs* xv (1961), 84-5.

[19] I. R. Hancock, 'Patriotism and Neo-Traditionalism in Buganda: the Kabaka Yekka ('The King Alone') Movement, 1961-1962', *J.A.H.* xi (1970), 432 note 42.

[20] Benedicto Kiwanuka, 'Address to the Annual General Meeting, 27 October 1962'; repr. in *The Democrat* (May 1969).

[21] Kabaka of Buganda, *Desecration of my kingdom* (London, 1967), 161-3.

[22] M. S. M. Kiwanuka, letter in *East Africa Journal* (February 1967), 5.

majority over both KY and UPC in the 1962 elections. Why did DP lose? There seem three basic explanations besides the one already mentioned (the indirect method of electing the new Buganda MPs through Buganda *lukiiko*). To start with, the *lukiiko* elections were too close in time to the territorial ones for Kiwanuka to be able to capitalize upon the anti-Buganda feeling outside Buganda that exploded in the aftermath of the UPC-KY alliance announced at the London conference.[23] Secondly, many local political networks outside Buganda seem to have been won over to UPC during the immediate run-up to the general election by the belief that Obote was a more likely winner than Kiwanuka because of KY support: here evidence from Bukedi district is probably not atypical. Finally, as in the 1961 election, UPC seems to have benefitted more than DP from the Asian vote.

After the 1962 elections, Benedicto Kiwanuka did not become one of the specially-elected members of Legislative Council as he might legitimately have expected. However, he was re-elected president of DP at the next delegates' conference, and thereafter he continued to play the role of agitator, albeit increasingly furtively as DP Members of Parliament crossed over to the UPC side in growing numbers and the Obote regime increasingly cracked down upon political opposition, first in the Buganda kingdom, then elsewhere in Uganda. After the toppling from power of Milton Obote, Benedicto Kiwanuka enjoyed a short period of prominence as Chief Justice, but his courageous defence of the rule of law in the face of tyranny caused him to be brutally eliminated by Idi Amin. Kiwanuka's words at the London conference of 1961 provide his political epitaph: 'I have expressed the views of democracy and nationalism . . . I have not compromised'.

The common assumption of scholars that DP was 'predominantly Catholic in leadership, inspiration and support' therefore requires considerable revision. The situation noted by Colin Leys whereby DP became 'a coalition of personalities and areas which, though certainly Catholic was no longer dependent on the Church for either leadership or funds' was one that seems to have come into being not at independence, but several years before when Benedicto Kiwanuka assumed the presidency of DP. Before and after this, the Catholic hierarchy in Uganda was concerned to defend its interests especially where church schools were concerned, and in the early 1950s the Catholic hierarchy may well have thought that these interests were best defended by supporting Catholic candidates at forthcoming elections. In 1961 the Catholic hierarchy in Uganda again threw its support behind DP, albeit

---

[23] B. D. Bowles, 'The Development of the Concept of Uganda as a Nation among Uganda Africans', PhD dissertation, Makerere University, 1971, 278.

this time at second remove (as is evidenced by Archbishop Kiwanuka's defence of democracy in Buganda and the remarks in *Leadership* magazine about what happened to African politicians who attacked the Catholic church). In 1962 this mistake was not repeated by UPC: though DP continued to be attacked at party meetings for its supposed sectionalism, there was no explicit attack upon church schools in the UPC manifesto.

After independence, there was a running battle over church schools, particularly in Buganda where the Kabaka's government allied with church authorities in Masaka and Rubaga dioceses to delay any takeover by the central government.[24] In the light of this alliance, Apter's remarks about the role of Catholicism in transcending ethnic ties in Ugandan politics ('Only the Catholic political groups have been able to call upon people's loyalties to lessen the effects of ethnicity'[25]) read somewhat ironically. But it is unlikely that it would have made much difference either to Uganda or to the Roman Catholic Church if Benedicto Kiwanuka rather than Milton Obote had won the 1962 election. It is unlikely that as tough a leader as Kiwanuka would have tolerated the continuance of extra-territorial control of Ugandan schooling any more than Obote did, and it is unlikely that Kiwanuka would have had much more political luck with separatist sentiment in Buganda. When Obote finally came round to organizing another general election shortly before his overthrow, the sort of support he evidently expected appears to have been very much like the sort DP had enjoyed at the 1961 election: little in Buganda or amongst the Asians, but substantial amounts elsewhere. Early in 1962 *Africa Confidential* suggested what might happen if DP won the forthcoming election:

> The indications are that Uganda's first year of independence will bring disappointment with lower incomes all round. There will be discontent as in Tanganyika, but if, as seems likely, DP are returned by a short head, they will not be able to rely on a one-party system to help them out. They may have to face a running fight in Buganda and from the UPC unless strong-arm methods are applied; and these, once started, may be difficult to stop.[26]

It was not to be so very different under UPC. Nor, for that matter, under Idi Amin.

---

[24] See Apolo Nsibambi, 'The Uganda Central Government's attempts to acquire effective control in administering education, 1962-70', *Proceedings of the Social Science Conference, Makerere, 1971.*

[25] Apter, *Political Kingdom*, 306.

[26] *Africa Confidential,* 3 February 1962.

The emerging pattern of Church and State co-operation in Kenya

JOHN LONSDALE, WITH STANLEY BOOTH-CLIBBORN
AND ANDREW HAKE.[1]

The historical and theological context of cooperation

Apart from the Roman Catholic Church, the churches in Kenya—and they are many—have historically possessed a very limited theology of secular power. The Catholic Church has moreover been inhibited from articulating its vision of the State and the right use of its earthly power by two historical circumstances at least, one general to Catholic missionary enterprise in Africa, the other particular to Kenya as a former British colony. For Kenya, in common with the rest of tropical Africa, has come within the orbit of Christendom too recently, too eclectically and too partially for the Church to echo, even unconsciously, old papal claims to mundane jurisdiction; and in colonial Kenya the majority of Catholic missionaries were not British but, rather, Italians, Dutch and Irish and as 'outsiders', reluctant to hold a public opinion.[2] This latter disability was shared by many Protestant missionaries, over half of whom have come from North America.

---

[1] This is a revised and amalgamated version of two papers originally contributed to the School of Oriental and African Studies' seminar on Christianity in post-colonial Africa, in 1974. We wish to acknowledge the helpful comments from members of the seminar and, from East Africa, of the Rev. J. Riddelsdell, then Acting Principal of St Paul's United Theological College, Limuru, and of Dr Kevin Ward, now on the staff of the Bishop Tucker Theological College, Mukono, Uganda, while exonerating them from all responsibility. It ought to be explained that the second and third of the co-authors were active participants in some of the developments described, as members of the permanent staff of the National Christian Council of Kenya. Their concurrence with the argument presented here is given in their individual capacity and should in no way be taken to represent the view of the Council. A more complete account of Christian involvement in the problems of Nairobi will be found in Andrew Hake, *African Metropolis* (Sussex University Press, 1977).

[2] An opinion expressed by the Vicar Apostolic of Zanzibar, 19 June 1934: National Christian Council of Kenya Archives, Race Relations Committee papers, file 2/A. And in Kenya the Catholic Fathers have never in recent years sought to sponsor a confessional political party like the Democratic Party in Uganda, although there was a missionary-sponsored Native Catholic Union between the wars in a situation when most political associations had affiliations with the Protestant missions.

Among the non-Roman denominations (and it is with these that the rest of the chapter is concerned) there have been two distinct theological positions, the conservative evangelical and the modernist or liberal, which were most fundamentally divided on the issue of the historical accuracy of the Scriptures. The conservative evangelical tradition has been the stronger of the two in Kenya and, in addition to its fundamentalist insistence on the strict authenticity of the Bible, has tended to place a strong, eschatological emphasis on individual salvation rather than social improvement in this world. To the conservative evangelicals their modernist brethren were distinguished by their emphasis on Christ as Perfect Man as well as God, their over-concern with ethics at the apparent expense of faith, their social rather than individual gospel. It is easy however to overdo the distinction and, in the case of Kenya at least, misleading to imply that the modernist missionary persuasion was necessarily more prophetic in its relationship to secular authority—at least before the 1950s, when African nationalism first effectively questioned the legitimacy of colonial rule. Until then the missionaries of both persuasions accepted that the colonial State provided a necessary and generally benevolent framework of order for their work.

When one examines their specifically evangelistic policies it is possible to argue that the conservative evangelicals were, in effect, more revolutionary in the social and political fields than the liberal modernists. For liberal churchmen who increasingly accepted the tenets of cultural relativism either tried to rephrase African custom in Christian terms, or, where this did not seem to be desirable, trusted in the gradual influence of 'civilization' on a society to erode it away. The evangelicals put more trust in the power of their converts' faith to confront and eradicate in themselves as individuals all adherence to practices which the missionaries held to be repugnant. The evangelicals therefore tended to challenge tribal authority—and the colonial stability which depended on it—in ways which modernists increasingly saw as unnecessary, perhaps even harmful, to the spread of the faith, and which government officials resented as being gratuitously offensive to African sentiment. As late as the 1920s some American evangelicals could see the tension between private faith and public 'improvement' in terms strong enough to justify refusal of the state's assistance to their mission schools.[3] But what enabled the two British societies, the Church Missionary Society and Church of Scotland Mission, to accept the state's aid in their educational

---

[3] For example, correspondence between the Friends Africa Mission and the government's Director of Education, 1924 to 1927: Kaimosi Mission Archives, file II/1/1. There was no necessary connection between a conservative evangelical theology and a poor educational system, as the Friends' own school at Kamusinga and the Seventh Day Adventists' schools in South Nyanza were later to show.

systems was not so much their modernism—for in the inter-war years there were still many conservative evangelicals among their leaders—as the colonial state's readiness to accord to them a quasi-established position in public life. The congregation at Nairobi's Anglican cathedral has been described, not inaccurately, as the colonial power at prayer; and at St Andrew's down the road would have been found many of its men of business.

Establishment imposed political obligations: it did not confer political licence. It was the duty of the Church, not to embarrass the state power but to influence it, to persuade in private rather than pronounce in public. Neither of the two Protestant theological traditions therefore encouraged the churches to play a prophetic role in society, to act as the public conscience of the State. The conservative evangelical position was at once too exclusive in its claims and too distant from the seat of power. This was most emphatically the case for the African independent churches, generally speaking of a fundamentalist persuasion, who were pre-occupied with the problems of evil, sickness and authority at the level of the congregation rather than the nation. The liberal position on the other hand, while by no means captive, was at least constrained by the rules of privileged access to the ear of the governors. At independence, the churches in Kenya would have assented more readily to the teachings of *Romans* 13 on earthly power than to those in *Revelation*.

This was not true of the National Christian Council of Kenya. In the early 1960s the NCCK had a wider church membership, and was much stronger in full-time staff and resources than its equivalents elsewhere in Africa.[4] This was a direct consequence of the Emergency years of the 1950s, when Inter-Church Aid (now Christian Aid), presented the Christian Council of Kenya (as it then was) with the external resources needed to meet the Christian challenge of post-Mau Mau reconstruction in the neglected pastoral fields of town and industry and in the political field as well, through the press. New missionaries were recruited, employed directly by the NCCK rather than by its member churches. Their theology was liberal, their gospel as much social as individual. Their work, in industry, in urban community development and in journalism, involved them directly in areas of public policy. It was in the decade preceding independence that there appeared to be the clearest evidence of the distinction between a conservative theology of Christian withdrawal from the world and a liberal theology of active social and political involvement. Relations between the NCCK and its member churches were not infrequently strained by ecumenical excursions into 'politics'. It is however open to question whether this division was

---

[4] Sixteen member churches were listed in 1961—a number which has been added to yearly.

attributable wholly to differing theologies. At least as important was the fact that the NCCK staff had no organic or historical connexion with the local environment. They were inhibited neither by the conventions of the colonial situation, nor by the politically divided traditions of rural congregations which were particularly a feature of Kikuyuland. The NCCK was free to be 'alongside' the new African politics—to the extent of appointing as its general secretary in 1962 John Kamau, who had spent three years of the Emergency in detention—in a way in which the local churches would have found difficult even if their leaders had thought it desirable.[5]

Kenya's post-war history had ensured that the mission churches would be more than usually closely associated with the colonial regime. Their African members in Kikuyuland, especially those whose faith had been deepened by the experience of Revival,* had been prominent in the initial resistance to the spread of Mau Mau and had then formed the nucleus of the Kikuyu Home Guard. A church dedicated to their martyrs was opened by the Archbishop of Canterbury. In the detention camps the churches were enlisted in the work of 'rehabilitation', which culminated in a cleansing ceremony in which the burden of repentance was placed squarely on the detainee. It was a rare Christian voice, black or white, which affirmed that this was a situation in which all were guilty; and it took a significant amount of moral courage for Christian leaders to denounce state terror against Mau Mau, whether casually employed by the security forces or institutionalized by the gallows. For a great many Christians the defeat of Mau Mau was a Christian victory; it demanded a great moral commitment. The churches were not well placed to detach themselves from the colonial definition of reality in order to consider afresh the moral claims of African nationalism when it returned in more peaceable guise. To most nationalists, the churches' blessings on *Uhuru* must have seemed too late to be wholehearted—and indeed there were not a few Christians, especially Kikuyu Christians, who feared that any renewed persecution by their former enemies would now be legitimized by the nationalists' assumption of state power.

The attitudes of political leaders themselves were, and remain ambivalent and self-contradictory.[6] They are naturally apprehensive about rivals in authority, conscious as they must be of the fragility of

---

[5] The NCCK's alignment was welcomed by Tom Mboya, in *Freedom and After* (London, 1963), p. 22. Individual missionaries found it easy to be on friendly terms with African politicians, many of whom were their former pupils.

*See above p. 74 and below p. 550.

[6] See for example Tom Mboya, who in the same breath complained that the churches were slow to take up African grievances under colonialism, congratulated them when they did, and warned the church after independence to 'preoccupy itself entirely with religious matters'. *Freedom and After* pp. 22-3.

state power. But this realization also makes them value the sacral supports the Church can give to the authority, not only of the State but also of the family—a nagging preoccupation at a time of rapid urbanization. Cabinet Ministers and other dignitaries spend much of their public time in opening schools, local leaders' conferences, or urban welfare projects, with speeches that extol civic and Christian virtues. Such occasions for public exhortation are particularly important in Kenya where the political party has been allowed to wither away; the church and other voluntary associations have inevitably become more instrumental to government in its efforts to enlist popular participation in 'nation-building' campaigns against poverty, ignorance and disease.

This wary government co-optation of the churches in the promotion of order and welfare has occurred in the almost total absence of any public, or for that matter, academic, debate on what can properly be called political philosophy. Anti-colonial nationalism in Kenya did not feel the need to justify itself in any terms other than what was widely accepted to be the self-evident right of its African peoples both to self-rule—a concept whose inconsistencies it was impolitic to examine too closely in a multi-cultural State—and to material improvement. To the extent that Kenyans had supported the nationalist movement the authority of the post-colonial State could be said to be derived from below, from the consent of the people. But even more than most nationalisms Kenya's had been divided not only by languages and cultures but also by an emerging social differentiation which issued increasingly in landlessness among the rural poor. The populism inherent in the state's authority has therefore more often been used by the State itself in order to blur, indeed to deny, social division, than critically examined by individuals in order to define the limitations on and accountability of the state's power.[7] Not until recently therefore—a point to which we shall return—have the churches been obliged to expound in any comprehensive way their own attitude to secular authority and obedience. The teleological assumptions of Christianity were not required to be spelled out, for lack of any clear ideological rival in nationalism. Nor, in Kenya, has socialism's variant of the ascending doctrine of secular power yet gained sufficient momentum to demand from the churches a considered response.

The institution which intellectually equips most young Protestant clergy for the new age is St Paul's United Theological College at Limuru, in the Kikuyu hills above Nairobi. And for St Paul's, as for other organizations, the nationalist and independence years were a period of transition and internal dissension rather than certainty. Around 1950 its theological training had emphasized the New Testament and individual

[7] See the discussion by John Saul on 'Africa', in G. Ionescn and E. Gellner (eds.), *Populism, its meanings and national characteristics* (London, 1969).

salvation; and in its teaching on the Old Testament the college seemed unaware that its prophets were critical of political systems. By 1960 a considerable re-orientation was under way, until in the 1970s the college's teaching on Christian responsibility within the political and social life of the nation was considered dangerously liberal by some of the older African clergy.[8] Here then was another reason for the hesitant voice of the churches on public issues in the first years of independence. It is likely to be many years before there emerges a distinctively Kenyan fusion of the intense personal experience of Revival which so often attracts men to the ministry, and the critical theology of St. Paul's.

The framework of cooperation

By 1963 about twenty per cent of Kenya's citizens would have claimed to be Christians; their churches were locally self-governing if Protestant, or fully articulated dioceses of Rome. Where congregations were multi-racial—as among the Anglicans, Catholics and Presbyterians especially—this fact had ceased to complicate the forms of church government. Missionary societies still had their local representatives, but they no longer occupied a constitutionally privileged position. And the connexions between the local churches and their former parents were of rapidly decreasing significance in the field of Church and State relations. Government's growing impatience with denominational particularism, especially in the educational sector,[9] soon demanded a larger role here for the NCCK.

The NCCK has now become the focus of cooperation between Church and State, not least because its functional agencies, the Christian Churches' Educational Association (CCEA) and Medical Association encompass both the Protestant and Roman Catholic Churches. Thus broadly based, the NCCK's focal position is reinforced by three considerations. From the government's point-of-view it removes from its dealings with the churches all the intricacies of denominationalism. Secondly, as the funnel for Christian aid from overseas the Council necessarily acts as the chief initiator, co-ordinator and guarantor of new forms of pastoral work. In an important sense the NCCK has organized cooperation not between the State and the Kenyan churches so much as between the State and external Christianity; the presence of its expatriate staff (as many still are) bears witness to the fact that Nairobi is a suburb of

---

[8] The original seminar paper by Lonsdale and Booth-Clibborn was in error in implying that the theological instruction of the 1970s had been unchanged since the 1940s and '50s.

[9] See Addresses by Elliot Kendall (Chairman of the Methodist Church in Kenya) and J. D. Otiende (Minister of Education) in *The Churches' Role in Kenya*.

Ecumenopolis, World City. To a great extent, like is therefore cooperating with like in that the state's links with international bodies, whether governmental or commercial, are often more tangible than its connexions with its own citizens, the poor especially. And so in the Church a dual form of life has emerged. The denominations, of which there are over fifty at work in Nairobi, provide a ministry to the human psyche as people undergo the stresses of rapid urbanization. Cleansing and forgiveness, assurance, direction and fellowship are offered and gratefully received by a significant proportion of the population. On the other hand the NCCK and its agencies relate to the structures of society, ministering to the departments of government, the media and industry. The Protestant churches have thus, broadly, split the functions of saving souls and serving the Kingdom and this, one can suggest as the third consideration which undergirds the role of the NCCK, most denominations have done with a sense of relief. The essential corollary has been that in matters of 'politics' the NCCK must not offend, too often or too directly, the more conservative among its member churches. In any case, the NCCK leadership's close association with the nationalist cause before independence has meant that it has tended to take an 'establishment' view of political problems thereafter.

The conditional nature of the relationship between the NCCK and the denominations, and the less conditional alignment between the NCCK and the new independent government together determined that the council should divest itself of its most salient public function, that of newspaper publisher, early in 1964.[10] Even then, the council dissociated itself from the now independent monthly, *Target*, when four years later it condemned the new party headquarters as a misuse of resources.[11] Disavowal of *Target* was the more surprising, given the freedom of worship and belief guaranteed in Kenya's constitution. This constitutional right may indeed be reiterated too often by members of the government to carry complete conviction. In 1973 the ban on the Jehovah's Witnesses for failure to honour the symbols of the State was also, although soon rescinded, a clear breach of the principle of religious toleration. There are probably rather few churchmen as yet who would confidently assert that freedom of worship is an inherent human right which it is government's duty unconditionally to protect.

It is in the educational field that the churches have, in a sense, lost most ground since independence. In the late colonial period most Christian denominations ran grant-aided schools, retaining exclusive

[10] For the details, see *Rock* No. 76 (March 1964), pp. 4-5.

[11] See *Target,* Nos. 45 and 46 (January and February 1968). The building originally designed as the KANU headquarters is now the Kenyatta International Conference Centre, home of the UN's Environment Secretariat.

rights of management under overall government supervision. With an eye on the future however, the CCEA persuaded several churches to put the management of their schools in the hands of committees which represented church, parents, teachers and local government alike. Some schools, in urban areas especially, were registered as CCEA schools; most, however, retained their denominational character.[12] Such was the closeness of the working relationship between the CCEA and the independent government's Ministry of Education that the 1968 Education Act came as less of a shock to Christian opinion than might have been expected. This formally transferred the right to management of all save 'special schools' (like the Blind School at Thika and other experimental projects which in government's view the church seems best able to pioneer) from the churches to the State. But the parochial politics of school management would change rather little. Written into the Act was the right of churches to representation on school committees and to consult the Ministry on staffing; the responsibility of the churches to draw up a syllabus for Religious Instruction and the right thereafter to visit schools to supervise that syllabus; and the right to free use of school buildings after school hours.[13] The General Director of the Mennonite Board for East Africa was certainly not alone in rejoicing that the Act was not loss but gain, in that it obliged the churches to minister more to their congregations now that the props of the school had been kicked away.[14]

The government had been very solicitous of Church interests in framing this Act. Why was this? Aside from the value which the State puts on Church support generally, the churches have very concrete resources at their disposal in the educational field. They remain important agencies for the recruitment of specialized expatriate skills; they can get financial support and staff for pioneer educational projects to which government feels as yet unable to devote public resources. The churches, so it is hoped, may instil in the teacher-pupil relationship a sense of moral responsibility which, if parental resentment is any guide, is too often lacking.[15]

---

[12] For some of the details see articles by F. R. Dain, Education Secretary of the CCK, in *Rock,* Nos. 19 and 20 (June and July 1959).

[13] As reported to the NCCK Annual Meeting, in *Target,* No. 50 (June 1968), p. 5.

[14] Bishop Donald Jacobs, in *Target,* No. 48 (April 1968), p. 17.

[15] For the often poor quality of the teacher-student relationship, see M. G. Whisson, 'The School in present-day Luo society', Cambridge Ph.D. thesis (1965).

Towards a Christian qualification of 'Nation-building': the crises of 1969-70

For the first years after independence the authority and structures of the Kenyan State increased steadily in power and mass, both absolutely, and relative to the churches. This was only to be expected. The Africanization of its personnel gave to the State an initially inexhaustible fount of patronage, its administration of loan funds and licences gave it a grateful clientele, on the land, in industry and countless small businesses. The State also gained enormously in ideological strength. For all the inequalities which flourish in Kenya's society, for all the corruption in high places both published and rumoured, Kenya's government has been more successful than many in Africa—and in obvious contrast with its neighbour Uganda—in preserving for its citizens that which most earns their allegiance, their peace and security. And in the concepts of 'nation-building', self-help and *Harambee*, the government deploys a powerful set of ideological symbols beneath which most people's aspirations can be accommodated—for at least as long as the commercial and land frontiers remain open to Africans in the wake of departing Asians and Europeans. Given the ruling dogma that the State exists chiefly to hold the ring while a congeries of potentially warring tribes is built into a nation by gradual accumulations of custom, commerce and exhortation, it is difficult to qualify these elements of the State's ideological charter without being accused of attempting to wreck the State itself. And if, as they increasingly accept, the churches are in society, they must surely be prepared to suspend judgement, 'at this stage of development', on the State institutions by which society is protected against itself. The pressures on the Church to conform to the State's definition of reality are perhaps greater now than they were in the colonial period.

But society is also in the churches. And society's divisions are reproduced within the Church in two ways. First, the overwhelming majority of Christians, like the majority of Kenyans, are poor, and poorly educated. In the rural areas the churches, especially the independent African churches, cater mainly for women—the people who must chiefly bear the strains of social change yet who are least regarded in the formal structures of society—since their men are so often absent in town. As the churches lose their reserved functions in schools and, to a lesser extent, in hospitals, so the ministry of the Word must increasingly be their sole source of authority. Yet in town the churches hold the attention of only a small minority of the new *élite*; for it is only recently that the churches have been able to match in their ordinands the quality of education demanded since before independence in the servants of the State. Next, like all other large organizations, the government included, the churches cannot escape the dilemmas of tribalism.[16] It is difficult to know in what ways the tribal composition of church leadership and membership has influenced the tone of relationships between Church and State. Two points may be tentatively suggested. The first stems from the fact that for historical reasons the Presbyterian Church is almost entirely a Kikuyu Church. Kenya has a largely Kikuyu government. And there have been signs that the Presbyterians have taken over from the Anglicans—with their more heterogeneous tribal composition—the position of quasi-establishment in terms of private access to the seat of power.[17] Secondly, in the churches more generally, there is a striking preponderance of West Kenya (Luo and Luyia) leadership—especially among the Anglicans, Catholics and Friends. It may well be that while their ethnic origin makes such church leaders more sensitive to the misuse of government power, they are, precisely for that reason, reluctant to speak out for fear of being dubbed 'tribalists'.

The churches' experience of their members' own poverty and cultural division prompted their material and prayerful support for the state's definition of 'nation-building' during the first years of independence. But it also gave a critical edge to their relations with government when official actions and inactions in 1969 exposed the shortcomings of 'nation-building' in the face of extreme poverty and extreme tribal chauvinism. This two-fold crisis, we would argue, initiated a long process of redefinition in Church and State relations, the eventual outcome of which is far from certain.

The churches' first concern was the relief of poverty. Through the NCCK they have acted as a broker between the different political levels and economic interests of Kenya, bringing together those who had previously lived in the sharply differentiated worlds characteristic of colonial society, to match up resources of skill, labour and capital which might otherwise have lain unemployed. The first such Christian initiative was taken at the time of independence to meet the plight of primary school leavers who could get neither secondary school places nor jobs. The churches set up a joint working party which soon drew in others, including representatives of government departments. Out of a long series of meetings came a variety of proposals,[18] the most fruitful of which was

---

[16] Tribalism may at times be manipulated to provide a political base, as argued for instance in Colin Leys, *Underdevelopment in Kenya* (London, 1975), pp. 198–206. But it would be a mistake to infer that 'tribe' has therefore no concrete existence; it is in a whole variety of ways the underlying metaphor of existence for most people, and not only Africans.

[17] This is to speak only of institutions: the Anglican Bishop Obadiah Kariuki is very close to the President, as his brother-in-law. No colonial bishop had so intimate a connection with a Governor.

[18] For which, see *After School, What?* (NCCK, Nairobi, 1966).

for village polytechnics—a term coined by the working party for rural centres which could offer two years' post-primary training in technical, agricultural and educational skills through which a living could be made in each particular rural area. By the end of 1972 the government was assisting sixty such projects, of which seventeen had been initiated with NCCK aid; this pattern of NCCK pioneering, followed by a hand-over to government, continues at the present time.

A later example of the churches' brokerage can be taken from higher up the educational system. Independence brought with it an enormous expansion of secondary schooling in the maintained sector and still more so in unaided *Harambee* or community self-help schools. Employers were trying to recruit more African secondary school leavers. It was soon apparent that there was a great disjunction between the quality of the supply and the nature of the demand. Employers complained of lack of motivation and skill in their recruits while being themselves subject to increasing criticism for failing to Africanize their management. But rapid school expansion necessarily depended on inexperienced teachers who had none of the knowledge or contacts to enable them to offer even minimal career guidance to many of their leavers. And so in 1967 the NCCK set up what has proved to be the first of a continuing series of Career Conferences, which have brought together career advisers from the schools, officials of the Labour and Economic Planning Ministries, and employers of every sort.[19] The churches had, from their relatively independent position, identified and done much to close a gap between the educational and formal employment sectors of the State and thereby helped to 'build the nation' in one of its more commonly understood senses, that is, the Africanization of the inherited structure of opportunity.

A very different example of the way in which the churches have helped to close a gap in the inherited framework of society can be seen in the relief and developmental work the NCCK has undertaken on government's behalf for the nomadic peoples of the arid Northern Frontier regions after the disastrous droughts of 1970-71. By 1972 K£75,000 had been committed to a variety of projects, from donors in many countries. The churches have been able both to supply individuals—for instance missionary doctors for government hospitals in areas where others were reluctant to serve—and to manage projects, like the development of settled agriculture around new boreholes.[20] A neglected sector of the population was at last being included in the nation.

---

[19] Reports on the Career Conferences from 1967 onwards were prepared by the NCCK.

[20] *Ready for Change: Development in Northern Kenya* (NCCK, Nairobi 1972).

In all these examples the involvement of the churches helped to bring about a certain redefinition of the problem. This was particularly so in the first case, where the problem of the unemployment of school-leavers was rephrased to emphasize the development of people, starting where they were, however humbly. Through all its initiatives the NCCK was working in harmony with the ideology and structures of the State. In 1969 however, the council's involvement with the shanty dwellers of Nairobi revealed rather sharply the limits of accommodation between 'nation-building' as the Africanization of an inherited opportunity structure and 'nation-building' as the redefinition of that structure in order to include within it the aspirations of the very poor.

Since the early colonial era there had been tension between the needs of new urban migrants for cheap housing and the determination of the authorities both to improve standards of shelter, security and sanitation, and to protect these gains from being swamped by fresh immigrants from the countryside. In the absence of sufficient accommodation provided by employers or municipality, the colonial solution had been a fitful resort to a combination of vagrancy laws and destruction of the shanty towns, in the hope that urban poverty would return to the countryside whence it came and where, it was argued with some justice, it had a better chance of relief. The 'problem' did not disappear with independence; it became worse. Rural landlessness increased with the twin growths of population and social differentiation; and colonial vagrancy or pass laws, the most hated symbols of oppression, could no longer be applied. In the decade before independence Nairobi's population was growing at an annual rate of 6½ per cent; in the decade thereafter the rate more than doubled, to 15 per cent. Of the several clashes between authority and poverty which ensued we may take the example of the destruction of Kaburini—'the graveyard', so called from its proximity to a cemetery—in which the NCCK and the City Council came to hold opposing definitions of the problem. By 1968 Kaburini had a population of 4,000; it lived by illegal brewing and was a convenient bolt-hole for fugitives, close to the city centre, and in particular for *pikipoketi*. Two fires in late 1968 and mid-1969 together destroyed over half the village's shacks. Living conditions became still more appalling, especially in the rains; some children died of exposure and malnutrition. The City Council hung undecided between order and humanity. It forbade any re-building by the squatters, but encouraged the NCCK and the Red Cross to help them with clothes, blankets and a soup kitchen; it supplied milk but refused to collect garbage; it disclaimed responsibility for sheltering any unemployed Kenyan who came to the city to squat, but talked of long-term plans for resettlement. The NCCK itself moved rapidly, under pressure of the squatters' plight, from a sudden awareness of the need for relief to a realization that relief alone, even in so extreme a situation, could serve only to pauperize its recipients. The NCCK's African social worker persuaded the people themselves, through an elected committee, to accept responsibility for running the soup kitchen, a nursery school, and the distribution of relief supplies. The NCCK then drew the University's Housing Research and Development Unit into discussions on the question of longer term resettlement. The Unit produced a five-year development plan in which a total of little more than K£100 per housing plot would be spent first on survey and site clearance, then, in sequence, on water points (later to be connected to each plot), roads, drains, street lighting and sewerage. The people would build their own houses and the whole cost of the scheme would be recovered from them, through water charges and rising monthly fees.

At the NCCK's invitation, representatives of central government and city council promised to look into the scheme and to do something. This they did. Early in 1970 a force of city council *askari* moved into Kaburini and started burning and destroying the houses. There was a public outcry, in which various government officials joined, and the city's welfare department embarked with the NCCK and the Salvation Army on a variety of short-term expedients, tented camps and so on, where living conditions were still less satisfactory than in the original shanties of Kaburini and which soon cost more than the resettlement programme proposed by the University's research unit.

This whole episode—and it was only part of a much larger problem—saw the churches, through the NCCK, taking the side of the shanty dwellers, labelled as thieves and vagabonds, illegal brewers and prostitutes, harbourers of rats and filth, a menace to society. On the other side, the establishment felt that they were upholding not only levels of health and decency but also moral standards which were gravely threatened. They were puzzled and disgusted that the churches should appear to defend immoral and illegal people. At root, this issue, like most others, was a theological one. Can any society accept people where they are, however far short they may fall from 'decent' standards of bourgeois or socialist morality, and work alongside them without opening the door to an uncontrollable flood of sub-standard behaviour in which many justifiable social norms become lost to view? Can the churches develop a theology of outstretch which holds on to both ends of this tension? It may be said that the Son of Man did just that, but if the churches try to follow, it may well be that the path will lead increasingly into conflict with the secular authorities, not only in Kenya but elsewhere in the Third World where poverty is so threatening in its degradation. For there is, as the churches everywhere are increasingly aware, a Fourth World, populated by those who are losing out in the Third World countries—those starving in famine belts, the inhabitants of un-controlled settlements like Kaburini, the unemployed, those who make shift in underworlds. The earlier examples of NCCK initiatives which we have quoted were instances of Christian contributions to Third World development, to 'nation-building'. But one can also see a rough pro-gression towards those who come lower on the list of public priorities in-cluding, in Kaburini, those whom the authorities would prefer to have out of sight altogether.

It was perhaps not coincidental that during the very period in which the NCCK was pressing for the claims of Nairobi's poor to be included within the politics of the nation, Kenya's churches were finding the voice to speak to a crisis which exposed the danger of the conventional political assumption that the building blocks of the nation were its tribes. In retrospect, the 'oathing crisis' of 1969 can be seen to be a watershed in the relations between the Kenyan State and the local churches. The details of the crisis are complex and but shadowily known but it was immediately clear that it presented a classic example of the demonic and destructive potential of political power within a fractured society. The government of Kenya was menaced by a two-fold cleavage opening beneath it. One growing division was within the ruling party, KANU, between the Kikuyu and the non-Kikuyu; the other was within the Kikuyu people themselves, broadly between those from Kiambu, the dis-trict nearest to Nairobi and best represented in Kenyatta's government, and those from Murang'a and Nyeri districts. The opposition Kenya People's Union, while strongest in West Kenya, had also enlisted the support of some Kikuyu, notably those who claimed to represent the cause of the landless poor; this emphasized to the government the dangers of its divisions within. Events moved rapidly toward crisis in June 1969 with the murder of Tom Mboya, who had to some extent held the ring between the two KANU factions and who was perhaps felt to be too powerful by some among the Kikuyu *élite*. Although it never emerged in court, it was universally assumed that the motive for murder was political. Mboya's Luo mourners were openly hostile to the Kikuyu. A general election was in the offing and the Kikuyu had already begun to close ranks. They did so now with renewed vigour. Who were the organizers of their unity is not known. But their method revived the fears of the 1950s. Very large numbers of Kikuyu were obliged to swear to keep the government of Kenya within the House of Mumbi (the Kikuyu Eve) and to swallow an oath of goat's meat and blood; a spittoon for the squeamish was provided at ceremonies which catered for the bureau-cratic *élite* in Nairobi. Many ceremonies were held near the President's home in Kiambu, with oath-takers arriving by the lorry-load 'to have tea', as the expression had it, 'with the President'.

Public criticism was initiated not by the churches but by a Luo MP in Parliament, despite the fact that those who were paying the price of resistance to the oath in beatings, intimidation and, eventually in one case, death were almost without exception Christians, individuals or congregations. Two weeks after the Parliamentary debate—during which government spokesmen had maintained a bland ignorance of oathing in face of the mounting evidence—the independent Christian monthly *Target*, now under its first African editor, came out in its September edition with a front-page editorial entitled 'Killing our Unity'. This condemned the tribally divisive nature of the oath and chided church leaders for failing to give any public guidance or support to those Christians who had to face its demands. The editorial was given added point by its juxtaposition with a photograph of the administration of the sacrament in Holy Communion, under the caption 'Taking the Oath'.[21] All the churches then followed this lead. It is doubtful whether their opposition had much effect on the course of the oathing campaign, since it appears to have achieved its objective of uniting the Kikuyu—including the poor of Kaburini and other shanty-towns—at the time the churches' protests reached their peak. The government did however take action against forcible oathing. It was probably prompted as much by fear lest this offend the Kalenjin peoples—who were the main political allies of the Kikuyu but resentful of Kikuyu land settlement in their area[22]—as by respect for public opinion as it was aired in Parliament, church and, belatedly, the secular press.

The statements of the churches in this period made clear, as had never been done before, the qualifications which were attached to the Christian's allegiance to the State. Most churches produced covenants or reaffirmations of their loyalty to Kenyatta's government; all were prefaced with a declaration that the Christian's first loyalty was to God and that worldly authority was derived from Him. It followed, as the Baptists' and Presbyterians' covenants put it, that the State was owed only 'such respect, service and obedience as is compatible with a God-fearing life.'[23] This proclamation of ancient Christian principles of political allegiance and resistance seemed to provide a release for an extraordinary upsurge of public complaint against the oathing and, more generally, tribalism and corruption in politics. However unintentionally and perhaps reluctantly, the churches for a moment found themselves at the head of a political opposition.

[21] *Target*, No. 65 (September 1969).

[22] *East African Standard* (EAS), 22 September 1969.

[23] J. Murray-Brown, *Kenyatta* (London, 1972), Appendix, pp. 328-30.

Conclusions

The most important aspect of the crises of 1969 for the theme of Church and State relations was the way in which the ministry of service in Kaburini and the ministry of prophecy against the secret oaths spelled out together, implicitly and explicitly, Christian qualifications of the 'nation-building' concept.[24] They were, moreover, authentically Kenyan qualifications, in at least three senses. To begin with, the hitherto characteristic partnership between the NCCK and the denominations in the field of Church and State relations was in 1969 reversed. In the ruins of Kaburini it was the ecumenical organization that was ministering to the souls and bodies of the poor. In the political crisis it was the local churches which defined the Christian's conditional obedience to the secular power; the NCCK as such had almost nothing to say. Next—a point that would scarce be worth remarking were it not of Kenya that we are writing—in both spheres African rather than expatriate convictions were those that carried the day. In Kaburini the African social workers took the crucial initiatives. In the oathing affair the Anglican archbishop, a missionary of long standing and now a Kenya citizen, nevertheless held that his African bishops had a greater right than he to lead opinion;[25] the editor of *Target* was African, as also the Moderator of the Presbyterian Church, the Rev. John Gatu.

Thirdly, and perhaps most importantly, the churches' response to the oathing crisis showed the peculiar strength of the conservative evangelical tradition in repudiating the supremacy of secular power—as incompatible with God's prior claims on Christian allegiance.[26] A 'National Covenant', the first critical Christian affirmation of secular loyalty to invite public support, was launched from the Baptist Church, a centre of middle-class evangelicalism in Nairobi, black and white. Henry Okullu, the then editor of *Target*, and John Gatu, are both strong members of the Revival brethren. Now, the political idiom of a young African state is very different from that of late colonialism, however powerful both may be in relation to the poverty and ignorance of most of those whom they rule. The common language of late colonialism was an overseas dialect of Western bourgeois liberalism, which accorded to the State enough power to ensure its citizens a rising level of prosperity and enlightenment in secure enjoyment of their property, but no more. The colonial State could most effectively be reminded of its highest duty in its

[24] From the viewpoint of Kenya's history the most important development in 1969 was the banning of the Kenya People's Union—something on which the churches had nothing to say.

[25] *EAS*, 9 September 1969.

[26] We are grateful to Dr Kevin Ward for alerting us to this value of the conservative evangelical tradition.

own language which, in the mouth of the church, was a liberal theology. The philosophical inheritance of the independent Kenyan State is at once more collectivist and more sacerdotal. It is only as a member of a collectivity that an individual can exist; and the rules of collective behaviour are best prescribed by a priestlike mediation between the present and the past, between the people and their forebears, which the elders are alone qualified to perform. That Kenya falls short of the ideal both by comprising a discordant collection of collectivities, its tribes, and by pursuing a capitalist path of social differentiation, means only that the ideal is the more insistently proclaimed as ideology, It is a very totalitarian view of the State (however weakly it may in fact be pressed) and the authority of its head is derived as much 'from above' as from below. It is, in other words, an authority peculiarly susceptible to the argument of other claims from above; it is an authority phrased more in the language of conservative evangelicalism than theological liberalism. And only with a common language is it possible to argue.

It remains to be seen whether the developing Kenyan evangelical tradition will in fact adopt a stance of 'critical solidarity' with the State. The indications are rather contradictory. In the events of 1969 their popular support witnessed to a considerable authority on the part of the churches—and it should be remembered that while KANU's membership remains rather static, new churches are constantly being consecrated in contemporary Kenya. As much as four years after the event both Gatu and Okullu were able to draw vigorous lessons from the oathing crisis, the one at St Paul's College graduation ceremony, the other in his cathedral pulpit.[27] It would seem unlikely therefore that it could be said of similar circumstances in the future—as it was argued by his most recent biographer of the crisis of 1969—that 'Kenyatta persuaded the churches in Kenya to go along with the [oathing] programme . . . on the understanding that it would be peacefully conducted.'[28]

Crisis is not however a normal condition, even in the Third World. In normal times it seems equally likely that the Kenyan churches may be so preoccupied with their own intense, revived, experience of Christ that they will fail to maintain an implied critique of the State, for want of a continuing commitment of their own to practical justice in society. That would certainly be a reservation held by Kenyan Christians of a more liberal persuasion, for instance in the University. And it must be asked whether, through a lack of direct involvement in works of 'improvement'

---

[27] *EAS*, 15 January 1974. The secular press did not report these statements directly but quoted them from the Christian newspapers. Okullu was at this time Provost of All Saints (Anglican) Cathedral, Nairobi.

[28] Murray-Brown, *Kenyatta*, p. 317. The statement does of course beg a large question.

on behalf of the Fourth World, the local churches may not forfeit the right to prophesy when prophets are needed. It is not sufficient for them to leave good works to the NCCK, since the Council seems—or so the experience of 1969 suggests—to be inhibited by its combination of overseas connections and locally 'established' position from maintaining a prophetic relationship with society. Indeed, the NCCK's co-operation with government in material development enables the Vice-President of Kenya to make such statements as that the church is 'part and parcel of Government', and without contradiction.[29] The indigenous Kenyan tradition of evangelical Revival, clear-sighted in crisis and prophetic in its defence of Christian autonomy when need arises, is, because of its very suspicion of hierarchy and organization, peculiarly ill-fitted to perceive, let alone guard against, such routine envelopment. It was not without reason that the Anglican Provost of Nairobi has warned the churches against the danger of living in 'the time of Constantine . . . who put the Church in his pocket by offering government protection'.[30]

[29] *EAS,* 4 February 1974.

[30] Henry Okullu, 'The Church and Politics', *East Africa Journal,* ix, 11 (Nairobi, November 1972), pp. 2-3.

Church and State in Zambia: the case of the African Methodist Episcopal Church

DAVID J. COOK

In a survey published in 1971 by the Mindolo Ecumenical Foundation[1] the five largest of Zambia's seventy-eight churches were reported to be:

Jehovah's Witnesses	130,000 members[2]
Roman Catholics	85,800
African Methodist Episcopal	50,000
African Reformed	36,000
(previously Dutch Reformed Church)	
United Church of Zambia	15,500

Figures of church membership may sometimes be misleading, but it is interesting for a country as much influenced as Zambia has been by mining, migrant labour, and the confrontation of diverse cultures in an urban setting, that a rough estimate should place two independent churches in a position of significant influence.[3] From the outset the African Methodist Episcopal Church (AME) in Zambia has been an urban body, spreading its membership through the artisans and clerks in the mine compounds, and planting new churches in the rural areas with the return of migrant labourers. It entered the country in a context of pan-African feeling, and its leading members during the movement towards independence contributed to, and were influenced by, the mounting tide of nationalism in Zambia. However, as I hope to show, the nationalism of the post-independence period, and the close contact of the church with government leaders in the new state have posed unexpected problems.

[1] Chester Woodhall *Churches and Development, Director for Zambia* (Kitwe, 1971), a survey made for the Mindolo Ecumenical Foundation. My own estimate for the effective membership of the AME Church in 1970 is 22,000. In the *Report of the Sixteenth Meeting of the Christian Council of Zambia* (Lusaka, 1975) the AME Church reported 43,022 members.
[2] This does not include the membership of the Independent Watchtower Church founded by Jeremiah Gondwe, said to be 4,000 strong in 1971 and to have risen to 19,000 by 1976. (*Times of Zambia*, 23 March 1976).
[3] The 1969 Census recorded a population of just over four million, of whom about one and a quarter million lived in urban and peri-urban settlements—one of the highest proportions of urban settlement in Africa.

Any account of the relationship between churches and the state, and churches and the Zambian people before independence, and therefore in a different way since independence, has to be related to the growth of a substantial white settler community in Zambia during the colonial period as the mining industry grew, to the uncertainty this created as to Northern Rhodesia's political future (whether with the black north or the white south) and above all to the emergence of a colour-caste society with its separate churches, schools, living areas, wage structures and pass laws. By the 1920s most mission churches could be clearly seen to be part of the white establishment. The cost of not conforming was shown as early as 1910 when the Anglican, Bishop Hine, refused to consecrate the new church at Livingstone, that his white parishioners had subscribed for, because they would not allow Africans to use it.[4] Over this issue he was forced to retire, a broken man, and a more accommodating successor let the matter drop. It was in this context that the AME Church became important in Zambia. It had been born out of protest in the USA in 1787 when the freed slave, Richard Allen, led a secession from the American Methodist Episcopal Church because of colour dis-crimination. From the time of his consecration as its first bishop, no white men held office in the church. It became an area for black initiative, successfully establishing not only a large church but also schools, colleges and universities governed by a new intelligentsia created through its education and religious discipline. Whilst these men were reaching out to Africa for a fresh identity and formulating pan-African ideas by the end of the ninteenth century, the first intelligentsia from the Protestant missions in South Africa, also caught up in the maelstrom of colour bar, looked across in expectation to USA.[5] In response to invitations from South African pastors who had formed 'Ethiopian' churches a few years earlier by secession from missions, the enthusiastic pan-African, Bishop Turner, crossed from USA in 1898 and received them into the AME Church. From South Africa it spread northwards remarkably quickly, reaching Zambia as early as 1900.[6] The policy of the church was that the pastors should remain strictly neutral in politics but there was a strong note of religious nationalism in Bishop Turner's charge to his evangelists:

The time has now come to replace [European missionaries] . . . Arise Africa, for Ethiopia is holding out her hands, not as supplicant, as the

---

[4] From the correspondence of Bishop Hine kindly lent by the Rev. J. Weller.

[5] Clearly expressed by the son of the founder of the Ethiopian church in South Africa in his biography of his father: *The Early Life of Our Founder* by the Rev. J. M. Mokone, (Johannesburg, 1935), who writes of 'the religious emancipation of the African Race'.

[6] Also the year of the first pan-African Conference in London.

white men call her, but to incite us to . . . conquer the first place among our people.

It was this mood of protest against white control that attracted King Lewanika of Barotseland to accept the church in 1900, and was the main reason why the British South Africa Company banned it from the territory.[7] Christian missions regarded the church then rather as established churches had viewed the Anabaptists in the sixteenth century and agreed with the ban.

It was again in a context of politics and colour discrimination that the AME Church returned to Zambia in 1931. During the copper boom, 1929–30, the first group of mission-educated Africans to gather in Zambian towns were establishing a network of welfare associations along the line of rail and beginning to use them to challenge urban colour bar and to negotiate with government and town management boards for some of the amenities such as sanitation and schools that their appallingly neglected compounds required. For such men the prospect of an entirely African-controlled church running its own schools and universities was exciting indeed. Largely due to the efforts of the government clerks, who had recently formed the Ndola Welfare Association, the government agreed to allow the church back into the territory, and it spread rapidly in the towns. For a period many of the welfare association leaders became self-appointed lay preachers.[8] The church grew partly because of its independence of European control and its closer contact than mission Christianity with popular culture. As one old pastor said, 'I joined because I am an African and want to be in an African church.'[9] The very loose links with the American church had left the way open for a good deal of traditional music and dancing to enter the church's liturgy in South Africa and this came north to Zambia and blended with local culture.[10] The people dance as they bring their offerings to the altar, and they dance at the end of the communion service. The warm, informal

---

[7] G. L. Caplan, *The Elites of Barotseland 1897–1969* (London, 1970), chapter 4; Walter Johnson *The African Methodist Episcopal Church in S. Africa with particular reference to Zambia* (Ph.D., London, 1971) pp. 357-61. Lewanika became Honorary President of the Negro Society for Historical Research in New York and two of his sons were honorary members. Compare also T. O. Ranger 'The "Ethiopian" Episode in Barotseland, 1900-5' in *Rhodes-Livingstone Journal* XXXVLI, June 1965.

[8] From the correspondence of Ernest Muwamba and Elijah Chunga, the Ndola founders, and from file ZA1/9/1/1 in the Zambia National Archives, Lusaka. I have discussed this more fully in 'Livingstonia Mission and the Formation of Welfare Associations in N. Rhodesia, 1912-31' in T. O. Ranger and J. Weller (eds.) *Themes in the Christian History of Central Africa* (London, 1975) to which Fr Adrian Hastings has contributed a biography of the Rev. J. L. C. Membe mentioned in this chapter.

[9] Personal interview with the Rev. Petro Simfukwe at Ndola, 30 December 1971.

[10] Personal interview with the Rev. Abiner Kazunga at Ndola, 30 December 1971.

atmosphere makes members 'feel at home' and uniformed organizations give women and young people the separate roles customary in village life and in independent churches elsewhere in Africa. Others joined for more consciously nationalistic reasons. The African National Congress leader, Harry Nkumbula, an ex-mission teacher, attending one of the church's Annual Conferences in 1953 said quite bluntly at that time of intense nationalistic excitement:

> I feel proud to see that today we have our own house in which to worship God by the black men. A man who is ashamed of his colour and race is not fit to live.[11]

But another expectation was better education. In a land so bereft of higher education as Northern Rhodesia then was, the church made immediate impact with news of its nine degree-giving colleges in the USA. The Rev. Hanock Phiri, who brought the first news of the church to Ndola, was regularly corresponding with his relative, Hastings Banda, now President of Malawi, then studying for his first degree in an AME college in USA. The church had established three colleges and many schools in South Africa, and Dr Coan, the Principal of Wilberforce College in Transvaal, did his best to assist the new schools founded in Zambia.[12] Despite this, neither the resources of the American church nor the meagre incomes of Zambian members could finance Phiri's bold plan to found one college in his native Malawi and two others in Rhodesia and Zambia.[13] One of the ironies of an 'independent' church in the colonial period was its inability to live up to its ideals for secular improvement because most of the wealth was in European hands. The mission churches provided the education and this was the main reason why the AME did not retain many of the ambitious intelligentsia that welcomed it so warmly in 1931.

The closest contact between the AME Church and nationalist politics developed during the struggle by African National Congress against the Central African Federation. When Federation was imposed against unmistakable African opposition, it was openly or tacitly supported by many mission leaders with the result that mission churches lost their more independently-minded members to the AME Church, which grew rapidly during the political polarization that followed Federation.[14] For a

[11] Minutes, N. Rhodesia Annual Conference, AME Church, held at Lusaka, 21 to 25 January 1953.

[12] J. L. C. Membe to J. R. Coan, 20 November 1951, with account of AME schools; and *Annual Report of the African Education Department* (Lusaka, 1945) with details of six of them, three of which were of sufficient standard to obtain government grants-in-aid. I have found about a dozen different schools in the period 1933–50, founded by AME congregations.

[13] Letter from H. M. Phiri to J. L. C. Membe, 25 September 1935.

[14] Only the Church of Scotland strongly opposed Federation in 1953. The Anglicans, Dutch Reformed Church and some Roman Catholics supported it

period the AME Church became virtually the established church of Congress Party. Its pioneer pastor, the Rev. J. L. C. Membe led the prayers at many Congress gatherings.[15] Kenneth Kaunda, the General Secretary of Congress, 1953-8, was a local preacher and choir leader at the Lusaka church. Wittington Sikalumbi, Vice-Chairman of Congress in 1953, was secretary of Broken Hill Church. A number of other prominent Congress officials were lay preachers.[16] But as the confrontation between Congress and the Federal government grew more violent, and many nationalist leaders, including Nkumbula and Kaunda, were imprisoned, the pastors feared a ban on the church itself. According to one source both Justin Chimba and Kenneth Kaunda were warned by their Presiding Elders not to preach 'political sermons'.[17] When Congress split in 1958, Kaunda's more militant party began to use tougher tactics to force the British government to intervene, and the AME Church found itself, with members in two bitterly opposed parties, obliged to adopt a more neutral line which reduced its influence between 1958 and 1964. The violent culmination of the political struggle was in any case a time of reduced support for all churches except for Alice Lenshina's.[18] It was then that the major mission churches realized the need to rethink their approach to Zambian nationalism[19] In December 1957 the Christian Council of Northern Rhodesia openly opposed the government's Federal Franchise Bill which the nationalists were attacking.[20] This was the first public sign of the Protestant missions' re-appraisal of Federation. It is significant that mission churches acting together in a Christian Council, and with powerful home churches behind them, could dare to stand out against a quite ruthless government in a way which an independent church like the African Methodist, that could easily be banned, could not

according to Lewis Gann, *History of Northern Rhodesia* (London, 1964) pp. 421-2.

[15] When Congress called a Two Day National Prayer, April 1953, in protest against Federation, only the AME Church unreservedly backed it and Membe preached to a large meeting in Lusaka on the text: 'Let no man despise thee or thy youth'—a brilliant reference to European disregard of African opinion over Federation. (Interview: Titus Mukupo, 2 June 1972, who heard Membe preach and was himself a young Congress member, and later an important nationalist journalist.)

[16] Interviews with Justin Chimba, 31 May 1971, and the Rev. J. L. C. Membe, 24 September 1971. Also Wittington K. Sikalumbi, *Before UNIP: The Development of Nationalism in Zambia* (Lusaka, forthcoming), and Minutes, Official Board Meetings, Broken Hill AME Church 1958.

[17] Walton R. Johnson, p. 390, quoting Justin Chimba. See n.39, below.

[18] The Lumpa Church rose to its peak membership of 100,000 at this time. Jean Loup Calmettes, *Lumpa Church, the Genesis and Development, 1953-64* (Ilondola Language Centre, Chinsali, Zambia, 1970), page v.

[19] See J. V. Taylor, *Christianity and Politics in Africa* (London, 1957); and Colin Morris, *Anything But This* (London, 1958); *The Hour After Midnight* (London, 1961); *The End of the Missionary* (London, 1962); *Nationalism in Africa* (London, 1963), which traces one church leader's re-appraisals.

[20] *The African Times,* 13 December 1957, and *ANC Official News,* December 1957, page 4.

afford to do. The AME Church, which had tried unsuccessfully in 1953 to enter the Christian Council, was admitted in 1957. As Membe informed his bishop later: 'that Body is the only strong body . . . through which all members of different denominations speak through to the Government'.[21] One of the effects of the political crisis which preceded independence was the drawing together of the churches and the acceptance of the AME Church into the religious establishment because African opinion began to count. At the same time the mission churches began to integrate their European and African churches and the Rev. Colin Morris and his colleagues successfully forged a link between Kenneth Kaunda and what became the United Church of Zambia in 1964. The significant feature of this new church was not only the merger of denominations but the coming together of white and African churches into a self-governing structure in which African leadership predominated. In the Roman Catholic missions a similar process of reappraisal and Africanization began.[22]

As Colin Morris wrote a few years later, this coming to terms with Zambian nationalism by the mission churches was practically 'an hour after midnight'.[23] Nonetheless, by independence the unique relationship of the AME Church with the nationalist movement of a decade earlier had ended. It was no longer the only church led by Africans and in close touch with Zambian politicians. The leaders of the United Church of Zambia were African and like the AME Church a number of its members were in the new government, including President Kaunda. At independence what Afrikaaner leadership remained in the African Reformed Church was replaced by Zambians and the first African bishops were appointed in Anglican and Roman Catholic dioceses.[24] Ironically, by contrast, the AME Church still had a non-Zambian bishop and an episcopal residence in Rhodesia with whose government Zambia was on the worst of terms. The institutions of the AME Church had developed in a period of pan-African nationalism, when black solidarity against colour bar had been the central theme. Pan-African feeling by no means ended at independence, and it has therefore been possible for the AME Church to be more resistant to change than churches with a more obviously foreign background. Nevertheless, since independence the AME Church also has been adapting itself to the new nationalism of a Zambian sovereign State. This

---

[21] Letter from J. L. C. Membe to Bishop Bright, 31 October 1960.
[22] In January 1958, for example, the Northern Rhodesian Bishops of the Roman Catholic Church issued a joint pastoral letter condemning racialism and segregation. Cited in Colin Morris, *The Hour After Midnight* (op. cit.) pp. 154–5.
[23] Colin Morris, (op. cit.)
[24] Personal interview with the Revd D. G. Whitehead in Lusaka, 26 March 1976.

has probably not been so rapid a process as the President would have liked.

There can be no doubt that at independence Kaunda had hoped for the formation of a national church more wide-embracing than the United Church of Zambia actually became, and was disappointed that neither the Anglicans nor the AME Church joined. His upbringing as son of a Church of Scotland minister had accustomed him to the idea of a national church. Church of Scotland missions pioneered national churches in India, China and Malawi and were a strong influence in the formation of the United Church of Zambia. The group of Methodist missionaries like Colin Morris and Merfyn Temple that supported Kaunda's party just before independence (and helped him to win political support from the more liberal element in the white minority) were also strongly ecumenical in outlook. It was at this time that Kaunda wrote:

> 'How can I believe in the sincerity of Christians who in Lusaka alone hold seventeen separate denominational services for Europeans every Sunday. This denominational idiocy is a terrible condemnation of Christianity and is a confusion to my people.'[25]

In 1969 when President Kaunda attended the African Methodist Annual Conference he warned its members that different denominations 'could lead to fanaticism—and religious fanaticism leads to deaths, untold sorrows and misery'.[26] Since then, with the split in the ruling party, August 1971,[27] and the creation of a One Party State, December 1972, the emphasis upon national unity and avoidance of civil strife has become even stronger.

But even although the AME Church did not enter a 'national church' at independence, Zambian nationalism has been the major influence upon its recent history. It has led to efforts to become more independent of the mother church in America and to increasing contact with other Zambian churches formerly regarded as rivals. One reason for this, of course, is the existence of the Zambian state as a new centre of identification, with its powerful symbols of independence, its programme of Zambianization of jobs, Africanization of street names and the mass media, nationalization of foreign firms and non-aligned foreign policy. Another has been the economic effects of independence

---

[25] Quoted from T. P. Melady, *Kaunda of Zambia* (London, 1964).

[26] *Times of Zambia,* 24 November 1969. Undoubtedly the reference was to the bitter struggle between the state and the Lumpa Church just after independence.

[27] When Simon Kapwepwe, Kaunda's long-standing political associate, resigned from the government and from the United Independence Party (UNIP) to lead a new political party, the United Progressive Party (UPP), and made a bid for the Presidency, which failed.

upon the AME Church, which has benefited from the general redistribution of income from European to African hands. At independence a number of the church's leading laymen and two pastors became government ministers and ambassadors. The shop-keepers, who were such a main-stay of the Copperbelt churches, also experienced greater prosperity particularly after 1966 when the Brown Commission recommended a 22 per cent wage increase to the copper miners and other wages rose proportionately in the towns.[28] Between 1964 and 1970 the real purchasing power of the urban employee increased by between one-half and two-thirds.[29] How these changes have affected the income of the AME Church may be seen from the following table summarizing receipts from the church's circuits and districts all over Zambia between 1954 and 1970. Receipts from various church organizations such as the Women's Missionary Society and the Laymen's organization are not included, so the figures do not represent the church's total income. What they do show is the fluctuation in support for the church by its local members.[30]

Table 1. *Contributions from Circuits and Districts to Annual Conference between 1954 and 1970*

	1954	1955	1956	1957	1958	1961	1965	1966
A.	£425	£566	£514	£724	£710	£776	£737	£1362
B.	100	133	121	170	167	183	173	316
C.	—	—	100	103.1	104.3	110.7	124.4	—

	1967	1970
A.	£1523	£1827
B.	358	430
C.	—	198.5

Data

A. Total contributions in £s sterling. The 1970 figure has been converted from kwacha (the new currency) at the original rate of 2K´=£1.

B. Total contributions based on 1954=100

C. Cost of living index of 'lower income group' where 1956=100, from *Report of the Brown Commission*, Appendix XVII, p. 161. The 1970 figure I have calculated from statements about real and money wages in the *Second National Development Plan*, (Lusaka, 1972).

[28] *Report of the Commission of Inquiry into the Mining Industry under the Chairmanship of Mr Roland Brown* (Lusaka, 1966).

[29] *Second National Development Plan, January 1972 to December 1976* (Lusaka, 1971), where real wages are said to have increased by one half. H. A. Turner's *Report on Incomes, Wages and Prices in Zambia* (ILO, Geneva, 1969) put it at two-thirds.

[30] Local income from circuits was taken to districts (Quarterly District Meeting), then by Presiding Elders of districts to the Annual Conference. The figures are taken from Reports of Annual Conferences.

Increase in a church's income may be due to increased membership or increased wealth of the same membership. In the absence of figures of membership, but from the growth in the number of circuits and pastors, I consider that the 75 per cent increase in the church's income between 1954 and 1957 was mainly due to increasing membership, and conclude that the church was growing substantially during its period of close alliance with Congress's early struggle against Federation and was making a contribution to Zambian Christianity that no other church could make. In the absence of other figures, one can only conclude that between 1958 and 1965 there was a period of relative stagnation. Earlier I have related this to the disruption of the church by the more violent culmination of the struggle against Federation, to the split in Congress (and in the church's lay membership) and to the revival of the mission churches. The marked increase in church income between 1966 and 1970 reflected not only a revival and expansion of church membership but also the emergence of something like a middle class within the lay leadership of the town circuits which has become an important new factor in the post-colonial period. This has helped to finance growth in the rural areas. It was there that the church had its largest membership in 1970—five-sixths were in rural circuits—but it was also there that members were least able to support themselves.

As Professor Turner has shown, although urban incomes have grown a good deal since independence, rural incomes have increased far less, and the dualistic economy of the colonial period has continued in a different form.[31] But through the centralized system of the AME Church a little of this urban wealth flows back to the villages. In 1970 nearly one half of the church's income in its central fund came from the urban circuits of the Copperbelt and Lusaka, and a good deal went out to supplement the small stipends of the rural pastors.[32]

The altered circumstances of the Zambian church since independence have changed its relationship both with its parent church in USA and with the conferences in Malawi and Rhodesia. The Malawi Conference had never been large probably because the Church of Central Africa Presbyterian (CCAP) was more advanced than most mission churches in the extent to which it was governed by Africans in colonial times. But the

[31] H. A. Turner (op. cit.).
[32] Financial and Statistical Report, South and North Zambia Annual Conference, 2-6 December 1970. It is from this report that I calculate the number of church members of regular standing to be about 22,000 in 1970. It should be noted that the main part of the pastor's income is paid by the local church and that wealthy town churches pay their pastors substantially more than the minimum. In 1976, during a period of financial crisis mentioned later in this chapter, the South Zambia Conference stopped the payments of supplements to pastors' salaries from the Central Fund. Only Presiding Elders continued to receive a payment from that fund to enable them to travel around their circuits to supervise their development.

conferences in Rhodesia had been so important that the bishop had placed his headquarters at Bulawayo after the South African conferences left the Seventeenth Episcopal District. Since 1964, however, the combined effects of political independence in Zambia and of UDI in Rhodesia have made the Zambian church the most influential in Central Africa. The economic side of this may be traced in the following table which compares the incomes of the five conferences in 1967 and their pastorates in the previous year. It will be noted that already the South Zambia Conference (containing the Copperbelt, Lusaka, and the line of rail) had larger economic resources than the whole of the Rhodesian church. By contrast with their Zambian counterparts, members of the urban churches in Rhodesia had experienced no redistribution of income in their favour but probably suffered some decline since UDI.

Table 2. Resources of the Conferences of the 17th Episcopal District[33]

Conference	1967 Income	National Total	Pastorates 1966	National Total
S. Zambia	£1567 ⎱	£2087	33 ⎱	70
N. Zambia	520 ⎰		37 ⎰	
S. Rhodesia	£514 ⎱		18 ⎱	
(Bulawayo)	⎰	£1136	⎰	42
N. E. Rhodesia	622 ⎰		24 ⎰	
(Salisbury)				
Malawi	£279	£279	33	33

Other factors were working in the same direction. After UDI American bishops found it difficult to get visas to enter Rhodesia. Between 1965 and 1967 Bishop Bearden was unable to use his episcopal residence at Bulawayo and lived in Lusaka, appointing the Zambian, the Rev. J. L. C. Membe, as his private secretary in place of the Rhodesian, Dr Tladi, who was unable, or avoided, coming to Zambia.[34] In 1971 Bishop Gomez had similar difficulties and used Lusaka as his base, between 1971 and 1972, although he did eventually obtain entry into Rhodesia for a few weeks in 1972.[35] At the Joint Annual Conference of North and South Zambia in December 1971 Zambian members recommended that if the episcopal residence in Bulawayo were to be

[33] Figures from Reports of Annual Conferences, 1966 and 1967.
[34] Reports of Conferences, 1965, 1966. Bishop Bearden understood that Dr Tladi was unable to come, but later it appeared that he may have avoided coming.
[35] Information from Bishop Gomez in Lusaka, 1971-2. The bishop's car and residence were being used by a Rhodesian church leader, 1971-2, who had connived with government officials to exclude the bishop from Rhodesia.

retained at all, it should in future be financed from Rhodesian and American funds, not from Zambian. With the bishop present, a resolution was passed that as the Zambian Church had the most members and Lusaka had already become the 'capital of Central Africa for OAU delegations, United Nations' agencies and the Non-Aligned Conference, it should become the seat of the bishop in the post-independence era.[36] At the earlier annual conference of the Malawi Church in 1971 it had been proposed that the episcopal residence be moved to Malawi. The Rhodesian Church wanted to keep the residence in Bulawayo.[36]

Underlying these differences was the steady formation within the seventeenth Episcopal District of three national churches with different problems and political loyalties, and perhaps the need for three bishops, having regard to the physical and political problems of travel between the three countries. As was to be expected, however, it was the Zambian Church with its larger resources that took the lead in pressing for the election of a local man, a Zambian, to be bishop of the seventeenth Episcopal District. This question of the localization of the bishop has been an important issue in the Zambian Church since independence. It was recognized by Zambian leaders that there were certain advantages in having an American bishop. He could stand above tribal and party political differences. He could present the world-wide nature of Christianity to local members. He could probably draw in more assistance from the American church than a local bishop might.[38] American assistance, which had been small in the early years, had increased a few years before independence. In 1961 Bishop Bright (with Bishop Jordan, one of the few really active bishops of the colonial period) introduced a system of minimum salaries, £8 a year for Presiding Elders in charge of districts, and £4 for pastors. His grant of £300 from American funds represented an addition of something like one fifth to the church's income. Bishop Bearden's £400 in 1966 constituted a slightly larger fraction. I do not know what assistance came with subsequent bishops, but whilst the resources of the Zambian 'middle class' have grown so have those of their Afro-American fellow members in USA and there has been a generally increased interest by the American Church recently in its African dioceses.[39] Obviously the American link was

---

[36] Joint Annual Conference, Ndola, 28 December 1971 to 2 January 1972, which I was kindly allowed to attend as an observer. Discussion on report of Standing Committee on the bishop's residence, 1 January 1972. One member of the committee was then a Cabinet Minister in the Zambian government.

[37] Statement by Bishop Gomez during the same discussion, 1 January 1972.

[38] The bishop's salary is paid by the American church, and he generally brings funds with him for the poorer pastors, and sometimes even gifts of clothes. (Personal interviews: Bishop Gomez, 1 January 1972 and Mrs H. Brookins, 28 March 1976.)

[39] Illustrated by the fact that one American church member, Dr Walton Johnson,

important. On the other hand, in 1971, during the relative prosperity of a copper boom, the Zambian leadership was convinced the time had come for a local man to be bishop. At this time I frequently heard it said by African Methodists that they should have led the way, not been the last to have a Zambian leader, and that few American bishops had spent their full four years of office in Africa, (more often it had been half that time), whilst less had bothered to learn a Zambian language. It was a view that reflected the increased self-confidence of the church's urban membership, and the growth of national feeling within the church since independence.[40]

Also important were the efforts of some of the ex-mission churches, with increasing local leadership, to meet the challenge of national social and economic problems.[41] What African Methodists in the Zambian government hoped to encourage was a large-scale commitment by their church, also, to community development projects, in co-operation with the government. The Rev. J. Siyomunji, Cabinet Minister for Western, and later Central, Province, and an African Methodist pastor, expressed this view in a paper entitled, 'The Role of the Church in a Developing Country', (20 November 1969), in which he urged his church to found agricultural co-operatives to raise rural living standards, and to initiate housing schemes to help the urban poor. To do this required a much larger income than the church had in 1969, and a higher level of management than brief visits by an American bishop could provide. Moreover, under the leadership of a Zambian bishop some of the well-educated members capable of organizing such projects, but then rather on the fringe of the church, might move closer to the centre, and the relevance of the church to its membership amongst the modernizing élite increase.

What the Presiding Elders were most concerned about was some means of training to prepare pastors to meet the challenge of rising educational standards amongst young people. The pastorate of the Zambian Church had always been a 'tent-making ministry'—pastors who financed themselves from secular employment and had simply the scriptures and their own religious experience to present to their fellow-men. The strength of the African Methodist Church had lain in these

has recently written a London University Ph.D. thesis (1971) on 'The A.M.E.C. in Southern Africa', and another is writing a history.

[40] Comments made in speeches by the Hon. W. Sikalumbi (then Minister of Land and Natural Resources) and the Rev. Mundia Wakunguma, respectively the lay secretary of the Conference and the Bishop's Vice-President, at the Joint Annual Conference, 1971-2, and repeated to me in conversation with approval by a number of the delegates.

[41] An interim report of this was given at the invitation of the Christian Council of Zambia by Chester Woodhall in his Churches and Development (August 1971) and is included as Appendix 15 in the Report of the Fourteenth Meeting of the Christian Council of Zambia (Lusaka, 1971).

fervent, conservatively-minded men of great character. They had largely created the church, and were still spreading it through the villages. Recent young entrants to the pastorate whom I interviewed between 1969 and 1972 were much the same as the older ones in this respect. In some cases their religious experience began with a dream. Generally their school education did not go far beyond the ability to read, and they had their own small plot in the village or a craft such as building or corn-milling to add to the 'minimum salary'. By contrast, more of the men in the towns had completed a primary school education and some had a few years at secondary school. Some had been clerks working in a mine or in government, or still were. Others ran small businesses. In their spare time some had taken correspondence courses from Wilberforce College or attended an evangelical Bible School. A handful of the leading pastors had actually studied at an AME college in the USA and completed a theological course, but bursaries from the American Church were infrequent and even to send one a year to USA was beyond the resources of the Zambian Church. The need was felt for some form of theological training in Zambia, and here, too, co-operation between the churches in some form of joint training centre seemed to offer the best way forward.[42] In other respects, also, for the AME Church co-operation with the other national churches, rather than separatism, was becoming a habitual policy.[43] Between 1973 and 1975, for example, the leading African Methodist layman, Mr Hosea Soko, served as chairman of the Christian Council of Zambia, and in 1975 Mr Wittington Sikalumbi, Secretary of the South Zambia Conference, and one of the most active laymen in Lusaka, agreed to serve as Vice-Chairman. The lay leadership, in particular, was steadily steering the church closer to other Zambian churches. But this was not the policy of the bishops.[44] Here, as in every

---

[42] The University of Zambia had no faculty of theology or philosophy. The United Church of Zambia had a small theological college at Mindolo on the Copperbelt, the African Reformed Church one in Lusaka. In 1972 the Anglican Church closed its St John's Seminary in Lusaka due to lack of funds and sought co-operation with other churches to mount a joint training centre. It seemed as if both the AME Church and the Roman Catholics would join such a venture, but a combination of clerical conservatism and the onset of the world economic depression in 1974 made this impossible. The AME Church between 1972 and 1976 obtained some training for its pastors from the Mindolo Ecumenical Centre, the International Training Centre in Lusaka run by the Farrar and McCabe families, and the United Church of Zambia college. (Information from personal interviews with the Rev. D. Whitehead, 26 March 1976, the Rev. David Simfukwe 25 March and 5 December 1976, and Mr McCabe and the Rev. T. Farrar, 25 March 1976.)

[43] For example the Rev. J. L. C. Membe was for some years involved with a Roman Catholic priest and a United Church of Zambia pastor upon a new translation of the Bible into Bemba at Mindolo Ecumenical Centre, an enterprise made possible by a long tradition of ecumenical activity in Zambia.

[44] Bishop Brookins (1972-6) on his arrival in Lusaka strongly attacked some of the other churches in some of his sermons.

other major issue, the unsolved problem of the church's leadership was increasingly felt.

The movement to have a Zambian bishop began soon after independence and came to a head after much discussion during Bishop Gomez' term of office. With some support from the Malawi and Rhodesia Conferences, the Rev. J. L. C. Membe, a Zambian pioneer known and respected in Malawi and Rhodesia, was elected at a meeting in Lusaka as the seventeenth Episcopal District's candidate for the four-yearly election of bishops by the General Conference at Dallas, USA, in 1972, which he and over thirty other delegates attended.[45] However, Bishop Gomez, who had been absent in USA at the time of Membe's election, did not accept the authenticity of his candidature, despite the fact that he came with a letter of commendation from President Kaunda, and, at the outset, the united support of the delegation.[46] Membe and the bulk of the seventeenth Episcopal District delegation soon realized that episcopal elections were controlled by the immense voting power of the American churches who were unlikely to support an outsider for such a highly prized position without very strong backing from Bishop Gomez.[47] Therefore they looked for another American bishop who was prepared to stay in Africa and develop the church rapidly with American funds to pave the way for a Zambian bishop at a subsequent election. With their support an energetic bishop, the Rt. Rev. Hartford Brookings, who had already made a name for himself in American dioceses, was assigned to the seventeenth Episcopal District. Meanwhile, Bishop Gomez had put forward the candidature of another member of the Zambian delegation, the Rev. Mundia Wakunguma, who had been his Vice-President and had deputized for him in his absence in USA. Wakunguma had been decisively outvoted by Membe in the Lusaka meeting, and received few votes at the Dallas Conference, but his unexpected candidature gave the impression that the seventeenth

---

[45] I was present at the election in Ebenezer Church, Lusaka. In the absence of the bishop, the Rev. Josephat Siyomunji, Cabinet Minister for Western Province, chaired the meeting. The two candidates were the Rev. J. L. C. Membe and the Rev. Mundia Wakunguma.

[46] Personal interviews with W. K. Sikalumbi 25 March and 6 December 1976, the Rev. David Simfukwe 25 March 1976 and the Rev. M. Wakunguma 26 March 1976. The arguments for electing indigenous bishops in the overseas Districts of the AME Church had already been cogently put by the Rev. F. H. Talbot of Guyana in the Sixteenth Episcopal District (Caribbean and South America) in *Voice of Missions,* April 1971, and Talbot was elected bishop of his District in 1972. I know from conversations with him that Bishop Gomez, who came from Trinidad, sympathized with localization but could not accept Talbot's view that overseas bishops should be elected locally and the election later ratified in USA. Hence he opposed the election of Membe in Lusaka. Only the General Council could elect.

[47] Personal interviews with W. K. Sikalumbi and the Rev. David Simfukwe (loc. cit.) In the General Conference held at Atlanta, Georgia, in June 1976, there were over 1500 certified electors, and probably only a few less in 1972.

Episcopal District was hopelessly disunited, and indeed sowed the seeds of future dissension.[48]

The failure to return with Membe as bishop was a disappointing blow to the Zambian church and there was some talk at first of refusing to accept Bishop Brookins.[49] However, an immediate crisis was averted by the fact that when he arrived he proved to be an eloquent preacher and strongly identified himself with the nationalistic, modernizing leaders of the town churches. He made it clear that he intended to spend his full four years of office in Africa, and he promised substantial financial assistance.[50] It was important also that he agreed to establish the assistance headquarters of the episcopal district in Zambia, not in Rhodesia, and a large house, standing in a forty-eight acre plot some twelve miles outside Lusaka was subsequently purchased for the bishop's residence, with plans to develop the site as a commercial farm and train Zambian farmers.[51] In 1974, as a result of his public support for the Zimbabwean nationalist movement, the bishop was prevented from visiting either Rhodesia or Malawi, and this concentrated his energies even further upon the new projects in Zambia. Apart from the farm there were two large-scale building schemes initiated on the advice of the Rev. J. Siyomunji and Wittington Sikalumbi. The first was to develop a valuable building site in a suburb of Lusaka near the International Airport to build one hundred houses and from the profits establish the church's finances. The second was the Bethel Project, a plan to build a cathedral church in the centre of Lusaka with an attached pre-school for seventy-five children and a secondary school for four hundred. A Bethel fund to obtain one-third of the required K250,000 from Zambian church members; the remainder was promised from America.[52]

Nevertheless, the failure to localize the bishop was eventually followed by a split in the church, whose significance it is still too early to assess,

[48] Personal interviews with W. K. Sikalumbi, the Rev. David Simfukwe and the Rev. Mundia Wakunguma, (loc. cit.). Unfortunately I have no account of these events from Bishop Gomez' view-point.

[49] I heard this personally just before I left Lusaka in 1972.

[50] Personal interviews with W. K. Sikalumbi, the Rev. David Simfukwe, (loc. cit.) Mrs Brookins, 28 March 1976 at the Bishop's residence, and the Rev. Chapala Banda, 28 March 1976 in Lusaka. Also a report in the *Mirror* (Lusaka) September 1974. The *Mirror* is a monthly inter-church newspaper produced by Multimedia, an ecumenical foundation.

[51] The *Mirror*, September 1974. From the report of the Afro-American pastor, the Rev. J. Langston Boyd who was appointed administrator of projects. A farm manager was hired to organize the planting of cash crops and poultry production. Also interviews with W. K. Sikalumbi (loc. cit.)

[52] The *Mirror*, September 1974, and personal interviews with W. K. Sikalumbi, the Rev. D. Simfukwe and the Rev. C. Banda, (loc. cit.). The houses were expected to sell for K2 million (about £1½ million). Due to the dishonesty of the contractor whom the bishop employed none of the houses had been completed by December 1976, but the church had substantial interest on a loan to repay.

but which must be placed in the context of loss of cohesion after the return of the delegation from Dallas without an authentic local leader. During the discussions which preceded Membe's election, ethnic and social differences were not far below the surface, but had been kept in check by the realization that the local candidate must go to America with united support, an understanding which might well have been strengthened by Membe's return as bishop. As it was, the delegation returned in a rising tide of recrimination and division between the original supporters of the Rev. J. L. C. Membe, who formed the bulk of the church in the Bemba-speaking Copperbelt and north, and the smaller party of the Rev. Mundia Wakunguma, a Lozi from Western Province, and Bishop Gomez' deputy, 1968-72. By 1974 the division had spread throughout the church, and when Bishop Brookins decided to transfer Wakunguma from Lusaka to a rural parish a substantial minority supported his refusal to obey the bishop, and left the church. In November 1974, with some two thousand supporters, the Rev. Wakunguma founded the African Methodist Independent Church, of which he became the first bishop. Significantly, it was the more conservative section of the AME Church that had broken away, that part which had resisted modernization, that disliked the strong Bemba influence both in Church and State, and cherished memories of a formerly independent Barotse kingdom. That the government recognized this dimension was shown by its refusal for a long period to register the new church as a permitted religious body.[53]

However, it would be wrong to view this schism in purely ethnic or tribal terms as some church members do. As Robert Molteno and others have shown, in present-day Zambia ethnic loyalties are used to obtain support in contests for power which have non-traditional aspirations.[54] Besides the total support of the many Lozi churches of Western Province, where only five members were reported by the *Times of Zambia* in November 1976 to have remained loyal to the AME Church,[55] the African Methodist Independent Church had captured many of the non-Lozi congregations in Livingstone, Southern and North-Western Provinces, and had been growing most rapidly in five centres in the multi-tribal squatter compounds on the edge of Lusaka. The appeal of its literature has distinctly been to the poor and downtrodden and against the 'urban intelligentsia', which it sees as manipulating the church to its

---

[53] Personal interviews with the Rev. M. Wakunguma and the Rev. C. Banda (loc. cit.) and the Government Gazette which published requests for licences from Independent Methodist churches which were not granted in 1975. Nonetheless they appear to have met for public worship in peoples' homes.

[54] Robert Molteno 'Cleavage and conflict in Zambian politics: a study in sectionalism' in William Tordoff (ed.) *Politics in Zambia* (Manchester, 1974).

[55] *Times of Zambia* 18 November 1976. It was one family.

own ends.[56] Equally important is the appeal of the new church to the older clergy who are afraid of the new ideas, and the new training programmes, Bishop Brookins and others have talked about, but which the younger, better-educated Copperbelt pastors have welcomed.[57] Finally, the split was precipitated by the bishop's decision to move Wakunguma from Lusaka, where he had a house and a relatively secure part-time employment in a College of Adult Education, to a rural parish where his church stipend would have been beggarly by comparison. It raised the whole question of the church's authority over a pastorate that was largely part-time or even voluntary.[58]

In some respects Bishop Wakunguma's Independent Church represented a return to an earlier form of the AME Church in Zambia, when, as he first experienced it in the colonial period, it had been a loosely knit group of independent congregations each expressing a different local identity and serving local needs with a self-help pastorate largely independent of central control. Since that time, the needs and ambitions of the laity in the towns have significantly altered. Leading figures in the church, after a period of nationalist revolution, have experienced participation in the management of a modern state with sophisticated bureaucratic systems and have aspirations to revolutionize mass living standards on a national scale. What these African Methodists are developing is a different kind of church, more national, more urban, more interested in reform than protest. But the problems of this kind of church in a developing country in a period of world recession are formidable. In June 1976 the thirty three delegates from the seventeenth Episcopal District that travelled to the General Conference of the AME Church at Atlanta, Georgia, found themselves 'victims of vividly exposed vexation'[59] when they learnt that Bishop Brookins, who had

[56] For example, the mimeographed document published in English, 16 February 1976, in reply to Bishop Brookins' invitation to rejoin the AME Church. Entitled, 'Reasons for Our leaving The AME Church and form the AMI Church', it complained of 'insults, demoralisation and despising used by the Bishop and his advisers a group of a few rich laymen, who hypocritically call themselves intellectuals, when in reality they are not better than ordinary Zambians'.

[57] This was mentioned by the Rev. D. Simfukwe, the Rev. M. Wakunguma and W. K. Sikalumbi in interviews (loc. cit.). The conservatism of the pastorate and tensions between them and better educated laymen were also given prominence by Walter Johnson in his study of the Lusaka Church a few years ago, cited in note 7. The African Methodist Independent apologia, cited in note 56, complained that the bishop and his advisers: 'in public meetings . . . have said . . . that they wanted young educated people and that the present leadership was out-dated, ignorant, too old and uneducated, and must be pushed out because they are feeding on the funds given by the people of God.'

[58] The AMI apologia, cited in note 56 asserted that most pastors earned only an average monthly stipend of K5 (or just under £4) so they could only be regarded as voluntary workers, and should not be transferred by the church from district to district by the bishop each year at the Annual Conference.

[59] The words of Wittington Sikalumbi, quoted from his *Brief Report on the 40th*

promised to stay in Zambia until the projects were completed sufficiently for a local man to be elected, had been re-assigned to a wealthy American diocese, leaving the Zambian church with crushing loans contracted with state finance institutions on the promise of funds from America which never materialized. A new bishop, the most recently ordained, had been assigned to the seventeenth Episcopal District.[60]

As much as any church in Zambia, the African Methodist Episcopal Church is in a process of becoming. Starting out as an 'Ethiopian' church which for many years was banned from entering colonial Zambia, after the ban was raised it was still distinguished for some years by the attentions of the Northern Rhodesia CID. It grew rapidly because it presented a Christianity that was relevant to the needs of African people, particularly the more ambitious and independent among them. It was sympathetic with their political aspirations and re-inforced them. Therefore, despite the formal neutrality of the pastorate, the church's relations with colonial government were generally somewhat uneasy. In this period, too, it was separated from much contact with mission churches. They disliked what was called 'poaching' and suspected its all-African management. But as mission churches began to respond more positively to their changing environment, the Christian Council ceased to be a 'mission club' and a wholly African church such as the AME Church was able to join. It was not, however, until political independence that the lay leaders and pastors became part of the new political and religious establishment. At this point Zambian nationalism became a more powerful force in the church than the older pan-African nationalism which had brought the church to Africa. A movement began to have a Zambian bishop and in other respects the church showed that it was evolving more into a national church seeking to solve its problems in co-operation with other Zambian churches that have similar needs. Though its financial resources have improved, the church is still poor by comparison with ex-mission churches. Five-sixths of its members come from scattered rural churches which in their small scale mirror the 'family' type institutions characteristic of village life. With their self-trained pastors these rural churches are very 'independent' in type, though intermittently assisted

Session of the General Conference of the AME Church, held at Atlanta, Georgia, 16-27 June 1976 (mimeo) page 15. On page 19 he comments: 'the unfulfilled promises made by the Bishop to assist us in financing the projects shall remain in our memories for many years to come'. Unfortunately, I have been unable to meet Bishop Brookins to elicit his side of the story.

[60] At the time of writing (December 1976) the newly appointed Bishop Thomas had not yet visited nor written to members of his new diocese although six months of his term of office had elapsed. (W. K. Sikalumbi, loc. cit.)

from the church's central funds. National feeling is strongest amongst the leadership and since independence there has been a merging at the top between church and government officials which make church-state relations an intimate affair at present. On the other hand amongst some of the rural churches sectionalism based upon ethnic and regional loyalties have contributed to the recent schism.

However, because of the change in the nature of the Zambian state, the major problem for the church has been how to adjust its relationship, based upon an earlier form of African nationalism, with the Mother Church in America. This has not yet been satisfactorily done. Nevertheless, despite schism and debt, the AME Church has continued to grow. The majority of the people in Zambia are still relatively uninfluenced by Christianity, and there can be no question about the AME Church's contribution to that challenge in villages and townships all over the country.[61]

[61] I should like to thank the many pastors and laymen of the AME and AMI Churches, whose kindness in answering my questions and giving me access to their Church papers has made this study possible.

Independent Churches and Independent States: Jehovah's Witnesses in East and Central Africa

SHOLTO CROSS

The Background

While the influence of the Watch Tower Bible and Tract Society (WTBTS)—or the Jehovah's Witnesses, as they have more familiarly been known since 1931—may be compared with that of the mission churches, in that like them it emanated from western Europe and America, it is distinct in two peculiar respects in its situation in Africa. Firstly, the WTBTS does not consider itself to be a church, or even a sect, but an organization. It believes that it is the religious duty of every member to attempt to convert non-believers (particularly the 'misguided' adherents of other faiths), yet it is not a missionary undertaking in the conventional sense. And it neither seeks any accommodation with the world or expects legitimation by the state. These features are consonant with the basic beliefs of the WTBTS that we are now living in imminent expectation of the 'end of all things' (the year 1975 is the most recently predicted date for apocalyptic happenings in a century of constantly revised analyses of Biblical chronology) when the Kingdom of God will be established on earth, to be ruled over by Christ and the witnesses of His truth amongst mankind, with the elevation to heaven of the 144,000 elect (Rev. xiv, 3). Temporal authority today represents the power of Satan, who is the invisible ruler of the earth, and when Christ and all His hosts defeat the powers of evil in the battle of Armageddon (an ongoing struggle symptomized by political turbulence on earth), temporal rulers too—including officers of the established churches ('Christendom')—will be cast into outer darkness. The WTBTS seeks to popularize this interpretation of the Bible, which is regarded as the exclusive truth, draw converts into a bureaucratically-managed and totalistic community, and passively to await the Kingdom. The conception of its religious function hence does not extend to medical, agricultural, or community development or the like, and since it views the state as fundamentally evil, it also requires its members to avoid all commitments to it other than the basic tributes of tax and keeping the peace. The Jehovah's Witnesses are a spiritual corporate organization, not a church.

Secondly, the WTBTS gave rise in central, although not in east Africa to an indigenous, Africanist millennial social movement, which provides contemporary Jehovah's Witnesses with a well-established history and tradition. Under the generic term 'Watch Tower', its characteristic ideas first entered Nyasaland in 1908 under prophetic African leadership, and were associated with resistance and rebellion to British colonial rule. Spreading with the diaspora of Tonga migrant labour over the ensuing decades to Southern and Northern Rhodesia, the Watch Tower movement acted as an early workers' movement, as a carrier of pan-Africanist ideologies, and as a vehicle for the expression of violent protest against foreign rule. Spreading into Angola and Mozambique it contributed towards the emergence of revolutionary nationalist movements, and in the Belgian Congo towards the formation of ethnically-based political parties.[1] The WTBTS repeatedly attempted to establish its control over the heterodox movements associated with its name, but with little success until the 1950s. And even then, as the following table shows, its period of legality in east and central Africa was a relatively short-lived one:

Country	Watch Tower first appears	WTBTS recognized	WTBTS restricted
Malawi	1908	1933	1967
S. Rhodesia	1914	1948	......
Zambia	1917	1948	1969
Tanzania	1919	1948	1964
Zaïre	1925	1959	1966
Kenya	1930's	1962	1973
Uganda	1940's	1948	1973

Despite these restrictions on its ability to organize, the WTBTS nevertheless accounts Africa as a continent where a major success has been made in increasing the number of Jehovah's Witnesses. About a quarter of a million of a global membership of 1.5 million Jehovah's Witnesses live in Africa. While there are less than 4,000 Witnesses in the three east African territories, 1.25 per cent of Zambia's population are members of the organization (about 130,000), and in 1943 there were approximately 60,000 in Malawi. A quarter of Zambia's Jehovah's Witnesses live in the Luapula province, which contains an eighth of the

[1] For a detailed study of the origins and expansion of Watch Tower in Africa, cf. Sholto Cross, 'The Watch Tower Movement in South Central Africa, 1908-1945', D.Phil. thesis, Oxford 1973.

national population, thus comprising what must be one of the densest areas of settlement of Witnesses in the world.

Recent Events

The relationships between the new African states and Jehovah's Witnesses consequently need to be seen against a background of a long and continuing involvement of this religion in changing Africa. The Watch Tower movement, as it is known today, consists not only in recruits to a bureaucratic sect managed from New York, but in long-standing members who have brought up their families as Witnesses. Certain areas of central Africa are steeped in a tradition that Watch Tower is not exotic and alien, but a local means of giving expression to hopes and grievances in opposition to the prevailing dispensation. In addition, there are a number of independent offshoots of the WTBTS which, although they may make use of the literature published in the Society's name, nevertheless regard themselves as fully autonomous and independent. Groups of independent Watch Tower adherents may be found today in the Central, Copperbelt, Luapula and Northern Provinces of Zambia, in Shaba province, Zaïre, in south-west Tanzania, and in eastern Angola. These are organized in village groups under prophetic leadership, and are often not distinguished in the public eye from the official movement. The Watch Tower, in other words, has a quality of grassroots, populist appeal which distinguishes it from most other fundamentalist sects and movements.

It would be short-sighted, of course, simply to perceive the popularity of the Watch Tower in terms of a voluntary association legitimating protest against central or local authority. Protest, and the urge to articulate it, emerges as changing social circumstances provide the individual with new aspirations which he feels powerless to realize through himself. The pace of social change has perhaps never been so rapid in central Africa as in this past first decade of independence; and the upheaval in expectations, the flooding migration to the towns, and the sudden inheritance of wealth and power by a new African *élite* have made the perceptions which contribute to the popularity of millennial ideas clearer and more widespread. The effect of membership of the Jehovah's Witnesses, as has been made clear in a number of recent studies,[2] has been to make it more possible for these new aspirations to be realized in practice. The Witnesses inculcate an ethic of social respectability, rather than necessarily one of economic achievement, and provide the believer with a closely-knit circle of fellows spreading not

---

[2] N. Long, *Social Change and the Individual*, (Manchester, 1968); S. L. Thrupp (ed.), *Millennial Dreams in Action*, (Comp. Stud. Soc. Hist., Supp. II, 1965).

only across the country in actuality, but at least in belief across the world. The tribesman may achieve literacy; as an economically aspirant person he is protected from the fear of witchcraft accusations designed to redistribute his wealth; and, upon his death, his immediate heirs can resist claims by the matrikin on his estate. He feels that he can understand the bewildering changes of the outside world in terms of an ideological interpretation which links innovation even at the most parochial level with the promise of ultimate salvation. The solidarity of the group is maintained and reinforced both by externalizing hostilities against the outside world, and by the central ideology which holds the state to be an institution of Satan, which may not command loyalty from the Witness, even though he is prepared to render unto it its due, according to his own perception of this.

While the Watch Tower thus has a long history in Africa, and is providing a basis for response to change in an ongoing fashion, the politicians too have often had a long acquaintance with the movement. As their perceptions of the problems of governing newly independent societies have altered, so too have their attitudes towards the Watch Tower changed. It is a truism that the political classes of the new African states achieved their initial prominence very often as a result of a mission education, but it is less generally recognized that it was particularly the mission graduate who was the firm enemy of the sectarian and fundamentalist small churches, which were sometimes perceived as rivals not only in spiritual matters. More particularly, however, it has been the understanding by African politicians of the goals they need to achieve which has led them into conflict with the Jehovah's Witnesses. The clashes and restrictions may be more accurately explained by an examination of the particular demands of politicians, I would contend, than by depicting the Jehovah's Witnesses as highly political movements in themselves. This is not to say that membership of a Watch Tower group does not imply the pursuit of certain ideologies which have political significance, nor that these have not on occasion actively provoked confrontation with the power of the State, creating self-fulfilling prophecies concerning martyrdom. But the course of events would appear to be determined more by the kings of the State than by the state of the Kingdom.

Zambia

The situation of Jehovah's Witnesses in Zambia provides an illustration of this. During the 1950s and into the early 1960s, the WTBTS under the branch chairmanship of H. W. Arnott succeeded in organizing the movement throughout the Federation, bringing most of the old independents within the effective control of the bureaucracy based on Salisbury and Kitwe. Assemblies were held at regular intervals attended by delegations from most countries in east and central Africa, and—apart from the question of whether these should be segregated or not—the Witnesses by and large kept out of the political disturbances which accompanied the transition to independence. Within two years of independence however, the groundwork for later clashes with the State was laid. With the transition from anti-colonial nationalism to the new politics of nation-building, President Kaunda's government placed a heavy emphasis on universal primary schooling, the singing of the national anthem and the chanting of political slogans concerning national unity at public functions, and the display of the Zambian national flag at all bomas and schools. Tribalism, disunity and a general lack of civic consciousness were held out in ministerial speeches and party propaganda as the major internal problems which have to be overcome in order that the pre-independence pledges of rapid advance might be fulfilled. Witnesses began to withdraw their children from school rather than see them forced to salute the flag and sing the national anthem, and by May, 1967, with over 500 children on the Copperbelt suspended from school, government officials led by the Minister for Education were warning Jehovah's Witnesses that they could expect to be banned.

Much of the hostility was directed at first against the European officials of the WTBTS who were criticized as being alien and hostile influences, perpetuating the ignorance of the Africans for their own sinister and neo-colonial ends. This of course was in accordance with the policies of the Mulungushi Reforms of April 1967, which looked forward to the Zambianization of all walks of life in Zambia—a policy of localization which met with a spontaneous acclaim from the mass of Zambians, whose enthusiasm for the United National Independence Party was hardly at that pitch of fervour which national politicans expected. The European officials of the WTBTS were expelled from Zambia in mid 1967, but the expulsion of children from schools went on. At this stage the police stepped in, and began to harass those Witnesses who refused to co-operate with national registration, vaccination programmes, and saluting the flag, and in a number of cases assemblies of Witnesses were broken up. A case was brought in the courts against this action, which appeared to have a chance of success. In September 1967, senior police officials and Zambian representatives of the WTBTS held a meeting at which it was agreed that harassment would cease and that the court case would be dropped.

During 1968 the dispute nevertheless escalated, with the role of ministers and police being taken over by party activists and senior politicians. A leading politician, Mainza Chona, set the tone by calling the Witnesses 'a party of abstainers'. From being a neo-colonialist influence that hindered development policies and the legitimate extension of state control, the image of the Jehovah's Witness now changed to one of a subterranean political party that sought to withold popular loyalty from UNIP. This was a period when Kaunda was attempting to realize his aim of a transition to a one-party state not by legislation from the top, but by popular acclaim. The general election of 1968 and the national referendum of 1969 were crucial steps along this road, and UNIP was in a state of constant mobilization during this period in an attempt to bring out a sufficiently large vote to ensure the smooth transition to a one-party constitutional order.

The tradition of political mobilization in Zambia—particularly on the Copperbelt—has been and is a violent one. The line drawn between card-checking campaigns and political blackmail, between sloganeering and intimidation and harassment, and between supervising the polling and beating up the opposition has not always been a clear one. Where a group as visible as the Witnesses existed, who neither were sacrosanct like the expatriates, nor led by a nationally important figure as were the African National Congress supporters, victimization might be expected. The position was exacerbated by the fact that not only was UNIP losing its exclusive control over the voter with the continuing support for the ANC, but there were also rumblings within UNIP, particularly in the northern provinces. Dissension had to be discouraged by sharp example. Members of the Watch Tower, who refused to buy party cards or register as voters, and on one notorious occasion, flaunted party discipline by walking past a voters' queue in the pouring rain with an elaborate display of umbrellas and indifference, provided an obvious target. In periodic outbursts of violence between July 1968 and January 1969, 45 Kingdom Halls were burnt, 469 houses destroyed, some K50,000 of cash and property looted, and a dozen or more Witnesses killed. In parts of the country, as at Samfya and Mansa in Luapula Province, Witnesses were forced to live in the bush, and the fact that they armed themselves with bows and arrows led to renewed fears that a confrontation of the proportions of the Lumpa[3] clashes would take place.

It was at this point that Kaunda entered the arena, hitherto occupied by such party hardliners as Mainza Chona, Fwanyanga Mulakita and Fines Bulawayo, and spent a day in conference with the Zambian WTBTS officials. As a result of the President's intervention, the policy of religious tolerance was publicly re-iterated, the ban on Witnesses

[3] The Lumpa church led by Alice Lenshina Mulenga was active in Northern Rhodesia/Zambia in the 1950s and 1960s , creating disturbances which led to armed suppression and mass arrests.

preventing them from entering markets, building meeting places, and attending religious services in each other's homes was removed, and members of the UNIP Youth were charged on various counts of assault and arson. Over the next two years, the intensity of this confrontation died down, but tension remained. A partial ban on the Witnesses was announced late in 1969 which prevents them from house-to-house canvassing, but their activities have nevertheless continued. Occasionally their meeting-places are destroyed, and police are reluctant to grant permission for the massive popular assemblies which are a feature of their organization. Yet the level of these conflicts has constantly sunk further away from the national arena to a parochial dispute involving local authorities and the police. The corresponding development in the national arena, of course, has been the externalization of the opposition within UNIP as the United Peoples Party under Simon Kapwepwe, and the declaration of Zambia as a one-party state.

An Overview

The argument, then, is that the evolving attempts of UNIP and its leadership to establish itself in sole command of the State brought about conflict with the Jehovah's Witnesses, at a time when intense political demands were being placed upon the country. This is not necessarily an argument that the conflict reflects cynical political expediency within the ruling party; to the extent that this existed, it conflicted with Kaunda's conception of the political life of the state. His view of the Witnesses, and the reasons for enunciating restrictions on them, were that they promoted divisiveness within the nation and represented a foreign influence, as they refused to participate in the national Zambian Christian movement favoured by the President. The Zambian case does suggest, however, that we should carefully examine the dimensions of political crisis within the State in attempting to reach a general picture of the situation of the Jehovah's Witnesses in east and central Africa.

The spectrum of possible bases for restrictions, persecution, and banning may extend from the cynical and expedient use of state power to eradicate the movement to restrictions which stem from a principled, ideologically-based conviction that Jehovah's Witnesses are so mis-guided as to be a danger not only to themselves but to others; and finally, perhaps, to paranoiac and demagogic policies which will not permit any opposition, and which see in any opposition the threat of revolution. As has been suggested, Zambia's response has veered between that of political expediency and legitimate concerns over the divisive consequences of their activity. The background of crisis was pre-eminently within the sphere of institutional politics, rather than economic or social upheaval.

The control of Kitawala in Zaïre has arguably been based largely on the politics of expediency, as President Mobutu has battled to outlaw purely local associations, which are blamed for the failure of national policies, the existence of corrupt politicians, and movements of opposition towards his rule. In Kenya, where the Witnesses number only a few thousand and have for the most part been particularly passive in nature, the recent banning would appear to be an easy way of gaining popularity by outlawing a minority group for a government which is considered generally to be too removed from the people. In Uganda and Malawi, however, the violence which Presidents Amin and Banda have unleashed against the Witnesses suggests that these leaders perceive the Witnesses as a genuine threat to their rule. Banda has sought to eliminate every vestige of opposition from Malawi, and consistently directed the MCP Young Pioneers against the Witnesses, such that by the end of 1972 some 20,000 refugees had fled into Zambia, and many hundreds of adherents had been killed. While Amin's actions may simply reflect the actions of the populist demagogue who buys time for his regime in a period of social and economic chaos by banning unpopular minorities, Banda's actions suggest the politics of the ageing tyrant, motivated chiefly by fear, who sees conspiracies around every corner. At the other extreme, President Nyerere's banning of the Watch Tower in 1968 stemmed from his impatience with any ideological challenge to his own conception of the establishment of the political kingdom.

Common to these states, however, have been national politics which have sought constantly for the centralization of power and the dominance of public life by a single, total institution. Because of its ideological attractiveness under current circumstances and its deep-rooted history in the area, the Watch Tower movement has run strongly counter to these absolutist tendencies. At critical stages in the political life of the new African states, the adherents of the movement have been perceived as a threat, and placed under restrictions which have little real relevance to their potential as revolutionary opponents of the state. Perhaps the WTBTS may take some comfort from the thought that given these centralizing tendencies, it is the established churches which are next in line for domination, should the politics of crisis so demand.

The State and Development Ideology [4]

While the open conflict between the state and such independent religious

---

[4] This section of the paper is an abridgement of my seminar paper 'The State, the Church, and Revolution in Independent Africa', delivered at SOAS, May, 1975, and also available for discussion at the Jos Conference.

groupings as the Watch Tower reveals clearly some of the political dimensions of the Church-State clash in Africa, this may perhaps be merely a preliminary skirmish to the confrontation between the one-time mission churches—many of which are now seeking to re-establish themselves as fully autonomous local entities—and secular authority. Adopting the same perspective as for the analysis of the Watch Tower, it may be contended as a corollary that the current adoption by many African churches of the priority of 'development' is far from being a real contribution towards material and spiritual needs, and indeed is a measure of their subordination to the state. In so far as the state's goals of economic development are objectively well-placed, an acceptance of direction by the churches may be unimportant, but the relationship between the state and the ideology of 'development' needs at least to be questioned.

As part of the process of centralization and the extension of control, the modern African state has sought to encapsulate voluntary associations within its party and bureaucratic structures—the best example being, perhaps, the elaborate rules for registration maintained in Zaïre, inherited from a Belgian colonial administration almost pathological in its fear of uncontrolled African activities. The new nationalism, arising from the attempt to transform anti-colonial solidarity into new forms of popular and emotional support for the leaders, has also helped to displace the church in a more subtle way: through endowing the new nation with mystical qualities and surrounding the leader and his utterances with an aura of reverence, the state itself is sacralized. Such policies emerge from weakness, rather than from strength; they are mounted in the face of highly fragmented and differentiated societies generally lacking a civic political culture. The state, then, is jealous of its authority and fearful of any undermining of its monopoly over the means of persuasion and coercion, and the function of prescribing national policy. These attempts to consolidate power are often legitimized in terms of development—a commitment towards economic and social goals, which has the further benefit of being expressed in the language of the professional world of the international administrator and the multifarious family of UN agencies.

The language and ideology of development thus not only constitute policies which objectively further the public weal, but are also—and perhaps predominantly—the modern form of a justificatory stance for the relationship between the state and the individual. To the extent to which the church unquestioningly adopts the language and priorities of development simply as a blueprint for economic growth, it may be discarding both its prophetic role and its capacity to further social revolutionary changes.

The example of the conflict over family planning lays bare one central issue of politics in those states which have directed themselves towards development as an overriding goal: where does the locus of moral authority lie? With civil authorities, or in those persons and institutions who care for the pastoral well-being of the people? It is only in a disestablished and secularized world, of course, that the problem can be posed in these terms, and it is a measure both of the fragility of the State and of the failure of the church to maintain credible moral leadership that each should feel it necessary to seek an exclusive voice in this field. Both in Zambia and Zaïre the debate between political and church leaders over family planning introduced the question of to what extent sovereign countries should accept external direction on policy issues of this sort; the terms of the debate were apparently more over who is master in whose house than over the substantive merits of family planning. But underlying the debate was the more serious question of the relative responsibility of church and state for the moral and physical well-being of the people. The recourse to dogmas of sovereignty and hierarchical ukases, it might be said, reflected competition for legitimate moral leadership rather than substantive disagreement.

In looking at the church in relation to the state and problems of economic development, then, we are looking not only at the classic problems of rivalry and competition for supremacy, but also at the clash between formal value systems. The development ideologies of most African states constitute one or other type of secular nationalism, embodying principles of economic rationality. Where these are expressed in quasi-religious terms—as in Zambian humanism—they tend either to be personalist philosophies, ideal statements with little reference to actual values and motivations, or simply ideological statements which are not operating as programmes. Tanzania has reviewed the real effectiveness of the *Ujamaa* policies as motivating factors; and the leadership codes which ask for a moral commitment to state goals do so mainly in terms of economic rationality. Even if we accept Weber's thesis on the mutual emergence of the Western ideas of progress and capitalist development with the Protestant virtues of thrift, sobriety, and investment, we must be aware of the way in which under late capitalism the value basis has shifted away from these formal religious values to more secular ideas of efficiency, profit maximization, and a belief in rational market forces. Where mission Christianity attempted simply to transpose the Protestant ethic in an attempt to make development happen, this could backfire—as it served to crystallize a rural and urban *élite* whose minds were fixed on the Western way of doing things, who had lost the ability to communicate and respond to rural society, and who came to be increasingly individualistic in their attitudes towards prosperity.This is the very situation, of course, against which modern rural development strategies are aimed.

The post-colonial states have in their own ideologies of development—which I have suggested should be read in connection with their attempts to legitimate the continuation of the political class in office—sought to secularize the idea of progress. Where does the church stand in relation to this? With the state monopolizing the field of policy, and attempting to increase its hold over the individual, it seems somewhat misplaced for the church to concentrate on formal religious values. It is generally debatable to what extent customary religions, such as those studied by Geertz and Bellah in Asia, did in any event contain the ideological seeds which helped the development process to be launched, and of course in Africa the historical origins of the dominant religious systems is very different.[5] Smelser has commented that 'insofar as religious belief systems encourage the break-up of old patterns, they may stimulate economic modernization. Insofar as they resist their own subsequent secularization, however, these same value systems may become an impediment to economic advance and structural change'.[6] If the church is not simply to be a conveyor belt for a spiritual version of rational economic motivation, inappropriate and class-based notions of the sanctity of property, or to provide a legitimatory service for the state in its demands for loyalty, what roles does it have to play?

Given the political dynamic of the current situation, it is clear that the church must challenge the idea that the state has the sole prerogative and responsibility over civic virtues. If this means adopting an 'anti-development' stance, it is probably a good thing. The church might learn from the emergence of 'sects', or the myriad of smallscale and unestablished religious groups in Africa, the nature of popular demands for a new moral framework. Urbanization from Abidjan to Lusaka has meant the extension of the city to the countryside, and of the peasant culture to the squatter settlements and bidonvilles. The problems of development are in many essentials the problems for this multitude of coming to terms with city life: the entry into relationships which go beyond the extended kinship network, the impersonalization of work relationships, and the lack of values to provide cohesion for mass urban living. Sects contain and display the duality of religious orientation to this-wordly and other-worldly goals in a very clear way. They provide a close-knit sense of community catering specifically for material needs

[5] Clifford Geertz, *Old Societies, New States*, 1966; R. N. Bellah, *Tokugawa Religion*, 1957. Also relevant is J. M. Yinger, *Religion in the Struggle for Power*, 1946.

[6] Neil Smelser, 'Mechanisms of Change and Adjustments to Change', in Finkle and Gable (eds.), *Political Development and Social Change*, 1966.

and ambitions, and some sects even have the air of being craft guilds, so specific is their orientation. Simultaneously, they maintain a fairly intense religious life, where day-to-day actions are subject to the guidance of religious authority, and prayer and ritual constantly reinforce the integration of religious values with public and private morality. It might indeed be argued that the explosion of sects in Africa today is a reflection on the incapacity of the quasi-established churches to cater for the emerging needs of the people.

If it is not to be forced to the sidelines by the political demands of the post-colonial state as simply a residual insititution catering for spiritual needs which are not generally regarded as having anything to do with building the foundations of a new society—a familiar picture in a number of countries—the church has, then, to be socially revolutionary. A contribution which particularly needs to be made is towards the establishment of a value system which will mitigate the consumption orientation and gross elitism of economic rationalism, and help to promote a style of development which is genuinely participant. Given the dominating concerns of most modern African states, I would contend, established status for the church would tend to jeopardize, rather than promote, the achievement of these aims. The historical power base in the metropolitan country and expatriate ruling community should not be exchanged for one in the new political class. To the extent that the church has to seek its own power base from which to resist the attempted domination and subordination by the state, this should not be within the ranks of groups with vested interests or regional demands, but at a popular level. The identification of basic needs, the mobilization of demands, and the communication of these to the state are the primary functions which the church should seek to fulfil.

Modern education among Freetown Muslims & the Christian stimulus

L. O. SANNEH

Entering upon Islam in Freetown is like walking through a minefield. The record of acute rivalry and internecine struggles makes it a special case in West African Islam. The divisive factors are alive even today, and an unwary student of the scene can, by probing almost anywhere at random, bring to the surface old quarrels and disputes which have their present day equally truculent varieties. Part of the explanation for the fragmentation of Muslim communal life is the strong currents of local drive and energy which, because they are often unco-ordinated and not precisely focussed, run at cross-purposes and generate tension instead of leading to communal efficiency. An important factor behind communal factionalism is undoubtedly the tribal or ethnic consideration, but that is by no means a sufficient explanation or even a consistent one. The divisions are deeply complex and alignments shift markedly across groups as well as within them, to such an extent that almost every major issue acquires the character of a separate and all-sufficient cause in itself: the *hajj*, election of community heads, or, more officially, tribal headmen, upkeep of the Muslim cemetery, the religious calendar—particularly at Ramaḍan—, hospitality to important Muslim dignitaries, and that fertile field of conflict, mosque-building, are some examples. Education, our chief concern here, is one such matter, and, like the other subjects of Freetown Islam, it has acted like a multiple time fuse, primed to go off every time the subject is brought up, and each time widening the rift between the factions.

The Muslim community, i.e. the informal conglomeration of community interests, at a very early date was concerned with Western (hereafter modern) education, and the colonial administration from the 1870s onward tried to bring Muslims the benefits of modern education through state sponsorship. Various schemes were launched which looked promising, but these invariably failed because of Muslim in-fighting and intra-ethnicity which flared up and engulfed the very projects designed to reduce tribal and other forms of local jealousy and conflict. It is significant, through a digression here, to see the extent to which Muslims utilized certain government institutions, such as the law courts, to compose disputes, even though the litigation process might actually exacerbate tension and harden attitudes, while other institutions like government schools and similar subsidized facilities were not taken advantage of to the same degree. The number of lawsuits and legal appeals and petitions which Muslims brought against each other bears tesimony to the endemic character of the splits in Freetown Islam. In the past the colonial administration tried to act as referee and help resolve some of the disputes, but some are still outstanding. It is of course misleading to try to suggest that the Muslim community, if such a homogeneous body can be pinpointed, was a disfunctional society, and indeed some of the disputes have led to the progress and extension of Muslim life in some parts. But this must be understood in the context of unceasing tension and conflict, and sometimes the process has even been in spite of the Islamic status of the protagonists. It is impossible to begin to understand present attitudes to modern education without a brief account of the historical background. My reliance on those who have worked before in this field will be obvious from the footnotes.

Muslim settlement in the Freetown colony[1] began at about the same time as the Christian presence. The original Muslim colony had as its nucleus liberated Africans who had been Muslim or had converted to Islam. It is customary to call these original Muslim settlers Aku, a term inadequately taken to mean Yoruba Muslims.[2] The earliest Muslim settlements were in the three villages just outside Freetown: Aberdeen, Hastings and Waterloo, but after about 1833 a large number of these groups migrated to Fourah Bay and Fula Town in the east end of Freetown.[3] From now on the border line between so-called Yoruba Muslims and the 'Natives' begins to look tenuous. Mandinka, Fulani, Susu, Temne and some other 'native' Muslims lived alongside the Aku,

[1] See Christopher Fyfe: *A History of Sierra Leone*, London, 1962; P. Kup, *A History of Sierra Leone, 1400–1787,* London, 1961.

[2] The nucleus of the Aku may have been Yoruba Muslims, but it is obvious that their number included Creole Christian converts. I do not know of any satisfactory explanation of how in fact this Yoruba nucleus was able to preserve its language and culture on slave plantations, particularly if dispersal of slaves was a feature of plantation life. If Aku is taken to mean Yoruba and that in turn is taken to mean Muslim, how does one designate Yoruba Christians among the Creole population? Michael Banton hints at the difficulty in linguistic terminology when he writes (*West African City*, London, 1957, p 153): 'Perhaps 5,000 Creoles would today describe themselves as Aku though the number who can speak Yoruba is much less.' In other words 'Aku' in fact comprises more than Yoruba-speaking Muslims. In the Gambia Aku is used to describe the entire Creole community, Christian and Muslim, with the latter being distinguished as Aku-Marabout.

[3] David E. Skinner: 'Islam in Sierra Leone During the 19th Century', Ph.D. thesis, Berkeley, 1971, p 142. This is a disappointing piece of work on a potentially fruitful topic. Poor documentation (there is no use of French or Arabic sources except in translation) and weak organization suggest it was hastily put together. I use it *faute de mieux.*

who themselves included Creole converts, in distinct pockets around the east end of Freetown.

The colonial administration, convinced of the need to pursue a policy of ethnic separation to preserve social balance in Freetown, acted between 1833 and the 1860s to prevent the Creole Christian community from being swamped by waves of local immigration, and since most migrants from the hinterland included important Muslim groups, this turned out to be the government's Muslim policy. However, the colonial authorities departed from this policy as abruptly as they had embarked on it, a change due largely to the efforts of Dr Edward Wilmot Blyden who, between 1870 and 1905, succeeded in obtaining both government and mission support for modern schools among Muslims. But the fragmentation of Muslim community life, which was not helped by the earlier official policy, exerted a negative effect on much of Blyden's initiatives, though impressive tangible results accrued from his work.[4] The Muslims in Fourah Bay, for example, split up into rival factions: the Haruniyah party led by the *Jama'ah* and the Suleimaniyah party led by the Tamba[5] men[6]. Although other issues lay at the centre of such divisions, the educational factor was the ostensible cause of the breach.

Temne Islam was similarly affected by endemic rivalries where the educational factor aggravated the forces of antagonism. A Temne educated at al-Azhar in Cairo founded the Almamiyah Society in an effort to contain the growing power of the Ambas Geda, led by S. B. Kamara, the colourful Temne tribal leader, better known as Kande Bureh. The Ambas Geda was a secret ritual dance society dedicated to the preservation of Temne traditional values in an urban milieu.[7] The struggle between the Almamiyah Society and the Ambas Geda was not a conflict between secularism and Islam, as has been suggested,[8] but simply a straight contest between styles of educated leadership. Another Temne leader, Shaykh Jibril Sisay, also educated at al-Azhar, found himself at the centre of Temne factionalism. After he established a modern school and appeared as the champion of educational advancement, the old *élite* in the Temne community decided to act in

[4] Skinner, 1971, 154–56.

[5] The word 'tamba' comes from a Mandinka phrase, *'tamba muru'*, meaning a 'two-edged blade which a man cannot squarely grasp.' It was applied to the Fourah Bay Muslim faction after a Mandinka mediation attempt failed. The factions became delicately poised for a confrontation. Leslie Proudfoot: 'An Aku Factional Fight in East Freetown', *Sierra Leone Bulletin of Religion,* vol 4, no 2, 1962, 86.

[6] Proudfoot, *op cit.*

[7] Michael Banton, 1957, 166–67. The word 'geda' is Krio, meaning an assembly, gathering or association, and indicates the eclecticism and aspirations of the founders.

[8] Proudfoot: 'Mosque-building and Tribal Separatism in Freetown', *Africa,* xxix, no 4, 1959, 410.

concert against one they regarded as an upstart. Shaykh Jibril was accused of misallocating funds donated for the school, and the issue became laden with political meaning. He was eventually tried and incarcerated at the Central Prisons for two years before the political scales were reversed and he was discharged. He was given a martyr's reward and sent to Cairo as Sierra Leone's ambassador, which post he held until recently.[9] The Temne community lost the school he founded and have not been able to replace it or found similar schools.

In the early 1900s the colonial powers encouraged the setting up of a school, identified at that stage with the Mandinka community. In 1905 the name of the school was changed from Mandinka School to Madrasa Islamiyah with the intention of encouraging other ethnic groups to send their children there. But the wider participation which the government hoped for never materialized and the school passed under a cloud, though it revived later under a different impetus.[10] Muslims also opened schools on their own initiative, and here again, as in the other situation, all such efforts were led by people who had to run the gauntlet of intense factionalism. In the 1920s and 30s Muslim efforts to create schools for their children were intensified, and out of this desire for educational improvement were born the two main rival groups in modern Freetown Islam: the Muslim Congress, followed by the rival Muslim Association. Within these two main factions were other competing alignments, so that no one set of factors or explanations can account for the complexities of Muslim attitudes. In 1922 Hadir-ud-Deen, as Secretary of the Muhammadan Education Board, proposed organizing Muslims into a unified body. Divisiveness was to be confronted directly. The result, a few years later, was the Muslim Congress, registered as a friendly society in 1932.[11] A Lebanese Muslim was instrumental in setting it up after correspondence with Jerusalem. The leading lights were Aku Muslims, though other ethnic groups were also active, for example, Almamy Daramé, the Mandinka Headman, who was among the original members.

The Muslim Congress filled two needs: it represented an independent Muslim initiative and it also provided a counterweight to the predominantly Christian influence in modern education.[12] The first object was, however, qualified by the fact that Congress received generous support from the Lebanese trading community.[13] Congress

[9] Interview with Idriss Alamy, an official of the UAR Cultural Centre, Freetown.

[10] Proudfoot, 1959, 407–8.

[11] Proudfoot: 'Towards Muslim Solidarity in Freetown', *Africa*, xxxi, 1961, p. 148.

[12] Ibid p. 155.

[13] *Op. cit.* During the visit in 1959 of Shaykh al-Hajj Cherri, an American Lebanese,

arranged for three local Muslims to proceed to al-Azhar for higher Islamic studies: Shaykh Jibril Sisay already mentioned, who was a student in the Gambia, Nazir Sahid and Abdul Karim Ghazali. The local Muslim newspaper which carried news of the scholarships ended with a moral piece: 'He who pursueth learning, walketh in the way of Allah.'[14]

But Congress again was wracked by divisions within the Muslim community. A break-away elitist group, the Muslim Association, was formed in April, 1942, with emphasis on primary and middle school for Arabic and Islam.[15] Its founder-president was Ahmed Alhadi, Master of the Rolls, Registrar and Administrator of Intestate Property, 'who developed a remarkable gift for legalistic formulation.'[16] The Association built a school at the foot of Mount Aureol, support for which was raised entirely from voluntary contributions.[17] Its first headmaster was a prominent Freetown political figure, Lamina Sankoh, formerly the Rev. E. N. Jones, an ordained Christian who eventually gave up the cloth.[18] At about the same time a new Muslim newspaper, the *Ramadan Vision*, was launched under the editorship of its proprietor, Abbas Camba, and this publication joined vigorously in the campaign for modern education among Muslims. Initially on the side of the Association, it advocated the strengthening of modern schools among Muslims and castigated Congress for its niggardly performance here. Within a short time of its founding, the Association was overseeing four schools in Freetown and one each in Aberdeen and Goderich.[19] Congress, however, continued to be active, and was in fact long to outlive its bitter rival. It held a successful fund-raising campaign at the Islamiyah School room on Sunday, 22nd August, 1943, where a large sum, including a single £200 sterling gift, was raised.[20] And like the Association the Muslim Congress was patronized by the Lebanese community and the government which was keen to encourage educational projects among Muslims.

It is clear that what united both the Association and Congress was their paramount desire to emulate Christian performance in modern education, for the overwhelming strength of Christian schools demon-

---

generous support was received for projects launched by the Muslim Congress.

[14] The *Ramadan Vision,* July, 1947, p. 4.

[15] Proudfoot, 1961, p. 151.

[16] Ibid p. 152.

[17] *Op. cit.*

[18] Interview, Abbas Camba, Freetown. A prominent street in the centre of Freetown is named after Lamina Sankoh.

[19] *Ramadan Vision*, August 19, 1944, p. 4.

[20] Ibid. p. 8.

strated where real power and influence lay. In this and other ways the Christian example was the direct, even if sometimes hidden, stimulus for Muslim efforts. But the Christian example, in spite of its obvious character, excited the spirit of factionalism among Muslims. The Association, fed by the *Ramadan Vision* with doses of sectarian indiscretion, openly derided the poor educational standing of Congress rank and file, and Ahmed Alhadi, A. F. Rahman and (now al-Hajj) Muhammad Mahdi, stood out on the side of the Association as the 'eager young men' of a new enlightened generation of Muslims.[21] These men were also prominent in championing a parallel educational development in the Muslim community to that which was taking place in the Christian one. It is ironic and perhaps inevitable that the Association as a Muslim organization should seek its justification in acceptance by the Christian community. An anonymous pamphlet, for example, widely attributed to Ahmed Alhadi, called attention to the contribution the church had made to the development of Sierra Leone, and emphasized that although Islam had called people to similar ventures of social improvement and nation-building, the actual contribution of Muslims in this field was paltry.[22] His own example of what Muslims could do did not rise above popular sermonising.[23]

The *Ramadan Vision* echoed such sentiments of emulating Christian example and declared, somewhat over-enthusiastically: 'Sierra Leone is witnessing the dawn of a new era in their (sic) awakening of higher education amongst Muslims.'[24] The credit for this was attributed to the 'spread of progressive ideas' among Muslims who had acquired the ambition to achieve equality 'with prominent members of our much favoured brethren the Christians.'[25] Another sign of the leavening influence of Christian example was the question of higher education for Muslim girls, although in the venerable Muslim tradition, the sanction and justification for this was found in the Qur'ān.[26]

The *Ramadan Vision* became carried away by its own enthusiasm. Its editor launched a colourful diversion and founded and became chief organizing secretary of the Fujalto Muslim Orchestra, intended to increase the pace of educational reform among Muslims.[27] The orchestra openly sought and received Christian assistance and blessing. Its Musical

[21] Proudfoot, 1961, p. 148.
[22] *Op. cit.*
[23] He dwelt on the Quar'ānic verse about man being a vicegerent of God (ii:28; xxi:105; xxxviii:25;xxxviii:25) and how man should be a partner with God in engaging in acts of creation in the world. Proudfoot, *op. cit.*
[24] *Ramadan Vision,* July, 1947, p. 2.
[25] *Op. cit.*
[26] Ibid p. 3. Qur'ān xxxiii:35ff (Flügel verse numbering).
[27] *Ramadan Vision,* July, 1947, p. 6.

Director was Mr C. W. Mann, a Christian organist at the prestigious Holy Trinity Church, Freetown.[28] The second performance of the orchestra was at Holy Trinity School during the *mawlid* celebrations.[29] Musical programmes included familiar *madīḥ* praise songs on the Prophet as well as some Christian music.[30] What seemed an enterprising if slightly unusual innovation in Freetown Muslim educational and social life ceased when the orchestra was disbanded following the withdrawal of its founder from active life.[31]

In the run up to independence (1961) education continued to play a critical role in the life of Freetown Muslims—and with no abatement of the factional spirit, leaving aside the activities of the Aḥmadiyāh Missionary Movement in Sierra Leone which will be considered separately. The prelude to independence found the Muslims increasingly out of step with their Christian counterparts. Not for the first time, some Muslim representatives at a public meeting pointed out the inadequacy of traditional Muslim education and recognized that political independence would reveal even more the inappropriateness of an al-Azhar type of training.[32]

In the Orthodox Muslim community—perhaps more on the fringes of it ideologically because of proven Aḥmadiyāh influence—one of the most ambitious educational enterprises was the educational work of the Muslim Brotherhood, *al-Ukhūwāh al-Islāmiyāh*, founded in Magburaka by al-Hajj Sori Ibrahim Kanu.[33] This movement is to be carefully distinguished from the politically militant *Ikhwān al-Muslimīn,* the Egyptian Islamic order normally associated with Muhammad Abduh(d. 1905).[34] The Muslim Brotherhood was founded in 1958, reputedly under the aegis of the Aḥmadiyāh[35], and soon after its creation it built its first primary school in Magburaka. By the time of the death of its founder in 1972 the Brotherhood had increased the number of primary schools to 38, of which only one was in Freetown, and three secondary schools, one

---

[28] Interview, Abbas Camba, Freetown.

[29] *Ramadan Vision*, July, 1946, pp. 5-6.

[30] Interview, Abbas Camba, Freetown.

[31] In actual fact the Orchestra continued performing long after the cessation of publication of the *Ramadan Vision* in June, 1948. It was run by the Fujalto Muslim Circle, a Fulani tribal association. The name 'Fujalto' was derived from Futa Jallon and Futa Toro where members of the Fulani tribal community originally came from. The Orchestra was finally disbanded in 1969 after many of its members left.

[32] Proudfoot and H. S. Wilson: 'Muslim Attitudes to Education in Sierra Leone', *The Muslim World,* vol 50, no 1 (January, 1960)

[33] Information gathered from Idriss Alamy, *loc. cit.* I visited Magburaka where Ibrahim Kanu is buried in an unmarked grave in the school yard.

[34] C. C. Adams:*Islam and Modernism in Egypt,* London, 1933, 1968.

[35] Humphrey J. Fisher: *Aḥmadiyyah,* London, 1963, 179.

each in Freetown, Sefadu and Magburaka.[36]   Most its educational strength continued to be concentrated at Magburaka although its secondary school in Freetown was flourishing with a record number of pupils in attendance at both primary and secondary level.[37] In Magburaka it also ran—and continues to run—an Islamics Institute which, unlike the primary and secondary schools, was staffed mainly by Egyptian teachers paid from Cairo.[38]

The Brotherhood Secondary school in Freetown is at 13 Berry Street, and was founded in 1969.[39] The curriculum includes modern secular subjects alongside Islamic subjects. It is co-educational, and the audit report for 1970/71 reveals it has 354 boys and 81 girls, though a slightly smaller number is given in the books of the school.[40] By 1975 its enrolment had more than doubled—with the attendant strains on space, facilities and staff. Another school with a strong co-educational and secular emphasis was the Wanjama Muslim Academy, which tried to produce candidates for agricultural training at Njala.[41] But the school hardly got off the drawing board before it was closed.

All this educational activity takes place against a background of intense factional rivalry. At a Muslim Meeting where the Supreme Islamic Council of Sierra Leone was created, the Muslim Congress came in for harsh criticism. It was taunted for its lethargy in modern education. It was pointed out at the meeting that there were 84 primary schools in the Western Area, i.e. the Freetown Peninsula, of which 33 were Christian schools and only one, a secondary school, could be credited to Congress, a meagre effort in its 42-year history—'Other than studying the phases of the moon and nominating imāms to officiate at congregational prayers, the Congress body—composed of Old Heads—', it is suggested, achieved very little by way of modern schools.[42] The

---

[36] Idriss Alamy, interview. A higher figure of 50 schools is given in a report of a meeting held at Kabala town on Sunday, 8/3/70. It says in the same report that some 150 more schools were planned. The meeting was organized by the Muslim Propaganda Regional branch.

[37] Idriss Alamy, loc. cit.

[38] The head of the Islamic Institute in Magburaka was until recently Shaykh Farūq. The curriculum is heavily committed to traditional Islamic subjects.

[39] Idriss Alamy, loc. cit.

[40] The Audit Report claims that of this number only 414 have paid their fees and 5 more were allowed to continue in deferment of payment. A/1 - 70/71, Audit Report. Fees collected for the third term of the 70/71 school year amounted to Le.5008:50, or £2504:25p sterling.

[41] A mimeographed prospectus was being circulated. Some copies in the files of Muslim Associations kept at the UAR Cultural Centre.

[42] Address given by Gibril Abdul Rahim to members of the Sierra Leone Muslim Community in Freetown, 12/7/70, at the Islamiyah School. Copies available in roneo.

'eager young men' of today carry this reproach to its logical conclusion by accusing Congress of being responsible for the relative backwardness of the Muslim community and for allowing the Christian community to dominate schools in Freetown and elsewhere. These sentiments lurk behind the anxiety of, say, the Sierra Leone Muslim Brotherhood, *Ukhūwāh al-Islāmiyāh,* which wants to dissociate itself from Congress. In a letter to the Sierra Leone Broadcasting Service (SLBS), the Secretary General of the Brotherhood expresses this position in forceful terms. The organizational model was here again the Christian example, with which the main part of the letter opens.

> For your information, the forming of the United Christian Council was only to unite all Christian Religious bodies and not with the idea of interpreting the individual educational policy and activities.
> Therefore the Sierra Leone Muslim Brotherhood does not and will not be prepared to pledge its responsibility to any Muslim organization in Sierra Leone. But it gives the full [sic] respect to the oldest Muslim Organization in this country, which is the S/L Muslim Congress when it comes to religious activities such as celebrations.
> But in the educational line, the SLMB does not and will never be prepared to surrender its rights to any other Muslim organization in this country, and as such, it will not be in our interest for any other Muslim organization to represent the SLMB in all Government affairs and it owes obligation to no other body as far as educational matters are concerned.[43]

The Muslim educational vanguard is being led by men who are also keen to shake Islam out of its torpor. Both the men educated at al-Azhar and those educated nearer home have found themselves joining forces against the conservative *élite* of traditional Islam. That Islam which spurns modern education, these reform-minded men are saying, is the Islam of the village and of ignorant leaders. In a play by Abdul Karim Ghazali village religion and its traditional stalwarts are pointedly caricatured when the Pagan priest and Muslim cleric are united in their disdain for modern education, represented in the dialogue by the clerk ('Clark') who butts into their conversation (the play is in the Krio language):

> (De Clark cam mix pan de tok.)
> Clark: M'hm mh, Pa nor mek dis man ton you lek how in day'o.
> Alpha: Me pekin, go sidom saful nar inglish book you sabi; you no sabi but god. Lef we leh we tok; way tin you day do sef not to trainin. Wen too big people day tok, you nor for put mot day.
> Merehsinman: Nar true word you tok so; dis book way den lan nor mek dem get trainin . . . . .

---

[43] Letter signed by Mr A. B. S. Conteh and dated 8/10/71. It was copied to the Aḥmadiyāh Missionary Movement in Sierra Leone.

Translation:[44]
(The clerk came to interfere in their conversation.)
Clerk: M'hm mh, Old Man, don't let this man make you into what he already is.
Muslim Cleric: My son, go and sit down to the English book you know how to handle. As for God you know nothing about Him. Leave the two of us to continue our conversation. In fact what you have just done is bad manners. When two elders are engaged in conversation you should not interrupt them.
Pagan priest: That's absolutely right what you said then. This modern education of theirs leaves them wanting in manners. . . .

It is said that when this play was performed before a local audience in Freetown, the Muslims, perhaps seeing the point, objected that this was a play about Paganism, not Islam.[45]

There is a rapid turn over in Muslim welfare associations, particularly those concerned with modern education. The Muslim Association, so strongly billed by people like Proudfoot for a promising future,[46] has long ceased to exist. Its challenge to the Muslim Congress was never a serious one in organizational terms, though its brilliant leadership under Ahmed Alhadi gave it a precocious strength. Too closely identified with the Creole Christian community, the Association proposed to fulfil a need in which it did not possess the experience and contacts of its Creole counterparts nor the support and understanding of the majority of the Freetown Muslim community. Squeezed between the two it mouldered away, and was in fact a spent force long before the death of Ahmed Alhadi in 1958. Fula Town Muslims also had an organization for running the Omaria School, opened with entertainment by the Fujalto Orchestra on 1st September, 1958. More from lack of support than from factional rivalry, the school was taken over by the municipal authorities. Abdul Karim Ghazali, very much the target of the Muslim anti-Israeli lobby because of his alleged contacts with Israel, teaches at the school.

Outside foreign support for Muslim efforts in modern education raises several different issues. The dearth of teachers in Arabic and Islam can be corrected by a supply of appropriately trained teachers from Egypt and elsewhere, as the case of the Muslim Brotherhood suggests. But if the aim is to train people who can fill jobs in the civil service and technical fields like agriculture, forestry, engineering and similar specialized areas, then should a Muslim school apply rigid religious criteria in its selection of materials, aid, pupils and staff? It is a pressing dilemma: if a school adheres strictly to traditional Islamic religious

---

[44] The translation is my own. The play was not translated into English.

[45] 'A Muslim Propaganda Play: De Man Way De Play Gyambul Wit God', in *The Sierra Leone Bull. of Religion,* vol 3, no 2, December, 1961.

[46] Proudfoot, *Africa, xxxi, 1961.*

formulae its capacity to make a meaningful contribution in secular fields will be correspondingly curtailed. On the other hand, if it is not necessary to insist on an exclusive Muslim identity then it seems superfluous to try to establish separate Muslim schools. Existing secular and government aided schools and institutions are better placed than any fledgling Muslim school, with a few minor exceptions. It does not seem to have been possible to resolve this problem which presupposes that the much wider issue of secularization and its significance for traditional religious structures has been confronted adequately. Both the older and the more recent Muslim organizations are characterized by their 'Islamism', i.e., an ideological commitment to Islam, with the difference that the more recent bodies stress the Pan-Islamic aspect. This has profound meanings for modern education. Modern Muslim schools receiving help from Arab countries are under constraint to submit to Arab political demands. Abdul Karim Ghazali's delicate position testifies to the reality of this problem. Another is the gift of books on Arabic and Islam from Israel, which touched off a flurry of activity in Congress circles, culminating in a general meeting of the Board of Imams on 6 August 1968. A petition was quickly drafted and sent to the Minister of Education, the press and other bodies.[47] It rejected the offer in disproportionate and highly charged language.

The Aḥmadiyāh contribution to modern education among Freetown and other Sierra Leone Muslims is unsurpassed in the history of Muslim contact with Western educational institutions. Originally stigmatized by the Muslim Association who in the main spurned them,[48] the Aḥmadī missionaries were cautiously received by Congress and they started work in Rokupr and Bo.[49] Their first school in Freetown was opened in January, 1959, and, like the others, it went onto the Government Assisted List.[50] The first secondary school was opened in 1964, and it has remained the only Aḥmadiyāh school there.[51] An off-set press has begun producing educational materials for use in schools, including a course in Qur'ānic Arabic for beginners.[52] The introduction of Arabic

---

[47] The Petition was the result of a circular letter addressed to various *imams* by Mr Ola Koromah. The letter-head was the S/L Muslim Congress.

[48] Proudfoot, 1961, 153-54, where the Association is reported to have co-operated closely with the Aḥmadiyāh Movement, but Fisher says only a couple or so of the Yoruba Muslims in Freetown joined the Aḥmadiyāh. Fisher: 'Aḥmadiyāh in Sierra Leone', *S/L Bull. of Religion,* vol 2, no 1, (June 1960), 1-10. Also Proudfoot: 'Ahmed Alhadi and the Aḥmadiyāh in Sierra Leone', vol 2, no 2, (December, 1960) 66-68, of the *Sierra Leone Bull. of Religion.*

[49] Fisher, 1963, 178.

[50] *Op. cit.*

[51] Mr Munir, Amir of the Aḥmadiyāh, interview.

[52] The off-set press operates from their head office: 6 Back Street, Freetown. A

teaching in schools is important for attracting children from the wider Muslim community. Previously the Aḥmadīs did not lay much emphasis on knowledge of Arabic, preferring instead translated work, and this caused loss of support from traditionally minded Muslims. With the new policy of teaching Arabic they should appeal to more and more Muslims, provided other considerations like politics, both local and international, do not interfere. Local political pressure could mount because of Aḥmadī insistence on avoiding direct involvement in popular political demonstrations of support or protest. International political pressure is beginning to be felt with Saudi Arabian and Pakistani opposition to Aḥmadiyāh Islam, regarded by both countries as heretical. Sierra Leone Aḥmadī face an up-hill task. Being a modernizing organization among local Muslims is hard enough, but to compound this with an avoidance of politics in a country which thrives on political manoeuvrings, plus having to face the counterweight of Saudi Arabian and Pakistani sanctions, is to raise a fundamental question about its survival in its present form. With the ban by Saudi Arabia on Aḥmadī pilgrims, the number of Aḥmadī Muslims who have remained unaware of the cleavage between Aḥmadiyāh Islam and Sunnī Islam will decrease. With financial support by orthodox Muslim countries like Saudi Arabia, Libya and Egypt the scales could be turned against local Aḥmadīs. The political implications of Pan-Islamism might force the government to bring Muslim activities and organizations under strict control, with all that means for Aḥmadiyāh political neutralism. The time may not be far off when Aḥmadīs are no longer able to straddle the divisions in Sierra Leone Islam, or even to profit by these.

Developments in other spheres of Islamic activity have emphasised the divisions among Sierra Leonean Muslims. By far the most important single external factor has been the involvement of oil-rich (and oil-enriched) states of the Middle East. But the dominance of Egypt before and after the boom in oil wealth has remained unchallenged. In 1961 Egypt began an educational mission to Sierra Leone. Today it has about 30 Egyptian teachers, paid from Cairo, teaching in the country. There are, according to officials at the Egyptian Cultural Centre in Freetown, 252 Sierra Leonean students in Cairo, most of them studying technical and similar subjects, although a number are at places like al-Azhar.[53] An estimated 15 Sierra Leonean students are in Saudi Arabia, and a smaller number in Libya. Morocco established an educational scholarship scheme in Rabat in the 1960s for Sierra Leoneans, but it was discontinued following student discontent with social amenities provided

bookshop selling these materials and school books and equipment is located at the same address.

[53] Kamal Lotfy and Idriss Alamy, interviews, UAR Cultural Centre, 8/4/75.

at the centre.[54] Another kind of contact is the one in which national Muslims are supported directly from the Middle East either as full-time missionaries or as grant-aided workers. Among the former is Shaykh Sallah Janneh, a graduate of the Islamic University of Medina and appointed missionary by Saudi Arabia to Sierra Leone.[55] Another is al-Hajj Abdul Rahman Kamara, supported by Saudi Arabia and once posted to Port Loko, a strong Muslim area.[56] The *imām* of the Hausa mosque, Malam Muhammad Bello, is also supported from Libya to help with some Islamic teaching.[57]

Support for individual Muslims is undertaken alongside support for local Islamic projects. Apart from the Aḥmadiyāh Movement, the Muslim Brotherhood, as already pointed out, is the organization most seriously committed to modern education. Five Egyptian teachers work at its school in Magburaka, plus two nationals. Enrolment in its schools in Freetown is now well over the 1800 mark.[58] Although suffering from bad organization and the legacy of the dominant personal leadership of al-Hajj Ibrahim Sori Kanu, support for the Brotherhood has not diminished. If it fails it will be for reasons other than support or finance.

Another organization prompted into prominence by political independence is the Muslim Cultural Society, though this particular organization took some time emerging, being founded only in 1973. In a public statement the organization wrote:

It was only after the independence of Sierra Leone and due to the broadminded and democratic policy of Government that Muslims attained their lost rights.

. . . We are proud to say that our Government under the able and dynamic guidance of our beloved President Dr Siaka Stevens has always given assistance and patronage to Muslims, so that they can fulfil their religious obligations.[59]

In spite of its self-confident claims, the Cultural Society is a newcomer to the hurly-burly of religious politics in Freetown. It has three primary schools with a pupil enrolment of 380.[60] It has the makings of a library of

[54] It is said that the students complained about the practice of strict seclusion of women which prevented contacts at their centre. Kamal Lotfy and Idriss Alamy, *loc. cit.*

[55] Information provided by the UAR Cultural Centre and other sources.

[56] *Op. cit.*

[57] *Op. cit.*

[58] I myself saw students from the Brotherhood schools on public parade at the Elizabeth Playing Fields in Freetown, during the *Mawlid al-Nabi* celebrations on Monday 24/3/75. The precise figure was supplied by Idriss Alamy who used to be an Auditor of the Brotherhood schools.

[59] Article in the Freetown *Daily Mail*, 24/3/75.

[60] *Op. cit.*

Islamic books at its centre for cultural activities.[61] Here it is only duplicating the fairly good library facilities of the Egyptian Cultural Centre on Pulteney Street in Freetown, although in the latter case poor shelving makes for difficulty in finding books. The Cultural Society also organizes classes in Qur'ān reading at their centre.[62]

The Kankele (sometimes also Kankaylay) Muslim Society has a similar history to the Muslim Cultural Centre. The word 'Kankele' is derived from the Mandinka, '*kang kili*', meaning 'one voice', unity, solidarity, thus illustrating the Mandinka origins of the Society. It was founded by al-Hajj I. B. Turay, one-time Propaganda Secretary of the Muslim Congress. He is the father-in-law of Shaykh Sallah Janneh. On 3 November 1974, the foundation stone was laid of a centre which, it is hoped, will house some 2,200 students, all girls, after completion. On this day the Kankele organizers collected £4,531 sterling in donations from individuals and branch offices. It is estimated that the centre itself will cost £150,000 sterling to build.[63] At the moment its headquarters are at 135D Kissy Road, and meetings are held in the Magazine Cut area of East Freetown.

The Kankele Society, in one aspect of its activities, brings two themes of this paper together into sharp focus, namely, the matter of Christian example and stimulus, and, secondly, of outside foreign support. In a letter addressed to President Anwar Sadat of Egypt, al-Hajj Turay drew attention to the urgent importance of education for Muslim girls and women, because of the comparative Christian excellence in this area. He was anxious that in time Muslim women should compare favourably with their Christian counterparts. Because of the confidential nature of this letter I cannot quote any part of it here, but it is worth noting that there are only six female students in Cairo, three of whom are the Razzaq sisters from Hastings, near Freetown.[64] The letter was accompanied by an architect's plan of the proposed building. No precise figure was quoted in the letter concerning the cost of the building and the appeal for funds was couched in general terms. There is a good chance that Egypt will respond. But there could be difficulties, one internal and the other external. The Kankele have appealed in the same terms to Saudi Arabia for funds without acknowledging this in the letter to Cairo. It is unlikely that these and similar possible sources will be unaware of each other over this matter and this could inhibit outside support. The internal difficulty

---

[61] *Op. cit.*

[62] *Op. cit.*

[63] Information from the files of the Muslim Associations, UAR Cultural Centre (with Idriss Alamy).

[64] *Op. cit.*

could arise out of increasing government involvement in local Muslim organizations to try to bring them under check. Muslim organizations appealing directly over the head of their government to foreign governments could quickly assume, or be alleged to assume, a political character.

Competition for support from the Middle East is rife among Freetown Muslims and this has driven the factions apart, paralysing national umbrella organizations like the Supreme Islamic Council and causing a flare up of individual associations led by younger men. This is another of the divisions in Freetown Islam: younger men with some modern education are impatient with the old *élite*. What feeds this smouldering discontent with the old is the prospect, among other things, of wresting power and control from traditional centres of power by appearing as successful men in the modern world with the ability to utilize international channels of contact. The traditional *élite* are keeping their powder dry against the day when the present proliferation of young talents will be a spent force and familiar patterns of the old *élite* re-assert themselves. At the moment the two sides live and let live.

By carrying over competitive factionalism into international politics in dealings with Arab governments, Freetown Muslims have introduced political calculations into their activities. This has caused the government to step in decisively. Muslim pilgrimage is now directly controlled by the government. The Supreme Islamic Council is under close government supervision. The organizational power of Muslim groups which enables them to campaign on a national basis to recruit new members and collect funds is anxiously watched by the government. Perhaps it was to allay such government suspicions that local Muslim organizations decided, after a particularly successful fund-raising compaign, to hand over the proceeds amounting to £22,000 sterling to the government. The government reacted by putting up air fares for the pilgrimage, and used the occasion to assert control over the entire pilgrimage organization.[65] In June 1975, a delegation of the National Executive of the Sierra Leone Muslim Pilgrimage Movement, led by Hajji Dankay Kabia, went to see the President to try to regain control of pilgrimage affairs.[66] The Saudi Arabian ban on Aḥmadī pilgrims may further complicate relations with the Sierra Leone government. Visits by Arab government officials is another potential area of conflict, for Muslim organizations would want to capitalize on such visits for their own sectional interests.

But in the final analysis what is of material significance for the

---

[65] Idriss Alamy, interview. See also *We Yone* newspaper, 11/6/75, and the *Daily Mail* and *The Nation* of the same date.
[66] The daily papers quoted above.

configuration of religious life in Freetown is not external foreign involvement which merely influences existing local factors, but the internal balance of forces. The most important element in this respect is the ethnic/linguistic factor. All the main ethno-linguistic groups of Freetown have their own separate adult evening schools. Of the 15 such schools only two are designated as 'All Tribes', and two others are described as mixed.[67] The Temne, Susu and Limba each have two evening schools. The Loko, Aku and Fula each have a school, with the Fula forming important minorities in two other schools, the *Taqwā* and the *Falah*.[68] The preponderance of such sectional interests in Sierra Leone Islam means that local Muslims are a long way from organic unity. Muslims in fact seem prepared to take sectionalism for granted and are concentrating their energies on ensuring a flow of funds from outside. It is difficult to foresee a time when Arab support can be important enough to be used as a lever to force Muslims to unite more. Fragmentation seems necessary to the vitality of Freetown Muslim life and an inalienable part of it.

A final theme is the continuing dichotomy between the Islam of Freetown and other urban centres and the Islam of the village, a dichotomy which is rapidly diverging through the impact of modern education on the younger generation of Muslims. In colonial times, rural Islamic interests maintained a stronghold on Muslims in Freetown through the institutionalization of traditional structures of authority. The system of 'Tribal headmen' and the ancillary organizations related to it, on which the colonial bureaucracy structured its relations with the various communities, embodied and perpetuated the power of 'village' politics. But such structures are archaic in an independent Sierra Leone, and national politics have destroyed the built-in mechanism of protection for entrenched interests. Hence the proliferation of numerous little groups organized by men who had been powerless within the traditional set up and who are now aware of the advantages which modern education gives them. They are swiftly challenging the authority of the custodians of 'village' values by throwing down the gauntlet on issues like modern schools, girls' and women's education, modern techniques of religious propaganda, adult literacy classes and modern social amenities. Clearly they have an advantage over the older men.

There is also a marked change in the attitude of the younger men, for

---

[67] Official files of the Muslim organizations, UAR Cultural Centre.

[68] The names of the schools, with tribal affiliation in parenthesis, are: Madrassah al-Imāniyāh (Temne), Nūr al-Islām (Susu), al-'Amāriyāh (Aku), Māqāmāt al-Islām (Temne), al-Almīniyāh (Limba), al-Madīnah al-Munwarah (Limba), Hayāt al-Islām (Susu), Dār al-Ḥadīth (All Tribes), al-Salafiyāh (All Tribes), al-Hudā (Loko), al-Rashād (Fula), Taqwā and Falāḥ (both mixed) and one school each in Kabala and Wellington.

example, towards the Arabic language. The Hausa *imām* is trying just as hard as the graduate of the Islamic University of Medina to speak fluent English. All the organizations led by these men publish primarily in English.[69] The religious life is explained and studied through the medium of English. There is a critical objection to the use of amulets and traditional methods of healing and other forms of therapy. These educated young men show little regard for their so-called crystal-gazing elders. They argue, in an almost exclusive way, for the use of modern skills in the understanding and propagation of Islam.[70] In meetings where the old and young are present the tone of discussions can be particularly vitriolic or else, in moments of supreme self-restraint, sullen. A casual glance at the official records of the organizations reveals this same atmosphere of mistrust, with skirmishes over minor details and at the least provocation.[71] Modern education has laid a charge along the trails of Freetown Muslims. The new generation of modern educated Muslims who are holding the fuse wires appear to want to increase the charge and shorten the wires. But what is beyond their control is the ability to hasten the older Muslims towards a final confrontation. Both have their strengths and at present both fit naturally into a pattern of delicate poise characteristic of Freetown Muslim life.

[69] One of the most ambitious ventures in this field is the Muslim Missionary Pioneers Association, organized and directed by a young convert from Christianity, al-Farid Ibrahim Cole. It has been producing a number of mimeographed pamphlets called the 'Islamic Education Series', devoted to a modern interpretation and defence of Islam.

[70] In one meeting of the Muslim Congress the younger men argued in favour of countering hostile Christian propaganda against Islam with a systematic exposition of Islamic teachings. Senior elder officials felt called upon to defend their own position here, for they became suspicious that it was being suggested that such a task was beyond their competence—as their reaction in fact appears to confirm. It was clear that the meeting was wielding a many-sided weapon which could be used against their opponents at the risk of an equal amount of injury to themselves.

[71] A celebrated case of hair-splitting was the attempt by Ahmed Alhadi to define in highly legalistic language the separate functions of the Almamy and the *Imām,* and ending by saying both officials have joint responsibility for the internal administration of their community. Proudfoot (December, 1962), p. 81. A different matter concerns the cashing of a cheque drawn on the account of Sir Banja Tejan-Sie, then Governor-General. The cheque was made out to Mr L. S. Fofana and given to Arun al-Rashid, a pupil of the Muslim Brotherhood Secondary School at Berry Street of which Mr Fofana was a former' Principal. It is not clear what the money was for, but al-Rashid cashed the cheque and with the money paid his school fees, presumably on the understanding that he was being supported by Sir Banja. This touched off a dispute and an enquiry was held. It had triggered a bitter feud involving the Brotherhood school and people connected with it. This was in December, 1970.

In the present circumstances Freetown Muslims will continue to be open to the influx of new ideas and fresh initiatives, especially in modern education. A dynamic situation has been created by the competition and jockeying for position and advantage among the ethnic groups and between the generations. Voluntary organizations multiply rapidly, partly to compensate for the ban on political organization under the continued National Emergency, but partly also to exploit the energies generated by ethnicity and the universal desire for the advantages of modern education. That is the crucible in which the new Islamic consciousness is being formed. Ironically, the factors, such as ethnicity, which have enabled Freetown Muslims to mobilize support are the forces preventing a maximum realization of Muslim potential. Their experience, when this has been carefully organized and articulated, could prove a model lesson for Muslims elsewhere.

Islam in Nigeria: changes since independence

A. R. I. DOI

Anything that is living in space and time must experience changes whether perceptible or not. Religion is also a living thing and is changing with the great revolution in the life of men who follow it. In Nigeria, political and social changes have come about as a result of the past colonial rule and its deep impact on Nigerians as a whole, followed by the independence of Nigeria and democratic government by Nigerians, the Nigerian civil war as a result of secession and finally the changing military rule up to the present time. These factors have brought a succession of political as well as social changes. With these came secularism, the neutral policy of the government between the religious groups, an increase in Western technological education and an emphasis on industrialized society and the growth of new urban centres which really produce a social revolution in Nigeria. When Nigerian society is undergoing great changes, it is only natural that the religious outlook of Nigerian Muslims is bound to change. There are times when the traditional value system creates resistance to change. But with the passage of time, the same people begin to accept change consciously or unconsciously.

In Nigeria, as in other parts of West Africa, in the early stages of the expansion of Islam, Islam provided believers with a Universalist religion, an Islamic social and religious pattern, and an attitude of cultural and religious superiority over Pagans. But they could not live on the sense of superiority alone. For a time, particularly in the former Northern Nigeria, Muslims even responded by a self-protective withdrawal but to their own disadvantage. This policy of isolation could not work successfully because it proved impossible to insulate the inhabitants of the Northern Region completely. The southern Muslims, on the contrary, were deeply influenced by Western education. They reacted against medieval thought and acquired Western education, became teachers, doctors, government officials, trade unionists and politically conscious élites.

In the six Northern states, therefore, the powers of resistance have ensured that the process of change has been gradual, restricted in operation, and allowed to influence only a limited sphere of life. Hence gradually they gave way, for no people in modern Africa can completely immunize themselves against the penetration of the new forces, especially now that they are finding themselves lagging behind the more open societies in educational, economic and political development.

Changes in Muslim Education:
As can be well understood, there existed hardly any liaison between the early Islamic and the Western systems of education.[1] With the independence of Nigeria, things changed a great deal. In 1954, the government introduced a scheme by which untrained junior primary school teachers attended bridge courses at the school for Arabic studies in Kano, and between 1954 and 1961 more than two-thirds of all primary school teachers received this training, which helped them to improve their positions and raised their standard of education. In the year 1960 the School of Arabic studies organized a post-secondary course in Arabic and Islamic studies as a preliminary to the establishment of the Abdullahi Bayero College. In this way a concerted effort was made to direct some of the students from the '*Ilm* schools and Higher Muslim Institutions towards university and post-secondary modern education. The then Northern Region Ministry of Education and Abdullahi Bayero College of Kano, which is part of the Ahmadu Bello University, led the working out of a comprehensive plan whereby the traditional system of imparting Arabic and Islamic education was contacted at various stages and channelled towards the inevitable Westernized system, so that a general uniformity at the level preceding the university was attained. The School of Arabic studies at Sokoto also made a start in this direction.

A serious disadvantage for the students coming from the Higher Muslim Institutions was their lack of knowledge of English and modern school subjects. As far as their knowledge of Arabic and Islam was concerned, they had a solid traditional background. In this way, the studies of Arabic and Islamic institutions were for the first time raised to a degree level, alongside other modern studies.

In the south a similar attempt was made to raise the poor status and standard of Arabic teachers by introducing the diploma course in the Department of Arabic and Islamic Studies at the University of Ibadan. Candidates for this course are largely drawn from the Qur'ānic schools which are sometimes named by their proprietors as '*Ma'had*', Institute, or '*Kulliya*', meaning a College. At this Department, a sound training is given to these students in Arabic, Islamic studies, history and English

[1] Cf. Hamidu Alkali, 'A note on Arabic Teaching in Northern Nigeria', *Kano Studies*, 3, 1967, p. 11.

language. Thus their standard of education is improved a great deal, but it does not really give them any better opportunity of employment nor a higher salary since this diploma is not recognized by the Ministry of Education.

The Muslim intellectuals have realized the importance of the Western derived education especially in an age of industrialization and scientific and technological advances. They felt that they were lagging behind in the effective participation in the administration of government. They also needed Muslim lawyers, doctors, engineers and educationists. They wanted to achieve this aim without changing their religion and culture. They felt a need to combine a sound Muslim education with an equally sound education along Western lines. This gave rise to a new enthusiasm in Muslim circles. Within the ranks of orthodox Muslims a number of organizations sprang up especially to develop Western derived education within a Muslim context. The two most dynamic and the largest of these organizations are the Jamā'at Naṣril Islam functioning in the Northern states of Nigeria and the Anṣār-ud-Deen society.[2] In a booklet published by this society, they have defined their aim thus:

'Prior to the inauguration of the society, only two or three Muslim schools were being run. The Christian Missionaries, on the other hand, dominated the educational life of the country, and pressure was being exerted on some of the Muslim pupils attending the Christian schools to convert to Christianity'.[3]

In the early thirties, the Native Administration also created several schools in response to an appeal by non-Christians.[4] The Anṣār-ud-Deen society, Aḥmadiyāh Movement, Zumratul Islamiyya and other Muslim organizations established both primary and secondary schools in Yorubaland. More recently, two secondary grammar schools have been opened by the Anṣār-ud-Deen society and the Aḥmadiyāh Movement in Islam in the Mid-Western State of Nigeria. The number of such Muslim schools is increasing gradually as the Muslims realize the importance of Western education. All these schools, both primary and secondary, insist on imparting Arabic and Islamic education as subjects. The environment of the schools is kept Islamic so that 'Muslim children could gain a Western education without parents being concerned about Christian proselytizing.'[5]

---

[2] Ansar-ud-Deen means the helper of the religion.

[3] Ansar-ud-Deen Society pamphlet issued on 1 June 1961, pp. 2-3.

[4] Archibald Callaway, 'Education expansion and the rise of youth unemployment in the city of Ibadan', p. 193.

[5] Ibid.

At present, courses on Arabic and Islamic studies are taught up to degree level in the Departments of Arabic and Islamic studies at the Universities of Ibadan and Ahmadu Bello. Similarly, Islamic theology, Islamic philosophy and Islamic history are being taught at the University of Nigeria, Nsukka, and Universities of Ife and Ibadan in the Departments of Religious Studies. The new Universities in Sokoto, Maiduguri and Jos have also degree programmes in Islamic studies.

Through Western education Muslims have introduced new schemes to improve their conditions of living, opened dispensaries and hospitals, schools and agricultural programmes and thus the influx of new ideas has accelerated. They send their young men and women for higher education in the well-established universities in Europe and America. Muslim youth also have realized that it is necessary to understand the new world into which they are being drawn and therefore come into opposition to the remaining few traditionalists who seek to retard this process. Nobody could have imagined, barely twenty years ago, the ʿUlamā persuading Muslim parents in the northern states to send their sons and daughters for western-oriented education along with some Islamic teachings in the modern grammar schools, the teacher training colleges and universities. But today, it is a reality. The Grand Kadi, the Sarkin Muslimin of Sokoto, and the Emirs continue speaking on the need of modern education for Muslims. Many new primary, secondary and grammar schools, teacher training colleges and colleges of arts and sciences have been opened by the governments of the northern states of Nigeria, but they have made sure that Islam is taught in all these institutions as one of the subjects. Recently some of the states have taken over the voluntary agency schools established by the various Christian missions and have changed their Christian names into local names and in some of these institutions Arabic and Islam are being taught as required subjects.

Education of women has also begun, but it will be long before the effects are seen. Recently during a meeting with Alhaji Shehu Ahmad Said Galadanci, the Provost of Abdullahi Bayero College, I was given an interesting account of how some Kano Muslims were afraid to send their daughters to a school which still bears a Christian name. (Kano State has not changed the names of the voluntary agency schools). Alhaji Galandanci convinced them that their daughters would not be forced to be converted to Christianity since he himself was a member of the new governing board and his daughter also attended the same school. It was only after such persuasion that they began to send their daughters to the school.

Changes brought about by external religious, social and political influences:
In independent Nigeria, contacts have increased with the outside world in general and the Muslim world in particular. The Arab influence has increased a great deal, especially as the number of Muslims going for pilgrimage to Mecca and Medina has multiplied beyond all proportions in recent years. In the year 1973 48,981 Nigerian pilgrims went to Mecca and Medina. It may be assumed that the most far-reaching and rapid changes that have affected Nigerian Muslim society have been those associated with contact with the wider Arab and Asiatic Muslim world and its way of life. During British rule, as J. S. Trimingham has said,

'The British tried to prevent Nigerian Muslims, especially the few educated ones, from having contacts with Egypt and other Muslim lands. These have been dissuaded from accepting offers of bursaries to study at the Azhar or modern Egyptian Universities'.[6]

But this isolation did not succeed even then. 'All the same', says Trimingham, 'they have not been able to prevent a minority from gaining wider contacts in ever increasing ways. These factors are operating to draw West African Muslims out of their isolation—an isolation, however, which is still very real'.[7] But this isolation, which before the independence of Nigeria, was 'still very real', is rapidly being eradicated.

After Nigeria achieved independence, a number of Muslim countries especially from the Middle East, began to show a keen interest in the affairs of Nigerian Muslims. On account of their oil boom, the currency reserves of the Muslim Arab countries are going higher and higher. At times one feels that they are puzzled as to what to do with their petro-dollars. Apart from a number of economic development plans in their countries, they have tried to imitate the activities of religious bodies like the World Council of Churches, Caritas and other organizations and have started Islamic missionary activities in various parts of Africa. Apart from purely religious gains, they also try to achieve some political advantages through their aid. At present, the Muslim envoys living in the Lagos metropolitan area are invited to the Islamic functions and celebrations. Some of them regularly attend Friday and ʿId prayers with local Muslims. In this way they come closer to Nigerian Muslims and at times travel in the Federation visiting Muslim organizations, distribute books and pamphlets on Islam, offer financial help to some Muslim educational organizations and give help in the building of mosques and

---

[6] J. S. Trimingham, *Islam in West Africa*, OUP, 1959, p. 218.

[7] Ibid.

schools.The largest contribution comes from the Saudi Arabian government in the form of Arabic and Islamic teachers, often graduates of the Medina University in Saudi Arabia, who are appointed in various Arabic and Qur'ānic schools in Iwo, Ilorin, Ibadan, Lagos, Kaduna, Kano and other places. It is difficult to estimate the role played by such Arabic scholars since they are often handicapped in expressing themselves either in English or the local languages. Besides this contribution, some local students are given scholarships to study Islam in Saudi Arabia and, on their completion of their courses, such graduates are employed in their home countries to teach Islam and Arabic language, the language of the Qur'ān. Such students can really render a great service in the work of dissemination of the pure Islamic teachings unlike the syncretic elements taught by the Alufas and Mallams.

It should be remembered that these teachers and missionaries sent by Saudi Arabia are the puritans taking the Qur'ān and the Ḥadith of the Prophet as the only authority in respect of the Sharī'ah. As a result they invite Muslims to follow the *salaf* and not to imitate the later interpretations and additions in the matter of Islam. The Nigerian Muslims are Mālikī (i.e. the followers of Imām Mālik) and at times find it difficult to understand the puritan teachings of these visiting 'Ulamā.' Besides, the Tijāniyya and the Qādiriyya Ṣūfī fraternities are very strong in the length and breadth of Nigeria. The chanting of the Tijāniyya litanies in mosques after prayers is commonly practised, and the Tijāniyya followers believe that the Prophet himself comes in their gathering during this practice and sits on the white sheet spread in the middle. These 'Ulamā' from Saudi Arabia consider this practice as a devilish innovation *(Bidᶜāt al-shaiṭāniyya)*. Some Alufas or Mallams just ignore their teachings and the same is the case with common Nigerian Muslims.

Egypt also sends scholars from al-Azhar University for the same purpose, some of whom teach in Ilorin where an affiliated Arabic and Islamic school is established known as *Madrassa al-Azhariyya*. There are others who teach in secondary schools in Lagos, Ibadan, Kano, Kaduna, Zaria, Sokoto and other places. They also face the same language problems but their presence encourages the local Mallams. Egypt also offers scholarships to Muslim Nigerian candidates to study at al-Azhar .

Another help that the Saudi Arabian government offers in the field of the advancement of Arabic and Islamic education in Nigeria is by giving financial support to a large number of *Madrassahs,* i.e. the Arabic colleges and institutes. They are also supplied with the Arabic and Islamic books needed into those institutions. Libya is another Muslim country which has started helping on similar lines recently. A Saudi Arabian delegation which visited Ibadan recently has taken over the entire running expenses of the Arabic Institute of Ibadan where the students will be offered free places without any payment of fees.

Islam and secularism in Nigeria

Before we embark on our discussion of secularism and its effects on Nigerian Muslims, it is essential for us to consider how secularism has influenced Muslims in some other Muslim countries as well as multi-religious countries. Secondly, we ought to consider whether the concept of secularism in Africa and Asia is really the same concept as is current in the West or is it different?

Secularism in Africa would not change Islam nor its doctrine or institutions, but it would certainly change the religious domain which would help to restrict and narrow the sphere in which Islam can mould the lives of its followers. The concept of secularization as it evolved in the Western world would certainly not apply directly to Muslim countries of Asia and Africa nor would it apply in the professed secular countries like India where a number of religions are practised and seventy million Muslims live as a minority. We must take into account the difference of basic conditions between the West and any given country in Africa or Asia. Let us examine two cases of Muslim countries—Turkey and Pakistan.

The greatest enthusiasm towards secularism was shown in Turkey once the seat of the Islamic *Khilāfat* (Caliphate). It was not directed towards denouncing Islam as a religion but to right the wrongs done to Islam which was practised as if it was a 'cult of the misfits' and a religion of tomb and hero worshippers. The Turkish model of secularism is considered as extreme by a number of Muslim scholars today. Kemal Ataturk was so much dazzled by Western civilization that he wanted not only to accept the good points from it but discarded every good point that Islamic civilization had contributed. As Niyazi Berkes has said, he began to think seriously 'not only of the inadequacy of their own system but also the efficiency and superiority of their adversaries who happened to belong to a different civilization and religion'.[8] The Turkish secular state has survived till today, but the notion of secularism taught by Ataturk has undergone a great change. There is Islamic revivalism in Turkey—mosques are full of devotees, recent election results have shown pro-Islamic tendencies, a very large number of Turkish pilgrims are seen in Mecca and Medina every year, but the *tekkehs* have not been revived nor has there appeared any change in the policy by which Turkey is a secular state.

[8] Niyazi Berkes, 'Historical Background of Turkish Secularism', in *Islam and the West*, ed. N. R. Frye, The Hague, 1957, p. 49.

When Pakistan was carved out of India as a Muslim state, its first leaders did not mean it to become the stronghold of a theocratic society, but the constitution called it an Islamic state, its philosophical basis being the monotheistic idea which would lead to a basis of nationhood situated on a common outlook of life and a common culture.[9] Perhaps the same notion can be applicable to the Muslim countries in the Middle East where 'secular' forces are at work, but their concept of secularism would be different from the one evolved in the Western world.

Now let us take the case of a secular country like India which is multi-religious. Although the Indian constitution declares India a secular country, secularism has another meaning from that current in the Western world. In the Indian situation and Indian context, secularism only implies a neutrality towards religions. By declaring India a secular state, it merely meant that 'religious matters were wholly referred to the respective Hindu, Muslim, Sikh, Christian, Jains and other religious communities'. The majority of the "Ulamā' in India and the Indian Muslim masses accept secularism identified with the 'secular state' as long as it denotes the state's neutrality in the sphere of religion.[10] But if secularism becomes 'anti-religion', for example, when it demands a share for man in what properly belongs to God, most Muslims will hesitate if not refuse to take such 'secularism' as a way of life. The Indian Muslims fear at times that in the name of 'secularization', 'they will eventually have to forget their religious past, give up the institution of *Sharī'ah,* and cut themselves off from their history.'[11]

Nigeria is a country where Islam, Christianity and African traditional religion are practised today. The government of Nigeria is secular almost in the same way as in the case of India which we have just discussed. Secularism here also implies only neutrality towards religion and religious matters are referred to the respective religious communities. In the Northern states of Nigeria, the Sharī'ah system of law is still largely practised by Muslims, but the Yoruba Muslims are more 'secularized' and do not insist on being governed by Sharī'ah law. The government does not interfere in this regard. The government does not favour one or the other religion. But at the same time it does not hinder religious progress and the individual and communal efforts made by the adherents of each religion for the advancement of their religious educational and social institutions patterned on the outlook of their faiths.

But this does not mean that there have been no disruptive tendencies

[9] Cf. R. A. Butler, 'Secularizing Trends in West Pakistan', *Al-Mushir* RawalPindi, January-February, 1971, vol. XIII, Nos. 1-2.

[10] Cf. Mushir-U-Haqq, 'Religion, Secularism and Secular state—The Muslim Case', *Religion and Society*, vol. XVIII, No. 3, September 1971.

[11] Ibid., p. 40.

leading towards the secularization of life in some degree among the educated class who have adopted Western culture. In the Northern states the Islamic culture is dominant in the life of people while Western culture affects only certain spheres of life. Even those northern scholars who go to Europe or America for higher education and become thoroughly acquainted with Western secularist culture come back more often than not with a much greater degree of modern Islam-consciousness. In spite of their acceptance of Western values, they engage in a subsequent apologetic and controversialist dialogue attacking Western culture, Western secularism and create an offensive mood toward the West. I have noticed this attitude in various northern Nigerian Muslim intellectuals during conversation with them. This is not a new attitude as a similar mood is seen in the Middle Eastern countries, India and Pakistan in varying degree.[12]

On the other hand, one can see a marked difference in this attitude adopted towards Western civilization by the Muslims living in Southern Nigeria, i.e., the Muslims living in Yorubaland, Auchi, Agbede and other areas. It is here that Muslims have acquired a more secular attitude towards religion as well as Islamic culture and civilization. Perhaps one would agree here with J. S. Trimingham that this change in attitude is due to the fact that in the former there is a long established tradition of Islam while in the latter Islam penetrated mainly in the last centuries.[13] Whatever may be said of the Southern Muslims who according to Trimingham are 'ready to come to terms with present realities and have proved more adaptable',[14] there has emerged a new enthusiasm since the independence of Nigeria for reviving old Yoruba traditional culture, traditional cults, Ifa oracles, traditional medicine, fortune-telling of the babalawo (the father of the sky), and what one of my friends recently described as Orunmilaism.

As a result of social change, much of the old traditional beliefs and practices have gone, though a great deal remains either visible or potently under the surface. As Parrinder says, 'much of the old faith of centuries has crumbled and disappeared. But much remains under the surface and continues to influence men's thinking. It is a mistake either to look at the religion as if nothing has happened, or to treat it as vanished without a trace.'[15]

Whatever may be the effect of secularism on individual Muslims or the

[12] Cf. Fazlur Rahman, 'The Impact of Modernity on Islam' published in *Religion Pluralism and world Community; Inter faith and International Communication, NUMEN*, vol. XV, Leiden 1969; also cf. W. C. Smith's *Modern Islam in India*, 1943.

[13] Cf. Trimingham, op. cit., p. 204.

[14] Ibid.

[15] Parrinder, Geoffrey, *West African Religion*, London 1961, p. 187.

Muslim societies in the Northern states of Nigeria and the south, the facts remains that the religious neutrality policy of the Federal and state governments has proved beneficial to Islam as well as Muslim educational institutions. This policy has given freedom to Islam to further its cause and in a way it has imposed restrictions on Christianity which had so far dominated the educational and social scene of the country. Some of the Muslim organizations laid down in their constitutions that their aim was to remove the educational imbalance between Muslims and Christians and wanted to remedy the situation by opening new educational institutions where Muslim children would get the Western-derived education without being converted to Christianity, the fear that the Muslim parents always had while sending their children to the schools run by the Christian missionary societies. It is interesting to note that the increasing degree of 'secular' spirit has helped to shape a new brotherly and friendly outlook among Nigerian Muslims. The impact of this factor is seen more in the south of Nigeria than in the Northern states. The Christians and Muslims and in some cases even pagans have adjusted themselves, they live together under one roof, join in the celebrations of ʿId al-Kabir, ʿId al-Fiṭr and Christmas together, without looking down upon each other's personal beliefs.

We cannot overrate the importance of modernity on Islamic societies. As Fazlur Rahman puts it, its impact on Muslim societies can be seen coming in successive phases.[16] It is true that while much technological development takes place in Muslim societies, this does not imply that to an equal degree modernizing processes take place on an intellectual and social level. There is no doubt a growing but gradual impact that can be seen in growing scientific skills, the introduction of constitutional government, some change in traditional habits of thought into a modern world-view, the introduction of political reforms and an adjustment to new norms and some degree of change in understanding an act of God.

The Northern Muslim also knows well enough that changes do occur, despite the axiomatic 'changelessness' of his society. He is no more a mere 'gambari', he has begun to think and plan ahead. Changes have been brought about by epidemics and cattle diseases and the recent drought in parts of the Northern states of Nigeria. Certainly these are sent by Allah, but men can at least act in a co-ordinated manner to combat this havoc and try to prevent or change its effect and it is only after then that they should accept the will of God. The North-Central Commissioner for Education, Alhaji A. Rafindadi recently said that 'the present drought in some parts of the country is not so much an act of God, as an omission by man'.[17] They do realise that it would not help

16 Fazlur Rahman, op. cit.

17 See *Daily Times*, Thursday, 17 January 1974.

just sitting idle and blaming God for consequences by saying *Komi sai Allah* 'everything is in the hands of Allah' and *Abar ma Allah,* Man has always had to adjust to his physical and biological circumstances. Periods of drought, dust storms—all may alter behaviour in particular localities. Biological factors such as disease, death and population density exert their influence upon the pattern of social life as well as their religious outlook.

Indigenization and National Integration

As pointed out by Trimingham, one of the greatest advantages that Islam has in West Africa is that it has become an African religion and that its missionaries for centuries have been Africans[18]. The indigenization programme of religious personnel, if at all it comes in force, will not in any way affect the Muslim 'ulamā' except the Aḥmadiyāh missionaries belonging to the Qadiani group which insists on having the Amir-in-charge of the mission sent from Rabwah in Pakistan.

It is true that as a result of the indigenization decree of the Federal Military Government, many Lebanese and some Syrian Muslim businessmen are leaving Nigeria. These Lebanese businessmen have spread through many parts of Nigeria and most of them are either Muslims or Christians. Most of the Muslim Lebanese[19] came from the south of Lebanon and belonged to the Shiʿite sect of Islam. They seldom took any interest in the Islamic affairs of the local people. Since their presence played no major role in the advancements of Muslims, their departure will certainly not have any significant effect on the local Muslim communities and their religious affairs.

In 1967, Col Ojukwu attempted the secession of the Eastern region from Nigeria as an independent Igbo homeland and named it 'Biafra'. As a result, the country was plunged into civil war which brought a great deal of misery to millions of innocent Nigerians. The entire Eastern region became a war torn area and civilians had to flee from place to place in search of safety. Ojukwu and his colleagues had tried to give the war a religious colour and some misguided foreign reporters even went as far as saying that 'it was a war between the Christian Ibos of East and the Muslims of the North', which was wholly untrue.

The propaganda in the so-called 'Biafra' was also based on a similar line. I have read the issues of the *Nigerian Outlook,* an Eastern

---

[18] Cf. J. S. Trimingham, *The Christian Church and Islam in West Africa,* S.C.M. Press, London 1955, p. 9.

[19] I made enquiries in the Lebanon Street in Ibadan and most of the Lebanese Muslims I talked to were more interested in their business rather than in religious matters. The same is also true of the Christian Lebanese.

government newspaper which later became *Biafra Sun*. The articles also referred to the war as a religious strife. Some European countries and foreign missionaries were also involved in the war simply because they thought that it was a religious war and wrongly believed, and their news media misinformed the world, that there was a plan of 'genocide of Christian Ibos'. As a result, some mosque buildings in Nnofia, Ibagwa-Nkwo, Onitsha and other places were partly damaged during the war. On Ojukwu's orders, some Muslim male members were taken away from Ibagwa-Nkwo to Enugu and they never returned. They are presumed dead. Many Igbo Muslims tried to run away from their home towns and villages and kept in hiding. Many of them changed their Muslim names into Christian and these were published in the *Biafra Sun*. The non-Igbos were asked to quit 'Biafra' irrespective of their religious adherence. Thousands of Hausa, Fulani, Nupe and Yoruba Muslims who had lived with the Igbos for many years also left to return to their place of origin. In short, the civil war seemed to give a heavy blow to Islamic activities in the former Eastern region.

The civil war ended in 1970 and the Federal Military Government gave general amnesty to all. Nigeria later became a twelve state federation in which the former Eastern Region was divided into three states: Rivers state, South Eastern state and Igboland became the present East Central state. The migrant Hausa, Fulani, Nupe and Yoruba communities formerly residing in that area and who had fled their homes as a result of Ojukwu's orders came back as soon as the situation returned to normal. They began to repair their damaged houses, mosque buildings and Qur'ānic schools. The Igbo Muslims came back from their hiding. Some of them who had changed their names, renamed themselves with Islamic names.

After the civil war, when the task of rehabilitation and reconstruction began, the people of the area who had been misguided by false propaganda in the name of religion could now understand the situation better. They could realise that it was not a religious war and that Muslims did not want to 'exterminate' them, nor was Islam based on any such inhuman ideology.[20] In the words of Kingsley Anyasi, 'the last civil war in the country has had one notable effect on the attitude of Ibos towards religion and politics. It has broadened their thinking and set their minds free. The Ibo is no longer prepared to take things for granted.'[21]

Another factor which has helped further Islamic expansion after the

---

[20] After 'Biafra' was declared, the late Prof Kala Ezera, then Dean of the Faculty of Social Science, delivered a lecture in which a copy of the Qur'ān in hand he declared: 'This book teaches that unless a Muslim kills a non-Muslim, he cannot be a true Muslim.'

[21] Kingsley Anyasi, op. cit., p. 11.

war is the presence of Muslims in the Nigerian army. Those areas in Igboland which had not seen any mosque building or any form of Islamic activities before now have an opportunity to witness Muslims praying and practising the tenets of Islam in the army mosques temporarily erected by the soldiers in the length and breadth of East Central state wherever they have encamped. This is the usual practice in the army that wherever they are stationed, they cater for the spiritual needs of their personnel by building churches and mosques. Since the Eastern region of Nigeria is predominantly Christian, people are familiar with Christian rituals and the functions of a church building. But with the coming of the army in order to maintain law and order, the Muslims among them began practising their religion. The Nigerian army is still stationed in various places in that area and wherever there is an army camp, invariably there is erected a mosque which has a direct or indirect impact on the local people living in that area.

> Sheikh Abdul Gaffari Emetumah, an Igbo Muslim leader, said recently: 'In the state (East Central) Muslims were brutally tortured by 'Biafran' soldiers because of their religious belief and many of them were in detention throughout the war. We were made to believe that the war was a religious one between the Christians in the Eastern state and the Hausa Muslims from the North and Yorubaland. We were however surprised after the liberation of our area, when an army Imam, Alhaji Major Bello of Third Marine Commando, spoke to us and made us realize that Islam is not meant for any section nor was it restricted to any region.
> He told us that we were free to practise any religion of our choice, adding that we all worship the same God, though in different manners. With this some of us who had lost hope of the survival of Islam in the state, were inspired and we started a small brigade to propagate the Islamic religion in the Iboland.'[22]

Many Igbos began to accept Islam. 'Before the war', says Kingsley Anyasi, 'many an Ibo student sponsored wholly or partly by his Christian parents would not be courageous enough to think of shaking off the religion of his father. Neither would he think of taking sides with a political party or organization which his parents opposed. But the situation has changed tremendously.'[23] A female Igbo Muslim under-graduate said: 'You could not blame us. National events and developments were in the past in favour of protectionism by pronounced religious-cum-tribal identification.'[24]

The Jamaᶜat Naṣril Islam, a powerful Muslim organization whose

[22] See *The Nigerian Islamic Review*, July 1973, p. 17.

[23] *Spear* magazine, op. cit., p. 11.

[24] Ibid.

headquarters is in Kaduna, has played a great role in the expansion of education among Muslims as well as spreading Islam. It runs a large number of Muslim schools and trains and sends out missionaries to preach Islam. The Sultan of Sokoto Sir Abubakar, *Sarkin Muslimin*, i.e. the leader of the Muslims of Nigeria, is the president of the organization and Alhaji Ibrahim Dasuki, who was turbanned in 1972 as the *Baraden Sokoto*,[25] is the secretary of this organization. Since the civil war this organization, whose activities were formerly restricted to the Northern states of Nigeria, has extended the sphere of its programmes in the southern parts of Nigeria and has recently established branches in Lagos, Benin, Enugu, Calabar and Port-Harcourt. During visits to Benin and Enugu in 1973, I found that the Jamāʿat Naṣril Islam has organized very many activities and has become popular in those areas and a large number of indigenous people have become members. In Enugu, a recently converted Igbo Muslim leader, Chief Suleiman Onyaema, is the president of the branch of the Jamāʿat Naṣril Islam. He has converted a large number of Igbos to Islam who have become members of this organization. In 1973, Alhaji Dasuki toured the Midwest, East Central and River states of Nigeria with some executive members of the Jamāʿat Naṣril Islam and said at a reception given in his honour by the Lagos branch of the organization that 'over five hundred Ibos were converted to Islam'[26] during this visit to East Central state.

Some of those who accepted Islam some years ago at the hands of Shaikh Ibrahim Nwagui have now started Islamic activities in their respective areas of origin and influence. Alhaji Tijani Akubuo takes a keen interest in the Islamic affairs in his home-town of Orlu. Before the war, H. E. Kamil al-Sharif, the former ambassador of the Hashimite Kingdom of Jordan, had donated a large amount of money to build Orlu Islamic centre. It contained a beautiful mosque, library, conference room and guest room. The centre was damaged during the war but has been re-opened recently where prayers are conducted on Fridays. The centre needs immediate repairs. Since Alhaji Tijani Akubuo runs his business in Onitsha market, he is mostly away from Orlu. In his absence, Mohammad Okagba looks after the Islamic centre. These two Igbo Muslim leaders have also built small mosques in the compounds of their houses. These mosques are used as *ratibi* mosques where people living in the nearby quarters offer their daily prayers five times a day.

Recently some new Islamic centres have begun their activities in Awo-Omama, Umuafor Akabor Oguta, Igbere, Abiriba, Umuahia, Awka,

---

[25] *Baraden Sokoto* conferred on Alhaji Dasuki is one of the earliest traditional titles used to honour staunch Muslim leaders who were prepared to sacrifice themselves and even their households for the spread of Islam.

[26] *The Nigeria Islamic Review*, July 1973, p. 3.

Aba, Awara Ohaji, Umuapu, Obokofia Egbema, Umudike, Mbaise and Izombe. Alhaji Sufiyan Agwasim, who was a staunch Roman Catholic before he accepted Islam in 1935, is an Igbo leader who runs a consultative Islamic society, named Jamaʿatu Muharrar-ul-Musulumi. Shaikh Abdul Gaffari Emetumah from Umafor Akabor Oguta is the secretary of this organization. Alhaji Agwasim originally came from Awo-Omama but made Aba the centre of his activities. These Igbo leaders travel in different Igbo towns and villages and preach Islam and gain new converts. In Owerri, Yesufu Awah accepted Islam as early as 1935 and now works as the *Ladhan,* i.e., the muezzin of the Owerri central mosque. Yesufu Awah, Maman Naibi and Shaibu are the Igbo Muslim leaders in Owerri who are actively engaged in preaching Islam to the Igbos living in the neighbouring villages.

Similarly the oldest Muslim area in Nsukka division, where an Islamic centre was functioning before the war, has once again resumed Islamic activities. The two Islamic schools at Ibagwa-Nkwo and Enugu-Ezike have been repaired and have started Islamic teaching programmes. A new Islamic society named 'Muslim Community Society of Nsukka Division and Akpanya' has been formed recently under the presidentship of Ilyasu Eya, an Igbo Muslim from Enugu-Ezike and its secretary is Abdullahi Adekwu another Igbo Muslim from the same area. The society manages the spiritual and social affairs of the Muslims, irrespective of their tribal belonging, living in nine villages: Ibagwa-Nkwo, Enugu-Ezike, Ibagwa Ani, Ogurugu, Ethe, Alo-Agwo, Unadu, Akpanya and Obukpa. The Muslim children of these villages attend the Qurʾānic schools situated at Ibagwa-Knwo and Enugu-Ezike. Ibagwa-Nkwo is an old centre of Islam with three mosque buildings one of which is a central mosque. There is a great deal of harmony among Muslims of different ethnic groups and the Christian Igbo population. With some friends from Medina University, I visited this area in 1972 and a rousing welcome was given to us by all the Muslims and their Christian Igbo chief since I had spent two years (1965-67) before the war teaching at the University of Nigeria, Nsukka. The present Chief Imam of Ibagwa-Nkwo is Mallam Ndan Jega, an old Nupe scholar from Bida, and the Chief Imam of Enugu-Ezike is also a Nupe, Mallam Adamu Ibrahim. Muslims living in the neighbouring nine villages assemble for their Friday prayers (*ṣalāt al-Jumʿah*) in these two central mosques.

The new supreme Islamic Council for Nigeria
The year 1973 marked an important event in the history of Islam in Nigeria. For the first time, Nigerian Muslims from all states within the Federation and different ethnic groups have united under one umbrella.

In August, 1973 a Muslim unity conference was called at Kaduna attended by Muslim organizations from the northern states as well as the southern states of Nigeria. It was, as reported by Alhaji Saka Fagbo, Director of the Muslim Information Centre at Lagos, 'the culmination of many years of tireless efforts to get Muslims in this country under one central organization.'[27] In the past, there did exist a gulf between the Muslims in the north and those living in the south, but this new body set up the three point aims and aspirations for the supreme council 'to cater for the interest of Islam throughout the Federation; to serve as a channel of contact with the governments of Nigeria on Islamic Affairs, where necessary, and to serve as the only channel of contact on Islamic matters.'[28] The new organization is called Nigerian Supreme Council for Islamic Affairs, its president is Alhaji Sir Abubakr, the Sultan of Sokoto, and the secretary general is Alhaji Ibrahim Dasuki, the *Baraden Sokoto*. There will be four members from each state of the Federation, to be appointed by the Islamic organization in the state. One of the objects of the council is 'to cater for and protect the interest of Islam throughout the Federation.'[29] The establishment of the supreme council augurs well for the progress of Islam in all parts of Nigeria, including the Igboland. The Supreme Council of Islamic Affairs will be under the leadership of the Sultan of Sokoto, Sir Abubakar, who is usually called the *Sarkin Muslimin,* the spiritual leader of the Muslims.

In the past there were, and even still are, many Jamāᶜahs societies or Islamic groups in the north, but they existed in isolation. In the early fifties, efforts were made to form central organizations and some such bodies did even emerge, but 'they were no more Nigerian than in name or through their impressive letter-headings.'[30] Jamāᶜat Naṣril Islam then provided an umbrella for the massive Jamāᶜahs of the Northern states, galvanizing the fold into action in the religious and educational spheres and providing a bridgehead and contact point with the rest of the Muslim world. In the southern part of Nigeria the move towards unity was kept alive by a number of organizations like Anṣār-ud-Deen society, Nawair-ud-Deen society and personalities like Alhaji A. W. Elias, the Baba Adini of Lagos, Alhaji Babatunde Jose, Alhaji Kensington Momoh of Midwest and Shaikh Ibrahim Niasse Nwagui, the Igbo Muslim leader from East Central State.

The council's first assignment seemed to be in the field of education. A delegation headed by the Grand Kadi of the Northern states, Alhaji

---

[27] *Daily Times*, Friday, 17 August 1973, p. 14.

[28] Ibid.

[29] *The Nigeria Islamic Review*, September/October 1973.

[30] Ibid.

Abubakar Gummi, made representation to the government of the Western State on the withdrawal of Higher School Certificate courses from the Ijebu Muslim College. When the last Ramaḍān fasts were observed, it was announced in all federal and state media of information, particularly the network of Radio Nigeria, Radio-TV Kaduna, NBC/TV, WNBS/WNTV, Midwest-TV, *Daily Times* and other national newspapers. Similarly ʿĪd-al-Fiṭr was also observed almost unanimously on the same date throughout the federation. But the perennial problem came up again in the southern part of the country at the time of observance of the ʿĪd-al-Kabīr. There has never been a problem in the Northern states since they accept the authority of the Sultan as their spiritual leader and observe their festival on the day declared by the Sultan. Even the Northern Muslims living and working in the South also obvserve their festivals on the same day as their Northern brethren do in the Northern states. But on the ʿĪd al-Kabīr, in spite of the announcement made on radio, the Yoruba Muslims celebrated their ʿĪd al-Kabīr a day earlier than in the Northern states. On asking some Yoruba friends, I was told that since the ʿĪd al-Kabīr was celebrated in the Northern states on Friday, there would be two *Khuṭbahs* (sermons delivered on the same day—one *Khuṭbah* during the ʿĪd prayer and the other in the Friday prayer at noon. Some *Alufas* (Yoruba ʿUlamā) scared the Chiefs, leaders and the Chief Imams saying that if two *Khuṭbahs* were said on one day, the Chiefs, leaders and the Chief Imams would die within one year of witnessing the two *Khuṭbahs*. Thus ʿĪd al-Kabīr was not celebrated on the same day in the country. This incident illustrates some of the difficulties facing the council, and it is too early to judge its success.

The Aḥmadiyāh problem in Nigeria

Although the Aḥmadiyāh movement was brought into Nigeria around 1916 by the late Alhaji L. B. Agusto, QC, it mainly spread in Lagos and Western States of Nigeria. It has recently been engaging the attention of a large number of readers of the national newspapers in Nigeria.

Nigeria was the largest centre of the Aḥmadiyāh before the present crisis began about two years ago. One might ask why some of the staunchest Aḥmadīs have become so vocal all of a sudden about the Aḥmadiyāh 'problem' which was never a problem in this country.

In 1916, a group of educated Nigerian Muslims wrote and invited Aḥmadiyāh into Nigeria 'without fully considering its claims and purports.'[31] Alhaji L. B. Agusto, one of these young men who went to Britain for higher studies, came into contact with the Aḥmadīs there;

---

[31] I. A. B. Balogun, 'The Ahmadiyya Problem in Nigeria', *Sunday Times*, 20 January 1974, p. 10.

once he understood the claims of the Aḥmadiyāh he returned home only to withdraw his membership of the movement, and he began an Islamic group named Jamāʿatul Islāmiyya in Lagos.

The Aḥmadiyāh Movement then split in 1940 into the Ṣadr Anjuman Aḥmadiyāh (Qadiani) and the Aḥmadiyāh Movement in Islam (Nigeria). The first mentioned is also known as the Aḥmadiyāh Muslim Mission whose headquarters has, subsequent to the partition of India, been removed to Rabwah in Pakistan. Their Amir-in-charge always is a Pakistani sent by their *Khalīfatul Masīḥ,* i.e. the Caliph of the Messiah (Ghulam Aḥmad).

The members of the Aḥmadiyāh Movement are led by a Nigerian and it has no connection with Rabwah, the Aḥmadiyāh headquarters. The Aḥmadiyāh Movement, therefore, is not regarded as true Aḥmadiyāh which say they must take a new oath *(bīʿat)* of allegiance to the successor to the Messiah, i.e. *Khalīfatul Masīḥ.* The Aḥmadiyāh Movement's present leader is Chief S. L. Edu, who recently wrote in the *Sunday Times* of Nigeria about the belief of his group concerning Ghulam Aḥmad. He said:

> My movement had stated its beliefs and these had been published many times in the national papers. The Executive Committee of the movement had published its decision on the desirability of changing its name so as to differentiate it from that of those who believe that there will be another prophet after our Holy Prophet Muhammad.[32]

The Aḥmadiyāh Movement, it is true, has published several times in the Nigerian newspapers that they do not believe in Ghulam Aḥmad as a prophet but they do believe in him as a promised Messiah and the Mahdī. Dr. Ismail Balogun who renounced Aḥmadiyāh wrote recently censuring the Aḥmadiyāh beliefs and suggested that in order to remain Muslims, and be universally recognized as such, Aḥmadīs will need to shelve their alien ideas of Islam; otherwise the majority of the Muslims will be justified to declare them and all those who bear the name Aḥmadiya as outside the abode of Islam.[33] Similarly, a very strong article was written by Alhaji Saka Fagbo formerly a great supporter of the Aḥmadiyāh Movement with a startling title: 'Ghulam Ahmad was a false prophet and a sinner.'[34]

Recently there has been a crisis in the Aḥmadiyāh circles in Nigeria. This crisis came about when the Executive Committee of the World Muslim League at its meeting held in Mecca, Saudi Arabia from Saturday October 3, to Sunday October 18, 1970, examined the copies of

[32] A letter by Chief S. L. Edu, 'Case of the Ahmadiyya Movement', published in *Sunday Times,* 3 March 1974, p. 4.

[33] Balogun, op. cit.

[34] *Sunday Times,* 17 March 1974, p. 13.

the English translation of the Holy Qur'ān sent by an Aḥmadī from Pakistan, Mirza Mubarak Aḥmad. The 'Ulamā' discovered that the translation marred the majesty of the Qur'ān and contained distortions of its meaning to justify the Aḥmadiyāh claims. The translator had resorted to strange renderings of the text which were incompatible with the well-known teachings of Islam and the commentaries of the great scholars of the Qur'ān.

The Secretariat duly passed the translation to the Cultural Sub-Committee of the World Muslim League for close examination. The report of the Sub-Committee's observations on the translation were submitted to the Supreme Council of the League which unanimously resolved 'That the purported translations of the Qur'ān by Aḥmadiyya organizations are false; that the Muslims in Muslim and non-Muslim parts of the world should be warned to refrain from using these translations; that the League's verdict should be promulgated by all possible means to all Muslims and other Muslim organizations are specially admonished to do their best in this regard in the interest of the Qur'ān to protect it from the evil onslaught of this errant group.'

On the basis of these decisions, the Saudi Arabian government decided that since Aḥmadīs are disbelievers, they should not be allowed to go to Mecca to perform their pilgrimage. It instructed its embassies all over the world not to issue the Ḥajj visas to the Aḥmadīs. This brought a great commotion in Nigeria. The Aḥmadīs stormed the Saudi embassy in Lagos,[35] and

> the commotion caused inside the embassy building reached a point that the Lagos State Commissioner for Information and Tourism, Alhaji Alade Odunewu, the Principal Secretary to the Head of State, Alhaji Hamzat Ahmadu, and the President of the Aḥmadiyya Movement in Islam, Alhaji S. L. Edu, were hurriedly telephoned by embassy officials to come to appease the angry pilgrims[36].

In spite of all this, they were not given visas for the Ḥajj.

The Saudi Arabian Embassy in Lagos has introduced a new measure to check whether the intending pilgrims are Aḥmadīs or true Muslims. Every pilgrim should get the signature from the Imam of the mosque where he offers prayers declaring that he is not an Aḥmadī. Then the visas will be granted. This brought about the present Aḥmadiyāh crisis in Nigeria. Many Aḥmadīs, in spite of their allegiance to the Aḥmadiyāh Mission or Movement did not know the actual beliefs of the Aḥmadiyāh. As Dr Balogun writes:

---

[35] *Daily Times*, 20 December 1973, p. 2.
[36] Ibid.

Even though Aḥmadiyya has been in this country for close to 60 years, I make bold to say that up till now the vast majority of the adherents of the organization, both within the movement and the mission are still in the dark about the details of its teachings as well as about its purport. For example it was only very recently when stiff opposition to the Aḥmadiyya started to rear its head in this country, that certain high ranking Aḥmadīs knew for the first time that Mirza Ghulam Ahmad had claimed to be a prophet. There are many members of the two groups today who become members only because they were attracted by the organized ways in which the groups carried out their functions.[37]

Once the crisis began, people wanted to find out more about the Aḥmadiyāh claims. It was during this period that a large number of pamphlets began to pour into the country exposing the Aḥmadiyāh claims as well as defending the same claims. Some people had become members of the Aḥmadiyāh simply because their children attended Aḥmadiyāh schools. Some people thought that the only difference between the Aḥmadiyāh and the non-Aḥmadiyāh was the Aḥmadīs folded their arms at prayer while the non-Aḥmadīs in Nigeria, who are predominantly Mālikīs, did not do so. When Nigerians went for the Ḥajj, they saw the majority of Muslims in Mecca not folding their arms since the Ḥanafites, Shāfiʿites and others do not fold their arms. Thus many Muslims erroneously thought that the Aḥmadiyāh who insisted on folding arms were correct while the others were wrong. Now they have begun to realize this practice makes no difference to the acceptability of prayers and both are correct.

The crisis continues. Some Aḥmadīs have asked people to rethink their position: 'We must, however, ascertain,' says Dr Balogun, 'where our loyalty lies: is it parochially to Aḥmadiyya or generally to Islam? I am sure that all Nigerian Aḥmadīs will answer in favour of Islam.'[38]

There have come about a number of changes since independence of Nigeria both in the general attitude of Muslims and the manifestation of Islam in this country which could be the subject of a whole book. I have not enumerated and commented ·on many other social institutions. I think, however, that an outline has been sketched, albeit lightly, to give some picture of the myriad of changes that have been brought into the entire life of Muslim Nigerians since the independence of Nigeria, when technology is introduced, adopted and diffused and modernism is finding its way in the traditional African society of yesterday.

[37] Balogun, op. cit.
[38] Balogun, op. cit.

Part II: Traditional Religion and Christianity: Continuities and Conflicts

Introduction

EDWARD FASHOLÉ-LUKE

Independent Africa presents pictures of diversity, unity and variety. The independent nations have had similar colonial experiences and Christianity has advanced in many of these nations through Western missionary endeavours. Since Christian theology arises from the lives of the various Christian communities, the emerging Christian theologies in independent Africa have shown remarkable points of congruence, as well as radical points of divergence. This is precisely because Africa has a rich and varied complexity of cultural, economic, political, linguistic, social and religious ideas, practices and rites.

Christianity in Africa is increasing by geometrical progression, and the forecast for the future growth of the Church in Africa is bright. This situation has not led to complacency however. Missionary methods and motives for evangelism have been, and are being, subjected to rigorous scrutiny and critical review. If the activities of Western missionaries are being criticized by African Christians, this is not because Africans are ungrateful or have failed to appreciate the significant contribution and the tremendous sacrifices that Western missionaries have made towards the development of African nations. Rather it is because we want to get the records straight and to move from the realms of hagiography to the field of solid church history. When it is suggested for example, that there was a remarkable coincidence between Christian missionary advance in Africa and Western colonial expansion, we are simply stating the facts of experience and not necessarily passing any value judgement on the activities of Western missionaries. Western missionaries stressed aspects of discontinuity between Christianity and African cultures and traditional religion to such an extent that they excluded the aspects of continuity between Christianity and African cultures and traditional religion. They condemned without proper evaluation African religious beliefs and practices, and substituted Western cultural and religious practices. This had the effect of making it impossible for a person to be a Christian and remain genuinely and authentically an African. The real tragedy was that Western cultural imperialism was imposed by Western colonial power. Moreover, some Western missionaries were racists, and supported the policies of the colonial powers in West Africa, who systematically removed Africans from positions of authority in the civil service, and replaced them by Europeans. Not only that, but the same patterns of behaviour were seen in the churches. Furthermore, in South Africa, racial segregation was enshrined in legislation, in the name of Christian civilization, and Africans were subjected to discrimination, humiliation and oppression. These are all facts of experience, which have to be chronicled and studied, even if we do not do this with the cool objectivity of the computing machine. In any case, Western missionaries have had opportunities to say what they think about Africans and they have done this with frankness and without calculating the consequences carefully. It is now time for Africans to speak about Western missionaries in Africa, and all that we request is that we be allowed to do so with the same frankness and clarity with which Europeans have spoken about Africans in the past.

It is also clear that despite the political independence of many African nations, the churches still operate on a dependence/domination axis and are still the agents of Western colonial mentality and cultural imperialism. Too many of the mission-founded churches are content with imported theologies, patterns of ministry, church structures and architecture, liturgies and spirituality. It is true that we must endeavour to maintain the tension between the particular and the universal, but Western theologies and culture must not be regarded as representing the universal, as was done by Western missionaries before the dawn of independence. It is precisely for this reason that the All African Conference of Churches Assembly in 1974 called for a moratorium on funds and personnel from outside Africa. The violent reaction of Western missionaries and churches to this call is an indication that they have still to be liberated from the ideas of cultural imperialism and colonial paternalism.

The economic, political and social situations in Namibia, South Africa and Zimbabwe deserve special treatment and have produced distinctive black theologies of liberation, which have been defined as theologies 'of the oppressed, by the oppressed, for the liberation of the oppressed'. Unfortunately Christians in the independent states of Africa seem to believe that oppression is confined to these countries. They thunder from their pulpits, and shout in their newspapers, vehement criticisms of neo-colonialism, minority regimes in southern Africa and apartheid; but they fail to see the oppression of blacks by blacks in their own countries. In many independent African states, military regimes rule and are kept in power by sheer brute force. Corruption and bribery are rife. The rich get richer through the exploitation of their poor black brothers. Ethnic group feelings are exploited for political and economic gain. All these evils are real in our African independent states and unless Christians in these countries condemn them with equal vehemence, they will not be qualified to condemn the evils perpetrated by white racists in southern Africa. It is clear that African Christians in independent states must first remove the mote in our own eyes, that we may see clearly to remove the beam in the eyes of the imperialists, neo-colonialists, racists and illegal minority regimes in Namibia, the Republic of South Africa, Zimbabwe and elsewhere. The point must be emphasized that African independent states need theologies of liberation as much as, if not more than, the blacks in the occupied territories of southern Africa.

Now, because of the peculiar economic, political and social conditions in South Africa, there has been a tendency to suggest that non-blacks must not participate in the creation of black theologies. However, we are convinced that the Christian Gospel is for the oppressed and the oppressor alike; no one can be excluded from the Kingdom of God manifested in Jesus Christ. Indeed, this is a genuine insight of African traditional ideas of community, where no one is excluded from the community. Furthermore, the term African, as Harry Sawyerr has shown, is a mythological term, indicative of love for the continent and commitment to an ideal. It is this definition of the term African that has been the motivating force of those who organized the seminars on Christianity in Independent Africa and the conference in Jos, Nigeria in 1975. The papers read at the conference were by Africans and non-Africans and these joint efforts symbolize our commitment to the African continent. As in all collections of essays, the length of the essays is uneven and their quality unequal; they show the various methodologies, viewpoints and preoccupations of the writers and in some way point to the rich complexity of Christianity in Independent Africa. The editors may be accused of perpetuating cultural imperialism, because the seventeen papers in this part have been prepared by nine African and eight European scholars. Our only response is that the criterion employed in the selection of papers for publication has been excellence and African Christianity demands that we use no other. Not all the papers read at the conference in Jos or in the seminars in the various centres in Africa and Europe have been published, but our accusers can take comfort from the fact that the entire project was predominantly African. They must also remember that to escape the dependence/domination axis, we must be prepared to provide our own funds; for self-government and self-support are inextricably linked together.

Bishop Desmond Tutu's paper claims that African Theology had previously failed to provide a sufficient cutting edge to approach the conflicts and injustices of contemporary African societies, but he also says that African Theology has performed a good job by addressing the split in the African Soul. Here, Bishop Tutu declares, Black Theology has some lessons to teach African Theology. Fr Magesa's attempt to devise the kind of cutting edge requested by Bishop Tutu, comes out in his adaptation of the model of a Theology of Liberation to the needs of Tanzania. Professor Ranger's wide ranging paper discusses various possible patterns of relationships between Government, Church and African Tradition. He notes that often the churches are conservative and traditionalist, while the followers of African traditional religion may be innovative and progressive. Government may be either. But basically, Professor Ranger insists these are not three wholly separate bodies which conflict or collaborate at their margins, rather they are overlapping influences on a single set of people. Conservativism and radicalism run through every major segment of African societies and valid Theologies of Liberation have to be sensitive both to the inherited oppressiveness of the past and the new oppressions of the present. Theology in Africa cannot be simply radical any more than it can be simply traditionalist, and, with classical confidence, Fr Sempore draws together the totality of the task which has finally to be embraced within a *Theologia Africana*.

Dr Kibicho asserts the continuity of one God across religious conversion in Kikuyu experience; this is paralleled by Dr Setiloane's South African study of the sense of an enduring religious and cultural identity among Sotho-Tswana. Dr Gaba's analysis of the Anlo Ewe concept of salvation provides a striking West African example of a rounded religious sense of a particular people revealed in their prayer forms and sacrificial ritual. This very real theological continuity between old and new has certainly not lessened the tension which goes with a discontinuity in cultural, moral, religious and social practices, a discontinuity sometimes required both arbitrarily and ignorantly by early missionaries in Africa. Dr Waliggo enquires into some of the areas of tension in Buganda. He shows that the best missionaries were well aware of the problems here and were anxious not to demand too great a cultural break; indeed they might take a more lenient view than the African priests who followed them applying the missionaries' principles even more uncompromisingly. Mr Dinwiddy approaches the same tension from a different angle and through different glasses, by examining the way in which contemporary African fiction portrays the rough missionary 'boots' stamping hard across the sacred places of tradition.

In some sense the very concrete material of these five studies, drawn from different parts of Africa or from the field of recent literature, is tentatively drawn together in a more general discussion on models of conversion, of continuity and of syncretism by Professor Peel. No study of the Christianization of Africa can afford to ignore other large scale instances of conversion to be found in various centuries and continents, and his chapter raises some fundamental questions concerning the nature of Africanization.

If Western missionaries frequently undervalued African recognition of the one God, they were nevertheless correct in appreciating that the presence and activities of spirits were often in practice a matter of greater immediate concern. Spirits can be of many sorts, some ancestral and some not, and they call for a very varied pattern of human response. The question of possession is only one part of this field. It is nevertheless an important part and itself complex enough. Spirit possession may be likened to a sickness, whether recurrent or non-recurrent, of which the victim needs to be relieved, but it may also be the recognized tool of a ministry with either public or private functions. Canon Barrington-Ward shows from a Nigerian example how patterns of spirit possession reflect wider social stresses and Fr Singleton suggests how in one type of situation the sufferer may be assisted.

If spirit possession can be a very personal problem, it is then also likely to be somehow symbolic of the wider state of the body politic. Here as elsewhere religious belief and pastoral care can never be very far removed from the public tensions of the secular order. If African theologies must delve deep into their traditional roots, they are summoned to look equally firmly at the contemporary state of African societies: racial conflicts, the increasing imbalance in the great majority of states between the rich ruling *élites* and the poor illiterate masses; various species of modernization and development policies, some hailing from the Eastern Communist countries and some from the Western capitalist countries. African theologies must take a careful and penetrating look not only at Zambian humanism or the different models of African socialism, but at the Zairean implementation of *authenticité* and the Mozambican commitment to scientific Marxism. It may well be that in the coming years the significant divide within the ranks of theologians will be between those who find the *raison d'etre* of their endeavour primarily in the dialogue with African tradition and those who find it within a radical struggle for a new society freed from poverty and oppression. Until now, if African theologies of East and West Africa have leant in the former direction, the emergent 'Black Theology' of the South has begun the formulation of a challenge from the latter viewpoint. It is a challenge which takes suffering and sin very seriously indeed and which finds therein a new centrality for the person of Christ. 'How like us He is, this Jesus of Nazareth', writes Dr Setiloane, 'Beaten, tortured, imprisoned, spat upon, truncheoned, denied by his own and chased like a thief in the night. Despised, and rejected like a dog that has fleas. For NO REASON'.

The Christian Church has perenially been recognized as a community of prayer, and as exhibiting a way of life which is sustained by the experience of prayer, both communal and personal. It has normally been in prayer formulas—its eucharistic canons, doxologies, litanies and hymns—that its most sure self-interpretation is to be found. Christian Africa is certainly no exception to this; indeed in West Africa so powerful is their stress upon prayer that many of the independent churches have come to be known generically as 'praying churches', the Aladura of Nigeria. But prayer was nothing new to Africa. Dr Gaba's study of salvation among the Ewe is a study pre-eminently of prayer forms, one example among a number of the growing recognition of the crucial importance of the prayer language of traditional Africa. It is therefore fitting that our final section be concerned predominantly with some patterns of worship and spirituality which have emerged in various churches and parts of the continent.

Fr Shorter discusses a number of more literary expressions of Christian spirituality in recent years and suggests a contrast between the 'ready made' spiritualities which missionaries tended to bring with them, deeply experienced but rather rigid, with a more fluid contemporary picture. This, of course, is true not only of Africa. It is widely characteristic of the contemporary church, that the rather fixed patterns of doctrine and institution, as well as of spiritual life and ascetical discipline, are today undergoing major revision, as many long-maintained certainties are questioned and new sources of inspiration discovered. Bishop Sundkler discusses the rich liturgy of George Khambule's 'convent' type of church in South Africa and compares it with the spirit of the Balokole in East Africa, so much more clearly in the Protestant evangelical tradition. The prayer of the Balokole appears to be one point, as 'Black Theology' interpreting a condition of sin and oppression is another, where the Christ enters most decisively into current African religious experience. The challenges and opportunities facing another significant sphere of contemporary African spirituality are described in Dr Weinrich's analysis of three diverse monastic communities, selected from the many who have recently been developing the contemplative tradition in Africa.

'The Church of Jesus Christ on earth through the Prophet Simon Kimbangu' is of peculiar importance for African Christianity, not only because of the most remarkable history of Kimbangu himself and his disciples, not only because of its very considerable size and organizational stability, but also because of its rich prayer life combining an original liturgical cycle and many devotional and ascetic practices peculiar to the church with a profound commitment to traditional Christian orthodoxy. We are fortunate to have Pastor Ndofunso's account of this new, yet already mature, corpus of African Christian spirituality. Here, if anywhere, one may be able to look for a synthesis, profoundly Christian and unquestionably indigenous. The last few years, since the Second Vatican Council, have witnessed a remarkable transformation of the liturgy of the Roman Catholic Church in many parts of Africa, but in few places has there been so serious an endeavour to renew the Roman Catholic tradition of worship within the African cultural context as in Cameroun; so it is valuable to have Fr Abega's account of the liturgy of Ndzon-Melen, based on his personal experience and involvement.

These selective and limited studies of African Christianity in the modern era are but pointers to a vast if still poorly charted reality. The intention of all those engaged in this project is to suggest in a tentative way some of the very varied growing points in the intellectual and spiritual maturing of the Christian churches in Africa, a maturing without which institutional and numerical progress would be no more than a hollow sham. It is also our hope to give fresh impetus to the quest of the churches to discover how they can be authentically African and yet remain integral parts of the universal Church.

Whither African Theology?

DESMOND M. TUTU

Without rehearsing a great deal of ancient history, it is still useful to examine the antecedents of African theology, because these help to explain its most important features. It is true to say that most of what is subsumed under the heading 'African Theology' is the result of a reaction against cultural and ecclesiastical colonialism. Most of it certainly predates the agitation and struggle for Africa's liberation from colonial domination. But the two movements are very intimately linked. This connection reflects the unfortunate unholy alliance between the political, economic and cultural hegemony of the West on the one hand, and the missionary enterprise on the other. While we cannot undo history, we must nevertheless still record our conviction that it was a great pity that Christianity was brought to largely unevangelized Africa by persons whose countries were riding on the crest of a wave of almost unprecedented prosperity and expansionism.

Men became missionaries from all kinds of motives, most of which were undoubtedly beyond reproach. But they would have to be persons of heroic sanctity had they not been tainted by the arrogance which was the almost invariable concomitant of a dominant culture. Only the exceptional among them would realise that Christianity and Western civilization were not coterminous; that the credal expressions and liturgical forms which the missionary brought with him were not to be confused with the eternal Gospel. It seems clear that Christianity unlike, perhaps, Islam, is not a success religion. Jesus Christ died an ignominious death on a cross. He had eschewed the path of a victorious and militant Messiah. Somehow Christianity tends to become distorted whenever it is associated with power and triumphalism.

Olfert Dapper, writing in the seventeenth century, was expressing the view of many a non-African when he said:

> No one, however thoroughly he has enquired, has ever been able to trace among all the Kaffirs, Hottentots and Beachrangers, any trace of religion or any show of honour to God or the devil.

No less a person than Robert Moffat in the nineteenth century echoed Dapper's words when he declared that:

Satan has employed his agency with fatal success, in erasing every vestige of religious impression from the minds of the Bechuanas, Hottentots and Bushmen; leaving them without a single ray to guide them from the dark and dread futurity, or a single link to unite them with the skies.[1]

To most of the missionaries those whom they were to convert were indeed benighted pagans whose way of life was thoroughly uncivilized and, therefore, irredeemably heathen. So the missionary would set himself the task of demolishing everything, so far as he was able, from their dark past. It is this missionary attitude and method of working which Parrinder describes when he contends that:

The old attitude of missionaries was usually destructive; the indigenous religion was not studied, it was not thought to have any divine revelations or inspiration, and little effort was made to use any part of it as a basis for fuller teaching. But it is not necessary to deny that the old religion both taught some truths and produced some spiritual values and living.[2]

Of course, not every missionary adopted this root and branch condemnation of things African, nor must we seem to give the impression that we are denigrating the entire missionary enterprise. We take off our hats to the missionaries for their superlative labours in education and medical care particularly. The missionaries were bringing the light of the Gospel to the dark continent. These poor native pagans had to be clothed in Western clothes so that they could speak to the white man's God, the only God, who was obviously unable to recognize them unless they were decently clad. These poor creatures must be made to sing the white man's hymns hopelessly badly translated, they had to worship in the white man's unemotional and individualistic way, they had to think and speak of God and all the wonderful Gospel truths in the white man's well proven terms.

It is odd that such a fundamental error was made when people like Robertson Smith had long ago written:

No positive religion that has moved man has been able to start with a *tabula rasa* to express itself as if religion was beginning for the first time; in form if not in substance, the new system must be in contact all along the line with the old ideas and practices which it finds in possession. A new scheme of faith can find a hearing only by appealing to religious instincts and susceptibilities that already exist in its audience, and it cannot reach these without taking account of the traditional forms in which religious feeling is embodied, and without

[1] Quoted by E. W. Smith (ed.), *African Ideas of God*, London 1961 ed., p. 83.
[2] Ibid, p. 239.

speaking a language which men accustomed to these forms can understand.[3]

African theologians have set about demonstrating that the African religious experience and heritage were not illusory and that they should have formed the vehicle for conveying the Gospel verities to Africa. And they showed that many of Africa's religious insights had a real affinity with those of the Bible. In many respects, the African was much more on the wave length of the Bible than the occidental ever was. The African understood more easily in his bones, as it were, the meaning of corporate personality, for instance, than the more individualistic Westerner. It was shown time and time again that the African sense of the numinous, his awareness of the proximity of the spiritual, his attitude to death and disease, in all these ways, he was far closer to the Biblical thought patterns than Western man could ever hope to be. It is true that there were differences in detail in the subjects as studied in various parts of Africa. But, by and large, it was legitimate to generalize and speak of African as an inclusive term. This anthropological concern of African theology has been an important achievement to chalk up. It was vital for the African's self-respect that this kind of rehabilitation of his religious heritage should take place. It is the theological counterpart of what has happened in, say, the study of African history. It has helped to give the lie to the supercilious but tacit assumption that religion and history in Africa date from the advent in that continent of the white man. It is reassuring to know that we have had a genuine knowledge of God and that we have had our own ways of communion with deity, ways which meant that we were able to speak authentically as ourselves and not as pale imitations of others. It means that we have a great store from which we can fashion new ways of speaking to and about God, and new styles of worship consistent with our new faith.

The fact is that, until fairly recently, the African Christian has suffered from a form of religious schizophrenia. With part of himself he has been compelled to pay lip service to Christianity as understood, expressed and preached by the white man. But with an ever greater part of himself, a part he has been often ashamed to acknowledge openly and which he has struggled to repress, he has felt that his Africanness was being violated. The white man's largely cerebral religion was hardly touching the depths of his African soul; he was being redeemed from sins he did not believe he had committed; he was being given answers, and often splendid answers, to questions he had not asked. Speaking about this split in the African soul, J. C. Thomas writes:

The African in fact seems to find himself living at two levels in every

[3]W. Robertson Smith, *Lectures on the Religion of the Semites*, London, 1889.

aspect of his life. Firstly there is the western influence on 'him from two different quarters: that is the influence inherited from the period of colonial rule; but also the inevitable influence of post colonial industrialization and education. Secondly there is the influence of his traditional culture and upbringing that gives many Africans the sense that they have a unique culture of their own which gives them an identity as Africans. Yet it appears inevitable that some areas of traditional culture will be abandoned if African states are to become self-sufficient economically and so free of dependence on foreign aid and trade.[4]

It is a remarkable tribute to the grace of God that Africa has managed to produce Christians of outstanding character when the odds have been so much against them. One of the main achievements of African theology has been to draw attention to this religious schizophrenia and to attempt to remedy it, mainly by rehabilitating Africa's rich cultural heritage and religious consciousness. But is this alone sufficient?

A major criticism levelled against African theology is to say that theology can never be ethnic. If it is, then a grave distortion must have happened. There is only one faith and, therefore, it is a serious aberration to try to nurture a particularist theology instead of holding out for an ecumenical and universal one. This criticism is often made as well by Africans who are apprehensive that a peculiar theology will mean that theology could so easily be turned into a chauvinistic tool by unscrupulous politicians who desire a supernatural sanction for their secular and often Machiavellian machinations. These theologians fear that they would have succumbed to the ever present temptation to pay the tribute to Caesar which rightly belonged only to God.

This is indeed a real risk—one knows only too well how religion has supported quite reprehensible situations in the past as well as today; and it is indeed right that the exponents of theology should remain ever on their guard. But the root fear is based unfortunately on an erroneous concept of the nature of theology. In our view, theology is a risky, albeit exhilarating business of reflecting on the experience of a particular Christian community in relation to what God has done, is doing and will do, and the ultimate reference point is the man, Jesus. Thus theology must necessarily be limited by the limitations of those who are theologizing—ethnic, temporal, cultural and personality limitations. This means that theology must of necessity be particularistic, existential and provisional. It must glory in its in-built obsolescence because it must be ready to change if it will speak meaningfully to the situation which it addresses. There must then be a plurality of theologies, because we do

---

[4]J. C. Thomas, 'What is African Theology?' *Ghana Bulletin of Theology*, vol. IV, No. 4, June, 1973, p. 15.

not all apprehend or respond to the transcendent in exactly the same way, nor can we be expected to express our experience in the same way. And this is no cause for lament. Precisely the opposite—it is a reason for rejoicing because it makes mandatory our need for one another because our partial theologies will of necessity require to be corrected by other more or less partial theologies. It reinforces the motif of inter-dependence which is the inalienable characteristic of the body of Christ. It is after all the Gospel of Jesus Christ which is eternal; man's response is always time-bound and his theology is even more so. The former is what ultimately gives Christianity its universality. Of course theology will have universal elements because there are certain constants such as the recalcitrance of human nature and the thirst for self-transcendence.

Another criticism is that all indigenous theologies tend towards what the Latin Americans call domestication. Indigenization encourages a too facile and cheap alliance between culture and Christ. It is true that Christ comes in fulfilment of all the best aspirations of African culture, but equally he stands in judgement over all that is dehumanizing and demeaning; and several elements in the African *Weltanschauung* can be so labelled. But such a fault is of course not peculiar to African theology and can be laid at the door of most theologies unless they are constantly on the alert not to neutralize the scandal of the Gospel; and one must needs exhort African theologians to exercise vigilance that they are not caught napping.

A more serious criticism is that indigenization has tended to be far too concerned with the past and consequently has given the impression that culture was a static thing. This is too anthropological an approach. The call must be for a theology that realizes that culture is dynamic and changing and so must realign itself to this ever-changing context. Hence we are hearing more and more of contextualization rather than indigenization (both extremely inelegant words). Theology has to take its context seriously while holding faithfully to its text, if it is to speak relevantly to that context. And it is perhaps in this area that African theology has performed least satisfactorily. Thomas in the article previously referred to is probably right to say:

> This process of Africanizing Christianity can only be done, however, if both traditional religion and the doctrine of the Christian churches are examined carefully and systematically and the areas of agreement and conflict are carefully defined and demarcated. It is a tragedy that in just these areas African theologians are producing works which are superficial and unscholarly.[5]

African theology has failed to produce a sufficiently sharp cutting edge.

[5]Ibid, p. 21.

It has indeed performed a good job by addressing the split in the African soul, and yet it has by and large failed to speak meaningfully in the face of a plethora of contemporary problems which assail the modern African. It has seemed to advocate a disengagement from the hectic business of life because very little has been offered that is pertinent, say, about the theology of power in the face of an epidemic of coups and military rule, about development, about poverty and disease and other equally urgent present day issues. I believe this is where the abrasive Black Theology (as practised in Southern Africa), an aspect of African theology, may have a few lessons for African theology. It may help to recall African theology to its vocation to be concerned for the poor and the oppressed, about man's need for liberation from all kinds of bondage to enter into an authentic personhood which is constantly undermined by a pathological religiosity, and by political authority which has whittled away much personal freedom without too much opposition from the church. In short, African theology will have to recover its prophetic calling. It can happen only when a radical spiritual decolonization happens within each exponent of African theology. Too many of us have been brainwashed effectively to think that the Westerner's value system and categories are of universal validity. We are too concerned to maintain standards which Cambridge or Harvard or Montpellier have set, even when these are utterly inappropriate for our situations. We are still too docile and look to the metropolis for approval and permission to do our theology, for instance, in a way that will meet with the approval of the West. We are still too concerned to play the game according to the white man's rules when he often is the referee as well. Why should we feel embarrassed if our theology is not systematic? Why should we feel that something is amiss if our theology is too dramatic for verbalization but can be expressed only adequately in the joyous song and the scintillating movement of Africa's dance in the liturgy? Let us develop our insights about the corporateness of human existence in the face of excessive Western individualism, about the wholeness of the person when others are concerned for Hellenistic dichotomies of soul and body, about the reality of the spiritual when others are made desolate with the poverty of the material. Let African theology enthuse about the awesomeness of the transcendent when others are embarrassed to speak about the King, high and lifted up, whose train fills the temple. It is only when African theology is true to itself that it will go on to speak relevantly to the contemporary African—surely its primary task—and also, incidentally, make its valuable contribution to the rich Christian heritage which belongs to all of us.

The continuity of the African conception of God intó and through Christianity: a Kikuyu case-study.*

SAMUEL G. KIBICHO

Christianity in independent Africa needs to be well rooted in the African soil of African traditional religion. This rooting of Christianity in African culture is already happening. For instance the use of African music in worship is now accepted by most churches. Examples could be given of other aspects of the traditional culture which have managed to continue into Christianity whether with 'official' consent or not, e.g. polygamy, woman-to-woman marriages, the traditional practice of magic and medicine, the traditional African concepts of and belief in God, the spirits, and so on. Above all, this chapter points to an urgent need for a thorough re-examination of the whole question of the relation between Christianity and African traditional religion (to be referred to from here on as ATR). A great deal of confusion still prevails on this question.[1] I was talking to a minister of the Presbyterian Church of East Africa (PCEA) not too long ago about some of these points, especially on the question of whether the Kikuyu knew the One True God, the Father of our Lord Jesus Christ before the coming of Christianity: this minister was in agreement with me on this question, but he felt it was a rather radical position and he was not free to express it openly.

The most basic question in this connection, which we need quickly to ask and answer for ourselves is the question: 'Was the God of ATR, (known by different names, such as *Nyasaye, Were, Mulungu, Mungu, Asis, En-kai, Akuj, Tororut, Ngai,* etc) the One True God whom we Christians worship in Christianity, the Father of our Lord Jesus Christ? If so, as most African Christians believe, did our forefathers really know

---

*This paper was first presented at a seminar on 'Christianity in Independent Africa', held at the University of Nairobi in mid-January 1975. It was presented again (with some revision) at Jos. Further minor revisions have been made for the present publication.

[1] Idowu, for instance, points to this confusion in relation to Christian evangelism right from its beginning in Africa. See E. Bolaji Idowu, 'Introduction', in *Biblical Revelation and African Beliefs*, ed. by K. A. Dickson & Paul Ellingworth, (Maryknoll, New York: Orbis Books, 1969), p.13.

him adequately for their religious needs (salvation), or was their knowledge of him only partial and preparatory for the coming of the full revelation in the Christ of Christianity? What was the view of the missionaries on these and related questions when they introduced Christianity to Africa? What has been the view of the African believers in both religions? And what is our own view especially from our own empirical study of ATR and within the context of the African experience.

Another important question related to the above one is: 'What has been happening to ATR since it was invaded by Christianity and other modern alien religions and forces? Is it really dying out so fast and with hardly a fight, as statistics from mission Christianity indicate?' In a recently published book, the following statistics for Kenya are given: in 1900 professing believers and practitioners in ATR formed 95.8% of the population, while Christians were only 0.2%; in 1962, ATR—37%, Christians—54%; in 1972, ATR—26.3%, Christians—66.2%. By the year 2000, these statistics go on to predict: ATR—8.4%, Christianity—83.4%.[2]

I must stop the list of questions here, for those related to this subject are very many. I should also hasten to add that even the ones we have raised cannot all be dealt with in such a brief space. I do hope, however, that the point has been well made: that in our thoughts about Christianity in Independent Africa, the place to begin is the question of the relationship between Christianity and ATR, and particularly the relation of the *Mungu* of ATR and the God and the Christ of Christianity.

What this chapter is suggesting (and it is based on an empirical study of the question at issue) is that contrary to the view of missionary Christianity, which I describe as one which assumes a radical discontinuity, and which has been accepted unquestioningly as the 'orthodox' view, as is the case with much of what goes for Christian theology which in truth is only Europo-American theology, what we actually have is a radical continuity of ATR, particularly of the African conception of God, even into and through Christianity. As indicated in the title, the Kikuyu conception of God is used as a case-study.

A brief description of the Kikuyu conception of God
Like most African peoples, the Kikuyu had a basically monotheistic conception of God. This is an important point when we come to consider the relation of the African conception of God and the Christian one. The

---

[2] *Kenya Churches Handbook, Development of Kenyan Christianity, 1498-1973*, ed. by D. B. Barrett, G. K. Mambo, J. McLaughlin & M. J. McVeigh, (Evangel Publishing House, Kisumu, 1973), p. 160.

chief name for God is *Ngai*. This name is derived from the infinitive *kugaya* (to divide or distribute). It signifies that as the Creator, Sustainer and Ruler of all, God is the Ultimate Giver or Distributor of all things and talents to all men, who are his children, as he wills. From this same sense, God is also called *Mugai*, a synonym of *Ngai*, but with an added note of intimacy.

Other names included the following ones: (2) *Mwene-Nyaga*: i.e. the Owner of Brightness or of the Sun, and of all great mysteries. These mysteries are symbolically represented by the Sun and by Mount Kirinyaga, the mountain of mystery and the main holy mountain of the Kikuyu. This mountain was also God's main temporary abode when he came down on his regular inspection tours. (3) *Nyene*: i.e. the Great Owner. A human owner would be described as *mwene*. *Nyene* in this case is the superlative of *mwene*, and signifies that God is the Owner of all things. (4) *Murungu*: the meaning is not clear, but signifies the attribute of incomparable greatness and power, or omnipotence. (5) *Githuri*: i.e. the Great Elder, (this one is rarely used) (6) *Baba*: i.e. Father. It is normally used in combination with *Ngai*: thus, *Ngai-Baba*, i.e. the Father-God.

Other attributes of God were expressed in beliefs and sayings such as the following ones: (1) God lives above the skies, but he is also everywhere (omnipresent). (2) God is the most powerful, '*Ngai niyo nguru*,' (almighty). (3) No one has ever seen God (invisible, spiritual, hidden). (4) God is the greatest or the ultimate mystery. (5) God is the most unique: he is in a class all by himself: he has no father, nor mother; no wife, nor family nor relatives. (6) God has no beginning or end, '*Ngai ndiri githia kana githethwa*' (everlasting or eternal). (7) God is one for all men. A few comments may be needed here to elaborate further on this belief: Kikuyu religion differed from that of their neighbours (Kamba, Maasai, Dorobo, etc.) in its methods of prayers, ceremonies and sacrifices (*Kirira na magongona*). But God was the same for all. A change from one religion to another did not involve a change of God. This is a very important point when we come to discuss Kikuyu conversion to Christianity. (8) God is both removed, hidden, far from men, and at the same time close to them (i.e. transcendent and immanent). He has given men reason (*meciria*), and knowledge of right and wrong, through which they are to order their lives in community without having to bother God unnecessarily. As one saying goes, '*Ngai ndagiagiagwo*,' i.e. God is not to be pestered. In other words, they were not to refer every little thing to him. Otherwise, they also knew that in everything they did, God was helping them to help themselves. As another saying goes, '*Ngai ateithagia witeithitie*' i.e., God helps those who are helping themselves, or God helps men as they are in the process of helping themselves. Again, they knew he was the Ultimate Sustainer and Controller of all things, and the Ultimate Determiner of men's destiny. He desired to see good, harmonious relationship, between all in the community, in love and justice, in mutual respect and concern. He punished and rewarded people according to their deeds. But above all, they knew he is a benevolent God, and the people could always approach him in prayers and sacrifices, mostly communally but also individually whenever they were in need or difficulty which they could not meet through the other human resources he had given them. They prayed to God not only in times of need, but also in thanksgiving, e.g. at harvest time, and also to ask for his blessing and guidance in relation to all important occasions and undertakings (including such things as journeys, building and moving to a new house, raids, all public meetings, parties, dances, cases, contracts, etc., etc.).

We could say a lot more on the Kikuyu conception of *Ngai*, but this very brief summary will be enough for our purpose. Note what we are saying: that this conception of God continues to the present day even into and through Christianity. It is still the basic conception of God for all Kikuyu believers, including Christians (radical continuity).

The relation of the Kikuyu Ngai *to the God of Christianity as the missionaries saw it*
The missionaries to the Kikuyu came round the turn of the century, mainly from Scotland, England, Ireland, Italy, France and the USA.[3] One important point to keep in mind when we consider their impressions of African religion and of African culture in general is that they were greatly inhibited in their perception of God in ATR by a number of factors. I shall mention two of these factors which are closely related. The first of these factors was the prejudices which they brought with them against the African peoples and against African religions. These prejudices were well expressed when they described the African peoples, as savages, primitives, the lower races, etc. and their religions as primitive religions, paganism, animism, etc. The second factor was the evolutionary view of the human races and of their religions, a view which was then quite popularly held. Africans and their religions were regarded as being at the bottom of the evolutionary ladder, while people of European origin were at the top. Therefore colonization was interpreted (and still is in Rhodesia and South Africa) as a divine mission to help advance these savage races in the scale of humanity, or to civilize them. In this divine mission (the 'White man's burden'), colonialism and

---

[3] See Roland Oliver, *The Missionary Factor in East Africa*, (Longmans, London, 1952).

Western Christianity saw themselves as united. And of course, when the chips were down, especially in the issue of Uhuru, the missionaries sided with their kith and kin, with very few notable exceptional cases. Hence, the Kikuyu coined the now well known proverb to express this fact: *'Gutiri Muthungu na Mubia'* (Between the settler and the missionary there is no difference). The following rather lengthy quotation from Bishop Walter Carey's *Crisis in Kenya* provides a good illustration of what has been stated above. Carey was an Anglican missionary to Kenya, according to his own description of himself. Formerly he had been Anglican Bishop of Bloemfontein in South Africa, before he retired to Kenya. He was writing in reaction (Western Christian reaction?) to the Mau Mau guerrilla war of liberation. He was addressing the public in the home country, Britain. Note the burning issue: Were the Africans ready for independence?

'If prep. school boys are ready for a trade union, then are these Africans at present. Till they are, we have to trust to long-term schemes of true education . . .

I have said that the settlers will never quit: they will either live here or be buried here, but they will never go . . . Nobody here is terrified of Mau Mau; we trust our Governor and Government and simply take as little notice as we can. Many carry guns, and I, who cannot afford a revolver, have an iron bar by my bedside which I would use to protect my wife. But if we stay—we lead. There is nobody else here at present to lead these Africans from savagery to civilization except us. If, and if, Africans can rise from mere cleverness (at best) to responsibility, to hard work, truth-telling, wise leadership—then good luck to them, we will help them and be glad to do it. Men can be partners. But as far as we can see ahead, there is nobody of that calibre—not one.'

Carey goes on to suggest that the only way these Africans are ever going to rise in some form of civilization is through the proper kind of education, which means education by contact with persons of character. Thus every European is an educationalist, even the settler. Therefore they had all to be very careful how they behaved before the Africans. Otherwise 'these primitive souls', who are a God-given responsibility to every European in Kenya, 'will learn to be immoral, Godless and unspiritual too . . . What a 'white man's burden! But it is inescapable . . .' Western civilization was built on 'Christian ideals, Christ's example and precepts, God's grace and given by the Holy Spirit in the World and in the sacraments of Holy Church . . .' Therefore,

I want these Africans to be educated: but it must be education by Christian teachers in Christian principles, and in a Christian atmosphere. Otherwise you will create mere clever savages . . . Only by the sort of character which Christ alone can give can we raise these folk out of the jungle.

But even with this kind of education, it will take a long time. For the Kikuyu particularly, who were found 'practically useless' even for slaves, it would take 'not less than 200 years.'[4]

Of course, we should not dwell too much on such attitudes as here expressed, especially if we have now passed that stage. But the question is: have we passed that stage? Aren't there distorted, evolutionary views continuing, especially in our theology? And also in colonial mentality in relation to our attitudes towards our culture, and our religion, i.e. our self-image? The worst type of colonial enslavement is the cultural-spiritual one—where the colonized is given a distorted image of himself and of his God by his oppressor and he accepts that image, and continues with it unquestioningly, despising himself, his culture and his religion and slavishly aping the culture of his colonizer. This is why we have to keep examining such images expressed in such otherwise repulsive terms. It is 'not yet Uhuru' (as Odinga phrases it) until we free ourselves fully, not only politically and economically, but also culturally and spiritually.

Let me pause here to warn that when we read such stuff by Bishop Carey and others, we should do so with a great sense of humour and with a forgiving heart. There is a story, I think a fictional one, of an African student in a US college in the 'deep south' (where there used to be a lot of segregation and discrimination against blacks, and also a lot of Christianity, the so-called Bible Belt). One day, he was reading in the library and for the first time he came across these derogatory terms by which Europeans and Americans described Africans. He got so angry, for a moment he forgot where he was. Suddenly, he threw the heavy volume he was reading at his imaginary enemies, as if they were actually there before him. The book landed on another student who was reading on the opposite side of the table . . . The student he hit was a black American, and the only other black in that whole college. I shall leave you to draw your own moral from the story.

To go back to our main point here: We are emphasizing the fact that the missionaries were greatly inhibited in their perception of both African religion and African humanity as a whole, by their prejudices against them, and also by the then current evolutionary view of the human races and of the religions. But as time went on, and after their

---

[4] Bishop Walter Carey (Missionary in Kenya), *Crisis in Kenya, Christian Common sense on Mau Mau and the Colour-Bar* (A. R. Mowbray & Co Ltd, London, 1953), pp. 12-30. His bluntly extreme views were immediately denounced by the CMS in Kenya, but the CMS did not repudiate his claim to be an Anglican missionary there. See *African Affairs*, 1953, April, p. 95.

initial shock was over, the missionaries started to appreciate and to acknowledge the fact that Africans had a better idea of God than had been generally assumed. The missionaries now began to have some very positive things to say about Kikuyu religion. Their negative evaluation however, continued to predominate. A few examples will serve to illustrate this:

One CSM missionary by the name of Alexander Y. Allen, wrote back home to Scotland soon after his arrival in 1903, about his first impression of the people. He had just been to a large religious gathering which included many 'heathens' at the Kikuyu mission. He wrote:

'I had come prepared to be very much shocked with the people and was very much agreeably surprised to see many faces full of character and intelligence.'[5]

A. R. Barlow, another well known Scottish missionary among the Kikuyu wrote in *Kikuyu News*, 1908:

'The Kikuyu have a wonderful system of sacrifice, perhaps almost unique among the tribes of East Africa . . . There is a distinct difference between the sacrifices to God and those to the spirits, showing that the Kikuyu's idea of the Deity is not so vague and so confused with that of the spirits of the departed as it has been supposed to be the case of many other tribes.'[6]

Fr Cagnolo had a very positive evaluation of Kikuyu monotheism which he regarded as good proof of the universality of the idea of God and of religion. He wrote:

. . . Since our arrival among these people, we found that the Kikuyu believes in a Supreme Being, spiritual, Ruler and Governor of the universe. He believes also in the survival of the soul. Like all the other Bantu tribes, they distinguish exactly two orders of ultra-mundane beings: *Ngai*—with the singular only—as Supreme Being and Source of all things, and the *Ngoma* or the innumerable spirits of the dead, with no connection with God, but in connection with us.

They do not know the forms and features of the Supreme Being, nor did they ever attempt to make material representations of Him . . . The Supreme Being is believed to be good *per se* and generally He is not invoked. Only in cases of public calamities, epidemics, droughts, mortalities, is God had recourse to in public prayers and sacrifices . . .

In times of misfortune, or public calamity, the Akikuyu do not imprecate, much less do they blaspheme God, who allows such evils; but with all compliance that borders upon fatalism, they simply say:

[5] Alexander Y. Allan, 'Letter from A. Y. Allan', in *Kikuyu News*, No. 6, Sept. 1908, p. 8.

[6] A. R. Barlow, 'A Sacrifice for Rain', in *Kikuyu News*, No. 3, May 1908, pp. 1-2.

'It is God's will'.

Cagnolo concludes his description by saying that the new doctrine of Christianity 'found a suitable soil for its growth', in Kikuyu 'monotheism, therefore the graft took hold and thrived.'[7]

Despite positive evaluations such as the two quoted above, the negative evaluations continued to predominate. Four deficiencies in the Kikuyu conception of God were especially stressed by the missionaries: (1) Vagueness of the conception and reality of *Ngai*. (2) Confusion of the conception of *Ngai* with that of the spirits. This is the deficiency implied in the term 'animism,' which is still used to this day by some Western missionaries and scholars to describe African religion.[8] (3) Remoteness i.e., *Ngai* was almost totally removed from their day-to-day lives. Instead, the spirits (*Ngoma*) and the taboos (*migiro*) occupied the greatest place in their religion and in their lives. This remoteness of God showed itself especially in what the missionaries regarded as an extremely low and depraved morality—especially in evil dances, songs, rites and ceremonies. Here the total depravity of original sin with its accompanying virtual abandonment by God was, they thought, most clearly manifest. Mrs H. E. Scott described the Kikuyu moral code as 'entirely non-moral'. Barlow stated that 'it may be doubted whether (the Kikuyu) possesses a moral conscience'.[9]

Cagnolo quotes the Rev. P. Perlo, the earliest missionary of the Consolatas who had arrived among the Kikuyu about 1902, and who therefore, in Cagnolo's words, had had the opportunity of witnessing 'in its crude reality the atrocious and pitiful conditions of the Akikuyu'. After describing the extreme depravity of their morality and of their whole culture, Perlo concluded:

> How could morals be found among this people who in their age-long abandonment have become so corrupt as to raise practices openly immoral to be a social institution? . . . In short, every moral principle in which our civilization glories and which our religion commands is here, at least in practice, simply reversed in its terms: and that is enough to argue that whatever inference is drawn in this connection it must always confront us with a state of things essentially deplorable, barbarous, inhuman.[10]

The conclusion of the missionaries (which they thus convinced

---

[7] C. Cagnolo, *The Akikuyu*, (The Mission Printing School, Nyeri, 1933), pp. 26–28.

[8] Cf. *Kenya Churches Handbook* (1973) p. 160.

[9] Mrs. H. E. Scott, *A Saint in Kenya, A Life of Marion Scott Stevenson* (Hodder & Stoughton Ltd, 1932), p. 159. A. R. Barlow, 'Good and Evil in Kikuyu Mind,' *Kikuyu News* No. 37, August 1952, p. 8.

[10] Cagnolo, *The Akikuyu*, pp. 253–7.

themselves was supported by empirical evidence) was that despite the vague idea of God (*Ngai*) which they had, the Kikuyu, like other Africans, were in actuality almost totally ignorant of the One True God, the Father of our Lord Jesus Christ. This verdict of the missionaries is well expressed in a CSM missions booklet in which a summary of 'native life' is given. The summary gives a very bleak picture of the native life, and it concludes:

> Yet amid all this bleakness, there is a thread of gold, a vague yearning after an unknown God of whom they are so ignorant that they can hardly be said to worship him.[11]

This quotation also indicates well the relation of the *Ngai* of the Kikuyu religion to the God of Christianity as the missionaries saw it. The Kikuyu had this vague, confused and corrupted idea of God, their *Ngai*. As among other people the world over, to whom the true revelation of God in Jesus Christ had not reached, God in his mercy and providence had preserved this vague idea of Himself. This idea, however, represented simply a strong yearning, like that of a child's yearning, which, because of the child's ignorance, leads him to grope in the dark for he knows not what. If no grown-up is around, the child may end up putting into his mouth any object that comes his way, and with it he may rest contented as if his yearning has finally and truly been satisfied. Needless to say, this may, and often does, lead to grave consequences. This was the case with Kikuyu humanity, as suggested to the missionaries by the bleakness of their social and cultural conditions. Thus, the erroneous and dangerous ideas and practices and customs they had grasped in their ages-long groping in the dark during this 'their long abandonment' (to use Cagnolo's phrase), had to be replaced with the right objects deriving from the revelation of God himself through Jesus Christ.

This explains why conversion to Christianity had to involve the abandonment and renunciation not only of the traditional African ways of worship, sacrifices to *Ngai*, communion with the ancestral spirits and other holy rites—but also the abandonment and renunciation of African cultural customs and practices including songs and the dances. All of them together were referred to as 'things of the devil' (*maundu ma ngoma*). Almost the whole of the traditional African culture was seen as being under the kingdom of the Prince of Darkness, and the African peoples were summoned by the missionaries to come out of it completely, root, stock and branch.

The following stanza from one of the earliest Christian evangelistic

[11] *The Mission of the Church of Scotland in Africa: A Booklet for use of Study Circles Reading the Text-book 'The Future of Africa' by Donald Fraser* (Edinburgh: Church of Scotland Mission, n.d.) p. 214.

hymns which we still sing in church to this day will serve as an illustration here. It goes as follows:

Andu a Gikuyu, ukai kuri Ngai
Andu a Gikuyu mutiuke kuri Ngai
Andu a Gikuyu ukai kuri Ngai
Mwone Mwathani witu[12]

Translated

People of Gikuyu, come to God!
People of Gikuyu, oh, do come to God!
People of Gikuyu, come to God,
And see our Ruler!

It sounds as if the Kikuyu people had suddenly turned atheists! The implication was that God was only to be found and seen truly in Christianity, not in the traditional Kikuyu religion and culture. Conversion was described as leaving the things of the Kikuyu (*gutigana na maundu ma Ugikuyu*) and, when one backslided, it was said that he had gone back to Kikuyu things and customs (*gucokerera maundu ma Ugikuyu.*

In the light of the above discussion, the relation of the Kikuyu *Ngai* to the Christian God as the missionaries saw it may be described as one of 'fulfilment through radical discontinuity'. This means there is hardly any continuity from the African conception of *Ngai* to the Christian conception as the missionaries saw it, and also according to the doctrine of so-called General and Special Revelation.

This is clear in the missionaries' explanation of why they chose to continue the use of the Kikuyu name *Ngai* for the translation of the Christian name, 'God'. In his book *The Work of the Christian Church among the Kikuyu* Bewes (a CMS missionary), explains that what they adopted was the name only, because 'the content had to be different'.[13] The new content was to be supplied from the Biblical story of salvation in which alone God has revealed himself fully and salvifically. Bewes goes on to explain that this was, therefore, the basic task of the missionary;: to get across to the people 'the Christian message, to live and to preach the story of God's great love and of God's great salvation among a simple pagan people, to whom it was news indeed'.[14]

This doctrine of radical discontinuity between the African conception of God and the Christian one has been accepted unquestioningly as the

[12] *Nyimbo cia Kuinira Ngai* ('A Book of Hymns in the Kikuyu Language and Supplement') (London: S.P.C.K. 1955), Hymn No. 60.

[13] T. F. C. Bewes, *The Work of the Christian Church among the Kikuyu* (London, Royal Institute of International Affairs, 1953) p. 317.

[14] *Ibid.*

orthodox Christian position, as it is thought to be in accord with the predominant Christian doctrine of revelation, i.e. the General and Special Revelation doctrine.[15] According to this doctrine of radical discontinuity, African traditional religion is presented as a religion through which the African people were merely groping in the dark for an unknown God, 'of whom they were so ignorant that they could hardly be said to worship him'. African traditional religion therefore was seen as undeveloped and incomplete: its main role was that of preparing the ground for the coming of the full revelation in Christianity. This is the way we who have grown up in Christianity have been trained to think about African traditional religion and its relation to Christianity. Thus, Prof Mbiti states: 'Christianity should be presented as the fulfilment of that after which, in all its richness, African religiosity has groped'.[16] The Rev R. Dain in further emphasizing this point, continues to comment, in his book *Luke's Gospel for Africa today*: 'African Traditional Religion should be seen as a preparation for the Gospel'.[17] I feel that this attitude towards African traditional religion as shown above is a relic of the old prejudiced, evolutionary view of African religion. Further, it is strongly refuted by the empirical evidence of what the African conception of God actually was, and what it has continued to be to this day even in its confrontation with Christianity and with other forces of modern change.

The radical continuity of the Kikuyu conception of Ngai as seen in the response of resistance and struggle against the evil of colonial enslavement
In their response of resistance and struggle against their powerful and ruthless invaders and oppressors, the Africans manifested and asserted a radical continuity of their conception of God. This is because from the very beginning of British invasion and occupation of their land—in the

---

[15] For some discussion of this doctrine, see for instance: John Baillie, *The Idea of Revelation in Recent Thought* (Columbia University Press, New York 1956); D. Kirkpatrick, ed. *The Finality of Christ*, (Abingdon Press, Nashville, 1966); H. Kraemer, *Why Christianity of all Religions*, trans. by H. Hoskins (Westminster Press, 1962); H. R. Niebuhr, *Radical Monotheism and Western Culture* (Harper & Brothers, New York, 1960); Karl Rahner, *Theological Investigations* Vol. V, trans. K. H. Kruger (Hebicon Press, Baltimore, 1966); Owen C. Thomas, *Attitudes Towards other Religions: Some interpretations.* (Harper & Row, New York, 1969); W. A. Visser't Hooft, *No other Name; The choice between Syncretism and Christian Universalism* (Westminster Press, Philadelphia, 1963).

[16] J. Mbiti, in a lecture to the Christian Churches Educational Association of Kenya in 1969, quoted by R. Dain in R. Dain & J. van Dieper, *Luke's Gospel for Africa today, a School Certificate Course based on the East African Syllabus for Christian Education* (O.U.P., Nairobi, 1972) p. 6.

[17] Dain, *ibid.*

days of Waiyaki and all through the period of our colonial enslavement, through the times of Harry Thuku and his Young Kikuyu Association, then the EA Association, the KCA and Kenyatta, the Kikuyu Independent Schools and Churches movements, and finally the Mau Mau guerilla war of liberation—all this history of struggle for truth, justice and *uhuru*, was made with God as the Africans saw him from within their traditional faith. Like the leaders in the traditional society, the leaders of these movements were both and at the same time religious and political leaders. The same was true of these movements: they were both and unitedly political and religious.

Whenever they were faced with a calamity, it was the traditional African custom always to beseech God in prayers and sacrifices, asking him to save them from the calamity. But at the same time, they did all they could to help themselves the best they knew how, using their God-given wisdom (*meciria*), and other talents, including magic, for they believed, as a traditional Kikuyu proverb states—and one which Mzee Kenyatta likes to quote often—'God helps men when they are in the process of helping themselves,' (*Ngai iteithagia witeithitie*).

European invasion and occupation of their land was the greatest calamity which had ever befallen the Akikuyu. I am told that when this calamity appeared, their first act was to beseech *Ngai* (*guthathiaya Ngai*), in a great sacrificial ceremony. The ceremony also included the ritual of

smearing the eyes of all the people including women and children, with the raw fat of the sacrificial lambs (*mathunya*). This was because their eyes had seen an extremely strange and ominous phenomenon. The uncanny colour of the strangers seemed to spell out the ominous nature of their advent.[18]

Again the Akikuyu had received divine forewarning of the coming of the white strangers and of their invasion and occupation of the land, through the prophecy of the great Kikuyu seer, Mugo wa Kibiru.[19] The prophet had advised them, among other things, to be very cautious in dealing with the white strangers, for they were a treacherous and ruthless people who would not hesitate to annihilate the whole nation with their powerful magic sticks (guns), at the slightest pretext. Finally, the prophecy had foretold that upon the fulfillment of certain signs and conditions which the prophet gave, the land would be freed from the tyrannical rule of the white strangers. The Mau Mau freedom fighters made frequent reference to these prophecies of Mugo wa Kibiru,

[18] Joseph Karanja Kahiu (of 'Matiba' age-set): personal interview, South Kinangop, 1969.
[19] *Ibid.*, see also J. Kenyatta, *Facing Mount Kenya, The Tribal Life of the Gikuyu* (Secker & Warburg, London, 1938), pp. 41-4.

especially in the famous Mau Mau hymns. They believed that things were going exactly according to the prophecies. By 1952 they could discern some of the signs foretold by the great prophet, and they were sure that the time of their freedom was at hand. Their unshakable faith in the *Ngai* of their forefathers who had thus spoken to them through his great prophet, Mugo wa Kibiru, gave them great hope and strength to continue their struggle for justice and *uhuru* even against what looked like impossible odds.

One point needs stressing once again here: the leaders and participants of these protest and struggle movements, from Waiyaki to Mau Mau, freedom fighters were among some of the most religious and God-fearing men and women in Kenya, in continuance of African traditional religion. This includes those who were also Christians, and they were many, including the topmost leaders: Field Marshall Dedan Kimathi and General Stanley Mathenge. They even kept their European Christian names! But in opposition to colonial missionary Christianity, which at this time was preaching non-involvement in politics and obedience to the colonial government which they said had been ordained by God, the Christian Mau Mau freedom fighters held on to the traditional African conception of God, which they also believed to be the true Biblical conception. It should be noted that they even read portions of the Bible, prayed in both Christian and traditional ways, and made reference to Jesus Christ, while they were in the forest! Their God they believed was the One True and Supreme God who was well known and worshipped by their forefathers. (Radical continuity). He was, above all, the Sovereign God of love and justice to all. In any dispute, therefore, such as the current one between themselves and the Europeans, He was on the side of justice. They were therefore sure that He was on their side, and that He would help them ultimately to win victory over their oppressors. And sure enough, He did.

The following stanza from one of the Mau Mau hymns depicts well their faith in *Ngai*, the One True God known and worshipped by their forefathers. It went as follows:

Hoyai ma (pray earnestly)
Thaithai ma (beseech truly)
Ni amu Ngai no uria wa tene (for God is the same one of ancient times, i.e. the *Ngai* of the forefathers of old).

It is clear from what has been stated in this section that the African conception of God was not just a vague and confused idea, nor was it a static conception. God was a real and living force, close to the people. He was involved in their history, though always shrouded in mystery, and their vision of him was capable of adaptation to the changing situations of their history. But all through the vast changes which had overtaken them, they had no doubt that God was the same *Ngai* who was well known, worshipped and trusted by their forefathers of ancient times.

It should also be noted here that the African conception and vision of the One True God as represented by the religio-political movements of protest and struggle for justice and *uhuru*, stood in judgement over the European Christian conception and vision of God represented by missionary colonial Christianity. Each of these two groups of monotheists claimed to be guided by the One True God (*Ngai*) in their views and actions in relation to the life-and-death issue of colonial-enslavement and the related question of liberation. Missionary colonial Christianity, with very few exceptional individual cases, sided with the colonial oppressors and taught the oppressed believers non-involvement and obedience to the colonial government. Kikuyu monotheists in the protest and struggle movements, on the other hand, believed that God was guiding them to continue the fight for justice and *uhuru* until complete victory was won: God was helping them in their fight because he is above all the God of love and justice to all. It is clear that colonial Christianity (i.e. a Christianity which supports colonial-enslavement *de jure* or *de facto*, and of which the Kikuyu said: 'there is no difference between the missionary and the settler'), had lost the reality and the vision of the One True God. At this juncture of the meeting of the two streams of revelation, the vision of the One True God was to be found among the believers in the *Ngai* of African Traditional Religion.

The continuity of the Kikuyu conception of Ngai into and through Christianity, as seen in the Kikuyu response to the evangelistic efforts of the missionaries
A similar assertion of a radical continuity of the Kikuyu conception of *Ngai*, such as we have seen in the above section, is manifested in the Kikuyu response to the evangelistic campaigns of the missionaries. What attracted the Kikuyu converts to Christianity in the first place was not a new or a better-known God presented by the missionaries. Rather it was education (*githomo*) and the social progress, security and other related benefits which it promised amid the utter uprootedness and dis-orientation in which the Kikuyu suddenly found themselves as a result of British colonial invasion and occupation of their land. It was this incentive of education (*githomo*) and the accompanying benefits, which, beginning around 1911, after about twelve years of evangelism, changed the Kikuyu response to the missionary evangelistic efforts from one of complete indifference to one of insatiable enthusiasm.

Dr Arthur very early noted this fact. In 1908 he wrote that it was not 'the desire to know God' or to adopt Western Christian morality which attracted the Kikuyu to the missionaries. Rather, said Dr Arthur, it was the socially beneficial and progressive things they could get through them, especially through the education being offered at the mission.[20] On the same point, Roland Oliver comments:

> It is significant . . . that the first expression of interest by the Kikuyu in the activities of the C.M.S. occurred in 1909 in the shape of a desire for the knowledge of reading and writing as accomplishments connected with the most highly paid employment on the newly established European farms.[21]

Again, stressing the same point, conversion to Christianity was referred to as *Guthoma*, which literally means 'to read' or to 'become a literate'; to backslide was referred to as *guthomoka*, i.e. to revert to illiteracy. The converts to Christianity were called *athomi* i.e. literates, the rest were called *Agikuyu*, i.e. the people who remained in the Kikuyu culture.

The main point which needs stressing here is that as far as the converts or non-converts to Christianity were concerned, God (*Ngai*) was never an issue. Despite the strange doctrine about the Son of God who became man, died and rose again (an element however which the Kikuyu could accept as part of the mysteries of the new religion), the *Ngai* the missionaries preached was the same *Ngai* whom the Kikuyu had always known and worshipped. The things the prospective converts to the new religion were required to abandon and renounce included beliefs and practices relating to the departed spirits or *ngoma* (despite the corresponding doctrine of the communion of saints in the new religion!), other traditional customs and rites, their methods of prayers and sacrifices, and their dances and songs. *Ngai* was not among the elements of their traditional religion to be left behind. They moved with him into the new religion, or rather he was the same one worshipped in Christianity. He was the one guiding and helping the progressive among Kikuyu to seek the new education for their benefit and for the benefit of their people who were already experiencing great suffering under the new yoke of colonial-enslavement. Getting as much education as possible soon came to be regarded as a sacred duty, because the far-sighted Kikuyu who had the welfare of the nation at heart, were quick to see that besides liberating the people from ignorance and superstitions (especially in the field of medicine), education was also to be the new weapon with

[20] J. W. Arthur, 'Dr. Arthur's Circular Letter, No. 5', *Kikuyu News*, No. 1, March, 1908, p. 6.

[21] Roland Oliver, *The Missionary Factor in East Africa*, p. 199, quoting C. Granston Richards, 'History of the C.M.S. in the Highlands,' (unpublished manuscript, n.d.)

which they would ultimately liberate themselves from colonial enslavement.[22] Among the early converts to Christianity were such progressive youths as Harry Thuku and Jomo Kenyatta (then known as Johnston Kamau), and others who would eventually become leaders in the struggle movements for justice and *uhuru*.

In his autobiography, Thuku makes the following comment which emphasizes the point made above, that God was not an issue for these young Kikuyu progressives who decided to join the new religion of the white man. The issue rather was the cultural things and customs besides the religious ceremonies and sacrifices which they were required to renounce and abandon. 'Some people' Thuku writes, 'when they become Christians, including myself, were no longer interested in Kikuyu things.' Kenyatta however, he adds, was different, for 'he kept some things of Kikuyu tradition.'[23] Similarly, the controversies which led to the establishment of the Kikuyu Independent Churches and Schools had nothing to do with the God-issue. They were all on cultural-political issues. Education was also a main issue, because the independents believed that the missionaries were in league with the settlers to control and limit African education (one main reason for having segregated schools!) so that Africans could remain for ever a source of cheap labour for the settlers. So, the Kikuyu independents started their own schools, and later built their own churches to go with the schools. The missionaries, of course, saw the independents especially the KCA as agents of the devil opposing God himself. Against this misconception, one of the KCA Christians who called themselves *Gikuyu Karinga* (i.e. authentic Kikuyu) voiced the feeling of all the Kikuyu independent Christians when he retorted: 'We are anti-mission, not anti-God.'[24]

[22] Cf. one popular song especially in Kikuyu Independent Schools Association (KISA) Primary Schools in the 1940s and early 1950s, which went as follows:

> Korwo ni Ndemi na Mathathi
> Baba ndagwitia kirugu
> Njoke ngwitie itimu na ngo
> Riu, Baba,
> Ndagwitia githomo.

Translated:

> If it were (the ancient days of) Ndemi
> and Mathathi (i.e. the oldest Kikuyu age-sets remembered.)
> Father, I would demand of you 'Kirugu'
>   (i.e. a warrior-strengthening feast).
> Then I would demand of you a spear and a shield.
> Now (however), Father
> I demand of you education.

[23] Harry Thuku, *An Autobiography* (O.U.P., Nairobi, 1970), p. 6.

[24] Carl G. Rosberg Jr. & John Nottingham, *The Myth of Mau Mau, Nationalism in Kenya* (Praeger, New York, 1966), p. 126.

Concluding remarks: The new in the New Religion was recognized and accepted

In conclusion it should be emphasized that the radical continuity of the Kikuyu conception of God into and through Christianity, and also through the religio-political movements of protest and struggle for justice and *uhuru*, as described above, should not be construed as implying that there was nothing new in Christianity. The Kikuyu converts of both kinds (nationalists and missionary-oriented), recognized very well that Christianity was a new and alien religion, with its own scriptures, creeds, history, symbols and mythologies of redemption, holy rites and ceremonies, etc. These elements were different, but the basic conception of *Nagi* they saw as being similar. As already stated earlier, this was not something new to the Kikuyu. The other nations which they knew, the Kamba, the Maasai, and the Dorobo, each had their own distinctive mythologies, symbols and holy rites and methods of prayers and sacrifices. Yet, the Kikuyu believed that they all worshipped the same One Supreme *Ngai* (*En-kai* in Maasai, *Ngai* in Kikamba). Moreover, even in these traditional societies, one could move from one community of faith to another (e.g. from Kikuyu to Maasai and *vice versa*). This was also true even within the Kikuyu nation because there were two communities of faith. One of the two groups called themselves the 'Agikuyu of Maasai or Ukabi tradition', while the other group followed the Kikuyu tradition proper. The former group then followed patterns of sacred rites and ceremonies believed to have originated from the Maasai, although they were not identical with the Maasai proper patterns of rites, etc. The Maasai ones were also believed to be less rigid and less demanding than the Kikuyu ones. The main point being made here, however, is that movement from one community of faith and sacred rites to another was not something new for the Kikuyu. Again, such movement from one sacral tradition to another involved a solemn ceremony of adoption to the new community of faith. It also involved a ritual cleansing (ritual vomiting, i.e. *gutahikio*) from and renunciation of the old tradition of mythologies, rites and sacrifices, as the candidate was initiated into the new community of faith. The whole rite was known as *Guciarwo*, i.e. 'to be born' into the new community of faith.

The Kikuyu converts to Christianity saw their movement from their traditional religion to the new one in a similar manner. And, as we have already seen, besides other factors, the new religion was the only way of getting the one thing the Kikuyu progressives desired most: education and other related benefits. Again, as a religion it proved to be better suited for the new modern era especially to the progressives, and since the basic structures of the Kikuyu religion had been destroyed by colonialism, Christianity and Islam offered perhaps the only choices for those progressives who wanted to continue in their beseeching and worship of *Ngai*. In addition, it made it possible for them to join with other monotheistic believers in *Ngai* from other groups, to form larger nation-wide, and even continent-wide communions of faith—a most desirable thing in the modern era especially in their continuing struggle for justice and *uhuru*.

It should be noted here that many of the older folk and illiterates continued in the old religion, with the necessary adaptations. But they too, when you ask them, feel that the God they worship is the same God (*Ngai*) who is worshipped in the new religion of the educated (*Dini ya athomi*).

The main thing then and the one that mattered most in relation to their conversion or non-conversion to Christianity was that the God they continued to worship in either the new religion or the old religion was the One *Ngai* who was well known and worshipped by their forefathers of ancient times (*Ngai o uria wa tene*).

Stanley Kiama Gathigira, a well known elder in the PCEA, and one of the oldest writers on Kikuyu religion, very early protested against the view that the Kikuyu did not actually know God before the coming of Christianity, i.e. against the view we have described in this paper as that of 'radical discontinuity' from the *Ngai* of Kikuyu religion to the God of Christianity. He wrote:

I know that some of the people of the races which have immigrated to this country say that the Kikuyu worship (or pray) the spirits (i.e. ngoma) and that the Kikuyu do not know the One True God. This is not true; such people (say so only because they) do not know well the customs and traditions (or religion) of our nation.[25]

A radical re-interpretation of Christianity, and of its view of ATR and other religions is called for

The radical continuity of the African conception of God as argued in this paper should form the foundational basis of African Theology, i.e. a theology which is a reflection on the One True God in his relation to man from within the African knowledge and experience of reality, and in his own history from the pre-modern to the modern times. It is also clear that it should lead to a radical re-interpretation of such major Christian doctrines as revelation, salvation, evangelism, that of Christ, and the Christian view of other religions.

The kind of reinterpretation called for is perhaps as radical as that which took place when Christianity moved from the Jewish soil of its

---

[25] Stanley Kiama Gathigira, *Miikarire ya Agikuyu* (Equatorial Publishers, Nairobi, 4th reprint, 1968), p. 29, my translation.

cradle into the Greco-European soil. I think however, that the Greco-European re-interpretation went too far into Greek metaphysics and theological exclusiveness—to the extent that the Jews (the tribesmen of Jesus, the founder of Christianity!) felt and still feel left out. The radical re-interpretation now called for by Africa (and I think also by the rest of the so-called Third World), will be in the opposite direction: away from Greco-European metaphysics and at the same time into more inclusiveness. With this kind of reinterpretation, even the Jewish believers in the One True God might feel included as would be the believers in the same One God within the African traditional religion both past and present. As this paper has shown, this radical re-interpretation of Christianity in Africa has in fact been taking place since the introduction of this new religion into Africa. It is represented in the belief of African believers of both religions (African traditional religion and Christianity)—that the God preached and worshipped in Christianity is the same God (*Ngai, Nyasaye, Asis, Mungu*, etc.) who was fully-known (to the extent that any humans can know God), worshipped and trusted by their forefathers in the traditional religions in ancient times. As the Mau Mau monotheistic believers expressed it in their hymns: '*Ni amu Ngai no uria wa tene*;' (i.e. for God is the same one *Ngai* of ancient times).

It should finally be stated that the kind of re-interpretation indicated here would not lead to a watering down of Christianity as some might think. On the contrary, it should lead to its enrichment: it should make it more truly universal in its theology and in its general vision of God, because the vision of God of a big section of a basically monotheistic humanity (hitherto excluded) will now be included in its theology. It will also make Christianity more open to the visions of God of other religions, thus making a fruitful and meaningful dialogue with them possible.

Man's salvation: its nature and meaning in African traditional religion

CHRISTIAN R. GABA

My purpose here is to investigate the nature and meaning of man's salvation in the traditional African *milieu* using an ethnic group as a case study. The specific material for study is the formal expression of man's religiousness characteristic of this group especially as it is visible in worship. This line of investigation is prescribed in terms of one of our main preoccupations: the relationship of Christianity and other ideologies. How should Christianity operate in independent Africa, indeed in any given historic or cultural context, to make life meaningful, especially within its own dimension alone, so as to justify its claim to universality? There is yet another important reason for pursuing this study in the way it is done here. It is to discourage the rather facile generalizations without enough evidence on behalf of all traditional Africa and to encourage students of African culture to opt for the moment for studies that aim at investigating aspects of African traditional life and thought in particular societies. These studies, it is envisaged, will eventually lead to more authentically representative generalizations for traditional Africa than is being done at present. The particular African ethnic group for study here is the Anlo Ewe people of West Africa.

The Anlo Ewe word which the English word 'salvation' translates in this study is *Dagbe*. This word belongs to the ritual rather than the ordinary sphere of life. It may, however, sometimes appear outside ritual circles. Even here the ritual connotation is never absent because it always expresses a prayerful wish for the promotion of human well-being. A glance through the present writer's work[1] reveals that abundant life rather than salvation is used to translate *Dagbe*. This is mainly because in the milieu of those for whom *Dagbe* has existential relevance, abundant life is a more expressive rendering of the concept than the word salvation. Bolaji Idowu observes that the Hebrew concept of *Shalom*, understood as total well-being in body, mind and soul in relation to

---

[1] *Scriptures of an African People*, NOK, New York, 1977. Except where otherwise stated, Roman numerals followed by the Arabic ones refer to quotations from this book.

personal, domestic and societal issues, is a goal of African traditional religion in general.[2] Total well-being, thus understood, best conveys to the inquirer what the word *Dagbe* seeks to express. In fact salvation is used in this study to translate *Dagbe* simply because it is the word that is generally employed in religious and theological circles to designate man's religious concept that is being considered here.

Unlike some other Anlo words[3] *Dagbe* does not lend itself to an easy etymological analysis. It is one of the words which do not appear to have ever given rise to etymological speculation among the Anlo Ewe people. Perhaps this is because the condition of human life it portrays is so obvious in any saying or action in which it occurs that any etymological speculation on it is rendered unnecessary. To gain an insight into the Anlo view of man's salvation, one requires a good grasp of the concept of *Dagbe*.

In Anlo thought *Dagbe* comes from God. This is clearly revealed by the following ritual utterance:

Take them [the offerings] to the abode of Mawu, the Creator and in return bring to us everything that makes for abundant life. LIX, 18, 20. (cp. XXI, 34-35).

Other ritual utterances seem to suggest that it is rather the deities[4] and the ancestors that grant man *Dagbe*. Two examples of prayer offered in the shrines of the deities vividly illustrate this view.

O Grandfather Nyigbla; today we have gathered in your sacred grove. Give life to all your male servants. Give life to all your female servants too. Grant abundant life and prosperity so that we continue to serve you. LXXXIII, 10-13.

Asitenu, owner of abundant life, owner of money, owner of success, [grant that] she may know nothing short of abundant life and prosperity. LXVI, 1-4, 19-20.

We may also draw attention to the whole of chapter XXIII of the writer's *Scriptures of An African People* which is an example of the general intercessory prayer that opens worship in the shrine of the ancestors. No reference is made in it to God even though the entire prayer is aimed at

---

[2] Idowu, E. B. *African Traditional Religion* London, 1973, p. 46.

[3] See e.g. the following studies by the author: (a) 'An African People's concept of the Soul', *Ghana Bulletin of Theology*, Vol. 3, No. 10, June 1971, (b) 'Sin in African Traditional Religion', *Ghana Bulletin of Theology*, Vol. 4. No. 1, December 1971.

[4] 'Deities' in this paper refers to the multitude of spirit beings who exist side by side with God and the ancestors in the Anlo concept of the sacred.

the realization of *Dagbe* in the life of lineage members and their well-wishers.

These passages from Anlo sacred utterances present some uncertainty in the thoughts of the investigator as to the real source of *Dagbe*. But this does not seem to be so with the Anlo people themselves. Admittedly the sacred utterances make both God and the lower spirit powers that operate through the deities and the ancestors the origin of *Dagbe*. This is because the object of any direct and organized cultic attention in Anloland is either the ancestors or the deities and never God. Then also, even though God is regarded as the Creator of everything that exists, and is in personal relationship with all men, yet he has appointed the deities and the ancestors as his representatives in the world of men. So that even though the Anlo people are aware that God is the real source of *Dagbe* and that the ancestors and the deities must receive it from him before passing it on to men, yet they explicitly address the deities and the ancestors at times as the 'owner of abundant life' [LXVI, 1] in their capacity as the representatives of God. In fact it is pertinent to remark here that the worshipful lower spirit powers qualify for cultic attention simply because they bear a representative relationship to God who is the ultimate goal of all worship. One only needs to watch an Anlo man when he is really at his wits' end spontaneously calling on his object of worship for succour so that he may have *Dagbe*. It is God rather than the deities and the ancestors that he directly appeals to. Moreover it should be remembered that the sacred utterances from which these passages are quoted do not constitute reasoned and clear theological statements but extempore expressions of religiousness. Therefore the Anlo concept of *Dagbe* reveals that in the thinking of this African people God is the source, the ultimate source precisely, of man's salvation.

Anlo traditional thought also holds that God offers *Dagbe* to all men regardless of their moral standing. Every form of formal worship in Anloland involves the sharing of a communal meal but it is to festival communal meals that special attention is drawn at this point. These meals are of two types—the general and the special. The general is taken by all people that are present during the sharing of the meal. This meal can even be taken home to those who, for good reasons, are unable to present themselves at the shrine. To partake of this meal, one does not need any serious self-examination on moral grounds, in fact one does not need it at all. Chapter LIX of the author's text of Anlo sacred utterances is an example of the prayer that accompanies the general communal meal (cp. Chap. LX). This chapter is one of the longest ritual utterances recorded but nowhere in it does one find even the slightest imprecation against one's enemies. This is not coincidental but purposeful. It is intended to convey the idea that, regardless of their moral condition, all men in this world are God's children and therefore qualify automatically for the enjoyment of *Dagbe* which worship, as it is visible in the sharing of this particular communal meal, confers. By this humanity, then, every human being in Anlo thought qualifies to participate in the salvation that God offers to men.

However to qualify for participation in *Dagbe* is one thing and actually to participate in it is yet another thing. Even though the good that *Dagbe* is believed to unleash on humanity as a whole is within the reach of every man, yet to appropriate *Dagbe* in one's life demands a personal decision. This is the concept that the second type of the festival communal meal ritualizes. The meal may be a special beer brewed personally by the priest himself or a blood meal that is prepared with pieces of the sacrificial meat cooked in the blood of the sacrificial animal. This special communal meal is shared only by those who have seriously examined themselves and come to the conclusion that they have satisfied the moral demands of the Anlo society. It is unlawful for and, therefore, extremely dangerous to the well-being of a person who realizes that he is morally unhealthy but participates wilfully in this meal. The prelude to a typical Anlo prayer is intended to remind worshippers of this cardinal requirement for effective communion with one's object of worship and, for that matter, for full participation in *Dagbe*.[5] With the sharing of this special meal, then, goes a personal appropriation of the benefits that *Dagbe* brings to man. So that another important element in the Anlo concept of salvation, as this is revealed by their concept of *Dagbe*, is that salvation is intended for all people that on earth do dwell. But the individual's realization of salvation demands a personal decision. A personal response to one's object of worship is indispensable to man's salvation in Anlo life and thought.

The human condition in which *Dagbe* is realized must not know anything that destroys life but must constantly overflow with all the good things of this life. Three passages from Anlo worship are quite illuminating here. The first is a recital which the priest uses to welcome worshippers to the place of worship:

You shall never worship trouble;
You shall never worship poverty;
You shall never worship sickness;
You shall never worship death;
It is only Grandfather that you shall always worship.
May he provide a firm support before you;

[5] For a fuller account see the author's 'Prayer in Anlo Religion', *Orita, Ibadan Journal of Religious Studies*, December 1969.

And also behind you;
Should the heat of misfortune surround you,
May it all be turned into abundant life for you.

LXXVI

The next passage is what the priest says to dismiss the congregation after worship:

Priest: Gathered as we are here today,
Grandfather, it is life we desire.
Here is the life!

Congregation: *Akufia! Akufia! Akufia!*

LXI, 40, 45-7

The last passage to be noted here is what the priest says immediately before the immolation rite in the sacrificial drama.

All the members of the *Vifeme* clan say:
If trouble seizes them,
May trouble leave them alone;
If poverty seizes them,
May poverty leave them alone;
If sickness seizes them,
May sickness leave them alone;
If death seizes them,
May death leave them alone;
But if abundant life should ever seize them,
May abundant life seize them and cling very firmly
    to them forever.

X, 6-16.

The immolation, it must be noted, is the culminating point of worship signifying complete human self-dedication to the divine in return for which man must enjoy divine protection which manifests itself in the enjoyment of *Dagbe* in all its forms. It is apposite here to note in detail the condition of life that *Dagbe* confers. This is expressed in the following passage:

Bless those who have no children with plenty of children and grant an increase to those who already have them. Grant good health to the farmer that . . . the harvest [may] far outweigh his labour. When the fisherman goes out in his canoe . . . allow [him] to catch only the edible [fish] and very plentifully. Help our traders too that they may also succeed in all they do . . . Let no one die prematurely. It is for good health that we pray . . .
Good health to all; Long life and prosperity to all.

LXXVII

One can say that human experiences like poverty, trouble, sickness and death, 'indeed all manner of misfortunes' (LXVIII, 5), suggest the absence of *Dagbe* from the life of man and that a life that enjoys good health and immeasurable success in all endeavours right through life and eventually ends in ripe old age (XXXVI, 55) is the life that provides proof for participation in *Dagbe*. Perhaps one can safely say that salvation in Anlo thought implies deliverance—deliverance from all material misfortunes for an unrestrained enjoyment of material prosperity in all its forms.

It should however be noted that in Anlo thought there are spirit powers that are regarded as essentially evil and these operate through human agents known as sorcerers or witches. In the Anlo *milieu* man's experiences involving evil spirits are as real as those involving the good ones. In fact they constitute perhaps the principal element that renders life a meaningless riddle in this African society. Then there is also the concept of destiny. According to this view the day-to-day experiences of man are part of his life's plan prearranged for him by God before his birth. And misfortunes also form part of a man's destiny. Thus the ills of life do not always signify man's unwillingness to participate in *Dagbe*. In other words, even though salvation in Anlo thought implies deliverance from all material ills, yet an unrestrained enjoyment of material prosperity is not a necessary index to the realization of the deliverance that indicates salvation.

The concept of destiny seems to suggest God as the cause of man's misfortunes since it is God alone who prepares the individual's destiny for him. But the concept of *dzitsinya* in Anlo thought attempts to qualify this position. *Dzitsinya* means conscience in English. It is regarded as the little bit of God that enters every individual at birth as the life-soul. In functional differentiation, *dzitsinya,* as conscience, acts as the voice of God in man, forewarning him before he plunges himself into any situation that may make or mar him.[6] Any experience of man that is favourable or unfavourable to him is regarded as a direct result of the individual's reaction to his conscience. So misfortunes may form part of a person's God-given destiny. Yet according to the Anlo conception of conscience the ills that man suffers may be his own responsibility. Therefore man rather than God is made directly responsible for those ills that signify the loss of salvation. Simply stated, in the Anlo scheme of salvation God is the origin of all things in the world but man is blamed for his inability to attain salvation.

Even though evil in the form of suffering is not incompatible with the sufferer's right relationship with God, yet moral evil definitely is. The individual who opts for a life that brings misery and woe upon his fellow men is godless, in fact, irreligious, simply because God is a moral being

---

[6] The Anlo word for conscience, *dzitsinya* is very informative. Literally it means 'the heart that informs before hand'.

always on the side of fair play. It is in this light that imprecations, which form quite a substantial part of Anlo prayers, must be understood.

> May the wicked people perish in twos and threes (i.e. in large numbers).
>
> XXVII, 33.

> Those who may scheme that [your] children and grandchildren should not live, may they become the victims of their own machinations and perish in large numbers.
>
> XLV, 30-35.

> Should anyone undermine him that he should fail in his employment, may that person utterly fail in any venture.
>
> XX.

These three passages reveal that moral evil, in the estimation of the Anlo people, is that which leads to the personal loss of salvation. All those who perpetuate moral evil must not enjoy material blessings but suffering even to the point of complete removal from society through early death. In short, wicked people must not enjoy the blessing conferred by *Dagbe*. Therefore another important element that features in the Anlo scheme of salvation is that suffering does not necessarily imply the loss of salvation but suffering is a necessary part of a wilful loss of salvation. All wicked people who, by their own act, are not in a right relationship with God, must constantly be under the scourge of material failure because this is regarded as God's punishment for the ungodly life. But interestingly it is not uncommon to find those who, after a serious self-examination, cannot pin-point any moral evil in their lives that could lead to the loss of salvation generally suggesting that they may have done some wrong which they themselves may have forgotten and which is responsible for their loss of salvation. As an illustration, one may refer to a sufferer's willingness to submit to the performance of rituals that typify an atonement for wrongs that he has done. This definitely questions the belief that suffering is not a necessary part of a personal loss of salvation. But it does serve as a way of emphasizing the finite and dependent nature of man on God. It also shows that the Anlo man does not take chances in his attempt to realize salvation.

The Anlo scheme of salvation does not assign the sinful to a perpetual loss of salvation. There is enough provision made for participation in salvation once more by those who have lost this opportunity. The prelude to Anlo prayers is apposite here. This divides society into two on a moral basis and then reminds worshippers of the fate of both the morally bad, i.e. the sinful, and the morally good, i.e. the faithful. Worshippers must declare themselves as the faithful so as to qualify for worship. In other words, all the sinful people are always reminded during worship that they must, and can, give up their sinful ways in order to qualify for an effective participation in worship for which they have, on their own accord, presented themselves. But the clearest illustration of the point being made here is provided by the general communal meal already discussed. That all people can participate in this meal regardless of their moral standing shows that the sinful are not assigned to a permanent damnation in the Anlo scheme of salvation. The door for re-admission into the company of the faithful for the attainment of salvation is always very widely open to all those who, by their own action, have forfeited the opportunity of sharing in man's salvation. This re-admission is effected through sacrifice.

The sacrifice in question here is the *nuxe* type of sacrifice. *Nuxe* is made up of two Anlo words: *nu,* a noun, means a thing; *xe* is a verb which means to pay or to prevent. *Nuxe* means either to prevent a thing from happening or to pay a price for something. By means of *nuxe* sacrifice, the Anlo people seek to pay the requisite price for their sin so as to remove the ills of life that have resulted therefrom, or to prevent the evil results of their sin from manifesting themselves in human affairs.[7] Relevant to this study are the following elements that form part of *nuxe* sacrifice.

The sacrificer formally announces his purpose for coming into the divine presence to show that he has come to a personal realization of his state of numinous unworthiness and that he is willing to be made worthy again. The following passage is an illustration of what the sacrificer says as he presents himself for *nuxe* sacrifice:

> Every year brings me the same round of misfortunes. . . . [I] consulted the diviners and I was advised to perform some rites. For the rites I must obtain cowries . . . the basic fruits of the earth . . . white clay . . . gin . . . chicken . . . soft drink. . . . . As I present myself before you, Vizaze, all the misfortunes that are after me, grant that they all leave me alone.
>
> LXIV.

The sacrificial victim is used to wipe the body of the sacrificer either by himself or by the officiating priest. A ritual recital accompanies this act:

> I wipe away death . . . sickness . . . poverty . . . trouble . . . indeed all manner of misfortunes from the person of me, Naki. May the days of my life here be long and full of prosperity and peace. May my earthly life reach its natural evening safely.
>
> LXVIII.

In this rite the individual identifies himself with the sacrificial victim in

---

[7] For a fuller account see the author's: 'Sacrifice in Anlo Religion', *Ghana Bulletin of Theology*, Vol. 3, Nos. 5 and 7, 1968-9.

order that the latter may take the place of the former. The victim also takes away the sacrificer's sins and their evil consequences as he transfers them to the victim by wiping his body with it.

The priest then cuts off the pieces of the string used to tie the victim as he addresses the sacrificer thus:

All strings that bind you to death, . . . sickness, . . . poverty . . . trouble . . . [and] . . . all misfortunes . . . All these I now cut off from your person.

LXX.

This is a ritual of absolution. Its aim is to bring into the experience of the sacrificer the fact that his sinful state that prevents him from participating in salvation has been removed and that he is once more qualified for a life that locates itself positively in the divine presence.

The sacrificial rite culminates in the immolation. Here a poignant petition is presented by the officiating priest on behalf of the sacrificer to his object of worship thus:

Naki's fervent prayer [is] If sickness . . . trouble . . . poverty . . . death . . . any manner of evil . . . seize her may . . . they leave her alone. But if abundant life should ever seize her, O grant that abundant life may seize *Naki* and cling very firmly to *Naki's* person for ever.

LXX.

As the words 'very firmly for ever' are pronounced the sacrificial victim is immolated and given to the deity. If it is an animal, the entire blood is given the deity, except where part of it is to be used in preparing the special meal that is not lawful for the sinful to share. In *nuxe* sacrifice where an animal victim always features the head is always offered to the deity with the words:

As long as one offers the head of an animal, one's head can no longer be claimed. Today I have offered the head of a chicken in exchange for her head. Henceforth her head is fully her own.

LXXV.

This recital very explicitly states that the sacrificial victim has completely taken the place of the sacrificer, and that, even though self removal from the divine presence through sin leads to the death of the wrongdoer, yet a timely realization of one's shortcomings leads rather to the death of a substitute that is acceptable to the deity and ultimately to the salvation of the repentant wrongdoer.

Parts of the sacrificial victim are presented not only to the tutelary deity of the sacrificer, but also to all other spirit powers both good and bad—to the bad so that they leave the person of the sacrificer and to the good to re-instate their protective presence. The rest of the sacrificial animal is then shared with fellow worshippers. This signifies a reunion with the deity on the one hand and with the community of the faithful on the other.

Sacrifice has been considered here in some detail because of the central place that it occupies in the Anlo scheme of salvation. In fact so central is sacrifice in the formal expression of the Anlo conception of man's religiousness that it alone could be studied for gaining a reasonable insight into the Anlo concept of salvation. If it is stated that the Anlo expression of man's religiousness is intensely ritualistic, here is some justification for it. This analysis of one type of Anlo sacrifice reveals that worship, as formal expression of man's religiousness which leads to man's personal realization of salvation, is an activity in which the believer actively participates. The believer is made to dramatize that which he is in need of; namely his total well-being that extends even beyond the grave.[8] In fact prayer alone, as typical of what is said by man in his attempt to realize salvation, is not sufficient to enable religion to provide man in Anlo traditional society with a meaningful response to life. It must go hand in hand with action which is visible in sacrifice. Sacrifice and prayer always go together in Anlo religion and typify the mobilization of all man's faculties in his search for salvation as a meaningful existence. Thus at the end of worship the Anlo man heaves a sigh of immense satisfaction which is a manifestation of the integral response that is indispensable for the religious life. In short, a very concrete expression of man's religiousness is a *sine qua non* that makes salvation meaningful in the Anlo *milieu*.

The attention given to evil spirit powers in *nuxe* sacrifice reveals that in the Anlo *milieu* they are real and that their reality affects the Anlo man's life. In fact so real are witches, for instance, in the life of the Anlo people that quite expensive *nuxe* sacrifices are offered as holocausts to make life meaningful. Moreover one only needs to take a casual look at Anlo life in general to see how preoccupied the people are with obtaining supernatural help that will grant them protection against evil forces especially those that manifest themselves in witchcraft and sorcery. Any meaningful scheme of salvation that wants to operate in the Anlo *milieu* must fully reckon with this Anlo belief.

The analysis of sacrifice in this study also reveals an intense use of ritual, yet sacrifice as ritual is not considered as mechanically effecting salvation in man's life. It is quite true that a meticulous performance of

---

[8] In Anloland the hope for a blissful after-life in the company of one's ancestors is a condition for the godly life on earth and the actual experience of a blissful life after death is *Dagbe*, i.e. the realization of salvation beyond the grave.

sacrifice unleashes salvation on all and sundry in Anloland. But it must be remembered that for a personal appropriation of salvation the sinful must not only publicly confess his sins but also solemnly promise to pursue henceforth what is of good report in the thinking of the Anlo people. And when the man in search of salvation is required to observe that which is of good report constantly in his life before his salvation is assured, then morality is given a central place in this religion having been made a prerequisite for the realization of man's salvation. It also makes the one who ultimately grants salvation and his representatives in the world of men moral beings as well. It is not therefore unknown to the Anlo man that it is the pure in heart that shall realize salvation.

Finally it has been noted that salvation is deliverance and this deliverance is from material ills in all manifestations. Peace, on this score, can be equated with material contentment. Even though there exists a belief in innocent suffering in Anlo thought yet the existence of this belief does not seriously question the view that on the whole the Anlo concept of salvation suggests an inseparable link with material prosperity. However it must be quickly emphasized that this link is not materialism because matter does not have the final say; strictly speaking it has no say at all in human existence in Anlo thought. We can say that this concept of salvation is the Anlo version of man's religious conceptualization of the totality of existence in the sacred presence where no destructive forces can dwell. This view presents salvation as total well-being of life in its individual as well as its corporate dimensions and this is reflected in all spheres of human existence. Human existence, in the language of Mircea Eliade, may comprise sacred and profane dimensions.[9] But in the Anlo *milieu* there must be a total dissolution of the sacred and the profane, of spirit and matter, before human existence can be realized. In short, this concept of salvation which links salvation with material prosperity is the way that the Anlo people seek to objectify a universal human concept in the *milieu* of religious man—any religious man—of salvation as the totality of involvement of the totality of being in Being.

What relevance, then, has an analysis of man's salvation in a comparatively insignificant traditional African *milieu* for an important and international religious culture as Christianity in Africa today?

'If you want to teach Kofi Arithmetic you must know Arithmetic and Kofi.' This is the first principle of teaching I was made to learn in the Teachers' College. To my mind this is a very useful principle in all cases of human communication. He who wants to put something across to others must definitely know what he wants put across. He must know his

---

[9] See his *The Sacred and the Profane*, New York, 1961.

subject matter. But of more importance is the communicator's knowledge of his hearers. In fact many bad communicators are usually not people who do not know what they wish to communicate but more often than not they are people who do not know their hearers adequately. The result is that all that the communicators struggle to make meaningful to their audience remains meaningless to them largely because both speaker and hearer operate on different wavelengths. Christianity, as a universal religion, involves communication. Therefore the Christianization process requires a good knowledge of those who are to be Christianized. But a greater knowledge of one's hearers is demanded in the Christianization process than in, say, classroom teaching, because the ultimate goal of Christianization is to evoke from the Christianized the response that will make them find human existence and its myriads of riddles entirely meaningful within the Christian perspective *alone*. The knowledge of one's hearers that Christianity needs in Africa is not that which takes a giant stride over all Africa, but that which painstakingly investigates the various smaller groups that make up the African situation. This is because the Christian objective is to make each single individual to respond to the Christian message. And the knowledge must also be of contemporary societies. This study exposes what, in the thinking of Christianity's hearers, makes life meaningless. Christianity must attempt to make life meaningful for its hearers within its own system if it wants to win the complete allegiance of its hearers.

Besides all this, this study reveals the nature of religion, of formal worship, in the life of an African people. This will enable the agents of the Christianization process to adopt for the Christianized a form of expressing the Christian conception of man's religiousness that approximates to the local conception of worship but with the central core of the Christian message in full view.

Finally this analysis of the concept of salvation exposes a scheme of salvation that is quite meaningful for those who belong to the *milieu* of which the salvation forms part. Objectively and dispassionately considered, this analysis of salvation reveals that the religion of which it forms part, to echo Joseph Kitagawa, is a culturally conditioned form of man's universal experience of, response and commitment to ultimate reality, which deals with universal human themes.[10] One easily discovers striking similarities which provide useful points of contact for presenting one's message. But it is precisely these points of contact which make an agent in the Christianization process ponder seriously over the whole

[10] Kitagawa, J. M. and Mircea Eliade, eds., *History of Religions: Essays in Methodology*, Chicago, 1959, p. 28.

missiological and evangelical enterprise; whether, in the light of his present knowledge of the religion of those he is to Christianize, dialogue rather than an impatient attempt to convert all his hearers should not be his guiding principle, and whether it is still right for him to consider all those who want to remain in their own religious persuasions as eternally damned. This in fact is the challenge that faces Christianity in Independent Africa as a religious faith that lays claim to universality. And not only Christianity but also all other universal religions as well as ideologies which are seeking for a foothold not only in Africa but in any historical or cultural context other than that in which they originate. Perhaps the general principle that will make anyone, particularly the Christian, to face this challenge squarely anywhere in the world is discerned in Carl Hallencreutz's comments on Chenchiah's contribution to make Christianity meaningful in the Hindu *milieu*. He said:

As a basis for mission this view implied that the Christian-Hindu relationship should not be understood in terms of confrontation between religions. Chenchiah pleaded instead that what was involved in the 'new creation in Christ' should be worked out from within the Hindu context. The Church's task in India was to offer a powerful Christian atmosphere within Hinduism and a practical means to implement this principle was to develop Christian ashrams.[11]

---

[11] Carl F. Hallencreutz, *New Approaches to Men of other Faiths*, WCC, 1970, p. 35.

How the traditional world-view persists in the Christianity of the Sotho-Tswana

GABRIEL SETILOANE

'To tell the truth, *Moruti, ngwan'ake*[1], the missionaries have not taught us anything new about God and his workings with man and the world'. So replied an old MoTswana woman to my question after a long discussion concerning Tswana herbs which she used to cure children's illnesses. The question I had asked was: 'What do you see as unique in what the missionaries have brought to us?', all the time my purpose and aim being to assess Tswana Christianity to-day.

'All they have taught us; the only thing they have introduced to us', she added, after a slight pause, caused, perhaps, by her realization of my astonishment at her first statement, 'is *tlhabologo*' (Civilization, meaning, in fact, material progress in the style of the West).

This old lady was a full member of the Methodist Church in that southern Botswana town. She was well-renowned for her zeal in the faith and her witness to the saviourhood of God through Jesus Christ, to which she was known as a powerful witness in evangelistic campaigns and Easter rallies. But she also secretly practised as a herbalist, specializing in the treatment of children's and infants' illnesses. 'Secretly' is not quite right: in fact, it was a secret only to the local minister, who was a young man and a stickler for the 'Methodist Laws and Discipline', and who would have dragged her before the church courts to strip her of her membership. She prized this membership. She was also a Class Leader and a committee member of the Methodist Women's Prayer and Service Union (Manyano). At first she had withheld against me, suspecting that I was a 'spy' from the church officialdom. Now that she was relaxed and able to call me *ngwan'ake* (my child), even though she still respectfully called me *Moruti* (minister, padre) she could even sadly express her disgust at the short-sightedness of the church officialdom which was not able to see that this now 'secret' activity of hers was, in fact, a form of prayer life for her and the fulfilment of her Christian commitment. For, like the other *dingaka* (medical practitioners) I had met before her, she understood her

---

[1] *'Moruti, ngwan'ake'*—lit. = 'Minister, my child'. Rather unusual, as *'Moruti'* is an address of respect, and *'ngwan'ake'* of endearment.

knowledge of healing and its successful practice was 'a gift of God', and not just acquired skill or wisdom.

Her statement about the impact of Christianity on Tswana life and understanding of divinity struck me as an echo of what a Tlhaping nobleman had told Moffat some hundred and fifty years before, not a hundred miles away from the same spot:

> Munameets, though an early friend of the mission, the travelling companion of Mr Campbell, and one of the most sensible and intelligent men of the nation, than whom no one at the station had enjoyed equal privileges, made the following remark to the writer in his usual affectionate way, not long before his death—'Ra-Mary, your customs may be good enough for you, but I never see that they fill the stomach', putting his hand on his own. 'I would like to live with you, because you are kind, and could give me medicine when I am sick . . . Perhaps you may be able to make our children remember your *mekhua* (customs)'.[2]

Since then Moffat's assessment of African reaction to Christian teaching has been corroborated by missionaries and Westerners, even to this day, whenever they are free and by themselves: viz:

> Although they have received much instruction, they appeared never for one moment to have reflected upon it, nor did they retain traces of it in their memories, which are generally very tenacious. Accordingly, those who, at an early period, made professions to please, died as they had lived, in profound ignorance.[3]

All too often African resistance to Western religious concepts and understanding has been supposed to be restricted to these earlier periods of the missionary enterprise and, today, to the so-called Independent Churches. In 1961, introducing his paper on 'The Concept of Christianity in the African Independent Churches', Bengt Sundkler remarked to the contrary:

> We shall deal here with what is officially known as the 'Native Separatist Churches'. This does not mean that, somehow, we already know what the concept of Christianity is in missionary-controlled

---

[2] R. Moffat: *Missionary Scenes and Labours*. London, 1842 p. 246 (Munameets should be 'Monwametsi' 'do not fill the stomach'—they do not satisfy, they are insufficient for life; mekhua (customs): 'Religion' is a European term. What the missionaries imparted was always understood as their 'way of life' (mekhua—to follow Moffat's spelling), equivalent, and in competition with, '*mekgwa ya Gorr'a rona*' = the ways of our fathers, i.e. African traditional religion and practice. It would appear that Moffat left out some very vital sentence following 'when I am sick'. The sense requires that there should follow 'But I still cannot accept your *mekhua*'.

[3] Ibid. same page.

African churches. For, although one is inclined to assume that the more or less prescribed form of worship and the translated catechism in the latter churches are an assurance of their orthodoxy, it is not only in groups separate from mission control that new ideas, ideologies and emphases have emerged. In the mission churches, too, there is constant, albeit unconscious, re-interpretation of the Christmas message, with new emphases and accents.[4]

There has been more to it than just 'new emphases and accents'. There has been a whole new setting in which the 'Christmas message' has been understood, a different world-view and approach to life and things around. Before the African countries became independent and their inhabitants could walk upright among the peoples of the world, before the missionaries lost grip of the 'control' they had on the African church life, these sentiments were muffled, practised in secret, or banished to the then so-called 'Separatist Churches'. These days, however, it is more and more recognized, albeit very late, and tragically too slowly, that:

. . . at least of equal importance is the study of religious life and thought of the millions of African Christians who belong to the more orthodox Catholic and Protestant churches. Where do these many Christians fit in the spectrum between the old African traditional religions and the thought-world of the New Testament? One interesting question here is whether one can discern a pattern of continuity or discontinuity between the past and the future.[5]

Africans themselves, seem to be more and more up and ready to say how they experience more a continuity than a discontinuity. And these are African Christians who stand high in the Councils of the Church as devised by the West.[6] Whenever they are called upon to confess their Christian faith in the presence of men, they are quick to declare, now, that:

Before doing this (i.e. saying what the faith is which is actually in us) we should like to reflect further on hope as this is experienced in the traditional religions of Africa, in so far as this hope is not just something our peoples once had in the past, but is a conception of life which influences the attitude of the modern African . . .[7]

[4] *African Studies*. 20.4.61. p. 203.

[5] Per Hassing in preface to M. J. McVeigh: *God in Africa*, Hartford, U.S.A. 1974, p. xix.

[6] See in particular: P. Ellingworth and Kwesi Dickson: *Biblical Revelation and African Beliefs*, Lutterworth, London, 1969, and add to the list the Rev. Dr E. Mveng, S.J., Cameroun, Lecturer in Theology; Pastor Seth Nomenyo, Togo, Theol. Secretary of CEUAA.

[7] WCC: Faith and Order Commission: *Giving Account of the Hope in us*. Documents for Discussion, p. 51 'Report of the Yaounde, F. & O. Seminar'.

For:

> Because of the cultural form in which it is clothed, the Christianity of the missionaries cannot be assimilated, nor can it help (our) people to face up to difficult situations.[8]

The West, or Europe may be able to set up clear lines of demarcation, and explain what they mean when they use the word 'religion'. For Africa, religion or religious considerations enter into and influence all spheres of life. Therefore, can we speak about 'The Wholeness of Human Life'.[9] Space will not allow that we, in this paper, attempt to show how Africa has reacted at every point of its meeting with Europe. However, this emphasizes the fact that every point of such contact, even when it has been at the most mundane materialistic level, has had religious effects. Consequently, African scholars and thinkers about religion say openly, these days, that:

> The result of the encounter between Africa and the Northern Hemisphere world has been considerable frustration for many, perhaps for all Africans, *at every level*.[10] (My italics).

But for the purposes of this chapter we shall have to select some examples.

Marriage: Africa v. Europe

Even before the question of polygamy is raised, the understanding of what marriage is all about, posed by Europe through what has been called 'Christian or legal civil marriage', has, ever since the beginning, been contested by Africans, as single persons and in their institutions. In southern Africa churchmen of very high standing have gone to all lengths to circumvent the demands of the 'mission controlled' Church that there be no exchange of *lobola* (bride-wealth) in the marriage of their children. Their understanding of *lobola* as *the* seal of marriage, more important even that the Church ceremony and the minister's blessing, has persisted (perhaps 'unconsciously' as Sundkler says), sometimes even when they themselves are ministers and priests. For, there is more to the exchange of *lobola* than meets the Western eye. As

---

[8] Ibid same document, p. 47.

[9] Report of the WCC sub-unit on Dialogue with People of Living Faiths and Ideologies Consultation held in Ibadan, Nigeria, September, 1973. The report is entitled 'The Wholeness of Human Life: Christian Involvement in Mankind's Inner Dialogue with Primal World-Views', S/E 52, vol. ix/4/1973.

[10] Report of WCC Faith and Order Consultation, Accra, 1974: 'Uniting in Hope'. WCC Geneva, 1975, p. 33.

the Third Assembly of the All Africa Conference of Churches meeting in Lusaka in May 1974 has so clearly emphasized, for Africans marriage is still a union, not only between two persons, but of two or even more family groups. The Assembly seemed of unanimous opinion that so it should remain.

But there is even more to the *lobola* and the festivities of the African marriage than just the union of the two or more family groups. In the rituals and the slaughtering of beasts small and large, during the negotiations and after, by either side (and this is still done by Christians too), the ancestors, who are part of the family, are invoked. Without their blessing and goodwill, the success of the marriage union would be in jeopardy. This is still so strong in the minds and emotions of the people that responsible parenthood will risk a dishonest attitude to the requirements of the Church in order to be in good relationship with the ancestors.

The Ancestors

I discovered how emotionally even I am still attached to my ancestors when I noticed for the first time that, in publishing my meditation: 'I am an African', as an example of the expression of Christian sentiments in the African context, the World Council of Churches, Publication Department, had omitted the portion which deals with the ancestors. 'To take the ancestors away from an African', remarked a Ghanaian woman—herself a member of WCC staff and a daughter of a very highly-placed Christian minister, 'is robbing him of his personality'. I felt happy at this corroboration of my deepest feelings. Few ethnographers and observers of the African scene have remarked about the persistence of the role the ancestors play in African life even after acceptance of Christianity, the pursuit of university studies to the highest of levels and sojourn abroad.

It often seems as if these attainments increase the cords by which Africans are bound to their ancestors: 'I came to the University's degree conferment ceremonies' a world-famous African professor of theology said to me. 'My son is receiving a PhD in Physics. It is important that I be present at this son's academic attainment: He is my father, you know'. (Meaning 'He is named after my father.') Therefore, showing respect to him is, in fact, to continue to show respect to the deceased father. Another professor of theology in an African University, a Christian minister, born and raised in a manse, relates how, on returning home after studies in the USA and at Oxford, his parents slaughtered a beast and, in the traditional fashion, called the whole family to welcome him back. This ceremony, called in Sotho-Tswana, *Pha Badimo*, thanksgiving to the ancestors, presupposes their presence, and it is they who, in fact, welcome back the returning member of the family. 'If I had said "No" to this', the professor goes on, 'I would have been understood to disown myself and my family, living and deceased'.

Nor is he alone in this understanding. This presence of the dead is felt all through Africa in spite of Christianity and Western sophistication. (The very professor quoted above prides himself in the fact that he is equally at home among his people in Africa as he is in Europe, especially England).[11] It is presupposed and taken for granted in all meetings between Africans—as when I was pick-pocketed on a Johannesburg suburban train. I felt the hand slip into my back pocket where I had the paper money. The train was packed, and I cried out 'Who is that?' When I was able to turn round the money was lying on the floor of the compartment. No one could be charged with having done it. I was glad I had my money back. So were my fellow travellers. They congratulated me: *'Hadimo ba gagu ba na le uena'*—your ancestors are by your side. In spite of the fact that I was in my clerical attire as it was Sunday morning and I was on my way to lead a service, they did not say, 'Your God, or your Christ was by your side'.

> Ah . . .yes . . .! It is true.
> They are very present with us . . .
> The dead are not dead, they are ever near us;
> Approving and disapproving all our actions,
> They chide us when we go wrong,
> Bless us and sustain us for good deeds done,
> For kindness shown, and strangers made to feel at home.
> They increase our store, and punish our pride.[12]

Life is more than physically perceived

'Main Killer of Blacks is Hypertension' stands a headline in the *Star*, a reputable evening paper in Johannesburg, dated Saturday, 13th July, 1974. This is the finding of a professor of African Medicine at the University of the Witwatersrand, Harry Seffel:

> 'He blamed the high incidence mainly on psychological stress to which the urban African was exposed. Among these stresses he listed ancestral spirits (!), Tokoloshi . . ..'[13]

It is quite understandable that bringing such a world-view into a late

---

[11] The question is whether the Europeans also accept him as fully 'European'.

[12] This is what the WCC editors omitted from my 'I am an African'.

[13] *Tokoloshi* is a medium of the witches, notorious in Southern Africa. The word used by a white man is shorthand for 'The African's unseen world'.

twentieth century metropolis, such as Johannesburg, should bring about complications. This accounts for the increase in the consultation of *dingaka* in the urban setting over against in the settled traditional setting of an African village. Consequently, many rogues and charlatan bogus *dingaka* prosper in the cities more than in the rural areas.

The main point here is that the Africans 'world' of witchcraft (I use this word without derogatory sense it often carries in the literature of Western scholars) and related ideas concerning the cause and cure of illness, does not leave him when he enters the city. So it should be. For all this is based on an understanding of a relatedness of persons in community, which is foreign to the European ideas, and the principles on which urban life is founded. Another expression of this search for a fullness of life, as is known in the traditional setting, is the Independent Churches. Bengt Sundkler, Fred Welbourn, B. A. Ogot and other writers on the subject, witness to this hunger for 'A Place to feel at Home'[14] of the African in a Western-type city. He comes with a different set of values and understandings and is frustrated that they no longer seem to hold. Therefore he looks for crutches. The Western-type church does not help. Often he discovers that the bogus *ngaka* also does not. This, to me, accounts for most of these churches being against the use of *ditlhare*, medicine, of any kind.

The Independent Churches

But there is, according to my reckoning, more to the Independent Churches than their study so far, from Sundkler to the present day, has acknowledged. Often they have been seen as an arena of catharsis for the politically oppressed, an interesting sociological phenomenon, and all kinds of reasons have been found to explain their cause, from Zionism, Pentecostalism and all kinds of heretical sects from abroad, to Ethiopianism and African nationalism locally. Seldom have they been seen for what they are, viz., attempts, however crude and untutored, of the African genius to hold its own, a preserving of the African indigenous understanding of the workings of divinity (or shall we straight away say 'GOD'?). In this way they form the vanguard of African resistance to the corrosion caused by Western theological teachings on the 'ways' of religious thinking and practice (the ritual, the dance, etc.) which takes place in the so-called 'mission controlled' churches. For, when one of Sundkler's 'Bantu Prophets', in an effort to account for why he hived off, declares, 'Our greatest problem is this:

[14] This is the appropriate title of Welbourn and Ogot's book on the 'Independent Churches in Western Kenya', OUP, London, 1966.

never to be treated as a human being',[15] he is uttering a deeply theological statement. Indeed, such a statement could be seen as wax to a political fire which is already smouldering, especially in southern Africa. But if we remember that the word he must have used would be UMUNTU (Person), and we understand that UBUNTU (Zulu), BOTHO (Sotho-Tswana) or UBUNTUNGUSHI (Bemba) is a concept much deeper than the European word Person or Personality can translate, meaning the very essence of being, the equivalent of 'the soul' in Western Christian language, we shall realise that we are dealing with deeper things when we speak to Independents. In his own way, therefore, the Independent Churchman was attempting to fit his theology of MAN, learned from his mother's knee, with his every-day life's experience in his contacts with the West, and found that it denied him this humanity.

'What more shall we say?'

Space does not permit that we should treat all the areas of resistance to which African world-views are holding tenaciously against the impact of Europe. But there are many more, such as the few I will now mention.

The attitude to cattle is a clear example. Among pastoral African peoples like the Sotho-Tswana (and even the Xhosa) of South Africa, where Westernization, education and the money economy have not removed the deep urge for a man to own cattle. Observing jokingly to a friend, a high official of an African university in southern Africa, that he was going to his cattle post on a Sunday morning and not to the church service, I was dumbfounded when he replied, in much more serious vein than I had spoken, 'What shall we say? Is it not perhaps a way of worshipping, too, for as one sees these cattle one praises God deeply for his gifts'.

Initiation, especially among the Xhosa and the Sotho of southern Africa, is another example. Here the greatest breach of the Christian code, the words heard most when Christians confess to their priests or ministers, are: *Ngwan'ake o titimetse*—My child has run off to the initiation school. Often the parent could have connived at it, or even aided and abetted. To put an end to this unnecessary compulsion of the people to live a double life, the Methodist Conference in South Africa was, in the late 50s, persuaded to appoint a commission to study 'Christian Life and African Life and Custom', the hope being that perhaps material might be gathered to remove the outdated regulation which made a parent punishable when his child went to the initiation

---

[15] In an address at a Consultation on the Independent Churches at Mindolo, 1962.

school. As convener and chairman of the commission, I was inundated with letters from an unexpected quarter: African members of the Church who resented this threatened digging into the private lives of themselves and their families. 'It will reveal too much of our ways of life to the white people'. Some Conference-appointed members of the commission, ordained ministers, refused to serve on it, either from private conviction or for fear of going against general public opinion.

Land was not only the property of the living, but of the total community of the living and the living dead. The latter's good disposition made possible rain in season, the harvest and plenty for all. When one understands what religious undertones are associated with land, how, therefore, the place of man's birth and upbringing is 'a holy place', because there he meets his ancestors, only then will one be able to comprehend the depth of insult and the feeling of being raped and dismembered of the victims of wholesale removals of villagers and townspeople in southern Africa, whether it be Mozambique, Rhodesia, South West Africa (Namibia) or South Africa itself. It is this kind of despoliation and desecration of the people's very sanctuaries and shrines, which leaves wounds which ages will not heal easily. For when the Bantu say of themselves or one to another that they are *Mwana we mvu*—son of the soil—it is so. They are tied to the soil, body, mind and soul. A child's umbilical cord is buried into the soil, the same soil into which his ancestors are buried, thus linking him to them there where they are. If he is removed permanently from that place the cord which ties him to them is broken. Old people in southern Africa often say, 'Is it a thing to be wondered at that our children are as wayward as they are, stealing, murdering, raping and doing things which are contrary to Botho/Ubantu'. For Africans understand very deeply the Jewish exiles' cry of shock when their Babylonian captors asked them to sing their beautiful songs and play for them on their harps: 'How can we sing the songs of the Lord in a foreign land?' (Psalm 137.4.)

Conclusion

In this paper I have attempted to avoid the use of the word 'religion', or even to deal with specifically religious ideas of the Africans. It is because I am myself of the conviction that the concept 'religion' is a Western phenomenon, defining the deity (GOD) whether it be a Supreme Being, Father, Brother or Mother, and even capable of dying. To do this in this paper would be importing foreign categories and trying to force the African understanding to stand or fall according to whether they make sense to them. Besides, it is the proper manner of the African understanding, especially the Sotho-Tswana, not to try to measure

MODIMO (THE DEITY);[16] nor was MODIMO ever conceived of as a 'person', as the concord of the word indicates even to this day. MODIMO, translated GOD by the missionaries, was always the numinous, *Ungeheure, mysterium tremendum et fascinans* of Rudolf Otto.[17] I have often remarked how, to this day, an African church service properly conducted still captures this mood, and is charged with an eerieness which one finds with difficulty in any other church worship setting. For—

> . . . we must acknowledge that the dialogue with the primal world occurs not only outwardly . . . but also inwardly when both the institutional structures and individual lives of Christians in the older churches . . . the primal inheritance is operative here also in varying and largely unknown degrees. Past attitudes towards African primal religions have been such that it has been exceedingly difficult to acknowledge this inheritance . . .'[18]

But now African Christians, especially those in positions of leadership[19] seem to be determined to express their Faith without denying their origins. This is the 'African Identity' in church and religious circles which first hit surface at the WCC Conference of the Commission of World Mission and Evangelism at Bangkok, December, 1972—January, 1973, continued to express itself in unmistakeable language in the bid for 'Africanisation' at the 'All Africa Conference of Churches' Third Assembly in Lusaka, May, 1974, and came up again under the title 'A statement of African Challenge' at the WCC Faith and Order Consultation at Accra, July-August, 1974:

> . . . for all Africans, even after many years of Christianity, and standing fully within the Christian Revelation, the spirituality and world-view of their fathers is still very present. We feel, therefore, that all the expressions of the Christian Faith up to now, from whatever area which makes up the Christian Church (Orthodox, Roman Catholic and Protestant) do not speak to us at the depth of our situation, past, present or future. However, when we come to the Crucified One straight out of our cultural and historical situation, it is

---

[16] The translation of the Sotho-Tswana MODIMQ with 'God' could be a devaluation, especially these days when Western theological concepts have reduced the activities and spheres of the latter. MODIMO is a much wider, deeper and all-embracing concept. Until Christian theology is ready to accept this as the concept for its 'God' too, it is a mistake to translate MODIMO by 'God'. For this reason, to do justice to the Sotho-Tswana concept, I translate MODIMO with 'DEITY' or 'DIVINITY', meaning the total sphere encompassed by either word.

[17] *Das Heilige*, Marburg, 1917, *ubique*.

[18] 'The Wholeness of Human Life', (see above, note 9), p. 2.

[19] See note 6 above.

then that He has meaning, and becomes not only *our* Saviour, but also Saviour of All Mankind. He then helps us to see God as the One and Only, the Inscrutable and Incomprehensible. For, from our unique heritage, we bring the view that God is UVELINGQAKI, One whose beginning or end no man can know or describe, UNKULUNKULU, a Power greater than all powers; MODIMO, that which permeates all and gives it life and LESA, the ground of being of all that is.[20]

---

[20] WCC Faith and Order Commission: 'Uniting in Hope', p. 34.

Ganda traditional religion and Catholicism in Buganda, 1948-75

JOHN MARY WALIGGO

The presence of traditional religion within Christianity is widely felt throughout black Africa. The independent churches show only one side of it. The mission churches manifest the other side. While the former churches have attracted much attention from scholars, the latter have not. It has thus seemed as if within the mission churches everything goes on much in the same way as in the 'mother' churches of Europe and America. A study of Catholicism in Buganda shows that this is not so. In this short chapter three points will be dealt with: first an examination of the causes for the revival of the forces of traditional religion during the last two decades; second a consideration of some of the ways in which this movement has manifested itself; and finally an exposition of some of the views of old Catholics interviewed with their suggestions for a solution to the present crisis and a few tentative approaches for Africanizing Christianity put forward by some of the clergy and young lay *élite*.

The tensions between traditional religion and Catholicism in Buganda have existed from the very beginning of the Catholic presence in the country. If, in fact, the church's policies were to be judged only by the degree they have succeeded in either eliminating or weakening the Ganda customs, ceremonies and superstitions which were declared incompatible with Catholicism, the conclusion would be none other than that the church has badly failed. Traditional religion has not always been on a diminishing rate among Buganda Catholics. Twice before 1948, during Mwanga's war of independence 1897-1900[1] and the Bataka land question 1920-7[2], it had become stronger at a time when missionaries and Christian chiefs were congratulating themselves on having obtained effective control over it.

The traditionalist movement which exists in the Buganda Church today began to regroup itself in 1948—the year of the Bataka agitation

---

[1] Mwanga's war was the last powerful attempt by traditionalists to restore the pre-eminence of traditional religion.

[2] This period witnessed violent attacks on the Christian landlords who used their private *mailo* land to impose on their tenants the Christian moral code.

popularly known as 'Bataka BU'.[3] Until that time the Catholic Church had not experienced a breakaway church within its ranks in Uganda. The Protestant Church had had two, and a third—the Balokole movement—in the form of revival within the 'Church of Uganda'.[4] But in 1949, the local Catholic community of Kirumba village in the very heart of the 'Catholic' province of Buddu had become in several aspects, separatist. Its 'Son' Ssemakula Mulumba, who at one time had been a religious brother, was sent to Britain to plead their land case,[5] having realized that the British administration in Buganda and its allies—the Christian chiefs—were not prepared to do justice to their discontent.

Although the Bataka movement had started as a socio-economic and political outburst, it soon became or was forced to become anti-Christian owing to the close historical link between religion and politics in Buganda. By challenging the Christian chiefs and landlords who from 1900 had been given quasi-dictatorial powers in their own estates and districts, the Bataka soon found themselves at loggerheads with church leaders. The presence of an African bishop—Dr Joseph Kiwanuka—did not help to calm down the situation. The church and the colonial rule had become inseparable in the eyes of these people in exactly the same way as the church had identified Mwanga's supporters as rebels not only against the British administration but also against the Christian churches.[6] The results were as disastrous now as they had been fifty years before. The villagers of Kirumba refused to send their children to the Catholic mission schools of Matale and Kirumba itself. They built their own school by self-help. It looked poorer in every respect than the mission ones. It was made of mud and reeds and thatched with grass. But it was 'their own'. 'The whitemen', declared Kabuubi of Nkoni, 'can never teach real knowledge to our children. They don't want to make them wise. We shall do that ourselves.'[7] Gradually they declined from going to church, and as priests, catechists and chiefs began to look at them with a sinister eye, the Bataka began as well to regard them as the enemies of the 'black people'. To them, all the different types of leaders

---

[3] 'Bataka BU' meant what Mulumba had asserted: that Buganda from time immemorial belonged to the Bataka—the clan-heads of the people. See S. Semakula Mulumba, *Bataka Uganda ne Endagano yo 1900*, pp. 42-4.

[4] Malaki church in 1914, Orthodox church in 1929, the Balokole movement in the 1930s.

[5] Mulumba remained in Britain until 1971.

[6] Bishop Streicher's attitude to the revolt. He had excommunicated its leaders and suspended all Catholics who joined it from the sacraments. Streicher to his missionaries, 8 December 1896, and 1 February 1898.

[7] Interview 18 November 1973.

were mere tools of the British administration, determined to oppose the interests of the commoners. They logically began to look for consolation and remedy in the traditional religion and its complex ceremonies. They did not ask that their names be removed from the mission baptismal registers, they did not set up a church of their own. Their determination was to remain Catholics but at the same time use traditional rites allowed or condemned by the church to further their cause. Had there been a religious charismatic leader among them, it is most likely that they would have formed the first breakaway church from the Catholic communion in Uganda. In the eyes of priests and devout Catholics, however, the Bataka of Kirumba were in many ways 'out' of the church.

The outward signs that marked out the supporters of 'Bataka BU' were first developed in Kirumba. In addition to an independent school, their houses had 'BU' scribbled on the front walls using chalk or banana fruit. Men grew long hair and beards, while women left their nails uncut and reverted to wearing the traditional bark cloth. The *lubaale* cult became popular once more as did the traditional rites surrounding birth, marriage, sickness, death and burial. The fame of the heroes of Mwanga's war was revived.

The Bataka movement was not restricted to Kirumba or to Buddu province. It spread widely in all the twenty counties of Buganda, finding eager supporters of all religions in each. Everywhere it went, its supporters manifested a greater reliance on traditional religion and a mistrust of church leaders and the direct successors of the 'heroic' Christian chiefs. The governor's unsympathetic attitude to the Bataka cause only helped to strengthen their movement by bringing to its support the African Farmers' Union.[8] As long as Ssemakula Mulumba remained in London as the Bataka's representative, enthusiastic supporters continued to have faith in his powers and collected money regularly to maintain him there. They wrote to him explaining their situation in Buganda and avowed that only their obtaining full justice would bring their movement to an end. Although Bishop Kiwanuka's banning from the sacraments of five of the Bataka leaders in Buddu proved a strong warning to their supporters, it did not stop the movement.[9]

With Governor Cohen's decision in 1953 to exile Kabaka Mutesa II, the Bataka protest became stronger and won support from an overwhelming majority of the Baganda. In the exile of the king, the Bataka pointed out, none could fail to see the misrule of the British

[8] D. A. Low, *The mind of Buganda*, London, 1971, p. 142.

[9] Interview with Benedict Nsigalira Bbotera, Buddu, 7 June 1973.

administration. It was expected that the churches and the Christian chiefs would once more rally their support for the governor so as to maintain the former alliance. But on'this issue, allegiance to kingship transcended the social and religious divisions in Buganda. Although most church leaders were cautious in avoiding utterances that would annoy either side, Fr Timoteo Muddu of Kabuwoko,[10] Buddu, who lived near the birthplace of the Bataka movement, openly supported the traditionalist opponents to the governor's decision. Like them, he grew a beard and let his hair grow long as the visible sign of national mourning. The wearing of bark cloth by both men and women became more widespread throughout Buganda.

Since it was the whites who had exiled their king, several Baganda Christians logically concluded that the prayers and forces of the Christian (white) religion were incapable of bringing him back. In a mass movement they sought help from traditional religion. Kibuuka, the god of war in former times, reappeared in a young 'priest' who was a Catholic. Having been brought up in a very devout Catholic family, Kiganira had rebelled against the religion of his parents and sought refuge in the old.[11] The new 'Kibuuka' took his abode in a large tree on Mutundwe hill near Kampala. It was here that thousands of people, most of them Christians, flocked daily to pay their respects, offer sacrifices and prayers for the solution of the national crisis. The churches proved powerless in preventing their people from making a 'pilgrimage' to Mutundwe. The administration, after weeks of procrastination, finally found an excuse to arrest the new 'Kibuuka'. The whole episode, however was most disheartening to the churches and the administration who thought that the Baganda had by this time been 'civilised'. The well-known diviners and traditional *Mandwa* (priests) in Ssese, Kyaggwe and Buddu counties were now frequently visited and begged to apply their powers for the return of the king. The most popular song of the time spelt out people's confidence in their traditional religious forces: *Abamutwaala be balimuzza* (those who exiled him, will themselves bring him back). When finally Mutesa returned to his kingdom in October 1955, several Baganda attributed their victory not so much to their Christian prayers as to the forces of traditional religion. Weeks before his arrival, numerous traditional 'priests', diviners and medicinemen began to arrive in the capital with their traditional symbols of power. While some waved rosaries or Bibles in welcoming Mutesa,

[10] Fr Muddu later left the priesthood and now teaches in a private school in Kampala.

[11] Interview with Yozefu Kasumagizi, the father of the 'priest' of Kibuuka, 8 February 1974 at Kyamaganda, Buddu.

others waved amulets, traditional 'horns' or medicines. Those wearing bark cloth or animal hides mixed freely with pupils in coloured uniforms, women in cotton *busuuti* and men in white tunics. Traditional revival had taken place and the churches saw no way of checking it. Everywhere Mutesa went to visit his people, the new strength of the traditional religion was clearly evident.

Before this traditional revival had had a chance to abate, nationalism had appeared on the scene from 1955 onwards. The more the administration arrested and exiled nationalist leaders and the more the churches joined the administration in shouting 'communism, communism', the more the common people sympathized with the nationalists and started to turn more to traditional religion as the 'safe' force during times of crisis.[12] This movement reached its climax in 1961 when 'Kabaka Yekka' (King Alone movement) was launched to fight the elections in Buganda in competition with 'national' parties. Two years before the birth of 'Kabaka Yekka', Augustine Kamya, a Catholic, had staged a most successful boycott of Indian goods using traditional means of winning support among the commoners, which were used by the organizers of 'Kabaka Yekka' from 1961 onwards with a similar success. By failing to reckon with the forces of traditionalism and nationalism, the Catholic church had, as it were, encouraged many of its members to choose the old rather than the new faith in their struggle for independence. From 1961 villagers were regarding 'Kabaka Yekka' as the surer means of preserving the throne than the national parties which had the backing of the churches.

When Archbishop Kiwanuka published his pastoral letter in October 1961 recommending Catholics to support national parties as opposed to populist movements such as 'Kabaka Yekka', many of his people turned a deaf ear to his advice.[13] He began to be regarded as one of the arch-enemies of the throne. Mutesa's arrest of the archbishop's vicar general only helped to confirm that belief in the minds of most commoners. It was only a matter of months before the staunch supporters of 'Kabaka Yekka' began to feel they were regarded as undesirable within the church. When the young charismatic Catholic politicians, Francis Walugembe and Ed Lubowa, took the banners of 'Kabaka Yekka', they appealed to Buddu Catholics in a traditionalist manner. They not only wore bark cloth at political rallies but also sang

---

[12] Most ordinary Ganda portrayed a type of nationalism that was limited only to the independence of Buganda and the preservation of the monarchy.

[13] Despite a wide diffusion of the archbishop's message, it seems that most Catholics voted for the Kabaka Yekka, although this view does not take into account the fact that the elections may have been rigged.

litanies of praise to traditional gods of the kingdom in somewhat the same way as Nkrumah had secularized the Christian 'Our Father' for his own praise. Once more, traditionalism had triumphed both socially and politically. Sacrifices were offered at cross-roads in several areas of Buganda by baptized Christians. Christianity, the people seemed to believe inwardly, was still a 'white' religion which could not be relied on in a crisis.

With the country's independence in 1962, the church's moral power over its members was further weakened. Several people believed that independence would bring recognition to all types of religious worship, including traditional religion which had been forced into the background by the laws and attitudes of the early Christian chiefs and landlords. The insecurity of the Ganda throne and the central political control by non-Ganda politicians provided the two basic threats which had to be met by a stronger reliance on the forces of traditional religion. The organization of the movement of Ganda to Ndaiga in the 'lost counties' between 1962 and 1964 in order to out-number the Nyoro in the impending referendum relied heavily on traditional devices.[14]

Three other issues weakened the church after independence: first was the nationalization of church schools, second, the great exodus of the people from villages to towns and, finally, the political instability in the country. From the very beginning, education had remained in the hands of the missions. Almost every educated Ganda had at one time been a mission pupil. Until the early 1950s the churches had had great influence in the way schools were administered. Moral and religious training had been stressed. From the late 1950s, however, the influence of the ecclesiastical education secretaries, the fathers-in-charge of mission schools and of headmasters who were submissive to church directives began to fade away. By 1966 the main Christian influence in schools was found in Parents' Associations.[15] The emergence of urban private schools in the 1960s and 1970s gradually eliminated the influence of parents as well.

The exodus into cities and towns especially by the youth in search of new jobs and opportunities has been a general characteristic of all independent African countries. Unfortunately in Ugandan towns jobs were very limited in number and the cost of living high. This created a situation in which most town people felt insecure. Few wanted to return to the rural areas. Reliance on traditional charms to fight insecurity became the answer. Traditional diviners and sorcerers readily moved into

[14] Interview with Petralina Malibano, Bisanje, Buddu, 4 March 1972.

[15] Several such Parents' Associations were set up to act as pressure groups to the government on the subject of schools.

towns to be of service to those who needed them and also to share in the profits created by the new demands. The areas of Bwaise, Katwe, Kisenyi—all near Kampala—became new homes for traditional medicine men. At Kampala car and bus parks, men and women openly sold medicine for good luck, to find a job, to get a house, to pass an examination or interview, to find a lover, to oust one's boss, to be promoted at one's job and to become rich quickly. Nine miles out on the Entebbe road there lived (still lives) one of the most powerful medicine men to whom politicians went to ask success in their careers. University students were not contemptuous of this traditionalist movement. Several of them sought out local medicine men for the same reasons as the less educated.[16] What was going on in Kampala was also found in other towns of Uganda. Only the forces of traditional religion seemed to possess the symbolism and philosophy which people understood and which were able to appeal to the educated and less educated alike. The political insecurity from 1966 created fear among the Ganda. The state of emergency in the kingdom, the abolition of the monarchy, the death of Mutesa in exile, the banning of political parties, the increase of unemployment and the fall in the prices of coffee and cotton all combined to bring deep disillusion among the people. Moments of fear have always witnessed greater reliance on traditional religion in Buganda. Many Ganda refused to believe that their king had really died in England until they saw his body in 1971. Several young Christian men and women were initiated in traditional religion and constituted as 'priests' in predominantly Christian villages. Among all Catholic initiatives to meet the post-independent situation, two have great relevance to the present theme. One was intensified devotion to the Baganda martyrs,[17] the other devotion to St Jude,[18] the patron 'of hopeless cases'. The former was endorsed by the entire church, the latter was private. The great appeal of the latter devotion among men of all religions and especially those living in towns and involved in the modern sectors of economy, indicates beyond doubt the mixed feelings with which Christians and non-Christians are using it for different motives.

The increase of traditionalism in rural areas was attributed to four

[16] Interview with J. C. Kiwanuka, Kampala, 6 June 1974.

[17] From 1964 when the Uganda martyrs were canonized, devotion to them was intensified. The last ten years have seen attempts by the people and church leaders to make this devotion answer some of the urgent prayers of the people and to calm down their fears.

[18] This devotion is new. It started around 1971 at Naguru in Kampala. The way in which its promoter, Mgr Kanyi, has shaped it, explains much of its appeal to the people. St Jude has become a problem solver, a Christian diviner, and a disposer of favours needed.

main causes by my informants. Several stressed the existence of non-Ganda in their areas. Some of these are feared and suspected of possessing stronger charms which could be used against the Ganda. This has led to their seeking out new ways of protecting themselves against the 'imagined' foreign 'horns'. Second, many old people who lived under the rule of the 'heroic chiefs' pointed to the un-Christian rule of the present generation of chiefs. The former had used laws and their own personalities to stamp out traditional religion and its allied forces. 'Now everyone does as he likes', complained Bagenda, 'what can you expect'?[19] The force of this argument can only be understood when one realizes the enthusiasm of the former chiefs who fought for their religion and became determined to use their victory for the spread and strengthening of Christianity. In so doing, however, they only succeeded in driving the traditional religion into the background from where it would emerge when time allowed. Third, some Catholics have suggested that the present church leadership is less effective in dealing with Christians who carry out condemned traditional practices than the former one. They recall the missionary period and that of Bishop Kiwanuka when disobedience to church laws carried strict punishments.[20] Since many Christians dreaded being excluded from the sacraments, they tried then to conform to the regulations. Catechists were powerful in villages, able to pull down traditional shrines, and burn traditional religious relics. Today, their influence is diminishing. Some of them are not socially accepted in the areas they work in, some lack the necessary religious knowledge to command respect. A few are suspected of carrying out occasionally the same practices which they condemn in others. Fourth, priests are criticized for failing to pay regular and long visits to catechist centres to know the people, and of doing away with the religious sodalities of men, women, girls and boys through which people's faith was strengthened and useful discussion held. They are also accused of weakening the former Christian substitutes for the deep-rooted traditional rites. The practice of blessing pregnant and newly-delivered women is disappearing, the use of holy water to dispel evil forces is declining, and the popularity of religious processions is withering away. The vacuum created by the removal of the former Christian substitutes, old Catholics argue, has been to the advantage of the growth of traditional religion. However, according to the evidence that has been available to me, the fundamental mistake of the church has been failure to understand the nature and force of traditional religion, failure to come to the rescue of Christians who live in two world views

[19] Interview with Yoanna Bagenda, Kkoki, 19 March 1974.

[20] H. Streicher, *Statuts Synodaux du Vicariat de l'Uganda*, Villa Maria, 1923.

that conflict, failure to see the diversity of traditional religion which varies according to ethnic groups, traditional skills, geographical settlements and the length of time that Christianity has been in the area. There has also been a lack of creativity in proposing experiments that attempt to answer the present needs of the people. The church has continued to use disciplinary measures against those who divert from the defined positions, without understanding enough their fears and anxieties. It has failed to discover or work out a theology of the 'weak' who cannot or frequently fail to reach the ideal. It has finally failed to start a meaningful dialogue with the ordinary Christians at the grass-root level of the catechist centres on this vital issue.

The suggested attempts for a solution

Any attempt to arrive at a happy solution of this problem will have to take account of the fact that the dichotomy between traditional religion, culture and Christianity is seen in a different light today from that of the past.[21] By becoming a Catholic in the first fifty years of the church in Buganda, a person accepted to become a 'new' creation in the waters of baptism and the assembly of Christians. He embraced a 'white' religion (*eddini ey'ekizungu*), received a 'white' name (*erinnya ery'ekizungu*) and was prepared to obey all that his new condition imposed on him. It was not possible for him to understand all that the new religion taught or why it condemned this and left that in his own traditions. True enough there were frequent failures in fulfilling all that the new religion demanded. But each failure was 'sin', a defect from the set norms, a lapse into the former ways of 'Satan'. One thing that seemed very rarely to have appeared was syncretism among Ganda Catholics. Their consciences had been scrupulously formed. In carrying out traditions or customs that society, clan, family or one's inclinations demanded, a Catholic felt he was committing a sin against his new religion. He rarely excused himself but would humbly go to sacramental confession before receiving Holy Communion. That was an age of complete uniformity and conformity throughout the Catholic world. The oneness of the church did not allow important adaptations or appreciations of non-European cultures and traditions in the spiritual formation and worship of Catholics. Canon law, church statutes, decrees from Rome, 'universal' theology gave the norm for churches everywhere.

Ever since Vatican II, the issue of the relationship between Africanness and Catholicism has been seen in a new light. The question now posed is

---

[21] Pope Paul's letter to African Christians '*Africae Terrarum*' of 1970; Pope Paul's address to African bishops at Kampala, June 1969.

'Has an African on becoming Christian, to give up all his long heritage in order to be a good Christian?' In other words, is there a way in which one can be truly Catholic and authentically African at the same time? The force of this question is undeniable today in Buganda where, despite a hundred years of effective Christian presence, the tensions between traditional religion and Christianity have been on the increase rather than decrease. Whereas the missionaries and the first generation of Buganda church leaders worked unceasingly to divorce tradition from Christianity in order to produce 'pure Christians', the present generation of church leaders have to address themselves to a reconciliation of tradition and Christianity wherever possible in order to produce an 'undivided Christian', and 'un-uprooted African' while at the same time avoiding creating a syncretistic Catholicism.

From 1965 the Catholic Church in Buganda began gradually to Africanize the liturgy. Hymns with Ganda melodies are sung everywhere in church. Drums are becoming more and more popular in churches. Family masses are said at important social occasions. In the 1970s the two Catholic dioceses in Buganda held important synods to plan for the future of the church. Their conclusions show great efforts being made to evangelize the townships, to increase the participation of Christians in the vital aspects of church life, to organize the youth, to promote the image of catechists, to raise the standard of religious education in schools and to carry on useful dialogue with Christians of other churches. These are signs of vitality within the church. However, a fundamental issue—the relationship between traditional religion and Catholicism—has not been faced. The obstacles in the way of our Christians receiving sacraments have neither been examined nor removed. The overall aim of the recent synodal decisions seems to be that of restoring the former vitality of Christian life, and not of finding a new one. The adaptation in the liturgy would have a deeper significance if the philosophy on which it is based is well founded and truly represents the cosmological view of the Ganda.

The solutions suggested to deal with this problem, which is causing so much internal spiritual pain among Christians, fall into two distinct categories. The old Catholics and some of the old clergy and catechists want to see the church return to its former rigorism in stamping out traditionalism. But many of the young clergy, a few of the old, and several of the young lay *élite* advocate a radically new approach. The former wanted all those who publicly perform condemned traditional ceremonies to be given public penances and the same to apply to those who consult diviners or use evil charms. The long religious instructions should be restored. 'These days,' declared catechist Tito, 'young people know very little about their religion.'[22] The decline in the practice of Christianity is seen as the main cause of the new strength of traditional religion. 'The church,' stated catechist Yoanna, 'is making everything too easy for the people. But the more it does that, the more it shows it has not understood the Baganda.'[23] If only priests preached longer sermons on Sundays and during Lenten retreats condemning traditionalism, if the former religious sodalities were restored to their initial vitality, if priests paid more visits to the ordinary people in the rural centres, traditional religion would be weakened. Asked whether they believed their suggestions would really solve the problem, none of them was too optimistic, for as Mutawonga asserted, 'whatever is ancestral in a Muganda will never completely die away'.[24] Thus, although, there are some elements to be considered and applied in these suggestions, that approach cannot go deep enough to the roots of the problem. Moreover, it has been the method used so far with only limited success.

The second approach suggested, which finds support in several recent writings on Africanizing Christianity, seems to promise greater rewards. The first step in this approach is a serious study of the cultures and traditional religions of the people in the different parts of Buganda, avoiding generalizations and concentrating on smaller entities which portray unity in lifestyle. Such a study would take account of people in different traditional occupations such as fishermen, hunters, bark cloth makers, blacksmiths, pastoralists and agriculturalists. A serious attempt would be made to discover the relation between 'culture' and traditional religion, for if Christianity is trying to fight culture, then it is on a dangerous and impossible task. Second, there would be an attempt to separate ceremonies from 'superstition'. The former would then in one way or another be incorporated into the church having been 'purged' of certain elements that are strictly incompatible with the true spirit of Christianity. The reasons for this are simple. Ceremonies are very important to any people. They are often social, as opposed to individualistic, practices. Their meaning and symbolism appeal greatly to the people, and if their deeper meaning is found, it will very often be compatible with Christianity. Their incorporation within Christianity would be the most significant step towards ending the existence of 'divided Christians' and a sign that Christianity is by nature a religion for all cultures.

Two minor pre-marriage ceremonies taken from southern Ganda

[22] Interview with Tito Zabasajja, Villa Maria, Buddu, 8 September 1973.

[23] Interview with Yoanna Bagenda, Kkoki, 19 March 1974.

[24] Interview with Petro Mutawonga, Nkoni, 19 January 1974.

may help to indicate the problems which African theologians have to confront today. Before a bride leaves her family, she sits on her father's and mother's lap three times. The meaning of the ceremony, as explained to me, is to tell the girl that henceforth she was no longer a 'baby'. She is going to become a mother and that requires her giving up childish ways. Secondly, the ceremony is the solemn form of saying goodbye to the girl and to reassure her of her parents' love which often may not have been manifested so externally. Finally it is a reminder to the girl that although about to marry, she would always remain a member of her father's clan and would have a place to return to should her marriage prove unsuccessful. This rather commendable and innocent ceremony acquired through time another motive which slowly obscured the original ones. Today, most parents who perform it do so under the belief that its omission would make the marriage of their daughter unsuccessful. This extra motive induced the church to discourage and often to condemn the ceremony.

A second example from the same area creates even greater problems to an African Christian reformer. Before a bride leaves her parents' house, her mother or paternal aunt throws three sticks in her way as she moves towards the doorway. As she jumps over each stick, the mother or aunt picks it up and ties it on her bark cloth girdle for future preservation. The meaning of the practice is to ward off evil charms which hostile people might put in the bride's way in her new home. Having been 'symbolically' bewitched by her dear ones, the bride feels immune to the evil medicines of her future enemies. The belief in witchcraft and powers of sorcery is still very strong. Several deaths and sicknesses are attributed to such powers. As long as such beliefs create fear, parents seem determined to continue protecting their daughters with traditional devices.

If African theology is to have relevant impact, it must start with issues such as these which seem common in all Black Africa and which demand serious local studies before they can be successfully solved. The aim of Africanizing Christianity must be clear: It is to make Christianity feel at home in Africa and to make African Christians worship God using all their cultural richness. While the means to achieve this aim may differ from area to area, some must be common to all: the use of serious study of cultures, creative experiments, and discussions at the grass-root levels. Africa has to find the men and women to do this job. This is not a task for theologians alone but for all who work in such sciences as develop our understanding of man and his environment. It is also important to keep the element of time in mind. A successful marriage between Christianity and traditional religions and cultures must take a long time to be planned before it is consummated. Short-lived experiments cannot provide useful conclusions. Time is needed to plan, to launch experiments, to assess their success before proceeding to the next stage. Finally, none can try to solve this problem without adequate freedom from the 'mother' churches and local church authorities. Freedom is what African church thinkers, planners and leaders need most. Once that is obtained—and there is much liberty already allowed within the church—Catholicism in Buganda, and indeed in all Black Africa, will start to revive and catch up with the radical changes that have taken place in Africa since independence.

Christianity having been based on 'God made Man' can never get away from the continuous process of 'incarnation' into all cultures as long as its essential message is kept. African theology will have reached the end of its first stage on the day that African Christians cease to regard Christianity as a 'white' religion and see it as part of them. Only then will Christianity be assured a permanent future in Africa, and only then will African Christianity have something vital to contribute to the world. Instead of driving away people from the sacraments, we need a new approach that will invite them back. Instead of a theology of the 'ideal' and for the ideal, we need one for the 'weak'. Instead of sticking to bygone solutions of the missionary era, we need a thorough re-examination of the past with a view to planning the future. Finally instead of building new experiments on generalized studies, we need far more case studies and effective dialogue with the people at the grass-roots.

Missions and missionaries as portrayed by English-speaking writers of contemporary African literature

HUGH DINWIDDY

Boots over deserts over seas over
    seven-fingered seas,
Over smell of the seventh desert
    among reedy spaces . . .

Behind the walled gods
    in market,
boots over mandos
and byelaws thereto appended
    by Leidan,
Archtyrant of the holy sea.

Christopher Okigbo, who was killed in October 1967 at Nsukka, wearing the uniform of a major in the Biafran Army, wrote these lines. They are found in the first part of a longish poem, 'Heavensgate', and the 'boots' referred to are seen as missionary boots. The 'sea' is a place of purification, and the 'walled gods' and sacred places are the very stuff of Igbo religion. Over these an alien religious law has been imposed: it is the missionaries 'that pulled us through innocence', trampling as they went, and burning, 'by red hot blade on right breast', the Christian crucifix—it is these who have left a 'scar'. 'Flannagan/Preached the Pope's message . . .' in Okigbo's 'Limits VII' and it came

    from frame of iron,
    And in mould of iron . . .

And the catechist, Kepkanly, a present day John the Baptist, ('Heavensgate') came

    with bowl of salt water
    preaching the gambit . . .

And, at the end of the section,

    O solitude within me
    remember Kepkanly.

It was the absolute way in which Christianity was presented that made Okigbo feel himself to be an 'exile' in his own land. 'There are here', he writes in 'Heavensgate', 'the errors of the rendering' and the movement of his poetry is a tracing of the paths of his interior return from exile.

I am the sole witness to my homecoming.

'The artist', writes Soyinka in *Transition 31*, 'has always functioned in African society as the recorder of "*mores*" and of the experiences of his society, and as the voice of vision in his own time.' Okolo, in Gabriel Okara's novel *The Voice* (1964), is trying to find a way of doing this:

> 'Our father's insides always contained things straight. They did straight things. Our insides were also clean and we did the straight things until the new time came. We can still sweep the dirt out of our houses every morning.'
> 'But the heap of dirt is more than one man's strength, Okolo. It may bury you.'

A similar feeling of individual helplessness seems to have struck the Rev. Ajayi Crowther, but from a directly opposite point of view, in 1844, well before he became a bishop, when he was helping at Freetown to prepare the Abeokuta mission. There 'in the Circular Road, behind Barrack Hill, was a notorious party of Shango worshippers'. On being challenged by him 'one Sunday morning, about service time,' they declared in 'their defence . . . that their gods were inferior deities commissioned by the great God to superintend inferior matters on earth. Having received the same from their forefathers, they insisted upon their worship as they found it was good for them.' He records this episode in his *Experiences with Heathens and Mohammedans in West Africa* (1892). In effect, on returning the following Sunday, he declared himself 'defeated', for, in defending themselves further, the noisy and perhaps drunken Shango worshippers, included the reminder, in Crowther's words, 'that the gods against whom I spoke were the gods of my forefathers; and that I could not dare to oppose the worship of the gods at Abeokuta'. Thus does he underline a dilemma presented in the work of many subsequent African poets and novelists.

It was, however, 'Bishop Crowther and his able and persistent fellow workers on the Niger' whom Dr Edward Wilmot Blyden chose to praise in the celebrated lecture delivered in Lagos in 1891, the year of Crowther's death, on the subject of 'The Return of the Exiles and the West African Church'. It is they, says Blyden, who 'on the Niger have laid the foundation of an African Church', but it was the strong opposition to African church leadership by expatriate missionaries in the 1880s and 1890s that considerably affected the way in which Christianity continued to penetrate West Africa. In the same lecture Dr Blyden referred to this new kind of expatriate leadership as 'foreign props and support' and asked whether 'our children will be able to maintain these alien and artificial arrangements'.

It is against the type figure of 'Kepkanly', seen as a product of the changed missionary attitude, and, in the Roman Catholic mission field, against what we could now categorize as Tridentine attitudes, that contemporary African writers have slanted their critical and sometimes caustic pens. They are 'the children' of Dr Blyden, whose reputation had greatly extended in the 1950s and 1960s, and they have written in these decades for the most part mockingly of the effects on their people of these 'alien and artificial arrangements'.

Towards the end of John Munonye's first novel (1966), *The Only Son*, Fr John Michael Smith has joined, in the 1930s, a recently founded mission at Ossa in Eastern Nigeria. His fore-runner, Fr Patrick Ryan—still at Ossa—had distinguished himself by throwing handfuls of pennies to the curious Igbo crowd that assembled on his arrival.

> 'Look at this white ichneumon fly who throws his own charm at people!' they sneered. Some said: 'He thinks we are so wretchedly poor as to be bewitched with money!' They abandoned the coins and went away—to the great delight of the smart ones among the newly converted Christians who quickly snapped up the coins.

Fr Smith, in his late twenties, was seen by the Christians as a 'well-fed priest' . . . While the natives said he was a wealthy man. 'He looks,' said they, 'like one fed by many wives.'

The author permits himself a flash-back.to Fr Smith's seminary in Ireland where the Father Superior is made to lecture to him thus:

> 'In this our early phase, with so many Christian denominations literally pouring into that pagan world, our first emphasis must be on statistical successes. We must bring the word of God to as many as possible at the same time. We want on our side the vast numbers who in Africa of the future will sustain the church with their numerical strength. Call it vote of the masses if you like. In pursuit of that objective, I'm afraid we've got to be impatient with the culture of the people. There just isn't the time to sort out first and label their customs as acceptable and unacceptable. To be ruthless in our method and yet successful in our aim, we must ensure that all along we present to the people good tangible evidence of the advantages of Christianity.'

The young seminarian is permitted to challenge this competitive doctrine, naming the utter need for sincerity of belief, but is reverently squashed by the dictum, 'we are on virgin soil, very vast too, and we want acres and acres of it to ourselves'.

Thus are the 'boots' exhorted to trample and Patrick Ikenga, born in 1927, into a Christian family is shocked to watch his Christian boy companions, with or without boots, kicking over *aja* sacrifices against evil spirits set up in little clay bowls by afflicted villagers, near the small railway town of Kafanchan. They contained 'a combination of cowrie shells, needles, banana stems, palm oil, strips of white, red or black cloths and pennies and halfpennies'. After washing the money the boys bought fried bean-cakes at the market and reminded Patrick that they were all Christians, 'who no longer shared a belief in these sacrifices'. Onuora Nzekwu's *Blade among the Boys* from which this episode is taken, traces the tortuous career of Patrick Ikenga up to his dismissal from a seminary—after two years—for making a girl teacher (who is betrothed to him traditionally) pregnant. It is again, a book set in Igboland at one stage further on the path of missionary progress than John Munonye's *The Only Son*. In the latter book we note the savage parental horror when sons in the neighbourhood sneak away to attend the newly created mission school.

First Machie, the misfit goes, then Ibe, 'only son's' best friend. 'I will grind his feet in a mortar' . . . 'May thunder strike you [Ibe] dead if you are here again' . . . 'I will cut off his lips with a knife' . . . 'I'm glad you (only son) have left the evil thing called Machie'. And, finally, to Ibe, 'Come here again and see if I won't crush ripe pepper into your eyes and nostrils. As for taking my son to that place, you will never succeed.'

Chiaku, the widowed mother of Nnanna, the only son, is the speaker. But Nnanna begins to feel a 'sense of inferiority' when secretly meeting Ibe and despite traditional 'packets' at Nnanna's head at night, the chalk lines drawn at the entrance to his hut, Nnanna joins the school.

Chiaku and her allies decide not to use violence against the mission, for 'such action would certainly invite a gruesome carnage from the Commissioner's soldiers at Ania'. Hence, in the event, the expensive skills of Ezedibia, the village doctor, and Chiaku's tearing of Nnanna's hair and ears, do not deflect him from his determination to learn the white man's magic.

'The worst thing about it is that children relish it', said Idimogu, father of Ibe, 'and these same children will one day be the fathers and mothers of the land!' Thus, in time, did a mission bell come to be recognized as 'a fact of life' in Nade.

It was said by the village elders—to sustain their morale—that it was not the 'favourite children' of their fathers who joined the school, and we note at first that the 'Kepkanlys', the African catechists and teachers, are ex-slaves. The teachers in primary schools are depicted as being inordinately brutal in their use of the cane, and both, like the ex-slave

George, remembered at Nade as 'a lunatic orator', are thought to have 'that veneer of education that was considered sufficient to preach the word of God': these are the new John the Baptists 'preaching the gambit'.

Two other ex-slaves David and Dominic were George's first converts at Nade, and, promptly, after their baptism, they destroyed the village shrine set up to Igwe, 'You who own heaven and earth', in the words of Chiaku. Twenty nine days later David and Dominic were found dead in their houses, struck down, it was reported, by the god, Igwe, himself.

It was Joseph, George's successor, who started the school and had forty boy pupils in the first four months. An early clash came over the discipline of secrecy traditionally enforced upon the young men initiated into the practices of the masquerades. Joseph, coming from Okpa, thirty miles away, where customs were different, was completely deceived by his pupils from Nade, more than half of whom absented themselves from school during the period of the can-carrying masquerade races.

Patrick Ikenga at the age of thirteen, in *Blade Among the Boys*, also has a problem at the time of the masquerades in his village of Ado. For him 'It was the flogging rather than the generally accepted theory that masqueraders were dead men come on a visit to the physical world that terrified him and limited his movements round the village'. It is noteworthy, nevertheless, that while waiting in dread before his initiation, he prays anxiously to the Christian God to 'give him courage in his coming hour of trial'.

The novelist does not reveal what thoughts brought Ikenga to this act of prayer, but in the context, it could be interpreted by an Old Testament concept of the superior power of Jehovah. Indeed, it could be seen as something similar to that identified in the Rev. Samuel Johnson's account of the defence of Abeokuta against the Dahomians on 3 March 1851. 'Even as it was,' he writes in *The History of the Yorubas* (1921), 'many eye witnesses do aver that what contributed most to their safety was confidence in the presence of missionaries in the town. "The God of the white man", said they, "is on our side".'

It is not too surprising that Kihika, the bold leader of Mau Mau, in Ngugi wa Thiongo's novel, *A Grain of Wheat* (1964), should be 'moved by the story of Moses and the children of Israel which he had learnt during Sunday school . . . As soon as he learnt how to read Kihika bought a Bible and read the story of Moses over and over again, later recounting it to Mumbi (his sister) and any other persons who would listen.'

A frighteningly bizarre episode in the village square follows a week after Patrick Ikenga's initiation. Masqueraders were dancing in the square and chasing uninitiated boys with their canes, when, along one of the paths leading to the square comes a foreign lady missionary. She is the headmistress of the local school and has with her six of her girls marching in pairs.

'Quicken your steps girls,' the missionary called to them, 'or we shall be late returning to the compound.'

'We are afraid,' one of the girls answered.

'Don't be afraid. The boys won't hurt you as long as you stand by me.'

'It's not the boys. It is the masqueraders we are afraid of.'

'Nonsense. You know that they are just boys wearing some silly garb. You shouldn't be afraid of them.'

'Eh!' the girls exclaimed, horrified.

'Now hurry or you·shall all be punished for disobedience.'

'Let's make a detour,' one of the girls pleaded. 'We know much safer paths.'

'No more of this nonsense,' she ordered. 'You'll do as I say. No more talking now. Hurry.'

It is utterly forbidden for women to witness the masquerading spirits, but when the girls fled to hide their eyes, they were threatened with dismissal from the school, while the missionary, after declining offers of help, suffered the terrible canes of the masqueraders.

'If only the lady had exercised some tact.' Thus ran the verdict of the village, but it was not the verdict of the newly ordained local priest whose sermon in Ado church deplored the shameful brutality shown to our guests and benefactors. All the village gave 'in return for all the schools the missionaries had built for them, all the education they had given them, and all the hospitals and doctors they had provided them with were insults, violent attacks and intolerance . . .' Thus are 'the errors of the rendering' apparent on both sides.

It is Ononye, Patrick Ikenga's uncle, and the person deputizing for him as 'Okpala', chief priest of the lineage, who explains, early in the book, that 'Christianity has developed only fibrous roots' in its adherents. To them 'it was only a means to an end, a must, if one had to have education—the gateway to prosperity—they tried to accommodate both the new and the old religions, professing one hypocritically in the open and sincerely practising the other in secret for fear of the epithet "uncivilized" being applied to them.' Thus, in the eyes of the novelist, have his people accepted the 'good tangible evidence of the advantages of Christianity'.

Meanwhile, to the mission authorities, education was seen as 'a useful guide to baptism, synonymous with conversion'. Thus, within the system, 'the baptism certificates were a kind of identity card', and admission to a school was determined by the age at which a boy was baptized. At the beginning of the school year Fr O'Brien, in *Blade Among the Boys*, turned away all the non-Catholic applicants—'yet it was known that, in the football class, boys from various Christian denominations could be found', for all of whom 'it was compulsory' to attend all religious services in the college chapel. To the general body of non-Catholic applicants Fr O'Brien gave the advice, 'if you are keen on coming to this school, then become a Catholic and return for admission next year.'

Patrick found himself to be one of the forty accepted entrants out of the two hundred or so who applied, and, within a fortnight of admission received twelve strokes of the cane for being a member of the 'orchestra'—a purely social body—which enlivened a local funeral. Fr O'Brien, however, judged such an engagement to be idolatrous. Patrick's chief flogger was Mr Ndibe, the son of a domestic slave, now a teacher, who at the end of Patrick's first year, gave him thirty-six strokes for killing a ceremonial goat for another funeral.

From many sources comes the complaint that missionary teachers of all kinds hated questions. In Okot p'Bitek's *Song of Lawino* (1966), from Acholi, Uganda, we find,

> Protestants and Catholic priests
> Are all the same—
> They do not like questions.
>
> When they mount the rostrum
> To preach
> They shout and shout
> And most of what they say
> I do not follow.
> But as soon as they stop shouting
> They run away fast,
> They never stop a little while
> To answer even one question . . .

Patrick's question to one of the fathers, 'Is it right for a man to be forced into the observance of his religious duties?' gives him the reputation of being a dangerous student and draws from the father the tough rebuke, 'Who cares what the students feel about it. Beggars must not be choosers. You either have education on our own terms or quit . . . As for you, if you ever become a priest, remember that it is the wish of the Church that you do not argue about your faith.'

It was over a penance to write out the *Pater noster* sixty times—Patrick wrote it sixty times in English instead of Latin—that Fr Gerard, his Latin teacher, lost his temper and, over which, Patrick was expelled from his school. Patrick's mistake is described by the Rev. Principal as 'a dirty trick to play on a priest of God making him lose his temper'. The principal, in admonishing Patrick, continued, 'You fail to appreciate that Father Gerard left his beloved ones thousands of miles away to bring you some light in this darkness in which you live.'

It was to bring the light of Christ to the darkness of Isolo, in T. M. Aluko's *One Man, One Wife*, (1959), that Pastor David, with his black book, 'Bibeli Yoruba' and prominent white collar visited the Odan tree in the village square, and the house of the priestess of Shonponna, god of smallpox. There was no prospect of trampling on the tree, but it underwent a vigorous kicking without any noticeable response from the spirit of the god of Isolo. 'There is no salvation in the worship of trees and rivers', declared Pastor David. Here, and in the parish of St Jude at Idasa, the Christian emphasis is on 'Christ, our Royal Master' leading against the foe, for,

> My foes are ever near me
> Around me and within . . .

'From the simple timber lectern Pastor David surveyed his congregation.' He judged them 'ready to receive the Word. This he let them have in his powerful emotional voice.'

'The Christian was a soldier'—thus ran his theme—'fighting against the desires of the flesh, which were invariably in conflict with the things of the spirit.' T. M. Aluko traces the emotional strains and fluctuations caused by the introductions of Bible Christianity, with all its literalness, to a polygamous world governed by the spirits of the Yoruba. The Christian standards set are too high for Mr Royasin, sole teacher and catechist in Isolo. He lives in 'the modest but neat Mission House' on 17/6 a month, a sum which Pastor David has steadfastly refused to increase, and which was thought to be comparatively lucrative in 1922. Royasin is rated an important man.

> The wizard who knows the White Man's secrets,
> The wizard who reads telegrams and writes letters,
> The wizard who understands and speaks the White
>   Man's strange tongue.

It is he who seduces the promised wife of a young villager and is publicly disgraced and hence is no longer in a position of 'envied honour and prestige in which pastors, catechists and school teachers constantly basked'. In returning from St Jude's, Idasa, where he had handed in his resignation, he finds the mission house burnt to the ground with all that he possessed in it.

Aluko's character, 'Bible Jeremiah', is the eccentric village elder who insisted on applying 'the incomprehensible standards of the new faith to the day-to-day administration of the village'. In opposition the other elders of Isolo, all of whom—except Jeremiah—belonged to a powerful secret cult, concluded during a smallpox epidemic, that 'we have offended the great Shonponna' . . . 'We have allowed the crazy new faith to estrange many of our young men and women from the worship of the mighty Shonponna' . . . 'Why do we talk of prayer when prayer has failed to stop the epidemic?' These are the words of the church elder, Joshua, son of Fagbola, mighty warrior, who declares the new faith has made the men of Isola into women. But it is Shango, god of lightning, who, in awful retribution, strikes him dead as he strides into the night after pronouncing his brave words. Known formerly as a 'pillar of Church and State', it was rumoured he had admitted to living a double life, and, because of the manner of his death, it was immediately known by all that he was a thief. From this his son Jacob is to suffer permanent disgrace.

The old ways remain powerful, and, in Nzekwu's *Wand of Noble Youth* (1961), the '*iyi ocha*' curse on a pregnant woman eventually causes the daughter of her womb to commit suicide on the day of her Christian wedding. Her suicide is caused by the jealous action of a rival suitor, and, in Francis Selormey's *The Narrow Path* (1966), a schoolgirl is killed by witchcraft following the boast of her mother that she had come top of her class.

When Mr Royasin fell from grace he complained of 'the all too narrow path of moral conduct' laid down by the new religion, and letters of protest flow from his pen to My Lord, the Bishop, the Governor and King George V. The same 'narrow path' is the theme of Selormey's book set among the Ewe people of Ghana. Indeed, the theme is central to every novel that treats of mission education.

Patrick Ikenga, when a child, was told of the nakedness and honesty of his forbears from the hills, and that 'none, except the newcomer, paid their nakedness any attention'. We note, however, that Nnanna, the only son, from a similar background, after a few weeks at school, 'turned his back abruptly on the two sins: a pagan feast and a naked female'. So strict were the Basel missionaries in Ghana, 'much too thorough in the wrong directions—they wanted to educate the mind, the heart and the soul, but not the body'—that reaction and not submission was bound to be the outcome of their teaching. Thus does Cameron Duodu in his *Gab Boys* (1964), set in Accra, anatomize the upbringing of Kwaku Sefa a product of 'this strict discipline enforced by the Germans' that made their pupils 'libertines the moment they got the chance . . . in the holidays'.

Thus Kwaku 'determined that for every nail the missionaries drove into his flesh, he would take out twenty'. So when he went home during the holidays, he drank not only palm-wine but '*akpeteshie*', and smoked pipes not cigarettes, and slept not only with young girls, but also with grown-up women, some of them married. Okigbo has a phrase in 'Heavensgate' about the 'white buck and helmet', and there are other symbols for missionaries , 'that had pulled us through innocence'. As Onuora Nzekwu writes of Patrick Ikenga, 'A considerable amount of force had been used to make him and thousands of other children at the mission school at Ado and elsewhere practise their religion, perhaps by the clergy, certainly by the schoolmasters'.

In an autobiographical sketch of his mission school experiences published in *East African Childhood* (1967), edited by Lorene K. Fox, M. Nzioki from Machakos, Kenya, recalls, when a student at Makerere University, a weekly episode in his second year at primary school.

On Monday mornings before class started Father Layton would come round with a stick to punish the little 'shenzis' who had not attended the Holy Mass. He would enter a classroom and, in accordance with the custom of the school, all pupils would stand.

'How are you, Father?' The pupils would greet him.

'I am quite well, ' Father Layton would reply.

Then silence till the 'Mzungu' said 'Sit!' The teacher in the classroom had no authority.

Not everyone would sit down. Those who had failed to attend mass were left standing. This was how we had been trained by our teacher, Mwalimu Paulana. He always told us, 'God is everywhere and sees you when you tell a lie.'

'Are these the Shenzis, Mwalimu?'

'Yes, Father,' the trembling Mwalimu Paulana would say.

Then the offenders would be caned in front of us, after which Father Layton would move on to the next classroom to execute this Monday morning's engagement . . . Then Mwalimu Paulana began the religious period. We were told about the Faith, taught the so-called truths . . . But still, to some of us, there remained room for doubt that the faith was taught us in the proper way.

Yet I loved learning, in spite of the fear.

Nzioki's school career ends with a night raid at his secondary school of the Father's veranda, and the throwing of four sofas over a cliff. 'At seven o'clock we boarded a bus and took off, some to return the following year, others to go on to town.'

Continuing sections of each book that presents mission education treat of the reaction in town to the missionary training. The 'Gab Boys' of Accra are 'a whole pack of lads', none older than twenty, 'our imaginations fuelled to combustion point by many action-packed American films . . . we had no creative occupation to provide an outlet . . . We respected nothing and nobody.'

'We are Pusupusu boys. Okay. There are Kibi boys, Asiakwa boys, Apedwa boys, Accra boys, Tamale boys . . . and also girls!' One of them sits in a law court unemployed and combing 'through the flat top of my Abidjan hair-cut' trying to look tough. He has been 'arrested for not paying land poll'. In the court the spokesman, like a linguist of old, urges that 'this kind of justice which came out of a book written by people following another country's traditions' is too rigid. 'The law my father knew and my father's father knew was one of the heart. One of the whole soul—one which did not depend on written words but upon realities, upon demeanour, upon circumstances. It was a law of the times, it wasn't written and therefore wasn't rigid.'

The mission and the state are seen to combine in the 'civilizing' process, and the men of God are thought to have betrayed their charges to the state. Thus, in the memory of the Asolo of Isolo, in *One man, One Wife*, 'When we, in our camp, refused to listen to the White Man, it was a big clergyman, that begged us to listen to him. It was he who persuaded us that the White Man was our friend . . . that was the beginning of our slavery in Adasaland—our slavery to the cunning White Man . . . We were sold to the White Man by the clergyman.'

The classic historical moment of missionary 'betrayal' is described by Stanlake Samkange in his *On Trial for my Country* (1966) which presents the trial, in the next world, of Lobengula. In this, John Moffat, chosen by Cecil Rhodes as negotiator, on the strength of his father's friendship through missionary work with Mzilikazi, makes a treaty of friendship with Lobengula and eases the way for the Rudd Commission. 'This close friendship between my father and the white man made it imperative for me', Lobengula explains, 'to treat uJoni like my brother and accord to him the rights and privileges of princes of royal blood.' When questioned about the Moffat Treaty by the Rev. F. W. Rhodes, father of Cecil Rhodes, Moffat is made to admit that Lobengula did not know that he was approaching him as 'a servant of the Queen', and that his treaty was 'just as fraudulent . . . as you and your friends claimed the Boer Grobler's treaty had been'.

When the Siriama Protestant Mission came to the Kikuyu ridges in Ngugi wa Thiong'o's *The River Between* (1965), it was said to have increased the already existing enmity between Kameno ridge and Makuyu ridge, and, as it grew at Kameno, it brought many white men to the hills, from which followed fears of a government post being set up on Makuyu. From here it was expected the ridges would be ruled and taxed, fears of which were thrown back in the form of accusations at Joshua, the Kikuyu Christian, left in charge at Siriama. 'Joshua did not mind this. He himself knew what a government was, having learnt about this from the Rev. Livingstone. He knew it was his duty as a Christian to obey the Government'. Obedience was the cardinal virtue in missionary teaching. 'Obey your father', Miriamu, Joseph's wife, taught her children. 'She did not say it harshly or with bitterness. It was an expression of faith, of belief, of a way of life . . . she had learnt the value of Christian submission' . . . But the command to obey one's parents was usually given in sterner tones. Thus, at the age of nine, Kofi, son of the headmaster of the Catholic primary school at Ho in Selormey's, *The Narrow Path*, is publicly given twenty-five strokes, and one for the Kaiser, by his father for breaking the Fourth Commandment.

The excessive use of force in mission schools is shown up in several books to be, to say the least, from the Christian side, counter-productive. In Amu Djoleto's *The Strange Man* (1964) Christian submission is portrayed as the moral goal, but Mensa, on arrival at his primary school on the outskirts of Accra, 'did not talk like a mission-school-trained child.'

'A mission-school-trained child must hesitate and, if necessary, beg for forgiveness whenever his elders were angry with him. No matter whether he was right or had a good excuse to give, once his elders, whether rightly or wrongly, thought he was wrong and were displeased with him, he must cower in tears and plead that he would never do anything wrong again. He must start every sentence with ''please'' whether or not the word was idiomatically or contextually appropriate. He must not look an elderly personage straight in the face and tell him no, if that were the truth. The truth was what his elders wanted to hear and he must say it in abject self-abasement. No doubt there were many grown-ups who had been so trained, who said yes, when they should say no. Men who tried to please anybody in authority and inevitably carried through life a personality which was colourless, futile, spineless, time-serving and oft-times dangerous.'

The statement that brought forth this careful analysis by the author was Mensa's reply to the question of an elder, 'Are you a spoilt child?' which was, 'I'm not a spoilt child. I don't steal fruit like your children do.' Mr Lomo, the elder in question, the headmaster, and Mensa's uncle had a system among his pupils of public trial before execution in which the quick-tongued were awarded the accolade of being potentially civilized persons. Mensa 'spoke freely like an uneducated boy from an uneducated village, a sign of total backwardness that could not be countenanced' and, if allowed to flourish, 'would give a lot of trouble to a civilized society'. A good educational system would make a boy as docile as possible, and turn him into 'a good diplomatist who would say he was not aware of something, not because he was not really aware of it, but because he could not be proved to be aware of it; he must be the kind of boy who should specialize in manufacturing white lies as a means of profiting from life . . . The good life demanded lying'. Thus it became more important to use 'the right language' than to speak the truth. To be thus was to respond successfully to the threat of punishment. Mensa must be trained to rid himself of his uneducated attachment to truth or 'he would embarrass organized society and organized society must survive not on occasional honesty but on endemic subtle lying.' Mr Lomo, after anatomizing Mensa's 'essential weakness', was confident that he could train him to become a Christian gentleman. And the eleven rules of the house are the 'frame of iron' in which the process is to take place.

Yet Okolo's claim, in Okara's novel *The Voice*, that 'our fathers' insides always contained things straight', and that they consequently did straight things, is open to question by the inquiring novelist. When Ezeulu, chief priest of Ulu, sent his son Oduche to church in Achebe's *Arrow of God* (1964), he did so in response to a changing world and after five years of thought.

'I want one of my sons to join these people and be my eye there' was his justification against the opposition of Oduche's mother for sending the boy to the mission. 'If there is nothing in it you will come back. But, if there is something there, you will bring home my share. The world is like a Mask dancing. If you want to see it well you do not stand in one place. My spirit tells me that those who do not befriend the white man today will be saying *had we known* tomorrow.'

Oduche was younger than the other Christian converts of Umuaro, being only fifteen or sixteen, and John Goodcountry told him and the others how the early Christians of the Niger Delta had 'fought the bad customs of their people, destroyed shrines and killed the sacred iguana. He told them of Joshua Hart, his kinsman, who suffered martyrdom in Bonny. 'If we are Christians, we must be ready to die for the faith,' he said.

'You must be ready to kill the python as the people of the rivers killed the iguana. You address the python as Father. It is nothing but a snake, the snake that deceived our first mother, Eve. If you are afraid to kill it do not count yourself a Christian.'

Thereupon Oduche, perhaps a budding martyr, perhaps a budding diplomatist, chose the smaller python from the roof of his mother's hut and put it to suffocate in his newly made wooden box. He did not wish to kill it outright with his stick.

'This whole conflict makes you grow into a timid person incapable of fearless decisions and actions.' The voice is again Patrick Ikenga's, and he talking to the girl, Nkiru, to whom he had been betrothed by their families. 'It colours your outlook,' he continues, 'until you move out of it into a neutral zone; in this case Lagos . . . Gradually you stop going to Church and you're not bothered . . . you find traditional elements are gone too from your life, though not as distantly as the Christian ones. Then you try to embrace Christianity of your own volition, as you should have been allowed to do from the start, and you find that your grudge against its exponents clouds your vision.'

We are back with Dr Aggrey's famous sermon of the 1920s that contains the story of the eagle, reared by 'a certain man' as a chicken. On being urged by a visiting naturalist to stretch forth its wings and fly, it did so only on the third attempt by the naturalist when he made it look at the sun. 'My people of Africa,' concluded Dr Aggrey in the 1920s, 'we were created in the image of God, but men have made us think that we are chickens, and we still think we are; but we are equals. Stretch forth your wings and fly! Don't be content with the food of chickens!'

Today there are many novelists, like Ngugi wa Thiong'o who share with Ikenga too many emasculating memories of a mission upbringing to permit anything but a merely verbal acknowledgement of Christianity couched in Biblical phrases. Stated in its bleakest terms Ngugi presents the case for such persons in his essay, *Church, Culture and Politics* (1972):

> The European missionary had attacked the primitive rites of our people, had condemned our beautiful African dances, the images of our gods, recoiling from their suggestion of satanic sensuality. The early African convert did the same, often with even greater zeal, for he had to prove how Christian he was through his rejection of his past roots.
>
> So that in Kenya, while the European settler robbed people of their land and the products of their sweat, the missionary robbed people of their soul. Thus was the African, body and soul, bartered for thirty pieces of silver and the promise of a European heaven.'

In the book, *Blade Among the Boys*, a conversation takes place between Christians attending a sacrificial offering at a shrine.

> 'You know,' added an ex-school-teacher, 'you are sinning against the first commandment which enjoins you to have no other God but Him.'
>
> 'There is only one God,' answered a student of the Holy Trinity College, taking up the defence. 'He is the one we all worship. The only difference is that in the Church our prayers are directed to him

through foreign saints, but here we approach Him through our ancestors who are our own saints.'

'Don't blaspheme!' another boy whispered urgently into his ears.

The concept of 'adaptation' has its problems and a new kind of missionary is unsympathetically described by Peter Palangyo, writing of Kachawanga, a post-Independent Tanzanian village, in *Dying in the Sun* (1968). 'He is an amicable Catholic father, the type who plays Christ all his life, with that golden beard . . .' He examines the masquerade mask hanging over the grave of an ancestor buried several years ago. 'There is so much to be discovered in Africa', he says.

'This tree springs from deep down so many African civilizations, a symbol, a witness to the fact I have always believed that you were superior to us long ago and that the pride of your superiority made God smite as he smote the Gomorrans. Yes, this archaeological mushroom is a miracle, a most holy miracle, praise be to the Virgin, and that is why we are building this Church here as a humble acknowledgement of entreaty.'

This curious, not very well digested product of anthropology, with hang-ups of the narrow way, and with the substitution of sentimentality for love can be put beside another type of missionary priest that has seldom caught the eye of the novelist. The old Father Superior of a village mission in Northern Rhodesia, as described by Dominic Mulaisho in *The Tongue of the Dumb* (1971), is a man of love. He recognises love even in 'pagans', and firmly states his point of view to the irascible Fr Chipwanya, a Polish priest, who habitually criticizes him in the mission for his doctrinal laxity. Brother Aruppe, an African, has just been killed by a lion while attending to the mission chickens at night.

'Father,' he said again, after swallowing even harder, 'let me be frank with you. These pagans loved Brother Aruppe as one of them. What did you do for Brother Aruppe? You treated him worse than a leper. You goaded him at table, at prayer, even in his sleep. Now he is dead. Only yesterday you emptied a jug of dirty soapy water on his head. All in the name of Christianity no doubt. Have these pagans done any such thing to you?'

This was the last straw. Father Chipwanya shot off, shouting, 'You'll see, you'll see!'

To prevent the lion, killed shortly after Brother Aruppe's death, from haunting them, the village pagans requested permission to bury its head separately from its body. Father Chipwanya curtly referred them to the old priest who replied significantly.

'My children, only Our Lord Jesus Christ could rise from the dead. But if that is your wish, do as you please. Sergio, our cook, will give you the tools.'

'May Jesus Christ be honoured,' said the people in chorus.

This novel is set at a time just after the Second World War.

One of the themes running through John Munonye's book, *A Wreath for Maidens* (1973), which portrays many of the ills in Nigerian Society that caused the Biafran War is, by contrast, the goodness of individual missionaries.

Fr Long, principal of Christ High School in Oban (Enugu), 'could tell you the family background of almost every student . . . He handled them with both sympathy and firmness . . .' He hardly ever carried a cane but instead would remind his staff that just as the pen was mightier than the sword, so also examples were a more positive and more effective instrument than the cane.

When the two leading theorists in the book—old friends from the University of Ibadan—are discussing which foreign nationals should be asked to leave the country, to the question whether priests, nuns and doctors should go, the reply comes,

'Don't be silly! You know whom I have in mind. The commercial and diplomatic and foreign aid people, who usually have hidden roles.'

In another part of the book the same two persons are talking with others at a political party committee meeting.

'Some of these missionaries are excellent men.'
'Maybe. A few individuals in whom the chord of humanity still vibrates!'
'Force of conscience—no more! They are atoning for the ills perpetrated on our race by their uncles.'

These points of view can be seen as a means of preparing the reader for the death of Fr Leo, a person who occupies in all a mere half page at the very end of the book. The scene is set on the battlefield in the Biafran front line.

Then a Catholic priest came along.

'Officer, do you mind, I would like to administer the last Sacrament to some of the wounded.'
'Go ahead, Father,' the lieutenant gave his consent, though adding that he personally did not believe in anything called Sacrament . . .
They got the lieutenant. They got the priest too. Terrible! . . .

In hospital, Medo, the teller of the tale, reflects:

'I was awake once more. I was no longer thinking about Anibado (his enemy); it was now the priest. His image floated before my eyes—the serene look, even in death, the resigned, forgiving attitude; the blood patches on his chest. He was a young man, perhaps my age. And an Englishman. Father Leo had been born in London, then reared in

Liverpool. That morning, he had spent hours distributing salt and medicine to his fleeing parishioners; and then, when it was noon, he volunteered to go to the front to attend to the dying. So much was loaded into that brief account. Indeed one could expand it into a book. I could perhaps do it myself. Yes, I would try to fathom his inner self, tear open his heart and explore the nature of his calling, leading to the last and supreme act of his self-immolation.'

In the solitude of his mind another memory lay.

The Christianization of African society : some possible models*

J. D. Y. PEEL

My aim in this chapter is to stand back somewhat from detailed and local concerns, and to try to see the process of Christianization from a remoter perspective, incorporating materials from various parts of Africa. In this attempt to survey the boundaries of the forest, rather than to examine the particular trees, I shall make use of a comparative sociology. The Christianization of Africa is a case of a more general type of process that has occurred to other peoples at different times and places: the gradual supplanting of local or ethnic religious identities by the world religions. By 'ethnic religion' I mean one that is peculiar to a linguistic or cultural area, expressing the particular forms of its social life and natural environment, such as the original traditional religion of every people: the early Romans, the Anglo-Saxons, the Arabs before Muhammad, the pre-colonial Yoruba or Kikuyu. Such religions have no scriptures, though they may have extensive oral literatures, and usually no prophetic or conversionary aspect. So much are they taken for granted, like the air itself, by their adherents, that there was often no distinct word to cover all the connotations of 'religion'. It was missionaries of Christianity and Islam who talked about 'religion' and asked themselves which practices of the 'pagan' constituted their 'religion', and so needed to be abandoned on conversion.[1]

'World religions', like Christianity, Buddhism and Islam, are based on the salvationary message of a particular historical prophet or teacher, addressing himself to an audience in potential spiritual crisis.[2] The message is recorded in scriptures by followers who seek to convert the

---

*This paper was originally given at the Ibadan seminar on 1 May 1974.

[1] Thus in many African languages the word now rendered 'religion' does not properly refer to the traditional cults, but only to Islam and Christianity (e.g. *ddini* in Luganda, *esin* in Yoruba.

[2] This perspective is essentially that of Max Weber, especially his *Sociology of Religion* (trans. E. Fischoff, 1963), as adopted in my 'The Religious Transformation of Africa in a Weberian Perspective', *Acts of the 12th International Conference on the Sociology of Religion* (1973), pp. 337-352.

rest of humanity. The world religions arose among peoples who had lost the relatively sure reality of their traditional social order; and they have ever since found the readiest converts among peoples who, through trade, wars, migration, the creation of larger political units or the development of wider markets, have lost this security. Later the world religions spread to the settled agricultural populations and a more 'traditional', locally-rooted form of the world religion grows up—e.g. the Monophysite Christianity of the Amhara peasantry in Ethiopia, the Buddhism of Burmese villagers, the 'folk Catholicism' of southern Europe, the rural Islam of Turkish peasants. But historically, the adoption of a particular world religion has stamped civilizations for centuries, giving a distinct cast to the institutions and life of their peoples.

Religious change in nineteenth and twentieth century Africa has been first and foremost of this kind: the spread of Islam and Christianity, at the expense of the traditional, 'ethnic' religions. But there have also been other elements: changes within the ethnic religions, modifications of the world religions as originally presented by their carriers, secularist modifications of all religions in urban and multi-religious contexts. The non-African observer of this extraordinarily rich religious scene is struck by two contrasting features.

Firstly, there are frequent parallels between aspects of contemporary African religion and other historical situations—for example between the urban Aladura congregation and nonconformist ones in early nineteenth century England, or between the type of religious situation described by Bede (talking about the conversion of the pagan Anglo-Saxons) and that in the diaries of the early pioneer missionaries in nineteenth century Africa.[3] These parallels make Africa of potentially very great value in the reinterpretation of other or earlier Christian epochs. Many of the great Christian classics—St Augustine's *Confessions* or Wesley's *Journal*—derived from social situations which have far more in common with contemporary Africa than with contemporary Europe. So many aspects of the African situation are more universal than seems at first.

On the other hand this needs balancing with the recognition that in its totality the African situation is unique. Partly this derives from the particular cultural heritages and historical experiences of different African peoples, above all, for our purposes, the close connexions between Christianization and the colonial episode in African history. Partly also it derives from the fact that, even where historical parallels can be drawn, they are here combined in unique ways. So contemporary

[3] This point is made at greater length in my *Aladura : a Religious Movement among the Yoruba* (1968), chap. 9.

African religion expresses both the dilemmas of recent conversion from ethnic religions and also the responses to rapid, quasi-industrial urbanization.

The question, 'What is happening to Christianity in Africa today?' suggests we need some more general model to which we can relate our particular observations. I shall try to do this by tracing historical parallels and establishing the points of similarity and difference. The two general areas, to be considered in sequence, are, firstly, the process of primary religious conversion, where the arena is the language area, kingdom or people to which an ethnic religion corresponds, and, secondly, the further development of Christianity, in more heterogeneous arenas, such as the nation, the city and multi-ethnic contexts.

Though the process of primary conversion is now substantially complete in many areas of Africa (such as southern Nigeria), we cannot understand further developments without knowing why primary conversion occurred. There are remarkably few studies which attempt to explain, and not just describe conversion. Christians and Muslims tend to assume the natural superiority of their religions, and regard their triumph as inevitable, once obstacles are removed. Anthropologists have written little about conversion among the peoples they have studied. Many authors, especially those hostile to Christianity, see conversion as an inevitable part of colonialism or as proceeding from crudely material motives. But negative parallel cases render this insufficient. Why should conversion to Islam also occur under colonialism, often closely related to Christian conversion, as the Ijebu case shows?[4] And why should British colonialism and missionary control of education *not* have led to widespread Christian conversion among Hindus and Buddhists in India and Burma? This suggests that we need to look at the character of the 'ethnic religion' as well as the social context of conversion.

The Christianization of African and certain other areas of the Third World in the nineteenth and twentieth centuries has been the fourth great age of Christian expansion, and we should compare it with the other three: that within the Roman Empire, before Christianity became the official religion in 310 AD; the expansion among the neighbouring pagan peoples outside the Mediterranean basin, between 310 and c. 1300, especially north-west to the Germanic peoples, north-east to the Slavs and south-east to the Ethiopians; and thirdly the sixteenth and seventeenth centuries in south and central America where the surviving

---

[4] Ijebu is one of the Yoruba kingdoms which was conquered by the British in 1892 and subsequently experienced a mass movement to Christianity. But equally, though less remarked on in the literature, there was a movement to Islam. For more detailed analysis and comparison with Buganda, see my 'Conversion and Tradition in two African Societies', *Past and Present* (forthcoming 1978).

indigenous peoples were converted to Roman Catholicism as part of royal policy.

Remote though these epochs may seem, Christian expansion in Africa has something in common with each of them. It resembles the first in that the first converts have mostly been drawn from the socially marginal or outcast, not the rulers or agricultural masses, but migrants, traders, ex-slaves etc. It resembles the second in that Christianity has faced similar ethnic religions, of small kingdoms or groups of clans; and some African kings and *élites* (e.g. Tswana, Ganda or Barotse) have actively sponsored it, as a form of cultural advancement and a way of association with larger power centres, just like the petty Anglo-Saxon kings. The resemblance with the third period lies in the association with European colonial expansion. But whereas the 'most Catholic Kings' of Spain and Portugal strenuously promoted Christianity, the major colonial powers in Africa supported it much less directly (and sometimes, in Islamic areas, actively discouraged it).

These parallels should serve to underline the variety of factors involved in Christian conversion. Some of these are intrinsic to a religion, such as the superior appeal of its theological character in particular social contexts. Robin Horton's work has been very suggestive here.[5] He shows how a very general feature of African cosmologies is the relation between the Supreme Being and subordinate deities; and how greater emphasis is placed on the Supreme Being by those societies and individuals with the greatest experience of extra-local relations, such as traders and nomads. Christianity and Islam have an appeal for their more detailed teaching in this area, and are found to be attractive to people in this situation.

Other factors are less intrinsic to the religions, such as the power or advantages accruing to members, ranging from regulàr attributes like writing or medicines, often combined, to features almost accidentally associated with them: the control of guns which Christians possess, a trading network (like that centring on cattle and beef in West Africa) controlled by Muslims, freedom from the authority of chiefs or elders, education and lucrative employment. Usually these elements are inextricably blended, and it is often best to see conversion as the search for a new identity, embodied in the membership of an attractive reference group: 'enlightened' young men, socially competent in new ways, possessing new and attractive life-styles, and holding out the promise, as it were, of being the wave of the future. People may join for one reason and then be influenced by the group in new ways. Conversion

[5] Especially his 'On the Rationality of Conversion', *Africa* XLV (1975), pp. 219, 373.

of other social categories, not so initially attracted (like women, farmers, chiefs) will occur as the converts rise to positions of power. Accompanying this will be a certain adjustment process, as the faith of a pioneer minority becomes a more easy-going majority religion.

However inevitable or necessary the conversion-process, once it has occurred, may seem to us to be, we must never forget it is governed by the reasons or criteria of value of the converts. They are not automata, but become Christians because in some way Christianity fulfils some traditional criterion better than the ethnic religion: it may seem more consistent with experience, more rational, more in tune with the spirit of the age, more powerful, more morally uplifted, etc. It is essential to understand these criteria, as they are likely to continue to underlie Christian profession. Moreover, the converts do not accept the missionary package lock, stock and barrel: they select and they make their own decisions about what is important and what is not. The shallowest misunderstanding of African Christianity (which one hears both in religiously conservative European circles and among anti-Christian Africans eager to play down the extent of Christianization) is that Africans are not 'true Christians' because they don't accept all the missionary package. It is quite unfair to call the Ijebu pioneer Joseph Odumosu, for example, a 'superficial Christian' because he remained polygamous and practised native medicine; for he and his kind expended much time, energy and money on distinctively religious activities like prayer and preaching.

This 'give-and-take' of conversion has, in my view, been much more successfully realized in the practice of ordinary Christians than in the writings of religious intellectuals, which, in their general contentions, have shown little change from the 1840s to the 1890s to the 1960s.[6] In general terms—with which no one could disagree—they argue that Christianity must enter, and be permeated by, African culture; that the indigenization of African Christianity must not be hindered by its European cultural trappings. The problem is to determine what is

---

[6] For example compare the general lines of argument in E. B. Idowu's *Towards an Indigenous Church* (1965) with those of Bishop James Johnson and the leaders of the African churches in the 1890s (on which cf. E. A. Ayandele, *The Missionary Impact on Modern Nigeria*, 1966, esp. Chap. 8). The African ecclesiastical radicals of the 1890s could justly invoke the philosophy of the great Henry Venn, C.M.S. secretary from 1841, as Ajayi shows in *Christian Missions in Nigeria* (1965). There is even the paradox that the intolerant G. W. Brooke, who played such a baleful role in the disruption of the Niger Mission in the 1890s, stressed the same general point: that Christian missionaries should 'adopt African customs . . . dress in Native clothes, eat Native food, live in Native style houses and teach in Native fashion' (J. B. Webster, *African Churches among the Yoruba*, 1964, p. 8). For a useful recent discussion of some of the problems, see Aylward Shorter's *African Culture and the Christian Church* (1973).

authentically African and yet not 'pagan' and what not.[7] Too much of the debate has focussed on rather superficial aspects of culture, like names, dress or styles of architecture. Do the style of St John's Cathedral or names like Frederick Kumokun Haastrup[8] really indicate Ijesha Christianity is not indigenized? If so—since these charges are not usually made against Islam—what about the Kano mosque, or Yoruba Muslims with names like Yesufu Rasak and Salawu Wahab? The most dynamic and successful church at meeting the religious needs of urban Yorubas—the Christ Apostolic Church—has been relatively indifferent to such superficial tokens.

The heat generated by such discussions is significant, however. Up to a point, it is always a problem to strike a satisfactory balance between the universality of a world religion and the peculiarities of a national culture. English Christianity is as English as it is Christian, Persian Islam is as Persian as it is Muslim. The intensity of the debate among African intellectuals relates, I believe, to two features of Africa's historical situation: firstly the need to rebut the extreme cultural depreciation of the colonial period, and secondly the highly problematic character of 'African' or 'Nigerian' culture, which is desired as a basis of continental or national unity but where there is such diversity in the traditional ethnic cultures.

The other aspects of the cultural dialogue is the bogey of 'syncretism', a concept favoured by anthropologists of the old 'culture-contact' school and by some European analysts of independent churches, as peculiarly applicable to Africa.[9] But if it means 'a mixing of ideas and practices from different sources', it is by no means peculiarly African. For no adherent of the world religions anywhere, derives all the furniture of his

---

[7] 'Pagan' is not here a sociological category and it is not synonymous with what I have called 'ethnic religion'. It is a necessary religious category of both Christianity and Islam, referring to those elements of the traditional or ethnic religions that must be deemed incompatible with them—largely the cult of ancestors and deities other than the Supreme Being. Other parts of the traditional religious culture are not only compatible with the world religions, but are actually a criterion underlying conversion to them.

[8] Haastrup was a former Lagos merchant who was elected Owa of Ilesha as Ajimoko in 1896, thus becoming the first Christian Yoruba crowned ruler. He actively sponsored Christian and educational initiatives, and may justly be compared with such other pro-Christian kings as Lewanika of the Barotse kingdom in Zambia or Khama of the Ngwato.

[9] E.g. J. C. Messenger's, 'Religious Acculturation among the Anang Ibibio', in W. R. Bascom and M. J. Herskovits, Continuity and Change in African Cultures (1959). Even B. G. M. Sundkler's classic study, Bantu Prophets in South Africa concludes with 'syncretism' as the key to the phenomenon and the claim that 'the syncretistic sect becomes the bridge over which Africans are brought back to paganism' (2nd edn. 1961, p. 297).

mind from his religion. Man's beliefs are nearly always syncretistic, in that their content shifts in response to new experiences, and that some attempt is made to harmonize old and new. The African convert continues to hold a great variety of ontological beliefs (ranging from beliefs about witchcraft, say, or about the healing properties of plants) on which Christian profession does not at once impinge. Moreover he must have some sort of orientation towards other spiritual entities: are they non-existent, or to be identified with devils, or with saints, or do they continue as before? In some areas, as regards the Supreme Being for example, a real syncretization or blending of beliefs from old and new sources, may occur. Elsewhere, what usually seems to occur is a compartmentalization of practice, without syncretism of ideas, but with attempts to avoid embarrassing clashes of context: Ifa might be defined as 'Yoruba philosophy' rather than 'religion', or churchwardens may go 'like Nicodemus', to consult the *babalawo* privily. Systematic syncretization of belief, like the Oba of Benin's Aruosa cult,[10] seems to be rare. It is certainly unhelpful and simplistic to see most independent churches as syncretisms of Christian and traditional religious belief, except in so far as they think religion should concern itself with healing and prophecy.

At this point I should stress our sociological ignorance of just what people do believe. A strange mixture of individual beliefs might emerge, but no stranger than what has emerged from recent studies of belief in seventeenth century England (then Christian for 1000 years)[11] or from contemporary opinion surveys. If a Yoruba Christian believes in reincarnation it is likely to be put down to 'syncretism', but what about the 10% of the British population who, according to a recent survey, believe exactly the same?[12]

When we consider the further development of a world religion in a society, one simple model or yardstick tends to be applied. It was that of the missionaries and of such African Christians as the Rev. Samuel Johnson when he expressed the hope at the end of his great history of the Yorubas, 'that Christianity should be the principal religion in the land—paganism and Mohammedanism having had their full trial.'[13] The

---

[10] This is a reorganization, by the Oba of Benin, of the cult of Osanobua, the Supreme Being as conceived by the Edo, incorporating both traditional materials and some Christian liturgical practices; see M. R. Welton, 'The Holy Aruosa (or Edo national church of God): Religious Conservatism in a Changing Society', *Practical Anthropology* XVI (1969), pp. 18-27.

[11] Keith Thomas, *Religion and the Decline of Magic* (1971).

[12] Surveys reported in D. A. Martin, *Sociology of English Religion* (1969).

[13] S. Johnson, *History of the Yorubas* (1921), p. 642.

nineteenth century missionaries, whether Protestant or Catholic, came from countries which had been profoundly and exclusively Christian, but where the authority of religion had already been greatly weakened by urbanization (and the consequent loss of the parochial control of rural society), by secular working class movements and by the growth of secular knowledge and science. 'The Sacred Canopy' of society was no more. But the missionaries aspired to create in Africa a piously observant Christian society like that which they believed pre-industrial Europe had had. Their model of religious change, still often used to gauge their success, was from the conversion of a pagan people to an African folk-Christianity as there had been a European folk-Christianity. Cardinal Lavigerie of Algiers seems to have planned his evangelization strategies with the trajectory from the pagan Frankish kings to St Louis of France in mind! For a while, the Catholics attained something of this kind in Rwanda see above, pp. 243-5), and the Church Missionary Society entertained similar, but less realistic, hopes for Abeokuta in Yorubaland.

But because Christianization came at the historical juncture that it did, bound in with colonial social changes that were linked with Europe's own industrialization, things couldn't be like that. Christianity came with pluralism and secularism. Still, how far have African societies become Christian? This, of course, depends on the criteria used. Williamson, writing about well-evangelized southern Ghana, where around 70% of the population declares itself Christian to the census-takers, still speaks of 'an overwhelmingly non-Christian population'.[14] There is no single 'correct' criterion—rather all the following levels have their significance: those who declare themselves Christian in censuses, those who are 'members' by the churches' criteria (which vary considerably from highly inclusive R.C. ones to very selective Baptist or Methodist ones), those who adhere in any way to local congregations, those who participate in any religious activity at all. Census figures apart, my own impression is that African Christianity in such areas as southern Nigeria presents as much social penetration as Christianity almost anywhere.

But perhaps statistics of individuals' practice are not so relevant to the definition of 'Christian society'. Those who feel hesitant about applying this label in Africa (except perhaps to the Ethiopians) seem to feel that it is more a matter of the 'framework' of society being Christian, as it was in medieval Europe, rather than of church institutions being influential

---

[14] S. G. Williamson, *Akan Religion and the Christian Faith* (1965), p. 17. Cf. John Dunn and A. F. Robertson's anthropological-historical judgement of Ahafo, by no means the most developed Akan sub-group, as 'now a much more predominantly and vigorously Christian area than, for example, the United Kingdom', indeed the site of a 'Christian ideological triumph' (*Dependence and Opportunity*, 1973, pp. 124-5).

or many individuals being churchgoers. To talk of 'framework' implies a virtual monopoly in practice of one faith and the public use of the faith as the exclusive source of moral and political legitimation: e.g. stealing will be held to be wrong because of the Eighth Commandment. Is this happening, or likely to happen, in Africa? This needs to be considered from two angles: the elimination or survival of the traditional ethnic religion, and the effects of modern pluralism and secularism.

Where world religions become social frameworks, two things must have happened to the old ethnic religion. Firstly, it must be eliminated: its shrines destroyed, its congregations dispersed, its priests dispossessed, its revenues taken away, its deities denounced as devils, forgotten or turned into fairy-story figures like Jupiter and Venus. This may be done deliberately by the authorities (as where the rulers embrace the new religion, like the Christian Anglo-Saxon kings, or the post-Jihad rulers of Hausaland, or the Christian *élite* in Buganda), or may occur by creeping neglect, which seems more common. Unfortunately, modern research has done little to document this: the students of traditional cults talk more about what exists than about what has recently disappeared. Secondly, elements of the old religion are incorporated, in suitable Christian or Muslim dress, in the local form of the world religion; as when Muhammad 'Islamized' the Kaaba (a large fetish-rock) at Mecca or when churches in Europe were built on sacred hill tops or on the sites of pagan temples. We should not forget that the name of the greatest festival of the Christian year, in the English language, commemorates a pagan goddess of Spring! In this way, spiritual power is appropriated, but the appearance of a rival source of legitimacy disappears. This seems to have happened rather little in Africa, though there are some instances in that rather untypical case, Buganda.[15] Even where churches in Yorubaland were set on forbidden sites or *igbo igbale* (like C.A.C. Oniyanrin, Ibadan or Otapete Methodist Church, Ilesha) this was not done to defeat the old religion by annexing the power of its sacred spots. Whereas in Brazil and Cuba Catholic saints took over some of the attributes of Sango, Obatala, Ibeji etc., this has not happened in Africa, except with the Supreme Being.[16]

A third possibility is that the ethnic religion may survive, attenuated

---

[15] Cf. *Proceedings of the C.M.S.* (1903), p. 122: a church is erected by the chief on the site of the destroyed temple of one of the old gods, Nende, whose priest had been the chief's father.

[16] An intriguing exception, reported in J. O. K. Olowokure's Ibadan MA thesis, 'Christianity in Ijeshaland' (1970), p. 122, is the reported identification of Jesus Christ with the *orisa* Oluorogbo, who is said to have been sacrificed for the safety of the people of Ile-Ife and subsequently deified (see E. B. Idowu, *Olodumare*, 1962, pp. 204 ff and M. A. Fabunmi, *Ife Shrines*, p. 9).

perhaps but recognizably itself; and so far this is what has happened. The survival seems most important in two areas: public festivals and magico-medical services for individuals. How *religiously* significant the festivals are is hard to say. Ogunba concludes his very fine study of Ijebu masquerades by being rather cagey, for he stresses their popularity 'particularly if one regards them more as a social and artistic institution.'[17] What is in the mind of active Christian *obas* like the Timi of Ede or the Owa of Ilesha as they celebrate their Ogun festivals? If they are continued for socio-cultural reasons, like much European folklore, or are reinterpreted merely as historical commemorations, they stop being 'religion'. But I would hesitate to believe that this is the case yet. They retain importance, I suggest, not merely because of some continued belief in the power of the old gods, nor yet because of potential tourist value, but because no other religion or sect can claim for itself a monopoly in expressing community feelings. That is to say, they can survive because of the pluralist religious situation—even though the vast majority (e.g. 92% of Yorubas, 98% of Ijeshas) claim adherence to religions which say, 'Thou shalt have no other gods before me!'

By 'pluralism' I mean a situation where there is choice between several competing religions, as against one where one religion has such a monopoly that all serious controversy takes place entirely within its ranks. Pluralism exists in two historical modes: firstly, when a world religion is first emerging (as in the Roman Empire) or when it is gaining converts—here, by definition, there must be choice between religions; secondly, after the fragmentation of a previously dominant religion, under conditions of modernization and migration to towns (as in post-Reformation Europe or America). The first kind of pluralism is quite compatible with wide-spread belief in spiritual or mystical forces, a personalized view of nature, belief in miracles and witchcraft, and an absence of any fundamental critique of religion as such. But the second tends to be found with a mechanical view of nature derived from science, the removal of religion from many areas of life, a secular attitude to what were previously 'religious' problems, and often indifference or even widespread hostility to religion as such.

What makes the future of the African situation very hard to predict, is that here we find both sorts of pluralism. Although, in my view, religious pluralism in Africa is most often combined with a profoundly spiritual world-view, it is unlikely to lead to a new orthodoxy, or the establishment of one particular church or religion as the dominant framework. For in any kind of pluralist situation, particular religions

[17] O. Ogunba, 'Ritual Drama of the Ijebu People' (Ibadan PhD thesis, 1967), p. 320.

must justify themselves to outsiders (especially those whom they wish to convert) by criteria outside themselves—criteria which tend to be secular or at least pragmatic. Hence we find in the towns, where religious pluralism is most marked, the following kinds of feature: a lot of shopping around between religions, the attitude that all religions are doing the same thing, a view of religions as competing for 'customers', the assessment of religions in terms of pragmatic or 'this-wordly' benefits. These were often the criteria that originally underlay conversion; and they make existing religions continuously subject to the same criteria. This explains the startling successes of some American evangelistic groups in cities like Lagos and Ibadan. For coming from a country which, despite its greater wealth, strongly resembles Nigeria's religious pluralism, they possess a strong 'consumer-orientation' which brings some success in the religious market-place. A further consequence of pluralism will be that Nigeria's fastest growing churches, the Aladuras, are justified (at least in their adherents' eyes) so much by the appeal to practical results—fertility acquired, health regained, examinations passed, witchcraft conquered—that they must be very vulnerable to the better provision of more reliable methods for attaining some of these ends.

However, this is too much like trying to see through a glass darkly. Religion has much wider appeal than this, and there is need for more studies that treat, not of particular churches, but of the whole range of religious expression within a community or area. Two pioneer studies of this kind might be mentioned: firstly, Murphree's study of a Shona chiefdom in Rhodesia, which analyses the way in which the four principal religions (Methodism, Roman Catholicism, Vapostori or Apostolics and traditional) actually dovetail with one another, meeting the complementary religious needs of different categories of the population.[18] Secondly, a rare example of a social survey of attitudes, there is Deniel's book on religion in Ouagadougou, capital of Upper Volta, which exemplifies a number of the points I have made about religious pluralism.[19]

A final point of a negative nature is suggested by the overall theme of this series of seminars—Christianity in Independent Africa. It is that political independence, as such, has made small difference to the situation of Christianity. The processes of change that affect religion—increases in numbers of adherents and clergy, the Africanization of hierarchies, urbanization—are more gradual than the

[18] M. W. Murphree, *Christianity and the Shona* (1969).

[19] R. Deniel, *Croyances Réligieuses et Vie Quotidienne à Ouagadougou* (Etudes Voltaïques, 1970).

steps of political change. Ecclesiastical decolonization, if one can call it that, began much earlier and has continued longer. The whole process of transformation is far from complete and its outcome is not to be predicted. But I hope that by drawing appropriate historical parallels, and establishing some of the basic sociological processes, we may better understand both the common and the unique features of Africa's experience of Christianization.

'The centre cannot hold . . .' Spirit possession as redefinition

SIMON BARRINGTON-WARD

The Isoko[1] of mid-western Nigeria were migrants from Benin who, in the early eighteenth century came to the western delta of the Niger to occupy the last land left available by other settlers; to the south and west are the Urhobo, closely linked to them by ties of culture and language, and the Itsekiri; and to the east and north are the western Igbo. Their whole society and culture was thus never strongly integrated. The formation of new communities and cults was a continuous feature of their history. They were loosely organised into ten major groupings, each linked to a founder who had given his name to the group and later to its central town. Within these were breakaway sub-groups with their own 'towns' and from these further independent 'villages' had grown up. In the early twentieth century settler communities from a range of such groups formed along the shores of the creeks, for trade and fishing.

Their social and religious structure was ultimately modelled on that of Benin. Originally each new '*Ovie*' or ruler of a separate grouping was supposed to have returned to the palace of the Oba of Benin to recognize his father's skull in the great chamber and to receive his state sword. He ruled with a council of elders who were drawn from the whole society of recognized adult men. Under these were a series of age groups. The Ovie's central settlement had its satellite quarters, and each quarter its extended family compounds. Independent groups quite often broke away to make new settlements.

Spiritually, all these sub-groups owed allegiance to the same central divinities. There would be the founder and fathers of the whole grouping, guardians of the town and all those originally linked to its founder, the founder and fathers of the quarter or the independent village, and the fathers of the extended family household. (There was a subordinate cult of the mothers for wives and daughters, but the society was patrilineal.) Then there was the Spirit of the land again worshipped by the whole grouping, sometimes associated with earlier inhabitants, the

---

[1] The earliest and best ethnographic study of the Isoko was made in 1933 by Dr James Welch in an unpublished PhD thesis for Cambridge University. He gives there some of this story, but most is as I received it from oral tradition.

Erohwa, amongst whom the Isoko had settled and with whom they had intermarried, or further up the river the western Igbo. Then there was Oghene, the framing and overarching firmament, maker of earth and sky, remote and abstract 'the one no-one knows'. With Oghene a tenuous relationship was maintained through the Oyisi tree planted in the family compounds or in the quarter. Indirectly linked to Oghene was the personal creator spirit, typical of other West African societies, who gave to each child particular personal characteristics and a particular destiny.

But other more extra-social Spirits, more various and sporadic, often associated with the wilderness or water or with particular natural features, identified themselves with particular forms, quarters or families originally often through the possession of a particular individual. Such Spirits bestowed particular skills or inspired particular institutions in a given grouping. They had their own particular moral and ritual requirements through which the group which adhered to them were defined: for example, respect for a certain animal, or refusal of certain foods. They had their own shrine served, and their own festival observed, by the group to whom they were linked, with their own songs and dances. From time to time, a new Spirit, with new rituals, rules, special songs, dances and even associated physical substances, would disclose itself through possession in a fresh act of definition. It disclosed itself through dreams, visions, voices, even through a traditional healer (*obueva*), who declared its nature and intentions to the sufferer whom it was seeking to possess. A new category was thus created, both divine and human. A new line was drawn. The Spirit thus disclosed had a dual role. It could account for a new set of phenomena, a new series of incidents, which were thus comprehended and incorporated into the whole body of folk knowledge. It could also give identity to a new social grouping. From the time that the Isoko first arrived in the new environment, new phenomena and new social groupings were naturally a frequent occurrence. Indeed the new Spirit cults seemed to multiply at the points of greatest conceptual and social confusion, where the boundaries were weakest; for instance in an area near the shores of tributaries of the Niger, such as the town and clan of Aviara, where trade links and water travel brought in more strangers and where there was a great number of independent villages.

Some degree of actual 'spirit possession' or ritualized disassociation attributed to a divine visitation was, of course, as in many other societies associated with the more central, public and institutional acts of worship. The Ovie was ritually possessed at an annual festival by one of the Spirits of his forebears, just as the priest of the land would be possessed during the 'blessing of the land' at the beginning of the dry season. But these were formal occasions at which every action of the possessed was prescribed by tradition and critically observed by the elders. Every step in a series of elaborate dance sequences was predictable and recognisable. The possession could itself have the air of a conventional compliance with custom. Even if it had often considerable reality and force, the past weighed as heavily constraining as the ceremonial headdress, the beads and the ornamental sword.

Spirit possession in a less controlled and more dramatic mode was more associated with the more individualized and free-ranging private Spirits and their cults.[2] Here also was a degree of convention and prescription, the more so for the longer established, which had by now become increasingly public property. First they became associated step by step with the possessed person's family, it might be, then, if a theoretical and social need were being fulfilled, with his quarter and so eventually with the town or clan, at which point they had some official status. Some such Spirits, associated say with a specific aptitude for a new style of fighting or for some new craft or psychological skill, became associated with certain town groupings. The process by which they had first been acquired became a legend. The story might begin with an account of the possession of an individual, often after an illness, by the particular Spirit, a particular style of possession perhaps re-enacted during the particular Spirit's festival. In certain towns particular *sacra* associated with such a Spirit (sometimes objects carved with a skill now lost) are still today brought out for the occasion amidst a distinctive ritual sequence, reminiscent of traditional festivals maintained in certain English towns.

Legends confirm the way in which the private and sporadic has thus become public and regular, the peripheral become central. One of the most famous such Spirits, Eni, a water spirit, was said to have possessed Uzee, the founder of the Isoko town grouping Uzere. The possession probably helped to define him and his followers as a migrant group distinct from others. It also clearly enabled them to cope on behalf of all the migrants with a new high incidence of witchcraft attendant on the whole new venture of migration. Uzee and his people were empowered to bring suspected witches to Eni and have them tested and if guilty, put to death. It is said that when Uzee tried to settle his people near Isseleuku, among western Igbos, Eni forced him on to Erohwa country where he

---

[2] I am here employing the same contrast as Robin Horton in several of his Kalabari studies, notably 'Types of spirit possession in Kalabari Religion', in J. Beattie and J. Middleton (ed), *Spirit Mediumship and Society in Africa*, London, 1969. A similar contrast is taken up and worked rather hard by I. M. Lewis, *Ecstatic religion*, London, 1971.

founded Uzere. Not long after, Eni revealed himself to a member of the group at a large wet season lake near Uzere, now called Lake Eni. There the famous annual witchcraft trials took place at which women from all over the midwest and beyond were paddled out into the lake and thrown overboard, only the innocent reaching the shore. At this festival of Eni, the Ovie of Uzere, clad in the special red robes which he had assumed after a formal cleansing and anointing, being possessed by the Spirit, danced and then presided over the sending out of the boats. What had once been a 'private' water Spirit in another part of the country had in the course of migration and settlement become the central cult of the Uzere clan and the basis of their town's fame and prosperity, overshadowing the cults of founders and ancestors.[3] Such a process of public 'institutionalisation' of private cults has been repeated in Isoko history in a wide range of contexts. This kind of development was to take on a new significance with the advent of Europeans and of a more drastic disintegration than Isoko had yet known.

Response to radical change

From the 1880s on, European influence first really began to make itself felt in Isoko. In 1888 the whole area reverberated to the echo of Royal Niger Company gunboats firing on Patani as a reprisal for Ijaw raids on a 'factory' further down the river. Not long afterwards on the Isoko riverside at Asaba Ase, the company set up another factory or depot. From the early 1890s CMS missionaries from Onitsha first began to penetrate. Henry Proctor started work at Patani. A community of Sierra Leoneans and 'educated' Nigerians (Saros) had meanwhile been growing up at Warri. They started a church there and before long its influence began to be felt among the Urhobo. In 1904 the government set up a court at Asaba Ase. A few isolated Isoko began to be caught up into the new way of life and glimpses of white intruders became more frequent. Two cataclysmic events followed. In 1905 an Urhobo newly-appointed 'chief' at Warri, whose aunt had perished in one of the Eni witchcraft trials, led a military expedition to Uzere to close down the ceremony once and for all. In 1908 a Niger Company agent began to introduce the palm-oil trade, revolutionizing the whole economy and way of life of many Isokos and encouraging a new kind of individual competition and new sources of wealth and power outside the traditional

---

[3] Oral tradition in Isoko strikingly confirms a hypothesis of Horton ('Types', p. 47) as to the way in which Kalabari spirits may have become part of the officially established 'village heroes' as he calls them. The Spirits may have 'stayed incubating on the sidelines until, at some time of social upheaval and change requiring new interpretative concepts, they came out to make grander claims for themselves'.

framework. New communities from mixed town and family groupings sprang up along the waterside for trade and fishing. The new money began to be used more widely. Roads, official rest houses, courts with court clerks from Sierra Leone or Yoruba country were installed. Two punitive expeditions revenged attacks on clerks and other breaches of the peace.

Obviously, over this whole period from the 1890s to 1910 or so Isoko central institutions and cults took quite a beating. It was said that 'Oghene was sleeping'. The power and authority of elders and rulers and hence of ancestors and town founders and official Spirits were said to be on the decline. Even the demands and food regulations of the more private peripheral Spirits were felt to be irksome.

In this situation, from the 1880s on in fact, new Spirit possession cults, with some of the same patterns of revelation through illness, dream or vision, which had characterized their predecessors, began to emerge. These new divine powers had different features, appropriate to changed circumstances. First they were nearly always transcultural, spread over a wide area and often coming from the already disturbed Urhobo or Itsekiri areas. Their songs contained Urhobo, Itsekiri and even Yoruba words. Secondly, they were invariably directed towards healing, cleansing away evil and either killing or purifying witches. Thirdly, they sat even lighter to existing structures and could tend to detach their adherents from all other customary obligations. One theme of their songs was the claim to surpass in power and authority all other spiritual beings. They also therefore tended to create a new community cutting across town, family and even society boundaries and set over against the rest of the world. Furthermore, they had caught on to the general sense of expectancy and new potential in the air and could claim to be introducing a new age.

Moreover, with the shaking of central institutions and the opening up of a wider world, categories were tending to become confused, boundaries weakened, and the world was being flooded with irreducible novelties such as the new currency, wealth and power and the new technology, which broke the conceptual and social nets of the culture and over which tradition and conventional wisdom had no control. There were new types of tension and new expressions of rivalry and mistrust. There were so many comings and goings breaking the frontier between the known and unknown world. Theft, dishonesty, adultery and all forms of sorcery and secret malice were said to be on the increase. New poisons and evil materials from outside sources were coming into use. New kinds of witchcraft were said to have come in from Asaba Ase, so that flying witches, symbolically freer and more penetrating than the old were-animal type, were said to be meeting in trees to offer their own kin for consumption by the coven. The fading of the former means of protection, let alone an event like the closing of the Lake Eni cult, added to the sense of all barriers being broken down.

At such a time the need for Spirit possession rituals and cults as a means of redefinition is clearly crucial. In the intensity of a new revelation, new lines could be drawn and new categories[4] created, and as in the past the new entities were many levelled. They created new Spiritual beings, which coped with and corresponded to new states of affairs, new circumstances and made a place for new social groupings. Thus the cosmology, the environment, and the society all interact and changes at one level are bound up with corresponding changes at another. Out of the intuitive unconscious interrelation of these three, a new vision and a correspondingly new pattern of social relations struggles to come into being.

So the succession of variations on this theme began. A series of very similar Spirit possession cults spread one after the other in different areas, each rising to its climax, gathering in an increasingly large number of adherents and after all beginning to fail and fall back before the next comer. The cult would develop from the centre at which the founder was first possessed and then be passed on by him or her to numbers of would-be apostles who arrived to receive the same possession and its accompanying symbol, it might be a chalk or a staff or a fan. Then the apostles in turn went off and set up their own centres. On market days the adherents of such cults would dance in bands carrying their emblems or wearing their particular dress. Such cults were often described as a 'dance'. Members of some of these movements wore red robes like those associated with Eni. Those coming to be healed or to be tested for witchcraft coming near the dance would be seized by the Spirit and possessed. They would then sometimes before or after eat the chalk, be touched by the staff or whatever. The guilty would either collapse or be cured. Theft, adultery, malice and mistrust were also said to be cleansed away. The cult would help its members to love one another. One 'dance' (Igbekwa) was indeed specially for women. It originated in Kokori in Urhobo country. It was led by a priestess to whom the corpses of witches said to have died from the 'dance' were supposed to be taken to be buried with all their property in the 'bad bush'.

The most famous and long lasting of all these new cults up until the 1920s was Ugo from Ubogho (again in Urhobo country nearer to Warri and the West). Ugo was quite elaborately organized. Priests received

---

[4] Obviously here I am drawing on Mary Douglas's (*Purity and Danger*, London, 1966) insight into the connexion between categories and boundaries and purity, which the Isoko evidence bears out strikingly.

both staff and special chalk from the centre. Witches, thieves, adulterers and liars were detected and killed. The founder was a fisherman. His original vision was of Ugo handing him a sacred gourd which could be used in the dance. The dress he and his followers adopted was red and the link with Eni was made explicit in Isoko. 'Ugo grow up as Lake Eni was dying'. 'Ugo was much heard of like Lake Eni.' 'When witches and thieves were being killed at Ubogho the worship spread more widely than any before it since Eni.' In Uzere itself, as will be seen, the proponents of Ugo were actually known as 'the sons of Eni'.

Perhaps it is not surprising that like some metaphysical and social cuckoo's egg inserted into this succession of Spirit possession cults sweeping through Isoko, Christianity first entered the area in a similar guise. The fact that it was not previously known in any other way, but here as on the Ivory Coast, came in first through local prophets, seems to put paid to a good many complicated theories about so called breakaway churches in other areas and to go some way to confirm Robin Horton's picture of Christianity as a catalyst.[5] But the way in which it happened also qualifies his picture somewhat as will be seen. The first clear identification which the Isoko made of this worship was not with Oghene but with the new 'unofficial' cults. The compelling power of the new worship and the way of life that went with it was attributed to its Spirit Egode, Jesukrisi, Churchi or even Mission. It was, characteristically, spread by a woman from another culture, this time Ijaw, being brought by her from Patani where she had been seized by the Spirit while attending the services of the CMS missionary, Henry Proctor. This possession had a remarkable effect on her, liberating from the Ijaw 'peripheral' spirit of which she had been a zealous medium and from allegiance to the other Ijaw central cults. It brought her a new healing.of ailments, healthy children and even to her Isoko husband exceptional catches of fish. Her two symbols were a bell and a book, effective enough without the addition of a candle in driving out all other Spirits from those who came to her. She and her family with other young adherents, from no one kinship group or quarter, broke away from the riverside town clan of Igbide and created their own settlement by the water's edge whence news of the power of this new cult spread inland along the trade routes between 1911 and 1912. At the same period, another woman, Emado, brought a similar cult from a western Igbo market town back to central Isoko. This worship, for which palm leaf shelters were constructed with box altars and in which Bibles were used as fans during the dance, was known as Enuwa Almighty One and

---

[5] R. Horton, 'African Conversion', *Africa*, XLI, 2 April 1971.

'Jesuskrisi'. 'It prevented all witchcraft and poison and drove away all other Spirits.'

In Uzere itself, a court clerk, an educated Urhobo man with a harmonium and a small library in his house, taught some of the lads for a time, leaving an identification in their minds between the wider world and its civilization, which he urged upon them, and the new Spirit movement which the boys called by the Yoruba word for the overarching divinity 'Oluwa'. When the boys met with the movement from the waterside they at once made the link and were for the first time actually possessed by the Spirit. Together with that whole generation of disciples they also found healing immunity from witchcraft and from the power of all other Spirits now seen as inimical and hostile.

In 1913 a missionary from CMS, J. D. Aitken, made the first of a number of visits, culminating in his being sent to reside in the original waterside community from 1918 on. Through his coming, the identification was first made for many between the new cult and Europeans. 'Then we first knew that this was an Oyinbo (European) thing.' The prominence of Bibles ('book'), of the bell and even in one place of the use of letters of the alphabet in worship had already provided symbolic hints. Now the identification was explicit and clear. Indeed it was to provide reassurance of roots in reality and in the wider world during a period of bitter conflict between the waning Ovies and elders in several Isoko towns and the young upstart adherents of the new cult, now gathering momentum and proving both exclusive and aggressive. Significantly the elders brought in Ugo, the flourishing Spirit possession cult, which they could identify with Lake Eni, to reinforce all traditional central cults and to deal with the whole parallel issue of the adherence of Christians to the town community as a whole. As a result, after physical violence, the sharp redefinition became complete and a number of new Christian settlements were founded. Ugo was here seen as the deliverer of all central Spirits and unofficial Spirits from the polluting power of the Christian cult. Intervention by missionaries eventually won legal protection for Christians. There followed a mass movement into the new church which went on until the late 1920s. Subsequently the church's increasing association with the new government and its taxes, its ever more European dominated organization and its new role as a means of access to education, European type medicine and the rationalized culture accompanying both, changed the nature of its significance. The enthusiasm of earlier days waned. After 1925 it was said that theft, adultery and conflict had entered the church. Witches were alleged to abound there, concealing themselves more effectively within the new organization. Only at this period was any real connection made with Oghene, when the popular movement was waning and Christianity had itself become, as it had been for the court clerk and his ilk, more of an aspect of European civilization.

But the sequence of successors to the old unofficial Spirit cults has continued both within and beyond the church. Most widespread is a cult arising in the early 1930s and surviving to this day, along with a multitude of smaller movements, called Igbe. Igbe like the others was a Spirit possession cult offering healing and cleansing in exchange for exclusive acherence. The founder, influenced by the more recent missionary efforts at linking Christian faith to Oghene, insisted that Igbe was the one eternal God who made all and who alone should be worshipped, but who was previously unknown either to African or European. The temples of Igbe are large whitened courtyards suggesting a possibility of Islamic influence, though the whiteness of the interior and the priests' robes is the traditional colour of purity and integrity. Outside the temple are piles of discarded charms, emblems and carvings of every kind of traditional religious observance public or private. Ritual language and concepts reflect Christian practice.

Church revival movements began with the 1928 'Holy Spirit' movement centred in Urhobo country at Warri, an attempt to reject Europeanized influence and to cleanse the 'impurities' of the church already referred to, as well as representing one particular person's struggle for power. In the 1930s, again, a possessed catechist denounced witches from the pulpit and held secret communion services for suspected women with a traditional witch-finding brew. In the post war period came a succession of new denominations, notably the pentecostal Christ Apostolic Church, the Cherubim and Seraphim and a number of freelance prophets and healers ascribing their power to some form of Christian spirit. There was a spirit movement emanating from Aviara, a strong centre of Christianity early on, led by a peripatetic preacher called Adam. Most recent of all is a consciously pentecostal revival within the main (Anglican) Church led by two sons of early Christian leaders, one from Aviara, working through Scripture Unions, Sunday Schools and Youth Clubs. The leaders were excommunicated by the Bishop of Benin for 'unorthodox' teaching and practice. One feature of their movement is Baptism in the Spirit accompanied by healing and cleansing. Thus the original pattern of the 1880s has been steadily and continuously developed and is still going on. It is interesting that from Aviara emanates a legend, still extant, of a lost Bible, far fuller and richer in content and consequences than the present version in use, which was originally given (even miraculously disclosed as a bound volume) to

Isoko Christians, but was then taken away and either lost or destroyed by the missionaries. What is the real significance of this symbol of a quest, indeed of the whole sequence of possession cults from the 1880s to the present day?

Spirit Possession as Definition

There must always be a degree to which the state of disassociation or of suspension of normal consciousness, bound up with the experience of alleged possession by a spiritual entity from beyond one's self, involves the suspension of ordinary norms, categories and limits. There must be, at least to an extent, a kind of mental and imaginative melting down culminating in a reformulation. Perhaps there are analogies here with the creative process itself. Indeed this is where the limitations of Robin Horton's extremely illuminating intellectualist approach seem most marked. He compares a traditional cosmology like that of the Kalabari to a scientific model and this is an attractive idea. But he seems to take too little account of the way in which, in a small scale localized society, religion, art, science and politics could all be one. And not only in such a society. The creative process in science itself is a much richer more imaginative and intuitive affair than older understandings of scientific method would admit.[6] It is not even true that scientific orthodoxy once arrived at is so freely open to change. Margaret Masterman's analysis of the way in which such orthodoxies come into being draws analogies from the emergence of religious themes or ikons.[7] In this sense there could be analogies to be drawn, both from Robin Horton's models and from Godfrey Lienhardt's images.[8] Out of the fading and breaking down of such a model or pattern of images, a creative consciousness in any given society, troubled by a quest for clarification and integration, grappling deeply with reality, can be overwhelmed as if from beyond itself by the sudden awareness of a new form, re-creating the whole field of experience on which it has been brooding. This reintegration, given in a moment of insight or ecstasy, can be abortive, or can, like the key structure in some new evolutionary phase, be the seed of a new pattern—not just a new theory, but at that primary stage at least a new 'theoria', as Eastern mystical theology termed it, a new vision.

A parallel process can take place in one's re-conceiving of one's identity and one's relationship. This is implicit in the approach to

[6] Cf. M. Polanyi, *Personal Knowledge*, London, 1958; P. B. Medawar, *The Art of the Soluble*, London, 1967.

[7] M. Masterman in *Theoria to Theory*, Vol. I, October 1966-July 1967, Cambridge.

[8] R. G. Lienhardt, *Divinity and Experience*, Oxford, 1961.

'madness' of the so-called 'antipsychiatry' movement.[9] Here states akin to disassociation or possession can offer a period of intense personal redefinition, out of the midst of which a new configuration, a new whole, a new centre and new boundaries can be disclosed.

Spirit possession is pre-eminently a liminal experience in Van Gennep's and Victor Turner's sense. (See below, pp. 540-1) Harriet Sibisi has described the possession experiences of a potential medium in Zulu society driven like many another before her into the wilderness by her spirit, into the void which is the prelude to new definitive action in a new role.[10] There is a sense of the dissolving and reconstituting of the essential structure of a personality or a society in so many varying accounts of possession experience: 'Take me, Break me, melt me, fill me . . .!'

'Public' and 'Private' Possession Cults

Robin Horton first made clear a distinction, developed by many others since, between what have been called public and private possession cults. Isoko society had this variation. It would seem that the redefinition process had a different outcome in the two settings. In the first formal, official and central possession was essentially a regular seasonal climax in which weakened cosmic, social or environmental boundaries, rubbed away somewhat by time and circumstance were re-drawn and confirmed. Here the melting was essentially a refining and clarifying of the existing grid. Hence the precise re-enactment of tradition. If there was any development to fit new situations it was unconscious and unintentional. In theory at least, traditional concepts and relationships were firmly rearticulated in the white heat of the possession experience. The Spirits quickened the central institution.

In the second, the whole *milieu* was different. Women, younger or more obscure men, or perhaps a disintegrated town group constituted spheres in which there was a search for a new focal centre and new boundaries, a quest for new lines of demarcation, which could, especially when handed down, assume their own imitative shadow forms. Food abstentions and other observances were a means of identification. But there was also scope for creative innovation. Each new private possession cult had in it the possible seeds of a new revelation to the whole society. In this liminal situation, norms might be suspended for a quite dramatic letting off of steam, a melting down of received rules and

---

[9] E.g. R. D. Laing and T. Esterson, *Sanity, Madness and the Family*, London, 1961; M. Barnes and J. Berke, *Two accounts of a journey through madness*, London, 1971; M. Barnett, *People not psychiatry*, London, 1973.

[10] H. Ngubane (H. Sibisi), *Body and Mind in Zulu Medicine*, London, 1977.

categories. Moreover, just as every new model, every new image or idea aspires to its centre and tends towards the greatest possible control over the material to which it relates, so each new spirit as it grasped its adherent might seek to some extent at least to offer a new centre and new boundaries as comprehensive as possible.

In normal times, the strength of the public corporate central framework severely restricted the extent to which most 'private' Spirits could approach the centre. Just occasionally, as with Eni, a Spirit of sufficient capacity for social reorganization, of sufficient utilitarian and explanatory power, might advance the centre and become coterminous with the central pattern, redefining the very nature of the community, e.g. in the settlement at Uzere. It is in the more marginal, less centrally involved sectors of society that new experience can be accepted and new social possibilities proferred. Thus amongst the Kalabari 'the heroes and other big spirits' were possibly 'originally introduced to the community as minor or water spirits on the heads' of Spirit possessed women mediums, so that 'they stayed incubating on the sidelines until, at some time of social upheaval and change requiring new interpretative concepts, they came out to make grander claims for themselves'. Thus the Kalabari may have provided themselves with 'new spirits to meet new challenges to their way of life'.[11] It is amongst the group who are seeking social and personal redefinition that cosmic and environmental redefinition will come most easily. They after all have least to lose and are freer to feel around them. Similarly amongst the Tonga,[12] the Masabe, private and individual Spirits, can, like Mangelo, aspire to such proportions that they may actually impinge on the public and communal basanqu ritual and begin to develop into community spirits. Similarly amongst the Lugbara, Adro, the spirit of the wild, presses through a variety of prophets his drive towards 'an attempt to re-form the basic principles of social organization'.[13] Perennially it has been the role of such cults and of their adherents to be a means of innovation and of response to historical change. In some societies it is not clear whether they were even present save at times of radical modification. Were there always Masabe among the Tonga, Amandike among the Zulu, Mbandwa among the Nyoro? Or, is the presence of such spirits among the Isoko and the Kalabari, or JokReba among the Alur a sign of a different kind of society?

[11] Horton, 'Types of spirit possession'.

[12] E. Colson, 'Spirit possession among the Tonga of Zambia', in Beattie and Middleton.

[13] J. Middleton, 'Spirit possession among the Lugbara', in Beattie and Middleton.

Liminal Periods

But the moment for those waiting on the sidelines for the 'idea whose hour has come' arises when, as in Isoko in the 1880s and just after, central institutions are discredited and their focal point in doubt, their boundaries broken down, and the nature of the whole society and of its universe is suddenly in question. Given a vacuum at the public centre the opening is there for any of a number of newly disclosed powers from the private sector to fill the gap. Even while the centre still appeared strong, the sensitive spiritual seismograph had registered the shock and the more perceptive and farsighted were feeling for new possibilities. Hence Robin Horton's report that in the 1890s when the principal New Calabar town 'hero spirit' was calling for the death of Christians and the end of their religion, 'the spirit of one of the best known (woman mediums) was telling people they should all join the Church since the spirits were weak and their day was over', an intuition at the periphery running counter to the centre.[14] Amongst the Yoruba in Efon, Alaye the medium of a forest spirit was likewise the first to proclaim the death of the old religion and the birth of the new. It is not clear how far the Aladura movement was preceded by new Orisa-style cults of a similar kind. In the Akan area there was apparently a sequence of new Spirit possession cults parallel to those in Isoko. From 1855 such cults were offering healing and witchcraft cleansing: in 1889 Dodowa a tobacco concoction cult; in 1905 Bakwe commanding all to join its ranks and 'love one another'.[15] Then, analogous to Ugo, there was the Mando cult in vigorous but apparently unsuccessful conflict with William Wade Harris, product of a Christian possession experience, like the pioneers in Isoko. Subsequently, like Igbe and the other Isoko movements in the church, we have in Ghana and the Ivory Coast the Spirit churches founded by 'apostles' of Harris who sought their power from him and a new kind of Mando in the form of Tigari still active to this day. In the Congo, there is the whole Ngunzist sequence, with its precedents in the seventeenth and eighteenth centuries, from Kimbangu to Matswa Andre, the Khaki movement and others outside Christianity but with Christian borrowings.

And there are all the Central and East African sequences of witch finding and healing movements placed in a succession by the careful work of historians like Terence Ranger and his school (see below, pp. 490-8). Always there is the same sense of a quest for redefinition and new demarcation satisfied by membership of the cult, the identification with all that is within and the repudiation of those without. The cleansing ritual again and again is a ritual of inclusion and exclusion. There is an

---

[14] Horton, 'Types of spirit possession'.

[15] H. W. Debrunner, *Witchcraft in Ghana*, Kumasi, 1959.

expulsion of evil from the body individual and corporate. Evil itself consists in the breakdown of boundaries under the weight of alien intrusion. 'The evilness consists not so much in the Spirit itself, but in the confusing of categories. Evil Spirit is Spirit out of place'.[16] New cults provide new categories and new definitions of good and evil Spirit as well as friend and alien. Through the dance and the trance, a new centre and new boundaries struggle to be born. Indeed as the whole culture passes through the liminal crisis of death and re-birth, the bounds of each cult reach out in an attempt to comprehend the whole community and its total experience offering a new centre and new boundaries potentially coterminous with a renewed society. Such a glimpse of reintegration was, presumably, the lost Bible which the Isoko Christians are still looking for.

Inclusion or Exclusion

But of course it is the necessity for the cult to exclude so much that constitutes the problem. The redefinition is too drastic for an increasingly complex and pluriform social situation. The more modern spirit possession cults have tended towards the exclusion of all who are not with them. The new 'dances' in Isoko, before Ugo, tended to repudiate other obligations, e.g. to ancestors or town founders, if not with the obsessiveness of Bakwe in Ghana or Mɐngelo among the Tonga or many of the witch-finding cults in Central Africa, e.g. that described by Audrey Richards in which, as at the Temple of Igbe in Isoko, all former sacred objects of whatever character, from the most trivial charm to the emblems of one's guardian Spirit or one's ancestors, were lumped together as evil and burned.[17] Ugo, it is true, was brought in to help press the displaced divinities back on to their thrones, but one suspects that it was at a price. It was a neo-traditionalist reaction at best.

Essentially there seem to be very varied modes of redefinition at work in Spirit possession cults. When the new 'form' emerges, it may repudiate all innovation and seek to redraw the old boundaries, like Ugo, or Watuwa Mungu among the Kikuyu in the 1930s, offering at best a symbolic modernity.[18] Harriet Sibisi suggests that the new Zulu possession cults were a series of efforts to withstand and repel the intrusion of novelty in the shape of first, in Ndiki, the new migrant

[16] H. Ngubane (H. Sibisi), op. cit.

[17] A. I. Richards, 'A modern movement of witchfinders', *Africa*, VIII, 1935, 448-61.

[18] J. M. Lonsdale, 'A Political History of Nyanza, 1883-1945', University of Cambridge, PhD thesis, 1965.

peoples from the North, second in Ufufunyaree of a desperate host of multi-racial invading Spirits, distorting traditional Zulu life and needing to be cleansed out.

Again it may repudiate all traditional Spirits and all other new patterns of life drawing a line round all those outside the new worship. The rituals and moral code of many of the new Christian movements seem designed to this end. The prophet, like the more rigid missionaries, treats all other would be divinities as demonic. He burns sacred objects and destroys the past with the same conviction that all is to be replaced, as when Nonqause urged the Xhosa to destroy their farms and their cattle. This was the attitude of the great majority of these new Spirit possession cults to all alternatives. It was the attitude of Garrick Braide, the new Elijah of Horton's Kalabari of 1914-15, of William Wade Harris and of all the Isoko apostles. As in Milton's Ode to the Nativity, the Spirits flee from their groves and shrines before the oncoming tread of the new power. Satan recruits to himself all the preceding divinities in the area.

The cult may have to fall back into a reluctant acceptance of plurality, as presumably occurred among the rival Spirit cults of Voodoo in Haiti (originally themselves Vodun, the private Spirits belong to a wider system) or their like in Brazil. In the midst of such plurality, as among the Tonga Masabe or the Nyoro Mbandwa, doubtless certain cults are waiting on the sidelines for the moment at which they can make their bid for the centre.

All this seems to me much nearer the real spiritual picture than Horton's speculation.[19] There he suggests that the High God of tradition has now come into his own as the power related to the wider world. But it looks rather as if we still see in many present day societies in Africa and elsewhere, a vacuum at the centre and a jostle of spirit cults around the periphery, one of which from time to time may make a bid for domination in the sudden offer of a new 'theoria', a new 'rough beast slouching off towards Bethlehem to be born'. Since every culture abhors that kind of vacuum at the centre, the constant sequence of efforts at inspired redefinition are bound to be continue.

Far from the identification of spirit cults and universal God having been arrived at, with or without the assistance of Islam or Christianity, I do not believe that it has yet, truly, at the spiritual and imaginative springs of our being, ever been made. For the Isoko, as for other societies in Africa, the emergence of a Christian 'possession cult', like Egode, Aladura, or Kimbanguism, seemed at first uniquely fitted to achieve this identification, to occupy the centre and reintegrate the culture. Such a cult offered new access to Divine Power, a new way of

[19] Horton, 'African Conversion'.

living and relating to others and a new future surpassing all that local cults could offer. Its songs alone made this plain, let alone the quality of its corporate life. What was more it not only sprang spontaneously from local roots, it was also 'an *oyinbo* (European) thing'. It had the seeming capacity to initiate its members into a new world-wide community, to intepret the forces at work in the life of a new society and to draw new universal boundaries. In the event, however, it was never really both intensive and inclusive enough. It never succeeded adequately in bringing its private religious resources to bear on the public world, the political and economic world. Robin Horton's account of an appropriate modern faith suggests a separation of communion, still in his view the role of religion, from prediction control, now the role of natural science. This is not a separation which any genuinely Christian vision of life can afford to make. Yet it is a fair criticism of much modern Christian spirituality. Even less than the romantic movement or the successive waves of Utopian revolution counter-culture and the like, have any Christian movements of renewal or revival yet succeeded in both interpreting and/or inspiring a society which is technological, complex and pluriform.

Can any such movement offer a convincing patterning of the whole of life? Can it provide the incentive for the constant reshaping of a continuously modifying and varying society? Can it convey such a sense of possession by a transcendent, universal, personal, ultimately mysterious love, breaking through from beyond ourselves, as to win overwhelming assent? Even to make the transformation of our world seem a final possibility? That would be the kind of redefinition of man for which not only the Isoko are still searching.

Spirits and 'spiritual direction': the pastoral counselling of the possessed

MICHAEL SINGLETON

The modern historian can write about European witchcraft crazes with a degree of detachment which the contemporary anthropologist, participating observantly in a sorcery scare, can rarely emulate. No matter how eloquently the former expresses his indignation at the clerical obscurantism which, in collusion with popular incredulity, sent thousands of innocent old women to a fiery end, he will still be raking over coals long spent in his own culture. The latter, on the other hand, *experientia propria constat*, is likely to have his own fingers burnt when the smouldering fires of suspicion flare up into accusations of witchcraft amongst the people whose social drama he is sharing. At the very least, he can no more remain indifferent to the visibly inhibiting effects of his people's idioms and images than he can fail to be moved by the manifest economic and political injustices done to them by individuals or institutions. This is perhaps especially true of the ethnologist who is also an ecclesiastic.

The apostolic anthropologist's position is as difficult as it is delicate. Mistaken by his fellow missionaries for an anthropologist, his parishioners take him to be an apostle. He himself fondly imagines that the latter are not far wrong, for the insinuation which hurts him most is that his apostolic activities are a mere front to accumulate field material for his academic pursuits. It is consequently intended that this contribution be read as an illustration of how apostolic and anthropological aims can converge harmoniously into a helpful pastoral strategy. At present the colonial administrator is accused of having applied anthropology so as to alienate the people from their best and long-term interests. There are those who fear that ecclesiastics now abuse ethnology so as to enslave the people to a particular church. May this essay also illustrate that, on the contrary, pastoral anthropology enables people to make their own that measure of Christian freedom in keeping with their capacities.

The Wakonongo, a branch of the Nyamwezi, in West Central Tanzania, to whom I ministered for three years, were bedevilled by *majini* spirits. As a Catholic priest amongst an almost totally Catholic population, I could not simply be content to analyse spirit possession from the socio-economic and historico-cultural angles. The people would not have understood, even less appreciated, my standing aloof from an issue which affected the community's life so intensely. This is not the place to discuss the sociological setting of the phenomenon—largely the local equivalent of Women's Liberation—nor to detail the cultural context—Islamic idiom superimposed on a traditional spirit cult. I prefer to outline here, how, after what seemed to me a sufficiently prudent and protracted investigation of the phenomenon, I came to involve the spirits in the psychotherapy of the possessed. Perhaps the most convenient and convincing way of explaining the procedure is to present a case study.

In the summer of 1972, N.,—let us call her Anna—the grand-daughter of the old headman with whom I was staying, turned up unexpectedly from her father's place some 200 miles away. She was pleasant and friendly, a smiling, uninhibited extrovert. A fulsome frame belied her early teens, betrayed, at times, however, by a girlish giddiness and candid coquetry. Her industriousness and readiness to help won her elders' approval. Her gaiety and good humour endeared her to her companions. I, for one, assumed Anna to be in the best of spirits.

All was not well however. It soon transpired that Anna had fallen out with her father. He had matched her to a cattle-rich neighbour and the marriage beer was already brewing before she had plucked up sufficient courage to decline her intended husband. Understandably, neither he nor her father were particularly pleased. Anna, however, held out against their exasperated entreaties and declared her intention of going to seek some respite at her grandfather's.

She seemed at first to have put behind her the worst of this distressing experience. During the day she worked whole-heartedly with us in the fields and in the evenings joined light-heartedly in the talk around the womens' fires. But her buoyant spirits did not last. A couple of days after her arrival, while bathing behind the hut prior to retiring for the night, she was heard sobbing. Worried, the womenfolk went to investigate and found Anna lying in a coma-like trance, quite incapable of coherent speech. No one doubted what had happened. She showed all the signs of having been possessed by a spirit. Wrapped in a blanket and still heaving heavily, she was ferried on the back of a bicycle to Wakamando's, the woman heading the *majini* cult guild. By chance, I happened to be there, having spent the evening at Wakamando's compound, assisting at the expulsion of a spirit and recording *majini* songs. The session was over and we were about to disperse when Anna was brought to us. Still lost to the world, she was seated on a special stool, neither recognizing me nor replying to my greetings. (To be exact I surreptitiously pinched her bottom to make sure she was not having us on but got no reaction!)

Preparations went ahead for treating the victim with the same no nonsense matter-of-factness which characterizes our casualty wards. A pot of herbal remedies was boiled to steaming point and placed between her feet. A blanket was pulled over her head and down to the ground. Anna rocked to and fro, inhaling the fumes from the pot, puffing occasionally on a hemp-stuffed pipe. Two young men began rhythmically to shake rattles close to her ears, while the dozen or so women present took up the repetitive *majini* songs, calling on the spirits to put in an appearance and be appeased.

Wakamando, who had been busy selling paraffin to a late-night customer in her husband's shop, came forth, put out her cigarette, seated herself on a block of wood facing Anna and summoned the spirits to declare their identity and intentions. When it became apparent after some minutes that a spirit was about to speak, the singing was stopped. The exorcist enquired after its name, provenance and purpose. The first spirit was followed shortly by another. In hysterically high-pitched tones they stated that they had been sent by Anna's father and fiancé to make her pay for infuriating the one and slighting the other. This seemed too much for Wakamando or rather for her own spirit, for he took possession of her and scathingly apostrophied Anna's spirits saying: 'You are not genuine spirits! Why do you torment this poor creature? She has done nothing deserving of capital punishment! What can we do for you? How long are you going to stay with your victim?'

Cowed by this imperious onslaught, Anna's spirits wiltingly acknowledged that Wakamando's spirit had a point and agreed to reconsider the terms of their mission. They would be content to trouble her for a while but, as she was obviously not entirely to blame, would stop short of killing her. (The spirits' initial intentions are usually lethal and part of the exorcist's art consists in negotiating a pardon.) They would eventually return from whence they had been sent. Meanwhile, however, deferential and preferential treatment in the shape of certain foodstuffs and ritual observances would be necessary. They then took their leave of us for that evening. Anna came to her senses and was restored to her attendant relatives, subdued but not shattered. She walked quietly home with us and slept soundly till the morrow.*

Even an amateur student of human behaviour would be able to transpose these rather exotic events and esoteric expressions into a more

---

* I have simply given the gist of a long and complex ceremony, dispensing with details of ethnographic interest, accentuating those of sociological relevance.

straightforward psycho-sociological key. In effecting such a transposition I do not want to imply that the people had no clue as to what fundamentally was at stake in spirit possession. Many a modern expert gives the impression that the people do not really know what they are talking about. You might keep dreaming of crawling into caves, the psychoanalyst knows you want to get back to the womb. Traditional theologians have told me that my psycho-sociological reading of possession is reductionist. The accusation would stick better if it could be proved that the people believed in spirits in the same hypostatic, substantialist fashion as the theologians themselves. My honest impression is that the theologians are saying far more than the people ever intended to say. My sincere conviction is that by making sense of Anna's case in the language of my own culture I was saying no more nor no less than what the Wakonongo were saying in the language of their culture.

Anna is but one of many young girls in modern Tanzania confusedly caught between two moral codes, the old and the new—which is not to say, absolutely, the good and the bad. On the one hand, the whole weight of ancestral tradition is behind her father. In rural Africa one does not lightly oppose parental authority. Anna, moreover, had not only failed in filial piety but had also seriously jeopardized her chances on the marriage market. African males—as two personal enquiries have proved—want respectful and submissive wives. Women known to be headstrong and self-willed are avoided like the pest. On the other hand, first the Church and then the Party have preached the equality of men . . . and women. Through schooling, religious instructions and the mass media, young women have been made aware of alternative forms to customary marriage. Girls know that in theory their destiny is theirs, that they and they alone should decide with whom to spend their lives.

The new code, however, has not yet crystallized into a 'collective representation', the ideal of individual freedom is still not incarnate in social structures. Consequently, no small degree of maturity and sophistication together with a large dose of courage and conviction are needed to stand out for one's future rights against prevailing patterns. Still young and unsure of herself, Anna's plucky stand was weakened by secret misgivings as well as the risk of serious consequences. The momentousness of what she had done finally caught up with her and she caved in. However, while her mind could no longer stand the weight and worry of her thoughts, deep down in her heart she felt not entirely to blame.

It was not only Anna's own spirits who expressed all this but also those of the exorcist herself. They could not deny that Anna had in a sense sinned. Her father and her fiancé had a case. But it was not so strong as to render her specious. Though the spirits would reluctantly have to make the point for which they had been bought and sent, they would not now execute their mandate to the full.

In plain, psychotherapeutical English: a personal problem of this magnitude cannot be solved in one summary session but must be thrashed out thoroughly until such time as the patient comes to terms with her predicament. In more esoteric, psychoanalytical English: Anna's spirits were speaking on behalf of elements buried in her subconsciousness, if not in the Freudian 'id' then at least there where the fresh seeds planted by the Church and the Party were struggling to find a way through the top soil of tradition. Wakamando's spirit echoed Anna's but also went on to put them in their place and, more importantly, before representatives of the local community. The exorcist's advice, or rather her spirit's, was basically sound: while the victim might have done wrong she certainly did not deserve the degree of punishment contemplated by those wronged and should eventually be left in peace. Which is the same as saying: while it is true that children cannot question parental authority with impunity but must pay the price, physically and psychologically for doing so, times are changing and the younger generation should be allowed a greater say in its future, especially in so important an issue as marriage.

Having come to know Anna intimately—within the limits allowed by my celibate state of course—I was as pained by her troubles as the rest of her relatives. She was more than merely another intriguing case of spirit possession, worth a page or two in my field-notes. She needed help as much if not more than the kids who came daily to have their tropical ulcers cleansed. But what could I do? A simple enough question to ask but a complicated one to answer. Should I as an anthropologist do anything? Should I not let nature take its course? As an apostle what would the Roman Church allow me to do in any case? The church does not like her missionary priests meddling with medicine let alone psychology and, as those who have seen *The Exorcist* will realize, permission for a regular exorcism is not readily given. What would the parishioners, even supposing they were unanimous in their interpretation of possession, expect me to do? To be honest, these are questions I ask myself now long after doing what I did. When the soul needs first aid as urgently as the body one does not stop to theorize.[1] Nevertheless, before

---

[1] This was not the first time we had been obliged to improvise, cf. 'The public confession of an extempore exorcist', *African Ecclesiastical Review*, 5, 1975, 1-6.

accounting for what in practice I did, it is not without interest to examine what in theory I could have done.

First I could, as many an expatriate is tempted to do, declare myself unable to judge about, even less interfere in, native affairs. This diffidence can be doubly motivated. On the one hand there is the missionary whose respect for local culture is coupled with a sinking suspicion that there are elements therein which are mysteriously impermeable to the outsider's understanding. Thus does many an article in the popular missionary magazine conclude with a question mark: perhaps witches do exist after all, perhaps the Devil is still operative in the Dark Continent? On the other hand, is the missionary who feels that phenomena such as witchcraft or spirit possession constitute so much superstitious nonsense, more or less deliberately perpetrated by mercenary-minded practitioners. Have they not been marginalized out of existence in civilized countries? Such a man either keeps his opinions politely to himself or publicly ridicules the people's in the hope that they will come to their senses and realize that they are gullible victims of figments invented by their own too fertile imaginations. If the first type of missionary often mystifies what is straightforwardly meaningful—witchcraft does exist but as the expression of stress—the second usually fails to do full justice to the seemingly bizarre—spirit voices are no more peculiar than the voice of conscience. The first attitude overshoots the mark, the second falls short of it. Evil spirits exist in Africa but as expressive of social evils larger than the individual man and not as the embodiment or equivalent of the Schoolmen's Devil. Some of the spirits' features might be figments of the imagination but they are also factors of fissures in the social fabric.

Secondly I could, as African priests I knew tended to do, consider the whole affair as endangering faith and morals because of diabolic origin. Either I could believe that those participating in the spirit possession cult were more or less deliberately dabbling in devil worship—in which case I could have nothing to do with them but seek rather to prevent others from falling into Satan's snares—or I could take pity on the people and proceed to exorcize them as victims of diabolical possession—but obviously in the context of an authorized Christian ceremony and not that of the pagan cult itself. The unimpeachable simplicity of both approaches stems from the same fideistic fundamentalism. The people as well as the Bible are taken literally at their word. There are spiritual beings not only because Christ assumed there were but because the people say there are. Spirits are for real. So far so good—but can a contemporary Christian not go a little further and locate this spiritual reality within the horizons of credibility set up by the human sciences rather than within the increasingly implausible philosophical perspectives which posited the existence of incorporeal intelligences? As the recent Roman document on the Devil demonstrated, faced with the increasingly incredible likelihood of spirits ever having existed in their own right, ecclesiastical authorities fall back on a 'take it or leave it' fideism: whether you like it or not, the existence of angels has been revealed.

The thorough-going fundamentalism of the extreme evangelicals which admits of no exceptions is more convincingly consequential than the mitigated fideism of the main line Christians. For the former, all Christ's miracles really happened, from the truly sublime such as the raising of Lazarus or the feeding of the 5000, to the somewhat ridiculous like his cursing the fig tree or conjuring a coin from the fish's mouth. Consequently, if spirits exist exactly as the Africans say they do, there is no reason not to accept that some Africans can metamorphose themselves into lions, since this fact is asserted with as much conviction as the former. Once, however, it is conceded that some miracles are perhaps symbolic inventions and that some items of native belief can be equated with psycho-sociological phenomena, then the theologian and the human scientist can strike out together in search for the criteria of ultimate credibility.

In between dismissing spirits as pure figments of the imagination and believing in them as independently existent, ethereal beings, there is a middle road other than that of heretical hypocrisy. One can act as if the spirits were real not merely to humour the fantasies of sick minds but because in a psycho-sociological sense they are real. The idiom of spirit possession can be interpreted downwards towards situations of stress and the like, rather than upwards into the realms of philosophy, theology or the concording of revelation with other religions. The credibility of this hermeneutical exercise depends more on practical than theoretical considerations. As Occam said: Don't multiply where you can subtract. I had six years of philosophy and four of theology behind me when I arrived in Ukonongo but I found my three years of sociology more than sufficient to make satisfactory sense of spirit possession there. To those who imply that I make mere symbols of the spirits I would reply the 'mere' is too much: the spirits are symbols, period,—symbols with lives of their own, but symbols all the same.

Thirdly and finally I could have done what in fact I did do. The following morning I called casually on Anna and asked her how she felt. She was much better but could remember little of the previous night's proceedings. Consequently, I went over the whole seance with her, repeating exactly what the spirits had severally said. I added that I approved of the way Wakamando's spirit had roundly and soundly dealt with her own. She should not, I suggested, be unduly afraid for the future nor over-remorseful about the past. After all, had not her spirits agreed, under pressure, that she was almost without fault. Had they not decided to only half execute their mandate and, provided they were not spurned or neglected, to stay but for a while?

Anna and the other members of her family present listened attentively to a tape-recording of the session, nodding their heads in approval of the manner in which Wakamando's spirit had handled the situation masterfully. The spirits had spoken leaving no further room for doubt as to the source of Anna's woes. But more importantly still, they had been spoken to in no uncertain terms. The situation was under control, under the community's control, the outcome promised to prove a happy one.

Had I been in Europe I would have been tempted to solve the problem differently. In the privacy of some presbytery parlour or in the even more secretive setting of the confessional, I would have sought to reassure a girl in Anna's predicament that, though she should perhaps have been a little more tactful towards her father and fiancé, she should not be too apprehensive about her future. If I was a good spiritual director, I would be able to draw such common sense advice from out of my *dirigée*'s own hesitant convictions. It was indeed thus that I at first tried to help the possessed face up to their personal problems. The Africans would listen respectfully up to my reasonable counsels but leave me less than reassured. My advice was sound enough but despite my priestly prestige was not persuasive enough by half.

Then it dawned upon me that my counsels, which corresponded to the possesseds' own persuasions, would gain in credence if they echoed those of the spirits themselves. I felt that by explicitly introducing the spirits into the context of spiritual direction the chances of obtaining satisfactory results would be greatly increased. Whenever the occasion arose I would attend a spirit session and reinforce its efficacy by relaying the proceedings to those most concerned. I not unnaturally found that the spirits were able to persuade the possessed as to the nature of his or her problem and the steps needed to remedy it, far more than I could ever have hoped to left to my own devices. Client-centred therapists[2] would not have been surprised to discover that the spirits showed themselves to be better spiritual directors than myself!

---

[2] At the time I had no more heard of Carl Rogers than had Wakamando. It was native intuition that she, and by congenital indolence that I, consistently chose to act 'upon the hypothesis that the individual has a sufficient capacity to deal constructively with all the aspects of his life which can potentially come into conscious awareness.' Hence it was spontaneously that she, and deliberately that I, saw it as our function to assume, in so far as we were able, 'the internal frame of reference of the client, to perceive the world as the client sees it, to perceive the client himself as he is seen by himself, to lay aside all perceptions from the external frame of reference while doing so, and to communicate something of this empathetic understanding to the client.' C. R. Rogers, *Client-centred therapy*, Boston, 1951, p. 24 and 29.

The churches, the nationalist state and African religion

TERENCE RANGER

Since the attainment of independence in most of black Africa the churches have faced two crucial questions. What should be their relationship to the new ruling regimes? And what should be their relationship to the spiritual traditions of Africa? These questions have been answered on the assumption that the churches, the rulers of the new nation states, and the leaders and followers of African religions have quite distinct and separate identities. And at various times and places they have been answered in terms of all three of the possible permutations.

The churches have sometimes feared a hostile alliance against them of the other two parties, the nationalist state and a revived traditional religion combining to take their revenge on past missionary arrogance. Alternatively, the churches have sometimes discerned the opportunity to ally themselves with the modernizing nation state so as to sweep away the remaining survivals of traditionalism. Finally, some people within the churches have argued that they should stand aside from secular modernizing development and concentrate upon meeting the spiritual needs of the mass of Africans. In order to do this, it is argued, the churches need to respect, or more often to co-opt and transcend, the forms and assumptions of traditional religion.

Nationalism and traditional religion against the churches.
The first of these permutations—an anti-church alliance of nationalists and believers in traditional religion—once appeared a likely enough possibility. Nationalist intellectuals savagely criticized the denaturing effect of missionary teaching and glorified what they took to be the spiritual assumptions of the past. In some of the crucial moments of the independence struggle church members believed themselves to be in very real danger from the attacks of nationalist militants who had turned for inspiration towards African religion, or what were regarded by churchmen as debased versions of it.

This was alleged to be the case during the Mau Mau emergency in

Kenya. More recently many people have detected the same sort of situation in Southern Rhodesia. An African Anglican priest has written about what he calls a revived 'heathenism' in the eastern districts of Rhodesia; about the destruction of churches in the African rural areas during the in-fighting between the rival nationalist parties; and about the return of those who are hostile to the church to ideas of spirit possession.[1] His analysis has been confirmed by an anthropologist who quotes nationalist songs glorifying the spiritual leaders of pre-colonial Zimbabwe and who writes: 'Spirit mediums are effective as a focus for nationalist sentiment because they bring the past to the present . . . and are unequivocally opposed structurally to Christianity'.[2] As mass nationalism has developed into a guerilla war many observers have asserted the same interplay. The guerillas 'have frequently sought the help of mediums urging them to approve of their cause and asking for blessing for their presence in the area and for spiritual protection'; the guerillas are said to have named their campaign zones after senior spirits; spirit mediums are said to have based themselves in guerilla base camps and to have broadcast messages of support for the guerillas over Zambian radio; Basil Davidson has remarked that loyalty oaths taken by guerillas in the names of the great spirits Chamenuka and Nehanda reveal 'a truly impressive' continuity with the pre-Christian past.[3] At least one African Christian minister has been executed by guerillas for suspected collaboration with the white security forces[4]

Yet in the result of the nationalist victory in Kenya, this threatening combination turned out to have very little substance. The Kikuyu who run the new nation are very much the product of Christian education and share most of its assumptions—a Kenyan government spokesman told coastal women who were protesting against the arrest of a leading witchcraft eradicator that they would do better to become Christians and learn how to develop.[5] It is true that in Kenya the Mau Mau fighters were defeated and independence was handed over by the British to the mission-educated élite. But other ruling nationalist élites of a rather different background turn out to share a common lack of sympathy for

[1] Reverend S. Madziyere, 'Heathen practices in the urban and rural parts of Marendellas area', Themes in the Christian History of Central Africa, eds. T. O. Ranger and John Weller, London, 1975, pp. 76-82.

[2] Peter Fry, Spirits of Protest, Spirit-Mediums and the Articulation of Consensus Amongst the Zezuru of Southern Rhodesia, Cambridge, 1976, p. 120.

[3] Basil Davidson, The Africans. An entry to Cultural History, London, 1969, p. 255; Martin Meredith, 'Raising the sacred spirits of war', The Sunday Times, 23 January 1977.

[4] Kees Maxey, The Fight for Zimbabwe, London, 1975, pp. 118-9, 135.

[5] Cynthia Brantley, 'The Giriama and witchcraft', forthcoming in The Problem of Evil in Eastern Africa, eds. T. O. Ranger and Sholto Cross.

traditional religion.

In Zaïre, for example, President Mobutu has announced a Return to Authenticity which sounds at first hearing like a real attempt to implement a nationalist alliance with traditional religion. Mobutu lays stress on 'African authenticity in a national rather than an ethnic context'; he 'seeks to awaken Zaïrean people to their origins and ancestral values'. But Zaïrean traditional belief displayed 'bewildering diversity'. 'Recognising this, for Zaïrean authenticity to be nationally rather than ethnically orientated, it has stressed the common negritude of a Supreme Being as a major source of inspiration'. Yet since 'the localized traditional concepts of God are very limited', the common negritude of the Supreme Being is in fact expressed through the three great church confederations recognised by the Mobutu regime, the Catholic, Protestant and Kimbanguist churches. Mobutuism does not really draw upon traditional insights. Its philosophical support comes rather from African Christian theologians who have produced generalized models of 'African religion' and then adapted the confessional statements of their churches to express a national authenticity.[6]

Mobutuism can derive this sort of conceptual support from the Christian churches and not from traditional religion. Its view of the other functions of religious associations also favours the great church organizations. Churches 'are required to prove their contribution to economic development . . . to fulfil conditions that include possession of a bank account worth $200,000, a clergy with a four year diploma in theology . . . and a plan and budget for educational programmes'.[7] Mobutuism 'challenges any form of absolutism that would seek to impose ethnic norms simply because they had worked in their original environment'. In so doing it turns its face against the spokesmen of traditional religion and against the prophets of the African independent churches. 'Now that we are free', says the prophet Mabwaaka Mpaka Gabriel, 'the government has forgotten us, forgotten that they owe their power to the prophets. So we say, "Very well, do it your way, see what a mess you get into". Which is why the Congo is the way it is'.[8]

Another variant of this pattern can be seen in the very different nationalist movements of ex-Portuguese Africa. These movements have

[6] J. R. Howell, 'The Theological Development of the Church of Christ in Zaïre in its ethnographical setting', MA thesis, School of Oriental and African Studies, London, 1976.

[7] Bennetta Jules-Rosette, 'Ritual Contexts and Social Action: A study of the Apostles of John Marangue', doctoral dissertation, University of California, San Diego, 1974.

[8] Mabwaaka Mpaka, 'A Prophet dictates his Autobiography', in John Janzen and Wyatt MacGaffey, eds., An Anthology of Kongo Religion, Lawrence, Kansas, 1974, pp. 53, 55.

their own heritage of negritude poetry. 'As a young brother of an old land', wrote Marcelino dos Santos, 'let us go, lifting in broad hands our father's heritage, and with the leaves of the heart carry on man's work, the great design of life'.[9] When Cabral spoke of a reconquest of history, it sounded once again as though he was talking about a return to the values of tradition.

But he was not. The liberation movements of Guinea and Angola and Mozambique have lived and fought among the people of the rural areas. They have had to try to understand the beliefs and attitudes of these people. Cabral himself called for an attitude of respect. 'Another aspect which we consider very important', he said, 'is the religious beliefs of our people. We avoid all hostility towards these religions, toward the type of relationships our people still have with nature because of their economic underdevelopment . . . We are proud of not having forbidden our people to use fetishes, amulets and things of this sort. It would have been absurd, and completely wrong, to have forbidden these. We let our people find out for themselves, through the struggle, that their fetishes are of no use.'[10] The beliefs of the people, then, are not to be arrogantly swept aside. *But* the beliefs of the people offer nothing of use for the future. A great revolution in consciousness is required, which will transform, through the struggle, the beliefs of the people. Rational self-help will replace belief in the action of spirit. When Cabral talks of a re-conquest of history what he means is that Africans must again control the forces of production; and this in turn means a transformation of African thinking, an annihilation of tradition.

Thus when the guerillas in Angola and Mozambique have encountered traditional religion, or independent churches of the Spirit type, they certainly have not attempted to harness them. They have recorded them in a rather puzzled way, and rejoiced at every evidence that the struggle is undercutting traditional modes of thought.

As to traditional beliefs and witchcraft', says Seta Likambuila of MPLA about eastern Angola, 'we have been trying to educate our people about these things and have abolished certain practices. At first certain foolish witchdoctors tried to witch our guerillas or use their magic against the Portuguese . . . but their magic didn't work and we have managed to convince most of the people that it is only through fighting with weapons that we can defeat the Portuguese. Some religious leaders also tried to prophesy military events . . . But their prophecies don't come true and we explain to the people that believing

---

[9] Marcellino dos Santos, 'Here we were born', *When Bullets Begin to Flower*, ed. Margaret Dickinson, Nairobi, 1972, p. 77.

[10] Amilcar Cabral, 'Towards Final Victory', January 1969, in *Revolution in Guinea*, London, 1969, p. 129.

these things can be very dangerous to the liberation struggle.[11]

In the light of all this it seems very probable that the Rhodesian nationalist movement will develop in the same sort of way. Ndabaningi Sithole has called upon the guerillas to dedicate themselves to the memory of the heroes of past resistance, many of whom were leaders of traditional religion, and Bishop Muzorewa invoked the same heroes in his opening address at the Geneva Conference.[12] Both men, however, are Christian ministers and have written eloquently about the contributions which Christianity has made to nationalism.[13] The radical guerilla movement is increasingly influenced by the approaches of FRELIMO. One can easily imagine a Shona spirit medium lamenting in future, in the same words used by Mabwaaka Mpaka Gabriel: 'Now that we are free the government has forgotten us, forgotten that they owe their power to the prophets'.

Alternative strategies for the churches.
In practice, then, the debate within the church has come to concentrate on the other two permutations. Some have argued strongly that the church should take every opportunity to ally itself with governments in the task of modernizing development. There has been a strong emphasis on church unity to match national unity. 'Don't forget', writes the Protestant church leader in Zaïre, Bediako, 'that the Lord expects you to love your country as He Himself when he knew that Jerusalem would be destroyed . . . A Zaïrean Christian must seek above all the good of his country'. 'There must be unity . . . The *ECZ* aims therefore to follow closely the command of Christ as stated in John 17, "Be ye One". Now these words were pronounced just before the arrest and death of Jesus Christ. In Africa words spoken by a parent or chief just before death are considered as his will and testament. Naturally, therefore, the words are obeyed.'[14] 'Excessive denominationalism is absolutely scandalous', writes John Mbiti about Kenya. 'It could well generate confusion and strife among Christians, and in the long run it will not be in the national interests of our country to tolerate and maintain this type of division

[11] *Interviews in Depth. Angola. MPLA. Seta Likambuila*, Richmond, 1974, pp. 24-6.

[12] Sithole's appeal is reproduced in Anthony R. Wilkinson, 'From Rhodesia to Zimbabwe', in *Southern Africa. The New Politics of Revolution*, London, 1976, p. 261; Muzorewa's speech is cited in *Free Zimbabwe*, No. 8, Nov/Dec., 1976, p. 4.

[13] See especially Ndabaningi Sithole, 'The interactions of Christianity and African Political Development', in *Historians in Tropical Africa*, eds. E. T. Stokes and R. Brown, Salisbury, 1962, pp. 351-64.

[14] J. R. Howell, 'The Theological Development of the Church of Christ in Zaïre'.

precisely when we are attempting to create national unity . . . Christianity must not be allowed to become a cloak and cover for divisiveness in the country'.[15]

It has been argued also that the churches have in fact been the true forerunners of the 'revolution in consciousness' which radical nationalists now desire.[16] It has been argued that the churches alone have the men, the equipment, the local knowledge and the good will to be able to offer systematic help with development. And if development or transformed consciousness involves the undercutting of traditional belief systems this cannot be helped.

Others have taken a quite different line. They have argued that the fact that the churches alone exist as a network apart from the agencies of government makes it all the more important that the churches should remain distinct from government. They have urged that however desirable it may be, development will create or intensify anxieties which it is the church's task to remedy. And they have argued that the anxieties of the people in the rural areas will inevitably be expressed within the traditional idioms, so that they can only be met by a church which takes these idioms seriously. These people recommend, therefore, that so far from the church triumphantly over-riding what survives of traditional religion and what has emerged as Christian transformations of tradition in the shape of the Spirit Churches, there must be a real effort to bring into the church the insights and instrumentalities of tradition. The church will then operate not against the nationalist government but away from it; not on the commanding heights of development planning, but in the village at the level of popular anxiety.

An eloquent recent statement of this view is Jacob Loewen's 'Mission Churches, Independent Churches and Felt Needs in Africa'. Loewen illustrates with some striking examples the continuance of anxieties, of witchcraft fears, of endemic disease. He illustrates also the continuing desire for spiritual healing, for cleansing from witchcraft guilt, and for prophetic leadership. The Spirit Churches, he argues, are meeting these needs through their 'intense desire to become authentic'; the mission churches in the rural areas are empty of comfort and all too often empty of people. They offer no answer to witchcraft fear; they have no belief in the possibility of spiritual healing; above all they do not offer prophetic leadership, but only *talk* about prophets, merely meaning people who can expound the existing scriptures and not 'people with relevant messages from God'. By contrast, Loewen urges, the spirit churches heal

---

[15] John Mbiti, 'Diversity, Divisions and Denominationalism', in *Kenya Churches Handbook,* Nairobi, 1974, p. 145.

[16] See as an example, *The Arusha Declaration and Christian Socialism*, Dar es Salaam, 1969.

and cleanse and prophesy. 'The whole African independent church movement is based on the concept of the prophet—men upon whom the Spirit of God comes in a special way and who have thus been empowered to deliver new messages from God . . . The (mission church) pastor learns more and more about God's written word, but few of them will be able to speak with prophetic authority as mouthpieces of God'.[17]

The choice between these two possibilities is not, of course, an entirely free one for the churches. Sometimes they may wish to participate in modernizing development but do not find the nationalist regime prepared to accept their help. This may turn out to be the case in Mozambique, where FRELIMO's educational policy statement accuses church schools of making man 'the subservient recipient of divine will' rather than 'being the agent of change in his society and environment', and declares 'the new revolutionary education in Mozambique' as 'aimed at forming a new Mozambican African personality, a New Man, free from superstitious beliefs, self-reliant and ready to make his scientific knowledge the basis of a new society'.[18] Sometimes, on the other hand, the choice of abandoning structure and attending to felt anxieties at the grassroots is virtually prohibited, as in Zaïre, by a more formal official definition of the church. But, broadly speaking, debate has hitherto moved between the one possibility and the other.

The false assumptions which underlie the debate on alternative strategies
I wish at this point to move this chapter in quite a different direction. I have been discussing the debate on the three permutations between church, nationalist state, and African religion, as though the three permutations had been correctly stated and stand as genuine alternatives. But I believe that the apparently clear cut choices which seem to be posed to the church do not in fact exist. I believe this largely because I think that the propositions depend upon two false assumptions about so-called 'traditional' religion.

One of these false assumptions is the idea of the distinctness of traditional religion from Christianity. The other is the concept of a total incompatibility between traditional religion and development. Each of the three permutations depends on the idea of African religion as archaic. The fear that African religion might combine with nationalism against Christianity is usually expressed in terms of 'atavism', or more politely in terms of 'revival'. The idea that the churches and the national

---

[17] Jacob Loewen, 'Mission Churches, Independent Churches and Felt Needs in Africa', mimeo., Lusaka, 1974.

[18] 'The Match that lights the Flame. Education Policy in the Peoples Republic of Mozambique', *People's Power*, No. 3, July-August 1976, p. 14.

regimes should combine to modernize usually casts African religion in the role of the reactionary influence—as a set of beliefs which confirm age-old habits of thought and work. Even those who urge that the church should seek to cater for the anxieties which have hitherto been met in African religion nearly always make the assumption that the church can take from a decaying tradition what she needs, can activate it and give it the capacity for life and growth.

I wish to argue counter-propositions which put the whole debate about the relationship of the church to nationalist governments and to African religious ideas in a rather different light. I wish to argue first that in most African situations Christianity and African religions are both parts of a single continuum of popular religious belief. I wish to argue secondly that there has been change throughout this continuum and that African religious ideas have responded to the problems of development and change.

Christianity, African religion and popular religion
There is a good deal of disagreement about the present influence of African religious ideas. On the one hand, Dr Sholto Cross, in a paper for the Jos conference, writes that

> the history of the church in Africa stands out in the history of the European expansion into the third world for its success in either bringing earlier religious systems fully within it or effectively wiping them out . . . Most of the rites and beliefs of earlier religions have been superseded.

On the other hand Okot p'Bitek insists that 'it is a fact that the vast majority of Africans today hold the beliefs of their religions. Christianity has barely touched the core of the life of most African peoples'.[19]

Clearly this is an argument which will be determined very differently in different places. There are some peoples, like the Giriama of the Kenya coastal hinterland, upon whom Christianity really has made very little impact, even though missionaries have been active in the area since the nineteenth century.[20] On the other side there are the Bakongo people of Zaïre whom Sholto Cross cites for an illustration 'in depth and detail (of) the process whereby Christianity has come to be the dominant popular religion'.[21]

[19] Sholto Cross, 'The State, the Church and Revolution in Independent Africa', SOAS seminar, 7 May 1975, p. 6; Okot p'Bitek, *African Religions in Western Scholarship*, Nairobi, 1970, p. 113.

[20] David J. Parkin, *Palms, Wines and Witnesses*, London, 1972.

[21] Sholto Cross, op.cit., p. 6.

I think myself that this sort of debate distorts the true situation. Bitek points out that 'many African Christians are also practitioners of their own religions', and uses this to substantiate his case that Christianity is a mere veneer over traditionalism. Cross refers to 'pagan survivals in grass-roots Christianity' in Zaïre, but regards these as insignificant fragments within a crucial Christian commitment. But the key point, I think, is not the determination of whether a man is really a Christian or really a traditionalist; the key point is that popular religion consists of both Christianity and African religious forms and ideas.

This is admirably expressed in Marshall Murphree's book on Christianity and the Shona. Murphree shows that it is only a relatively few people in eastern Shona society who are exclusively Catholic, Protestant, Vapostori (an independent church of the spirit type), or traditionalist. The majority of the population moves from one set of rites to another and selects from among beliefs. Murphree writes:

> There are in Budjga four religious orientations, each with aspects which attract certain segments of the Budjga population at the same time as they repel others, and none of them able to meet the whole range of religious needs in contemporary Budjga society . . . Each group is best understood as a modality on a religious spectrum which they all must share. No single one of them in itself represents "Contemporary Budjga Religion"; Budjga religion is the complete religious spectrum itself, of which they are only related parts. This view challenges the assumption that the religion of a society must be an integrated, logically consistent set of beliefs . . . There is such a thing as "Contemporary Budjga Religion". This entity is not the traditional religion of the Budjga of the pre-Occupation days, nor is it Christianity; these are only the component parts of a contemporary religion which by the circumstances of its development and environment is something different from, and more than, the sum of the two.[22]

This image of the spectrum can in itself be misleading if we imagine either that the proportions of the influence of the various 'modalities' remains fixed, or that traditional religion, the independent churches and mission Christianity are ranged along this spectrum in a neatly logical movement from small scale conservatism at one end to large thinking innovation at the other.

MacGaffey and Janzen, in their excellent anthology of Kongo religious thought, assume a position very similar to that of Murphree.

> Nearly everybody is at least nominally a Christian. But it is also true that nearly everybody believes in at least the possibility of witchcraft, and also in the possibility of divination and spiritual healing . . . It is

[22] Marshall W. Murphree, *Christianity and the Shona*, London, 1969, pp. 150-1.

our view, which we cannot do more than state here, that there is a Kongo folk religion embracing and transcending its particular manifestations in Kimbanguism, magic, divination, and many different ritual and organizational forms.

But their idea of the 'folk religion' is certainly not a static and neatly compartmentalized one.

The various denominations can be described as unstable precipitates of a popular religion which includes them. In times of crisis whether personal or national, Bakongo readily participate in rites of divination, pilgrimage and worship which they abandon when the crisis passes. Thus in 1921, and again in 1959-60, at the end of colonial rule, probably a majority of them could have been described as Kimbanguist enthusiasts.

At other times popular religion 'precipitated' a mass response to Protestantism, during the so-called 'Pentecost of the Congo', and later to the Salvation Army. At yet other times popular religion precipitated a mass enthusiasm for 'traditional' movements of healing.[23]

Hence the Catholic, Protestant, independent and traditional parts of the spectrum are not fixed; the precipitates are unstable. Moreover, we cannot safely assume that the various creeds occupy fixed ideological points on the spectrum, so that mission Christianity will attract people who want a 'scientific' explanation of events, an ideology of individual self-help, and so on, while traditional religion will attract those who long for a return to the small-scale, organic, communal world, with the independent churches providing some sort of conceptual bridge between the two. As Murphree writes,

> the application of the word 'syncretistic' to the independent groups implies that they stand at some mid-point along a continuum which stretches from the Traditional Religion at one end to the 'orthodox' churches at the other. But . . . at least on some points of doctrine the Vapostori are consistently more 'orthodox' in their Christian belief than members of the older denominations, while in the matter of polygamy, in ideal and practice, they are more 'traditional' than the Traditionalists. In Budjga . . . all the religious groups, from the Traditional Religionists to the mission-sponsored churches, are to some extent 'syncretistic'. In this they all reflect the process of modification and adaptation which is taking place not only in religion, but in the other institutions of Budjga society as well.[24]

Now, I would maintain that this model of a spectrum within which there is a constant reforming of 'unstable precipitates' is applicable not

---

[23] Janzen and MacGaffey, op.cit., pp. 3, 33.

[24] Murphree, op.cit., pp. 170-1.

only to the Shona and the Bakongo, two areas of intensive Christian-ization, but also many other parts of Africa. And I would also maintain that, if we adopt it, we are compelled to make considerable modifications in our discussion of how the church should relate to the nationalist regimes on the one hand and to African spiritual traditions on the other. Of course, the idea of the spectrum of popular religion still allows for the distinctness of the dogma and structure of one denomination as against the others—after all, the totality is not an 'integrated, logically consistent set of beliefs'. It allows also for competition, hostility and even overt aggression by the official representatives of one denomination towards another. It allows for the increasing influence of one 'precipitate' as against the others.

But in terms of the experiences not of denominations but of their members, we are dealing with a situation in which it is impossible to think of 'Christianity' having an autonomy from the totality of popular religion. For either the Bakongo or the Shona it is almost impossible to think of society either repudiating Christianity in the name of traditionalism or repudiating traditionalism in the name of Christianity. This would mean not merely civil war between factions, but civil war within people who are inhabitants neither of one or other faction but of the whole spectrum. In any case the autonomy of the Christian part of the total spectrum to move off on its own 'Western' modernizing lines, abandoning the other components to archaism is also an illusion. Janzen and MacGaffey tell us that the participants in the Kongo folk religion, Christians and non-Christians, 'the healers, their clients and their persecutors' alike,

> are all guided in their experience of the world by a system of thought that remains African and traditional rather than European and Christian. The persistence of traditional thought is not remarkable and calls for no explanation unless one first assumes that African beliefs must necessarily disintegrate in a world dominated by bureaucratic and capitalistic institutions. We consider that this assumption can never be made *a priori*; even if it were true, sociological inquiry shows that the impact of European institutions on Kongo life has not given rise to a homogeneous process of 'modernization'. The relations of European bureaucratic institu-tions and African customary ones in modern Kongo constitute a complex field marked by extensive inconsistencies and discontinuities. Within this field there has been no simple process of challenge and response between such clearly defined entities as 'Christianity' and 'paganism' but a complex interaction and adaptation continuously modified by political, economic and cultural factors.[25]

[25] Janzen and MacGaffey, op.cit., pp. 3-4.

Hence a proposition which sees the churches linked with the State in modernization against African religion seems unlikely and unconvincing—unless by churches we mean only the formal ecclesiastical hierarchies. But if it is true that popular religion, including Christianity, is 'a system of thought that remains African and traditional', it might be thought that the viewpoint of missionary radicals that the church ought to identify itself, with traditional insights by co-opting and transcending them, has much to be said for it. In this way it might perhaps be possible to permeate the whole spectrum with Christian values.

Yet this attitude also seems to me ill-founded. It depends on two erroneous assumptions about traditional religion. The first is that traditional religion is no longer really capable of meeting needs on its own. The second is that we know 'where' traditional religion is located and what it 'is', so that we can if we choose get to the same place and share in the same identity. But this overlooks the process of modification and adaptation which Murphree found taking place in all components of Budjga religion. Most often the churches in trying to adapt or adopt an aspect of traditional religion arrive at the place where traditional religion once was rather than at the place where it is now, finding themselves committed for decades to 'Christian' initiation, for example, at a time when traditional initiation is being transformed or abandoned altogether.[26] And even if a church, through acute and sensitive field study, managed to arrive at exactly the place where traditional religion currently is 'at', even this in itself is not useful unless we also know where it has been and where it is going. There is no use in adopting or adapting something which is at a point along a line of development unless we understand, or could duplicate, the dynamics of that development.

African religion and the dynamics of change

This brings me to the second, and more important, of my two counter-propositions—that African religion has responded creatively to 'development' and modernization. I wish to explore some of the ways in which this creative response has taken place and some of the directions in which it has moved. Before doing so, however, it is time to do two things. One is to abandon from henceforth the word 'traditional'. It is often convenient to speak of 'traditional religion' and there is no simple acceptable alternative. But the word is misleading if it implies immobility or even conservatism. So for the purposes of this section of the chapter I propose to use the term 'African religion', even though this is also

---

[26] Terence Ranger, 'Missionary Adaptation of African Religious Institutions. The Masasi Case', *The Historical Study of African Religion*, eds., T. O. Ranger and Isaria Kimambo, 1972, pp. 221-51.

misleading since plainly Christianity and Islam have become African religions too.

The second thing needed is to make some advance apology for going on to do what I have just been arguing is strictly impossible. I propose for some pages to isolate African religion from the total spectrum of popular religion, and to try to talk about the development of its ideas and forms in isolation from those of the mission and independent churches. This is certainly going to be an artificial procedure. But I think it is justified in view of the fact that so much previous literature does the opposite, concentrating on religious change as though it were the work exclusively of Christianity.[27] In a sense I am attempting to carry further into the twentieth century the 'thought experiment' proposed and conducted by Robin Horton in his 'African Conversion'.[28] Horton was trying to understand the change and development of ideas usually described solely in terms of conversion to Christianity, and in order to do so he undertook a 'thought experiment'. He set up the late nineteenth century situation, with all its colonial pressures, as it impinged on African societies, but excluded from the picture the factor of Christianity. How might African religion then have responded, he asked; indeed how did it respond below the observable surface of Christian activity? In the result, both on the basis of an experimental argument drawn from an analysis of the nature of African religion and on the basis of the scattered evidence, Horton concluded that African religious leaders themselves were independently moving in directions apparently similar to and congruous with certain aspects of the missionary message. In the same way I want now to exclude for a while what we know about Christianity as an agent of modernization, about its contributions to an ideology of individual self-help, about its enlargement and generalization of the spiritual principle. I want to ask what results we get if we look at the evidence we have for the state of African religion at various points in the colonial period and to ask whether what we see can be understood as a developing response to twentieth century social and economic change. I want to ask whether words like 'survival', 'continuity', or even 'revival', really describe the phenomena which have been observed.

I will borrow some sentences from a recent unpublished paper of Horton to send my argument on his way.

> I suggest that we should allow ourselves to be guided by certain principles of continuity and economy of intellectual effort which are accepted in the wider arena of the history of ideas. One of these is that where people confront new and puzzling situations, they tend to adapt to them as far as possible in terms of their existing ideas and attitudes,

[27] This is true, I think, of all the available single volume surveys of African religion.
[28] Robin Horton, 'African Conversion', *Africa*, XLI, 2 (1971), pp. 85-108.

even though they may have to twist and stretch these considerably in the process. Another is that when people assimilate new ideas, they do so because they make sense to them in terms of the ideas they already hold.

Hence an African people's capacity to respond to the colonial situation has to be seen largely in terms of the particular structures of the varying African religious systems and their different capacity for adaptation. 'Instead of being dominated by the notion of "impact", our thinking is now dominated by the notion of active, creative innovation'.[29]

'Active, creative innovation'—the words conjure up an image so different from that normally associated with African religion that at first a natural reaction is to question whether it could take place. We are used to the idea that African religion operated within very restricted horizons; that it met very effectively the needs of the face-to-face rural communities of pre-colonial Africa, but that it could not cope with the interaction with wider world. This, after all, is the argument of Zaïrean philosophers, who argue that spiritual unity at a national level has to be based on a Christian authenticity rather than on a traditional one. Once—so John Mbiti tells us—each tribal group had its own religion, co-existent with society: now the Kenyan nation needs a unified Christianity. And Horton himself writes of a 'way of life . . . dominated by subsistence farming' in which 'social relations are likely to be largely circumscribed by the boundaries of the local microcosm' and which produces 'a religious life in which a great deal of attention is paid to the lesser spirits, underpinners of the microcosm'.[30]

But this microcosmic model of African religion in pre-colonial times needs to be modified in two very important ways. In the first place we are becoming increasingly aware that religious allegiance was not bounded by the immediate local community and that individuals could be members of cultic associations which stretched over very wide areas. In the second place most pre-colonial African religions were conceptually two-tiered. In addition to the idea of the lesser spirits of the microcosm, there was the idea of the Supreme Being who underpinned 'events and processes in the macrocosm—i.e. the world as a whole'. When change comes to the microcosmic society; when men are involved in trade and migrant labour; then

> the social life of those involved will no longer be so strongly confined by the boundaries of their microcosm. Many of their relationships, indeed, will cut dramatically across these boundaries. Now when people come to try to conceptualise and make sense of these changes in their life, the structure of their cosmology will guide them in certain

[29] Robin Horton, 'Conversion. Impact versus Innovation', paper for the African Studies Association conference, Liverpool, 1974, pp. 3, 5.

[30] Horton, pp. 3-4.

definite directions. Specifically, it will lead them to pay far more attention than before to the Supreme Being. It will also lead them to a considerable elaboration of both the concept and the cult of this being.[31]

Horton's analysis suggests where we can expect to find some of the key innovators. They are likely to be prophets—in Loewen's definition, 'men upon whom the Spirit of God comes in a special way and who have thus been empowered to deliver new messages from God'. It was no accident that the last decades of the nineteenth century produced a flowering of prophetism in so many parts of Africa.[32] But this, too, we may find hard to accept. We are used to the idea that the Christian tradition has prophets but that the African tradition does not. Where do they come from, these African prophets who have been so striking a characteristic of African religion in the last hundred years? Perhaps, after all, they are a result of the impact of Christian ideas?

There is currently a good deal of work going on in East and Central Africa, and I have no doubt in other places too, which allows us to understand the provenance and mode of operation of African prophets. Of this work I wish to draw attention merely to one recently published example, Professor Peter Rigby's 'Prophets, Diviners and Prophetism: the Recent History of Kiganda Religion'.[33] Rigby is concerned to argue that 'the logic and rationale for prophetism in Kiganda society lies in the structure and development of Kiganda religion itself'. He argues that in the past Ganda religion operated on two levels: the public, national level and the individual, private level. Public religion was concerned with 'macro-time and . . . the commemoration and veneration of the past, the "golden age" of Buganda. The lesser rituals of divination and healing at a popular level exist in micro-time and are concerned with the individual's or small group's adjustment to the immediate past, the present and the future'. In public religion there was 'a premium upon orthodoxy'. But 'rituals of divination and healing . . . are highly adaptive and innovative. Since the diviners and mediums in Kiganda society are the ones who aid the common man to order and insure his future, it is *this* category of spiritual and religious officers and roles that are primarily oriented *towards the future*'.

The prophet is both an innovating figure and also one who can appeal to the symbols and prestige of the public tradition. 'The prophet achieves

---

[31] Horton, p. 4.

[32] A good deal of work is under way on nineteenth century prophets. An outstanding example is Kennell Jackson's doctoral dissertation on the Kamba. Professor B. A. Ogot is editing a book on East African prophets.

[33] Peter Rigby, 'Prophets, Diviners and Prophetism: the Recent History of Kiganda Religion', *Journal of Anthropological Research*, 31, 2, Summer 1975.

his exceptional status in structural terms by *transcending* the duality inherent in Kiganda religion . . . The prophet mediates between the "popular" and the "esoteric", the mass of the people and the political *élite*, between micro-time and macro-time, and between the past and the future'. Changes taking place in the twentieth century have made it easier for a prophet to emerge from the future-oriented ranks of the diviners and at the same time to capture the prestige of the national symbols. Economic and political change under colonialism has undercut the significance of Ganda religion at the public, political centre. 'The political importance of Kiganda religion lies now among the common people, not among the elite'. Hence a prophet whose main concern is to mediate change in the interests of the masses can do so in the name of great spirits and rulers of the past.

Rigby describes just such a prophet, a diviner named Kigaanira Ssewannyana, who exercised considerable influence in Kampala during the 1950s. Kigaanira claimed to be possessed by the spirit of Kibuuka, the Ganda divinity of war; he operated from Kibuuka's traditional shrine, and called on the people to return to their old gods. But so far from being a conservative or reactionary figure, Kigaanira was 'a new man', literate and widely travelled; he appealed to the urban masses of Kampala; and in his prophecies he proposed a series of new metaphors and symbolic statements designed to enable the Baganda to come to terms with the tensions of the late colonial situation. Rigby draws some general morals from all this. 'Religions, or any other set of beliefs concerning supernatural forces and powers, do not die out with social change and an increased sophistication in science and technology. They change and develop new forms and concepts'. The urban Baganda have been assisted in their adjustment to change by 'the viability and adaptibility of African religions, rituals and symbols'.

Rigby's paper was originally given at a conference on the history of East African religion, at which a number of other studies of twentieth century prophetism were presented.[34] There is not space here to summarize these other studies but it seems worthwhile to quote my own conference report.

The paper givers were arguing that the prophetic response to the twentieth century, even though it arose out of the dynamics of 'traditional' religion, nevertheless had the effect of bringing about major changes within that religion. The prophet was seen as not so much the defender of custom against the whites; indeed, the prophet was seen as often not primarily concerned with the whites at all. The

[34] Terence Ranger, 'Report on the Conference for the Historical Study of East African Religion', *African Religious Research*, vol. 4, No. 2, November 1974, pp. 40-1.

prophet's essential task was to create new communities of concept, to bring about a new balance within African religion. Thus prophetism has been a major agency for profound internal conceptual and structural change.[35]

Yet while prophetism has been—and still is—one major agency of change within African religion, it would be a mistake to focus on its dramatic and individual action at the expense of studying the much wider range of innovation. It is rarely possible to comprehend the overall or general direction in which conceptual change is going in a society merely by looking at the teachings of a prophet. The prophet's message is most often partial and provisional; in any case it is usually heard differently by his followers, who take from it what they feel they need; and unless we can see it in the total context of change it is often difficult to understand how it fits in. In the past, concentration on the prophet—the great 'witch-doctor' of earlier European texts—has served to melodramatize our view of African religion. Even now that we are getting much more internal and profound studies of prophets we must be careful not to allow their fascination to dominate our analysis. We need studies of the total movement of ideas; studies in which the prophetic movements are treated alongside other less striking but equally important manifestations of change.

The most successful such study with which I am familiar is Wim van Binsbergen's recently published 'The Dynamics of Religious Change in Western Zambia', a preliminary and condensed version of a much longer work.[36] Binsbergen describes the Ila prophet Mupumani, who began his prophetic career in 1913. Mupumani carried a message, entrusted to him by God. He announced that it was God alone who held absolute sway over life and death; that previous rites of mourning and of propitiation of spirits were irrelevant and absurd; and that the only effective response to affliction was the recitation of the formula, 'We are humble to the Creator of Pestilence'. In this way, Mupumani made God 'towards whom little or no ritual used to be directed, the immediate and exclusive focus of a new ritual and theology'.

This all fits in so well with Horton's analysis that one might be tempted to use Mupumani as summing up the major movement of Ila ideas. Yet in fact the process was a much more complex one. For one thing, the prophet's message was too austere for his followers. They re-interpreted it in terms of a promise of the return of a caring God, the end

---

[35] Ranger, op.cit., p. 41.

[36] Wim M. J. van Binsbergen, 'The Dynamics of Religious Change in Western Zambia', *Ufahamu*, vol. VI, No. 3, 1976, pp. 69-87. My citations, however, are from a longer unpublished version, 'Religious Change in Central Western Zambia: towards a synthesis'.

of death, the absence of witchcraft, the resurrection of the dead. And the movement thus having become a millenarian one, it suffered the common millenarian fate of rapid disillusionment. In this process the Mupumani movement was typical of Ila religious change—a series of innovations, responses, back-trackings, disillusion, and yet in the complex and dialectical way a slow, steady and regular change.

In the decades after Mupumani the area 'continued to seethe with religious innovation'. There were further prophets. There were so-called cults of affliction, in which it was believed that sickness was the result of possession by an alien spirit who had to be propitiated. There were movements of witchcraft eradication, which offered healing to the witch, protection to those who feared witchcraft, and the cleansing of society. These innovations were the work of three groups of inventors. One group were 'modern achievers', men who operated on the borders between traditional rural society and the European economy and who were acutely conscious that African religious beliefs offered no ideological support for their activities. A second group were the officers of the African religions themselves, who were equally aware of the gap which was opening between belief and socio-economic reality. 'Religious innovation becomes as imperative for them as it is for those spear-heading socio-economic change; they have to find new answers . . . to satisfy their own existential needs for meaningful integration of life, society and the universe.' The third group consisted of people previously subordinate, who saw possibilities of increased influence or prosperity as the ideologies which had supported previously dominant groups were undercut.

Binsbergen is here revolutionizing the older picture. In this older picture the 'modern achievers' were all thought to have abandoned African religion for Christianity; the established officers of African religion were thought to have done no more than to resist Christian influence and to persist with increasingly archaic rites and beliefs. The subordinate 'underlying segment' was thought to have remained in a state of confused bewilderment. Binsbergen replaces all this with a picture of 'seething experiment, innovation, spread, acceptance and rejection', largely within the framework of indigenous beliefs.

The particular forms that innovation took depended upon the identity of the innovator and the character of the experience of his audience. Yet there *was* slow, steady and regular change overall. Binsbergen lists this, and discusses the changes in much more detail and subtlety than is possible here. There was a change in the concept of time from 'the cyclical present' to 'the eschatalogical conception of time as drawing to an end in the future'; there was 'a decline of ecological concern in the religious system' as migrant labour became a more important source of male income than agriculture; there was a movement away from veneration of 'the supernatural entities recognised in the old religious system, predominantly the village dead' and towards 'universalist supernatural agencies', such as the stress on the supreme power of God, or the idea of 'abstract affliction principles' within the healing cults. There was a shift from ideologies of communalism and towards 'counter-ideologies of individualism', expressed most clearly in the healing cults, 'cults of egotism par excellence'. There was a shift away from the dominance of witchcraft fear and the use of the idea of the witch as the dominant explanation for affliction, and a shift towards the explanation of misfortune in terms of abstract spiritual principles.

What we have in this western Zambian case, then, is essentially 'one overall process of religious change', taking the form of a number of 'distinct movements, greatly overlapping in time, each of which manifests particular innovations.' The innovations remain within the African idiom of the spiritual, assuming the reality of spirit, assuming spiritual cause for suffering and evil, and assuming spiritual inspiration for prophecy. At the same time there is a movement towards a linear, future-oriented concept of time, towards the definition of more abstract and general principles of causation. And despite the emphasis on the individual—or because of it—what is taking place amounts to a 'religious reformulation of community'.

Binsbergen's analysis remains the most fully worked out but neither his western Zambian data nor his interpretation of it can be regarded as idiosyncratic. It is becoming clear that the overall process of religious and conceptual change in many other regions of East and Central Africa has taken place in much the same sort of way and moved in much the same sort of direction. I have myself recently begun a similar exploration of Shona ideas and practices in relation to affliction in which the varied but systematic development of more universal and abstract forces of causation and healing can be plainly detected.[37]

Conclusion

I have done some violence to Binsbergen in using him to carry out my version of Horton's thought experiment. In fact in his paper he does not exclude innovations of Christian character, just as these have to be included in any examination of the development of Shona ideas about affliction—or for that matter in any discussion of prophetism in

[37] Terence Ranger, 'The Healing of the Witch. Developments in Shona thought and practice', SOAS seminar, January 1977.

Kampala.[38] And of course once the 'thought experiment' has been carried through, and it has been seen how the apparently haphazard record of African religious development amounts to purposeful innovation, we must rapidly strive to integrate this back into the model of the spectrum and the metaphor of precipitation. It is not my intention to tot up points for African religion as against Christianity. Once I have been able to convince you of the capacity of the leaders of African religion to participate in innovation, then the many detailed recent accounts of the prophetic leaders of the independent churches are just as much to my purpose as Binsbergen's account of Mupumani. The point is that the religious formations at every point in the spectrum have been developing their ideas, symbols and rituals during the twentieth century.

I hope that my argument of the two counter propositions has done something to modify the way in which we look at all three of the original permutations of the relation of church, nationalist State and African religion.

Let us look again, in the light of what I have been arguing, at the evidence which seemed to support the idea of a nationalist traditionalist alliance against Christianity in Southern Rhodesia. I remarked earlier that it seemed unlikely that the nationalists would carry through such an alliance. But the point now is that it seems unlikely that the African religious leaders see the situation in that way either. The current activities of the Shona spirit mediums are usually spoken of as though they demonstrated an impressive 'continuity', or perhaps a 'revival' of traditional religion. In the light of the work of Rigby, Binsbergen and others we must surely wonder if these expressions are adequate. Binsbergen's work might lead us to look for an increase in the importance of those African spiritual leaders who speak for the High God or a direct spiritual intermediary; Rigby's work might lead us to explore the significance of the spirit mediums to urbanized Shona or to ask how far the mediums have been able to combine the authority and prestige available to them by appeal to the kingdoms of the past with the forward-looking perspectives of the diviners.

I have tried to explore some of these issues in my own work on Shona ideas of affliction. And fortunately we have the work of Dr Elleck Mashingaidze to help us to rethink the role of the spirit mediums in particular. Dr Mashingaidze has studied the spirit mediums of the Mazoe district, north-east of Salisbury. He emphasizes above all else their flexibility and adaptiveness. In the early 1890s they advised the Shona to

---

[38] Binsbergen discusses Ila participation in the Watch Tower movement and the commitment of some modernizing achievers to mission Christianity; Rigby describes Kigaanira's confrontation with an independent church prophet, whose spiritual power was popularly believed to have overthrown Kigaanira's.

listen to the missionaries, since they saw no clash of interest between the missionary preaching of the sovereignty and nearness of God and their own concern to develop new spiritual concepts. In 1896, however, faced with the profound disasters of human and animal plague and of human oppression, they developed an ideology of resistance and advised the people of Mazoe to drive out the whites. In the first decades of the twentieth century, adapting themselves to a situation of white power and economic change, they advised a selective adaptation and an exploitation of Western education. More recently some of them have supported the guerillas. And all the time, within the continuity of the spirit medium institution, modifications of myth and practice have been taking place: towards a more systematic conceptualization of the hierarchy of mediums; towards a divinization of the great spirits, like Chamenuka, and an emphasis on their intermediary role with God; towards a constant reformulation and extension of the prophecies of the most famous nineteenth century mediums of Chamenuka. As Mashingaidze writes:

> The role of traditional religion from the beginning of the encounter of the two systems was to moderate change that had become inevitable. Shona traditional religion remained the source of Shona constructive and creative response to Christianity and to European culture as a whole. It reminded the people that there was still room for accepting or rejecting certain aspects of the new order . . . Shona religion realised that by allowing certain changes it could make an important contribution to the culture of the new Mashonaland.[39]

In their interaction with the guerillas one could see the mediums as once again engaged in moderating 'change which has become inevitable'. But there is no reason to suppose that in so doing the mediums are demonstrating hostility to the other elements of 'the culture of the new Mashonaland'. Nor is there any reason to suppose that only this part of the total spectrum of contemporary Shona religion is responding with sympathy to the changes brought about by rural militancy. In his remarkable biography, *Obed Mutezo, The Mudzimu-Christian Nationalist*, Ndabaningi Sithole has described how his ZANU militant hero combined 'in his mind without sense of strain the dual loyalty to the *midzimu* (ancestor spirits) and to the Christ of the Methodist Church: the two were in no sense competitive'. Sithole has also described how Mutezo's nationalism is derived both from the confidence given to him by his ancestral spirits and from the ideas and organizational experience of his Methodist membership.[40]

---

[39] Elleck Mashingaidze, 'Christianity and the Mhondoro cult: A study of African Religious Initiative and Resilience', Limuru, June 1974.

[40] Ndabaningi Sithole, *Obed Mutezo*, Nairobi, 1970. The citation is from my own summary of the book's argument in my 'Introduction', p. 9.

If we turn to the second permutation—the possible alliance of the mission-seeded churches with the nationalist State in the name of development and against tradition—it is equally clear that some modifications have to be made. It is no longer so obvious that African religion has nothing to contribute to development, or that it cannot generate responses to enlarged scale. I favour myself a definition of development such as that advanced by Basil Davidson in his *Can Africa Survive?*, in which he places great emphasis upon the participation of the people themselves in change. And if development means a process whereby the people of the rural areas 'revolutionize their own consciousness' and develop conceptual formulations which enable them to take a lead in local economic transformation, then we have to look very closely at available mobilizing ideas. It is fashionable now to look at mobilizing ideas from outside, at what Davidson calls 'the transfer of understanding from the few to the many'. Of course Davidson and other liberation theorists do not think in terms of coercion and thought control from the top:

> the few have to transfer their convictions, their ideas about the present sufficient number of the many . . . This the few can do only by entering fully into the concerns and interests of the many. All these things they must share and understand and make their own, while at the same time adding their own vision and understanding so that the movement *moves*—and moves forward.[41]

In such a view of development, however much the few identify with the many, it is still the ideas of the few, ideas derived from Western education and from familiarity with the world revolution, which count. I wish to argue that among the important available mobilizing ideas there are also the sort of developments of concept and symbol which Binsbergen has described for western Zambia. The many have themselves, through modifications within African religion and by means of selection along the whole range of the popular religious spectrum, arrived at ideas appropriate in many ways to communal development. There are new concepts of time, environment, causation—all serviceable to development, and yet all mediated through popular religion and hence acceptable to the total community.

All this seems to me to throw real doubt upon the call for 'national' and united churches. It is a call which seems to rank the churches with changes from 'above' rather than as part of the process of change from

---

[41] Basil Davidson, *Can Africa Survive?*, London, 1975, pp. 168-9. For a much fuller debate on this issue see my original SOAS seminar paper, which drew on some of the same material as this paper but in the context of an argument with liberationist development theory; Terence Ranger, 'Consciousness, Liberation and Development: A Review', SOAS seminar, 7 May 1975.

below. It is a call which sometimes seems to spring rather from a desire for authority than from a commitment to liberation. The various mission churches in Africa had a great deal of authority; they were allocated monopolistic spheres of influence by the colonial regimes; they imposed upon their converts an ecclesiastical discipline long since defunct in Europe itself. But always below the surface was the seething of innovation and the movement of people to and fro along the spectrum. And today it is perfectly plain that Africans live in a situation of religious pluralism. The old monopolistic spheres have broken down; Africans no longer have to be a Methodist or an Anglican or a Seventh Day Adventist in order to obtain an education or to enter a hospital. Africans can choose among a variety of Christian churches and sects; a variety of indigenous movements; a variety of secular ideologies. The church cannot seek to close this freedom of choice in the name of national unity or of the special role of the church in development, since intellectual developments outside it are relevant both to development and to enlarged scale. The church, or so it seems to me, has to accept its place in the spectrum and if its influence is to grow within it then it must grow because the church succeeds in innovating in ways which offer more to individual need than any alternative.

And this bring us to the third permutation—the idea that the church should seek to play the role of African religion and so to minister to the real fears and needs of rural Africans. Here I need only refer back to my earlier discussion. There is no point in the churches seeking to become like some model or other of traditional religion. There is every point, however, in the churches seeking to understand in their own terms what the needs and fears of men and women are, and in seeking new ways of meeting them.

I can illustrate this briefly by reference to south-east Tanzania, where I carried out field research in 1975. The Anglican Church in that area had enjoyed a monopoly for a very long time; it had sought to enlarge the traditional sense of community on the basis of a network of Christian villages, which were consciously also part of the national and international church; it had adopted a systematic policy of 'adaptation' of traditional modes. In the last two or three years all this has broken down. The Tanzanian Government has taken over all schools and hospitals. It has moved people into relatively few large *ujamaa* villages, where Christians of different denominations live with Muslims and adherents of African religions. This regrouping has also undercut supposed traditional modes of Makua or Yao or Makonde ritual behaviour, since the villages contain peoples of all three ethnicities. The new villages offer in this respect plurality of choice, as well as an increasing familiarity with secular ideologies. They also generate a good many tensions, exacerbated by the compulsion employed to move people into them and by the drought and food shortages of 1974. In such a situation the various denominations do indeed form parts of a total spectrum of belief; they are indeed 'unstable precipitates'. In the last two or three years there have been two impressive precipitations of popular involvement. One of these has been mass resort in the new villages to rituals of witchcraft eradication and cleansing, in which very many Christians have taken part. The other has been the extraordinary mission of spiritual healing carried out by the late Edmund John in a series of meetings in Masasi Cathedral, to which hundreds of Muslims and other non-Christians flocked. Here there was a genuine choice of two kinds of spiritual cleansing. This responsiveness to what real people want rather than to abstractions of what we think they have always wanted or should want is the true challenge to the church.

Towards a theology of liberation for Tanzania

LAURENTI MAGESA

The sudden and thorough winds of change let loose by Vatican II and the changed outlook of the World Council of Churches threatened to shake conventional Christianity in Tanzania down to its very foundations. Today, these winds of change continue to impinge upon the praxis of the Christian faith here with ever greater urgency. Other factors have since come into play which serve to heighten the impact. The blow struck at the conventional Christian outlook—which can be summed up briefly as one of 'withdrawal' from the world—by Vatican II and the official stand of the W.C.C. on a number of questions was serious enough. But it would not have been fatal had it not been for the Arusha Declaration. This document started Tanzania officially on the road to Socialism or, to be more precise, *Ujamaa*. Looking back from the present vantage point, it is easy to see that the Arusha Declaration spelled the death knell of the attitude we have briefly called 'withdrawal'. Since 1967, the date when the Arusha Declaration was promulgated, it seems that the Tanzanian Christian experiences religious fulfilment more in the praxis of *Ujamaa* than in the traditional *loci* of God's presence. Of course, the ordinary Tanzanian Christian, being no theologian, does not express his experience in so many words. However, his behaviour and attitude leave one in no doubt whatever as to his conviction: where conventional religious practice does not reconcile with the present evolution of his *milieu*, the Christian in Tanzania opts for the latter. The fall-off in numbers at religious worship and the reception of the sacraments in the Catholic Church, for example, can be cited as indications of this. On the other hand, the increasing involvement in nation-building projects by almost every Tanzanian is taken as a sign that the country in general is being gripped by secularism. And so, quite a number of Christian religious leaders are anxious: is the Tanzanian Christian losing his faith and giving up his religion? The anxiety is real and not altogether unjustified. But positively it points to a need which can no longer be ignored.

The need, to which the current anxiety of the church leadership in Tanzania points, amounts to a new formulation (or perhaps a reformulation) of theology. We speak of theology as being a systematic reflection on the word of God as applied to people living in given circumstances. In other words, theology is a search of how God speaks to men in certain human situations. Now the politico-socio-economic situation—the only situation in and through which God ordinarily speaks to us men—is, as it were, turning full-circle in Tanzania. Hence a need for a new reflection on the work of the Spirit today, a new theology. The Latin American theologian, G. Gutierrez, explains:

> As a critical reflection on society and the Church, theology is an understanding which both grows and, in a certain sense, changes. If the commitment of the Christian community in fact takes different forms throughout history, the understanding which accompanies the vicissitudes of this commitment will be constantly renewed and will take untrodden paths. A theology which has as its point of reference only 'truths' which have been established once and for all—and not the Truth which is also the Way—can be only static and, in the long run, sterile . . . A theology which is not up-to-date is a false theology.[1]

There is a clear need of taking a different theological road in Tanzania. 'As there are many ways to get to Dar-es-Salaam safely and without harm,' a friend says, 'so, too, there are many ways to reach the Throne of Grace safely and without harm, without going via the well-trodden theological paths of Europe or America. The destination is indeed the same, but to get there it may be necessary at times to take different routes.'

It is only by interpreting the action of God in a language the contemporary Tanzanian can understand that Christianity will influence his life in any significant way. To-date it would seem to many that it has failed to do so. Among those who hold this view is Bishop R. Ndingi Mwana wa Nzeki of the Catholic Diocese of Machakos, Kenya. He says:

> To me it would seem that the reason for this failure lies not so much on not adapting good African traditions and values into Christianity, but more so in not making efforts right from the start to discover and develop African theology.
> . . . we (in Africa) are relatively free to create new theological structures and development and to elaborate new doctrinal formulations to our own Christian enrichment and to the whole Church of Christ.[2]

A Theology of Liberation

Let us submit right away that in the present circumstances in Tanzania

---

[1] G. Gutierrez, *A Theology of Liberation*, Orbis Books, 1973, pp. 12-13.

[2] R. Ndingi Mwana wa Nzeki, *Target*, 26 January 1975, p. 3.

only a theology of liberation centred on Christ will do. This will be a theology of a process of human growth brought about by 'the action of human freedoms enlightened by the rationality of the intelligence and immersed in the realism of a political policy.' This process of growth can only be realized through struggle against oppressive forces and structures on all levels of human life in order 'to generate viable structures of freedom, creativity, and communication'.[3] A theology of liberation, therefore, will have to take history as an instrument of liberation.

> To conceive of history as a process of liberation of man is to consider freedom as a historical conquest; it is to understand that the step from an abstract to a real freedom is not taken without a struggle against all the forces that oppress man, a struggle full of pitfalls, detours, and temptations to run away. The goal is not only better living conditions, a radical change of structures, a social revolution; it is much more: the continuous creation, never ending, of a new way to be a man, a *permanent cultural revolution*.[4]

A theology of liberation for Tanzania will have to take shape along those lines. In its beginnings it will have two characteristics: it will be a reaction and a response, necessitated by the religious and political situation in which Tanzania was and, to some extent, continues to be. By reacting against alienating situations it will, paradoxically, indicate routes of liberation to be adopted by the church. Thus it will be a positive response to unique human experiences in Tanzania.

As a 'political' or 'liberating' theology, it will not be out of step with the Holy Scriptures, rather it will be at the centre of the meaning and significance of the New Testament. For, in our study of the New Testament, it is essential to realize that:

> The preaching of Jesus was certainly political, having reference not merely to morals but to the concrete polity of man. It was in another direction, not aside from politics but within and beyond politics that the fulfilment came, that the Kingdom came.[5]

Our theology would fail us if it failed to bear this witness of Jesus. 'When our theological account of what Christ was doing has the effect of making us indifferent (i.e. 'withdrawn') to what *in human terms* he was after (i.e. involvement in human life), then the theological account is simply the cloak of agnosticism'.[6] This only emphasizes what we have

---

[3] René Laurentin, *Liberation, Development and Salvation*, Orbis Books, 1972, pp. xii-xiv.

[4] G. Gutierrez, ibid., p. 32

[5] S. Moore, *No Exit*, Darton, Longman & Todd, 1968, pp. 15-16.

[6] S. Moore, ibid., p. 17.

already mentioned: that the requirement of a relevant theology of liberation for Tanzania is both to interpret life and to give it a sense of direction. It is to tell the Christians what God is saying to and requiring of us in the present human situation. It is continuously to teach Christians what modern educators have called a Christian 'critical awareness' of history.

A Theology of Culture

But, in the formulation of a liberation theology for Tanzania, where could we look for inspiration? In the present Tanzanian environment, a theology of liberation will necessarily be a theology of a new culture.

A new cultural reality is emerging in Tanzania today. While it would not be correct to say that the pre-independence cultural patrimonies—customs, institutions, languages—have disappeared, it is true that they are going at an unprecedented rate and large parts of the patrimony of any given tribe do not have the place of honour they held before. One need only mention language as an example. To the younger generation—30 and below—the tribal languages count for very little. Swahili, the country's national language, is steadily but surely replacing them. In this dynamic formation of a Tanzanian culture, one would be closer to the truth, however, to say that the movement, the dynamism, is one of fusion or symbiosis. The old patrimony of each tribe is being blended (sometimes intentionally, other times imperceptibly) with new, or what could be called 'foreign' values, producing a reality, though neither completely old nor totally new, but really Tanzanian in flavour. And the latter is what matters most of all.

The pervading influence in this cultural evolution is the government, or to be more exact TANU, the party. Today TANU's policy of *Ujamaa* and self-reliance is the driving force behind all aspects of life of the Tanzanian—morals, social organization, economic life, education and, as can be inferred, language both in the ordinary sense (Swahili) and in the wider sense of the word (symbols and symbolisms). All this means that a political theology aiming at human liberation in Tanzania today must be keenly sensitive to the dynamics of culture. It must be, as we have said, a theology of this new Tanzanian culture.

In simply political terms the new Tanzanian culture comes as a response to oppression. It is only just over a decade ago that Tanzania became a free country. Colonialism has not been forgotten and the alienation suffered during that period is all too vivid in the people's mind. At that time the Tanzanian was conditioned, as it were, to see himself only as a member of a tribe and to esteem the tribe over the nation. Consequently, there was no unity. Physically he was often used (as an instrument) to produce wealth for the colonial masters. He was thus made to consider himself an inferior being. Psychologically he was, so to speak, permanently in trauma. He distrusted himself and lacked initiative. The truth was always the master's. The master was always right.

This situation is far from completely gone. Political independence alone does not bring self-confidence to a people to whom human dignity and self-respect have been denied for almost a century. More important is psychological independence and it takes a cultural evolution or revolution to make people psychologically free. Thus the development of a new culture in Tanzania. The emphasis is on human dignity and national unity.

A theology of culture, if it is to be liberating, must therefore seek to transform this new culture, by transforming the whole church, into a force for human liberation. The question to ask at this point, however, is: although it is a response to an oppressive situation, is the emerging Tanzanian culture domesticating? Is it alienating? To what degree need it be conformed to the Gospel, to Christ himself?

Theological Ambiguities

That question leads us straight into one of those areas in theology which we could appropriately call 'grey areas'. These are problems in theology for which—however much one would like to—one cannot get an either-or solution. The question of war has been one such theological grey area for a long time. Another is the question of violence. And most recently, brought into open and ferocious debate by Pope Paul VI's encyclical *Humanae Vitae*, contraception, abortion, euthanasia.

The setting is the same when the patrimony of a people is being supplanted with new values, sometimes even by conspicuous force against the will of the people concerned. One is led to wonder whether this process is not in itself oppressive, whether the church should not raise her prophetic voice against it? This is what is happening in some areas of life in Tanzania. Is it not therefore a challenge which the church in Tanzania should and must meet?

There can be no denying that it is. Theology must help the church to face the situation. But it must be repeated that the situation is simply ambivalent: this we must admit before all else. One sees the development of the new Tanzanian culture as very desirable; but one could also view the suppression of the old culture as oppressive. The ambivalence is clearly shown, for example, in the following words of President Julius Nyerere, the chief architect of the new culture of Tanzania. In reference to getting clean water for the Maasai, a non-farming, cattle-herding people of northern Tanzania who live in obviously unhygienic surroundings, he said:

> People tell me, 'The Masai are completely happy.' I tell them, 'It's not a question of whether they are happy! But . . . there is a difference between clean water and dirty water. My problem is to get that (Masai) women clean water.'[7]

Theologies which deal with human life cannot escape such theological grey areas. A theology of liberation for Tanzania is no exception. However, we are not at an impasse. There are realities in Tanzania which point to a possible solution, at least for the present. We could go about it by asking: If TANU's policy of socialism and self-reliance is the driving force in the formation of the new Tanzanian culture, what are its aspirations? What are its aims? What is its praxis? Are these aspirations, aims and praxis fundamentally liberating or alienating? What area needs most the redemptive powers of the Good News of human liberation (i.e. Salvation)?

These are big questions and in a paper like this we cannot treat them adequately. Suffice it to give a brief review of the basic aspirations and aims of *Ujamaa* and the means now used to reach these aims.

Ujamaa: Aspirations, Aims, Means

It is necessary to mention right away that, as it is understood in Tanzania today, *Ujamaa* is a vision of man which is flexible and eclectic rather than a hard-core doctrinaire ideology. The basic and most important aspiration of *Ujamaa* is the dignity of the human person and the society he constitutes. The purpose of the Arusha Declaration, of *Ujamaa*, as President Nyerere explains, is man:

> For in Tanzania which is implementing the Arusha Declaration, the purpose of all social, economic and political activity must be man—the citizens, and all the citizens of this country. The creation of wealth is a good thing and something which we shall have to increase. But it will cease to be good the moment wealth ceases to serve man and begins to be served by man.[8]

Deriving from that basic aspiration there are those of sharing of all national resources and responsibilities at the national level; equality of all men; freedom for all; and development for the ultimate progress of the person.

Inherent in the Arusha Declaration, therefore, is a rejection of the

---

[7] W. E. Smith, *We Must Run While They Walk*, Random House, 1971, p. 4.
[8] J. K. Nyerere, *Freedom and Socialism*, O.U.P., 1968, p. 316.

concept of national grandeur as distinct from the well-being of its citizens, and a rejection too of material wealth for its own sake. It is a commitment to the belief that there are more important things in life than the amassing of riches, and that if the pursuit of wealth clashes with things like human dignity and social equality, then the latter will be given priority.[9]

The aims of *Ujamaa* are much like its aspirations. It aims at creating a society without classes where, as the saying goes, 'all are for one and one for all'. This means unity and sharing of the riches of the nation. All citizens are invited to take an active part in the political life of the nation. They have the right and responsibility to do this in order to reach the aspirations and aims through the hard work and sacrifice of all.

A truly socialist state is one in which all people are workers and in which neither capitalism nor feudalism exists. It does not have two classes of people, a lower class composed of people who work for their living, and an upper class of people who live on the work of others. In a really socialist country no person exploits another; everyone who is physically able to work does so; every worker obtains a just return for the labour he performs; and the incomes derived from different types of work are not grossly divergent.[10]

The above sound like, and indeed are, universal socialist ideals. One would therefore want to know what is peculiarly African in *Ujamaa*. What liberating values could a political theology draw from it?

As against the abstraction of other socialisms, *Ujamaa* is existential and personal. It stresses participation in reality. It is a child of a culture which prefers the symbol to the abstraction. It underlines the necessity for its success of that attitude of mind to treat all fellow human beings as kinsmen. Persuasion rather than coercion is used to get people to cooperate and to share their responsibility. Men are values in themselves and they may never be used as means for economic progress. The sole criterion of progress is the inclusive need of society and of the individual person.

In short, the message of *Ujamaa* is one of brotherhood, development, economic justice, equality, freedom and the continual betterment of the human person. And all these are empirical dimensions of salvation.

The Gospel Tidings and Ujamaa
The brief review we have given of the basic aspirations and aims of *Ujamaa* puts us into a position to affirm with Fr N. Bevan that at the

[9] J. K. Nyerere, ibid.
[10] J. K. Nyerere, ibid., p. 233.

very least the spirit of the Tidings of the Gospel and that pursued by *Ujamaa* are not antithetical but identical. There is therefore no reason for the Christian not to accept the vision of *Ujamaa*.

But must we not go further and say that this vision *must* be held by Christians? These are Christian principles even if the Christian lives in some other nation, or if the policies of our nation were to change, because the aspirations of Ujamaa express the spirit of the Gospel.[11]

With the spirit of the Gospel *Ujamaa* rejects as bourgeois: (1) Order which is understood as immobility or the preservation of the *status quo*. This may be, in actual fact, established disorder which degrades the human person. For it, even spiritual values could be used 'as a cover for evils of both the economic and political disorders in society . . . hiding (as it were) a corrupt merchandise by putting a noble label on it'.[12] (2) The separation of spirit from matter and thought from action. In *Ujamaa*, this is a betrayal of the human being and in the Christian religion it is a betrayal of the Incarnation. Both amount, in theological terms, to a gross misunderstanding of God's saving action in the world.

Again, like the Gospel, *Ujamaa* affirms:

(1) A constant vigilance and struggle against any socio-politico-economic deformations. (2) The necessity and importance of the human community. (3) Commitment to the world. (4) Interest in persons. (5) Inner conviction as against niceties of externals only: *Ujamaa* is an attitude of mind.

Practice versus Theory

Up to now we have been considering what we have called aims or aspirations of *Ujamaa*. We have therefore been in the realm of theory. But what about the practice of *Ujamaa*? Are we perhaps being guilty of glorifying the theory of *Ujamaa* and ignoring the area that counts most—the area of practice? For, liberation, if it is to mean anything at all, must be an experienced reality. And if *Ujamaa* has liberating values in theory, it must make them real in practice.

One must mention and emphasize here that in any society there will always be tensions between theory and practice. This is the human situation which any theology of liberation must recognize and work against. Just as professing to be a Christian does not guarantee sanctity, all the citizens of a nation do not adhere to socialist aspirations in practice simply because that nation professes to pursue these aspirations. Abuses of practice will occur. They must even be expected and so

---

[11] Fr N. Bevan, unpublished lecture.
[12] Fr N. Bevan, ibid.

prepared for. In Tanzania as well there are abuses of the practice of *Ujamaa*: dishonesty, opportunism, coercion and so many others. Christians, however, must avoid two temptations: to remain neutral and do nothing about these abuses, or secondly, to reject *Ujamaa* because of some mistakes and injustices in its practice.[13]

The praxis of *Ujamaa*, then, needs most the redemptive awareness of the Good News. The function of a political theology or a theology of liberation is to synthesize the action of God in the day-to-day happenings, in the 'signs of the times' for the benefit of the church. Theology must inform and lead the church to be sharply critical of any alienating tendency in the praxis of *Ujamaa*. It is the Christian community's task to witness to the shortcomings of any social or political programme. But because the aspirations of *Ujamaa* are fundamentally Christian, our criticism will be one of solidarity.

It follows, then, that the most immediate task for theology to act as a liberating force in Tanzania is to show to the church in this country the importance and primacy of involvement in all sectors of national life. Ultimately, this means involvement in TANU and politics. The bishops of Tanzania urged Christians to do precisely this in their pastoral letter, *Peace and Mutual Understanding*, published in 1972. They said:

> Politics is a pathway of Christian commitment because we discover daily that change in the quality of our life is influenced by political action. . . . Let us not as Christians be content to be bystanders. . . . All who have the ability must use their gifts in the service of others.

The end in view should be to bring the Good News of Christ—the good news of liberation from disease, ignorance, poverty and oppression—to bear on the whole nation via the participation of the Christian Church. This is the transformation of humanity from a sin situation unto a situation of grace, into the Image of God. This is the work of Christ himself:

> The spirit of the Lord is upon me,
> For he has anointed me.
> He has sent me to bring the good news to the poor,
> To proclaim liberty to the captives
> And to the blind new sight,
> To set the downtrodden free,
> To proclaim the Lord's year of favour.
> (Lk. 4:18-19)

To give direction to the movement of the church towards this end, as we have noted in passing, requires a synthesized liberation theology of

---

[13] Fr B. Joinet, adapted from speech, Kigoma, July 1971.

doctrine, worship, sacraments and structures. Prior to this, however, or rather in the process of doing this, we must have a liberating pedagogy.

Pedagogy : A New Catechism?

In the pedagogical field, the work that has been done in Holland is pioneering. A few years ago, a new catechism—popularly known as the Dutch Catechism—was published there. Its publication raised a flurry of strong comments for and against it. The excitement has completely subsided now, but the catechism itself, despite its imperfections, remains a monumental achievement in the field of catechetics anywhere in this century. It is a pointer in the right direction for any efforts in the future.

In saying this I am by no means recommending the Dutch Catechism for use in Tanzania. For one thing, like every other book, it has its roots deeply in a place and culture. For another, it is conditioned by a certain focus. Both of these, in the case of the book in question, are far different from the Tanzanian reality. I am only saying that the spirit and the pedagogical method of the catechism strike a match. Both could be used profitably as bases on or from which to build a suitable catechesis and to develop a meaningful catechesis for Tanzania. Let me explain briefly.

The pedagogical approach of catechesis in Tanzania to date was, I think, alienating. It looked upon the catechumen and the Christian as children who had to be provided with food already chewed. It assumed that truth was a finished product to be handed over to those who did not have it. It did not consider truth as something to be achieved stage by stage by personal search. And since catechesis was deeply steeped in Western theological concepts and notions—which theological concepts and notions were deemed higher and better than any of their Tanzanian counterparts—the alienation of the Tanzanian Christian became complete. This sort of catechesis made him a stranger in both worlds: he felt at home neither in his Christian commitment nor in the traditions of his forefathers.

The approach of the Dutch Catechism would be liberating in that it would try to present the message of faith not as cut and dried information about God or things pertaining to him. Liberating catechesis understand that revelation is really God making himself known, unfolding himself, as they say, (not things about him) in people's daily lives. And so Christians, as indeed the whole human race, have to search for him in various ways.

In Tanzanian circumstances, I will point to the method currently used in the Adult Literacy Campaign as a fine example of pedagogy suited to Tanzania. Here, quite rightly, the student is asked to take himself seriously and to embark on the road of personal and social betterment. A relationship is established from the very outset between learning to read and write and the actual life experience of the student concerned. It is, in the final analysis, a sort of 'do-it-yourself' project. It seeks to awaken the critical awareness of the student and to lead him to ask more and more questions. The right questions are more important than the answers![14]

Catechesis in Tanzania could emulate this method to advantage. The idea is to relate the Divine message of the Gospel to the contemporary human experience and to set Christians on the quest for God there. If the quest is sincere, every Christian will encounter God in his own way. It is a slow and painstaking task but it is the only truly Christian way. What is important in the quest is the encounter—which is also a lifetime process—and this encounter can take place only in real life. Any presentation of doctrine, then, which would show the people that their life is the working ground for God's self-revelation would do infinitely more good for the Christian Faith than any amount of information about God to be memorized and forgotten not long afterwards. Doctrine is only a fingerpost; every Christian has to do his own walking.

It would be premature at this stage to attempt an outline of the themes to be treated in catechesis in Tanzania. Two things, however, must be said right now if the mistake of the traditional European-American inspired catechisms, of presenting information about God, is to be avoided. First, catechesis in Tanzania must not anchor itself on the question: 'Who is God?'. This question alone creates an attitude, a way—and a wrong way at that—of looking at religion and life. It takes God out of human life and makes him an object of study. It completely undermines the necessity of the never-ending search for God. Consequently, it makes religion peripheral in human life instead of it being central. In Africa everything has a religious significance. Here lies the significance of the Incarnation.

Secondly, and this flows directly from what has just been said, catechesis in Tanzania must avoid what Freire has called the 'banking' and Jean-Paul Sartre the 'digestive' or 'nutritive' approach. We must discard this attitude of contradiction between teacher and student, catechist and catechumen, priest and congregation so prevalent in our catechesis to-date.[15] If a new catechesis in Tanzania starts by successfully avoiding both of the above pitfalls, it will walk on firm ground.

---

[14] This is, in essence, the method of 'Problematization' or 'Conscientization' developed by the Brazilian educator, Paulo Freire, *Pedagogy of the Oppressed*, Penguin, 1970, p. 56.

[15] The logic of this oppressive attitude has been noted by Freire, pp. 46-7.

Laurentin, Gutierrez, Dom Helder, Segundo

Consideration of a theology of liberation for any of the so-called Third World countries necessarily entails reference, however brief, to the work that has been done along that line in Latin America. The Latin American theologians and churchmen—René Laurentin, Gustavo Gutierrez, Dom Helder Camara, Juan Luis Segundo, to mention only a few of the well known ones—have pioneered this theological development. I do not intend to go into a lengthy discussion of any of their work. I only mention them to acknowledge the debt of inspiration that any emerging liberation theology—and especially this paper—owes them. But, while we are at it, we could perhaps ask and try to answer one important question: How would a Tanzanian theology of liberation differ from a Latin American one, or any other?

First of all it must be said explicitly that theologies of liberation will differ from nation to nation, from country to country, from culture to culture. This is simply because the human reality, the environment at any given time, differs from place to place. The degree of oppression, that is to say of sinfulness, in structures, institutions and societies—which political realities therefore need the liberating power of the Good News—is also different. All these, then, call for different theological responses in form and degree to make them instruments of human freedom in given *milieux*.

It is in this respect that theologies of liberation in Tanzania and Latin America will differ. The Scriptural background—continually enlightened by modern scholarship—will be the same, but tactics of involvement, encouraging proclamations, denunciations will, of necessity, take different forms. While, for example, the current theology of liberation in Latin America will condemn and urge political action against domination of Latin Americans by capitalist exploiters at home and abroad—as Gustavo Gutierrez shows in his classic, *A Theology of Liberation*—liberation theology in Tanzania today will do the opposite. It will insist on alignment with government action aimed at human freedom and it will show the theological insight of the aspirations and aims of *Ujamaa*.

Let it not be thought, however, that we are suggesting any exclusivity in liberating modes of action: that liberation theology will always condemn in one place and affirm in another. By no means. On the contrary, practically everywhere, with only a difference in degree, it will have to do both. For, Christ's Kingdom, though come (i.e. beginning here), is eschatological. For liberation theology, the most important thing everywhere, in all cases and at any time is theological perception which necessitates 'a great familiarity with the Bible, a deep insight in the concrete cultural and sociological situation, and a sound theological thinking to make the bridge between both'.[16]

A political theology or a theology of liberation anywhere is a theology of Gospel responses to actual human situations. It deals with real needs of people, people who are suffering the effects of what is so rightly called 'institutional or established violence'. It is therefore less theoretically oriented than practical, combining pedagogy, critical reflection and praxis together. In one word, it is a prophetic theology—prophetic in the Biblical sense of the word. And as Bishop Trevor Huddleston wrote 20 years ago:

> Prophecy is still a function of the Church: prophecy in its true (i.e. Biblical) sense, that is. It always amuses me to hear discussions on the hoary old problem of religion and politics and to think what such discussions would have meant to men like Jeremiah and Amos and Isaiah and Ezekiel. For in fact half their time was spent in trying to bring home to the men of their day the fact that God was directly concerned in the way society was organized: in the way wealth was distributed: in the way men behaved to one another. In short—in politics.[17]

The contemporary experience of Tanzania is prophetic in precisely the above sense. It is an experience of freedom, self-confidence and general human betterment. In a big sense, it is an experience of liberation from the alienation engendered by colonialism. The Spirit is gradually creating men into the Image of God. Essential now is a theology which will inform Christians of this movement of the Spirit and warn them of tendencies to move without him. For Christians are those who know the action of God. All men may—and indeed do—experience the same reality, but Christians should see more in reality. This means proper guidance. In Tanzania, proper guidance would be provided by a theology of liberation for Tanzania.

[16] S. Moons, 'Liberation or Salvation', *Service*, 1974, p. 57.
[17] Trevor Huddleston, *Naught for your Comfort*, Collins, 1956, p. 239.

Conditions of theological service in Africa: preliminary reflections

SIDBE SEMPORE, OP

For the past twenty or so years, a handful of African intellectuals, clerics for the most part, have been vividly aware of the necessity of theological thinking undertaken in Africa itself by Africans. The urgency of such indigenous thinking arises not only from the internal logic of the Gospel as it gradually takes root and develops within a population, but also from the discrepancy which suddenly appeared in the nineteen-fifties between the intention of the foreign evangelizer and the evangelized African. The twilight of French and English colonialism was at that time casting deeper and deeper shadows over Christian consciences both in Europe and in Africa itself, where the suspicion began to be felt of some undisclosed connivance and complicity with the colonizer on the part of the evangelizer. The picture of an African church constructed and directed by missionaries suddenly revealed its defects and contradictions, and a certain number of Africans began to point them out more or less bluntly.[1] The more fully aware among the Christians realised that very shortly there would be a need, not merely to replace the missionaries pure and simple, but also completely to rethink in depth the very subject of evangelization. This could not be undertaken without explicit recourse to theological thinking.

Catholic and Protestant thinkers then took up the task of clearing the way for a truly African perspective on the Christian message. Their theological preoccupations and points of view had necessarily been affected—and circumscribed—by the colonial context and the missionary view of the problems, from which they were trying to break free. In their pioneering work they were obliged to take as their point of

---

[1] The trial of the missionary and the missionary church has been a favourite theme for a certain number of African writers, such as Mongo Beti, F. Oyono, and, much more subtly and radically, V. Y. Mudimbe in his recent novel, *Entre les Eaux. Dieu, un prêtre, la révolution*. On the part of African priests, the most hard-hitting criticism was that which F. B. Eboussi recently launched against the entire missionary effort in an article published in *Spiritus, no. 56*, May-Aug 1974, with the title, 'La démission'.

departure the colonial and missionary foundations, at that time still relatively stable, in an attempt to reach a new politico-theological level, as the evolution of Africa demanded. The two-fold reaction against colonial domination and missionary hegemony has taken two roads; on the one hand the road of the cultural ideology of Negritude, and on the other that of Adaptation as a theological concept applicable to the whole African church. This idea of Adaptation, bequeathed by the missionaries, and taken up by, among others the authors of the collective essays, *Des prêtres noirs s'interrogent*, published in 1956[2] has since been transformed into 'African Theology' as conceived first of all by people such as Mulago, Tshibangu, and Sawyerr.

The majority of these early African theologians have since developed further, thanks to the new currents of thought to which political independence and, in the Catholic context, the Second Vatican Council gave birth. It is true that some of them have had trouble freeing themselves from the reflexes acquired in the colonial, preconciliar period.[3] This shows that this theology already possesses a history in Africa and that for the last twenty years an African theological tradition with distinctive, fixed features has been in existence. Like any true tradition, it constitutes a point of reference, not a norm. The work of breaking new ground undertaken by these pioneers still needs to be pursued today, but under different conditions and in other ways.

Here I appeal to the rising generation, with a sensibility and training unmarked by the colonial and preconciliar legacy, to keep its distance from the theological tradition founded by its elders, and to build with its own hands a theology faithful to the demands of the Gospel, and at the same time faithful to the needs of the present and the aspirations of the Africans of today. Such a theology can germinate and flourish only in certain conditions. After indicating the area of enquiry open to the African theologian today, I shall attempt to isolate some of the subjective conditions which seem to me to be essential if we are to create a favourable climate for theological research.[4]

---

[2] *Des prêtres noirs s'interrogent, Coll. Rencontre, no.47, Paris, Cerf, 1956.*

[3] Thus for example the tendency to reflect by reaction against or opposition to the white world is still strong in many African theologians; similarly the tendency still to study the problems of the fifties. The recent pamphlet of Tshibangu, *Sur le propos d'une Théologie Africaine*, Kinshasa 1974, succumbs to this temptation by committing African theological reflection to the debatable routes of Senghor's Negritude, the Vitalism of Bergson or Blondel, and the theory of Participation, preached by a certain Ethnology.

[4] I hope the reader will excuse the too exclusively Catholic references throughout this study. It is merely a point of departure which admits its limitations, but does not mean to be restrictive.

The area of enquiry

The area of enquiry for a theologian cannot have limits determined *a priori*. Nothing human can escape being put into some sort of relationship with God and consequently nothing human can escape theological research.[5] It will be the task of each theologian to situate his research in his own particular context and direct it towards the most urgent sectors. If, however, I were to designate the constant factors for theological activity in Africa, I should reduce them to the following few schematic indications concerning the religious legacy, the cultural contribution and the socio-political context of Africa.

A look at the religious past of Africa is necessary in order to comprehend better the present with all its nuances, and direct the future. Today the phenomenon of religion is the object of profound and methodical study and research on the part of scholars from every background. The incidence of religion in the life of Africans today, and the forms they have used in the past to express their religious vision thus constitute for the theologian a vast field of investigation and a fertile soil for a meeting ground between the Gospel and the African desire for a God of joy.

The human contribution of African cultures should not escape the interest and attention of the theologian. Our way of being man, of living the human experience, should not remain the object of the tactless stare of the foreign ethnologist; it is from within that we must undertake and pursue the quest for our cultural identity as men. The Christian message only takes form and strength from its encounter and critical dialogue with a given culture. It aims to become the thread of the human fabric which unfolds within a whole culture and it is very important for any theological project that this human fabric be evaluated.

The socio-political context waits impatiently to be the object of serious theological consideration. The Kingdom of God in travail in our continent confronts the successive social and political mutations which constitute for the African both an opportunity and a risk. The church could become culpably marginal in this new Africa should it fail to make a theological investment in the testing times Africa is now traversing. The real problems of the African today are equally social, political and economic. Without worrying unduly about whether we are engaged in 'Black Theology', 'Political Theology' or the 'Theology of Liberation', we must not hesitate to bring theological consideration to bear on the

---

[5] We must react strongly against the tendency to confine African theological activity to the realm of liturgy or the study of traditional African religions; profound and positive study of our African religions and the development of African liturgies are of the utmost interest to the African theologian, but they cannot claim exclusivity, or even absolute priority, as against other theological *loci*, which may be just as important and just as urgent.

most sensitive points in African life, at the very heart of situations in which the African is struggling for his food, for his liberty and for his dignity.

Conditions of theological service

Let us now tackle the subject of the conditions of theological service in Africa. Theology and theologian are words which have come to us after a long journey through time and space. If they are to be utilized in an African context, it is absolutely essential that we must redefine them for ourselves.

There are almost as many theologies as theologians, and the extreme difficulty in which one finds oneself when trying to give a definition of theology is easily comprehensible. Yet from Origen to Saint Augustine, from Thomas Aquinas to Schillebeeckx, from Suarez to Rahner, from Luther to Barth or from Meister Eckhardt to Küng we can distinguish common family traits, a constant feature: one finds in them, as in all authentic theologians, a continuing concern to reconcile the elements of the Faith with the actual experiences and demands of the human spirit, with its eternal thirst for reasons. To see more clearly, more deeply, more justly; this is the ambition of the office of theologian, carried out in so many different ways by so many theologians. It must be admitted that any science has its counterfeits and its failures, and the history of theology, both Eastern and Western, contains fine examples of theological sclerosis, parrotry, formalism and fanaticism. However this is not to deny that throughout the centuries of the history of the Church there have been those Christians, whether famous or not, who have refused to be superficial relayers of the Message, and have striven to penetrate its spirit and bring all their faculties to bear on the study of the Message in relation to the needs of their contemporaries.

This is the way that I view, schematically, the nature and purpose of theology throughout the history of the Church, in order that they may be redefined in an African context. The most essential feature of theology, its office of studying and reaching a deeper understanding of the message with the aim of helping men to adjust better to the demands of that Message, will naturally be found in any true theological enterprise in Africa. But it will have to become incarnate, live the life of our flesh and our blood, feed on our concepts, conform to our ways of thought. In this sense theology, like Faith, must Africanize itself, take up residence among us, share our preoccupations, our questionings, our destiny.

An African Theology?

Since I have just mentioned the Africanization of theology, I cannot ignore the much debated question of an 'African Theology'. For the last fifteen years the topic of the development of an 'African Theology' in Africa has often been raised, particularly among African priests and ministers. In congresses, meetings, *colloquia*, reviews, etc., every tone from calm, objective discussion to passionate, angry demands has been used to justify the need for an 'African Theology'. Arguments, sometimes of epic dimensions, have set African partisans of this theology against its adversaries, generally European, the most famous being that between Tshibangu and Vanneste, both teaching at the National University of Zaïre.[6]

This controversy about the legitimacy of an African Theology arose in the general context of demands and affirmations which engaged the whole of Africa in the fifties and sixties. The impact of independence and the perspective of the Council liberated forces which had lain dormant in the fields both of politics and religion, in colonial, missionary Africa. The distance that the clergy wished at that time to put between themselves and the former evangelizing power is not unrelated to that of politicians regarding the former tutelary power.

Thus I freely admit that at a given moment in our history, during the Romantic period[7] through which our church has passed, we experienced the need for struggles and slogans to make clear our determination to take charge of the future of our church. We needed to decolonize ourselves spiritually, to shake off the psychological yoke which kept us bowed before the theological 'imperialism' of the West. We no longer wanted to think by proxy; we no longer wanted our theological bread to come to us ready-cooked in European and American ovens. From being mere consumers we wanted to become producers of theology, our own theology. Therefore we had to demand loudly the right to put our own label on what we produced.[8] We were indeed fighting for a principle. The

---

[6] The debate about African Theology was opened in 1960 by Tshibangu and Vanneste in the *Revue du Clergé Africain, no.4,* T.15, 333-52. In the same *Revue*, B. Studer with 'Encore la Théologie Africaine', *R.C.A.* 16, 1961, 105-29, and A. Ngindu with 'Unité et Pluralité de la Théologie?' *R.C.A.* 22, 1967, 593-615, contributed their point of view. Finally Tshibangu and Vanneste again confronted each other on the same theme at the time of the Fourth Theological Week at Kinshasa in 1968 with precisely this title: 'La problématique d'une Théologie Africaine'.

[7] A time of demands, affirmations, defence and illustration of the African personality.

[8] Inevitably, however, much naïvety crept into this race for an 'African Theology'. Some, for instance, seem to think of it merely as a listing of 'African values', the 'uncut stones' of missionary terminology. Those necessary elements for any valid theology, good exegesis of the Holy Scriptures, and sound knowledge of the history of the church, were often left on one side.

controversy has moreover been useful in helping to highlight the impreciseness of the terminology used on both sides, and in unmasking the sophistries which slipped too easily into the debate. Terms such as 'theology', 'African', 'Catholic', 'Western' are dangerous short cuts which hide a mountain of ambiguity and imprecision. They are coloured and given different meanings according to the origin of the protagonists, their previous training, the problems of the time, and the essence of subjectivity.

Today, as I have already remarked, there has been a considerable evolution in Africa both on the ground and in the mind. To argue everlastingly about the 'to be or not to be' of an African Theology is to beat on doors already broken down.[9] It is no longer a matter of whether an African Theology has a rightful place in the Universal Church; today it is a matter of setting ourselves without delay to the difficult task of embodying, acclimatizing and coming to a deeper understanding of the Christian Message on our African soil, making use of our own resources, of the authentic riches we possess, having faith in the Holy Spirit and our own capacity for meditation.

The African theologian

Therefore rather than an African Theology, it is African theologians that we need. That Africa lacks theologians is a well known and serious fact. Yet the strengthening of our church demands the active participation of everyone, and in particular that of those topographers of the Faith who, while yet struggling on the ground, are able to step back a little in order to make a more accurate estimate of the depth of the field. The need to sit down and take stock, strongly recommended in the Gospel for those who wish to build in a responsible manner (Luke 14,28), will only be realised in our church if there can be found in it a certain number of theologians devoted specifically to the task of continuously reevaluating the foundations of life and faith.

The task facing African theologians is complex; to devote oneself with the necessary firmness to theological work in Africa, some degree of vocation and preparation for it is required. Indeed seen as an aspect of the whole range of church activities, the work of the theologian is a ministry, a 'deaconship' or a dynamic research service which makes the

[9] Mudimbe, in the novel cited above, makes clear his irritation with interminable arguments about African Theology: 'Some fellow priests believe in the possibility of an African theological road . . . Among them, thought precedes action. It is as if Plato, before beginning his work, had announced that he was going to create Greek philosophy.' (Op. cit. 47.) Contrary to Mudimbe, I believe that these discussions were not entirely fruitless at the time, but agree with him that they have become fruitless today.

theologian a servant with the specific duty of serving his brothers by deepening their understanding of their Faith. The task of the theologian within the church is therefore a service instituted, or rather inspired by the Holy Spirit to meditate ceaselessly on the inexhaustible riches of the Faith, and to make it incarnate in the successive historical conjunctures faced by the Church in its long march to a Somewhere. It can therefore be seen that such a 'deaconship' has no place for amateurishness, fantasy or superficiality, and that a call both from the Holy Spirit and from one's circumstances is required for dedication to it.

In my attempt to sketch a portrait of the African theologian, I shall restrict myself to the following characteristics.

A servant. First and foremost the African theologian is a servant,[10] a Christian who wishes to make his contribution in the place where he lives; to explore and clear the way for an ever more authentically African Christianity, one that would be truer, more faithful to the Holy Spirit, and more heedful of the requirements of Africans. He must never exchange the modest role of servant for that of master, and in this respect the African theologian is clearly differentiated from his former Western colleagues. In the past theologians in the West have frequently felt that they were part of the 'magistracy' of the church because of an obstacle between research and teaching. Historically this can be explained by the fact that the episcopal hierarchy gradually turned away from theological research so that they could devote themselves to the administrative affairs of a diocese, leaving to theologians the task of searching the Scriptures, and interpreting the foundations of the Faith. It can also be explained by the fact that virtually all the theologians in the West were members of the clergy, and thus presented themselves before the laity as their masters in doctrine, in theology, members of the 'teaching church'. Here in Africa the theologian must strive to repudiate magisterial attitudes and doctoral mannerisms and appear in the simple garb of the seeker, as one who has chosen to seek and scrutinize the Faith and remain amongst men. Far from being a salesman of doctrine, he must be content to become a servant who, in all honesty and truth, seeks because he does not possess, discusses because alone he cannot suffice, and shares because he does not hoard. He must always be aware of the danger of theological *hubris*, that pride which can so easily turn a theologian into an omniscient, omnipresent oracle.[11]

[10] Again it is the ready pen of Mudimbe which exposes this characteristic in the words of his priest-hero: 'I was the master. Or, to employ a fine theological euphemism, I was a servant. A powerful servant.' (Op. cit. 50.) This 'power' of the theologian can make itself clear particularly in the self-satisfied display of titles, references, and other academic qualifications.

[11] We must not exchange complacency for pusillanimity; to be a servant does not mean becoming the slave of accepted formulae, or the griot of the ancestors' authority.

Committed and responsible. This danger of pride will be less of a hazard to the African theologian if he himself always takes care to live according to what he teaches or proposes. He must show himself to be the servant of the Faith that he is studying in his own everyday life. Theological service commits the theologian to leading an ever more demanding and authentic life of faith, so that he must strive as hard as he can in his own life to narrow the gap which so often exists between the theological word and the deed of the Christian, between a wonderful language and a life which takes no part in it. 'They say and do not': this reproach which can be addressed to any Christian who gaily confesses his faith without bothering to translate it into practice, would be a terrible accusation for a theologian who was ready to clear a path for others without venturing upon it himself. Amongst us in Africa thought and life have always been united, and wisdom has been the fruit of their indissoluble union. Whether expressed in fables, stories, proverbs and maxims, or lyrically in prayers, incantations and poetry, thought acted as the mainspring of life. In the same way theology will become wisdom and will be the mainspring of Life for the African Church and particularly for the theologian. Art for art's sake was a possible attitude in poetry; theology for the sake of theology is properly a non-sense. Even if it be admitted that the theologian must be prepared in some measure to relativize the results of his research, he must nevertheless not affect indifference, detachment or neutrality with regard to what he says. He cannot be content with being, in the words of Senghor 'the man who describes the straight road, but makes his way by winding paths' (*Hosties Noires*). He must also remember that 'it is intolerable to ask others to get wet while remaining dry oneself'.[12]

The theologian's commitment and sense of responsibility towards what he says and writes will shield Africa from being encumbered with a pseudo-theology making a jigsaw puzzle out of the articles of Faith and philosophical theorems. This determination to promote a dynamic, responsible, committed theology will have an influence even on terminology. For the more the theologian secretes 'theology' as one secretes a foreign body, the more esoteric will be his terminology, so that it becomes an insulator or protective screen between himself and 'the people', and then theology is no longer in the service of the community or the Church, but merely a collection of initiatory texts solely for the eyes of the members of a caste. On the other hand if the theologian aims to promote a living theology in the service of his brothers, he will make himself adopt a simple, sober terminology.

Loyal and critical: In the service of the Faith and its incarnation in Africa, the African theologian must be in the thick of things, participate

[12] Y. Congar, *Au milieu des orages*, Cerf, Paris, 40.

with his whole being in the cares of his church, experience them fully, feel solidarity with its doubts, gropings and hesitations, in a word, be completely a son and member of his church. To experience solidarity is to work from within, to act as a loyal member of the church and accept marginalization only if all else fails.

But this fundamental solidarity of the theologian with his church, his people and his country must not become uncritical, since he has a new perspective brought about by the slow maturing in his mind and heart of the Gospel message. The critical, prophetic duty of the Gospel must play a vital role in the theological enterprise in Africa; for, as has been well said, 'The Gospel is not neutral'.[13] To speak is to take up one's position in the name of the Gospel. This duty of criticism does not apply to relationships brought about by destiny, for this is where the Gospel become incarnate, but to relationships which are the result of compromise or complicity, for this is where Sin is most effective. To have a critical attitude towards one's community or one's country is not to be a candidate for excommunication or expulsion, even though at times these eventualities may arise when reprisals are taken. To have a critical attitude is simply to take the Gospel seriously and accept the ruptures it entails. This implies a rejection of blind loyalty due to blood or interest as a valid criterion for judgment or for action.

In this respect, a speculative theology comfortably ensconced in untroubled concepts, content to nurse the credulity of some, or pander to the good conscience of others, could never be any use for Africa.[14] Theology is an unsentimental confrontation with reality, the whole of reality. Thus no proper theological work can be carried through today in South Africa without some analysis and denunciation of the doctrine of *apartheid* and its consequences, in the very name of the Gospel message. In the same way Zaïrean theologians cannot remain indifferent to Authenticity and Mobutism. In Tanzania, Guinea, Ivory Coast or Madagascar, theology has to take up a stance in regard to the official framework of the life of the. people: *Ujamaa*, Marxism, Capitalist liberalism, or *Fokonola*. To talk of God to a man in his place and time, necessarily requires some critical reference to these space-time coordinates which very frequently give shape to aspirations, and dictate the attitudes adopted.[15]

Free to serve: The matter which I must now emphasize, since it appears

---

[13] The title of a recent work by F. Biot.

[14] In saying this, I have no intention of condemning healthy theological speculation, essential if one is to avoid the danger of a shortsighted, 'practical' theology. But this 'speculative' theology, according to the etymology of the word, should be 'mirrored' in the Gospel, and 'reflect' the pre-occupations of the African people.

[15] I do not mean to say that all theologians should transform themselves into critics of their societies, and prophets to their communities. I simply mean that theologians

to me to be vital for the possibility and carrying out of theological research in Africa, is the question of the liberty of the theologian. The last few decades in the life of the Western Church have shown all to clearly what it has cost the best Catholic theologians to carry out research from which everyone benefits today. Times have changed, and the freedom for research in theology is at present an acquisition which nothing, in principle, should compromise.

On 10 July 1969, Pope Paul VI, talking on the theme of the liberty claimed in these days, said, 'Liberty must not be confused with ideological and religious indifference, and still less with systematic individualism, or with irresponsibility, caprice and anarchy.' Then he added these words laden with meaning and with great implications:

We are about to see a period of greater liberty in the life of the Church and, consequently, for everyone of her sons. This liberty will mean fewer legal obligations and fewer internal inhibitions. Formal discipline will be reduced, the element of arbitrariness will be abolished, as will all intolerance and absolutism. The positive law will be simplified, the exercise of authority tempered, and the sense of Christian liberty increased.[16]

The Pope's astonishing words, inviting all Christians to rediscover the true liberty of God's children with no need for legalism or intolerance, appear to me to have a particular relevance for those charged with the delicate responsibility of bringing Faith and the world face to face in a frank, exigent dialogue. On the one hand scholars must avoid 'ideological indifference, irresponsibility, caprice, and anarchy'; on the other, the guarantors of this liberty for research, the authorities of the hierarchy, will condemn 'arbitrariness, intolerance and absolutism'. It would be easy to understand these words in one way or the other. I shall merely draw from them a few conclusions with regard to the liberty for theological research in Africa on two levels: at the level of the universal church, we need to know whether the particular churches of which it is composed really have sufficient freedom to manoeuvre (freedom *for* our church); at the level of the particular African Church, we have to learn how far we ourselves are ready to guarantee the theologian his freedom for research (freedom *in* our church).

At the level of the universal church, the question which first springs to mind is this: will the African Church be granted sufficient liberty to express and formulate in its own way its own view of what the problems are and its own theological vision? Or will it be obliged to suppress its personality and be a servile follower of what is told her by her sister-

must also explicitly take on this critical and prophetic duty in the midst of their people.
[16] See: *Document. Cathol.* No. 1545 (3-17 August 1969), 706.

churches of East and West? Here we rediscover the problem raised above by those in favour of an African Theology, and it has already been stated that the problem can no longer be seen in these terms, at least at the level of principles. Again it was Paul VI who declared at Kampala: 'It is possible for you to remain sincerely African even in your interpretation of the Christian life; you will be able to formulate Catholicism in terms completely appropriate to your culture.'[17] We have to admit, however, that in practice the possibility of eventual conflicts with Rome may paralyse or inhibit the progress of our theological creativity.[18] We must take care that our conception of and innate respect for the 'chief' does not prevent us from being ourselves, and henceforth clearing a path for Christianity that only we can discover. Thus in practice we shall be able to justify and deserve the theoretical liberty we enjoy within the universal church. We are neither Eastern nor Latin, and our church has no desire to be Greek or Latin, it is enough that it is Catholic and African, with all that that implies. This plurality of ways of being, officially recognized in the universal church, will at times give rise to tension, since centuries of conditioning towards uniformity will not disappear in a day;[19] but we know that through the ages the Holy Spirit has presided over the loyal, difficult discussion conducted between individual churches to absorb or reduce the inevitable tensions arising from plurality. The unity of the Church exists in the plural, for every *credo* is a polyphony.

At the level of Africa itself, the question of liberty of research in theological matters is in danger of becoming a more pressing problem. It is to be expected that the activity of African theologians, committed to the prospect of opening up new roads, will meet with resistance and opposition within our churches themselves. In the Catholic context one thinks naturally of the ecclesiastical hierarchy, and the delicate problem of the relationship between the episcopate and the scholars.[20] When

[17] One should not see these words of the Pope as a 'permission', which might 'permit' us to be ourselves in Christ, but as an urgent encouragement. We must not look for justifications or for foundations of African theological reflections in the 'overtures' of the West.

[18] This reflex is much too frequent among those of us who, while being Catholic, have difficulty in reconciling our communion with Rome and our union with the Holy Spirit, the source of life and activity. Communion with 'Peter' must not go so far as to cause that petrification of the spirit which is the cause of so much obstructionism and conformism.

[19] Thus, for example, possible modifications which could be introduced by us in the materials of the Eucharist, the sacramentalization of polygamous unions, conditions for divorce, the ordination of married men . . . or any other point of pastoral practice or the formulation of doctrine, could doubtless arouse opposition from abroad, or put difficulties in our way. But the unity of the Church is created from the unstable equilibrium which exists between the churches and witnesses to their vitality and originality in the Spirit.

[20] It goes without saying that in making such a clear distinction between bishops and scholars, I am making an oversimplification in order to make the case clear. A

talking of the commitment of the theologian, I stressed that he must avoid irresponsibility; he commits himself through his work according to his temperament and education. On his side, it is to be hoped that episcopal authority will not be used ill-advisedly. The possible inadequacies or exaggerations of certain theologians should be tracked down and countered by arguments of a theological nature, not by argument from a position of authority. The role of a bishop is that of a supervisor, who watches over the welfare of all and supervises the progress and dynamism of communities. In respect of theological work, the role of the episcopate is to stimulate and to regulate, encouraging the authorities to promote research and guarantee the freedom of the scholars; if need be, to rectify without ruining the work. An authority which is not upheld and an authority which is too interfering are two contradictory aspects of the same deficiency in the episcopal role; both fail in their duty to stimulate and regulate the research of the church, the one by default, the other through excess. Thus to be fruitful, relationships between bishops and theologians should depend not on force, but on trust. Trust is necessary for the settlement of disputes, which are bound to arise, given the limitations of both parties, and also the inherent difficulty of any theological undertaking. One must persuade oneself that 'the difficult problems posed today cannot be reduced to a subversive enterprise; everything is not *instituted* and *given*, and research is needed',[21] with all the risks that entails. The psychosis of error and the panic-stricken fear of heterodoxy are contrary to a loyal, clear-sighted search for the truth of the Gospel. The obsessive cult of the correct formula leads directly to formalistic dogmatism.[22]

A man of dialogue: Free to serve, while making use of temperate audacity and rigorous honesty in his investigations, the theologian can never forget that the systematic method, which threatens all such undertakings, could lead him inevitably to refuse the necessary dialogue

bishop who is both pastor and theologian, like so many Fathers of the Church, has become an ideal difficult to achieve nowadays, at least in the Catholic Church, on account of the numerous changes of context and mentality which have taken place in the history of the church since those days. The distinction between bishop and theologian is *de facto* and not *de iure*. In Africa many bishops are very well equipped for theological work, but very few of them can find the time to devote themselves to it properly.

[21] Y. Congar, Op.cit., 57.

[22] Mgr Edelby, with humour and seriousness, said: 'It is neither possible nor desirable never to err in theological research, for that would mean that one was marking time, making no progress. It is better to err while seeking, than not to seek in order not to err! . . . At all cost we must defend total freedom of expression within the Church, provided it be sincere. This freedom will naturally imply the possibility of error . . . God himself was prepared to tolerate the possibility of error in man when he gave him his freedom.' (in: *Inform. Cath. Intern.* No. 287, 1 May 1967, 32).

with other scholars and ministers, and turn him into an intransigent doctrinaire. To be open to discussion is a precondition of healthy theology. The diversity of African theologies and theologians makes it necessary to set up an organization for permanent discussion, where different ideas meet, correct each other and complement each other. Truth cannot be appropriated; it is 'bargained for', and I consider extremely important the will and capacity to introduce discussion and negotiation as principles of communication and a means of arriving at a greater degree of truth. This presupposes that each theologian should be prepared to criticize himself, and be criticized.[23] By the very fact that he makes proposals without imposing them on others, the theologian must be prepared to make his research relative, trying to find in others the share of truth he hopes for. Guehenno found an admirable expression for this demand made on the scholar: 'Let us have clear ideas; let us express them with all our strength. That is the job of our courage. But in the same way as one leaves a margin by everything one writes for second thoughts, corrections, everything not yet decided, truth for which as yet we only hope, let us leave around our ideas the margin of fraternity.'[24]

Ecumenical by conviction: Finally, the African theologian will be a Christian, open to the ideas of others. His theology must extend hospitality and friendship to all true values. Any self-sufficient theology is bound to become bloodless. To think that one can treat as unimportant acquisitions gained by others beneath our skies would be to fall into puerile fantasies. An obtuse theology, which, in the name of Africanness, refused to borrow from Eastern or Western thought, should the need arise, would certainly decline into sterile religious folklore. True goodness, especially theological goodness, acknowledges no country. It would therefore be useless to close one's mind systematically to other theologies, and adopt towards them an aggressive or defensive attitude, on the pretext of preserving one's identity. The African theologian certainly has the duty to take as his starting point above all African questions and ways of seeing the problems, to make the utmost use of the African materials at his disposal, to make available the results of his research to his African brothers, as a matter of priority; but while thus engaged, he cannot refuse, if need be, to have recourse to non-African helpers, and in all critical freedom make use of the experience of

---

[23] Apart from J. Mbiti's attempt at a critical evaluation of a few African theological works (in: *Spiritus*, May-August 1974, 'La Théologie Africaine', 307-332, an article which unfortunately does not mention the work of Francophone African theologians), it must be admitted that there is as yet no critical dialogue between African theologians. The circumstances of congresses and *colloquia* are too ephemeral for true in depth exchanges of view, even though the interpersonal contacts thus brought about are worthwhile and useful.

[24] Cited in Y. Congar, Op.cit. 56, note.

others to corroborate his own.[25]

This ecumenism of theological thought will also prove its worth in the approach to African realities. Thus a Catholic theology which refused to welcome the spiritual and human values contributed by the African religions, Christian denominations, independent or dissident African churches, Islam, or any other religious movement, could not claim to be really Catholic. A theological vision should strive to embrace the phenomenon of religion in all its facets. A tropical or equatorial theology cannot come to birth and grow without taking note of the luxuriant religious vegetation which hems it in on all sides and constitutes, as has already been remarked, a necessary theological locus. Coexistence and contact with the varied forms of religion and Christianity are a permanent call to open-mindedness and welcome.[26]

In collaboration with lay people: This African theologian, as just described, will he necessarily be a cleric? In principle the reply is only too clear: theology belongs to the whole of God's people, and is not the property of clerics alone. Therefore as far as possible we in Africa must end the connection between theology and the clergy which has been operative in the West. This connection is the result of the fact that, especially in the Middle Ages, the philosophical and literary culture necessary for a theology of the scholastic type was the lot of the clergy alone, who formed the intelligentsia of the time. This *de facto* monopoly led the clerics to forge for Western theology an ultraspecialized vocabulary, a veritable jargon, to which access was gained only through the universities or, later, the seminaries.

Today it is more widely realised that the active participation of lay members in the whole life of the church, including theological research, would give the church a much more dynamic appearance, and protect it from all forms of clericalism. So we must hope that our church benefits from research undertaken both by clerics and lay people. Thus there might come into being a real thology of the church, built by the whole of God's people.[27]

[25] The ecumenical attitude of the theologian does not confine him to the role of a mere borrower; a real dialogue can be instituted with, for instance, Western theology, whose most recent tendencies seem to throw down a radical challenge to our research effort. Such an in-depth dialogue would be of benefit to both sides. In any case it would enable the African theologian to take advantage of the dilemmas and exhaustion of Western theology.

[26] On precisely this point of ecumenism, the theologian can be of great help to the pastor, who, despite himself, often tends to adopt a purely negative attitude towards the diversity of beliefs. He will make·an effort to show that the overture in question is in no way connected with the tactical, condescending attitude which sees African religions as a vast quarry of uncut stones to be exploited, or other Christian confessions as prodigals lacking repentance.

[27] At the last Vatican Council, Cardinal Lercaro considered the problem in these

In the present state of affairs it seems unlikely that this desire will be realized, in that lay people capable of embarking on a theological type of reflection certainly exist, but rarely show themselves. The image of the priest as the only specialist in religious matters still holds sway in our minds, and encourages reflexes of monopoly on one side, and passivity on the other. There is a great need of lay people capable of making a contribution to the confrontation betwen Faith and the cultural, professional, political, economical and social problems of modern Africa. Their place in these various *milieux*, in conjunction with their professional skills and the strength of their faith, would enable them to conduct a demanding dialogue between the Gospel message and the African world. But rapidly made secure or marginal by the present pastoral structures, they leave uncultivated gifts and aptitudes which could be of tremendous service to the African Church.

One possible way to arouse a current of theological interest in Africa with the participation of lay people would be to set up a close collaboration between clerics and lay people in one field of research. It could be done, for example, by the formation of small cells, small groups where clerics and lay people working on the same research subject would give each other a helping hand and assist each other quite openly. Such work teams would have the advantage of being homes of research where lay people could openly express and freely develop the questions and answers they carry inside themsleves concerning the Faith, the Church and society. Clerics would learn to simplify their theological language, and experience more directly the demands of the African cultural and professional world.

Can any conclusions be drawn? These thoughts were intended merely as an introduction. In making a rough sketch of the African theologian as I envisage him, my main aim was to appeal urgently to young people who hesitate to commit themselves to theological research. May these few lines provide an introduction to a fraternal dialogue with them.

terms: 'We must suggest to lay people that they have the courage to devote themselves to the study of theological questions by serious scientific projects. I am not only saying that lay people should generally have some theological education (which, unfortunately, we often set at too high a level); on the contrary, I am thinking of something much more important, not indeed for all lay people, but certainly a great many . . . The Church needs a large number of lay theologians, trained in theological doctrine in a strictly scientific manner. This was the situation in the Church before the ecclesiastical sciences became the monopoly of clerics; and this is still the situation today in the Orthodox church and some Protestant communities.' (*Orientierung*, Zürich, 15 May 1968, 104).

Recent developments in African Christian spirituality

AYLWARD SHORTER

The author of the article on Spirituality in *Sacramentum Mundi*, the Encyclopaedia of Theology, complains that there is a 'banality' and an 'anaemic unreality' which is almost always connected with the word 'spirituality'.[1] One can sympathize with him and suggest that, at the outset of a chapter such as this, it is necessary to say what we mean by 'spirituality'. In recent Christian usage the word has come to have a personal—even an inward—emphasis, associated with phrases such as: 'the interior life' or 'the life of the soul'. In its origins spirituality was a more dynamic and outgoing concept. Primarily, the word is a Christian one, deriving from New Testament ideas such as *pneuma* and *spiritus*, and referring to the life-force which stems from God and which vivifies the baptized Christian. Through his union with Christ, the Christian enters the sphere of the spirit, and the term spirituality betokens his personal relationship with God, the core of his existence as a Christian. According to early Christian thinking, therefore, spirituality is not a theory, a *gnosis* or esoteric knowledge, but rather it is an encounter with God in life and action.

Spirituality can, by extension, be applied to every religious system, in the meaning of 'living religion' or 'religion in action', and in this sense one is referring to a dimension of life that transcends and reinterprets all relationships and experiences. It is really Heiler's definition of experiential prayer—that continuous mode of living which for the religious believer is a living communion with ultimate reality, usually conceived as personal and present in his experience.[2] Prayer as a living communion with God, divinities and spirits is to be distinguished from formal prayer, or prayer as communication, whether it be spontaneous or secondary, expressed in words, symbols or in contemplation. A study of prayer and prayer literature, therefore, provides a key to prayer as communion or to spirituality which is the essence of religion and the

---

[1] Sudbrack, J., 'Spirituality', in *Sacramentum Mundi*, 1970, Vol. VI, p. 149.

[2] Heiler, F., *Prayer; A Study in the History and Psychology of Religion*, London, 1932, p. 358.

foundation of worship. Spirituality, therefore, is not concerned with dogma, ritual, moral codes and religious structures as such. Nor, on the other hand, is it solely interested in personal convictions and charisms. Rather it is the area of tension between the two and the emphases which are made now on one aspect, now on another. It is the tension between activity and contemplation, between enthusiasm and legalism, as well as between the individual and the community. It depends, to a certain extent, on differing theological and cosmological pictures and on the believer's social conscience.

It is easy to appreciate that different ages, places and cultures have their own spirituality, and that the same can be said of religious movements and their founders. In the Christian tradition one can speak of the medieval spirituality, the spirituality of the reformation or of the Spanish mystics. Different spiritualities go by different names: pietism, revivalism, quietism or the Benedictine, Franciscan, Dominican and Ignatian spiritualities, to mention only a few. It is also possible to speak of differing spiritualities in the religious cultures of traditional Africa, and even to observe historical changes and developments in their spiritualities. The development of African Christian spirituality, particularly in the post-independence era, is one aspect of the encounter which has taken place in Africa between Christianity and traditional religious cultures. This chapter, then, will attempt to make some general observations about the spirituality of African traditional religion and the ways in which this has modified the forms in which Christian spirituality came to the continent. In particular we shall look at specifically African contributions in the shape of religious movements and writing.

The Spirituality of African Traditional Religion

One cannot begin to speak about the spirituality of African traditional religion without confronting the methodological problems involved in the study of African religious traditions. Personally, I do not accept that anyone can make general statements about African traditional religion without first establishing that the different religious systems in the different parts of the continent are related or comparable. Furthermore, I do not think it meaningful to speak about a basic African world view, or a fundamental religious philosophy underlying the different religious manifestations, unless the existence of such a world view or such a philosophy can be clearly proved through systematic comparative analysis.[3] On the other hand, I would be the first to agree that we are far

---

[3] John Mbiti speaks of a single, basic religious philosophy in his *African Religions and Philosophy*, London, 1969, p. 1. John V. Taylor speaks of a basic world view in his *The Primal Vision*, London, 1963, p. 27.

from being in a position to make such an analysis, but I would not, however, condemn the student of African religion to a rigorous particularism on that account. I believe that it is possible to rise above the level of the particular study even now. In the first place, there is the possibility of the kind of limited comparative study proposed by the late Sir Edward Evans-Pritchard in his Hobhouse Memorial Trust Lecture.[4] This envisages an intensive comparison between systems that are structurally, culturally and environmentally similar, a comparison that pre-supposes historical interaction between peoples and groups of peoples. One would then be studying variations between systems that are basically similar and subject to the same historical influences. The historical study of African religion is certainly making great strides and is revealing how widespread certain religious ideas and institutions are.

The question then arises whether one can go further and establish a series of categories based on such intensive comparison. So far, the kinds of categories that have been established have not taken full account of historical factors. Goetz sets up his categories on the basis of an analysis that traces religious elements in a culture down to the living experience of a particular environment and of a particular social ecology.[5] Mary Douglas applies Bernstein's ideas about the influence of language on culture to the influence of social categories on African ritual, theology, cosmology and morality.[6] This is a beginning, but when we do have some fairly presentable categories, then it should be both possible and worthwhile to carry out thematic studies in which certain themes are examined according to their variations in the different categories. Instead, therefore, of studying the differences in systems that are basically similar, one is studying the treatment received by certain common themes in systems that can be shown to be different. I feel that this will probably be the limit to which the study of African traditional religion as a unity can be taken.

For the present, therefore, a thematic study is entirely tentative, based as it is on categories that have yet to be perfected and to gain acceptance. A fundamental theme in the spirituality of African traditional religion is that of man's share in the creative process through his experience of life and the transmission of life. This is not seen as an expanding programme of world conquest, since African religious systems did not

[4] Evans-Pritchard, E. E. Y., *The Position of Women in Primitive Societies and Other Essays in Social Anthropology*, London, 1965, pp. 13-36.

[5] Goetz, J. and Bergounioux, F. M., *Prehistoric and Primitive Religion*, London, 1965.

[6] Douglas, Mary, *Natural Symbols*, London, 1970.

possess the requisite social or theological scale for such an idea, but it is seen as a share in the activity of a divine life-giver, and it is beautifully expressed in the recorded prayer and religious poetry of a number of African peoples. In the words of a Rwandese mother, her child is 'the field that we share with God (*Imana*)'.[7] It is obvious that such ideas flourish in societies with a theistic outlook and which are weakly structured. It is also appropriate in more strongly structured societies where the concept of the spirit-intermediary, particularly the lineage-spirit or ancestor, is strong. It is less well emphasized in societies where group loyalties are not so strongly stressed and where greater importance is attached to the ways in which the individual relates to others in categories focussed on himself. In such situations, achieved rank and status have a greater importance and there is usually a strongly structured, hierarchical or centralized society. The theological model here is one in which, not only is the supreme being outside the direct experience of the believer, but he has, in the traditional mythology, a tense and equivocal relationship with other spirits or divinities.

Another theme, and one which has a similar pattern of distribution, is that of memorial. This is the concept of effective commemoration or anamnesis. African traditional spirituality is frequently focussed on the idea of continuity with the past, a continuity which renders prayer and moral action effective. This is especially the case in the theistic systems where people are conscious of the need to be in harmony with their ancestors and to carry out the rites of their ancestors in the places established by them. This imitation of the ancestors is a pledge of future divine favour. Where the ancestors are themselves intermediaries, they are a living pledge of divine favour and prayer is addressed wholly or primarily to them. However, in this theme historical factors, in many cases, play a more important part. For some groups specific historical events are endowed with religious significance and are remembered and celebrated as an integral part of religious worship. A good example is provided by the Luo of Kenya and Northern Tanzania many of whose religious beliefs and practices cannot be understood without reference to their migrations in the sixteenth century, a historical fact which was decisive for their actual identity and location.[8] Memorial plays a definite role in the more strongly structured, hierarchical societies, but here it usually centres on the cult of historical personalities whose remembrance is imbued with religious or moral values.[9]

[7] Guillebaud, R., 'The Idea of God in Ruanda-Urundi', in Smith, E. (ed.), *African Ideas of God*, London, 1950, p. 197.

[8] cf. Ogot, B. A., *History of the Southern Luo*, Nairobi, 1967, Vol. I, *passim*.

[9] cf. the cult of Kintu and Mukasa in Buganda, Uganda.

Traditional African spirituality is typically communitarian, especially in those systems characterized by intermediaries and by a relatively theistic theological model. This is less true in unstructured societies with a personal religion and it may also be so in the more person-orientated, hierarchical society. A communitarian spirituality means basically a greater emphasis on action than on reflection, but traditions of asceticism and of silent contemplation are nevertheless found inserted into the celebrations of the community. It is important also to remember that 'community' in traditional Africa is not simply a community of the living, but one which transcends death both through the immortality of what John Mbiti has called 'the living dead' and by the transmission of life to subsequent generations.

We must be content with this somewhat bare, thumbnail sketch of spirituality in the religious traditions of Africa, and consider now its impact on Western Christian spirituality as brought to Africa in the nineteenth century.

Christian Missionary Spirituality

Christian missionary spirituality is essentially a spirituality of action, the more so in the early stages of the mission. This is true of most church traditions. The Jesuits who gave impetus in the sixteenth century to Catholic missionary activity, and, in the eighteenth century, indirectly to the first Protestant missions, called themselves 'contemplatives in action'. The Moravians, who were among the pioneer Protestant missionaries, saw their Christian commitment essentially as a missionary commitment. It was no accident that Cardinal Lavigerie, the founder of the White Fathers, gave his missionaries an Ignatian (Jesuit) spirituality. His first idea was to model his missionary society on the missionary monasteries of the European 'Dark Ages', but it soon became apparent that, if he wanted Christian influence to permeate the scattered settlements of Equatorial Africa, Benedictine 'stability' would be a hindrance rather than a help. It was for the same reason that the Benedictines of Songea (Tanzania) and the Trappists of Mariannhill (South Africa) were obliged to modify the monastic way of life. The emphasis in nineteenth century missionary spirituality, as it came to Africa, was Evangelical and Jansenistic. It attributed great importance to personal piety, and to the union or friendship of the soul with Jesus Christ. Piety was, furthermore, expressed through rules and observances, fidelity to which was considered a normal test of sincerity and even of sanctity. Christian spirituality, at that time, was almost aggressively zealous, infected with varying degrees of intolerance and bigotry. This aggression, however, was basically a form of defence, and early missionaries had built up a mental picture of themselves as forming a bulwark against a raging sea of diabolically inspired paganism. Their mission stations were to them oases of tranquillity and good order in a desert of immorality and lawlessnes. Their spirituality was somewhat inward-looking, in spite of the great stress on activity. It was also a spirituality that tended somewhat towards Manicheism, towards a separation of spirit from matter and a condemnation of the latter. It was a spirituality of great courage, stoicism and personal conquest, and one that set a premium on work and professional competence.

In many ways the spirituality that characterized the Christian missionary expansion into Africa was the antithesis of African traditional spirituality. While it was perfectly true that Christians were mostly prepared to accept a diversity of Christian spiritualities, and therefore to envisage the eventual development of an African Christian spirituality or spiritualities, they did not attempt to understand African traditional religious ideas as a coherent system, worthy of respect. Their prejudice was partly due to the reigning theology of salvation, and partly to the dispersed and fragmented character of African traditional religion itself which contrasted with the impressive religious cultures of Islam, Hinduism, Buddhism and other world religions. Moreover, the human sciences and the scientific study of religion were as yet undeveloped. The spirituality taught in the mission schools, in the seminaries and theological colleges was basically the same, Western model, nourished by ascetical practices invented in Europe and by spiritual literature written in Europe. Later on, as travel and communications improved, the visits of European and American evangelists and retreat-givers became a regular feature. It was some time before missionaries began to consult their own Christians and to notice any evidence of a distinctive African Christian spirituality.

'*Africa's Old Testament*'

Frequent early attempts to describe African spirituality took the form of a comparison with the Biblical spirituality of the Old Testament. As salvation theology developed the notion of a *praeparatio evangelii*, it became fashionable to say that Africa had had her own Old Testament, preparing her for the announcing of the Good News in modern times. One of the best of such studies was that made in 1956 by Jean-Claude Bajeux: 'Mentalité noire et mentalité biblique',[10] and the same theme has recently reappeared among the Black Theologians, with Bonganjalo

---

[10] Bajeux, J-Claude, 'Mentalité noire et mentalité biblique', in *Des prêtres noirs s'interrogent*, Paris, 1956, pp. 57–82.

Goba's: *Corporate personality: Ancient Israel and Africa.*[11] One can be pardoned, perhaps, for thinking that the similarities adduced by these writers are a trifle obvious, based as they are on characteristics shared by preliterate societies all over the world. There is an exasperating tendency in much African religious writing to proclaim the obvious as being uniquely African, and to ignore original insights. Nevertheless, the exercise of comparison in this case can prove to be a useful starting point for further discussion. Like the ancient Israelites, people in traditional Africa were close to nature. Like them too, they saw divine power at work even in secondary causes. The Bible is the product of oral tradition, similar, in many of its literary forms, to the oral traditions of Africa. The Bible uses concrete imagery and symbolism, rather than the language of philosophy or rational analysis. So, too, do the oral traditions of Africa. In the Bible we find institutions and values comparable to those of traditional Africa, values of the family, vital values, hospitality, the corporate personality and so forth. There are, of course, areas of difference and divergence on which the authors do not dwell. We do not, for example, find in the Bible the same vital relationship between the living and the ancestral intermediaries that we find in Africa. Nor do we find in Africa the experience of a God intervening so closely and so constantly in the history of the nation—particularly of its political institutions. However, the point is taken that, by and large, Africans are at home in the Old Testament.

The question then arises: Are we to assume that Africa must forever remain in the Old Testament? Or is she to emerge into her own experience of the New Testament? The answer of a very important section, if not of the majority, of independent church movements is that they are happier with an Old Testament spirituality. Harold Turner allots second place in his typology of African Independent Churches to churches of what he calls 'Hebraist' type.[12] Whereas, the churches of Christian type are not theologically or religiously distinct from the parent mission bodies, the Hebraist churches reveal considerable originality in adapting aspects of Old Testament belief and practice to traditional religious ideas, while representing a break with the past in many respects. Turner describes two main types of Hebraist Church, the Israelitish and the Judaistic. The Israelitish type sees God as loving and co-operative, speaking through a founder or prophet. While magic and idolatry are strongly condemned in these churches, joy is the predominant

---

[11] Bonganjalo Goba, 'Corporate Personality: Ancient Israel and Africa', in *Black Theology*, Basil Moore (ed.), London, 1973, pp. 65-73.

[12] Turner, H., 'A Typology for African Religious Movements', *Journal of Religion in Africa*, 1967, Vol. I, fasc. 1, pp. 1-34.

characteristic of their spirituality, frequently expressed in the sacred dance. The Judaistic type of church emphasizes laws and taboos. Stress is placed on asceticism, on repentance and on suffering. All of these churches are very concerned with the supremely important values of life and health, and this is true in general of African religious independency which interprets Biblical events and even Christian sacraments in terms of healing from a complex of sickness, sorcery and sin. The scholars who have compared the Biblical and African mentalities ignored the important theme of memorial. Not so the Hebraist churches which have, by and large, made a highly successful marriage of tribal and Biblical history and topography.[13]

The comparison of African and Biblical mentalities, therefore, has not been an idle or irrelevant piece of speculation. On the contrary, it would appear that to many Africans the Old Testament has offered a new means of expression for their traditional religious spirituality.

Bantu Philosophy and the Jamaa Spirituality

The *Jamaa* movement in Zaïre (then Congo) flourished in the 1950s and 1960s, but it had its roots in the 1940s with the publication of Placide Tempels' reconstruction of Bantu Philosophy.[14] The work of Placide Tempels and of disciples like Alexis Kagame generated well merited excitement in the 1940s and 1950s. With Aristotle and Aquinas as guides, they explored the abstract content of certain Bantu languages and constructed a European type of philosophy on the key concept of 'vital force'. It is difficult to do justice to the impact made by these ideas on writers and thinkers at the time—particularly Christian writers and thinkers in Africa. One after another, African theologians took over and developed the theme of 'vital force' with a succession of variations and applications. It was Tempels himself, however, who drew conclusions from his own philosophy for spirituality in Africa.

The spirituality which Tempels developed and described was called by the Swahili word *jamaa*, 'family' (not to be confused with the more famous Tanzanian political philosophy *ujamaa*, 'familyhood').[15] It was based on the three fundamental aspirations of the Bantu which Tempels had identified. These were: the desire for life, the desire for fecundity and the desire for vital union with the sources of a stronger and fuller life. These are very general aspirations, but they are certainly

---

[13] Sundkler, B. G. M., *Bantu Prophets in South Africa*, Oxford, 1961, p. 291.

[14] Tempels, Placide, *La philosophie bantoue*, Elizabethville, 1945.

[15] Tempels, Placide, *Notre Rencontre*, Léopoldville, 1962.

fundamental ones, which Tempels, as a philosopher, was right to notice. He was also certainly right in stressing that the Bantu desire for a fuller life is not merely concerned with physical life, but also with spiritual, moral and social aspects of life—with success, influence, social esteem, sharing and human fulfilment. Tempels insisted again and again that *jamaa* was not a lay apostolate movement, like the Young Christian Workers or the Legion of Mary. *Jamaa* had no structures, no programme, no rules or manual. *Jamaa* was to be an idea, a spirit of encounter and mutual self-revelation between priest and people. Tempels envisaged small groups of priests, each with his *baba* (fathers) and *mama* (mothers), a kind of spiritual family based on reciprocal understanding and shared prayers. The aim was freedom and spontaneity, a personal encounter which would enrich all concerned.

In his writing about *jamaa*, Tempels insisted again and again that he was advocating spiritual friendship and spiritual community—a relationship that must bypass sensual attraction. *Jamaa* was to be a union, not of bodies, but of souls. Using the images of the 'New Adam' (Christ) and his spiritual encounter with the 'New Eve' (Mary), or of the traditionally spiritual love of St Joseph for the Blessed Virgin, or even, on occasion, the example of the Blessed Trinity, Tempels strove to make the point that human love was ultimately spiritual and that it could even be expressed bodily, without a union of bodies in the sensual or sexual context. The aim of *jamaa* he summed up as 'to be' and 'to be perfectly'.

Tempels' anxiety about a possible misunderstanding proved to be well founded. His highly mystical ideas proved impossible to realize, and the ideal of spiritual friendship is, as spiritual writers know, an ideal fraught with possible ambiguity even among dedicated people. To advocate it as an ordinary channel of lay spirituality was asking a great deal. A basic problem was the desire for complete spontaneity that contradicted the cultural symbol of the family which was used to give expression to the new spirituality. A family possesses a structure, and relationships, even deeply personal relationships, have to be defined in terms of that structure. Moreover, whether one likes it or not, there are rules, 'do's and don'ts' for working in groups. Tempels constantly repudiated any idea that he was the leader of a movement or that reference should be made to him for the introduction and running of the *jamaa* groups. However, it soon became obvious that he was alone the repository of the *jamaa* idea, and that the whole idea was doomed to failure without the presence and support of his charismatic personality. *Jamaa* was, perhaps, a dream impossible to realize, but it proved the point that spirituality is not fundamentally philosophy, but a dimension of real, everyday living.[16]

Victor Turner's Concept of Liminality

Traditional African asceticism was associated with the celebration of the great drama of life and death in the rites of initiation, or rites of passage. It was Arnold van Gennep who gave us this concept of passage, analysing its stages as phase of separation, liminal phase and phase of incorporation.[17] Victor Turner, the social anthropologist, enlarged on van Gennep's ideas. Working from the material he collected among the Ndembu of Zambia, Turner developed the concept of the liminal phase, the realm of cultural ambiguity to which initiates belong.[18] Liminality is the antithesis of status. Its attributes are transition, homogeneity, equality, poverty, humility, sexual continence, silence, acceptance of suffering, obedience and sacredness. It is one of the most fundamental manifestations of the sense of community, and it is sacred, displaying the sacred power of the weak and defenceless. The liminars, or threshold people, experience the well-springs of freedom and humanity, understanding, through their common experience and through the common reactions which they learn, that human life is something profoundly shared. They are also, says Turner, a mirror held up to society itself, enjoying a more or less explicit prophetical role. The liminal state can also be more or less permanently institutionalized in the form of secret societies, mask societies and so forth.

Turner's description of liminality reaches almost mystical heights and he has no hesitation in comparing the African experience with Western Christian monasticism, with the common life introduced by St Benedict, with Franciscan poverty and with Hindu and Buddhist mysticism. Social anthropologists have been rightly suspicious of general comparisons like these, made over immense distances of time and space. However, the concept of liminality is attractive and does have obvious application to the 'Pilgrim Church' of the Christian tradition, as well as to the ideals and rules of life of Christian religious congregations. It is an idea that

---

[16] Fabian, who studied the *jamaa* movement at the end of the 1960s, insists that Fr Tempels remained in complete, if remote, control of the movement from Europe. However, his research shows how the movement became a highly structured association with a strong emphasis on *mafundisho* or teaching. It also interpenetrated an unofficial shadow *jamaa* that was heterodox and which, at times, practised sexual communalism. The texts given by Fabian in the appendices certainly betray an undesirable and overt sexual symbolism. It is small wonder that large sections of the *jamaa* fell foul of the Catholic hierarchy in Zaïre. Moreover, it seems that while the movement was extremely successful in the heterogeneous mine compounds of Katanga, the *jamaa* philosophy was less attractive to those practising their own traditional cultures in their homelands. c.f. Fabian, J, *Jamaa, A charismatic movement in Katanga*, Evanston, 1971.

[17] Van Gennep, A., *The Rites of Passage*, London, 1960.

[18] Turner, V. W., *The Ritual Process*, London, 1969.

should be helpful in trying to give expression in Africa to the social role of religions. As yet, however, it does not seem to have received very much attention outside the academic circles of the anthropologist and student of religion.

Christian Spirituality and African Humanism

African spirituality can, in a sense, be said to have stolen a march on African theology in post-independence Africa. We have already noted a pre-disposition among missionaries towards African spirituality, whereas the nature and method of African theology is still a matter for heated debate. The Roman Synod of 1974 highlighted the debate between those who did, and those who did not, want a culturally diversified theology. In any case, in the midst of all the talk of African theology, precious little theology is actually being written by Africans. It has even been suggested that Africans are fundamentally uninterested in theology,[19] and the studies of Tanner and Deniel exemplify the emphasis traditionally placed on morals, rather than on dogma, by Christians in Africa.[20]

In the meantime, an African spirituality has flowered in the new humanism which accompanied and followed the achievement of political independence. This humanism was firstly a political philosophy, but it was never an atheistic humanism. It was expressed in political ideals such as the Negritude of Senghor, the Humanism of Kaunda and the Doctrine of *ujamaa* of Nyerere. As such, it tried to impart a new application and a new dynamism to the human values of the ancient village world of Africa—particularly to the idea of co-operative living, and to the idea of human life as essentially shared and communitarian. These ideas harmonized with, if they were not (as they sometimes were) influenced by, the writings of the Christian scholar and spiritual writer, Teilhard de Chardin. At any rate, the Christian resonance of such philosophies was soon appreciated by Africans, sometimes almost to the verge of fanaticism, and the claim was even made for them that they represented an African way of living the Christian Gospel, completely in harmony with the Christian communism of the primitive church. Both Kaunda and Nyerere themselves can be said on occasion to have become spiritual writers, emphasizing the spiritual dimension of human personality and

[19] Turner, Philip, 'The Wisdom of the Ancestors and the Gospel of Christ: Some notes on Christian Adaptation in Africa', *Journal of Religion in Africa*, 1971, Vol. 4, fasc. 1, pp. 45-68.

[20] Tanner, R. E. S., 'Extempore Prayer among Adolescent Sukuma in Tanzania', *Nairobi Workshop in Religious Research*, (mimeographed), 1968, pp. 391-6; Deniel, R., *Croyances Religieuses et Vie Quotidienne*, Paris-Ouagadougou 1970, p. 299.

the need for Christian movements of liberation and protest.

In fact, the post-independence accent on development and communal living at village level was accompanied by a Christian rediscovery of human values. Both the Second Vatican Council (1962-1965) and the Fourth Assembly of the World Council of Churches at Uppsala (1968) placed the emphasis on man and upon human culture and development. The face of the missionary church had also changed. Not only was Africanization gaining momentum, but the churches were increasingly involved in every aspect of development. Coupled with this was an increasing emphasis on the local church and the local community. Africa began to experience the introduction of the contemplative religious life—the witness of being, rather than doing—a far cry from early missionary activism.[21] Greater spontaneity was encouraged, not only by liturgical renewal and creativity, but by the spread of pentecostalism and charismatic movements. In many ways, the gulf between the spirituality of the old Africa and that of Christianity was being bridged.

It was characteristic that the successors of Placide Tempels should turn their backs on metaphysics and concentrate on values. One of them, Dominic Nothomb, published a remarkable essay on African humanism in the year the Vatican Council ended.[22] The book was inspired by the author's own missionary experience in Rwanda, and its expressed aim was to show how African values harmonize with Christian values or call for further fulfilment in Christianity. Even so, an attentive reading of the book reveals that it nevertheless owes a great deal to the earlier metaphysical stage and to the latter's underlying linguistic analysis, rather than to the methods of structural anthropology.

It is in the area of African creative writing that there is most hope for a developing Christian humanism. Political independence not only brought humanistic political philosophies into their own, it also gave encouragement to their literary counterpart, a new output from African authors writing mainly in English and French. This new literature was written for the *élite* and for a readership abroad, but it is already beginning to make itself felt through school syllabuses which introduce a large number of secondary school students to the ideas of these writers. The authors of these novels and poems are mostly unsympathetic to Christianity, preferring to idealize the religiosity of African tradition. At best they value the Church's humanitarianism; at worst, they condemn her cynicism and iconoclasm. (See above, pp. 426-42.) In this assemblage, those who proclaim the possibility of a synthesis of the two

---

[21] cf. Bouaké Declaration of the Monasteries of Africa, in Peifer, C., *Monastic Spirituality*, New York, 1966, pp. 375-6. See also below, pp. 554-5.

[22] Nothomb, D., *Un Humanisme Africain*, 1965, Brussels.

spiritualities—that of Christianity and that of African traditional religion—are rare indeed. But the fact is, they are there. A few writers exist who have a more penetrating and more positive understanding of Christianity and who definitely reject the all too common academic view which sees the Christian and the African identities as incompatible. Two outstanding examples are Camara Laye and Michael Kayoya.

Camara Laye's strange, mystical book, *The Radiance of the King*, was first published in French as long ago as 1956.[23] Nine years later it appeared in English and immediately went into several editions. Although he is a self-confessed Muslim, Laye is obviously strongly influenced by Christian ideas. Interpretations of the book differ. If it is not an account of man's searching for God, it is an account of his searching into the mystery of his own being—which is probably the same thing in the long run. The story is of a young, white man's quest for serenity and fulfilment in the service of an African king. In a way, the book celebrates many of the attributes of liminality as described by Turner. The king is surrounded by mystery, glimpsed at a distance at the beginning of the story, and sought by the hero for the rest of the book. One by one, the veils are lifted, as mystery succeeds mystery, beginning with the journey to the mysterious 'South' ('The South is everywhere') where men can shed their status, their artificiality and their inhibitions. The hero discovers peace through the self-surrender of love, through abnegation, nakedness, emptiness and hunger, and it is the 'adorable fragility' and purity of the boy-king with his far-off smile and mysterious omniscience that draws the man into his embrace—to be enveloped forever. Another variation on that ancient theme of the power of the weak. *The Radiance of the King* is a modern expression of the kind of interior quest which constitutes the prayer of African religious tradition, the gradual divesting of self which terminates in the eternal silence of God.

Less sublime, but no less thoughtful is the poetry of Michel Kayoya, the young priest so tragically put to death in Burundi in 1972. Kayoya's *My Father's Footprints* appeared in French in 1968 and again there was a long lapse of seven years before the English translation was published.[24] A second book, *Between Two Worlds* appeared in French in 1970, and an English translation is in preparation.[25] Kayoya examines the

---

[23] Laye, Camara, *The Radiance of the King*, 1965, London.

[24] Kayoya, M., *My Father's Footprints*, Nairobi, 1974, tr. by Aylward Shorter and Marie-Agnes Baldwin.

[25] Kayoya, M., *Between Two Worlds*, in process of translation by Aylward Shorter and Wandera Chagenda. Original French edition: *Entre Deux Mondes*, Bujumbura, 1970.

philosophies of Capitalism and Marxism and rejects both. Finally, he opts for a Christian reawakening of his own African culture, a rediscovery of humanity in African terms. The themes of African traditional spirituality are all there: life-communion, closeness to nature, divine power present in secondary causes. Like Camara Laye he sees human development as a quest, a conquest of self. Atheism is firmly denied. Becoming a Christian means becoming more fully a man—since manhood is now assumed by God in Christ. It also means, because of the African philosophy of humanism, becoming more truly a *Murundi* (citizen of *Burundi* and member of the *Barundi* people). Kayoya frequently refers to the necessity of dying humanly, dying well. In this, he has added his own personal witness to his writings.

Conclusion
The main difference between the spirituality of the missionary era and that of the post-independence era, is that the first was lived uncompromisingly by those who preached it. Indeed, it was the mainspring of their whole lives and of the lives of those who accepted their preaching. The new spirituality of the African Christian humanist is still largely theory. It lives on the printed page and in the lives of a relatively few dedicated individuals. It has not yet percolated downwards to ordinary men and women. The early missionaries had a whole edifice of spirituality behind them, ready-made and impregnable. The new spiritual synthesis is being slowly and painfully worked out. It is still far from gaining acceptance on a wide scale. Little by little, through religious education and preaching, the ideas may begin to influence Christians at large.[26] Probably, the majority of Christians in Africa are troubled by an unresolved duality in their thinking, an inability to make the necessary synthesis of Christianity and traditional values. Early attempts to offer a synthesis, like that of Placide Tempels, were too rarified and unrealistic. The Independent Churches—or at least the Hebraist section—offer a synthesis which does not take them out of the Old Testament. The new writers offer the best hope, if their ideas become known and are translated into action.

[26] Already ideas from Kayoya and Camara Laye have been used in new religion syllabuses for secondary schools in Africa: *Developing in Christ*, and *Christian Living Today*, London, Geoffrey Chapman. (Series completed in February 1975).

Worship and spirituality

BENGT SUNDKLER

'Spirituality' is not a term commonly used in Protestant theology. This does not of course exclude the existence of the fact, or facts, which this term may be supposed to represent. 'Religious experience', 'piety', or, perhaps most often, the wide concept 'life' ('spiritual life', 'Christian life') are words more often used by Protestants, also African Protestants. From the outset, the wide variety of expressions and traditions must be emphasised. We are looking in vain for a common formula.

Yet, when compared with Western Protestantism, African spirituality seems to suggest a common ground of experience, in the relatively strong corporate nature of the Christian life. Over against the individualism of the Westerner, community, fellowship and group feeling fill the African scene. This characteristic pattern of corporate worship shows through most vividly and dramatically in the life of the Independent African Churches, with their roots both in genuine African experience and in an archetypal inspiration of Biblical teaching.

'Spirituality', in this context, may be taken to mean something very different from the Western or Eastern idea and practice. It is not so much the 'still, small voice', but rather 'the storm' and, not seldom, 'the earthquake' (1 Kings 19), which typify the common worship and emotional experience of the group. The Zulu prophet is not the terminal receiver of his message but always a channel for the message to be transmitted to the church, and this message is in the process amplified by the participating mass experience.

There are exceptions to this enthusiastic outpouring of the Spirit. The thousands of Shembe's Nazarites, all in white, assembled in 'Paradise', (at Ekuphakameni, near Durban) in the Sabbath service of the annual 'July' festival sit very quietly in the ground. The singing—slowly and quietly rising and falling—reminds one of the slow but mighty swell of the Indian Ocean nearby. The style of worship is even today dominated by the personality of the founding Prophet (d. 1935) who, far from being the shouting and jolly Zion preacher, was rather subdued in presenting his message.

Shembe provides a beautiful solution of the tension between corporate participation and the individual's experience. In the worship as such, the individual is ideally not more than a molecule among the thousand and ten thousand of faithful at Ekuphakameni, the centre of the Church. But the daily family evening worship opens the door to the individual's meeting with God. The printed service—part of the Introductory chapter in the printed Hymnbook, *Izihlabelelo zamaNazaretha*—has 36 short paragraphs (3-4 lines each). No. 35 says:

'For Jehova visits his people in their sleep. You must look after your house (family) well, so that Jehova may not be angry in coming to you in the dream.' Matt. 2:13.

The dream experience is the individualized and interiorized continuation and adaptation of corporate worship. Here is of course 'spirituality', in Zulu or Swazi Zion, in that inner, more luminous world of the dream.

There is a difference between the charismatic group which functions as an 'open' congregation, with a somewhat floating membership, and the closed 'convent' type of church. As an example of the latter type we mention George Khambule's church (d. 1949). For many years, his church of some two hundred men and women lived together as a closed community. Khambule was highly creative with regard to new forms of liturgy. The point is that he could only function in this creative capacity as he had at his disposal an ever present group of faithful who could form chorus groups, etc.

Khambule's religion *is* worship, in the specific sense of corporate religious dramatic performance, in which prayer and praise are acted out by the whole community as a total, all-engaging drama. It must be kept in mind that the Saints were a closely-knit religious community, living together, working together and worshipping together at their Telezini Zion, directed by an authoritative, and indeed charismatic, leader who also was an imaginative stage-manager. Khambule had the gift of engaging everybody in active worship. This was also the means of evangelism: people joined him because they enjoyed playing their part in the great drama of Telezini.

An idea of this active and dramatic worship can be conveyed by some of his most representative liturgies, with the understanding that these, as a matter of course, were sung antiphonally, by leader and congregation. The contents of these liturgies are soon recapitulated. It is all about the communication between Heaven and Telezini. Against a solemn, backdrop of Paradise, with Jehovah well established in the centre and an occasional introductory reference to the Trinity, the core of the drama deals with Telezini, beginning with George Khambule's vision of Telezini from Heaven in 1920. This is the real centre of the doctrine. In the foreground, George Khambule as St Nazar and his Saints move and act as the chief players. Communication between Telezini and Heaven is reached through the Gates—the role of the Gate-keeper in Khambule's writings should be stressed—and by means of a 'heavenly telephone'. Then again, space is filled with the armies of Apocalypse: Angels, Creatures, Elders: all illuminated by an occasional flash of lightning, more Zulu, perhaps, than Hebrew.

The form of the liturgy is most interesting. It is all by way of sung responses, performed antiphonally by these highly musical Zulu men and women. It is as music that this liturgy lives and moves the hearts of the participants. There is a constant response and *interplay*—the exact word for what occurs—between the Priest and his Congregation, between the stage-manager and his cast. Sometimes the responses are very brief. At other times, the priest sings long passages from the Book of Revelation or from the hallowed tradition of Khambule's life, while the congregational response is perhaps reduced to one short line, sung with great enthusiasm.

In 1969 we heard Archbishop Sikakana as Leader sing one verse at a time from St John's Apocalypse. His little congregation of four or five, under the determined and energetic direction of the Archbishop's wife, would repeat the same holy words. This was not all: the Archbishop would sing one line, with strong emphasis. The congregation would respond with the same vigour; then—and this had a very moving effect—the Archbishop would repeat the singing of the words with a soft voice, as if whispering a great secret, and his wife and the congregation followed him. With innate discipline, they would enter into the secrecy of these holy mysteries and corporately whisper their joy at the Angels and Creatures and Elders, invisibly but certainly present, moving their wings softly.

This was also part of Khambule's considerable genius, for as the insignificant little group arranged a special service for the benefit of their white visitor, they were all aware of their fundamental debt to 'George', who had once conceived and created all these words and the liturgical arrangement of words, and the music, and their copes and mitres and staffs.

This effect was emphasized by the pattern of movements enacted by the Archbishop and his group. It perhaps goes without saying that in these actions they believed they were solemnly imitating the movements and mannerisms of the unforgettable George Khambule himself. I have often noticed how in these churches this jerky curtsy or that strange sound—howling, hawking—performed regularly by the group was at the same time an expression of an identification with the particular church founder, who perhaps unwittingly had introduced this step or sign or sound. Thus while leading the singing, Sikakana would hold his archiepiscopal crozier in his left hand, moving in a dancing rhythm, from time to time bowing deeply.

The 'Africanness' of Independent Nguni Churches appears particularly in the spontaneity of worship, with its rhythm and colour. Yet, in the midst of spontaneity there is rigid ritualization founded in certain verbal forms and bodily expressions. The ritualization is emphasized by the strictly followed forms of worship. There is in fact much more of printed or written forms of worship than one would possibly expect. Shembe's and Nzuza's printed hymnbooks (the latter not available to the public) are examples.

The development of a Church Year is also significant. 'iGoodi' (or Good Friday) is the name for the most important of church festivals, including Friday through Easter Sunday. This *triduum* with its vigils, and the identification during the vigil by each man and woman with the Golgotha drama, make this occasion much more important than it is within comparable mission churches. As a rule Christmas and Pentecost have never become nearly as important as this 'iGoodi' (or Easter Service). In Swaziland, the iGoodi has become a modern national festival, celebrated by all the Independent Churches, under Zionist leadership, and with King and Queen-mother taking an active part. The royal kraals of Lobamba and Lozitha are centres for this celebration.

The corporate nature of African worship, a developing emphasis on some rituals (e.g. the sacrament of Baptism and the practice of confession), and the recognition of dreams as a means of divine communications are also prominent features of African Protestant churches. Participating in a Presbyterian Sunday morning worship in Cameroun, I noticed that, after an introductory prayer, about one fifth of the large congregation rose to sing a hymn. After the Old Testament reading, a second fifth of the congregation formed themselves into a choir and sand a hymn. After the Epistle, a third fifth, after the Gospel and sermon the remaining parts of the congregation formed their particular choirs, contributing to the edification of the total congregation. In fact, the Sunday congregation consisted of a sum of choirs. During the week these assisted at weddings and burials and in a variety of other activities.

Also in Africa, Protestantism is a book religion. The role of the Bible as a book, read and to some extent assimilated, must be emphasized. The first Uganda converts became known as *abasomi*, Readers, i.e. people who could read books. The activity of the catechetical class did not consist primarily in the chanting of certain prayers and confessions but rather in the teaching of the art of reading so as to allow each individual—in principle, if not always in practice—to read the Bible on his or her own. 'The school in the bush' was fundamental for the evangelisation of the people. The personal experience of the Holy Scriptures was basic to the spiritual life of the individual, of the family worship, morning and evening, and of the congregational worship.

It was a daring road to take. It has even been suggested of late that the fact of Bible translation into a particular vernacular has constituted one of the foremost causes of the emergence of African Independent Churches. More important is the positive and constructive role of Bible reading for the spiritual nurture within mission-related Protestant churches. For the first two or three generations in a local church it was not so much the total Bible which was the basis of reference, but rather a selection of Old Testament stories together with the four Gospels. These formed the basis of texts for teaching in schools and preaching in church, repeated in endless, dramatic and captivating retelling in the homes and in local meetings.

The worship experiences vary of course greatly between different denominations and at different levels of education and sophistication. But it must be stressed that many specifically 'African' homiletic situations include an element of an almost electrifying 'give-and-take', a challenge and response between preacher and local group. And the more the congregation consisted of committed 'readers' with a living knowledge of Old Testament archetypes and New Testament parables, with an existential understanding of their message, the more this worship experience deepened and quickened the spiritual life of the group and of the individuals concerned.

The two sacraments, particularly baptism, form a solid foundation of the new spirituality. 'Thus we experienced our day of joy' was how Pastor Andrea Kadjerero, the first pastor of the Bukoba Evangelical diocese, referred to his baptism in September 1906. The general rule (with some exceptions) that Protestants in Zaïre and Congo (Brazzaville) follow Baptist practice has been of the greatest importance for the understanding of the Christian life: a very real personal decision was often taken and the filth of sin was washed away: a new person was born. Dr Andersson's conclusion for the Congo 'churches at the grass-roots' is representative for the whole continent: 'It is quite clear that for the catechumen baptism was both a moment of decision and a source of power to which he returned particularly in times of temptation and distress'.[1]

Regular communion is experienced as a personal strength and forms a deeply corporate experience. A disturbing problem about Holy

[1] E. Andersson, *Churches at the grass-roots*, 1968, p. 165.

Communion is, however, that admission to it is sometimes taken as a guarantee of moral blamelessness, and participation at the altar can accentuate an unmistakable Protestant tendency to moralism. This was brought home to me when reading the church council minutes at the Lutheran church at Ceza, Zululand. The secretary, a Zulu catechist, registered various cases of a breach of the sixth commandment (in the Luthran catechism) by simply quoting the person's name, adding 'C.D.6'. The formula 'X.Y., C.D.6' thus meant that X.Y. had transgressed this particular commandment in the church's discipline. But if the offender, after being under church discipline for a year or two and having been 'forgiven', repeated the same offence, the note in the council minutes was a brief, factual 'X.Y., 2.C.D.6'.

After the first one or two generations of a growing Christian mass movement, there was often felt a characteristically Protestant dissatisfaction with the church situation now interpreted as lukewarmness, 'coldness', or even 'death'. In certain countries—for example Madagascar, East Africa and Cameroun—there followed 'revival' movements which for some time injected a new spiritual dynamism, new 'life', into the body of the church. The Balokole movement in East Africa is a case in point.

The Balokole are an 'African' movement, yet related to a Western tradition. They have largely remained a dynamic revival movement within the mission-related dioceses and synods of Anglican, Presbyterian and Lutheran, etc., churches in East Africa. The movement cannot be understood—and should not be interpreted—without their historical roots in 'Keswick'. This was—and is—one of the evangelical 'Holiness' movements of the nineteenth century. It was in 1875 that R. P. Smith started a conference at Keswick (Lake District) which was to become an annual event. It was supported mainly by Evangelical Anglicans, not least by C.M.S. lay missionaries. Three C.M.S. medical doctors had been strongly influenced by Keswick before leaving in the 1920s for Uganda and Rwanda.

One could in fact lead this influence further back, to another C.M.S. lay missionary, George Pilkington. He was translator of the Ganda Bible, killed in the Sudanese (Muslim) mutiny of 1897, regarded as a martyr for his faith and thus related to the first Buganda martyrs of 1886. The rallying song of the modern East African revival movement, *Tukutendereza Jesu*, sprung from this generation of martyrs. It uses Luganda words. Once again in church history, words sanctified by the blood of the martyrs have been used as a *lingua franca* of the song of the heart. These beginnings in sacrifice and martyrdom gave their overtones to the life of the modern movement.

This movement began about 1930-5 in Rwanda and Uganda, and the three medical doctors already mentioned were part of these beginnings. William Nagenda of Uganda was one of its great African leaders. The movement influenced the Anglican theological seminary at Mukono and caused a revolt there. The whole final class at Mukono left the seminary just before ordination and thus spread the fire of the movement; but the movement remained a dynamic within the church, and did not—at least speaking in large terms—result in break-aways.

There arose theological tensions within the movement: between those who were supposed to represent spiritual 'activism' and those who taught 'spiritual quietism' ('Christ alone', 'Christ suffices'). This controversy in the cities and villages sharpened theological concepts and emphasized the need for Bible study.

The revival hit those churches which had been formed a generation earlier by impressive mass movements. The first generations had joined the church through Baptism and receiving a New Name and thereby overcoming a deep personal problem, that of *enshoni*, shame. At that time, it was regarded as a shame not to be modern, not to be able to read, not to have a new Christian or Muslim name. But the revival revealed a deeper need than that of conventional modernization and adaptation. Deeper than *enshoni* lay *ekibi*, guilt. That had to be 'thrown up', purged, confessed. Through public confession the individual experienced a sense of liberation and a new joy, a discovery that only now he or she had begun to know what real Christian faith was. Restitution became necessary. This experience was shared through open confession before the group.

Revival resulted in the forming of what was claimed to be somthing of a new clan, *oluganda*. They were 'brothers' and 'sisters' in this new clan, blood-brothers in Christ. The greeting *Tukutendereza* became the shibboleth of this blood-brotherhood. It was used only with reference to the brethren. If meeting with an outsider one preferred the ordinary more neutral greeting *Salaam* or *Orairotai*. The brethren formed teams of three—six—twelve—farmers, fishermen, carpenters, builders, businessmen—who might go away for weeks in order to witness.

The role of women in the Fellowship is a considerable factor. Revival has lifted hundreds of thousands of African women and given them a new role, a new sense of personal worth. I do not know of any other factor in East Africa which to that extent has served to emphasize equality between the sexes as Revival (see above, pp. 145-6).

Locally these men and women formed a '*Fellowship*': the English word was kept in the African vernaculars. The foreign English word as a term for deep spiritual communion had, I think, a double meaning: it emphasised the historical relationship with a Keswick revival tradition and set the revivalist group apart from the ordinary run of nominal Christians. It also seemed to symbolize the newly discovered universality of the Christian faith. The members of the corporate Fellowship took part in the ordinary church service on Sunday morning, but later the same day, Sunday at 3 p.m., had their very own meeting at the back of the church, the Fellowship. It lasted an hour and was devoted to confession or testimonies and to Bible study, often the sermon text from the morning's Matins.

Dr Kofi Busia of Ghana said, in the 1950s: 'The Church has remained an alien institution'. Revival seemed to overcome something of this alienness. As men and women were hit by the Spirit, they knew that this concerned them, and them alone. The Balokole revival is experiential religion. Revival translated and interiorized the conventional Jesus message into intimate personal terms. In the early years of the movement it acted as an 'anti-structure' tearing to pieces conventional patterns but also creative. But eventually, as leaders of the revival became bishops and local leaders of the churches, balance was regained: structure and form had reasserted themselves, now in a new shape.

As we have seen in the evening worship of Shembe's Nazarites, the dream takes this interiorization of religion one step further. It is necessary to emphasize the role of dreams as a means for the individual's appropriation of the experience of God's will. Consider two examples from leading personalities in East and West Africa.

At the beginning of the Balokole movement in the 1920s and 1930s dreams were often referred to. The late William Nagenda himself told me, in 1956, of a dream, significantly a dream about his mother. In his room he had a picture of Jesus with a crown of thorns. His Balokole friends when seeing this picture, asked him: 'Are you a Roman Catholic—you have a religious picture on the wall?'—'Oh,' he replied, 'but that is a beautiful picture of Jesus'.

Then he had a dream: he saw somebody bringing a photo of his mother. 'But I was dismayed, for on that picture she looked as if a very ugly woman. So in the dream I took the picture and threw it away'.

He then went to his friends and told them of his dream and asked them to give their interpretation of it. They answered: 'If you had understood Christ and known him personally in his real beauty, you would have understood. That picture of Jesus in your room is ugly. But Jesus Himself is a beautiful Saviour.'—'We prayed together. I felt such a heavy burden of sin that I was like a dead man. I could only throw myself upon God.'

Listening to the account of a great many dreams throughout the continent, I have been impressed by the role of the mother in a fair number of them. In an ethical conflict, she may appear as the arbiter.

Bishop Akinyele of Ibadan (Anglican) told me in 1953 of 'The most wonderful experience of his life', referring to such a dream in 1893, sixty years prior to our interview. In 1891 his mother had died. Three years earlier, in 1888, the little boy was about to leave the home in order to go to school where he was to stay in the missionary's house. 'The day before I left home my mother and I knelt together and prayed. She made me promise to do God's work in His church and not to aspire for worldly advancement.' The boy did well in school and in 1893 was told that he had been selected to become a 'private clerk' in the Governor's palace in Lagos. This was a very great and rare honour, 'a turning point in my life'.

'But then I had a dream. I saw my dead mother approaching me. She reminded me of my promise given many years earlier, to work for God and not for the world. I so much would have liked to have gone to the Governor—but for that dream!'

The following morning he was found weeping torn as he was between two loyalties. But the same day he decided to inform the governor that he could not come to him. He had to keep his promise to a higher authority.

To a much larger extent and on a much deeper level than is generally noticed, I think, the religious quest has a sounding board in the relationship with the parents, possibly, in the case of men, especially with the mother.

It is of course well known that in African Independent Churches, particularly of a charismatic type, dreams take on an authoritative and more or less self-evident revelatory function. In mission-related Protestant churches the role of dreams is nowadays treated as a problem. This also applies to the Balokole movement in East Africa. At least officially, they emphatically discourage dreams these days. The late William Nagenda told me: 'Satan too can inspire dreams. Then people will trust dreams more than their personal Saviour. Therefore we are against dreams'. So the debate about the spiritual reliability of dreams goes on. A Kuta pastor (Congo-Brazzaville) told me in 1953: 'There are two kinds of dreams. 1. Such dreams as refer to matters about which the dreamer had already thought before the dream. 2. Such exceptional dreams as refer to matters which one had not thought of before. The latter convey the calling of God'.

Western monasticism in independent Africa

A. K. H. WEINRICH

Monasticism as a way of life, in which men and women can dedicate themselves to live exclusively for God, is found among all great world religions, be these Hinduism, Buddhism or Christianity. It gives visible expression to a strong call experienced by its members to leave the wider society with its values and to set up small alternate societies based on the ideals and values of their religion. In the Catholic Church of the past, such monks and nuns were regarded as forming a spiritual *élite*. Today their *élite* status is queried, for the Second Vatican Council has abolished the traditionally accepted hierarchy of lay people, active·religious and contemplatives.

One of the key problems tackled by most monasteries at present is that of wealth. Religious, on entering their various communities, take the three vows of poverty, celibacy and obedience. Since over the centuries monasteries have often become rich, and since new monasteries are often supported by older monasteries until they become self-supporting, their members are able to live economically secure, though frugal, lives. This is the reason why the question of religious poverty has troubled many religious, especially in countries in which the general standard of living of the majority of people is well below that of the monks and nuns who make an explicit vow of poverty. To overcome the unease, spiritual interpretations of religious poverty have been advanced which state that individual religious are poor indeed, since all possessions are held in common by the community, or that religious poverty means above all inner detachment, not destitution. Still, these explanations have left many members unsatisfied and have induced them to search for a more authentic expression of their religious commitment.

In independent Africa a second problem has to be solved: almost all monasteries have been founded by men and women coming from Europe or America, and they have brought with them their own ideas of what constitutes monastic living, thus offering to young Africans a form of Christian dedication which is expressed in Western cultural values. Since few of these founders were trained in African anthropology, or in sociology which would have made them aware of the relativity of their own cultural values, they generally demand from the African candidates what no monastic community demands from European or American candidates, namely to give up not only certain human values which are to be offered as a special sacrifice to God, such as personal property, parenthood and free will, but even their own culturally conditioned way of thinking and feeling.

The seriousness of this situation has by now been realized in most communities and efforts are being made to rectify the situation. Political events have also greatly contributed to this change. During colonial days most religious foundations in Africa were of an active type, for missionaries belonged themselves to active congregations, and, seeing the need for more workers to spread Christianity, they either helped African men and women to found their own congregations—by 1974 there existed 108 such congregations of African women with over 9,000 members[1]—or they encouraged Africans to join their own missionary congregations. In the latter case, the life style was always European; in the former it was predominantly so.

Contemplative foundations in Africa were rare in colonial times and most were begun only after African countries had gained their political independence. Then, however, there was a sudden upsurge of contemplative foundations for women so that by 1974 some 110 monasteries existed. At a rough estimate, some 500 to a 1,000 of their members may be African; but no exact statistics are available on their racial composition. In most of these, African and European sisters live in common. It is in these communities that most experiments have taken place, both to give to the religious ideals brought from overseas an African cultural expression, and also to reduce the standard of living in the monasteries, making it more like that of the poor in African society.

The sudden upsurge of contemplative life has greatly surprised Western missionaries and responded to a deep need in many Africans. It was also a reaction against Western activism. Moreover, to the extent that the new monasteries, which mainly recruit their members from among the most educated strata of African society, also emphasize true poverty, they are also a reaction against the materialism of the new African *élites*.

In this paper I shall analyse how three monasteries of women in Africa—Cistercians in Uganda, Carmelites in Rwanda and Poor Clares in Malawi—have handled the two problems of cultural adaptation and religious poverty.

---

[1] See: Sr Anne Gregson, W.S., 'The African Sisterhoods' Paper submitted for discussion at the School of Oriental and African Studies in October 1974, p. 6.

A Cistercian Monastery in Uganda

Cistercians belong to the large Benedictine family which has its origin in feudal Europe and which, in spite of its adaptations through the centuries, has retained many traditions which arose out of the social conditions of the Middle Ages. Thus monasteries of this type have a matriarchal structure and are situated in rural areas. This allows the nuns to engage in agriculture and to be economically self-supporting. Such characteristics make a Cistercian community highly suitable to Ugandan rural life, for Uganda too has until recently been a feudal society.

In the early 1960s an African bishop in Uganda felt the need for a contemplative community in his diocese and, knowing of a successful Cistercian monastery of monks in Kenya, a monastery which has greatly contributed to the development of its neighbourhood through modern agriculture, contacted the monks and learned that a monastery of nuns in Holland was prepared to make a foundation anywhere in the third world. The Kenyan monks contacted the women's monastery in Holland with which their own home community was linked, and the nuns responded. In 1964 thirteen nuns arrived in Uganda and settled in 1966 on a 78 acre plot of land belonging to the local bishop, but which he left to them for their exclusive use. Seven of the thirteen nuns, however, left Uganda within the first six years for health reasons or because they could not adjust themselves to the climate. Cistercians think that a local community should have at least a dozen members and since the Dutch monastery could replace only two of the nuns, additional temporary help was received from a monastery in England and from a monastery in Belgium.

The first years were hard for the pioneers. From 1964 to 1966 they lived in a nearby parish house until their monastery was built. To speed the building process and reduce costs, the monastery was constructed of large hollow blocks and covered with a corrugated asbestos roof without an inner ceiling. The greatest problem during these years was water. The nuns fetched the water they needed from a nearby pool, just as did the African villagers. This water, however, was highly polluted and gave rise to frequent dysentery. The pioneers also suffered much from malaria. Their first concern, therefore, was to dig a pit in the swamp, and once this was done, they made the water available to the local people, although the water supply was far from adequate for both the nuns and the villagers. At the request of their physician they also improved the quality of their food, and so health problems were slowly overcome.

Some of the Dutch nuns had come from farms and so were well acquainted with the various branches of agriculture. In a truly Cistercian way, they at once began working for a living from the land. They decided to go in for dairy farming since this was less labour intensive than crop production. Some years after the arrival of the nuns, the monks in Kenya donated them an exotic bull and six milk cows, and since then the nuns have raised a fine herd of exotic and cross breeds. One of the nuns is an expert at dairy farming and has introduced Dutch husbandry methods. For example, she takes away the calves from their mothers a day after their birth in order to increase the milk yield of the cows. This greatly disturbs the African herdsmen who consider this practice immoral. The land given to the nuns by the bishop has proved inadequate for dairy farming. It has also the disadvantage that one part of about 20 acres is separated from the rest of the farm by a public road. African owned stock is passing there and the nuns fear that their cows may get ticks from African herds, passing on to them the fatal East Coast fever. In 1973 they lost twelve head of exotic cattle through this contagion and so they have taken strong precautions which so far have proved successful. The abbey's dairy products are impressive. All the cheese, butter and sausages eaten by the nuns are home made and of high quality.

The nuns have also planted a large banana plantation, because bananas are the staple food in this part of Africa. Bananas need much labour at certain seasons of the year, more than the nuns can afford to spend on economic activities because, like most contemplatives, prayer leaves them with only four to five hours a day for work. Hence they have employed African labourers, eighteen men and eight women. For some of these, particularly for men of Rwanda, they have built special brick houses where they can live with their families. Some still live in mud huts; but there are plans to replace these as soon as possible. These employees are each allotted a small plot to cultivate their own crops. As this description indicates, this Cistercian abbey resembles in many respects Benedictine abbeys in medieval Europe.

With the help of their mother house in Holland and of the monks in Kenya, but especially through their own efforts, the nuns in Uganda have been able to erect most of the buildings necessary to enable them to live a full monastic life as laid down in their rule and to provide themselves with the material necessities of life. Their heaviest outlay at present is the wages for their employees whom they pay four shillings each for a five-hour working day. This is fair by Ugandan standards. As a result of these efforts, the monastery was elevated in 1971 to the status of an abbey and was granted full papal enclosure. To be elevated to the status of an abbey, a monastery must have at least twelve members, six of whom must be finally professed; the community must have all the essential monastic buildings, such as a chapel, refectory and chapter room; the full regular life must be observed; and the community must be able to raise at least half of its revenue. The elevation to the status of an abbey and full papal enclosure are signs of the maturity of a contemplative community in the Benedictine family. The Cistercian nuns in Uganda reached this goal within seven years, in spite of great initial difficulties.

This achievement has been predominantly the achievement of the European pioneers. But the Dutch nuns did not come to Uganda just to establish another Cistercian abbey in a different continent; they came to offer their way of life and prayer to the African people. Hence they made efforts from the beginning to attract local women to join them. To attract educated Ugandans to the Cistercian ideal, the community issued a leaflet which is widely distributed in Ugandan high schools. It reads:

> The Cistercian nuns live their contemplative life of prayer, sacred reading, study, manual labour in silence, solitude and sisterly love. And yet: a contemplative life is not turned away from the world. It embraces the whole creation—but it embraces it in depth. The contemplative is not called to act on the surface of the political, social and economic life. She is called to bring the whole of the cultural life of man to its centre in Christ . . . A monastery is a 'Centre' for the realisation of God where the inner meaning of life, its dimension of depth, can be discovered.[2]

To understand the community which is so eager to invite African women, a short sketch of the Dutch nuns is useful. Of the eight pioneers, five were choir nuns and three lay sisters. Before the Second Vatican Council, this was the distinction made in most monasteries between members who, before they entered, had received a high school education or professional training and those who had come from manual occupations. The former were the full members of the monastery, bound to chant the Divine Office in Latin, the others were not obliged to take a full part in the liturgy and were responsible for most of the manual work. Since this distinction has been abolished, all members of the community take an equal part in the liturgy and in the various tasks which have to be performed in the monastery. This greater equality has been facilitated by the singing of the Divine Office in the vernacular, rather than in Latin. The language spoken in this Cistercian abbey is English.

The high proportion of original choir nuns has given to the community several members with a good intellectual formation, for three had been teachers before they entered, two social workers and one a nurse. Of the lay sisters one had been a housekeeper and one a seamstress; the other, who had been a teacher, had asked to be accepted as a lay sister for personal motives. African applicants are expected to have completed a minimum of four years secondary education. The community argues that this academic level is necessary to enable African women to study theology, Scripture and other religious subjects, which are considered

[2] *Our Lady of Praise*, Butende.

essential for Cistercians to penetrate deeply into the spirit of their order and so be able to live the contemplative life in its full dimensions. Sacred studies have always been highly valued in Benedictine monasteries.

Many African girls have applied for membership during the last ten years, and after careful selection seven have been accepted. Two of these have made their final profession, two are temporarily professed, one is still a novice, one an oblate and one is a postulant. This means that one of the Africans joined the nuns shortly after their arrival in Uganda, the rest joined later. Six of these seven sisters have the required educational standard, but for one an exception has been made because of her outstanding knowledge of the Bible; she is a living concordance. This sister had been engaged by a mission as an untrained teacher after completing her primary education. She was already 27 years old when she applied for membership and brought with her a good testimonial from her parish priest. The nuns therefore gave her private lessons to enable her to follow the regular religious instructions in the community. Once African girls have been accepted for training, they are given the same instructions as are nuns in Holland. Their postulancy, the initial testing period, lasts for one to two years, the noviciate itself lasts two years, and the time of temporary profession, during which sisters can still decide to withdraw, lasts from three to six years. Only after some six to ten years, therefore, does a Cistercian commit herself by solemn vows to stay in the monastery for life.

Postulants and novices are instructed in the liturgy, which fills many hours each day, and in sacred music, so that as soon as possible they can take an active part in the most important work of the Cistercians, the *Opus Dei*. During the noviciate they study spirituality, theology and scripture, as well as the history of their order and the obligations incurred by taking vows. The nuns continue these studies throughout their lives. This thorough training narrows the cultural gap between the European and African members of the community. Complete equality between black and white has been stressed. All eat and sleep in the same room and dress in the same way. This is quickly appreciated by the members who have grown up in a colony in which black and white lived differently. Yet the way of life at the abbey has remained predominantly European. The abbess is aware of this problem and looks forward to the time when life in the abbey will have become thoroughly Africanized. She has studied local customs, but thinks that changes have to be introduced by the African members themselves, once these have been deeply steeped in authentic Cistercian spirituality. She is convinced that only the indigenous people can Africanize monasticism, for if Europeans were to undertake this task, they would create an artificial and unauthentic version of African life. At present she considers it more important to make good Cistercians out of the African sisters. Since the Cistercian order is a thousand years old, she thinks in long epochs and is unhurried in her plans for the future of her particular community.

The atmosphere in this Ugandan abbey is best described in the words: humanity, common sense and reasonableness. Asceticism is subordinated to these values and severe external penances are discouraged. Instead everyone is expected to be punctual at community exercises, to help wherever help is needed and to treat everyone with love. One young sister who, whenever communal tasks had to be done, went into the chapel to pray, was dismissed as unsuitable for the Cistercian life. The Cistercian time table is demanding. Every morning the nuns rise at 4 a.m. and pray and read sacred scripture until 8 a.m. Then work begins until noon. Lunch is followed by a siesta and more reading and prayer. From 5 to 6 p.m. the nuns complete the work they started in the morning, and after supper domestic tasks, such as preparing the food for the following day, are carried out together. After eight o'clock the community sings the night prayer and retires for the night.

One of the oustanding characteristics of Cistercians is their rule of silence. Unlike most other monastic communities, which have regular periods of recreation incorporated into their daily time table, Cistercians have no daily recreation periods; they only have a communal recreation twice a year. Since the renewal chapters there is more scope for private talks. Friendships are not discouraged and a close friendship between an African and a European nun has been approved by the community, for it is thought that it has enabled the African to absorb the spirit of the order more readily and that it has taught the European to understand in greater depth the thinking and feeling of Africans. Every member is encouraged to talk freely to her superior. The abbess is always available to any sister who wants to speak to her. She is, in fact, the spiritual adviser of most nuns. Her maturity and well-balanced outlook on life have won her the confidence of her sisters and she herself reciprocates their confidence to the degree she judges wise. If she herself is in need of advice, she contacts the abbot of the Kenyan community. She also occasionally visits him to make a quiet retreat away from her community.

Although Cistercians value utter silence and physical withdrawal from the world in order to live lives of prayer and praise, the abbess does not enforce these rules rigidly. She believes that the situation of a monastery in rural Uganda calls for various adjustments. Thus she has never allowed a grille to be erected in her parlour because she considers it hurtful to African feelings, for she has observed how profusely Africans greet each other. She also allows her sisters to escort their visitors to the monastery gate, for she learned that it is an African custom to accompany visitors on their return journey. Visits outside a monastery are not normally allowed, but again the abbess has made exceptions. Once, when the father of an African sister told her that his daughter's aunt lay seriously ill, she allowed the young nun to visit her relative, for she surmised that in African custom this bond was so important that it justified waiving the rule. She herself too leaves the enclosure occasionally, when African villagers fall seriously ill and need hospital treatment. The nearest hospital is 15 km. away and no local transport except the abbey car is available to the people. She considers it a Christian duty to take the sick to hospital. She has also made some provision at the abbey for some first aid for the people and one of the nuns, who in the past was a social worker, is running a club for African women, teaching them hygiene, child care and domestic skills. All this means that human considerations outweigh strict adherence to rules.

The Cistercians in Uganda are open to change. There is nothing rigid in their way of life. The abbess is taking a long term view of the future. Together with the other Dutch pioneers she has laid a firm economic and spiritual foundation and hopes that the African members will build on it and slowly reshape the abbey according to their own cultural values. The abbess believes that even if the growth is slow—because candidates are very carefully selected—it will be solid, and unless external political events intervene, she expects a bright future for her abbey. The personality and vision of the abbess have to a large extent determined the shape of her community. For several years she has combined in her own person the offices of abbess and novice mistress, and even for one year that of prioress as well. This had become necessary because of extraordinary circumstances. Yet she had always been assisted by her council of four nuns. At the end of 1972 she could appoint a prioress, and in January 1974 a novice mistress. Both were taken from among the Dutch nuns. In November 1974 the first two solemnly professed African sisters were elected by the community to the council of the abbey. This is the first step towards a devolution of authority to the African members.

From a Western point of view this monastery has been highly successful. It is built on a sound economic foundation; a solid spiritual foundation has also been laid, and the first steps have been taken for a gradual but certain devolution of authority into African hands. Yet the African continent is not inclined to take a long term view as does the Dutch abbess. Africa is in a hurry and its political leaders and the people at large demand Africanization now. The problem of the distribution of wealth in society is also acute, and by Ugandan standards the Cistercian nuns are rich. Their community gives the impression of being a predominantly Western enterprise, and through the solid training in Western thought patterns the African members, once they take over the administration, may be reluctant to make more fundamental changes, such as may be required to root Christian monasticism deeply in African soil. African initiative has not been used to any extent to mould the community, and since its black leaders have first to be steeped in Western values, it is doubtful how effective they will eventually be in coming to grips with the new realities of Africa.

A Carmelite Convent in Rwanda

This convent is the only religious community I visited in French-speaking Africa. Unlike the abbey in Uganda which has been shaped by the policy of its foundress, the Carmelite convent in Rwanda has been shaped by later events and has taken on a totally different form from its original concept.

As early as 1934 some Belgian nuns made a Carmelite foundation in Zaïre, then known as the Belgian Congo, and in 1954 this community undertook a new foundation at Zaza in Rwanda. By 1962 the Rwandan community had grown in number and, in its turn, undertook a foundation in Zaïre. Carmelites desire to maintain a family spirit in their communities and so do not want their numbers to increase beyond twenty. Moreover, Carmelites value solitude and have preserved an eremitical tradition in their communities. By the early 1960s the Carmelite convent in Rwanda, situated in a remote rural area, consisted of a large brick building erected in colonial style, and the life of its members followed the traditional monastic pattern. The nuns owned a large plot of land which they had surrounded with a high brick wall to emphasize their withdrawal from the world.

Slowly but radically this traditional way of life was altered, partly because of the arrival of new members, partly because of the influence of the Second Vatican Council. In 1961 the foundress died. A new prioress was sent from Belgium who had already absorbed some of the new religious ideas then spreading in Europe. As the documents of the Second Vatican Council became available, she encouraged her nuns to study them carefully. In 1964 another Belgian nun arrived who, during the preceding two years, had helped to found a new monastery in Zaïre. She too was very concerned that religious life should be updated and made meaningful to modern women. In her youth she had studied the writings of St John of the Cross, and, being strongly attracted by his austere theology, had entered a Belgian Carmel in 1949. She found, however, that the great vision of St John had been smothered by legalism and so she asked for a transfer to Africa, hoping that in that continent she might find new possibilities of leading the religious life according to its original inspirations. She found in the prioress in Rwanda a kindred spirit and together the two nuns prayed and thought about the renewal of their Carmel. This nun later became prioress herself and novice mistress. Shortly after her arrival a French Carmelite joined the community. She too had asked for a transfer to Africa because she felt that the way in which the religious life was lived in France was unauthentic.

In addition to these Europeans, some African nuns lived in the original Rwandan Carmel; some of them were Tutsi, some Hutu. In the past the Tutsi had formed the aristocracy of the country and ruled over the majority of the people of Hutu stock, but at independence it was the Hutu who formed the government and took revenge on their former masters by barring them from educational institutions and public positions (see above, pp. 245-54). The first African nun who became prioress in Rwanda, however, was a Tutsi, a fact which was never commented on in the community, for tribalism was absent amongst the sisters. This nun had grown up in a rich polygamous family. When her father became a Catholic, he separated himself from all his wives but one, and in order to cope with the increased work in the home, he employed two Hutu servants. His wealth enabled him to send his daughter to a secondary school run by a teaching congregation of Rwandan sisters. This was at a time when higher education for girls was rare, because even today only nine per cent of the country's people are literate. After her schooling, this young Tutsi joined the community of the teaching sisters and made her profession with them. Five years later she saw the Carmelites passing through her town and was impressed by their simplicity and poverty. She was specially impressed by the work-worn hands of one nun, because these reminded her strongly of the hands of her own mother and grandmother, and so recalled her childhood in the village. Two years later her congregation was dissolved because it had very few members; she sought permission to join the Carmelites and was accepted. However, she had not expected the great emphasis on silence and solitude in the Carmel and it took her some time to adjust to these. About the same time some other African women joined the community. These had experienced a great love for prayer since childhood and they easily fitted into the spirituality of the order.

This group of nuns, Africans and Europeans, studied the Vatican documents together and were especially interested in the call to lead a truly poor life according to the Gospel. They realized that poverty was a relative concept and that their poverty had to be recognized as such by their neighbours. They therefore reviewed their communal property and came to the conclusion that two items—a harmonium and a refrigerator—were definitely above the means of their neighbours, yet until then they had considered both indispensable, because one was needed in divine worship, the main purpose of their lives, and the other was needed to preserve their food. However, since the ordinary people could not afford to keep their food in a cool place, they felt that they too had no right to do so. They therefore donated their refrigerator to a mission clinic and gave their harmonium to a parish church.

They soon found that in having given away these two items, they had become free. Their food did not go bad, for most of it consisted of bread, vegetables and bananas; and their liturgical life did not suffer either, for they now introduced local musical instruments, such as drums, tambourines and string instruments. At once their singing took on an African note. In their new freedom they subjected every item they possessed to a critical evaluation. Soon, therefore, they lived in an almost empty shell of a convent.

One day during this period of experimentation, the nuns received a visit from their local bishop and during the conversation he entrusted to them his need for a seminary, asking them to pray that some benefactor might be found to pay for it. The nuns prayed and at the same time continued their discussions about true poverty. One evening a European sister asked tentatively whether it would not be possible to offer to the bishop their convent as a seminary and to build for themselves a new one consisting of huts similar to those in which the village people lived. At this the African sisters were delighted and said that they had for a long time longed for this change, but that they had been hesitant to express their desire, fearing that such a radical change might be too difficult for the Europeans. The Europeans then tried to be more radical than the African sisters, for they suggested that their huts be truly poor; but the Africans maintained that this would not be acceptable to the people. They insisted that their huts be built of materials available to everybody, but that they be built carefully and beautifully, for otherwise the Carmel would lose the esteem of the people. An agreement was reached with the bishop and he accepted the convent property. The land was divided and the nuns began building their new huts. The people of the neighbourhood were startled at this development and many were critical, thinking that Europeans were making fun of African poverty. However, when they saw how beautiful the convent huts were, they changed their minds and instead of criticizing, some families began imitating the buildings of the sisters so that general housing standards in the area improved.

The convent was built by the nuns themselves and in 1972 it looked as follows. A bamboo fence, no brick wall, enclosed the property. Nearest to the gate was a large round hut which served as a chapel. The people entered it from the outside, the sisters from the inside. There was no grille separating the people from the nuns. Like all other huts, the chapel was built of clay and sand, and some cement was added in the flooring and on that part of the outside wall most often hit by the tropical rain. The roof was of papyrus reeds which grew on the property. It was rain-proof and has never needed repairs. The altar was made of unhewn rock, and little carved stools served in place of choir stalls. The walls were covered with African musical instruments.

Inside the enclosure a circle of huts extended on either side of the chapel. Each hut was divided into four triangular rooms, each with its own window and door. These rooms were furnished with a bed and a grass mattress, a little table, a chair and a washstand. In these rooms each nun prayed and worked on her own, and in fact most work was done in solitude. One of the huts was larger than the others and served as a refectory and chapter room. In one half stood a long table and stools where the nuns took their meals. In the other half stood a circle of little stools. Here the nuns met in the evenings to review their day and to pray the evening prayer together.

Outside this circle of huts were the guest quarters, a bakery and a kitchen, and adjoining these was a small vegetable garden, a chicken run and a large banana plantation. It was from these that the nuns obtained their food and earned their living. Their staple diet was bananas. Vegetables and eggs also contributed to their food. But they never ate meat and so their chickens were finally sold to the people. The nuns had no cows and therefore bought their milk from their neighbours. They also bought flour and sugar from a shop and with these they baked bread and biscuits for sale. From the sale of bread and some garden produce the nuns earned just enough money to purchase their own clothing and to pay wages to five hired labourers who helped them in the banana plantation, for the nuns found that hired labour was necessary if they were to have enough time for prayer. Yet their relationship with these labourers were not that commonly found between employers and employees, because the nuns worked side by side with their assistants. They had also adopted three poor families in the neighbourhood with whom they shared their daily meals. The clothing of the nuns was re-designed and made of strong but cheap locally-produced material. They greatly simplified their long Carmelite habit of the past and reduced their veils to little head scarves, resembling those worn by local women. This, however, was strongly criticized in Belgium when the Rwandan superior visited her home convent. The sisters in Rwanda agreed to enlarge their veils slightly, but they consented to no other alterations. Each nun possesses only one habit, and when it is washed, a blue overall is put on, such as is worn during work, until the habit has dried.

This simplicity of life satisfied the inner need of the European sisters and it also attracted African women by its novelty. As more and more applicants arrived, a new foundation was made in 1969 in Kigali, the capital of Rwanda. In 1972 both communities had thirteen members: in one were four Europeans and nine Africans and in the other three Europeans and ten Africans. In both communities, African and European sisters mixed on a basis of complete equality. The Africans are both Hutu and Tutsi, but no tribal feelings are ever expressed. This is significant because in the rest of the country tribal animosity runs high. Most of the Africans are junior members, who joined only after the far-reaching changes in the life style of the community had taken place.

Applicants to the Carmel have to have some secondary education, but occasionally exceptions are made. Thus when an orphan asked for admission, the community was at first reluctant to accept her because the young girl had not been to school and knew no French, and French is the language spoken in the community. But since the young woman was obviously eager to dedicate her life to God, the community thought that they might admit her as a lay sister; however, there was no need for a lay sister and the Vatican Council had anyhow eliminated this class of nuns. The young woman was allowed to live for some time with the sisters and slowly found her way into the noviciate where I met her as a very quiet but observant member. She would never have been admitted in the Cistercian community in Uganda.

Young women who are interested in the Carmelite life are invited to stay for one month in the guest quarters of the convent in order to observe the life of the nuns. If they give the impression of being mature, truthful and well-balanced women, willing to lead a community life, and if there are sufficiently educated, they are then invited to join the formal postulancy and noviciate. In 1972 the community laid great emphasis on education, because it was thought that a contemplative life could only be lived authentically if it was grounded on solid theology, and for this intellectual competence was considered essential. The nuns claimed that people who lack a solid theological foundation easily slipped into a false mysticism, and this they regarded as the ruin of contemplative life.

They also insisted on secondary schooling because all the books in their library were written in French; no literature in the vernacular was available. In fact, the community fought shy of the vernacular and neither the European nor the African sisters wanted to use it; not only because it would emphasize tribal differences between the Hutu and Tutsi, but also because a neglect of French would exclude the community from world literature, and everyone in the community valued French religious writings.

This great emphasis on French as the only means of communication had further ramifications. Thus all the African sisters denied any knowledge of their traditional religion and claimed that they were only familiar with the Catholic faith. They also denied any knowledge of tribal customs. They rejected every aspect of traditional religion as totally incompatible with Christianity. Never in English-speaking Africa have I encountered such a radical rejection of traditional values, and I think that it may be due to particular historic circumstances in Rwanda.[3]

If, therefore, the adaptation of monasticism to Rwandan life is considered at the time the sisters lived in their village convent, it must be stressed that external adaptation had been carried out to a very high degree, but that only a moderate attempt had been made to adapt monastic values to the spiritual values of African society. French language, French literature and French thought patterns prevailed and were valued as symbols of civilization and respectability. This mixture of material adaptation to African life and of Western values was visible in all forms of worship and in community living. Africans value companionship and desire to share their experiences; Carmelite spirituality, however, emphasizes seclusion. Hence, instead of working in common, Carmelites retire to the quarters of their huts and work in solitude. The superior of the Poor Clare monastery, discussed in the next section, said to me that she judged Carmelite spirituality unsuitable for Africans because of this insistence on solitude. African Carmelites also admitted that at least initially they had found this solitude hard. Twice a day, however, the community met to share their thoughts: after lunch the sisters relaxed together while they prepared the vegetables for the next meal or did some other light work. This half hour was often filled with laughter and sometimes with dancing. After supper the community met in the second section of the refectory hut for night prayer. This meeting included a public examination of conscience. In the past it consisted exclusively of an admission of faults, but since the spiritual renewal had taken place, it had turned into a revision of all aspects of daily life, including spiritual successes and ordinary problems of daily living. Hence the evening prayer extended into a spiritual discussion lasting about an hour.

The Carmelites' readiness to adapt externally, but to adapt internally only with reluctance, was still more clearly seen in the prayer life of the nuns. Most African people express their religion through dancing and verbal expressions. In Carmelite tradition, however, contemplative prayer receives precedence over liturgical prayer; this is one of the

---

[3] The anti-colonial Nyabingi cult with its many prophetesses was violently put down by the European administration. Out of fear that a charge of cult membership might be laid against them, Rwandan Africans went so far as to destroy even their ancestral shrines and to suppress any demonstration of their traditional religion.

greatest contrasts between the Benedictine and Carmelite ways of life. The day starts with the liturgical morning prayer. After Mass the nuns spend one hour in silent prayer. At Zaza some brought their prayer mats into the chapel and squatted on them, often bending their foreheads down to the ground and remaining motionless in adoration. The evening prayer is also followed by one hour of silent prayer and a second hour of spiritual reading. This hour can be spent either in the chapel or in the nuns' private rooms. All liturgical prayers were sung or chanted in French, according to French tunes, but accompanied by African musical instruments. Nobody seemed to notice this inconsistency and no attempt was being made to create or adapt local tunes for church music. Yet some bodily movement was encouraged during prayer; for example, during intercessions the nuns, standing in a circle round the altar, lifted their hands to heaven, and during the Magnificat the younger sisters danced in honour of the Mother of God. Again, therefore, an external adaptation had been welcomed, but no change was being made which touched on the deeper levels of thinking and experiencing the divine.

The question may be asked, how lasting a material adaptation can be if the deeper way of thinking and feeling, through which cultural values are expressed at their most meaningful level, are excluded from this search. The development of the convent at Zaza throws light on this question, for in early 1975 I learned from a European member that a year previously the sisters at Zaza had expressed a wish to amalgamate with their convent in Kigali because the surroundings of their rural Carmel remained too under-developed so that contemplative life became difficult. I do not understand the reasoning behind this statement, for Carmelites have always sought solitude, and an under-developed rural area certainly provided them with it. Still, the sisters moved to town. At the time this significant move was made, three Europeans returned to their original Carmel in Belgium and France, and only three remained. In 1975 there were therefore twenty-five African and five European Carmelites living together in Kigali. With such a small proportion of Europeans, Africanization became spontaneous. One European sister wrote that the huts had been a real experience in the life of the community and helped everybody to become simpler. They also enabled the sisters to share their life of prayer with the local people. Yet subconsciously it was realized that this external adaptation had not been the whole answer.

Some parts are rather revealing: the move to live in huts came originally from European sisters, though it was enthusiastically supported by Africans, with one reservation: not to build too simply. When the village experiment was abandoned, three of the eight Europeans returned to Europe. Can it be inferred that these had been prepared to live without all physical comfort, but still as Europeans as far as spiritual values are concerned? On the African side, there were nineteen members in the two convents of Zaza and Kigali in 1972 at the time of my visit; in 1975 there were twenty, i.e. only one more person had joined. Does this mean that after a short period of rapid growth, at the time when the experiment was novel and drew excited attention, Africans lost interest? Africans have always been familiar with village life; what the African sisters had longed for may well have been the deeper spiritual rapprochement to their own culture. The three Europeans who left Rwanda had been living in the village Carmel; those who had moved earlier to Kigali stayed. Also Kigali had at the time of my visit a European prioress. In 1975 an African prioress was elected. Letters from the Carmel indicate that Africanization at a deeper level is now taking place. In 1972, when I proposed such a transformation at a community meeting, it was strongly rejected.

From these changes I draw the conclusion that the desire for great poverty came predominantly from the Europeans; it may almost have been a kind of subconscious self-defence against giving up their own deeper cultural values. The African reaction seems to have been a longing for this much deeper adaptation, and I interpret the original enthusiasm of the African sisters for the village style convent as being motivated by the hope that it would be symbolic of deeper transformations. When these did not occur, they rejected the externals and set about to express their own religious needs, needs deeply rooted in their African culture, in all seriousness. It would be interesting to revisit this convent now to see what changes in depth have taken place. It is important to note, however, that poverty has been preserved in Kigali, for living standards there are not above those of the village Carmel, only the romanticism of the village is missing. Hence the Africans sacrificed no ideals when they moved to town.

A Poor Clare Monastery in Malawi

This monastery was founded by a woman with rare insight into the mentality of another people and with an appreciation for cultural values different from her own. Her own background greatly contributed to this, for she was born of a French settler family in Algeria with a militant Communist tradition, and she lived in Algeria when the local people became aware of their own national identity and strove for independence. Hence she must in many ways have felt marginal in the country of her birth, and such marginally-placed persons generally become detached and keen observers of social life. Her studies of philosophy and sociology further sharpened her insights, and so did her social work in the 'Casbah'. Being also a very gifted person, she was chosen by her community to make a foundation in Malawi, after a bishop of that country had approached her Algerian monastery to send sisters to his diocese.

With four companions this woman set out in 1960 to found a monastery in Lilongwe, then a sleepy provincial town, but now the capital of Malawi. She built an austere monastery which strictly reflected her view that the contemplative life had to be lived in strict withdrawal from the world. Hence she divided the monastic complex into three parts. The first consisted of a front garden, itself enclosed by a wall, through which visitors could enter a small white-washed parlour whose black curtains had remained drawn throughout my visit of several days. A grille separates the visitors' section of the parlour from that of the nuns. The abbess never encouraged visitors, but, following the traditions of both the Franciscan order and of African society, she nevertheless welcomed those who did come.

From this outer part of the monastery, visitors have access to a part of the chapel where they can attend the daily sacrifice of the Mass and most parts of the divine office. But the sisters' and the people's sections of the chapel are again separated by a grille, and a curtained partition shields the nun's choir from the view of visitors, except during Mass. This contrasts very strongly with the more integrated community of worshippers, both nuns and lay people, in the Rwandan convent.

Unlike the parlour, the chapel is a most attractive room, full of light and beauty. The wood of the altar, walls and stalls is painted in natural dyes found in the open countryside, but at first sight they give the impression of being inlaid with ivory and ebony. All designs are African. In the people's section of the chapel, benches stand parallel to each other, as is customary in Catholic churches, but in the nuns' choir, stalls stand along the walls so that the nuns always form a semi-circle around the altar. Drums and other African musical instruments are kept at the back of the choir.

The second part of the monastery consists of guest quarters and rooms for candidates who wish to join the monastery. The gate between this section of the monastery and the outer garden is always locked. It was in this section that I was given a cell. The cell was exceedingly narrow, with just sufficient room for an iron bedstead. In one corner was a tiny wash basin with cold running water. The bed had a narrow foam mattress and some blankets. I was told that I had been given an especially comfortable cell, for the nuns themselves have no bedsteads and blankets, but sleep on a mat, using maize leaves for a pillow. The guest wing also had a sitting-room. In this semi-enclosed section of the monastery was also a vegetable garden in which the nuns work. The nuns grow their own vegetables.

I was not allowed to enter the monastery proper which contains the living rooms of the nuns. I was told that the food of the nuns is exceedingly simple, consisting mainly of vegetables and maize porridge, the local African staple food. Most European food items now widely accepted by Africans, such as bread and cheese, had for a long time been cut out of the nuns' diet. Now the nuns are given loaves left over from guests. Their dress is very simple and they always go barefoot. Thus they live strictly according to the instruction laid down by their foundress in their ancient rule:

> I beseech and entreat my Sisters that they be always clothed in poor garments, for the love of the most holy and most sweet Child Jesus, wrapped in poor little swaddling clothes and laid in a manger, and of His most holy Mother.[4]

Poverty, to the Poor Clares, is something precious, something freely chosen for love of God, and it is never endured grudgingly. Poor Clares want their poverty to be real, but poverty, they believe, can be beautiful. Thus they have decorated their chapel, as I have already described, and every part of their monastery is kept spotlessly clean and attractive in its simplicity.

This material environment in which the nuns live their lives is culturally relatively neutral. The abbess explained to me in 1972 that her community was living in a town which was soon to become the capital of Malawi, and to build a monastery of huts would be objectionable to the local people. Brick houses were the norm in the evolving urban areas of the country and to be unobtrusive meant to build as simply as possible in the local style. But this did not mean that any luxury was permitted. Living conditions were utterly frugal, and apart from the regularity of meals and the provision of clothing, they were hardly superior to those of the ordinary people.

Like the Carmelites, the Poor Clares have also an eremitical tradition, but it is balanced by strong stress on community living. For this reason Poor Clares work and relax in common, but they have long periods of retreats and daily times of complete solitude. They carry out their tasks in large work rooms in utter silence. The abbess said to me that the African sisters came from villages in which privacy was unknown. They were used to live within the sight of all other villagers and to share with them everything that occurred. Coming from a Western background which stresses a certain reserve and privacy, she found this sharing very

---

[4] Quoted by Fr M. Francis, *The Right to be Merry*, London, 1957, p. 54.

hard. Her readiness to live her life in full publicity, as the Africans expected, shows the direction she has given in her monastery: it is to be an adaptation in depth, in which European members have to strip themselves of their own cultural heritage in order to be one with their African sisters.

Unlike the Carmelites in Rwanda, therefore, who began by external adaptation, the Poor Clares in Malawi began by an internal transformation of monastic life. Knowing that the best way to penetrate the thinking and feeling of another people is to speak their language, the abbess insisted from the beginning that the local language, Chewa, be the means of communication in the community, and all Europeans had to learn it. In fact, some of the French nuns were so intent on learning Chewa that they neglected learning English, the official European language of Malawi. Consequently several African sisters are more fluent in English than are some of their white sisters. It never concerned the foundress that this stress on the vernacular could have negative spiritual effects by making it more difficult for the sisters to read spiritual books in an internationally spoken language. All the sisters did learn some English and had at least a reading knowledge of it. What counted for her was that the Africans' religious experience was in African thought patterns, and these were expressed in their local language.

Most foundations of contemplative communities in Africa have considered education as very important, and since educational facilities are rare for African girls, there is generally a bias of recruiting nuns from among the new middle classes of African society. This has not been the case in this community, for the Poor Clare abbess did not insist on a secondary school education for applicants and played down her own intellectual achievements. But she saw to it that sisters were given the opportunity to continue their studies both before and after their temporary vows, and she laid special emphasis on the secular subjects of English and history. However, such knowledge was not considered necessary for admission to the community. Instead she claimed that a contemplative vocation was a rare gem which was either given by God or not, and which could not be acquired. She claimed that she recognized the presence of a vocation in an applicant by a special thirst for God. All the African sisters to whom I spoke stressed that since childhood they had sought to be alone with God; some added that they had had this longing even before they had become Christians. None of them had felt attracted to an active apostolic life, and since no contemplative monastery had existed in Malawi until 1960, they had been unaware that their longing could be fulfilled.

The abbess said to me: 'An African girl may enter an active

congregation and accept a European way of life, even though this is not too good for her as a person. But if an African were to enter a monastery, and if she were there forced into a contemplative mould evolved in Europe, her personality could be destroyed. Hence contemplatives in Africa, of whatever racial background they may be, must accept the African way of life as the mould of their own living.' She never lost sight of this insight and acted accordingly. She held that contemplative life in Africa had to be African in its inspiration and expression right from the beginning, otherwise later generations of nuns would reject the pioneers of the contemplative life as unauthentic ancestors. In this she differed strongly from the Cistercian abbess in Uganda who believed that only a future generation of African nuns could bring about an Africanization of the contemplative life.

Such a view poses challenges, but it also brings rewards. The adoption of the vernacular, for example, posed difficulties in the liturgy, because parts of the divine office had not yet been translated into Chewa. So the nuns and their friends sat down and prepared their own translations. Since the aim was not only a linguistic adaptation, but an adaptation in all the dimensions of divine worship, the nuns wanted their prayers to be accompanied by African music and African dances. In spite of the rich African cultural heritage in music and dance, the little church music which existed at the time in Malawi was not in the least influenced by African rhythms and tunes. Hence the nuns began composing their own tunes. Every day after lunch they came together to set new parts of the divine office to music and to invent new dances for the liturgy. By the time I visited them in 1972, they had almost completed the musical repertoire for much of the divine office. Their liturgy is a most moving expression of African religious thinking and feeling. All gestures have been Africanized and European gestures which have little meaning to Africans, such as a genuflection before the Blessed Sacrament, so common in Catholic worship, have been replaced by African signs, for example by a reverent bow and by hand clapping. The nuns did not evolve new liturgical forms for themselves only, and as people heard about these experiments, the nuns had gramophone records made of their music so that others can now make use of their music.

All this means that the abbess did not work for racial or cultural equality in her monastery, but for inequality: she wanted African cultural values to dominate; in fact, only these were officially accepted. No European woman was accepted on any other terms. This has greatly affected the composition of the community. In the early 1970s the monastery had fifteen African and four European sisters, plus the abbess. This means that no other European had been admitted to final vows by that time, only Africans had. In addition there were several novices and postulants. One novice was a European who had been a member of an active missionary congregation and had asked for permission to transfer to the contemplative life. She was still on trial at the time of my visit. Several other Europeans before her had attempted to join, but all had found a life which demanded the renunciation of their own cultural heritage either too hard, or they left on the recommendation of the abbess who made it clear to them that they were not suited for this way of life. All of these left before taking vows. As a consequence of this policy the community is predominantly African and all leadership positions are now in the hands of Africans. For several years the novice mistress and vicaress, that is, the assistant of the abbess, have been Africans, and since January 1975 the office of the abbess has also been handed over to an African nun who, though still young, is performing the abbatial duties most efficiently and with insight and understanding. As soon as the foundress had seen that an African was capable of taking over the leadership, she voluntarily withdrew from her office and left for France, where she is now living in a hermitage. This is the ultimate form she has chosen for her life which has always been devoted to an ever intenser search for total union with God.

The daily life of the monastery is in harmony with the ideals implanted by the foundress in the community and incarnated by the African sisters. The European sisters, unlike the Europeans in the Rwanda Carmel, have always remained in the background. They mix with their Malawian sisters as equals and never expect Africans to look to them for leadership or inspiration, as has been done by the Cistercians in Uganda and, to a lesser degree, by the Carmelites in Rwanda. To see to the various needs of the community, the sisters are grouped into small teams working together in the kitchen, garden or sewing-room. These groups are always racially mixed or all African, and they are not supervised by the European sisters. At periods of recreation, which are always light-hearted, the sisters often gather in the garden to chat, laugh and sing, because Poor Clares love nature, and so do Africans. Here, too, all mix as equals.

Yet the essential activity of a monastery is neither work nor recreation, but prayer. The life of prayer in the monastery alternates between silent contemplative prayer and solemn liturgy. Prayer is given preference over all activities and nuns are even allowed to interrupt their work for a quarter of an hour to pray in the chapel. The day closes with an hour of adoration before the Blessed Sacrament and the official night prayer of the church. During this night prayer sisters often prepare a special scripture passage, read it out to the community and then accuse themselves of faults contrary to its spirit. Other members of the community may afterwards add their own self-accusation. No outsider is allowed into the chapel during this time. The nuns feel that this openness binds them strongly together. After night prayer those who wish to continue praying may do so privately; some also get up in groups to pray together during the night. In this way the chapel has become the centre of the monastery, and this makes it clear to all that it is prayer which gives meaning to the life of contemplatives.

This description of the Malawi monastery shows that these Poor Clares have succeeded exceedingly well in integrating the religious life with the African way of thinking and feeling. Material conditions are considered of secondary importance and a brick monastery does not in the least disturb them as being less authentically African than huts. The integration of African values has occurred at a deeper level. Poverty too is observed, and this from a double motive: it is one of the outstanding values of the Franciscan spiritual tradition, and it is also essential for women professing poverty in an African state in which the majority of citizens are exceedingly poor. The devolution of authority into African hands has occurred fast. The result is that a monastery has been established which, though it has grown out of the Western tradition of monasticism, is in fact an authentic African expression of the monastic way of life.

CONCLUSION

One great concern which stirs responsible people in Africa today, just as it does in other parts of the world, is the problem of inequality. In the past it was racial inequality which preoccupied the people in Africa, because it created different classes of citizens. This problem is slowly being solved, but already a new problem comes to the fore: inequality in wealth. For in many African countries modern *élites* are emerging which take to themselves many of the privileges formerly held by European colonials. Consequently the rich still exploit the poor and human dignity is far from being universally guaranteed. In this situation the question may be asked whether monasticism knows an answer to this problem.

In all Catholic monasteries in Africa the racial question has some relevance and none of the monasteries I visited has ignored it. Of even greater importance is the related question of Western influence. This question has some meaning even in monasteries founded solely by Africans. For I found that in a Nigerian Benedictine monastery, founded by an Igbo woman without the help of resident European nuns, the way of life was strongly influenced by Western cultural values. The reason was that she had received her own training as a contemplative in Europe and that she has not yet learnt to distinguish which practices are essentially Benedictine and which are European expressions of the monastic life.

As far as the authenticity of religious poverty is concerned, perhaps the best measure is the degree to which nuns share in the poverty of their surroundings and show a solidarity with their poor neighbours, as has been done by the Carmelites in Zaza and Kigali, and by the Poor Clares in Lilongwe. For it is only when religious poverty is an expression of solidarity with the poor, that it can be seen as an eminently Christian virtue and as having meaning in modern Africa.

The value of education must also be re-examined, for in itself education is of an ambivalent nature. Nobody questions that a solid grounding in theology, which requires education, is very helpful for a deeply contemplative life, but what may be questioned is a one-sidedly Western education which makes a person marginal to his or her own culture and leads to a neglect, or even rejection, of African cultural values. For this will be harmful to the contemplative life. The Poor Clares in Malawi have circumvented this danger, and the African Carmelites in Rwanda seem to have become aware of it and to have taken steps to overcome it.

These issues, a solidarity with poor neighbours, recruitment among the uneducated as well as the educated, a careful use of education so that it serves cultural adaptation rather than discrimination, seem to be some factors which, when set within the wider context of religious dedication, are likely to determine whether a contemplative community has a message for its own country or not. Benedictines, Carmelites and Poor Clares have all their specific spiritual traditions which give a characteristic flavour to the religious life lived in their communities, but to African society as a whole these family differences may be of lesser importance than the overall message, namely that of a religious community's witness to transcendental values, expressed in a life style which incarnates them in a particular local culture. The present search by people for a more just and egalitarian society, which stresses the equal dignity of all persons, is also a factor which monastic foundations will only overlook at the risk of appearing irrelevant. Finally, new monasteries in Africa have to redress the previous unbalance, introduced into Africa by missionaries who, in their eagerness to spread the Gospel, emphasized the active apostolate so exclusively that they deprived the young African church of the rich Catholic heritage of contemplative living. It is only when action and contemplation are well integrated in a Christian community, that a local church reaches its full maturity.

The role of prayer in the Kimbanguist Church*

DIAKANUA NDOFUNSU

Early prayer among the Mukongo people before the prophet Kimbangu
Among the Musi-Ngombe tribe in Lower Zaïre, where the prophet
Simon Kimbangu was born, they have since ancient times recognized a
supreme God (Nzambi a Mpungu), a powerful, transcendent God
present through the heavenly bodies. The sun, on account of its
brightness during the day and its appearance every morning, represents
God. The other heavenly bodies, the moon and the stars, are God's
entourage.

The power of the supreme God is revealed through a supernatural
strength expressed in thunder and lightning, violent rain or the wind. In
this situation in former times men prayed, simply calling on the name of
God for protection. In joy and grief, or even in mourning, men
remembered God and cried out, pronouncing the all-powerful name. The
very fact of pronouncing the name of God shows particularly how
superficial was their knowledge of the supreme God. The second prayer
addressed to God is linked with the practice of magic (fetishes). One sort
of fetish made use of by this tribe (and in several other regions of Zaïre,
as well as other African countries) is called Mpungu, the name of the
supreme God. This fetish contained (or contains, if it still exists) a power
against sorcerers, to heal sicknesses and chase away evil spirits. The
Mpungu is able to solve many kinds of grievous problems for those who
come to make a complaint. The fetish-priest says a prayer in the name of
Nzambi a Mpungu, inserting the name and cause of the plaintiff; this
invocation to God is syncretized with an invocation to the spirits of the
ancestors. In this tribe this sort of invocation is called Nsibu. This
primitive form prayer was often accompanied by rites: a collection of
magical objects, various gestures, incantatory hymns etc.

This example teaches us why the prophet's mission would have been
impossible without the instigation of Jesus Christ. This ancient
knowledge of God appears difficult to erase, for we know that mankind

---

* A fuller version of this chapter was published in French by the Ecole Supérieure de
Théologie Kimbanguiste, Kinshasa, November 1975.

has a tendency to believe only in the face of concrete, visible facts. The arrival of the missionaries, accompanied by colonization, obscured the new knowledge of Christianity. The preaching of Christ was seen as another means of helping colonization to alienate men completely from their African identity. It was in this situation that Christ turned his face towards this people and chose the prophet Simon Kimbangu as his messenger to recall to the faith all those who might feel themselves touched by this message received from Christ.

The prayer which brings the dead to life

Before the birth of the prophet there existed, in his tribe, a supernatural force called Kimbangu. This force was invoked in a case of still birth. As soon as the baby was born the midwives placed it between the legs of its seated mother. The midwives cried aloud, calling on the name of Kimbangu and shaking a piece of cloth in the direction of the child to give it the air that would give breath if Kimbangu intervened. Here is the song of invocation: '*Ngudi didi muana, Kimbangu nza kunfidila yani*', which means literally: 'The mother has bewitched the (new-born) child, Kimbangu comes to give it back to me.' In the time of our ancestors, before the coming of the prophet, this force saved many children whose case seemed hopeless.

The origin of this invisible power, that our ancestors only knew through some innate revelation in the heart, is unknown. And it still shows how greatly God is love towards all. He extends his plan of salvation to the whole world, even to the least-known, obscurest corners of the globe. God is present through his Spirit which is active there, and comes to the help of this people. What is more He prepares in them a true coming of the Holy Spirit, whom God will put into a person called Kimbangu to give to mankind a new knowledge of God, to change the structure of his social and religious life, and to free mankind from the slavery of the material and spiritual world. This is the origin and the aim of Kimbanguist prayer, which consists in paying careful attention to the prophecies of the prophet throughout his mission, thanking God for the prophecies which have been fulfilled and asking him to fulfil those which remain as yet unfulfilled.

Kimbanguist prayer from 6 April 1921 onwards

The meaning of Kimbanguist prayer is to thank God through Jesus Christ for his great gift to us. This gift is the true Christ revealed through the Holy Spirit, who restored the prophet and clothed him in his power. The Spirit is made visible through the person of the prophet, who fulfils the following conditions: in him we now know that Christ is our only Saviour, and that he is stronger than the spirits, the Mpungus, and the other fetishes; we know that Christ is the only path that leads to eternal life. Through the Spirit of truth, the prophet Kimbangu gave us the knowledge of the Word of God, written in the Bible, which he left us for our inheritance.

We thank God that mankind in general, and the black man in particular has been unbound and made totally free spiritually and materially, and for the fact that the colour of a person's skin no longer constitutes a scale of values applying to the races of the world. It is in this that a prophecy made by the prophet Kimbangu in a symbolic form has been fulfilled; in his youth, he transformed a nut which had gone bad into one that was sweet and wholesome.

The prophet's prayer is based on the mission entrusted to him by Christ, and on his absolute certainty that Christ will support him and that he will emerge victorious from the traps set by his enemies. He cured the sick, raised the dead and drove away evil spirits; he asked everyone in the name of Jesus Christ to throw away the fetishes. He could do nothing unaided; Christ was the head of his mission through whose will he took action.

It was through prayer that he entered into contact with Christ, and asked for or received replies or instructions as to what he should do or not do according to the situation. It was in praying that he asked for helpers, and sifted the good from the bad. He did it by a simple game that Christ had revealed to him: he made them eat a bitter fruit. Those who ate were chosen, but those who refused were denied the priesthood.

The priesthood of intercession can be transmitted; God transmits it to the one who takes up his mission. At the time of his divine revelation, the prophet Kimbangu was also vested with the blessing of this gift from the Holy Spirit. He made many intercessions, as Moses interceded for his people of Israel, and as Jesus interceded on the Cross: 'Father, forgive them, for they know not what they do.' (Luke 23, 34).

When the prophet Kimbangu interceded, he did it as the representative of the people who had sinned. Here are a few of the objects of his intercession:

He prayed for the sick and the dead, for those who were falsely accused and for enemies. He also asked God for help, given the spiritual and material poverty of mankind.
He prayed for perfect unity among men, that there should be no more barriers or frontiers.
He prayed for those who plotted against him, as Saint Stephen had done. (Acts 7, 60)
He prayed that those who had understood the aim of his mission

should be steadfast in the faith, particularly the sacrificers (priests) in exile and other Christians, whose persecution had begun in 1921 and was to last until 1959.
He asked God to open the hearts of the unbelievers, so that they might accept the message of Christ.

Here is an extract from one of the prayers of the prophet Kimbangu:

I Thank Thee, Almighty God, Maker of heaven and earth. The heaven is Thy throne and the earth is Thy footstool. Thy will be done on earth as it is in heaven. Bless all peoples of the earth, great and small, men and women, whites and blacks. May the blessing of heaven fall on the whole world so that we all may enter heaven. We pray to Thee trusting that Thou dost receive us, in the Name of Jesus Christ our Saviour. Amen.[1]

The sons of the prophet are for us the vanguard of Christ. They are concerned with our spiritual and material problems. In them, the prophet still lives for us, and herein Christ manifests himself and continues his work in the strength of the Holy Spirit. Often they ask everything in their prayers, bearing everything for us, as though they were more guilty than we. They include in their prayers our supplications, and many different expressions of our weaknesses. We find below an extract from a prayer by his Greatness Dialungana Kiangani, the second son of the prophet, in commemoration of the death of their mother Mama Mwilu Kiawanga. In this prayer Tata Dialungana has not failed to mention the difficulties of the whole Kimbanguist community and all those who are not yet members of it. I quote from page 12 of the collection 'Office of the prophet Simon Kimbangu':

God, our Father,
    We give Thee thanks; through Thy love and through Thy mercy, hear our prayer! Thou wished us to be full of gladness; for in the midst of sin, Thou pardoned us; even though our sins were scarlet, Thou hast washed them away, Thou hast caused blessings to rain down, Thou hast caused Thy Holy Spirit to descend upon us, and upon the sermon we have come to hear: 'We will sell our goods to follow Thy pure pathway' (the theme of the sermon).
    God our Father, we realise for certain that this event, the death of Thy servant, resounds through the whole world; this is the fulfilment of the promise of Jesus. As Mama Mwilu comes to Thee we pray that Thou accept her.
    Father, grant us Thy abundant love so that we improve our actions, and the whole of our Christian life. We behave badly; direct our affairs, for we desire to conquer evil through the power that Thou dost give us. Give us Thy strength, so that we be not tried nor covered in shame. Grant us Thy power, because we have accepted the task of

[1] Quoted in M-L. Martin, *Kimbangu*, Oxford, 1975, p. 49.

leading all the world to Thee. Bless the deacons, bless the catechists, bless all Christians, bless the catechumens, and those who are not members of the church of Christ, bless the holy city of Jerusalem, and the city of Nazareth. May all be blessed in the name of the Father and of the Son and of the Holy Spirit who descended on the prophet Simon Kimbangu, the messenger of Christ. Amen.

Here is another extract from a prayer by his Eminence Diangienda Kuntima, the Spiritual Head of the Kimbanguist Church, uttered in remembrance of the prophet's death, in which he takes advantage of the opportunity to make a request for peace in the land, which the 1960 secessions had upset. This comes from 'Office of the prophet Simon Kimbangu', page 20:

In the name of the Father and of the Son and of the Holy Spirit that descended upon the prophet S. Kimbangu: God our Father, this is a great day; Thou hast willed that Thy servant should no longer remain in the state of an impure body; Thou hast changed it into a holy body. This is why we prostrate ourselves before Thee today, our Father, so that Thou may see what is troubling us.

Heavenly Father, our country is suffering; that is why we beg Thee, Lord, approach and draw near to us, and let us see Thy grace.

We ask for Thy help in our problems, in the name of the Father and of the Son and of the Holy Spirit who descended upon the prophet S. Kimbangu. Amen.

Worship in the Kimbanguist Church

The Church of which I am speaking here is not only a house of God, a temple, but above all the great community which continues to expand even today, from the day of Pentecost (Acts 2, 41) and the time of the first apostles in Jerusalem, right up to the present, despite the multiplicity of denominations.

The Church is the body of Christ; every Christian is a member of that body. God reveals himself to man; in response to this revelation, man adores God, serves him, and becomes a witness for him in a mission—which is a gift of the Holy Spirit—which he fulfils in giving worship to God. The rituals which accompany this worship are of a secondary nature; the Church must be led by the Holy Spirit.

The Kimbanguist Church has daily worship, in the morning and evening. It also recognizes important festivals commemorating past events. These events are taught by accounts which make known to us the work of the prophet and the first Kimbanguist Christians, and their perseverance in exile. Thus these events become a living teaching which revives the faith of the believers. The events of our history often have parallels in the Bible, which is the foundation of any Christian message.

Here are a few examples: the outpouring of the Holy Spirit reported in the Bible (Acts 2) brings to mind that new outpouring at N'Kamba, when the Holy Spirit began the work of Christ there on 6 April 1921, and Christ cured a woman in response to the prayer of the prophet S. Kimbangu. Christ is a suffering servant (Isaiah 53). All those who have followed him have suffered in his name. The prophet Kimbangu, the sacrificers and all who wish to be saved by Christ agree to suffer with Him. (The 'sacrificers' are the '*bansadisi*' (assistants) of the prophet.)

The Kimbanguist festivals are as follows:

On 24 and 25 December we joyfully celebrate the festival of Christmas, commemorating the birth of our Saviour. This festival coincides with that of the liberation of the Kimbanguist Church in 1959. On 25 December we have a special service of accounts. In this service the Spiritual Head draws up an accounts sheet of the moral and spiritual behaviour of the Christians, and announces a line of conduct to be followed, so that everyone behaves in a Christian manner. For example, the year of 1975 was proclaimed the year of love for one's neighbour; in every parish sermon and every general service the theme was love.

There are three principal festivals celebrated by the Kimbanguist Church to commemorate the events of its own history. The first is the festival of 6 April. It commemorates every year the start of the prophet's mission on 6 April 1921, a day on which there have been many miraculous deeds. These signs signify two things in our eyes: firstly they predict our total liberation, and secondly they celebrate the glory of God, manifested in the death and resurrection of His Son, Jesus Christ, since the 6 April coincides with the festivals of Good Friday and Easter Day. Secondly, the festival of Matondo—Collection—in July corresponds to the festival of the first-fruits which was celebrated in May or June (Leviticus 23, 9ff). Thirdly, the festival of 12 October commemorates the death of the prophet Kimbangu in 1951, and coincides with the feast of Tabernacles which was celebrated in October (Leviticus 23, 23-42).

We also have special services in the morning and evening of the following days:

27 April, the anniversary of the death of Mama Mwilu Kiawanga, the wife of the prophet, in 1959.
2 April, to commemorate the return of the prophet's mortal remains from Lumumbashi to N'Kamba in 1960.
We do not forget the birthdays of the three sons of the prophet, to thank God for continuing His work through them; for us they are the shepherds of the great flock.
Every Wednesday is devoted to church work and to prayer.

The Kimbanguists celebrate on Sundays (Acts, 20, 7), because it is the Lord's Day (Revelation 1, 10). This day is sacred to the Lord, and the faithful go to worship. In principle, the faithful should abstain from doing anyone a service in return for personal gain, from buying or selling, and from any work (Exodus 20, 8-10); for every Kimbanguist Sunday is devoted to prayer and worship: hymns, prayers, preaching, offerings . . .

The Kimbanguist order of service for Sunday is as follows:

1. Communal singing.
2. Prayer said by one of the congregation.
3. Reading of a psalm.
4. Singing of anthems.
5. Reading of verses from the Bible on which the sermon is to be preached.
6. Singing of anthems (continued).
7. Blessing of the children.
8. Offerings collected by the deacon.
9. Prayer and sermon.
10. Various announcements and greetings.
11. Closing prayer.

On each first and third Sunday of the month, a special service takes place that the Kimbanguists call the special service of *Nsinsani* (competition). The aim is to collect sums of money for the construction of our buildings, such as school buildings, churches, a clinic being built by the faithful, a reception centre, and so on.

The rites accompanying Kimbanguist prayer

Nowadays rites are no longer used to ensure that prayers are answered. In the Christian Church all rites should be preceded by absolute obedience to the will of God. Although they are essential for the worshipping life of the faithful, the rites must nevertheless be considered of secondary importance. It is essential for the Holy Spirit to dominate and direct the worship with its rites.

The Kimbanguist Church acknowledges a few important rites. The first is the Sacrament of Baptism. This takes place by the laying on of hands, and the raising of the neophyte kneeling in front of the pastor. The kneeling and raising of the neophyte symbolize his death and his resurrection in Christ. Baptism is our condition of life renewed, or a new birth. For us the baptism of water is a baptism of repentance to prepare for Christ's coming (Mark 1, 4). But since Christ came and died on the cross and rose again from the dead for the remission of the sins of the world, it is now the Holy Spirit who comes into the heart of mankind to reveal the possibility of repentance. If a person accepts this possibility, the Church receives him through the laying on of hands so that the Holy Spirit may dwell in him, without using water.

Here is a résumé of a baptism service in the Kimbanguist Church (see *Liturgie kimbanguiste*, p. 1):

After a short prayer suitable for the occasion, the pastor says: 'Jesus says to his apostles—and to us today—that He is the way, the truth and the life. No one comes to the Father but by Him; for as in Adam all mankind sinned, in Him it rediscovers eternal life.

Let us remember what John the Baptist said about the baptism of the Holy Spirit: I baptize you with water to bring you to repentance; but he who comes after me is more powerful than I, and I am not worthy to bear his shoes, and He shall baptize you with the Holy Ghost and with fire.

The Church of Jesus Christ today subjects you to baptism as She was commanded by the Messiah: Go, make disciples of all nations, baptizing them in the name of the Father, and of the Son and of the Holy Ghost, and teach them to observe all that I have commanded you.

Whoever believes in Christ, is baptized, and carries out His commandments has salvation; whoever does not believe in Him denies himself salvation. Repent, and let each one of you be baptized in the name of Jesus Christ for the forgiveness of sins; and you will receive the gift of the Holy Ghost. Rise then and be baptized for the remission of your sins by Christ, and glorify His name. (Acts 2, 38)

(Note: A pastor pronounces this baptismal formula a little apart from the others. The catechumens to be baptized, kneeling in a row, hold out the right hand to the pastor in front of them. After the pastor on one side has pronounced the baptismal formula, the others assist the new converts to rise.)

'Dearly beloved friend, I receive you into the assembly of Jesus Christ, the Saviour and Lord of mankind, for your eternal salvation in Him and through Him, in the name of the Father and of the Son and of the Holy Ghost.'

The closing prayer is as follows:

'In the name of the Father and of the Son and of the Holy Ghost, Lord Jesus, in obedience to Thy commandment, Thy Church has just proceeded to baptize those who have today accepted union with us, and agreed to bear every one his own cross towards Thee, that Thou may remember them and us in Thy heavenly kingdom of justice and glory. Protect them from all sin, and strengthen them constantly in their faith in Thee. Be their guide and protector at every moment and manifest Thy eternal love to them, as to us. In the name of the Father, the Son and the Holy Ghost.

May the grace of our Lord Jesus Christ, the love of God our Father, and the fellowship of the Holy Ghost be with all of us, today and for always! Amen.'

The Sacrament of the Eucharist

The composition of the elements of the Kimbanguist Holy Communion is authentically African. To represent the body of Christ, the Kimbanguist Church makes use of a cake made of maize flour, potato flour, and flour from raw, dried bananas; to represent the blood of Christ it uses natural honey diluted with water.

In the Kimbanguist Church, communion is only celebrated three times a year: in April (the 6th in principle), in October (ideally on the 12th), and on 25 December, on the occasion of the feast of the Nativity. 6 April is the anniversary of the beginning of Simon Kimbangu's ministry of healing and evangelism. Communion is celebrated both in memory of that date and Easter Day. 12 October is the anniversary of Simon Kimbangu's death in 1951.

After a religious service (the consecration of the elements of the Eucharist by His Eminence, the Spiritual Head of the Kimbanguist Church, or his representative), in which the sermon deals with the Communion, the Kimbanguists wishing to partake collect themselves in silence. On this occasion the pastors, deacons and deaconesses whose task is to distribute the communion are dressed in white.

Led by the pastor who presides over the ceremony, the people who are to distribute the communion go into the church or an enclosed area where the cakes and the honey are set out. There the pastor responsible for the distribution prays that the cake and the honey be transformed by the Lord into the body and blood of Christ. Then each takes a communion tray and moves towards the waiting Christians.

At this moment all kneel. A pastor among the communion team says another prayer, before reading the following text: 'The Lord Jesus, in the night that he was delivered, took bread, and after giving thanks, he broke it and said: This is my body, which is broken for you; do this in remembrance of me. In the same way, after having supped, he took the cup and said: This cup is the new testament in my blood; do this in remembrance of me, as oft as you shall drink it; for as oft as you eat of this bread and drink of this cup, you do show the Lord's death until he come. That is why he who eats or drinks the Lord's cup unworthily, shall be guilty towards the body and blood of the Lord. Therefore let each man examine himself, and thus eat the bread and drink the cup; for he who eats and drinks without recognizing the body of the Lord, eats and drinks a judgement against himself.' (1 Corinthians 11, 23-29)

After the reading of this text, two pastors say short prayers, and the pastor in charge then says the last prayer before the distribution of the communion; the Lord Jesus Christ is invited to come and partake of the Holy Sacrament with the congregation of his church, as he did with his apostles. After the prayer, the communion begins: the communicants stay kneeling in their places, and those making the distribution pass in front of them; the Christian first eats the body of Christ, then drinks his blood.

After everyone has communicated, the members of the team of distributors finally communicate themselves, and the ceremony is brought to a close by a final communal prayer said by the pastor in charge of the team.

The Sacrament of Marriage

Here is an extract from the declaration of His Eminence, published at the time of the liberation of the church:

'Kimbanguist religious marriage has its source and its end in God, the only foundation that can be laid down.

Indeed Holy Scripture tells us: "If the Eternal does not build the house, those who build it labour in vain." (Psalm 127, 1)

The essential and most important element in this marriage is the mutual love of the married couple, a love inspired by faith and noble sentiments, alone capable of uniting firmly the two partners and of granting them, not a perfect marriage, but the possibility of simply and humbly living a pleasant life together, in which there is giving and self-giving, forgiveness and the asking for forgiveness, in a spirit of self-denial, sacrifice and prayer.

This marriage is concluded when there is a solemn commitment by the couple toward each other, in front of a pastor, who proclaims the word of God to them, blesses their union and intercedes in their favour.

The religious ceremony takes place when the couple have fulfilled the requirements of customary law, which prescribes in particular:

1. That the engagement be announced with the full consent and in the presence of the parents of the engaged couple;

2. That the engagement should be publicly announced and officially recognized by both parties;

3. That the engagement be made public, the girl's dowry in the marriage be paid, with all the customary ceremonies which bring together the family and friends of the couple;

4. That the couple remain apart, and live according to the dignity and respect of traditional practices until the day of the religious marriage ceremony.

In order to preserve the unity of the couple and ensure the vitality of their Christian life, it is necessary for one and the same motive force to move the husband and wife in the same direction, in profound unity. This cannot be achieved if there is a spiritual divergence. In these circumstances the Kimbanguist Church advises the future husband and wife to seek unity in the Christian faith, in the communion of the Church, before their union.

Nonetheless the Kimbanguist Church tolerates, and even gives its blessing to mixed marriages (i.e. the marriage of Kimbanguists to believers of Protestant or Catholic origin), but only after deep consideration; for it is difficult for such marriages to encourage the faith of the husband and wife and ensure harmony in the Christian education of the offspring.

We adopt the same line of conduct in the matter of marriages between Kimbanguists and unbelievers, in accordance with the instructions of the Holy Scriptures in this respect (1 Corinthians 7, 12-15).

A marriage contracted within another religion is fully respected, that is to say that if husband and wife were married in the Catholic church, the Protestant church or the Salvation Army, and they subsequently become Kimbanguists, their marriage is valid and they are in order with regard to our religion.

Kimbanguist marriage is indissoluble. Separation of bodies can be granted if one of the parties has committed adultery (Matthew 19, 9).

It may happen that for some reason or other one of the partners may find a pretext for giving up their right at their request.'

Other Sacraments (or activities of a sacramental nature)
Instead of baptizing children, the Kimbanguist Church gives them a blessing; that is why the sacrament of confirmation does not exist in our church. We receive the faithful baptized in other churches with a prayer, but this is not confirmation as practised in other churches.

Unction of the sick: this is done, but instead of oil, we use the water of N'Kamba to pray for the healing of the sick, (James 5, 15). All Christians are commanded to pray for the sick, and all have the right to use the water of N'Kamba. But the laying on of hands is reserved for the Spiritual Head and the '*Bansadisi*', or in exceptional circumstances a pastor as substitute. As regards the other rites that we call sacramental, everyone has access to them if he feels a spiritual need. The church also organizes the burial of the dead.

Sacramental rites particular to the Kimbanguists: The blessing of the faithful by the Spiritual Head, by the laying on of hands; the consecration of houses and new cars; the laying of the first stone of a house, and the blessing of other objects by the water of N'Kamba (holy water). And we must especially make mention of bathing in the pool of N'Kamba. Nothing prevents a church introducing such rites which arise through its history and culture, and the understanding of the Gospel given by the Holy Spirit, provided that it does not forget its universality.

The times of Kimbanguist prayer
For the Christian, prayer is a compass which guides him throughout his life towards Christ. It is a fundamental action before all other actions.

The first prayer of a good Christian is to ask the Holy Spirit to intercede for him that he might pray better.

But when should one pray? Many people would like to pray, but cannot find the time for it. Modern man finds his time very full; we have become the slaves of time. How can we escape the rationalization of life? In *Le combat de la prière* Hans Asmussen poses the question: Will God forgive us the fault of having handed over to ourselves our days and nights?

This is the greatest struggle of the Christian in the modern world; is it really necessary to abandon our spiritual life in order to earn our living? In our church, many of our members employed in factories lack the opportunity to participate frequently in the prayer meetings and services organized by the church. In spite of this hindrance, these Christians do not feel deprived of the daily prayer, either collective or individual.

The time of prayer is not determined by the fact that prayer is an essential need in the life of the Christian. But the Kimbanguist Church has adopted the three times of daily prayer suggested in the Bible: in the morning, at midday and in the evening (in the afternoon at 15.00 hours, at the time when the daily 'evening' sacrifice was offered). This is the prayer attested by the most ancient witnesses (Cf. Joachim Jeremias, 'Abba, Jesus and His Father'). The psalmists make mention of these three times of prayer: 'In the morning I turn myself towards You and I look' (Psalm 5, 3).* 'It is a good thing to give thanks unto the Lord . . . to shew forth thy loving kindness in the morning' (Psalm 92, 1-2). These quotations allude to the morning prayer. At midday we can read Psalm 123, 1: 'Unto Thee lift I up mine eyes'. For the evening there is Psalm 4, 8: 'I will both lay me down in peace, and sleep', and Psalm 91, 5: 'Thou shalt not be afraid for the terror by night; nor for the arrow . . .' In his high chamber Daniel had windows that opened towards Jerusalem, and three times a day, he knelt, he prayed and praised his God (Daniel 6, 10).

The morning prayer is offered in a short service lasting twenty to thirty minutes. It has the following form:

1. Singing in unison (a song of thanksgiving, such as *'Ntondele kua ngeye Nzambi'*).

2. Prayer: The morning prayer contains the following elements:

a) To thank God who has protected everyone during the night: rich and poor, good and bad, great and small, black and white.

b) To intercede for three categories of people: firstly for those who have died during the night; that God the Father of all may forgive them, and accept those souls who have just appeared before Him, for they lived in a disordered world. Then we pray for those who are sick or in prison—for

---

*Verse references are to the Authorised Version of the Bible.

those who have been falsely accused and those who deserve their lot; we ask God to cure the sick and shorten the stay in hospital or in prison. Then we pray for those who form the community that is praying; that God may grant them strength and health to survive during the day and to persevere in the face of the hidden dangers of the day, and that He may also bless the day's labours.

3. Bible reading, prayer and preaching. (Here the Christians who have some knowledge of the Bible may be authorized to preach.)

4. Singing in unison (connected with the preaching).

5. Announcements by the pastor, deacon or catechist, and if necessary greetings to visitors.

6. Closing prayer: We thank God for the preaching that He has just blessed; we intercede for the three sons of the prophet, who have to bear a heavy burden in the church, and for all the leaders who help in this task.

The midday prayer is either individual or collective, according to circumstance. Often a bell is rung to remind the faithful, far and near, to participate in the midday prayer; if no bell can be rung, the faithful keep a close watch on the time, so as to be ready at the right time. We give thanks to God for protecting us during the first half of the day, and we ask Him what is His will, so that we may persevere until the evening. The midday prayer is not a service, but it is accomplished by the reciting of three prayers, and a song of lamentation.

The evening prayer is a short service, as in the morning; it consists of the following: singing in unison; prayer by a member of the congregation: we thank God for taking part in the day's activities and for protecting us from the dangers of the day. And we ask Him to extend his kindness until night. This is followed by preaching (various exhortations) and a closing prayer.

On certain days, such as Tuesday, Thursday and Saturday, the evening worship is replaced by choir practice, in which new songs are learned or old ones rehearsed, especially on Saturdays to prepare for Sunday.

The Kimbanguist Christian prays before undertaking any action. Before he eats, he prays to thank God, the master and friend of all, who provides nourishment for all the people of the earth, both good and bad. Before doing any service, a good Kimbanguist asks God to preserve him from all evil, he asks for strength, intelligence and wisdom so that he can perform his service well. He prays before going on a journey. The night before, and in the morning before getting out of bed, he prays to give thanks to God and ask Him for the opportunity to act well in the day which has just dawned. In the evening before going to bed, he asks for divine protection during the night. But above all he thanks God for a well-spent day.

The content of Kimbanguist prayer

The content of Kimbanguist prayer varies; prayer follows the history and development of the church. Events which happen to it give rise to prayers; and no event which affects the church is outside the scope of prayer. Thus it acts as a regulating mechanism in the situation experienced by the church. Here are a few examples of the changing content of prayer: the prayers during the clandestine period of the church were not the same as those during and after the liberation; the intercessions of the church that the country might achieve independence were not the same as those after independence.

In difficult circumstances, prayers are often lamentations imploring divine assistance, together with songs of distress. The same applies in mourning, or when the body is suffering (in cases of sickness). When feeling joyful, one prays to thank God, and one thinks of others. The songs which accompany these prayers are praises and thanksgivings.

Kimbanguist prayer begins with an invocation that is virtually uniform, wherever the Church extends: It begins by the invocation of the Trinity: 'In the name of the Father, and of the Son, and of the Holy Ghost.' Sometimes one adds: 'who descended upon the prophet Simon Kimbangu.' The prayer ends with the same invocation before the Amen. (See the prayer of His Eminence, page 581 above.)

This invocation is followed by a request, which depends on the good intentions of the person who is praying, and the current situation. The prayer ends, as described above, with thanksgivings and a closing invocation.

Kimbanguist song, choirs and music

The doctrine of Kimbanguist song is historical. At the start of the prophet's mission at N'Kamba, the songs utilized to accomplish the work of Christ were those of the Protestants. But the Protestants refused to sell their hymn books to the followers of the prophet. Saddened, Simon Kimbangu went apart to pray, laying before God this poverty in song, so deeply felt by his congregation. From that was born the gift of 'catching' the songs.

Kimbanguists catch songs in various ways: in dreams, and in visions in which they hear angels singing. As a general rule, once they have been caught, the songs are sent to an office, set up by the church called the Directorate of Kimbanguist songs, where they are studied and to some extent modified to give them a good meaning. Other songs are deleted, if the meaning of the song is not clear. The songs have to be examined to avoid those that may be inspired by the Devil.

Kimbanguist songs are primarily prayers. 'To sing is to pray twice'.

Prayer includes the whole of doctrine. Thus through their richness, Kimbanguist songs include the whole of Christian doctrine. They are living lessons, explaining and clarifying Biblical teaching. Three quarters of them are caught through divine inspiration; they can be found throughout Kimbanguist history. They contain: encouragements: '*A makesa ma Yisu*'; exhortations to perseverance; homage to God; certain elements which foretell the future, sometimes even dealing with the end of time. This type of song warns the faithful to be prudent in a given situation which may bear a resemblance to a recent event. They also commemorate the prophet's mission, and the love of God towards his creation.

Apart from their own songs, the Kimbanguists do not deny themselves the pleasure of singing other hymns in an ecumenical context, and rejoice if others sing theirs.

The Kimbanguist Church has a multiplicity of choirs; each parish possesses at least one. A choir that could be called a 'pilot' choir is the leader of all the other choirs. It is called the 'choir of leaders', and the people of whom it is composed are capable of leading a choir wherever it might be within the church.

The recently caught songs, arranged by the directorate of songs, are sung first by the choir of leaders, and then spread to all the other choirs. This choir of leaders operates at the regional level; each region possesses one which pilots the others in the same region.

Beside the leaders, there is another very important choir in the church, the G.T.KI., (Kimbanguist theatre group). The task of this group is to sing and bring to life the history of the Kimbanguist Church and Bible stories by means of theatre. Such groups, each comprising several members are found in each region of Zaïre and in all the countries where Kimbanguism has taken root. Their aim is to bring the events of the past to life, so that they can be relived in every generation.

There is also another method of singing the glory of God: music. Kimbanguist music is executed by: the band, a group of flautists, a group of guitarists, or a small group of people who accompany their songs with accordion players.

In 1921, when the prophet realized that his members seemed to be weakening because of the frequent arrests and other torments, caused by the colonizers, he took his disciples by night to a mountain in N'Kamba where they sang and prayed to God, and all saw the glory of God. (2 Kings 6, 17). And in this vision they saw the heavenly orchestra singing the glory of God.

This vision began to be achieved in 1960, when the church started a badly equipped band. But today, it is well equipped and I might venture to say complete. It plays religious songs, but in certain cases it also plays profane songs if it wishes, for example the national anthem, and other party songs (of the *M.P.R.*) and even those composed by our ancestors which contain words not unworthy of a Christian.

The flautists also comprise an authentic band, made up of flutes in wrought iron or bamboo, tomtoms and the big drum, made from native or imported materials. The group of flautists stands in for the band in case of absence or fatigue, especially on the occasion of Nsinsani Sundays, when music is played for six hours. (See above p. 583.)

The attitude of a Kimbanguist Christian during prayer

For Kimbanguists the Bible is the foundation of the divine revelation. It is the fundamental source of Christian doctrine. Certain attitudes originate in the practices of God's chosen people, the people of Israel.

The Kimbanguists remove their shoes for the entire duration of the service. This custom is also observed when one is in a place that has been proclaimed holy. For Kimbanguists N'Kamba is the New Jerusalem; for Jesus appeared there, and his presence represents the holy land of Jerusalem. That is why the land of N'Kamba is holy, for Jesus appeared there, and Kimbanguists remain barefoot in the holy city.

Kimbanguist prayer begins, as we have said above, by an invocation 'in the name of the Father and of the Son and of the Holy Ghost'. After this invocation we are assured of Christ's presence. That is why the place where the prayer is recited, wherever it may be, is declared 'holy', and one must take off one's shoes, as God told Moses (Exodus 3, 5).

The men also take off their watch, bracelet and hat (1 Corinthians 11, 4) to be unpretentious before God. The women cover their heads with a cloth (1 Corinthians 11, 5). For a Kimbanguist woman this attitude is not only observed during prayer, but is characteristic of her whole behaviour, and her everyday dress. Even in bed at night, she keeps her head covered.

The most suitable position for praying is a kneeling position, with the hands together in front of the chest. The supervisors who keep order during worship remain standing during the prayer to watch over the congregation, and for the same reason they do not shut their eyes.

Like the Protestants, Kimbanguists close their eyes for prayer, to avoid distractions and bring themselves into contact with God. And kneeling before him, we are unworthy to look at him; the head is lowered to show even more humility. Pockets are emptied of money and all other objects.

It may happen that in some cases it is impossible to adopt these attitudes during prayer, when among a non-Christian group for instance, or even among Christians, if one does not want to make oneself conspicuous, or whenever there is need of a short, quick prayer; in this case I pray discreetly without adopting any of the attitudes enumerated above. It follows that one can pray seated, lying down, standing, working, walking, or travelling. But as a general rule, one should subject one's body to some discipline.

Prayer in the face of obstacles or difficulties

At the beginning of his prayers, the prophet Kimbangu often made use of an expression which evoked the greatness of God in contrast to our terrestial state. He used to say: 'God, our Father, the heaven is your throne, and the earth is your footstool.' Formulated in this way, the words express the difference which exists between these two opposed worlds. Heaven, the realm of the Most High and all the saints, is a world of holiness, joy, richness, and eternal life; whereas the earth on the other hand is a world of sin, suffering, poverty and death.

Even though he is set apart to participate to some extent in the joyful life of heaven, the Christian still lives materially in the world where there is so much weakness and anguish. His poor faith is wavering; he is surrounded by all sorts of vexations. God demands that we obey His law, which is there to protect the faith of the Christian. But faced with the problems of life, the Christian's faith and obedience must proceed from his trust in God, so that believing, one requests the help of God to conquer one's unbelief. This request is the prayer we make to God, in the name of Christ, to ask for the things we lack, the possibility of victory, the strength, courage, serenity and prudence to confront the problems surrounding us.

Kimbanguist Christians live this same existence, surrounded by great problems, in their faith, and confess that God is the all-powerful Father, the Creator of Heaven and earth. They confess Jesus, the only Son of God, who suffered under Pontius Pilate, died on the cross, rose from the dead, and went up to heaven, and is seated at the right hand of His Father, who sent the Holy Spirit to us in the person of Simon Kimbangu, to come to our aid in our current situation. He strengthens us in our faith and our witness for Christ.

The regulations of the Kimbanguist Church

Kimbanguist Christians are obedient to the law that God gave to Moses to establish His covenant with His people. (Exodus 20, 1-17) But strict observance of the Decalogue is supplemented by the rules that Christ gave to his servant Simon Kimbangu to help us in this observance. These rules are as follows: Kimbanguists abstain from the consumption of alcoholic drinks. (Do not get drunk with wine; that is debauchery. On the contrary, be filled with the Holy Spirit, says the Bible, cf. Ephesians 5, 18). They also abstain from smoking any kind of cigarettes. They eat anything that is edible, but the meat of the pig and the monkey is forbidden. The reason why is the province of the prophet who knows the reasons for it. Often Mark 5, 1-13 is quoted, the story in which Jesus expels evil spirits from a man, and sends them into a herd of pigs. Attendance at a place where there is dancing is forbidden; and Kimbanguists themselves do not dance. They go to see films only of a religious or cultural nature, not those that shock. A good Kimbanguist avoids walking alone with a woman or a young girl for a considerable distance without a witness, so as to avoid the opportunity of falling into sin. Kimbanguists exclude all forms of polygamy (polygyny and polyandry).

If a Kimbanguist transgresses these rules, he is temporarily excommunicated. During this time, he is under supervision from the parish of which he is a member; they visit him frequently to admonish him, strengthen him and invite him continually to worship; for Christ is looking for his lost sheep. (Luke 15, 1-7).

Retreats and the spiritual life of the Kimbanguists
Like any other church, the Kimbanguist Church cannot declare that it is perfect, for the reason that, in its visible state, it is made up of members who are spiritually weak. The aim of the church is to be able to model itself on Christ, to try to be perfect; for it is the body of Christ and every Christian is a member of that body. That is why the whole church suffers, if but one of its members stumbles. Thus it has to watch over the whole life of the Christian. The church seeks those members who are lost to set them on the right road towards Christ. To reform its members, and urge them to conform to the pure, good life of the Christian, the church organizes retreats, in which the faithful are made conscious of their faults (sins) and seek to repent.

Retreats have their origin in the Bible; in the life of God's servants there often arise difficult situations which require concentration and perseverance in prayer. When this occurred they often withdrew far from the community to take refuge in the temple or on a mountain or in the desert. Let us remember the prophetess Anna who devoted her time to prayer and fasting (Luke 2, 37). Jesus passed forty days and forty nights withdrawn in the desert, praying and fasting, before beginning his ministry. Before his arrest he withdrew to Gethsemane with the disciples whom he loved (Luke 22, 39-45). The first Christian community, the one at Antioch, prayed and fasted (Acts 13, 2ff). The entire mission of the prophet Kimbangu was conditioned by retreats; he often withdrew by himself to pray and fast.

Retreats are a vital necessity of the Kimbanguist Church. When its members were deprived of their life of public worship, they used to go a long way from the village at night, to bring themselves into contact with Christ through songs and prayers. Each prayer meeting began with a confession of sin, to ask Christ for forgiveness before anything else, so that the meeting could be deepened spiritually.

The three sons of the prophet, who bear a heavy burden in the church, withdraw either together or individually, to consolidate their faith, and accomplish the heavy task of leading this great church of four million members.

I have already said that the Kimbanguist Church makes its way through prophecies. The retreat is one of the prophecies of the prophet Kimbangu; it was fulfilled in 1972. The Spiritual Head began by organizing a group of people who were thought to be spiritually worthy and capable of leading the retreats well. This group is composed of men, for leading the mens' retreat; in this group are only men, plus a few women to do the cooking—or even to preach; a group of women lead the women's retreat.

The retreats are organized every week in places specially prepared by the church, in such a way that the places for men and women are apart. They are organized in nearly all the regions of Zaïre, and in neighbouring countries. The number of participants varies between 50 and 500. The retreats open their doors to everyone, even though they are organized by the Kimbanguist Church; many Christians of other denominations are interested and come and participate, even some non-Christians and Muslims.

The retreats play a very important part in the church: they give the faithful the opportunity to concentrate on prayer, to try to find the right path to Christ through the teaching of the Bible, by Bible study and preaching, to confess their sins publicly and to have recourse to renewed spiritual strength. I could say that for us at present, retreats are an outpouring of the Holy Spirit of N'Kamba which is continuing, because men and women once more feel free, having cast aside fetishes and other magical practices, as in the time of the prophet Kimbangu.

The duration of the retreat is always three and a half days. It begins on a Tuesday evening and ends on a Saturday morning. One of its characteristics is a fast of from one to three days, during which people abstain from food and drink. This deprivation frees us from material cares and puts us in direct communication with Christ.

The programme of the retreat is very concentrated; in the mornings it begins with a service; then the participants are divided into groups of seven or nine people. These groups spread out in the forest for prayers. In these groups prayers are said in turn; often there is a cycle of nine prayers, interspersed with songs, confessions, and Bible study; for example, after three prayers, they sing or pass on to some other activity. After this cycle of nine prayers, there will be a message from one member of the group: an exhortation, a vision seen during the prayers, a response to the questions . . . The programme continues in this way until evening, when the leaders come and collect the groups and institute a strict check to find out whether, for example, someone is missing.

During the night, there are fixed times for prayer; as an example: about 20.00 hours there is a sermon; at 22.00 hours there will be three prayers and a song; the same thing at 3.00 and 5.00 in the morning.

Moreover at the retreat, everything—the visions, the dreams, the songs which have been caught, in every group and on each day—is set down in report books that are presented to the Spiritual Head of the Church or his representative.

All those who have participated in a retreat meet one evening a week of their choosing, at the parish level. In these prayer meetings, there are also group confessions of sins.

This method has greatly helped to fortify the faith of the members, particularly the young people, so that they persevere in prayer and in the life of worship. It is also a good way of deepening brotherly love, getting to know one another better, and getting to know Christ and serve Him more fully.

Liturgical Adaptation

P. ABEGA

This chapter merely provides some historical evidence on which later historians can build to trace the itinerary of the progress of Christianity in Africa. It deals with the experiment in liturgical adaptation in the parish of St Paul de Ndzon-Melen, in the southern suburbs of the town of Yaoundé, the capital of the United Republic of Cameroun. We will sketch in the historical background to this experiment, and will examine the Biblical foundations on which any authentic Christian experience must rest. The cultural model for this experiment will be presented in the third section. The description of the new liturgical rite will take up the fourth section, and in conclusion we shall attempt to show what are the fruits we expect from it for an authentic Christian life on African soil.

Historical background
We are all aware of the conditions in which our peoples were Christianized: through ignorance, dishonesty or scorn for the African, to whom they refused the status of a man, an adult, the missionaries acted as if the Black man was a *tabula rasa*, a grown up child, who had lived in a historical and cultural void. One could therefore instil into him any gesture or any symbolism one desired, with no fear of the consequences, no traumas, no regrettable confusion. In illustration of this, we should mention a gesture that was particularly offensive to us: the kissing of the cross or the altar. In fact among the Beti the cultural category of the kiss does not exist. But it was at all costs necessary to get the people to adopt it. To translate this idea, use was made of the Beti word for 'sniff', *nyumulu*. Now in Beti one only 'sniffs' something, if one wants to find out whether it is getting high. In this case how can one 'sniff' Christ? Did he smell bad? Who cannot see the stupidity of introducing a gesture completely foreign to the mentality of the people? Nevertheless our people began to 'sniff' Christ without much grasp of the symbolic category underlying the gesture. And even now many of our colleagues in the priesthood 'sniff' the altar, without asking themselves what this gesture might mean. We could recite a long list of such examples, but that is not the object of this paper. This example merely illustrates the discomfort that a certain kind of Christianity inspired in the more

thoughtful amongst us. The year which can be called the turning point was 1958, the year in which, newly armed with the baccalaureate, we entered the major seminary. That year we began to say out loud what many people were saying in a whisper, for fear of excommunication. And it was in 1958, at the major seminary of Otélé, that attempts at liturgical adaptation began seriously.

Religious singing was the first field of exploration. The lack of adaptation was here particularly evident. Most of the languages of South Cameroun are tone languages. The act of overlaying these languages with prefabricated Western melodies had the effect of completely upsetting the language, resulting in meaningless phrases, or even comical absurdities that rob prayer of its seriousness. An example: In Ewondo there are four homographic words in pairs. The first on a low tone and the second on a high tone give the following sequence: *O ne m'ben yéné ma ngó*, (you are good have pity on me). In the other sequence we have the first on a high tone and the second on a low tone and this gives: *O ne m'bén yéné ma ngo*, (you are a cudgel look at me poor sheathfish). Thus instead of the prayer of the first sequence, in the second formula we ask God to knock us senseless, since he is a cudgel and we are a fish. And it is the second meaning which prevails with the overlaid Western melody.

When it was decided to begin to restore order to the situation, Latin was still the obligatory language sung at mass. The first change was to sing Latin to African tunes as in the mass called 'the mass of the canoers'. The attempt to adapt some psalms to Camerounian tunes proved catastrophic. It was necessary to take a very dangerous step at a time when Rome still forbade the introduction of modern languages into the liturgy, and sing the psalms of the breviary in the Camerounian languages to Camerounian tunes.

This did not happen without encountering a great deal of resistance. I remember an amusing occasion when the parish priest stopped the seminarists in the middle of mass; when questioned by the seminarists after the mass, he replied: 'I cannot understand either the words or the music; it is nothing but shouting, there's no piety in it.' Yet the enthusiasm aroused at a popular level by these songs ought to have made him more circumspect. The movement, once launched, could only spread further.

One of our colleagues in the priesthood, Abbé Pie-Claude Ngumu, has made it his life's work. His task has been not only to enlarge the movement that had been begun, but to deepen it and make it ever more authentic. He was ordained in 1960, and made curate of the parish of St Luke at Tala. There he started a church choir, and since he possessed musical talent as a composer, he experimented with new songs for this choir. At this period he had the good fortune to arrange the enthronement of Archbishop Jean Zoa, the first Camerounian

Archbishop of Yaoundé, in the cathedral of Yaoundé. This event will long be remembered in the annals of the country for its originality, its authenticity and its magnitude.

After he was made curate at the Cathedral of Yaoundé, Abbé Ngumu founded the famous choir of the *Maîtrise de la croix d'ébène* at Yaoundé. This choir represented the Cameroun at the first Festival of Negro Arts at Dakar in April 1966. There it carried off the first prize for African religious song.

But the great turning point in this experiment occurred in 1968, when Abbé Pie-Claude Ngumu was made founding priest of the parish of St Paul of Ndzon-Melen with a mission to experiment with a new liturgy. It was granted to the author of these lines to participate in the creation of this new liturgy. Relieved from my duties as Latin teacher at the minor seminary of Mvolyé, I was made a curate to assist Abbé Pie-Claude Ngumu in the Ndzon-Melen parish in 1969. It was at our suggestion that he decided to introduce the dance as a necessary adjunct to our music. Our melodies are always rhythmic; while they are being played, those present have the greatest difficulty in stopping themselves from beating time with head, finger, or foot. So then we asked why this movement that people had so much difficulty in restraining should not be given free rein. Yielding to our requests in this matter was the starting point of that liturgy that has been so much talked about, the liturgy that is the pride of the Cameroun, and certainly marks an epoch in the history of the church. Since it was launched, this experiment has met with a varied reception: for some it constitutes an attempt to paganize Christianity; for others it is one of the finest achievements of post-conciliar Catholic Christianity. Since then, Canadian, French and Belgian television services have filmed it for themselves. It surprised everyone by its originality at the festival of Algiers. We could go on for ever listing individual favourable reactions. We will confine ourselves to quoting that of Alioune Diop who admitted, after being present at this mass, that he had communed in the great cry of Africa, acclaiming the Lord, beyond the Beti words which he did not understand. But to remove any taint of paganization of the church, let us look at the Biblical foundations for such a procedure.

The theological and Biblical foundations of this indigenization
The great mystery to reflect upon here is the mystery of the Incarnation. Coming from the right hand of the Father, 'the Word of God was made flesh'. Henceforth there exists in the person of Jesus the indissoluble union of two halves: on the one hand the Word of God sharing with the Father the absolute, the unalterable, the universal; on the other hand the

Son of Man destined to become universal, assuming through the ages the differing faces of mankind at all times and all places. At the historical level this man bears the face of a Jew, an Aramean—a face both historical and contingent, and an exemplar.

This face of the Jew almost concealed the true intentions of God in his saving action. Indeed from the very first Council of Jerusalem the question was raised as to whether every man had to become a Jew to have access to God's salvation. In the apostolic college there were many who fell into this heresy; they demanded circumcision, an essentially Jewish rite, as a condition of entry into God's new people.

But at every vital moment in the history of his people, God raises up the providential man, to keep the first aim in view. That man was the apostle Paul. This Jew, who had at first been so Jewish that he had persecuted the Church of Christ because he thought it anti-Jewish, this man who had received his revelation not from men, but directly from Christ, this man, I say, was the first to stand up and oppose this Judaization of the Christian from every people and from every age. And this means, in concrete terms, that though Christ is unchanging in his aspect as Word of God, his face as a Jew, on the other hand, must act as a pattern for all the faces Christ is called upon to assume in becoming incarnate in every people.

But how can this incarnation of Christ in every people take place? Christ remains present in his church through those means of contact which we call the sacraments, the means whereby he continues to place himself within the reach of men of all times and all places. Now if we go back to the source of the sacraments and observe them at their origin, Christ, who instituted them, did not fix the form of any sacrament. He did not say how any one of them was to be carried out. All the sacraments are instituted in principle. 'This is my body, this is my blood, do it in remembrance of me.' How? Nothing is said. For us, that means that Christ intended that each people should develop each sacrament with the gestures that spoke for it. So that although each people partakes of catholicity in its adherence to the principle, the way in which it carries out this principle in its life is, in essence, particular, and that is true of all the sacraments.

This incarnation, moreover, does not happen exclusively at the level of the sacraments; it also happens at the level of the perception of the message. The Gospel can be compared to a great musical instrument with a wide and varied range. On this instrument each people is invited to play, in its own register, a hymn of praise to the Eternal.

These ideas are confirmed by the apocalyptic vision of the final scene in Heaven. There Saint John shows us all the peoples of the earth gathered around the Lamb praising God, each in his own tongue, his own liturgy. These people come from everywhere. They are performing a miracle that is the reverse of the one at Pentecost. At Pentecost, the apostles were speaking one language, but those present heard them in their various languages. Around the Lamb of God each people speaks its own language, but the Divine listener hears only one and the same hymn of praise.

In short, since Vatican II, the church understands that it is one in diversity. It understands that catholicity, universality does not in any way mean uniformity. It understands that God's enormous riches have been shared out among the peoples; that we must not reject any of these riches. On the contrary we must set up *omnia in Christo*.

The basic cultural model

Therefore drawing on Beti sources, we had recourse to the traditional Beti assembly in our efforts to reorganize the Catholic mass. What form does this assembly take? The assembly (etógán, ekóán) is called by any member of the tribe who has a problem; this problem may be particular or general. Whatever this may be, this meeting is always informal at the time it is convened, that is to say that there is no fixed agenda. The members making up the assembly are informed then and there of the subject of discussion. And it is the member who has convened the assembly who informs the assembly about the matter in question, either in person, or through an intermediary he has designated. When everyone has understood the subject, they deliberate so that each can express his point of view. For those who have had the good fortune to take part in such meetings, it is a real pleasure to listen to these oratorical contests, where the arguments for or against a particular suggestion come into conflict. It is a true passage of arms, with proverbs flying back and forth like bursts of gunfire aimed at each member of the assembly. When all those wishing to make a contribution have expressed their point of view, the Ndzo rises to sum up the discussion, and proposes the solution or solutions decided upon. The people agree by various acclamations.

Then the convener gives a meal to the whole assembly. This meal has a two-fold significance. It signifies gratitude towards those who answered yes to his call for an assembly; he tries in this way to repay them for the trouble they have gone to on his behalf. The second dimension of this meal is one of communion. Indeed, communion at the family table is an outward sign of the communion of hearts over the proposed solutions. After this meal the members separate and return to their own homes. In short, the assembly comprises two parts: the shared word, and the equally shared meal. This two-fold communion in the word and in the meal also constitute the two dimensions of the traditional Catholic mass.

The presentation of the new mass

The traditional Catholic mass does indeed comprise the two dimensions of communion mentioned above, but it still troubled us in many respects. On the one hand, at the beginning of the mass, one recited many prayers without first knowing why one had been called together by God. Then the sentiments expressed are somewhat ill-assorted. A sentiment like that of praise can be found in the *Gloria*, the *Sanctus*, and in the various eucharistic prayers. Repentance for sin is found in the *confiteor, misereatur, Kyrie, Gloria*, some prayers from the canon, *Agnus Dei* etc. Lastly and most importantly this mass shows up a dichotomy in the manner of participation, the officiating priest on the one hand, and the congregation on the other. The Ndzon-Melen mass tries to remedy these deficiencies. The Melen liturgy conforms to a very logical, coherent internal structure, as we hope to make clear in the following brief description.

First the Melen liturgy has the intention of being a true action of the people of God, as is suggested by the etymology of the word *Leitourgia*. Through the choir of the choristers the people are closely associated with the action of the priest. When the priest presents the Gospel at the appointed place, the choir escorts him there with singing and dancing. When he has finished consecrating the bread, the choir runs up to join with him in acclaiming the Lord who has arrived in the midst of his people. Finally it is the same choir that guides the multitude of the faithful in making the required movements, and it is the choir which carries the people's offerings to the altar. In short, henceforth the dichotomy between priest and congregation is ended; actions carried out beside the people are no more. Everything is accomplished by the people, with them and in the midst of them. Here is a description of what happens.

The service begins with the acclamation of the book, out of which the word of God they are to share together will be taken. While the ministers are dressing, the balafons strike up the song and the people dance. The president brings the incense and censes the book. Then the cross is placed at the head of the procession, while the president takes the book, comes out first, and shows it to the congregation, who acclaim it with a splendid acclamation. The procession sets off with the deacon or master of ceremonies carrying the open book that the president has handed to him. He walks in the middle, behind the president, and from time to time one of the servers censes the book during the procession. When they arrive at the appointed place, the celebrant enthrones the book and all the ministers take their places.

After the enthronement of the book, comes the proclamation of the word. Leaving out all the introductory prayers, the commentator gives a short introductory talk to the congregation to herald the mystery of the day. The people sit down and listen to the three readings, interspersed with the coda of a tune played quietly by the instruments during the reading. This ends with the solemn proclamation of the Gospel and the final song of meditation takes us right into the word of the one who has called together his assembly. Then comes the homily, a sermon in the form of a dialogue between the congregation and the celebrant. After bringing to birth the truth of the day, with the maieutics of Socrates, the celebrant concludes this concerted activity with various recommendations.

Then there rises up, like a hymn of acclamation and assent, the song of the Credo (*m'ayébo*). During the singing the crowd bring their offerings to the designated place: money, plaintains, sweet bananas, groundnuts, yams, macabo, sugar canes, vegetables of all kind, eggs, chickens, kids etc . . . in short, everything that the Lord found good at the creation or which is the fruit of man's industry for his further development. At the end of the Credo those who are called reflect upon their conduct, reveal their intentions to the Lord both as individuals and as a community. A hymn of supplication has taken the place of the *Kyrie* (kud a bía ngól). Finally the celebrant concludes the whole of this first part by the prayer of the day (Collect). As can be seen, prayer forms a kind of conclusion to the activity as a whole, not an introduction as in the traditional mass.

The second part follows immediately: the preparation of the communion meal. The choir goes in a dancing movement to collect the offerings of the people to carry them to the altar. This procession of the offerings is one of the most moving parts of this celebration. The people, clapping their hands and bearing their offerings to the Lord's altar in all their brilliant colours, gives one momentarily the illusion of participating in a celestial liturgy. The priest blesses the offerings one by one as they are presented to him, and the choir carries them back to a specially prepared place round the altar. While the choir is going back to its place, still dancing, the priest arranges the eucharistic elements on the altar. With no other transition, he formulates the invocation over the offerings and strikes up the great hymn of the action of grace (Preface). At the singing of the *Sanctus* four to six young girls come around the altar at a dancing pace, like the ten virgins who had gone forth to await the arrival of the bridegroom. Then comes the consecration of the bread and the wine. These two actions are accompanied by shouts of ovation (ayangá) and applause (kób) from the crowd. At once several other members of the choir run forward to join the young girls, and with the entire crowd of people sing the hymn of praise. In this new liturgy, the *Gloria* has become a song of welcome, bursting with joy, from a people happy to receive at last their Emmanuel. After this song of praise, the choir dances back to its place. The canon continues until the singing of the *Pater noster*, sung by the whole congregation, which is followed by the prayer after the *Pater*. Then a last pause to own oneself a sinner and call upon the Lamb of God to bring us his peace. After the prayer asking for peace, the faithful greet each other by shaking hands.

Then follows the communion meal in which all are invited to participate, if not materially at least spiritually. It goes without saying that an exhortation to come and make one's communion would be superfluous, since in the traditional communion meal, it is taken for granted that one should take part in it. During the communion the people sing the Lord's blessings.

After the communion meal and the purification of the sacred vessels, the people of God dance to a song about the active power of Grace; and the whole of this part of the ceremony ends with the last prayer of the people. After this prayer the priest blesses the congregation, and gives them leave to depart. During the dismissal, the choir performs a last song, reflecting upon the work of Grace made effective in the course of the mass. Thus ends the great liturgy of Ndzon-Melen. It may last two hours or even three, and people never tire of remaining standing in order to be a part of this august assembly. In short, we have here a liturgy for and together with God's people.

By way of a conclusion

The Ndzon-Melen liturgy is a step in the direction of what is called the indigenization of Christianity, an expression popularized by the Catholic bishops at the time of their most recent symposium in Rome. What in concrete terms is meant by this expression?

We outlined above a preliminary approach to the question: Christ wishes to make himself the universal man, so that he can be reached by man, wherever he comes from, and thus be able to lay before him the message of salvation in the light of his own concepts. But what are the benefits of indigenization for someone who has accepted Christ's message?

Firstly indigenization puts an end to that dichotomy which a certain type of evangelization creates in any man: a life which can be called Christian, and another natural, profane life, as it were, separate from Christ. In Africa this dichotomy has not been seen, as it has elsewhere, in terms of a juxtaposition, but in terms of opposition and conflict. It is assumed that, since the missionaries regarded our traditional religion and our symbolic cultural arsenal as the work of the Devil, every time that the African reverts to curative or divinatory practices etc., he does what is fundamentally evil in the eyes of the Christianity he has been taught. But nevertheless his whole being continues to be influenced subconsciously by traditional rituals. Therefore there is a perpetual conflict between the human values instituted by our ancestors for the well-being of our society, and this Christian vision instituted by the era of the missionaries. Here we could quote the opposition between Christian marriage and traditional marriage; and the equally clear-cut opposition between the Catholic priest and the traditional priest who is called a sorcerer. Our aim is to take what is worthwhile from these traditional rites and characters, and integrate them into Christianity. By doing this we hope to overcome the conflict instituted in the past between traditional African people and Christ. We hope to overcome the dichotomy between the Christian and profane life, and recreate the unity of the person who has been baptized, who must be wholly Christian and wholly at home in his society. Christ will in this way create a twofold authenticity. We shall be authentically Christian and sons of God, and authentically men of our different lands in the image of the Son of God, who is authentically Son of God, and Son of Man.

The second benefit we anticipate is the Future of the Universal. When God creates man in his own image, he does not give all his attributes to every individual; he distributes them to each man according to his possibilities and his design (cf. the parable of the talents). When God creates societies, he creates them in the image of divine society. Without making more divine societies, he endows each society with certain values different from those of other societies. When each people eventually brings to Christ the values granted to it by the Creator, the uniting of these values will then be able to recreate on this earth the manifold, complex countenance of God. That is what some of us call the Universal. God alone is a universal factor. The other universal is gestating, gradually coming to birth wherever the various peoples of the world learn to contribute their different values to the common good and create a single value which will be the very image of God. This will only happen if everyone accepts the foundation of everything in Christ.

APPENDIX

Address by Professor E. A. Ayandele, Principal,
University of Ibadan, Jos Campus, on Sunday 31
August, 1975

Distinguished scholars and churchmen, I am extremely pleased to welcome you to the Jos Campus of the University of Ibadan. I venture to hope that, our elementary facilities notwithstanding, your important Conference will feel duly at home in this cosmopolitan seat of several Christian missions and crucial meeting point of the Cross and the Crescent.

A careful study of your list of participants reveals your laudable intention to have the widest possible cross-section of scholars and churchmen interested in the presence of organized Christianity in Africa. Firstly, there are non-African representatives of Christian missions, parents of the Western-oriented Churches in Africa. Naturally their stance in your deliberations might be affected by the metropolitan ideals and experiences, as well as the legacy of the made-abroad forms and formularies introduced into Africa by missions in the nineteenth century. Secondly, there are the predominantly elitist African representatives of Western-established Churches which in many ways are still doctrinally, culturally and ecclesiastically subservient to metropolitan headquarters in Europe or in the New World. True, their Western-established Churches have been striving to rid themselves of the incubus of made-abroad prefabricated cultural and ecclesiastical yoke, but quintessentially these African elitist leaders of Churches have yet to show that they are able, or willing, to fully understand the African *milieu* in which they should expect the Christianity of the Bible to be incarnate. Thirdly, there are the spokesmen for Pentecostal, or Spiritualist, or Aladura Churches, up to now held in irrational, uncharitable and jaundiced contempt by the more elitist Western-oriented Churches. The fact that they are being represented at this Conference largely by scholars who themselves are not members of those churches, is a clear evidence of the terrible division in Christendom. From the massive evidence that has been provided about some of these Aladura churches, one would have thought that there should be no more doubt that they are *ipso facto* legitimate branches of the Church Universal; that in matters of the spirit and in their greater closeness to the grass-roots, they have salutary lessons to teach the more elitist Western-oriented Churches. Lastly, there are the religiously indifferent, or hostile, scholars who have parodied Christianity in literary works, or have looked upon Christianity with harsh, patriotic eyes, as a negation or antithesis of national identity, or as a colonialist legacy, or as a veritable obstacle to achievement of nationalist goals, or as an archaic capitalist ideology incompatible with the proper evolution of modern Africa. Such sceptics and 'patriots' are the ardent apostles of secularism.

It is not my intention to pre-empt some of the themes you will be exploring in the next week. However, permit me, as a keen student of the Christianization of African peoples, to make a few observations on some aspects of Christianity in independent Africa.

The crucial contribution of Christian missions to emergent Africa south of the Sahara is only too clear from the prominence of studies on missionary activity in African historiography. To this day, the second decade of independent Africa, organized Christianity remains an effective force on the continent. And this in spite of the religious neutrality and ever increasing secularization of African States. Invariably religious minorities, Christian communities continue to be far more important in the social, political and economic life of society than is warranted by their statistical strength.

At this stage of consolidation of independence by African States there are pertinent fundamental questions worth asking by all truly concerned about the prospects of Christianity on the continent. Among the essential questions are: How Christian is Africa? How far has the Church been fulfilling a divine, as distinct from mundane, purpose in Africa? Of what relevance is Christianity to nation-building in independent Africa?

Many scholars and churchmen, I am persuaded, would spontaneously give unduly optimistic answers to such questions, convinced that the Church has not been doing badly at all, in any case not as badly as critics make out. Given the calibre and stature of the scholars gathered at this Conference I have no doubt that there will be no indulgence in mere platitudes and that, in the over-all and ultimate interest of the Christianity of the Bible in Africa, informed criticism will be welcome.

With every sincerity I bell the cat. Firstly, it seems to me that the balance sheet of the institutionalized Christianity inherited by independent Africa is one of assets and liabilities, perhaps more of the latter than of the former. Among the assets are: the permanence—as opposed to the ephemerality of earlier appearances—of Christianity, in the hands of Africans and, to some extent, its expression in ways distinctly African without impairing its universality and sublimity; the raising up, through their schools, of battalions of Western-style educated *élite*, without whose activities the termination of colonial rule and the emergence of nation-states would have been impossible—the Church for more than a century being the ideological vanguard; solicitude for the lowly and deprived in society, as well as for the diseased, through medical care; innoculation of individuals with philanthropic impulses and the concept of self-help.

These assets, which belonged to the now past romantic age of missions and churches, have been diminishing in value with the emergence of African States. For with its financial resources and political military power the State, in a way the Church cannot do, is able to mobilize the masses towards national goals with social welfare programmes much larger in scale than are within the reach of the Church, and without any religious or class discrimination. In other words in ways and to an extent that never was in pre-independence days the citizen, even when he is a Christian, is more conscious of the State than of the Church as his benefactor; feels more grateful to the State than to the Church; does not need to think that the Church or Christianity exists to become educated, Western-style, and accomplished in life. It is not an accident that from his pocket the Christian adherent is more willing to render unto Caesar the things that are Caesar's, but not necessarily unto God the things that are God's. More than in a potential fashion the African State is aggregating to the modern nation what Reinhold Niebuhr[1] spoke of as demanding the total devotion of its citizen—not to God what is God's and to Caesar what is Caesar's but everything to Caesar and lip service to God.

In my judgement the biggest loss of the Church to the State is what was their traditional greatest social asset—control of Western-style education. From the position of virtual, through involuntary, monopolist in the early days of colonial rule, the Church descended to the still gracious level of the diminishing principal in the sharing of the burden of education as the colonial period lengthened. But in independent Africa, in a matter of years, the Church has been relegated to playing a mere ancillary role, in most areas a mere agency for fulfilment of the no-nonsense secular social and cultural goals of the State. What a reversal of role within a generation! The State has become the real benefactor and dispenser of the greatest means for social, political and economic changes in Africa, thereby rendering the Church increasingly a lesser recipient of gratitude from the masses for social welfare.

The dismal picture does not end with the diminishing assets. As students of organized Christianity in Africa know only too well, the

---

[1] Reinhold Niebuhr, *Moral Men and Immoral Society* New York, 1932.

liabilities have remained aggravated in some areas. There is the issue of sociological splintering of social units down to the family level, as a result of conversion of individuals out of the family. There is the problem of the colonial, or neo-colonial, image—doctrinal, cultural and ecclesiastical—that still attaches to the Western-established Churches, an image that will never be effaced as long as the Church in Africa looks Londonward or Romeward or New Yorkward or Richmondward, rather than Heavenward through Africa. There is sectarianism, ideologically out of tune with the concept of national unity and the Pan-Africanism of the Organization of African Unity, a sectarianism quite often arising out of human-made non-essentials of religion.

How easily the Churches in the world generally, but in Africa in particular, are completely oblivious of the oneness of Christ, of His indivisibility. There is the age old problem of Christianity yet to endeavour rationally to become incarnate in African culture; of Christianity yet to be expressed in the deepest and innermost feelings of Africans, in the manner the so-called pagans express their spirituality through the gods. Lastly there is the fact that Christians, like Muslims and 'pagans', believe that their religion is superior to other religions. The only difference is that, in my opinion, Christians have been more guilty than the two other religious communities by being the most articulate in denigrating the others, adopting a negative and therefore unrewarding attitude towards Islam and African traditional religion, religions they little understand unto the present day.

No less disadvantageous is the fact that, in practical terms, the Church has lost its primacy as an arsenal of ideologies relevant to the building of modern African States. Except for its doctrine, in particular the centrality of the person of Jesus Christ, institutionalized Christianity preaches no ethical or moral values, or even the concept of Deity, not found in other religions. And largely because of the conflict that has at all times existed between precept and practice, between what the Christianity of the Bible says and its exponents and professors are observed by non-Christians to be practising, there is very little to distinguish Christians as a group morally superior to other religious communities in Africa.

Quite a contrast to the relative ineffectiveness of Christian ideologies in contemporary Africa is the captivating secularism of States. The national ideologies in African States are not to be misconstrued as other forms of religion, but as rival ideologies which the masses believe have greater immediate relevance to their lives and the evolution of the nation. It would be a defeatist, negative and empty self-consoling attitude for organized Christianity to decry the emergence of secular ideologies in a situation where the State does not proscribe religion.[2] It seems to me that the attitude of the Church to secular ideologies should be positive, in the sense of identifying the properties that make secular ideologies of ever greater appeal than Christian ideology, on behalf of which thousands of lives and millions of Naira have been spent in Africa since the middle of the nineteenth century.

The point that should pre-occupy Christians is how they are to recover their pristine pre-eminence as the ideological vanguard of modern Africa. However, that vantage position may have been lost for ever. This is because neither Islam nor African traditional religion, both of which claim no inferiority to Christianity, is yielding the ground. In Africa Islam has successfully proved the bugbear of Christian missions and the walls of paganism have refused to collapse Jerichowise. This point should be emphasized, if only to puncture the self-indulged belief of some protagonists of Christianity, who for generations have been predicting the decease of African traditional religion in favour of the Christian faith. Indeed Christians should deem themselves lucky that, by and large, African States pursue the policy of religious toleration, the real guarantor of the permanence of Christianity in independent Africa.

Apart from the danger of being outrivalled by secular ideologies like statism or socialism, the Church in Africa is a house divided against itself. In its evolution the Church has passed through a three-stage process, with unsavoury acrimony all the way. Western-established and Western-oriented churches were the first, monopolizing the field. They gave rise to the so-called African Churches largely because of the little relevance of their alien complexion, their obstreperous and adamantine refusal to pay due cognizance to the concept of African personality. But the so-called African Churches, themselves essentially chips from the old block, lacked the will and spirit to fulfil the declared purpose of their existence. Their elitist leaders were fecklessly enslaved to Western culture from which they were incapable of emancipating themselves. Consequently, doctrinally, structurally, liturgically and theologically they are neither here nor there. Finally, arising out of spiritual dissatisfaction with the former two, are the Pentecostal or Spiritualist Churches. These Aladura Churches, as they are generically labelled, are certainly closer to the grassroots than their more elitist predecessors. Their emphasis on things of the spirit, their freedom from the cultural, ecclesiastical and doctrinal yoke of the Western-established Churches and their relative worldly poverty, are characteristics that stand as a rebuke to their more elitist and more prestigious co-religionists.

---

[2] The case for a positive response to secularization, as providentially determined in favour of Christian theology, has been well argued in Harvey Cox, *The Secular City*, Penguin 1966.

The basic differences in the evolution of the churches in Africa underlie one of their major weaknesses—eternal division and endless fissioning. In independent Africa Christ is divided not only in the form of approach but in the way He is being interpreted. Ecumenism, basically a lip-service affair, hardly gets beyond the talking stage, at which level passionate acrimony forces each Christian community back to its isolationist sectarian shell. The legion sects and sub-sects that litter the continent demonstrably contribute to the splintering of African society.

Another major weakness of institutionalized Christianity in Africa, revealed in bold relief by researches, is its negativism about Islam and African traditional religion. Related to the bill they have paid for their assault on Islam in logistics, money and men—not to talk of uncharitable passion—Christian missions are perhaps the greatest Don Quixotes of our time. Charging at the windmills, Christian missions misdirected their energy and resources by seeking to convert Muslims, even when they knew that Christianity has never converted Islam. Adamantly impregnable and impenetrable in geographical areas where it had been supreme in Africa before Christian missions began their quixotic assault, the Crescent extended its frontier to 'pagan' areas during the colonial period, to the chagrin of Christian missionaries who began to chafe that the Cross was being outrivalled by a much less organized non-mission intensive religion.

As an academic I have often wondered the worth of researches about Islam and Muslims by non-Muslim scholars, mostly Christians! In contrast, Muslims have not been bothering themselves with negative energy on how to convert *Anasaras*. They recognize *Anasaras* as 'People of the Book', as enjoined by the Qu'rān, and become defensively aggressive only when their peace is being disturbed by *Anasaras* presenting to them what they are convinced is a religion inferior to Islam.

Even less easy for the Christian to understand than Islam is African traditional religion, about which non-pagan scholars have been pretending more knowledge than they ever could obtain. These non-pagan scholars fail to realize that there is more to African traditional religion than its observable external manifestations, its theology and cosmology, its philosophy, its organization and forms of worship. One stark truth is that 'pagans' are in no way anxious to be very helpful to outsiders by revealing to them the inner properties of their religion. In the light of this fact one must wonder whether Christians could justifiably claim that they have conquered 'paganism'. How could they conquer an enemy they do not know, except very superficially?

Indeed, for those who care to investigate, African traditional religion remains an instinctive part of most African professors of Christianity. Scratch the African pastor and you would discover that he has greater faith in the charms and amulets he wears surreptitiously and in the 'witch-doctor' to whom he pays nocturnal visits than in the Holy Bible and Jesus Christ; scratch the Christian medical doctor and you would discover that he pays greater attention to the diviner and the psychical fears instilled by his village *milieu* than his scalpel and the white man's tablets; scratch the prominent layman politician and you discover that his public bold face and animal courage are against the background of his secret endless grovelling before masters of supernatural forces in traditional society.

That purist and fundamentalist Christians should stop wishing away African traditional religion is clear from the brazen premature accommodation of the Church with indigenous and imported secret societies or cults, as well as with the institution of chieftaincy. With reference to chieftaincy titles—and I am not referring to the artificial ones manufactured for sale to the educated *élite*—how far could they be divorced from rituals of African traditional religion? As for the cults, they have definitely come to stay. The Church seems completely paralysed to take the obvious step, that is first investigate the theological implications of these cults and compatibility or otherwise with the Christianity of the Bible before accommodating them. As far as I know no genuine or sustained effort has been made to investigate them in relation to the Christianity of the Bible. So far, the attitude has been one of do-nothing or let sleeping dogs lie. Is it because, as it has been alleged time and again, ecclesiastics are members of these indigenous and imported cults? To an extent that must dismay purist believers, the cultic element has pervaded organized Christianity in Africa to the point that it is feared that a paroxysmal eruption would follow any attempt at investigation, not to talk of a purge!

I do not want to be misunderstood as pre-empting judgement on secret societies for fundamentalist believers, as I am one hundred percent ignorant about them. But I think the Church in Africa should take the bull by the horns by borrowing a leaf from the Roman Catholic Church which, at the expense of warfare with Freemasons in Europe, carried out several investigations, before concluding that Freemasonry was a conspiracy against the Church. The result: article 2335 of the Church's Code of Canon Law which automatically excommunicates Catholics who join the Freemasons and similar societies.

Lastly, one other longstanding obstacle that inhibits evolution of a firmly and deeply rooted Christianity in Africa is its imperialistic posture. True the Church has moved very fast to disinherit its colonial legacy, and Africans are increasingly the effective directors of the Churches. However, it behoves the metropolitan parents in Europe and America to put a complete end to proprietorial attitude and behind-the-scene subtle monitoring from metropolitan headquarters. From the point of view of Africans outside the Church, the imperialistic image of the Church will never disappear until Africans are in full control of all Church institutions, including the seminaries; until they do not have to refer to so-called spiritual or ecclesiastical superiors in Europe and America for directives or the final word on the affairs of the Church in Africa.

Disconcertingly the imperialistic stance of the Church is much more in evidence on the cultural plane. To date cultural imperialism pervades very many facets of organized Christianity in Africa—the priestly robes, liturgy, prayer-books, theology, hymnology, even mannerisms. Metaphorically most Churches in Africa believe, or are still being told, that unless Africans are first 'circumcised', that is adopt the non-Biblical cultural elements that Christianity had acquired in Europe or America, they cannot be saved! They have yet to learn the lesson of the first apostolic Christian Council at Jerusalem which forbids putting on converts a yoke which missionaries themselves would not bear. That yoke, I contend, is the cultural imperialism immanent in the forms and formularies, 'the non-essentials of religion', that have divided Christian communities in Africa into 'tribal' compartments of Methodism, Anglicanism, Presbyterianism, Catholicism and so on.

The Christianity of the Bible does not necessarily lose its universality or sacredness by bearing the imprint of the African, his emotions, his intense yearning to see God, through African-based forms and formularies which would elicit the best of his spiritual nature and resourcefulness. This is not just a demand, but a right—and that a right in the best interest of Christianity—that there should be African versions of Christianity, in the way there are European and American versions, not in disharmony with national aspirations and not paganized, in which the African would be able best to fulfil himself spiritually to the maximum of his endowment. As put succinctly by Bishop James Johnson earlier this century, in a manner reminiscent of Apostle Peter at that first Jerusalem Council:

> Christianity is a Religion intended for and suitable for every Race and Tribe of people on the face of the Globe. Acceptance of it was never intended by its Founder to denationalize any people and it is indeed the glory that every race of people may profess and practise it and imprint upon it its own native characteristics, giving it a peculiar type among themselves without its losing anything of its virtue. And why should not there be an African Christianity as there has been a European and an Asiatic Christianity?

Contributors

THE REV. P. ABEGA is a member of the Department of African Languages, University of Yaoundé.

DR A. E. AFIGBO is Professor and Head of the Department of History and Archaeology, University of Nigeria, Nsukka.

DR E. A. AYANDELE is Vice-Chancellor of the University of Calabar, and was formerly Principal of the Jos Campus, University of Ibadan.

THE REV. CANON S. BARRINGTON-WARD is General Secretary of the Church Missionary Society.

THE REV. CANON S. BOOTH-CLIBBORN is Vicar of Great St. Mary's Church, Cambridge. Formerly he was the founding-editor of *Target* in Kenya.

D. J. COOK is Senior Lecturer in History at the University of Zambia.

THE REV. DR C. M. COOKE is a lecturer at St. Patrick's College, Kiltegan, Co. Wicklow.

DR S. CROSS is a Lecturer in the School of Development Studies, University of East Anglia.

H. DINWIDDY was formerly Dean of the College at Makerere University and is currently in continuing education.

DR A. R. I. DOI is Professor in Islamic Studies at Ahmadu Bello University, Zaria. He was formerly Head of the Department of Religious Studies at the University of Ifé and taught at the University of Nigeria, Nsukka.

THE REV. DR E. FASHOLÉ-LUKE is Head of the Department of Theology at the University of Sierra Leone.

THE REV. DR C. R. GABA is Head of the Department of Religious Studies, University of Cape Coast.

DR J. R. GRAY is a Professor of African History at the School of Oriental and African Studies, University of London.

THE REV. A. HAKE is Director of Social Services for Swindon Municipality and author of a study of Nairobi, where he worked for the National Christian Council of Kenya.

THE REV. A. HASTINGS is a Lecturer in the Department of Religious Studies, University of Aberdeen. From 1973 to 1976 he was a Leverhulme Research Officer on Christianity in Independent Africa at the School of Oriental and African Studies, University of London.

THE RT. REV. P. A. KALILOMBE became Bishop of Lilongwe in 1972.

DR O. U. KALU is a Senior Lecturer in the Department of Religion, University of Nigeria, Nsukka.

THE REV. R. E. KENDALL is Director of the Community and Race Relations Unit of the British Council of Churches. Previously he was Africa Secretary of the Conference of British Missionary Societies.

DR S. G. KIBICHO is a member of the Department of Philosophy and Religious Studies, University of Nairobi.

SISTER ANCILLA KUPALO is training young sisters in her Community, the Sisters of Mary, in Kenya. She served as a staff member of the Pastoral Institute of Eastern Africa, 1972–1975.

DR I. LINDEN has taught at the Universitities of Malawi, Ahmadu Bello and Ifé. He is now working with the Catholic Institute of International Relations.

DR J. LONSDALE is a Lecturer in History at the University of Cambridge; Fellow and Tutor of Trinity College.

THE REV. L. MAGESA is teaching at Kipalapala Seminary, Tabora.

DR J. MFOULOU is *Maître de Conférences* in the Department of Sociology, University of Yaoundé.

PASTOR DIAKANUA NDOFUNSU is Chaplain and assistant-lecturer of the *Ecole supérieure de théologie Kimbanguiste* at Kinshasa.

THE REV. DR NGINDU MUSHETE is a Professor in the Faculty of Catholic Theology at Kinshasa, and Director of Research at the *Centre d'Etudes des Religions Africaines*.

THE REV. CANON DR J. A. OMOYAJOWO is a Commissioner in the Public Service Commission of Ondo State, Nigeria. Until September 1975 he was a Lecturer in the Department of Religious Studies, University of Ibadan.

KOFI ASARE OPOKU is Senior Research Fellow in Religion and Ethics, Institute of African Studies, University of Ghana, Legon.

DR J. D. Y. PEEL is Charles Booth Professor of Sociology at the University of Liverpool.

DR T. O. RANGER is Professor of Modern History at the University of Manchester.

DR L. O. SANNEH is a Lecturer in the Department for the Study of Religions, University of Ghana, Legon.

THE REV. DR S. SEMPORÉ, O.P. is engaged in pastoral and research ministry at Cotonou, and lectures in Scripture at the Faculty of Theology in Abidjan and at the Dominican Institute in Ibadan.

THE REV. DR G. M. SETILOANE is Senior Lecturer and Head of the Department of Theology and Religious Studies in the University of Botswana and Swaziland.

THE REV. DR A. SHORTER, W.F. was Director of research at the AMECEA Pastoral Institute. He is now at Kipalapala, Tabora.

THE REV. M. SINGLETON, W.F. is attached to the African department of the International Research and Information Centre, Pro Mundi Vita, Brussels.

DR F. C. STEADY was born in Sierra Leone. She received a D. Phil. from the University of Oxford in 1974, and has been a member of the faculty of the University of Sierra Leone, Yale University and Boston University.

THE RT. REV. DR B. SUNDKLER is a Professor Emeritus of the University of Uppsala.

DR M. L. SWANTZ is Lecturer in the Science of Comparative Religion at the University of Helsinki. She is also directing a research project on

'The Role of Culture in the Restructuring of Tanzanian Rural Areas'.

DR G. O. M. TASIE is Head of the Department of Religious Studies, University of Jos.

DR T. TUMA is working in Nairobi with the Association of Theological Institutions in Eastern Africa. Until 1976 he was Lecturer in Church History at Makerere University.

DR H. W. TURNER has been a member of the Department of Religious Studies, University of Nigeria, Nsukka, and subsequently at the University of Aberdeen.

THE RT. REV. D. TUTU is General Secretary of the South African Council of Churches. Formerly he was Director for Africa of the Theological Education Fund and Bishop of Lesotho.

DR M. TWADDLE is on the staff of the Institute of Commonwealth Studies, University of London. During the 1960s he was successively a schoolmaster in eastern Uganda, a researcher into local politics there and in Buganda, and a Lecturer at Makerere University.

THE REV. DR J. M. WALIGGO received a Ph.D. from the University of Cambridge in 1976 and has returned to the Masaka Diocese in Uganda.

A. F. WALLS is Head of the Department of Religious Studies, University of Aberdeen.

DR A. K. H. WEINRICH (SISTER AQUINA, O.P.) is Senior Lecturer in Social Anthropology at the University of Dar es Salaam.

Index

Abeokuta, 427, 430, 450
Abiodun, Captain, 102, 103, 106, 107, 108
Abolege, 225, 225n
Achebe, Chinua, 438
Acholi, 257, 432
Action Group, 197, 197n
Adaptation, 517; liturgy, 102, 103, 171, 422, 490, 541, 573, 597-605; Religious Life, 559-62, 564, 565, 568-70, 572, 573, 575; role of the Church, 501; structures of Church, 5, 6, 37, 38, 39, 59, 77, 88, 93, 95, 170, 170n; see also Culture, Christianization of African; Spirituality, African Christian; Syncretism; Theology, African
Adejobi, Adeleke, 54, 57
Adejobi, Mrs, 105
Africa Confidential, 264, 266
Africa Report, see 'Report on the Experiences of the Church in the Work of Evangelisation in Africa'
African Brotherhood Church, 45, 48, 53, 55, 56
African Christian Churches and Schools of Kenya, 46
African Independent Churches Association, 47, 58
African Methodist Episcopal Church (AMEC), 9, 12, 49, 51, 57, 158n, 285-303
African Methodist Independent Church, 300
African National Congress (ANC) Zambia, 288, 309
African Reformed Church (Zambia), 172, 173, 285, 290, 297n
Africanization, 13, 38, 59, 166, 253, 361, 411, 424, 569, 613; Government posts, 263, 275, 291; 308; integration, 290; leadership in Church, 4, 5, 6, 19, 21, 27, 28, 30, 32, 33, 61, 62, 68, 69, 80, 101, 202, 202n, 203, 203n, 239, 243 ff., 290, 296, 298, 299, 427, 453, 542; street names, 291; see also Adaptation; Authenticity; Culture; Christianization of African; Liturgy; Self-support; Theology, African; Spirituality, African Christian
Aggrey, Dr K., 115, 439
Agre, Bishop B., 42
Ahmadiyah, 14, 322, 322n, 324n, 326

326n, 327, 328, 330, 336, 344, 350, 350n, 351 ff.
Ajuoga, Bishop, 54
Akinsowon, Christianah, 54
Akan, 114, 117 ff., 450, 450n, 467
Aku, 317, 317n, 319, 337
Aladura, 96-110, 243, 453, 606, 610; attempts to unite, 99 ff., 109; see also Cherubim and Seraphim; Christ Apostolic Church; Church of the Lord
Alexandria Confession, 24
Algeria, 27, 450, 569, 570, 599
Alienation, 109, 190, 366, 367, 506, 507, 508, 511, 512, 515, 544, 578
All Africa Bishops' Symposium, (RC), 68
All Africa Conference of Churches, 19, 24, 45, 358, 406, 411
Allen, Richard, 286
Aluko, T. M., 433, 436
Alur, 466
Ambas Geda, 318
Americo-Liberians, 49
Amin, Idi, 255, 265, 266, 311
Anabaptists, 287
Ancestor Veneration see Primal Religion
Anglicans, 17, 18, 60-74, 98, 99, 102, 109, 139, 145, 152, 153, 153n, 155, 158, 165, 167, 168, 171 ff., 197, 199, 211, 214, 264, 268, 272, 276, 282, 284, 286, 290, 291, 297n, 374, 375n, 384, 447n, 450, 451n, 458, 461, 462, 550, 552, 561
Anglo-Saxons, 443, 444, 446, 451
Angola, 16, 17, 27, 305, 306, 482
Animals, sacred, 438, 456
Ankole, 257
Anlo Ewe, 360, 362, 389-401, 434
Anthropology, 170, 170n, 366, 440, 445, 471, 475, 480, 517, 518, 533, 540 ff., 554
Anyogu, Bishop John, 202n, 203
Aoko, Gaudencia, 53, 54
Apostolic Revelation Society, 54
Apostolics, see Vapostori
Arusha Declaration, 28, 484n, 503, 508
Ashanti, 49
Asians, 266, 275, 417
Assemblies of God, 157
Assembly of Zionist Apostolic Churches, 47
Association of Members of the Episcopal Conferences of East Africa (AMECEA),